# AMERICAN
# LEGISLATIVE
# BEHAVIOR
## a reader

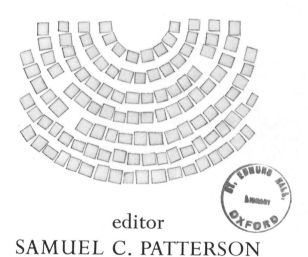

editor
## SAMUEL C. PATTERSON
University of Iowa


D. VAN NOSTRAND COMPANY, INC.
Princeton, New Jersey • Toronto • London • Melbourne

Van Nostrand Regional Offices: *New York, Chicago, San Francisco*

D. Van Nostrand Company, Ltd., *London*

D. Van Nostrand Company (Canada), Ltd., *Toronto*

D. Van Nostrand Australia Pty. Ltd., *Melbourne*

Published simultaneously in Canada by
D. Van Nostrand Company (Canada), Ltd.

Library of Congress Catalog Card No. 68-25816

21411

Bb

PRINTED IN THE UNITED STATES OF AMERICA

environment. Part II focuses on the recruitment, background characteristics, and individual adaptation of legislators. In Part III are presented analyses of some of the important aspects of formal and informal legislative structure, stressing committee structure, political party, leadership, and latent structure. Part IV brings together analyses of legislators' expectations and perceptions, providing definitions of the legislative role in various structural contexts. Communication is the focus of Part V, which includes studies of the relationships between constituents and legislators, lobbyists and legislators, and administrative officials and legislators in communications terms. Part VI is devoted to legislative Action, or decision-making, presenting analyses of legislative voting behavior in different legislative settings. Finally, Part VII deals with legislative behavior research in general, presenting selections relevant to analysis in all of the six perspectives on legislative behavior.

These behavioral perspectives of legislative systems together provide a coherent schema, represented in the diagram at left. Constitutional rules and doctrines, electoral requirements, and apportionment constitute the environment for legislative representation. Legislative actors, in the institutional structure of the legislature, communicate on the basis of their expectations and perceptions, and take action. This oversimplified schema provides an elementary theoretical skeleton, and the reader of the selections to follow will discover many nuances and complications as flesh, muscles, and vital organs are added to the skeletal framework.

S. C. P.

# Authors

CHARLES F. ANDRAIN is Assistant Professor of Political Science at San Diego State College. His major research interests are in the field of African political studies.

WILLIAM BUCHANAN is Professor and Chairman of the Department of Political Science at Washington and Lee University. He co-authored *The Legislative System: Explorations in Legislative Behavior* (1962), and wrote *Legislative Partisanship: The Deviant Case of California* (1963).

CHARLES L. CLAPP has served on the staff of The Brookings Institution, and as Legislative Assistant to United States Senator Leverett Saltonstall. He is the author of *The Congressman: His Work as He Sees It* (1963).

WILDER W. CRANE, JR. is Chairman of the Department of Political Science at the University of Wisconsin–Milwaukee. He has authored several articles in political science journals, and has written a monograph on *The Legislature of Lower Austria* (1962). In 1957, he served as a member of the Wisconsin Assembly.

DAVID R. DERGE is Associate Dean of the Faculties at Indiana University and a member of the Department of Government. His research papers have appeared in the *American Political Science Review,* the *Journal of Politics,* and the *Midwest Journal of Political Science.*

THOMAS R. DYE is Professor in the Department of Political Science at Florida State University. He is the author of a number of articles in social science journals, is a contributor to *Politics in the American States,* edited by Herbert Jacob and Kenneth N. Vines (1966), and is the author of *Politics, Economics, and the Public* (1966).

HEINZ EULAU is the author of many articles and several books, including *The Behavioral Persuasion in Politics* (1963), and he is the co-author of *The Legislative System: Explorations in Legislative Behavior* (1962) and *Lawyers in Politics* (1964). He is Professor of Political Science at Stanford University, and is associated with the Institute of Political Studies at that university.

LEROY C. FERGUSON is Professor of Political Science at Michigan State University. He is co-author of *The Legislative System: Explorations in Legislative Behavior* (1962).

WAYNE L. FRANCIS is Associate Professor of Political Science at the University of Washington. In addition to contributions in scholarly journals, he is the author of *A Comparative Analysis of Legislative Issues in the Fifty States* (1968).

CHARLES E. GILBERT is Associate Professor of Political Science at Swarthmore College. His work has appeared in the *American Political Science Review.*

RALPH K. HUITT is Assistant Secretary for Legislation of the Department of Health, Education, and Welfare. He is on leave from the Department of Political Science at the University of Wisconsin. He has written extensively about the legislative process in Congress, and has served on the staffs of then Senator Lyndon Johnson and Senator William Proxmire. He also has been Director of the American Political Science Association Study of Congress.

WILLIAM H. HUNT has done his major research work with members of the French National Assembly. He is Assistant Professor of Political Science at Virginia Polytechnic Institute.

MALCOLM E. JEWELL is Professor of Political Science at the University of Kentucky, and Editor of the *Midwest Journal of Political Science*. Among his scholarly writings are three monographs on the legislative process: *The State Legislature* (1962), *Senatorial Politics and Foreign Policy* (1962), and *Legislative Representation in the Contemporary South* (1967). He edited *The Politics of Reapportionment* (1962), and is co-author of *The Legislative Process in the United States* (1966).

CHARLES O. JONES has done extensive research on policy-making processes and on the Republican Party. His books include *Party and Policy-Making: The House Republican Policy Committee* (1964), *The Republican Party in American Politics* (1965), and *Every Second Year* (1967). He also has contributed papers to the major political science journals. He is Professor of Government at the University of Arizona.

DUNCAN MACRAE, JR. is Professor of Sociology and Political Science at the University of Chicago. The author of many articles for professional journals in the social sciences, he has written *Dimensions of Congressional Voting* (1958) and *Parliament, Parties, and Society in France* (1967), both major research reports on legislative voting behavior utilizing cumulative scale analysis.

JAMES G. MARCH is Professor of Psychology and Sociology, and Dean of the Division of Social Sciences at the University of California–Irvine. His contributions to theory and research on organizational behavior have been massive. Among a score of articles and books is his co-authored work on *Organizations* (1958).

DONALD R. MATTHEWS has written *U.S. Senators and Their World* (1960) and *The Social Background of Political Decision-Makers* (1954). He is also co-author of *Negroes and the New Southern Politics* (1966). At the University of North Carolina he serves as Professor of Political Science and as Director of the Political Studies Program.

LESTER W. MILBRATH is Professor of Political Science at the State University of New York at Buffalo. His research and writing have focused on political participation and lobbying. In addition to numerous professional articles, he has written *The Washington Lobbyist* (1963) and *Political Participation* (1965).

WARREN E. MILLER is Executive Director of the Inter-University Consortium for Political Research and a member of the Department of Political Science at the University of Michigan. In addition to his research on congressional representation, he has written very widely on voting behavior and elections. His contributions to the voting behavior literature include co-authorship of *The American Voter* (1960) and *Elections and the Political Order* (1966).

SAMUEL C. PATTERSON has written several articles and monographs, and is co-author of *The Legislative Process in the United States* (1966). He is Professor of Political Science at the University of Iowa.

LEROY N. RIESELBACH is Associate Professor of Government at Indiana University. He also has been on the staff of the Mental Health Research Institute of the University of Michigan. His articles have appeared in the *American Political Science Review* and *International Organization,* and he is the author of *The Roots of Isolationism* (1966).

WILLIAM H. RIKER is Professor and Chairman of the Department of Political Science at the University of Rochester. Among his extensive writings are two major books: *Federalism: Origin, Operation, Significance* (1964) and *The Theory of Political Coalitions* (1962). He is a frequent contributor to the *American Political Science Review*.

JAMES A. ROBINSON has made significant contributions to the study of Congress, especially in the realm of foreign policy-making. He is Professor of Political Science and Director of the Mershon Center for Education in National Security at Ohio State University. His books include *Congress and Foreign Policy-Making* (1967) and *The House Rules Committee* (1963).

SEYMOUR SCHER is City Manager of Rochester, New York. He has contributed scholarly articles to the major political science journals, especially focusing on legislative-executive relations.

DONALD E. STOKES is Associate Director of the Inter-University Consortium for Political Research, and a member of the staff of the Survey Research Center and the Department of Political Science at the University of Michigan. He has conducted research on legislator-constituent relations both in the United States and Britain, is the author of innumerable articles, and is the co-author of *The American Voter* (1960), *Elections and the Political Order* (1966), and a forthcoming book on congressional representation.

DAVID B. TRUMAN is Professor of Public Law and Government at Columbia University, and Vice-President and Provost of the University. He was President of the American Political Science Association during 1964–1965. He has written widely on political behavior, including *The Governmental Process* (1951), and *The Congressional Party: A Case Study* (1959).

JOHN C. WAHLKE, at the University of Iowa as Professor of Political Science, has made major contributions to the study of legislative behavior. In addition to scholarly articles, he is co-author of *The Legislative System: Explorations in Legislative Behavior* (1962), and *Government and Politics: An Introduction to Political Science* (1966). He also is co-editor of *Legislative Behavior: A Reader in Theory and Research* (1959) and *The American Political System: Notes and Readings* (1967).

# Contents

## PART V. COMMUNICATION

## PART VI. ACTION

## PART VII. RESEARCH

# Part I

# Representation

# Introduction

IT HAS BEEN commonplace for several centuries to characterize legislative institutions as being *representative* in some sense. A rather wide variety of doctrines of legislative representation has flourished over these centuries, but the concept *representation* is still not entirely unambiguous. Legislative representation may refer both to the individual legislator and to the legislative assembly as a whole. The individual legislator may be said to be a representative in at least three senses.

In the first instance, the legislator is a representative in the sense that he is appropriately *authorized* to act as a representative. In modern times, and certainly in the United States, legislators are authorized representatives by virtue of the implementation of constitutions and laws through the processes of election. In this sense, the answer to the question "Who is the representative?" becomes "Whoever has the constitutional-legal authority to act as a representative." In practice, this kind of Hobbesian conception of representation does not carry analysis of legislative behavior in the United States very far, since we are likely to begin by dealing with legislators whose authorization to act is not in question, having been conferred by political processes of long standing and established legitimacy. Questions about the authorization of American representatives arise mainly in connection with the mechanics of elections where contests develop over who was legally or honestly elected to take a legislative seat.

In the second sense, we may speak of legislative representation in *instrumental* terms. We often talk of legislators acting for or in behalf of constituencies. The legislator who is authorized to represent a constituency may or may not act in its behalf. If we ask "Who is the representative?" we may answer "The legislator who acts for his constituency." In the instrumental sense, representational behavior may take two general forms: agency and delegate. In their most extreme forms, agency representation implies the legislator who acts for his constituency without regard for the views of his constituents, while delegate representation implies the legislator who acts for his constituency only in terms of the wishes and demands of his constituents. These distinctions are part of the classical dialogue about proper representation, notably reflected in Burke's famous speech to his Bristol electors and in the debates of the First United States House of Representatives.

The third sense in which a legislator may be said to be a representative is *symbolical*. We may speak of the legislator as acting like his constituents, of being similar to them (and perhaps different from them) in some symbolically important ways. If we ask "Who is the representative?" we may respond "The

3

legislator who is a symbol of his contituents." Without suggesting metaphysical attributes, it may be said that the legislator represents his constituents in his manner, style, dress, socio-economic status, beliefs, and the like. Symbolic representation implies the legislator who expresses the character of his constituency.

Apart from treating individual legislators as representatives of constituencies, we may consider the representativeness of legislative assemblies. While it is quite possible to analyze legislatures in terms of the extent to which they are authoritative, instrumental, or symbolic, the collective structure and behavior of the legislature raises additional facets of representation. Focusing on the representative person in the context of American politics provides the perspective for analysis of the linkage between representation and responsibility, since American legislators are, at least potentially, held accountable at the polls for their performance. Focusing on the legislature as a whole opens the wider perspective for analysis of consent and compliance with collective decisions and policies.

The collective character of legislatures raises questions about representativeness which are somewhat similarly raised when dealing with a representative sample. The legislature sometimes is spoken of as a mirror, or microcosm, of the wider citizenry. Legislatures are often criticized on the ground that they are in some way inadequate samples of the population. Thus, American state legislatures were chastised for many years prior to *Baker* v. *Carr* because they did not adequately mirror state populations by the equal population standard. Despite some evidence which suggests that legislative apportionment may have little long-term effect upon policy outputs in the American states, people continue to attach importance to the equi-population apportionment of state legislatures, thereby underscoring the symbolic importance in the states of a legislature with equi-population representation.

Although elections constitute only one method of selecting and conferring authority on representatives, they occupy a place of obviously prime importance in discussing American legislatures. American politics operates on the basis of elected legislators, with appointment used in some states only to fill unexpired vacancies. The importance of popular elections in the development of American legislatures is nicely illustrated by the late nineteenth-century alterations in the method of selecting United States senators. Originally they were unequivocally chosen by state legislatures; however, by the time a constitutional amendment required the popular election of senators, they were already frequently popularly elected *de facto*. But just as districting and apportionment rules may produce representative assemblies that are skewed samples based upon the equal population criterion for evaluating them, so elections are not neutral in their effects upon the legislature. The representativeness of a legislature is likely to be heavily dependent upon the nature of the legislative election. Thus, legislative districts may be adequately equal in population but vary a great deal in the extent to which there is competition for legislative seats. Gerrymandering, electoral traditions, clustering effects, and the massive advantages of incumbency have meant that the vast majority of legislative districts in the United States are politically "safe." Significant inter-party competition is relatively unusual in legislative elections.

The regularities in the processes and results of legislative elections go quite beyond the stability of party or candidate success in legislative districts. The relation between election votes and legislative seats shows remarkable regularity, at least at the congressional level. But the extent of legislative electoral competition and the uniformity in the relation between votes and seats, and the impact of these structural factors on legislative policy-making, are only beginning to be studied systematically. The essays reprinted here suggest some ways in which the task of comparative systematic analysis of these phenomena can be carried forth.

# 1. Operative Doctrines of Representation *

## CHARLES E. GILBERT

The main point of this article is to identify some traditions of American thought that figure in analysis of the distinctively democratic aspects of government. The discussion is centered on doctrines of "representation." While that term has a generally understood meaning, its application in specific contexts depends upon values and expectations closely related to other largely procedural aspects of politics; and together these perspectives figure in appraisals and decisions of policy.

The "distinctively democratic aspects of government" have broadly to do, I think, with relations between public officials and the population. These can be conceptualized and described in terms of institutions, influence, identification, or exchange, and are so treated in various positive or empirical approaches. At the points where normative critique and empirical description join, the literature of American political science seems to have converged on several broad concerns that tend to organize and orient discussion—e.g., representation, responsibility, rationality, and lately, the "public interest," of which "representation" surely has the clearest empirical reference. These are overlapping or intersecting concerns. They emphasize different aspects of government and different blends of calculation and control (or intellectual *versus* institutional elements); but they do not refer to distinct phenomena, and they relate to common normative traditions.[1] Such terms are often, I think, of dubious utility because they tend to obscure the more detailed values at stake in action or discussion and perhaps thereby to discourage more pointed empirical inquiry relevant to those values. However that may be, the interrelatedness of these concerns and the broad relevance of "representation" can be briefly indicated.

There is a school of thought that would distinguish "representative government" from democratic government; but the term representation itself surely stands for a basic democratic relation. It may be regarded as expressive (symbolic) or instrumental, in the language of Parsons.[2] It may be virtual or actual (sanctioned). It may concern likeness of a wide range of characteristics of elected officials and constituents or it may relate merely to agreement on stated issues of policy; it may be a matter of psychological "identification" or of correspondence respecting explicit issues or interests.[3] Elections apart, proponents of "representative bureaucracy" have argued the actual or potential reflection in administration of broad socioeconomic strata, or a balance of concrete interests, or of basic constitutional traditions. All discussions of the subject deal, at least implicitly, with two of its

* From *The American Political Science Review,* Vol. 57 (1963), pp. 604–618. Reprinted by permission.

aspects: *what* is represented, and *how;* with the identification and evaluation of interests, and with the norms and sanctions affecting official behavior.[4]

Both "rationality" and "responsibility" chiefly relate to the *how* of representation. The critique and defense of the classical model of rational choice in administration have largely to do with the institutions in which ends are defined, the organization of search for alternatives and selection of relevant interests, the validity of abstract or *ex ante* expressions of popular wants, the superiority of long-run governmental leadership to short-run responsiveness.[5] The connotations of "responsibility" vary with the context: accountability, rationality, or effectiveness, or all these may be involved.[6] The classical, Benthamite democratic model emphasized *ex post* accountability through elections, assuming a simple governmental structure and a politics about limited, concrete, discrete concerns; once these assumptions are outmoded or relaxed we face the problem of appropriate indices of governmental performance beside simple and clearly sanctioned "accountability" and including norms relating to "rationality" and "representation." Finally, as "control" suggests the problem of responsibility, "calculation" points to the "public interest" issue. As the simple accountability model breaks down in, say, Anthony Downs's analysis and requires reliance on broad indices of governmental performance, so on, say, Kenneth Arrow's demonstration the problem of mapping individual preferences onto a social welfare function cannot be solved, given his conditions, except under special assumptions about how interests are to be identified and related by political processes; and with these assumptions we are back to doctrines of representation.[7]

The interrelation of these concerns will be apparent in the discussion of separate traditions that follows.[8] The traditions are primarily academic rather than popular. Some are rather distinct philosophical positions; but others are not. Despite the danger of ambiguity or misunderstanding it will be convenient to title the traditions: idealist, utilitarian, formalist, pragmatic, participatory, populist. These categories, it will be seen as the discussion proceeds, are not always mutually exclusive.

## I

The distinctive element of *idealism* appears to be that important values attach to the community and polity as wholes, or as complexes of institutions. Short of the entire community, high value inheres in organizations and institutions in which individuals cultivate common and usually non-material interests. The interests or goods preferred in idealism may be collective (inhering in groups) rather than common (reflecting agreement); but reducing this distinction is an important idealist objective; and the interests normally emphasized are the kinds of "goodness" that can be predicted *of* the community rather than located *in* the community.[9] They are ethical conceptions, better described as values than as interests.

Such values need social definition. If the logical method of idealism is dialectic, its preferred social expression is dialogue which, as a practical matter, requires some mix of political leadership and mutual discussion. The larger the society the more crucial the functions of leadership—not only the conduct of discussion and articulation of aspirations and agreements; but the conservation of authority by stressing collective purposes, obviating conflict by prompt action, or attending to interests not served by decentralized "social choice" processes. In such processes the electoral sanction helps encourage responsiveness and sensitivity in officials and participation by publics; but the direct or exact reflection of interests is impossible for the most important interests.

Where explanation is concerned, idealism bears on the fact of political obligation and the forms of political institutions rather than particular policy outcomes. Often its method is functionalism: it emphasizes "system values"; and its seeming tautologies sometimes refer to cumulative social processes. Popular aspirations are partially shaped by leadership; but leadership rests on authority, and authority depends upon faithful reflection of popular aspirations. The ambiguity of these aspirations requires ample official discretion. The important effects of social choice processes are those on the political system itself.

A somewhat more specific way of viewing the idealist tradition is to envisage the American President as Chester Barnard's executive presiding over an economy of incentives and contributions which, however, he can largely define and redefine by moral leadership.[10] This kind of organization theory also lends itself to utilitarian analysis, depending on the nature of the incentives and contributions. But the idealist can argue that, where moral leadership is heavily emphasized and accepted by all concerned, and where "identification" with either the "organization" or broad purposes is widespread, then executive discretion in defining purposes (values and obligations) tends to maximize both "efficiency" and "effectiveness" in Barnard's terms.

Another characteristic of idealism is its emphasis on "expressive" representation —on "style" rather than procedure or accountability to concrete interests or defined constituencies. This will be important if representatives are to have the latitude that the idealist accords them; then people can presumably look to such attributes as energy, decisiveness, or indicia from oratory or social position for assurance that candidates or officials share the proper image of the community as well as for clues to likely concrete choices. The importance of the idealist position here, I think, is its attempt to deal with those aspects of the political process where interests, ends, or values lack specificity; its valuing of representation in its non-sanctioned sense; and its recognition that representation must be virtual rather than actual in some degree. Generally, idealists want to enlarge those areas of politics whereas other traditions do not; but one suggestion of idealism for social science would be to try to identify the elements of "style" that figure in policy and electoral decisions.

I think the idealist tradition is not generally well thought of today. We tend to mistrust its ambiguity about leadership and responsiveness, to doubt that the same subtle dialogue and ethical argument are possible in the great society and in the small group and to emphasize, therefore, the electoral sanction and the specifics of instrumental representation rather than the diffuseness of expressive representation; we set more store by substance and procedure than by style; we suspect that unitary claims often mask sinister interests.

There is nonetheless an American idealist tradition, native or transplanted. De Grazia has described the effects of transcendentalism on the notion of "enlightened individualism" as a doctrine of representation; and the effects of German idealism on early American political scientists and their philosophical contemporaries is reflected in John Dewey's beginnings. Woodrow Wilson's encomium of the presidency seems an implicit expression of the idealist tradition with respect to representation, and Glendon Schubert has described some outcroppings of the tradition in modern writing on public administration.[11]

A strong modern statement is that of Joseph Tussman: the analysis begins with the "body politic" and turns on the relation between it and its members, between members and authoritative agents.[12] Membership implies in part a "recognition of some *common* or shared concern" as well as "that one's own interest constitute only a subordinate part of a broader system of interests"; it also involves some minimum moral commitment to the body politic (commitment to the moral beliefs of the body politic?), and some modicum of active participation to make authority acceptable. Agency (authority) involves "a task related to some aspect of the public good and . . . a measure of discretion." Government—authority and obligation—is the outcome of implied agreement: "only by dint of ceaseless devotion to the task of keeping the delicate structure of consent, participation, and authority in good repair can we save the claim of self-government from being a bitter mockery."

## II

The implications of the *utilitarian* tradition for modern democratic government are ambiguous, as chroniclers of British thought have often pointed out. At least three strains of utilitarianism appear to affect democratic theory today. Arbitrarily, I shall treat one of these as my "utilitarian" tradition, on the ground that the others are now largely merged in other traditions to be reviewed below.

All three versions have in common the definition of interests in "individualistic" terms. In one, the emphasis is placed on the primacy of the individual's preferences (as they have been represented since marginalism entered the utilitarian tradition), on the incommensurability and noncomparability of personal utilities, and on the inadequacy of any but the simplest and most perspicuous political processes and laissez faire governments for representing and aggregating individual wants. In this school of thought there is a strong presumption against governmental intervention and political action; its adherents are often styled "conservative" today although, historically, "liberal" is more apt. This is the view I shall term "utilitarian"; but two other versions should be distinguished from it: One can be called the populist aspect of the utilitarian tradition, which has emphasized the radical, reforming, and especially majoritarian doctrine of Bentham and James Mill.[13] Though stressing individualistic definitions of interest and "direct" representation, the emphasis on *equality* in this school evidently covered an assumption of sufficient agreement to enable majority rule to work. The final version of utilitarianism appears to stress central decision rather more than direct representation. This version is reflected in some of Bentham's writings on governmental reform and, in a sense, in the nineteenth century British administrative reforms. Interests are defined in terms of individuals; but the "greatest good of the greatest number" can be discovered by administrative management and central decision and the overview these afford. This is the notion of the "service state," and it would seem to assume substantial agreement on the needs to be met and the services to be rendered—on the scope and ends of state activity. Grant this assumption, together with governmental consolidation and electoral reform (enlargement of civic and official perspective, abatement of "vested" interests, and enhancement of competition and participation), and the identification of interests, including "externalities," by central administrators may be admissible; and it might be more accurate than majority voting alone because of its attention to externalities and intensities.[14]

It seems to me that *both* the populist and, let's say, the "centralist" versions of utilitarianism assume substantial, if implicit, agreement in the population on the ends and means of public policy (or on ends, with means of secondary importance); they are at the opposite extreme from idealism in discounting the problems of disagreement of dissensus and the need for elaborate political processes for the integration of interests. "Representation" is simple and direct and uninteresting; politics is at a minimum.

The distrust of complex political or representative processes is common to all three versions of utilitarianism; but with the critical difference that the first version is mistrustful of state activity as well. (This view may sometimes reflect ethical egoism rather than strict ethical utilitarianism, or an implicit or explicit analogizing from economic to poltical contexts.) Public action entails sanctions and "pains"; private interests belie the easy majoritarian assumption of agreement on ends and means. If implicit agreement or a simple felicific calculus won't work, then individual differences and social disagreement become crucial and *coercion* becomes highly probable in collective decisions. The concern with coercion is, I think, the central concern of utilitarianism as here defined; "liberty" is treated in negative terms as the absence of coercion, "equality" as the integrity and noncomparability of individual preferences—and it is these that are to be maximized. *All* representative or political processes, and thus *all* state activity, threaten these values, which can also be expressed as rationality and impersonality in governmental action (concerns close to the "rationalist" tradition below).

The modern centers of this utilitarian approach have been Vienna and Chicago; its chief exponents have been economists. It is, I think, most thoroughly set out in the writings of von Mises, Hayek, Henry Simons, and Frank Knight; and Knight will here be taken as its protagonist.[15] Four recurrent propositions in Knight's writings are characteristic of utilitarianism and illustrate the points made above; these are: (1) that even persuasion and salesmanship amount to coercion in their violation of the integrity of individual preferences;[16] (2) that the representative relation of "agency" can *never* be clearly defined politically and always gives rise to substantial discretion;[17] (3) that the proper condition of state activity is maximum agreement or consensus, which is *not* reflected or supported by the direct political or administrative action advocated by other versions of utilitarianism;[18] and (4) that heavy procedural safeguards, as well as high agreement, should accompany governmental action.[19] Knight's problem in all his recent writing has been to define the kinds of processes that will yield agreement with least "coercion"; no definite solution appears, but the discussion verges on idealism and shares the vagueness of that tradition while deemphasizing the role of leadership and representative processes that idealists often emphasize.

In politics, indeed, Knight turns out to be something of a Kantian: the integrity of personal preferences implies Kantian standards of conduct. The primary political problems are defined in largely Kantian terms: how to get agreement on ends; how to maximize the role of intelligence and rationality in defining collective ends and means; how to minimize coercion, including the manipulations of others' fields of choice.[20] The role of government turns out to be a hindering of hindrances; order and law are synonymous, ideally, with maximum freedom the first end of the state. Freedom and order are best reconciled through government by discussion in which, however, order rests heavily on habit and tradition, and in which the case for change must develop from rational discussion and demonstration; not from central decision or a simple aggregation of given preferences. The discussion is highly abstract and uninstitutional.

Utilitarianism offers a definite position on the identification of interests, but has little to say about aggregation in any political or institutional sense. The original Benthamite view, characteristically ambiguous as to egoism *versus* universalism, was that:

> each voter acts as a trustee for himself and for all the rest of the community in his exercise of the suffrage. Now if he is precluded from the possibility of promoting his own particular interest to the prejudice if the remainder of the universal interest by the manner in which his vote is cast (as by ballot), then the only interest of his which he has any prospect of promoting by his vote is his share of the universal interest. And for doing this, he sees before him no other possible means except voting for the candidate who is likely to render the most service to the universal interest.[21]

Early utilitarianism implied simple and centralized institutions and concrete, definable interests. Implicit in this is an emphasis on governmental *economy* and deemphasis of the public sector (explicit in Bentham and Mill) that would improve pure accountability because the presumption against public expenditures would narrow the alternatives for public decision. This thread in utilitarianism is emphasized in the tradition outlined above, which argues that intelligent electoral appraisal (either public interested or egoistic) and an accountable officialdom are *only* maximized as public action and alternatives are minimized.

The tradition dealt with here has had its major applications in public finance, where it has stressed the condition of individuals rather than collective benefits, together with governmental economy and the rationality and integrity of individual preferences. The other major elements of utilitarianism seem to have merged in other American traditions, and to have been dissipated in the process. The innovating thrust of the tradition shows up most sharply in pragmatism (below)—though the hedonistic point of it is qualified. The centralizing and synoptic strain has been largely assimilated to rationalism (below). The populist development will be dealt with separately.

### III

Idealism and utilitarianism can perhaps be regarded as the two basic traditions with respect to the definition of interest—one aspect of representation.[22] Nonetheless, I think two other traditions can be distinguished on this point; these are rationalism and pragmatism.

What I shall term the *rationalist* tradition is difficult to define and distinguish. This is partly because it is so widespread; probably it was the dominant tradition in American political science until recently, and perhaps, in a normative sense, it still is. It is less distinctive philosophically than the other major traditions, and it is not easy to identify in a word; in the following discussion the terms "formalism" and "rationalism" will be used interchangeably.[23] An important aspect of this tradition is its alliance with public law; a related aspect is its reliance on certain analytical concepts—such as "state," "sovereignty," political "authority"—from which it is difficult to eliminate the normative content. Formality is highly valued in governmental institutions because certain broad end values are in some degree "built in" and protected against perversion through interpersonal interaction. The tradition thus has in it a good deal of the "formalism" against which pragmatism revolted.[24] In its normative and analytic concerns, rationalism is more-or-less equivalent to "constitutionalism."

The formalism and formality in the tradition would seem to result from the way in which interests are defined. In Banfield's terms, the rationalist persuasion is "qualified individualistic"; that is, the ends of the polity are in the first instance those of individuals, but are selected from certain "appropriate" classes of ends.[25] In practice, these ends or classes of ends are hard to define and give rise to some of the classical problems of political theory—e.g., the meaning of "liberty." In theory, the ends or interests have often been designated "rights": indeed, one characteristic of the rationalist tradition is its historical tendency to define interests as rights or "natural rights." In modern theory these "rights" have often become "ends of the state"—e.g., security, liberty, justice, welfare, order—but these are ends of individuals, or imputed to individuals, satisfied through state action or inaction.[26] The shift of emphasis from individual "rights" to common "ends" has helped to reconcile state action with the liberal tradition and to obviate or obscure the difficult question of rights. Thus it has tended to separate the formalist tradition from the variant of utilitarianism emphasized above, and to relate it more closely to the other trends of utilitarianism.

This kind of definition of interests—one root of the rationalist tradition—raises several issues. One, of philosophical interest, concerns the intellectual bases of the tradition. I think these mainly lie in natural law theory which, while sometimes "naturalistic" in the meta-ethical sense, also emphasized a rational faculty by which ultimate ends are apprehended and applied. Formalism as here defined has close affinities with formalism in normative ethics though it does not imply such a position. Thus the rationalist tradition has inherited one important and distinctive orientation to the study of politics: a means-ends approach in which "rights" or "ends" are the starting point for the analysis of institutions; an important method of explaining or understanding "the state" or its elements is in terms of the ends of the state.[27] This approach entails the emphasis on formality and procedure already remarked, not only in a normative sense but also in empirical inquiry. Empirically, the purposive, means-ends approach suggests an emphasis on institutions, constructs and procedures that are often defined by their relation to general and abstract ends; normatively, attention is centered on this relation and the refinement and illumination of ends in terms of institutional means and conversely. The same goes for certain key concepts. Hence the traditional distinction between "power" and "authority" in which authority is tested ultimately by general, abstract ends and immediately by procedures reflecting these ends (historically, "rights" and "authority" were the main considerations in a more contractual view of political obligation). Hence, also, the distinctive concern of the rationalist tradition to segregate *public* and *private* ends in political action and to maintain the state-society distinction by formality and publicity. The distinction helps guarantee that the leverage of "authoritative" institutions will not be lent to private purposes, and that governmental action will—in part by publicity—be limited to areas of general agreement.[28] Hence, further, the rationalist emphasis upon clear definition and separation of institutional functions, upon separation of powers thinking and especially the policy (politics)—administration distinction drawn by Goodnow, Lowell, and Wilson. In part, the point of the distinction is to further synoptic and "rational" decision making through hierarchy; in part, I think, to see to it that certain institutions are clearly charged with the protection or promotion of certain set "ends"; and primarily to protect rights by checks and balances. A final consideration: often the rationalist tradition appears to place high value on a large measure of agreement or consensus. The reason for this is not obvious. It may be that sharp dissensus, or even a highly pluralistic politics, calls in question imputations of common ends or common understandings about procedures; the result is particularism in assertions of ends, and resort to "power" in political action at the expense of rights or ends assumed to be common.

It was mentioned above that the formalist tradition probably constitutes the mainstream of American political science; for many purposes it would be too broad and indiscriminate a characterization, but I do not think it is for the present purpose.[29] Indeed, on the normative side, this tradition certainly remains important; but, among other reasons, the difficulties it presents to distinguishing normative and positive inquiry have led to its repudiation by some as political *science*. The early "greats" of American political science were predominantly in this tradition: note Woodrow Wilson's emphasis on the constitutional "ends" of representative government; A. L. Lowell's insistence on substantial consensus as the condition of a "really public" public opinion; and Frank Goodnow's implicit concern with formality and procedure and explicit attention to publicity in politics and impartiality in administration.[30] Historically and *ad hominem* it is tempting to interpret the political science of these eastern academicians as a Brahminical endeavor to protect middle class, Anglo-Saxon amenity against the new political pluralism arising from late nineteenth century immigration, industrialization and urbanization; but Wilson, Goodnow, and Lowell did not invent the rationalist tradition: before them were the Founding Fathers. Turning to a recent and influential political scientist, much of Charles E. Merriam's writing can be construed as an attack on the empirical side of the formalist tradition; but only as an adjustment or adaptation of the normative side; certain problems generated by that tradition (*e.g.,* the public-private distinction and the definition of institutional ends or functions) were crucial to him, and some of the classical concepts (*e.g.,* state and sovereignty) remained at the center of his thought.[31]

To come at last to the question of "representation," I think it can be argued that this relation derives much of its status as a concept—or, more simply, as a concern and object of inquiry—from the rationalist tradition. This is probably because representation in the rationalist tradition is not direct; it is acknowledged that there is no permanent or mechanical solution of the problem of agency, and it appears in this tradition that a modicum of discretion is desirable. As Banfield points out, the "qualified individualist" position requires some latitude in the selection of ends by those in responsible positions; the abstract nature of the "ends" favored in the rationalist tradition requires a balancing of more parochial interests in concrete situations. Discretion, in turn, raises the problems of "responsibility" alluded to above, and it is in this connection that the rationalist emphasis on formality and publicity—on the distinction between public and private—is important. In summary, "representation" presents interesting questions of organization because of the twin necessities of discretion and control that are entailed in the rationalist tradition and the procedural and intellectual values that must therefore be balanced.

The large role of representation in rationalist thinking is evident in the opening pages of Woodrow Wilson's *Constitutional Government:* the history of constitutional government is the history of "political liberty," and political liberty is "the right of those who are governed to adjust government to their own needs and interests." [32] In changing circumstances this calls for constant adjustment between "the power of government and the privileges of the individual . . . :

> And so the growth of constitutional government has been the growth of institutions, of practices, of methods of performing the delicate business of maintaining an understanding between those who conduct the government and those who submit to it. The object of constitutional government is to bring the active, planning will of each part of the government into accord with the prevailing popular thought and need, and thus make it an impartial instrument of symmetrical national development; and to give the operation of the government thus shaped under the influence of opinion and adjusted to the general interest both stability and an incorruptible efficacy." [33]

This statement expresses aspects of rationalism already discussed: formality and impartiality in government; common understandings and ends in the population. To these are added Wilson's characteristic concern with leadership, energy, and efficacy as official attributes and national perspectives on policy, to which are related his well known views on the roles of president and parties. For Wilson, as well as for Lowell and Goodnow, "responsible" government implied rationality (means-ends, central, synoptic decisions), effectiveness (given agreement on ends and impartial administration of means), and adjustment between "opinion" and the "general interest." This adjustment is the job of political representation and implies discretion rather than direct reflection; responsible government means more than merely representative government.

The rationalist tradition approximates idealism at times in its emphasis on common ends, official discretion, and the practical importance of political obligation. The crucial differences are that ends are more specific in the rationalist tradition; that they are more clearly attached to individuals and are thus plainly common rather than collective; that more detailed attention is given to the organization and institutions of representation so that discretion, while necessary, is relatively narrow and clearly reviewable. Policy is penultimately referred to procedural standards. In order to foster an overview of common ends and to enforce "public" concerns where some private interests are leveraged, rationalism today usually leans toward more centralized and synoptic decision making, though this is a matter of context.

*IV*

The *pragmatic* tradition is a recent but extremely influential one. Historically, the philosophical tradition—the revolt against "formalism" or, in political science, against rationalism—may be seen as most influential; or it may be argued that the pragmatic tradition in political science, with its emphasis on group interests, was mainly a recognition and attempt at explanation of an altered political structure in the twentieth century. Probably both developments were important: it seems plausible to argue that American politics developed a pronounced economic pluralism with the rapid capitalization and industrial growth of the late nineteenth century and a more pronounced cultural particularism and class consciousness a bit later in the wake of the "rise of the city." If some rationalist writing can be construed as an effort to reverse or mitigate the resultant political tendencies, then the pragmatic tradition can probably be interpreted as an attempt to work with them rather than against them. Two other socio-political tendencies may have encouraged pragmatism: one is the increased importance of education and communication with urbanization; another the growth of governmental regulation and social service and the consequent concern to relate the specialist or expert to the public. Together these are the "problems" of *The Public and its Problems:* they call in question the rationalist model of agreed-upon ends, central and synoptic decisions, understood procedures, all consistent with the ready adjustment of government to popular preferences. On the other hand, the philosophical and intellectual history of pragmatism seem to have an independent importance in two respects: a change in *what* is valued accompanied by emphasis on "experimental" ethics and politics; and the beginnings of the "group approach" to politics in the development of "symbolic interactionism" in philosophy, psychology, and sociology.[34] Thus, both the *what* and the *how* of representation were reoriented in the the pragmatic tradition.

The discussion that follows is focused on John Dewey; but I do not mean to limit the pragmatic tradition to philosophy or philosophers. I think the tradition has been strong in political science, including much of what Glendon Schubert has recently called the "realist" position on the public interest and, in terms of empirical work, the pervasive "group approach" to politics. The characteristic outlooks on concerns relevant to "representation" seem, however, to be most clear in the writings of John Dewey—in particular in *The Public and Its Problems.*[35]

Dewey's work is certainly a rejection of rationalism; its relation to idealism and utilitarianism is less clear; but I think it can be taken as a combination and a qualification of both. Briefly and broadly, Dewey's central problem is to explain and justify (or, explain-and-justify) the emergence of "publics" and the incidence of state action. There are two lines of explanation: one runs in terms of "externalities" (the third-party effects of private transactions), and is cast in the utilitarian tradition; the other relies on communication and socialization (symbolic interaction), and largely belongs to the idealist tradition. Since Dewey's philosophical self-consciousness about both these traditions is a matter of record, his ambivalent approach is not surprising.[36] The general proposition suggests itself that Dewey was a utilitarian respecting the identification of interests and an idealist with respect to their aggregation; but it is not clear that he himself would have admitted the distinction, since it implies given interests independent of or exogenous to political interaction. As a political method, pragmatism appears to call for minimizing the role of *a priori* interests and maximizing the effects of political processes, so long as they are properly organized.

Dewey is generally felt to have been an especially ambiguous philosopher. His ambiguity about utilitarianism and idealism is especially important. The "first causes" of political action appear to be utilitarian.[37] But three symbolic interactionist modifications are crucial: one is the significance accorded to social determination of interests,[38] a second is the primacy and reality of groups in the study and understanding of politics;[39] and a third is the role of communication in defining and creating common interests.[40] When Dewey approaches these problems in terms of conventional philosophy the result is a doctrine of consciousness which, while akin to that of James, was heavily influenced by idealism and is highly social in nature.[41]

Pragmatism is thus distinct from utilitarianism and idealism, emphasizing neither concrete, parametric interest nor abstract, emergent ideals. Dewey argued that interests are changed by interaction which cannot be labeled "coercive," that ideals are only meaningful for *individuals* in *action,* and that general "ends" cannot properly be imputed to societies by philosophers—thus rejecting our three previous traditions. *The* political problem is not the guarantee and adjustment of "rights" nor the maintenance of authority and obligation nor the maximization of net pleasure; but is more nearly defined in utilitarian than any other terms as the progressive adjustment of interests that will afford maximum opportunity for individual expression and choice. Thus the main point is to improve political organization and communication so as to promote easy access, broad participation, and an adequate range and accuracy of information. Like a market, the political process facilitates trading and thus reflects intensities; unlike a market it should promote common social values at least to relieve externalities and perhaps for their own sake as well.

Three other aspects of Dewey's position are worth brief notice: the implications of "instrumentalism" for political science; his outlook on the public-private distinction; and his emphasis on process rather than structure.

Talk of "problem-solving" runs through Dewey's discourse and figures in the title of his most relevant book. The point is that questions of public policy are treated as discrete and immediate issues requiring adjustment rather than challenges to "rational" decision wherein choices must be made among complex programs in light of ultimate ends of the rationalist type. The issue here is not quite Weldon's "problems" *versus* "difficulties"; the point of instrumentalism is to obviate the formal fact-value problem by foreshortening means-ends chains, by depicting purposeful choice as a scanning of immanent consequences only, and by emphasizing an experimental or conditional approach to choice. It is a "scientific" approach to social choice in Dewey's sense of science as control (rather then prediction); it discards governmental divisions of labor in which some officials decide on "ends" while others deal in "means"; and its relevance to some current conceptions of "incrementalism" and "representative bureaucracy" is evident.

The erosion of the public-private distinction follows from instrumentalism: if abstract ends or endemic rights are discounted, then the rationalist reasons for distinguishing the two spheres are less important. "Publics" are formed when the "lasting, extensive, and serious consequences of associated activity" are perceived. They differ only in degree (of duration, extensiveness, and intensity of consequences) from "groups." *The* public differs only in degree in the opposite direction: it consists in a broader perception of consequences; it progresses from "society" to "community" through fuller communication and firmer understandings.[42] Nonetheless, the point of *The Public and Its Problems* is to argue that the public-private distinction is important; to redefine it in more realistic, less rationalistic terms; and to reverse the "eclipse" of the public in a pluralistic society. The question of *criteria* for the adjustment of interests is implicit in Dewey's statement of "problems" in terms of "externalities"; but his solution is to try to obviate serious problems by organization, communication, and interaction. If the political process works freely and reflects interests fully, it will sufficiently narrow the expert's discretion.

The shift of attention from structure to process stems from symbolic interactionism: individual interests and attitudes are principally shaped by interpersonal interaction in primary groups; shared interests or groups are created and maintained in the same fashion; "publics" and the political system also depend on these basic processes. Here again, Dewey can be understood to argue that secondary and political groupings simply reflect a balance of common and complementary over competing interests to which economic analysis would be most appropriate; but in the main he is concerned with the processes of interaction by which interests are altered and adjusted and these are primarily social-psychological in nature. A crucial consideration is that of constant change in interests. Formal institutions admittedly reflect more enduring interests or purposes; but they need not be represented as abstract or ultimate "ends," and are more realistically regarded as subject to redefinition and revaluation as a result of new transactions and interactions.[43] For political science, the most important result of the emphasis on "process" has probably been to encourage reliance on social psychological and small group models for characterizing key points in "representation."

From all this it would seem to follow that, for Dewey and pragmatism, formal, arm's length institutions of representation will not be favored. It does appear that *any* government is in some degree a "representative" institution:

A public, articulated and acting through representative officers is the state; there is no state without a government, but there is also none without a public. . . . By our hypothesis all governments are representative in that they purport to stand for the interests which a public has in the behavior of individuals and groups. . . . Rarely can a person sink himself in his political function; the best which most men attain to is the domination by the public weal of their other desires. What is meant by 'representative' government is that the public is definitely organized with the intent to secure this dominance. The dual capacity of every officer of the public leads to conflict in individuals between their genuinely political aims and acts and those which they possess in their non-political roles. When the public adopts special measures to see to it that the conflict is minimized and that the representative function overrides the private one, political institutions are termed representative.[44]

Both aspects of "representation" are here—the identification of interests, and the definition of "responsibility"—but the emphasis is on the "public interest" rather than the "responsibility" aspect. The "representative function" is to relieve or forestall externalities; the role of the representative for Dewey today would seem to be to signal the affectation of some by the activities of others, probably to reflect intensities of interest, and to effect satisfactory adjustments of interest. For the pragmatist, *the* political problem consists in the conflict of interests; the solution is twofold: "expertise," and creation of a "public" or "community" through improvement of communication and understanding. No *standards* for decision—either substantive or procedural—are proposed.

In construing interests as changeable and profoundly affected by social organization pragmatism has tended to press political analysis back to psychology and sociology and to discount political forms and their finality as norms. The tradition thus has little to say about procedure and "responsibility" because it mistrusts categorization and institutionalization of adjective or procedural values. On the instrumentalist view the values relevant to a particular problem are only developed, ordered, and clarified in the process of decision. Thus, the test of policy is necessarily more procedural than substantive, indirect rather than direct: maximize access, communication, participation so that individual choice is frequent, informed, influential, and broadly affected by the choices of others. Like instrumentalism in ethics, this tradition tends to view policy problems in specific social contexts over the short run, arguing that, under the foregoing conditions, free experiment will produce "appropriate" (for "correct) solutions. For the decision maker the implication is: consult; look to intensities and breadth of affectation; let the process and the private parties carry most of the weight of decision.

## V

Two traditions remain to be described; but the descriptions will be brief. One tradition will be termed the participatory; I have in mind theorists who emphasize the importance for democratic government of individual participation in groups and localities to the near exclusion of any attempt to represent a public at large. As a doctrine about *what* is to be represented this tradition sometimes reduces to pluralism, syndicalism, or a functionalist or producers' ethic, as it has in Europe. More often in America it has been a doctrine about the *how* of representation, asserting that compatible interests are only created through participation and interaction, and that arm's length representation and formalistic political processes frustrate integration and the continuing revaluation of interests by freezing certain interests in institutions. "The evaluation of interests involves the psychological development of an interacting people." [45]

Probably Mary Parker Follett is the foremost American exponent of this point of view and the most thoroughgoing.[46] In Follett the revolt against formalism is far more thoroughgoing than in Dewey; the fact-value distinction is expressly discarded, and publics are to be built up entirely out of face-to-face interactions rather than by the apparatus and officials of the "state." Consensus on the intellectual level is specious, arrived at "by virtue of the prestige of verbal argument which arrests the activity of your mind . . . the only real consensus is that which arises on the motor level." [47] The same considerations apply to consent as to consensus:

The theory of consent rests on the wholly intellectualistic fallacy that thought and action can be separated . . . that we think with our 'minds' and we don't. . . . Thus the fullest freedom in passing on policies is not self-government, because the participation has to take place further back, in the activity from which the policies emerge. . . . We cannot really carry out the will of another, for we can only use our own behavior patterns. . . . The 'will of the people' then is found exactly where our own will is found, in our concrete existence.[48]

Party as an agent and geographical constituencies as subjects of "representation" are out; they lead to "domination" or "compromise," but not to "integration." No parametric ends or interests are to be imputed to individuals or embodied in institutional forms; interests are at once created and expressed in interpersonal interaction, and abstract statements of ends and interests are either misleading of self-serving or both. There is no utilitarianism at all in Mary Parker Follett, but there is a strong affinity for idealism.[49]

Follett's is the most systematic and celebrated statement of the participatory approach; in her writing it is extended to the overall organization of "the state," whereas in other expressions it is usually limited to particular programs or aspects of government. In any case, the intent of this tradition is to minimize "representation" in the sense of the reflection of pre-existing interests and to maximize participation in processes by which interests are to be simultaneously created and expressed. The general result of this approach would be thoroughgoing decentralization of decision making to those immediately concerned; the question of how to deal with the third party effects of these decisions is postponed or ignored.

## VI

Finally, the populist tradition on representation may be briefly described. Readers are referred to Dahl's *Preface to Democratic Theory* for a rigorous and critical exposition.[50] For present purposes, its principal elements are its emphasis upon political equality and majority rule, and its insistence on direct translation of majority preferences into public policy. These two elements tend to reduce "representation" to a negligible role—as close to strict "agency" as possible. Values of procedure and style in governmental action are minimized; so is protection of any substantive or distributive values against majority action. Intensities, as Dahl points out, are not to count. The political process should be reduced, so far as practicable, to a series of electoral mandates; and it is to be hoped that politics and government can be so organized that the mandate will be clear and categorical. Neither political leadership nor responsiveness are especially valued, since both involve some discretion on the part of the "representative." If the participatory tradition is said to seek to minimize pre-existing interests and to emphasize interaction, the populist tradition may be said to do the opposite: it emphasizes the "given" interests of individuals and seeks to minimize aggregative processes. It has often been pointed out that this is an unrealistic position on at least two grounds: that some kind of political process and some alteration of interests is necessary in order to create majorities in a modern, pluralistic society; and that, in such a society, most people will not be willing to trust the concrete interests they indulge with high intensity to the disposition of majorities—people at large are not consistently majoritarians.

Indeed, there seems to be more of disembodied ideal and less of accurate description in the populist and participatory traditions than in any of the other views outlined above. As the populist tradition ignores the stubborn facts of pluralism, intensities, and the effects of interaction revealed by all our empirical work, so the participatory view seems unduly to discount the "externalities" of interaction and the demand for a modicum of foresight, integration, and protection of certain substantive interests by formal, procedural surrogates that makes at least the fiction of an overall "public" and a "sovereign" meaningful in a pluralistic society.

The populist and participatory traditions have something else in common which, I think, can best be described as an insistence on the "popularness" of political decisions, or what Ranney and Kendall have called "popular consultation." Often, when the strict majoritarian principles of populism or the functional premises of the participatory school are relaxed, the two traditions tend to converge. Both then emphasize governmental responsiveness to publics, or they emphasize leadership in behalf of a putative common public or "people." Then problems of "representation" reappear; but then our other traditions are also involved, and populism and participation are merely emphases.

## VII

What has so far been said seems to me to lead to several suggestions about "representation" and the broader relevance of the several traditions to inquiry.

1. The meaning of "representation" is not clear; otherwise the problems surrounding it would *probably* not receive such different treatment in the six traditions just discussed. I argued above that problems that are often discussed in terms of "rationality," "responsibility" and the "public interest" substantially overlap with those of "representation," and representation was there left undefined. If the term has a distinct meaning the core of it must be, as is often pointed out, in the literal sense of "present again"; but there are issues concealed in this. One issue is *what* is represented—whether abstract and ideal values referred to the community, ends presumptively common to all (or most) individuals, personal characteristics and tastes in infinite detail, or concrete wants and material interests. Closely related to what is represented is the question of *how,* in which a basic ambiguity is involved. Two kinds of processes figure in it: on the one hand those suggested by "identification" or "responsiveness"; on the other those intended by "control" or "accountability." In either case the representative relation may involve reflection of interests or characteristics in great detail or with broad discretion; but in one the interests are not thought of as concrete or clearly definable and in the other case they are; in one the relation is thought of as primarily psychological (intellectual or emotional) and in the other as physically sanctioned, ultimately. We often speak of the processes involved as informal or formal. Finally, with respect to either method of representation, there is the question of degree of discretion of the representative which, as Banfield has pointed out, also depends on what is represented.

Two aspects of what has been said require brief comment. One is that formal, electoral accountability may be employed to encourage closer "identification"; but it might also be argued that emphasis on electoral accountability discourages "genuine" identification. Second, one *might* feel more or better represented as a result of enlarged official discretion; this might be so (as idealists have argued) when concrete interests conflict but discretion allows officials to emphasize more abstract aspirations referred to the community; or where (as rationalists have argued) short-run claims can be resisted by officials until there has been time for deliberation and reflection.

Probably the basic ambiguity in the term itself has to do with the *how* of representation: in one view the method is virtual (resting on identification or responsiveness); in the other it is actual (entailed by physical control or formal accountability). Both are operative, necessarily in democratic political systems, and give rise to contrasting understandings of "representation." There is, however, a difficulty beside that of ambiguity, viz., that the detailed *reflection* of interests in policy is impossible when interests conflict. Thus the root notion of representation ignores the problem of aggregating interests, and the basic processes and relations of democratic government certainly cannot be characterized as, literally, matters of "representation." What *can* safely be said is that people are often concerned about the "representativeness" of 'governments and officials; that this (ambiguous) value figures in popular appraisal and thus the legitimacy and effectiveness of institutions; but the nature of this concern can't be pressed beyond the literal meaning of "represent."[51] It probably depends in part upon circumstances, including *what* is sought to be represented.

2. The issue between "representative government" and "popular government" seems to be largely a false issue today; surely Bentley and subsequent group theorists have been right in pointing out that democratic government is a congeries of controls, and representation, as Garceau has said, a continuum of interactions and decisions.[52] Probably the most important problems of representation today arise within groups rather than government and involve the adequate definition of "group interests" and control of discretion where there is little political competition and few standards for official conduct.

3. Two of the traditions outlined above are *primarily* concerned with "representation" in the root meanings just discussed. These are the participatory and populist traditions: the first strongly influenced by idealism (in the version treated here) and the second by utilitarianism in the ways in which they deal with the characteristic problems of the representative relation.[53] Both traditions tend to assimilate problems of aggregation to those of representation, or to discount or obscure the difficulties involved in aggregating interests. They thus appear to be the least realistic of the six traditions so far as the full range of democratic political problems is concerned; it was briefly argued above that they contribute less to explanation or understanding than the other traditions, although they express influential normative ideas or ideologies.

4. The question what is meant by the term "representation" seems of much less importance, given its ambiguity, than the question how it figures in one's approach to broader normative problems of politics. That is really the point of this survey. The first four traditions dealt with. seem to me to be important types of political theory and, provisionally, to be the viewpoints of most general application to government and policy, though I mean this only for American politics. I say "types of political theory," since they are not straight applications of ethical theories to political decisions but involve different "models" of democratic government and political processes.

One difference has to do with *what* is represented or embodied in policy. It is possible to distinguish between "values" on the one hand and "preferences" or "interests" on the other. In general, the idealist and rationalist traditions regard this distinction as important and argue that it is legitimate to postulate broad agreement on "values" of rather high abstraction as standards for appraising governmental policy and performance. The utilitarian tradition has emphasized preferences or interests; and the pragmatic tradition stresses the contingent and contextual nature of values which are thus discounted relative to immediate and tangible interests.

Another difference relates to the *how* of representation. Democratic politics can be conceived of as the identification and discrimination of interests, the communication of interests, the measurement of interests, the creation of generation of interests, the direct reflection of interests. One may also find room for the critical evaluation, enlightenment or enlargement of preferences or interests. Surely all these figure in politics; and they receive differing emphases in our "traditions." Some traditions are more relevant to some policies or political problems than to others. Their relevance seems likely to depend on such considerations as: whether discrete, concrete, or individual interests are clearly identifiable; the importance of intensities and of externalities; on whether enduring community ethical values are at stake, and how directly; whether ends are defined with sufficient clarity and agreement to permit a means-ends approach to policy; the opportunity for political favoritism; the availability of understood or expected procedures; the extent to which a traditional "right" is at issue; the threat to public "authority" from either dissensus or ineffective action; whether leadership seems essential if anything is to happen and the seeming importance to society of action; the importance of science, technology, or technique; whether affected interests can effectively compete for access or recognition; whether symbolic or "style" components of politics seem to be of popular importance; the risk of perversion of widely accepted ends to private purposes in the absence of safeguards; whether an "emergent" policy area is involved where wants are evident but inchoate—and so on.

5. While the traditions, as here defined, are primarily normative, they also offer contrasting descriptions of politics. Louis Hartz has written that the "images" of democracy have never squared well with reality; that, by a sort of dialectic, democratic traditions tend to deny what is right under their noses.[54] The traditions dealt with here are all "ideal" or at least hyperbolic statements about important relationships in democratic government, and are often attempts to correct or correct for unwanted or unwonted aspects of modern politics. These seem nonetheless to be some affinities between these traditions and some of our modern types of empirical inquiry about politics, which can be briefly suggested in conclusion. The point is not that normative and positive questions can't be distinguished—but only that certain normative concerns may predispose one to certain empirical approaches; and that a given empirical approach may yield research of more significance for some normative concerns than for others.

One positive approach to inquiry is cast in terms of simple "exchange" on the model of economic (price) theory, with no assumptions about the desiderata or counters of politics—except that the model works best where these are relatively concrete and discrete. Another prominent approach emphasizes "influence" in which sanctions—threats and deprivations—figure importantly. Both these models seem to have close relations to the utilitarian tradition. Another is the "group" approach, in which social psychological models and mechanisms of interpersonal interaction and "identification" are often basic, and which has close affinities with the pragmatic tradition. A final approach can simply be termed "institutional," though the term covers a lot of ground. Here inquiry is concerned to account not only for particular policy outcomes, or for characteristic outcomes, but for overall change or stability in the political system itself. Functional analysis is often part of this approach. In any event, in relating values to institutions it has to recognize official discretion, to describe the traditions that confine it and explain it, or which confirm or explain "authority." This general approach seems more closely connected with idealism and rationalism than with the other normative traditions, in that it finds more room for the factors and phenomena emphasized in those traditions.

A good deal of our empirical political science has come to emphasize the "influence" and "group" models either explicitly or implicitly. They are closely related to one another and to the economic model; exchange, threat, or identification (mutuality of interest) may figure as the fundamental processes in either.[55]

Generally, however, these approaches would seem to have most to say about the concerns of utilitarianism and pragmatism; while approaches emphasizing norms and institutions throw more light on idealist and formalist interests.

The main point of this paper was to identify some important intellectual traditions; these necessarily brief and general suggestions about their relevance for policy and empirical research may, however, be worth further development in democratic theory. As to policy, most of the "traditions," and especially the first four, apply to problems of government other than representation and indicate that different institutional arrangements may be appropriate to different spheres of action or decision. As to research: since "representation," despite its important role in democratic philosophies and practices, is unlikely ever to meet with common understanding as a concept, the empirical study of representative processes seems likely to be affected by commitments to these traditions; and their critical examination should therefore help to clarify research.

## NOTES

1. On "calculation" and "control," see R. Dahl and C. E. Lindblom, *Politics, Economics, and Welfare* (New York, 1953).

2. Talcott Parsons, *The Social System* (Glencoe, Ill., 1951), p. 400 ff.

3. Harold F. Gosnell, *Democracy: The Threshold of Freedom* (New York, 1948), ch. 8.

4. *Cf.* the discussions in A. L. Lowell, *Public Opinion and Popular Government* (New York, 1914), ch. 9; and H. Eulau, *et al.*, "The Role of the Representative . . .," *American Political Science Review*, Vol. 53 (1959), p. 742.

5. *Cf.* Norton E. Long, "Public Policy and Administration: The Goals of Rationality and Responsibility," *Public Administration Review*, Vol. 14 (1954), p. 22; C. E. Lindblom, "The Science of Muddling Through," *Ibid*, Vol. 19 (1959), pp. 79–88, and "Policy Analysis," *American Economic Review*, Vol. 48 (1958), p. 298–312; Jas. March and Herbert Simon, *Organizations* (New York, 1958), ch. 6.

6. J. R. Pennock, "Responsiveness, Responsibility, and Majority Rule," *American Political Science Review*, Vol. 46 (1952), pp. 790–807.

7. See Anthony Downs, *An Economic Theory of Democracy* (New York, 1957); and Kenneth Arrow, *Social Choice and Individual Values* (New York, 1951).

8. Thus, there will be some affinities with such discussions of these concerns as Alfred de Grazia, *Public and Republic* (New York, 1951); M. Meyerson and E. Banfield, *Politics, Planning, and the Public Interest* (Glencoe, Ill., 1954); Appendix by Banfield; Glendon Schubert, *The Public Interest* (Glencoe, Ill., 1959); and C. J. Friedrich (ed.), *Responsibility* (Cambridge, Mass., 1960); and it will be convenient to refer to these.

9. The distinction seems due to McTaggert; see C. D. Broad, *Five Types of Ethical Theory* (New York and London, 1930), p. 249 ff.

10. *The Functions of the Executive* (Cambridge, Mass., 1938).

11. *The Public Interest, op. cit.*

12. *Obligation and the Body Politic* (New York, 1960).

13. *Cf.* A. V. Dicey, *Law and Opinion in England in the Nineteenth Century* (London, 1905), on the "collectivist" trend in British thought; Samuel Beer, "The Representation of Interests in British Government: Historical Background," *American Political Science Review*, Vol. 51 (1957), pp. 613–650, esp. 635 ff. on the "Radical" model of representation; and Joseph Hamburger, "James Mill on Uni-

versal Suffrage and the Middle Class," *Journal of Politics,* Vol. 24 (1962), pp. 167–190, esp. 187 on the "populist" outcome of philosophical radicalism.

14. This brand of utilitarianism has probably been of some importance in the public administration movement in the U. S.—*cf.* the doctrine on authorities and special districts, on hierarchy and executive accountability, and on consolidation and enlargement of governmental units.

15. *E.g.* F. von Mises, *Bureaucracy* (New Haven, 1944); F. von Hayek, *Individualism and Economic Order* (Chicago, 1948); H. Simons, *Economic Policy for a Free Society* (Chicago, 1948); Frank Knight, *The Ethics of Competition* (New York, 1936); *Freedom and Reform* (New York, 1947); *Intelligence and Democratic Action* (Cambridge, Mass., 1960).

16. "Human nature is also averse to the mental effort of critically considering the possibilities and costs of change, especially the labor of appraising alternatives and reaching intelligent agreement on what is desirable. There is an almost instinctive appeal to force, including persuasion, one of its most insidious and dangerous forms." *Intelligence and Democratic Action,* p. 34.

17. "The mystery is not that representative institutions were discredited but that any other result could have been expected. The agency relation presents a problem for which there is no mechanical or intellectual solution, while direct democracy, on any considerable scale and with positive functions, is out of the question. . . . To substitute competitive politics for competitive business is to jump out of the frying pan into the fire. No possible 'machinery' will preserve responsibility without actual crowd rule, or will give political guidance . . . in the absence of moral leadership accepted as such by the masses." *Freedom and Reform,* pp. 29–31; and *cf. Intelligence and Democratic Action, pp.* 127–28.

18. *Cf.* the quotation above. "It follows that the ultimate task of *society as a whole,* as of government . . . is to create such individuals in such a total culture situation, that agreement on right ideals will be possible, and will be achieved by non-political processes." *Freedom and Reform,* p. 204.

19. *Ibid.* ch. 12 esp. pp. 355–56. *Cf.* von Mises, *Bureaucracy, op. cit.*

20. *Intelligence and Democratic Action,* pp. 124–25.

21. *Handbook of Political Fallacies,* ed. Harold A. Larrabee (Baltimore, the Johns Hopkins Press, 1952), p. 184.

22. *Cf.* Banfield, *op. cit.*

23. The most germane philosophical tradition seems to me to be the Lockean one described by Louis Hartz, *The Liberal Tradition in America* (New York, 1955). No single term occurs to me that does justice to what is described below: "liberalism" and "constitutionalism" are a good deal too broad and "proceduralism" somewhat too narrow. Since Schubert's writing on the "public interest" was referred to above I should point out that I don't use the word "rationalism" as he does; and this discussion should not be equated with his.

24. Morton White, *Social Thought in America: The Revolt Against Formalism* (Beacon Press Edition: Boston, 1957).

25. Banfield, *op. cit.* and *cf.* R. Brandt, *Ethical Theory* (New York, 1959), ch. 15, on "extended rule utilitarianism." Since the ends in these appropriate classes are often imputed to every one, or denominated "ends of the state," the line between rationalism and idealism is often a thin one in theory as well as in practice. Woodrow Wilson's discussion of the representative role of the American president was cited above as an illustration of idealism; yet Wilson as political scientist seems to belong to the formalist tradition, as will be argued below.

26. The five "ends" listed are those of Charles E. Merriam, *Systematic Politics* (Chicago, 1945), esp. ch. 2.

27. An important way, but not necessarily *the* way. The rationalist tradition may not be at odds with, say, "behaviorism"; *cf.* Merriam's writing.

28. *Cf.* the doctrine of "public purpose" in our public law and in the period of "revival of natural law theories," the "public" ends of the police power and the doctrine of "business affected with a public interest."

29. It is interesting that the tradition has been less dominant in English political thought, where both idealism and utilitarianism have been stronger.

30. Woodrow Wilson, *Constitutional Government in the United States* (New York, 1908); A. Lawrence Lowell, *Public Opinion and Popular Government* (New York, 1914); and Frank Goodnow, *Politics and Administration* (New York, 1900).

31. See esp. *Systematic Politics, op. cit.; On the Agenda of Democracy* (Cambridge, Mass., 1941); *Public and Private Government* (New Haven, 1944); and *The Role of Politics and Social Change* (New York, 1936).

32. *Constitutional Government,* p. 4.

33. *Ibid,* p. 14.

34. By "symbolic interactionism" I mean the common emphasis on socialization and communication in the work of, *e.g.,* James, Dewey, Mead and Cooley in the disciplines mentioned above. *Cf.* Fay Karpf, *American Social Psychology* (New York, 1932) for a summary discussion relating these developments.

35. New York, 1927. While the influence of this book is necessarily problematical, judging from internal evidence as well as from citation it was of enormous influence on political scientists trained in the 1930s and thus on the "group approach" to politics. Bentley's *Process,* of course, was published long before and is, indeed, a very different kind of book, despite some philosophical affinities between the two authors. I think it is arguable that Dewey's work has been the more influential in political science; but I do not know just how to argue the point here.

36. *Cf. German Philosophy and Politics* (New York, 1915); *Creative Intelligence* (New York, 1917); Morton White, *The Origins of Dewey's Instrumentalism* (New York, 1943); and White's discussion in *Social Thought in America, op. cit.*

37. "Conjoint . . . action is a universal trait. . . . Such action has results. Some of the results are taken account of. Then there arise purposes, plans, measures and means to secure consequences which are liked and eliminate those which are found obnoxious. Thus perception generates a common interest. . . . Consequences have to be taken care of, looked out for. This supervision and regulation cannot be effected by the primary groupings themselves. . . . Only the exigences of a preconceived theory would confuse the state with that texture of friendships and attachments which is the chief bond in any community, or would insist that the former depends upon the latter for existence." *The Public and Its Problems,* pp. 26; 27; 34–35.

38. "The underlying and generative conditions of concrete behavior are social as well as organic: much more social than organic as far as the *differential* wants, purposes, and methods of operation are concerned. . . . The desires, aims and standards of satisfaction which the dogma of 'natural' economic processes and laws assumes are themselves socially conditioned phenomena." *Ibid,* 103–4.

39. See esp. *ibid,* 19–27; 39–47.

40. *Ibid,* ch. 5; and esp. pp. 141–59.

41. *Cf. Human Nature and Conduct* (New York, 1922: Modern Library Ed.). p. 62 ff., and the closing chapter.

42. *The Public and Its Problems,* esp. p. 146. Dewey relied heavily on the type of community-society distinction stressed by Tönnies and Weber.

43. "The very fact that the public depends upon consequences of acts and perception of consequences, while its organization into a state depends upon the ability to invent and employ special instrumentalities, shows how and why publics and political institutions differ widely from epoch to epoch and place to place. To sup-

pose that an *a priori* conception of the intrinsic nature and limits of the individual on one side and the state on the other will yield good results once for all is absurd." *The Public and Its Problems,* p. 65. *Cf. Reconstruction in Philosophy* (New York, 1920); Beacon Press Ed., Boston, 1948), p. xiii.

44. *The Public and Its Problems,* p. 76.

45. Mary Parker Follett, *Creative Experience* (New York, 1924), p. 35.

46. See *The New State* (New York, 1918), *Creative Experience* (New York, 1924), and *Dynamic Administration* (eds., Metcalf and Urwick, New York, 1942). *Cf.* Henry S. Kariel, "The New Order of Mary Parker Follett," *Western Political Quarterly,* Vol. 8 (1955), pp. 425–40.

47. *Creative Experience,* p. 198.

48. *Ibid,* pp. 198–99.

49. This is recognized in Bosanquet's *Philosophical Theory of the State* (London, 4th ed. 1953), Introduction and Preface to the Third Edition.

50. Chicago, 1956.

51. The term "representative government" doesn't help us in construing "representation." Representative government sometimes simply refers to government by officials chosen in generally competitive elections; but it frequently further implies distance and discretion for representatives and is contrasted to "popular" government. On this interpretation, to be concerned for the "representativeness" of government is not necessarily equivalent to concern for "representative government."

52. Garceau, "Research in the Political Process," *American Political Science Review,* Vol. 45 (1951), p. 69. Bentley's summary discussion of this point is in *The Process of Government,* pp. 455–56.

53. There is considerable overlap here: some versions of populism appear to stem from the rationalist or even idealist tradition, simply placing greater stress on political *equality;* and the participatory tradition has, in some thinkers, close affinities with pragmatism.

54. Louis Hartz, "Democracy: Image and Reality," in W. N. Chamber and R. H. Salisbury (eds.), *Democracy in the Mid-twentieth Century: Problems and Prospects* (St. Louis, 1960).

55. *Cf.* George C. Homans, *Social Life: Its Elementary Forms* (Boston, 1961).

# 2. The Senate and American Federalism *

## WILLIAM H. RIKER

At Philadelphia in 1787 the authors of the Constitution invented a new kind of federalism. In previous federal governments, the participating states were no more intimate than permanent allies, and citizens retained a primary loyalty to local governments. The federalism of 1787 achieved a converse effect, however, for it subordinated the member governments and created a nation. Likewise, while the earlier federalisms were notoriously prone to muddles in policy and stalemates in action, the American form turned out to give reasonably effective government, even in the short run. For both its nationalism and its effectiveness, therefore, it found favor with constitution makers elsewhere: in the larger Latin American states, in most of the new nations of the British Commonwealth, in the Germany of Weimar and Bonn, even, on paper at least, in the Soviet Union and Yugoslavia. Probably the clearest demonstration of the prestige and utility of the American invention was the revision (in 1848) of the Swiss Confederation into a federalism patterned after the United States. The cantons thereby abandoned the one remaining survivor of the alliance type of federalism, represented in the middle ages by the Swabian, Rhenish, and Lombard leagues, as well as by the Swiss. And so it happens that about half the earth is presently ruled by federal governments—all of them reminiscent in one way or another of the Philadelphia invention.

What was the secret of this new federalism? Why was it so effective, so nationalizing that half the world has seen fit to borrow it? If the inventors themselves had understood exactly what they had invented, we could hope to answer these questions more easily. Unfortunately, however, the inventors were not quite certain what they had done and their confusion has been transmitted to scholars and jurists even in our generation. Many of the delegates were, of course, fully conscious that they had created a new political form. In the thirty-ninth *Federalist,* for example, Madison demonstrated that in the proposed Constitution the alliance type of federalism was systematically infused with devices borrowed from unitary governments. What resulted from this infusion was, he observed, something unique, so unique indeed that he had no word to name it. But although he and other delegates were proud of their invention, they could not state with adequate generality how their federalism improved on others. Even Hamilton, whose utterances usually displayed the systematic coherence of the doctrinaire, left diverse rationales unreconciled. In the fifteenth *Federalist* paper, for example, he implied that the essential merit of the new Constitution was its provision that the central government should

* From *The American Political Science Review,* Vol. 49 (1955), pp. 452–69. Reprinted by permission.

rule persons as well as states. In the seventieth *Federalist* paper, on the other hand, he suggested that the essential merit was a single executive, as against the collegiate form hitherto usually characteristic of federations.

Looking at the Philadelphia invention with the historian's advantage of hindsight, it is now possible to perceive the advantageous feature of the new federalism. After 165 years, it is clear that the Constitution was effective and successful because, in contrast to all previous federalisms, it made the central government formally independent of the states, leaving the states no effective constitutional means to control national decisions. By this standard we can distinguish two major types of federalism: one in which federal decisions are made exclusively through the machinery of the central government (this type we can describe as centrally-directed or centralized), and the other in which federal decisions are made, partially at least, through the machinery of local governments (this type we can describe as peripherally-directed or peripheralized). Centralized federalisms are, it turns out, just about as capable of effective action as most unitary governments and certainly as capable of creating a citizen loyalty. But in peripheralized federalisms, like the old Swiss Confederation or contemporary international organizations, where local governments by constitutional right take part in central decisions, direct the voting of their delegates to the center, form suballiances to control its policy, confirm federal decisions, and influence federal policy as much as does the federal government itself, there these local governments usually retain the primary loyalty of the citizen.

To say that the federalism of 1787 was centralized subsumes the statement of the fifteenth *Federalist* paper that the national government was to rule persons as well as states; one of the reasons the state governments could not, under the new form of federalism, control the federal government was that the states did not control the relation of citizens to the nation. Some peripheralized federalisms have permitted the federal government occasional direct contact with citizens (e.g., in military affairs and, rarely, in judicial affairs); but the American federalism allowed the central government to do almost all its business directly with persons—its taxing, its recruiting, its policing, its judging, etc. Hence the state governments were deprived of that middleman position which in peripheralized federalisms permits them to control the policy of the center. Similarly, to say the federalism of 1787 was centralized subsumes also the assertion of the seventieth *Federalist* paper concerning a single executive, for the collegiate executive in peripheralized federalisms has always been one major device by which the federated governments have controlled the federal.

In a variety of other ways, too, the new Constitution centralized federalism. For example, by the provision (Article I, Section 10) that "No State shall, without the consent of Congress, . . . enter into any agreement or compact with another State . . . ," it isolated state governments from each other. Thereby it forestalled formal factions among states, one of the most frequent occasions in earlier federalisms for devolution of authority to local governments. (Such factions were, incidentally, the characteristic defect of the Swiss Confederation.) Again, by the provision (also Article I, Section 10) that "No State shall enter into any treaty, alliance, or confederation . . . ," it forestalled formal intrigue with foreigners, intrigue which might force the whole federation into an undesired position. (Incidentally also, such intrigues were the characteristic defect of the Dutch Republic.) Both these provisions were copied, almost verbatim, from the Articles of

Confederation (Article VI), but in a centralized federalism they had a special force. They did not, it is true, prevent the Civil War, which involved a formal faction of states, or the Hartford Convention, which contained the threat of intrigue with foreigners; but they did enable the United States to surmount those difficulties in a way that centralized its federalism even more.

Altogether, therefore, the Constitution provided for a national government largely independent of the federated governments. It contemplated, of course, that the people of the states would control the national government. But it contemplated also that the control would be direct, not through the agency of state governments. Naturally, it did not forestall sectionalism; no constitution, federal or unitary, could do that. But it did arrange things in such a way that state officials had to use the political party, not state governments, to make their influence felt in Washington. Thus, although the constitutional system was undeniably federal, although the state governments continued to pretend to a vague sort of "sovereignty," still it was federalism with a difference: state governments, as state governments, could not hope to control national policy.

While we, with our longer experience and larger vocabulary, can thus identify the achievement of 1787 as a centralization rather than a peripheralization of federalism, the authors of the Constitution themselves were not aware that they had really shut off all circuits for states to direct the nation. Indeed, they thought that the Senate, at least, retained the peripheralized character of the Articles of Confederation. With two members from each state, members chosen indeed, by state governments, it embodied half of the so-called Great Compromise. It was the most important national institution so constructed,[1] and the founding fathers evidently believed that it was sufficient to maintain the principle. The delegates from the small states signed the Constitution as eagerly as did the delegates from the large and then went home to urge its adoption. Hamilton, much as he yearned for a unitary state, reconciled himself to the form of the Senate and rationalized it concisely and drearily in these words:

. . . the equal vote allowed to each State is at once a constitutional recognition of the portion of sovereignty remaining in the individual States, and an instrument for preserving that residual sovereignty.[2]

The Senate did not, however, have quite the anticipated effect. Except for the few occasions when sectionalism has been organized by state governments, the Senate has not been a peripheralizing institution. This failure of the Senate to represent state governments is a crucial constitutional development, for thus was achieved the centralizing purpose of the Convention of 1787 in spite of the miscalculation of the delegates. Indeed, this failure of the Senate is of equal and similar significance to the failure of dissident factions to carry through such states' rights programs as the Virginia and Kentucky Resolves, the Hartford Convention, or the Civil War—any one of which, if successful, might have peripheralized or entirely destroyed American federalism. But, although constitutional practice so significantly diverges here from constitutional form, the divergence has never been systematically examined. And so this paper is devoted to an examination of the development of the role of the Senate from the representation of state governments, which was the role initially intended, to the representation of the people of the states, which was the role finally played.

This change of role has two chronological phases. The earlier phase—and for that reason probably the more important—is the gradual failure of state legislatures to enforce their instructions to senators. The second phase is the gradual transfer of the power to elect senators from legislatures to the people, a transfer that starts with the public canvass and culminates in the Seventeenth Amendment. By the completion of these two changes, the Senate was divorced wholly from state governments and could not possibly have the effect that the founding fathers expected.

*I*

The Senate seemed in 1787 to be a peripheralizing institution because it was to be elected by state legislatures. Election by state legislatures implied accountability to them. And if that accountability had in fact come to exist, then the governments at Boston and Albany, Philadelphia and Trenton, Richmond and Charleston might very easily have forced the national government to refer its problems to them. State legislatures and the parties that preferred them to the national legislature did indeed try to enforce accountability by means of the doctrine of instructions. Hence that doctrine was, next to the method of election itself, the main avenue through which state legislatures pushed themselves into national affairs.

The idea that senators ought always to obey their immediate constituents is now almost forgotten. Only scholars still know that it was ever acted upon and few of them have studied the action systematically enough to recognize its significance.[3] State legislatures did indeed continue until 1913 to instruct their senators according to the traditional formula ("Be it resolved that our Senators in Congress are hereby instructed, and our Representatives are requested, to vote for . . ."). But by 1860 few senators felt bound by instructions; and, under the Republican centralism thereafter, they regarded them as mere expressions of opinion. Hence by long disregard the doctrine of instructions passed into obscurity, and in so passing freed the national government from the peripheralizing influence of the Senate.

The doctrine of instructions followed naturally from political institutions prior to the Constitution. Town meetings in colonial New England regularly instructed state representatives and continued to do so until the disappearance of the Federalist party in New England.[4] Elsewhere, voters ocassionally instructed by petition; and as late as 1835 Thomas Ritchie, one of the great Jacksonian editors, attempted to revive the practice in Virginia.[5] Delegates to the Continental Congress were often instructed; and since the Articles of Confederation (Article V) explicitly provided for the recall of delegates at any time, the instructions were easily enforced.

We have no clear indication as to the attitude of the delegates at the Constitutional Convention toward the practice of instructing, for the subject is not mentioned in any of the records. On the one hand, many delegates seemed to expect that the Senate would resist the democratic folly of more popular bodies; and this expectation implies that they did not anticipate that the popular bodies would regularly instruct and thus control the Senate. On the other hand, nearly all of them anticipated that the Senate would protect state rights; and it is hard to visualize any practical system of protection that did not include the doctrine of instructions. Regardless of the attitude of the founding fathers, however, state legislatures, accustomed to both giving and receiving instructions, continued to instruct senators after 1789.

But from then on instructions were less effective—and that is the reason why the Senate did not peripheralize American federalism. State legislatures lost the sanction of recall and the first Congress definitely approved the loss. The House refused by a large majority to add "the right to instruct" to the First Amendment, apparently because it seemed too "democratic" for the representative system and smacked too much of the localism of the Articles.[6] Similarly, when senators of the first Congress had occasion to discuss some of their many instructions, several Federalists argued that instructions "amounted to no more than a wish" and that legislatures were "only the machines to choose" senators, possessing no more right to instruct them "than the electors had . . . to instruct the President." On the other hand, William McClay, a proto-Republican, who had already tried to control the vote of his fellow Senator from Pennsylvania by getting the state legislature to instruct them, argued that responsible representation required obedience to instructions.[7] The Federalists, in the majority, clearly won the debate and thereby not only discouraged instructions then but also aligned themselves and their descendant parties against the principle of instructions forever.

State legislatures and the Jeffersonian Republicans, however, held tenaciously to the doctrine of instructions. The North Carolina legislature, for example, intending to rebuke Samuel Johnston's disobedience, invited him to render an account of the first Congress. He refused to attend and report to them and they refused to re-elect him.[8] With a strong sense of particularism, legislatures continued to expect that senators would obey frequent and detailed instructions. It was altogether appropriate, therefore, that the Kentucky Resolves of 1798, the great pronouncement of Jefferson's party, should take the form of instructions to senators.

Republicans were eager to make the doctrine of instructions work, for they believed that without it "the power of electing would be . . . incomplete, and the Senator, instead of being a servant, would be the uncontrollable sovereign."[9] But instructions were freely violated even then and needed a new sanction to substitute for the sanction of recall, which had so effectively peripheralized the federalism of the Articles of Confederation. So compelling was the need for a substitute that the whole subsequent history of instructions can be written in terms of the search for, the discovery and application of, and the ultimate disillusionment with, a substitute for recall.

In the absence of recall the most obvious sanction was refusal to re-elect, as in the case of Samuel Johnston. But it was weak: new majorities in state legislatures could not threaten a senator who, chosen by the old majority, knew he would not be re-elected anyway, or who, with a longer term than theirs, might hope for re-election and vindication from their successors. So, sporadically and in floundering fashion, Republicans and state legislatures alike searched for a better substitute. When several senators violated instructions in voting "not guilty" on the impeachment of Justice Chase, a constitutional amendment was introduced to rebuke them:

> That the legislature of any State may, whenever the said legislature shall think proper, recall, at any period whatever, any Senator of the United States, who may have been elected by them. . . .[10]

"Whenever. . . at any period whatever"—the redundance testifies to the passion, but the motion was tabled. Several years later the Massachusetts legislature (ironically Federalist) invented a better sanction. John Quincy Adams provided the occasion: though elected as a Federalist, he voted for the Embargo Act, whereupon Timothy Pickering, Adams' colleague and the leading Federalist senator, roused Massachusetts Federalism to win the spring elections in 1808.[11] The new Federalist legislature promptly censured Adams and, adding indignity to the rebuke, elected his successor six months ahead of time. Sensitive to the "accumulated personal malignity borne me . . . by those who rule the State," Adams felt compelled to resign.[12]

This was, so far as I can discover, the first instance of a forced resignation, the only substitute sanction ever used with any success. But it too was not nearly so effective as recall, for it worked only against men with a quick sense of personal honor and, even then, only when there seemed to be mitigating circumstances of party advantage. Explaining to Senator Anderson of Tennessee that he indulged his sense of honor only because Jeffersonians were five-sixths of the Senate, Adams wrote:

> If then I did abandon you, it was from the perfect conviction that you were too strong to need any asistance of mine. For be assured, if the odds had not been so unequivocally decisive, . . . highly as I reverenced the authority of my constituents, and bitter as would have been the cup of resistance to their declared will, I would not have yielded up my trust until the moment when it was taken from my hands. . . .[13]

The next instances of censures and forced resignations, involving David Stone of North Carolina and William Branch Giles of Virginia, occurred at the end of the War of 1812. These resignations signified little in the politics of the period, for neither was submitted until after the people ratified the censures by re-electing Madisonian majorities to the state legislatures.[14] But they counted much for developing the sanction, and Giles especially, publicly disavowing instructions even as he obeyed them, placed the subject in the forefront of party controversy. In the South, where forced resignation was most important, these two cases formed the tradition, thereby aligning conservatives against instructions entirely and setting a precedent on which radical Jacksonians could rely.

In the interim of incoherent issues and disorganized parties between 1815 and 1832 there were, so far as I can discover, no forced resignations. But they occurred often in the 1830's, when politics polarized around such events as Clay's motion of censure for the removal of deposits from the United States Bank, Jackson's extraordinary message in reply, and Benton's motion to expunge the motion of censure. As Jackson pointed out in his reply to the motion of censure, it would have failed if four Whig senators had obeyed instructions to oppose the restoration of deposits.[15] He might have added that it would have failed by one vote more had not Rives of Virginia resigned rather than obey instructions to support restoration. Jackson's emphasis on disobedience, however much he disclaimed any design "to interfere with the responsibility due from members of the Senate to their consciences, their constituents, and their country," was in fact intended to encourage state legislatures to instruct or instruct out of office every doubtful senator.[16] A Whig in Tennessee described the local agitation over Benton's motion thus, and his words concretely reveal the importance of the doctrine of instructions in a time and place of great Jacksonian influence:

> The "expunging resolutions" had been suffered to sleep in quiet in the legislature for the space of near a five-month. Meanwhile . . . no means were left untried to gain friends indoors and without. The people were invoked, and Gen. Jackson's reputation, like Caesar's pierced and bloody mantle, was held up before them. Public meetings were called and private memorials circulated. They sought to seduce the ignorant by misrepresentation, and to allure others by promises and flatteries. Gen. Jackson . . . did not think it out of the way to address himself personally, and by strong appeals, to many members of the legislature, and among them to some who must have been designated by some shrewd friend at Washington (the Speaker of the House [Polk], we suppose here), for they had never had the honor to see or be seen by the President, and were surprised—not flattered off by the distinction.[17]

Although the Democrats failed there, Tyler and Leigh of Virginia and Mangum of North Carolina resigned rather than obey instructions to vote to expunge, and were replaced by Jackson men. Since Benton's resolution passed by a vote of only 24 to 19, the three forced resignations provided the margin of success. This vote has often been derided as a "tinsel victory," but in fact it finished shaping the disciplined Democratic party which Jackson bequeathed to Van Buren and Polk. That instructions and forced resignations were crucial for the shaping testifies to the significant role they played in that era of American politics.[18]

But it testifies also, at the highpoint of instructions, to the inadequacy of their sanction. Although forced resignations, along with other Democratic victories, helped to expunge, they still were only half effective. The New Jersey legislature, for example, having instructed their senators to expunge, then requested them "to resign their seats . . . in case they should not think it proper to vote as above directed." [19] The Democrat of course obediently voted to expunge; the Whig disobeyed and refused to resign; yet two years later he was re-elected by the expanded Whiggery at Trenton. So it seems that resignations were not easily forced when senators sat for six years, state legislators for one or two. Nevertheless, in the South—where the people generally and even some Whig leaders thought that instructions were vital to popular rule—the substitute sanction worked fairly well. Consider what lies back of this advice given by J. H. Pleasants, editor of the Richmond *Whig,* to John Tyler when he and Leigh were instructed to vote for expunging:

> If you obey, dishonorable motives, the love of office . . . will at once be ascribed. A great clamor will be got up. with design to influence the elections in April, and they will be most perniciously influenced by it. If you *disobey,* and retain your seats, I do not hesitate . . . to say, that our hopes of carrying the State, spring and fall, will be annihilated at once. The cry of violated instructions is raised; false issues will again be made, and the true issues merged in them.
>
> You correctly say that, before that cry, false or fair, no man has been able to stand, let his popularity have been what it may. It overthrew us last spring, and will do it the next; . . . if you relinquish your seat, you give us the

argument of obedience . . . always influential. . . . You disarm the enemy and inspirit our friends . . . [with] . . . a sentiment of indignation. . . . Success in Virginia is the first thing to be considered. Success is secured by your resignation—defeat is entailed by your retaining your places. I am very sensible that, by resigning, you countenance dangerous heresies . . . but you are powerless to sustain . . . [our] . . . principles by holding on. You but strengthen the hand of the enemy. . . .[20]

Only in the South, however, did instructions thus influence elections and hence only there was forced resignation really effective.

Jackson's use of instructions was both the high point of their life as a custom and the beginning of their obsolescence. Always fertile in the generation of political devices, always convinced that custom was not a rope that bound him but the raw material for a whip that would fit his hands, Jackson transformed instructions into a device by which he, as a national leader, could control both state and nation. Instructions and forced resignations were too fragile to endure for very long after the transformation. The purpose that had formed them and encouraged their development was thoroughly peripheralizing. When Jackson made them serve a national, centralizing purpose, the political circles that had previously fashioned the theory and practice of instructions lost interest in them. Thus Jackson—who usually stood in theory for localism in government, but who in practice almost always centralized—here, typically, occasioned the decline of the one major instrument for state control of national policy.

Hence, after the flowering of forced resignations in the climate of the expunging resolution, the sanction was less used, perhaps because Jackson's successors lacked his prestige to manipulate state legislatures. Even in retirement, however, Jackson himself still made it work. Outraged by Tennessee's defection to the Whigs in 1836, he schemed to redeem it for the Democracy. He induced Polk to run for governor and after Polk's victory wrote exultingly to Van Buren:

. . . of course Mr. Foster [the Junior Senator] and his gagg law will not any more trouble the United States Senate—Judge White must resign, or he will feel the weight of instructions and a Senator elected over his head—the precedent set by our last Legislature [which instructed Grundy, a Democrat, to vote against the sub-treasury] will justify this procedure. My own opinion is, White will resign—Bell being disappointed in going into the Senate to fill White's vacancy, which was the price of his apostasy, if he is disappointed in getting into the Speaker's chair will resign or *cut his throat* in despair and disappointment; and this catastrophy will end the existence of bluelight federalism in Tennessee.[21]

Bell's throat remained intact, but White and Foster were indeed instructed out, by being required to support the entire Van Buren program.

Still the Jacksonian device of humiliating instructions did not catch on. It was never again successful in Tennessee and was used elsewhere only reluctantly. Thus the North Carolina Whigs, theoretically opposed to instructions, tried to force out Bedford Brown and Robert Strange with a resolution asking them to "represent the wishes of a large majority of the people of this State." [22] Although Brown and

Strange refused to treat this as an instruction, they did resign in 1840 to seek re-endorsement from the people—and did not get it.[23]

This was the last important case of forced resignation. Hence also it began the end of the doctrine of instructions, although some Southern senators did continue to regard even unpalatable instructions as binding. Senator Jarnagin of Tennessee, for example, voted under instructions for the tariff of 1846, but only after great pressure from President Polk himself and several of his emissaries.[24] Polk recorded his worries in his Diary:

> . . . My Private Secretary . . . informed me that the Bill . . . to reduce the tariff .had been [re-] committed to the committee on Finance . . . by a majority of one vote, Mr. Jarnegan [sic] having disregarded his instructions and voted with his Whig friends. Jarnegan holds the fate of the bill in his hands and there [is] no reliance to be placed upon him. He declared on Saturday last in the presence of the Cabinet . . . that he would vote for the Bill, and yet today he voted to embarrass and defeat it.[25]

Still, Jarnagin's reluctant "yes" on final passage carried the bill.

Even this obedience—in letter if not in spirit—could not last if the sanction disappeared; and that is just what happened. There were no clear cases of forced resignations after 1846. In 1849 Thomas Benton, Jackson's aide in organizing forced resignations, received and ignored unpalatable instructions. In the same year Lewis Cass, then the titular chief of the Democracy, was instructed to support the Wilmot Proviso; he not only disobeyed without resigning, but even persuaded the legislature to rescind its resolutions. Not surprisingly, therefore, John Bell of Tennessee remarked in justification of his disobedience on the Kansas question in 1858 that he found even "Democratic Senators obeying or disobeying instructions at their discretion." [26] In 1878, L. Q. C. Lamar of Mississippi disobediently voted against the Bland silver bill. A great outcry was raised about the violation; Jefferson Davis even broke the silence of his retirement to denounce Lamar and defend instructions as a principle of the old Democracy. Lamar stumped his state in 1879 and again in 1881 defending his course and was triumphantly re-elected.[27] Thereafter instructions were obeyed if palatable and unconcernedly ignored if they were not.

Instructions failed, I believe, through lack of a dependable substitute for recall. Forced resignations, the only available sanction, required that elections turn on the issue of obedience and that senators love honor more than office. By mid-century, neither requirement could be met. Voters quite reasonably refused to consider form more than substance; and the Democratic party that asked them to do so had for a time lost those states in which the technique was most popular. By mid-century, also, the Senate's prestige had risen so high that no man could lightly resign from it. From 1792, when Charles Carroll resigned, preferring to sit in the Maryland Senate, even from 1842 when Franklin Pierce resigned an office without a future in a city his wife disliked, the Senate's prestige rose steadily, as the statistics on resignation [28] show: from 1790 to 1819, 89 senators resigned; from 1820 to 1849, 91; from 1850 to 1879, however, only 34, exclusive of the seceders, who were also expelled; from 1880 to 1909, only 23; from 1910 to 1939, only 21. Also, a change had come about in the motives underlying resignations.

The prestige of the Senate had at first been little greater than that of high state office, but this was no longer the case from about 1850: from 1790 to 1849, 48 senators resigned to take state office; from 1850 to 1949, only eight. From 1850 to 1949, 50 out of 90 senators resigning took high office in the national government, while 20 more resigned for ill health or financial reasons. How could instructions be enforced when neither political principles nor personal honor could compel men to resign a valuable property?

Localistic sentiments were extraordinarily strong in the first half of the nineteenth century. Had they had adequate institutions, they might have succeeded in peripheralizing American federalism. It is, therefore, crucial good fortune that no effective sanction for instructions was ever developed. In the absence of a sanction, the device of instructions gradually ceased to operate; and only the constitutional method of electing senators remained as a method by which the Senate might peripheralize federalism. To the gradual obsolescence of that method also, we now turn our attention.

*II*

At the same time as instructions lapsed into obscurity, a new device began to appear for further separating national and state legislatures. This was the public canvass for seats in the Senate, a canvass, that is, of voters rather than of state legislators, a canvass in which candidates for the Senate helped elect those state legislators who were more or less formally pledged to vote for them. Prior to the 1830's, candidates for the Senate did not usually campaign until after the state legislature was elected, at which time they canvassed not the voters but the legislators. A master-servant relationship was thus established, except when, as rarely happened, the majority of the legislature chose a senator not of their own party. The senator, the servant, necessarily owed the legislators gratitude; but they owed him nothing—perhaps this explains why they felt free to instruct him so peremptorily. The rise of the public canvass for the Senate subtly changed this relationship. When a candidate for the Senate stumped the state in a campaign for the state legislators, he urged voters to vote for those candidates who were in turn pledged to vote for him for senator. Gradually, voters came to choose between rivals for the state legislature, not on the basis of their capabilities as lawmakers, but rather on the basis of the vote they would cast in senatorial elections. When this happened, each state legislator then owed his office less to his own merit and more to the merit of the candidate for the Senate with whom he was aligned. As a result, senators earned gratitude as much as they owed it. And, when gratitude flowed in both directions, senators depended less on state legislatures and in turn national government depended less on local government.

The system of public canvass for the Senate, both the product and the cause of popular excitement in campaigns, probably originated in the party turbulence of the 1830's. It received a fillip from the free-soil agitation of the 1850's, and matured with the development of rigid parties after the Civil War. Although possibly some candidates canvassed publicly earlier, the first instance I can find is the Walker-Poindexter campaign in Mississippi in 1834. Friends of Senator Poindexter, a Republican turned Whig, arranged for him to castigate Jackson at a series of outdoor banquets. At the first one, Robert J. Walker replied so effectively that the assembled crowd passed a resolution asking him to run for Poindexter's seat. Both candidates then canvassed the state, and, in striking anticipation of the Lincoln-Douglas campaign, met occasionally in debate.[29] The struggle between Democracy and Whiggery intensified the public canvass for the Senate, as well as all other sorts of campaigning. By 1841 the public canvass was so well established that Polk, as governor of Tennessee, refused to call a special session of the legislature to fill a Senate vacancy because "the members elected to the legislature in 1839 had not been chosen with the selection of Senators in view."[30] Doubtless this was merely a polite and politic way of saying that the Democrats were in the minority; but it is still significant that Polk could rationalize his interest with a reference to the public canvass.

It was the Lincoln-Douglas campaign, occasioned like earlier ones by a new minority and a split in the majority, that popularized the public canvass over the whole nation. In order to quell the Buchanan Democrats in Illinois, Douglas arranged for the state convention to endorse his re-election. Similarly, the Republicans endorsed Lincoln lest some of their legislators vote for Douglas in order to embarrass Buchanan.[31] Each candidate had, therefore, a pledged slate of electors. This was entirely new, for even the public canvass had not heretofore turned legislatures into mere electoral colleges. The correspondent of the New York *Evening Post* said it was "without a parallel" because:

> another instance can [not] be shown where two individuals have entered into a personal contest before the people for a seat in the United States Senate—an office not directly in the gift of the people, but their representatives.[32]

Inaccurate history, perhaps—but good evidence of the impression the campaign made. Some journals, like the Boston *Daily Advertiser,* were disturbed:

> It would be unfortunate for the social and industrial interests of the States, if this mode of electing legislators, solely and chiefly from regard to their votes for U. S. Senator, were to become general.[33]

And the Cincinnati *Commercial:*

> It is difficult to conceive of anything more illegitimate . . . the Senator . . . is the representative . . . of the state, as an independent polity, and not . . . of its individual citizens; and any attempt to forestall the action of the Legislature, either by party action or personal appeal to the people . . . is . . . an offense against the sovereignty whose freedom of action they thereby seek to fetter and control.[34]

Conservative disturbance did not, however, prevent the spread of the canvass, especially in states where the parties were in balance. The mechanics of re-election also encouraged it. Regularly, from 1790 to 1913, about 40 per cent of the senators won re-election and an even larger proportion sought it. Hence, gradually, most sitting senators came to be considered candidates for re-election. Once the public canvass operated, the parties solidified behind and against these presumptive candidates: thus John Sherman, for example, said that near the end of his fifth term in 1892, "I considered myself a candidate, without any announcement, and entered into the canvass as such."[35]

The combined effect of popular excitement and presumptive candidates is indicated by the history of elections in Indiana, one of the states really marginal in party attachment at the turn of the century. In the two decades, 1891–1910, there were seven regular elections. In every case the public clearly understood that the incumbent senator was a candidate. In three other cases—in 1896 when the Republican, Fairbanks, beat the venerable Voorhees, in 1908 when the Democrat, Shively, beat Hemenway, and in 1910 when the Democrat, Kern, beat Beveridge— the party out of power had clearly (if not always officially) nominated a candidate long before November. Thus in five-sevenths of the opportunities a candidate was in effect nominated before the state legislature was elected.

The endorsement of candidates in convention, the other new aspect of the Lincoln-Douglas campaign, was not, however, so readily accepted elsewhere. The Massachusetts Republican convention, fearing that conservative legislators would not vote for Sumner, did indeed copy the Illinois technique in 1862 and 1868.[36] But not until the mid-eighties, when the public canvass was quite frequent, did formal pledging again become popular. Then it spread widely and soon seemed an extra-constitutional means for popular election of senators.[37] In the election of William E. Borah in 1906–1907, both Republican candidates organized campaigns in every county of Idaho to elect a slate of county convention delegates.[38]

These devices, the public canvass and pledged legislators, were at their height soon after 1900. How well they worked is shown by the idiom: people spoke of the "election" of senators in November, when in fact only state legislators were then elected. Sometimes, of course, even candidates who had not campaigned tried to get elected by combining the minority with malcontents of the majority. Sometimes, as in Turpie's election in Indiana in 1887, the coalition succeeded; more often, as in Hanna's election in Ohio in 1898, it did not. And prolonged deadlocks —G. H. Haynes [39] counted 45 between 1891 and 1905—could often be broken only by ignoring the voice of the people. But despite these aberrations, the public canvass did work to free the senators from deep dependence on legislatures in at least half the elections in the turn of the century era.

The public canvass occurred, however, only when there was a sufficiently high degree of political excitement. If the excitement was lacking, as for example in Massachusetts, where the overwhelmingly dominant Republicans were wholly blind to any defect in the characters of Senators Hoar and Lodge, then senatorial elections reverted wholly to the legislature. The direct primary, however, formalized and generalized the public canvass. This device, which originated in South Carolina in 1888 and which spread rapidly through the Populist and Democratic South, was widely copied after 1903 (when Lafollette instituted it in Wisconsin) in the Midwestern and Northwestern states most deeply touched with progressivism. By 1910, 44 out of the 46 states had primary election laws and 28 of these provided in one way or another for the nomination of party candidates for the Senate at the party primary.[40] More than half of the senators could assert proudly, with Cummins of Iowa: "I was selected by a primary vote in *my* state." [41] The constitutional method of election could hardly serve a peripheralizing purpose when many senators believed they owed their seats, not to the state legislatures, but to the people.

Legislatures were not, however, formally bound by the primary results. The dominant party could, and occasionally did, ignore the primary in choosing the senator. But even this gap in popular control was closed by the invention of the Oregon system. It provided not only for senatorial nomination in primaries but also for a test of popular sentiment between the nominees at the November general election. Candidates for the state legislature could, if they chose, subscribe to a promise to vote for the candidate who won the test vote in November. In 1909 the Oregon legislature, a majority of which had subscribed to the promise, actually elected a Democrat, George Chamberlain, because he had won in November, 1908, even though the legislature was overwhelmingly Republican. (Eastern Republicans were inclined to regard this as the best possible argument against direct election.) Finally, fearing that even this method of "solemn promise" would not work—the fear indicates the extent of bribery in state legislatures during senatorial elections—Oregon amended its Constitution to require the legislature to elect the people's choice.[42] Thus, the Oregon system instituted a rigid pattern of popular election and excluded the state legislature from the selection of senators as far as could be done under the Constitution. It was copied in Nebraska and Nevada and would probably have been more widely copied had not the Seventeenth Amendment made imitation unnecessary.

## III

The Seventeenth Amendment completed the centralizing process that the public canvass began. The canvass had started to make the decision of the people a guide for the legislature. The system of pledging legislators, the direct primary, and finally the Oregon system, had each formalized the role of the voters a little more, until finally it seemed likely that the legislatures would select senators as mechanically as the electoral college selected the President. Thus these earlier reforms both occasioned the Seventeenth Amendment and anticipated its effects.

From the time that the public canvass became a fairly regular feature of senatorial elections (i.e., from the 1880's), there had been widespread agitation to amend Article I, Section 3. In the Forty-eighth Congress (1883–1885) there began a flood of proposals for popular election, in the form of memorials from state legislatures, petitions from private groups, and resolutions from congressmen. The agitation reached its high-point in the first session of the Fifty-second Congress (1891–1892), which received seven memorials, 54 petitions, and 25 resolutions on the subject. On January 16, 1893, the House actually passed a resolution to submit an amendment to the states—but the resolution never got out of committee in the Senate. The agitation levelled off thereafter, but persisted until the Amendment was finally and formally proposed in 1911. The House indeed resolved to submit an amendment in 1894, 1898, 1900, 1902 (unanimously), and 1911. On the last occasion, the Senate concurred.

It concurred because there was little point in holding out any longer. Thirty-seven state legislatures (more than the three-fourths necessary to adopt an amendment) had, by memorial to Congress or by institution of senatorial primaries, indicated that they no longer wanted to elect senators. Observe this colloquy, which occurred not long before the Senate gave in, between Senators Cummins of Iowa, a Republican progressive, and Heyburn of Idaho, also a Republican and by far the most dogged opponent of direct election:

> MR. CUMMINS. . . . the Senator from Idaho is insisting . . . that if the voters of the United States be permitted to say who shall be their Senators, then this body will be over-run by a crowd of incompetent and unfit and rash

and socialistic and radical men who have no proper views of government. I am simply recalling to his attention the fact that the people of this country, in despair of amending the Constitution, have accomplished this reform for themselves.

MR. HEYBURN. Like a burglar.

MR. CUMMINS. In an irregular way, I agree, but they have accomplished it.

MR. HEYBURN. Like a burglar.

MR. CUMMINS. And they have accomplished it so effectively that, whether the Constitution is amended or not, the people in many or most of the States will choose their own Senators.[43]

The accomplishment was a fact; hence Heyburn could not argue, he could only sneer. Like the Nineteenth Amendment—and possibly also the Eighteenth—the Seventeenth simply universalized a situation which a majority of state legislatures had already created.

Since the Seventeenth Amendment thus simply acknowledged an already existing situation, scholars and citizens alike have been unaware of its exact significance. Senatorial resistance to the doctrine of instructions was deliberately nationalistic. The opponents of instructions wanted to expand the role of the national government and to curtail the role of the states. The advocates of instructions were the states' rights parties. The failure of instructions was, therefore, a planned victory for centralized federalism—although not a conscious victory, for it came too slowly to be recognized by the participants. On the other hand, the Seventeenth Amendment, another very real victory for centralization, was hardly a deliberate one. Throughout all the agitation for the Seventeenth Amendment and its preceding reforms, no one—so far as I can discover—ever advocated them as a way to centralize federalism. The public canvass for the Senate was so natural a development out of other and earlier public campaigning that no one thought it needed justification. But if anyone had ever felt called upon to justify it, he would, I am sure, have described it as a democratic or popular device, which, intrinsically, it was. The same remarks hold for the extensions of the public canvass: presumptive candidates and pledged legislators. They were not justified; they were merely used, first because they were a new and effective way to win elections, later because they were simply a part of the procedure of campaigning. The direct primary for Senate seats and the Seventeenth Amendment were, however, elaborately justified. These were the dearest inventions of progressives to bring about a democratic utopia; these were the devices on which progressives in practical politics and progressives in universities thoroughly agreed. In consequence, they produced mountains of words in exhaustive and usually naive justification. But none of these justifications interpret them as devices to centralize federalism. It was, on the contrary, frequently asserted that the direct election of senators would peripheralize federalism, strengthening state legislatures by forcing them to concentrate on state business. It is difficult to understand how even the progressive propagandists imagined that depriving legislatures of their only control over national affairs would strengthen houses that were already decadent for want of a significant agenda. Instead, the reforms were justified simply but voluminously as extensions of democracy and as methods of avoiding deadlocks and bribery in senatorial elections.

Only the opponents of the Seventeenth Amendment understood its effect on federalism. In quite graphic terms Elihu Root, for example, described the control that state legislatures would lose. In 1911 the New York legislature still retained more power than most over the election of senators. Doubtless, therefore, the intimacy Root suggested was typical of other states only in an earlier era:

> Mr. President, this change [the popular election of Senators] would take the direct responsibility of Senators for their actions from the States [sic] legislatures to the people at the polls. The members of the State legislature . . . are familiar with the incidents and difficulties of legislation. They know how necessary it is that in order to accomplish beneficent results mutual concession shall be made. They know how impossible it is that any one man, or any one locality, or any one State can have all of its own way. When members of this body have to explain to the State legislature the reasons for their action, they meet minds that are competent and trained for the appreciation of their explanation. The people at large have far less understanding upon the subject that I am now speaking of than their legislature. . . . This will cease to be a deliberative body if every Senator has to convince, to explain to the great body of the people of his State every act he performs and every concession he makes.[44]

And he drew from his remarks a warning to the states' rights Democrats of the South, who provided the bulk of the votes for the Amendment:

> Let me tell the gentlemen who are solicitous for the preservation of the sovereignty of their States that there is but one way in which they can preserve that sovereignty, and that is by repudiating absolutely and forever the fundamental doctrine on which this resolution [to amend the Constitution] proceeds.[45]

But Root's understanding is not typical. Most opponents did no more than quote with pseudo-scholarship what the founding fathers had said about the Senate. Hence for all of its supporters and for most of its opponents, the centralizing effects of the Seventeenth Amendment went entirely unnoticed.

They were unnoticed because, by 1911, the state legislatures had lost all touch with national policy. By reason of the failure of the practice of instructions and by reason of the gradual mechanization of their part in the electoral process, the legislatures had been increasingly confined to the particular problems of their states. Hence the Seventeenth Amendment only formally excluded them from participation in national government. The actual exclusion, which the Amendment recognized and ratified, was the result of a constitutional evolution in process for the preceding 120 years.

## IV

By reason of the development described in this essay, the main peripheralizing feature of American federalism was excised from the Constitution. And that very excision had a centralizing effect, for it allowed other centralizing forces to operate with a minimum of restraint. The state governments of course remain to peripheralize federalism by means of their influence in political parties; but at least these governments cannot by constitutional right interfere with national policy. And considering that, compared with the national government, they have on the whole turned out to be far less efficient in aciton, far less competent in decision, and far less democratic in spirit, this change in the role of the Senate was surely good fortune for us all. Although we received it unconsciously, it seems important now to comprehend it rationally. Not only may we then defend our centralized federalism against the contemporary resurgence of peripheralizing measures, but also we may more wisely advise our imitators, especially in international organizations.

## NOTES

1. The electoral college should probably be interpreted as another peripheralizing institution, inasmuch as its authors probably expected that state legislatures would choose the electors. But it was largely accidental that the electoral college had this peripheralizing form; indeed the framers adopted it only because they thought there were worse disadvantages in all the other forms suggested. Although the state legislatures did usually choose the electors in the early years of the Republic, still the Constitution did not formally invest them with the duty. It merely said: "Each State shall appoint, in such manner as the legislature thereof may direct, a number of electors . . ." (Art. II, Sec. 1). Hence, because the form was accidental and the wording imprecise, the electoral college was quickly deprived of whatever peripheralizing character may have been intended. Another part of the Constitution that might have turned out to be peripheralizing was the ambivalent provision on state courts in the supremacy clause. But the series of decisions, beginning with *Martin* v. *Hunter's Lessee*, 1 *Wheat.* 304 (1816), which deprived state courts of any authoritative role in interpreting national law, eliminated that danger. The Second, Ninth, Tenth, and Eleventh Amendments were also quite clearly intended to peripheralize. They were not, of course, the framers' work and are not, indeed, in harmony with the original Constitution. By reason of the disharmony, perhaps, they (especially the Tenth and Second) have been more effective for peripheralizing than provisions of the original Constitution itself.

2. *The Federalist*, paper no. 62.

3. Almost the only discussions are: George H. Haynes, *The Senate of the United States: Its History and Practice*, 2 vols. (Boston, 1938), Vol. 2, pp. 1024–34; and William E. Dodd, "The Principle of Instructing United States Senators," *South Atlantic Quarterly*, Vol. 1, pp. 326–32 (1902). The latter is largely theoretical; the former gives a few examples.

4. Kenneth Colegrove, "New England Town Mandates," *Publications of the Colonial Society of Massachusetts*, Vol. 12, pp. 411–49 (1920); Colegrove notes that even in 1851 Fall River broke a senatorial election deadlock by instructing its representative to vote for Charles Sumner (p. 449).

5. *Ibid.*, p. 443; Charles Henry Ambler, *Thomas Ritchie: A Study in Virginia Politics* (Richmond, 1913), pp. 163–64.

6. *Annals of Congress*, Vol. 1, pp. 733–47, 1st Cong., 1st sess. (August 15, 1789). Seventeen state constitutions, mostly in New England and the Midwest, did eventually come to guarantee the right to instruct (Colegrove, p. 443); but, of course, this guarantee meant nothing if the national government refused to recognize it.

7. *The Journal of William McClay*, ed. Edgar S. McClay (New York, 1927), pp. 387–89 (entry of Feb. 24, 1791); see also p. 188 (entries of Feb. 6 and 7, 1790).

8. H. M. Wagstaff, "Federalism in North Carolina," *James Sprunt Historical Publications*, Vol. 9, p. 24 (1910).

9. John Tyler, writing in 1812, quoted in *The Letters and Times of the Tylers*, ed. Lyon G. Tyler, 3 vols. (Richmond, 1884–85, and Williamsburg, 1896), Vol. 1, p. 274.

10. *Annals of Congress*, Vol. 14, p. 1214, 8th Cong., 1st sess. (March 1, 1905).

11. Henry Adams, *History of the United States during the Second Administration of Thomas Jefferson*, 2 vols. (New York, 1902), Vol. 2, p. 240.

12. *The Diary of John Quincy Adams*, ed. Allan Nevins (New York, 1928), p. 57 (entry of July 11, 1808).

13. *The Writings of John Quincy Adams*, ed. Worthington C. Ford, 12 vols. (New York, 1914 ff.), Vol. 3, pp. 269–70 (letter to Joseph Anderson, Dec. 15, 1808). Adams also wrote in this vein to Senator Giles of Virginia.

14. Details of the resignations and the arguments for and against instructions are set forth in Dice Robbins Anderson, *William Branch Giles: A Study in the Politics of Virginia and the Nation from 1790 to 1830* (Menasha, Wisconsin, 1914), pp. 166 ff.; *The Letters and Times of the Tylers*, Vol. 1, pp. 273–75; and William Henry Hoyt, *The Papers of Archibald D. Murphey*, 2 vols. (Publications of the North Carolina Historical Commission, Raleigh, 1914), Vol. 2, pp. 1–6.

15. Peleg Sprague of Maine, Theodore Frelinghuysen and Samuel Southard of New Jersey, and Thomas Ewing of Ohio.

16. *Congressional Globe*, Vol. 1, p. 316 (April 16, 1834).

17. E. H. Foster to Hugh L. White, Feb. 26, 1836, quoted in Nancy L. Scott, *Memoir of Hugh Lawson White* (Philadelphia, 1856), pp. 337–38.

18. As the vote on the resolution to expunge indicates, the substitute for recall did sometimes work. Aside from the forced resignations already mentioned (Adams, 1808; Stone, 1814; Giles, 1815; Rives, 1834; Tyler, 1836; Leigh, 1836; Mangum, 1836), these resignations were also forced: Tazewell of Virginia, 1832; King of Georgia, 1837; Foster of Tennessee, 1839; White of Tennessee, 1840; Brown of North Carolina, 1840; Strange of North Carolina, 1840; Preston of South Carolina, 1842; Haywood of North Carolina, 1846. Several other resignations, submitted in similar circumstances, should be classed as "almost forced": Sprague of Maine, 1835; Porter of Louisiana, 1837; Black of Mississippi, 1838; Rhett of South Carolina, 1852; Berrien of Georgia, 1852; and Everett of Massachusetts, 1854.

19. *Congressional Globe*, Vol. 3, p. 159 (Feb. 1, 1836).

20. John Hampden Pleasants to John Tyler, Jan. 13, 1836; quoted in *The Letters and Times of the Tylers*, Vol. 1, pp. 524–25.

21. Jackson to Van Buren, August 12, 1839, Van Buren Papers, Library of Congress; quoted in Eugene Irving McCormac, *James K. Polk: A Political Biography* (Berkeley, California, 1922), p. 152. See also pp. 165–69.

22. J. G. DeRoulhac Hamilton, "Party Politics in North Carolina, 1835–1860," *James Sprunt Historical Publications*, Vol. 15, p. 51 (1916).

23. *Congressional Globe*, Vol. 7, pp. 110–11 (Jan. 14, 1839); Hamilton, *op. cit.*, pp. 51–70.

24. *The Diary of James K. Polk*, ed. Quaife, 4 vols. (Chicago, 1910), Vol. 2, p. 24 (entry for July 13, 1846); Vol. 2, p. 49 (entry for July 25, 1846).

25. *Ibid.*, Vol. 2, pp. 51–52.

26. Benton's instructions: *Congressional Globe*, Vol. 21, p. 98 (Jan. 3, 1850); Cass' instructions: *Congressional Globe*, Vol. 20, p. 432 (Feb. 2, 1849); rescinded, *Congressional Globe*, Vol. 21, pp. 702–3 (April 11, 1850); Bell's instructions: *Congressional Globe*, Vol. 27, p. 805 (Feb. 23, 1858). Bell's speech and Andrew Johnson's reply well summarize the arguments for and against instructions.

27. Edward Mayes, *Lucius Q. C. Lamar: His Life, Times, and Speeches*, 2nd ed. (Nashville, Tenn., 1896), pp. 330–48, 362–64, 395–411, and 441–42.

28. *Biographical Directory of the American Congress*, 1774–1949, H. Doc.

607, 81st Cong., 2nd sess. (1950), p. 952; Roy Franklin Nichols, *Franklin Pierce* (Philadelphia, 1931), pp. 106–8.

29. Henry S. Foote, *A Casket of Reminiscences* (Washington, 1874), pp. 217–19.

30. Quoted from the Nashville *Union,* April 1, 1841, in McCormac, p. 183.

31. Edwin Erle Sparks, "The Lincoln-Douglas Debates of 1858," *Collections of the Illinois State Historical Library,* Vol. 3, pp. 19–28.

32. Quoted by Sparks from the New York *Evening Post,* Oct. 21, 1858, on p. 540.

33. Quoted by Sparks from the Boston *Daily Advertiser,* Nov. 6, 1858, on p. 536.

34. Quoted by Sparks from the Cincinnati *Commercial,* Sept. 23, 1858, on p. 540.

35. John Sherman, *Recollections of Forty Years in the House, Senate, and Cabinet,* 2 vols. (Chicago, 1895), Vol. 2, p. 1118.

36. Moorfield Storey, *Charles Sumner* (Boston, 1900), pp. 233, 356.

37. John Haynes, "Popular Election of United States Senators," *Johns Hopkins Studies in Historical and Political Science,* Vol. 11, pp. 547–60, at p. 560. Haynes mentions especially the Democratic convention in Illinois in 1890 and the Republican convention in Minnesota in 1892, to which should be added as another outstanding example the Republican convention in Indiana in 1886. In the 1890's, these precedents were widely followed, and county conventions frequently pledged candidates for state legislator to a particular senatorial candidate. See Sherman, Vol. 2, p. 1118, and Mayes, pp. 433–34 and 446. In 1911, Senator Brown of Nebraska could say: ". . . it has been the frequent custom in States without primary election laws, as well as in States with them, to nominate candidates for the legislature, and in the nominating conventions pass resolutions instructing the nominee when elected to vote for some man for Senator." *Congressional Record,* Vol. 46, p. 2493 (Feb. 14, 1911).

38. Claudius O. Johnson, *Borah of Idaho* (New York, 1936), pp. 63–68. Borah did not introduce the device of pledged delegates into Idaho. He had in fact opposed it in 1894, when stalwarts first used it successfully.

39. George H. Haynes, *The Election of Senators* (New York, 1906), pp. 180–81.

40. *Congressional Record,* Vol. 45, pp. 7113–20 (May 31, 1910).

41. *Congressional Record,* Vol. 47, pp. 1742 (June 7, 1911). Emphasis is added because it is clearly implied in the original context.

42. Details of the Oregon system are set forth in *The Code of the People's Rule,* S. Doc. 603, 61st Cong., 2nd sess., pp. 33 ff. Details on its operation are readily available in *Congressional Record,* Vol. 45, p. 5827 (May 5, 1910), in a speech by Senator Jonathan Bourne, which is reprinted under the title "Popular Government in Oregon," *Outlook,* Vol. 96, pp. 321–30 (Oct. 8, 1910).

43. *Congressional Record,* Vol. 47, p. 1743 (June 7, 1911).

44. *Congressional Record,* Vol. 46, p. 2244 (Feb. 10, 1911).

45. *Congressional Record,* Vol. 46, p. 2243 (Feb. 10, 1911).

# 3. Malapportionment and Public Policy in the States[*]

## Thomas R. Dye

Commentators on state policy have often implied that malapportionment seriously affects the policy choices of state legislatures. In the literature on state politics it is frequently argued that there are important policy differences between urban and rural constituencies and that malapportionment, by over-representing rural interests, grants them a real advantage in policy-making.[1] It is also frequently predicted that reapportionment on a population basis will bring about noticeable shifts in many state policies.[2]

Malapportionment of state legislatures has been successfully challenged on the grounds that it denies to the citizens equal protection of the laws.[3] This challenge was essentially a normative one, stemming from deeply held values about political equality.[4] The merits of this type of challenge do not lend themselves to empirical verification. However, statements about the effect of malapportionment on public policy, and predictions about the policy consequences of reapportionment, can be tested empirically. Such tests, of course, in no way reflect upon the moral quality of the proposition "as nearly as practicable one man's vote should be equal to another's."[5] But they can help us to know what to expect in the way of policy changes in the wake of reapportionment. In the past, proponents of reapportionment have been very enthusiastic about its expected consequences. Having attributed a lack of party competition, unfair distributions of state funds, conservative tax schemes, unprogressive education policies, and penny-pinching welfare programs to rural over-representation, they naturally expect to see these conditions changed by reapportionment. Court-ordered reapportionment is viewed as a source of strength for state legislatures rather than an infringement of a heretofore exclusive prerogative of these bodies. Reapportionment, it is said, will help states come to grips with important domestic problems in the nation and reassume their rightful place in our federal system.

In contrast, a few scholars have sounded a note of caution regarding the expected consequences of reapportionment. On the basis of roll call analyses in the Missouri and Illinois legislatures, David Derge concluded that metropolitan and non-metropolitan legislators seldom opposed each other in unified voting blocs.[6] It is difficult to see how reapportioning legislatures to reduce rural over-representation would have much effect on policy-making, if we accept Derge's conclusions that only infrequently do rural-urban divisions influence legislative decisions anyway. Duane Lockard also entered a caveat about the consequences of malapportionment.

[*] From *The Journal of Politics*, Vol. 27 (1965), pp. 586–601. Reprinted by permission.

With specific references to conditions in Massachusetts and Connecticut he asked: "Do states with fair apportionment respond to urban appeals more readily? If anyone has made a systematic study of this, I am unaware of it, but limited evidence does not seem to indicate that the states with fair apportionment are any more considerate of urban problems than states with malapportionment." [7] Herbert Jacob was equally skeptical of the consequences of malapportionment. He computed rank-order correlation coefficients for the relationship between malapportionment and party competition, highway fund distributions, and certain welfare expenditures for the fifty states. On the basis of low coefficients, he concluded, "it is improbable that it (reapportionment) will substantially invigorate state governments or dissolve the stalemates which sap public confidence in them." [8]

The purpose of the study reported here was to examine systematically the impact of malapportionment on party competition and public policy in all fifty states. If the policy choices of malapportioned legislatures are noticeably different from the policy choices of well-apportioned legislatures, and these differences in policies can be traced to malapportionment rather than some other condition, then reapportionment can be expected to have a significant impact on state policies. However, if the policy choices of well-apportioned and malapportioned legislatures do not differ significantly, or if differences which do occur are the product of some condition other than malapportionment, then more caution is warranted regarding the policy changes that reapportionment may bring. The same test applies to expectations about the impact of reapportionment on party competition. Only if there is significantly more party competition in well-apportioned legislatures than in malapportioned ones, and this increased competition is attributable to apportionment rather than some other condition, is one safe in predicting that reapportionment will bring about greater party competition.

### Measuring Malapportionment

Several measures of the malapportionment of state legislatures are available. Perhaps the most common measure is the theoretical minimum percentage of a state's population that can elect a majority of each house.[9] The two minimum percentages for each chamber can be added to provide an index of malapportionment for the legislature as a whole. Percentages are additive in this case because the real denominator is the power of each house to influence policy and this is assumed to be real. In 1960 this index ranged from a low of 37 for Nevada with the least representative legislature to a high of 96 for Oregon with the most representative legislature. Hereafter this measure is referred to as the "index of representativeness."

Another index was devised by David and Eisenberg to focus on urban under-representation in state legislatures.[10] Because urban areas are most likely to be the subject of discrimination, the authors felt that urban under-representation should be a specific object of measurement, in addition to theoretical measures of representativeness. In order to determine the degree of discrimination against urban areas, David and Eisenberg computed the "value" of a vote cast in the largest urban counties of each state. First they computed the average population of a single member district in each state. Actual constituencies were then compared to these average constituencies: the "value" of a vote was represented by the ratio of an actual constituency to the average constituency in each state. For example, in a district with twice the population of the state's average district, the value of a vote would be .50. The "value" of a vote in the largest category of county in each state was computed for each house and then the measures for both houses were averaged to provide an "index of urban representation" for each legislature. In 1960 this index ranged from a low of .12 for Georgia, where the largest counties were most discriminated against in apportionment, to a high of 1.05 in Louisiana, where the largest counties were granted the greatest legislative representation.

A third measure of malapportionment is the technically sophisticated "apportionment score" proposed by Glendon Schubert and Charles Press.[11] The apportionment score combines inverted coefficients of variation for each state (divide the population of the average district by the standard deviation of all districts and subtract the quotient from 1.0) with statistical measures of skewness and kurtosis in the distribution of districts by size of population. The result is an index that measures the combination of variance, skewness, and kurtosis in the populations of legislative districts in each state. According to this scale, in 1962 Massachusetts, with the highest apportionment score, was technically the best apportioned legislature in the nation and Indiana, with the lowest score, was the worst.

All three of these measures—the index of representativeness, the index of urban under-representation, and the apportionment score—are used in this study. Each measure depicts a slightly different aspect of malapportionment; each results in a slightly different ranking of states.[12] The first measure focuses on the theoretical minimum proportion of a state's population that can control the legislature, the second measure focuses on urban under-representation, and the third measure focuses on the degree to which a state's apportionment scheme approaches the statistical concept of normality. In the analysis to follow we shall evaluate the political relevance of each of these measures.

### Measuring Public Policy

Measuring state policy choices is an even more difficult task than measuring malapportionment. In the 1960–61 legislative biennium, more than 104,000 bills were introduced in the state legislatures throughout the nation. Each bill rejected or enacted represents a separate policy choice. What policies are to be selected in order to assess the impact of malapportionment? It was decided to select 30 measures of state policy in three of the most important subject matters of state politics—education, welfare, and taxation. Education is the largest category of state spending. In fact, with the exception of national defense, education is the nation's largest public undertaking. The responsibility for this undertaking rests with the fifty state governments. Twelve variables reflecting important attributes of state educational systems were selected for analysis:

Public School Expenditures Per Pupil in Average Daily Attendance, 1960–61
Average Annual Salary Per Member of Instructional Staff, 1961–62
Male School Teachers as a Percent of Total, 1961–62
Pupil-Teacher Ratio: Enrollment Per Member of Instructional Staff, 1961–62
Percent of Elementary Teachers with B.A. Degree, 1962
Percent of Secondary Teachers with M.A. Degree, 1962

Drop-out Rate: High School Grads in 1963 as Percent of 9th Graders in 1959
Percent of Selective Service Examinees Disqualified for Failing Mental Test, 1962
Average Size of School District in Pupils, 1961–62
State Participation: School Revenues from State as Percent of Total School Revenue, 1961–62
Federal Participation: School Revenues from Federal Sources as Percent of Total School Revenues, 1961–62
Per Capita State Expenditures for Higher Education, 1961

Welfare expenditures are the second largest category of state expenditures. Although many state welfare efforts are federally assisted, responsibility for welfare programs and benefits rests with the fifty state governments. Ten welfare variables were selected for analysis:

Average Weekly Payment Per Recipient Unemployment Compensation, 1961
Average Monthly Payment, Old Age Assistance, 1961
Average Monthly Payment Per Family, Aid to Dependent Children, 1961
Average Monthly Payment, Aid to Blind, 1961
Average Monthly Assistance, Medical Assistance for Aged (Kerr-Mills), 1961
Per Capita State and Local Expenditures for Welfare, 1960
Per Capita State and Local Expenditures for Health and Hospitals, 1960
State Participation: Percent State Expenditures of Total Expenditures for Welfare, 1960
State Participation: Percent State Expenditures of Total Expenditures for Health and Hospitals, 1960
Federal Participation: Per Capita Federal Grants to the State for Health, Welfare and Related Purposes, 1960

Eight measures of tax burden and revenue structure in the states were also selected:

Total State and Local Tax Revenues Per Capita, 1960
State Revenues Per Capita, 1960
State Revenues as a Percent of Total State and Local Revenues, 1960
Percent of Total State and Local Revenues from Federal Sources, 1960
Income Tax Revenues as a Percent of Total Tax Revenues, 1961
Sales Tax Revenues as a Percent of Total Tax Revenues, 1961
Alcohol and Tobacco Tax Revenues as a Percent of Total Tax Revenues, 1961
Motor Fuel and Vehicle Tax Revenues as a Percent of Total Tax Revenues, 1961

All 30 variables were obtained for each of the fifty states.[13]

### Measuring the Impact of Malapportionment on Public Policy

The method chosen to assess the impact of malapportionment on party competition as well as state education, welfare, and tax policies was that of linear regression analysis. First, simple correlation coefficients were computed for the relationships between the several measures of malapportionment and the selected measures of state policy. These simple coefficients show the extent to which differences in policies among the fifty states are associated with malapportionment, but they do not deal with the possibility that some other intervening variables and not malapportionment, might account for these differences. For example, if it is shown that, in general, wealthy states are better apportioned than poor states, it might be that differences in the policies of well-apportionment and malapportioned states are really a product of the fact that the former are wealthy while the latter are poor. If this were the case, policy differences between the states might be attributed to wealth rather than malapportionment. Other intervening variables might be urbanization, industrialization, or the educational level of the state's population. Several studies have shown these socio-economic variables, all of them interrelated, to be associated with variations in state policies.[14] In order to isolate the effect of malapportionment on state policies from the possible effects of socio-economic variables, it is necessary to control for these latter variables. This required that partial correlation coefficients be computed which would show the relationship between malapportionment and the several measures of state policies while controlling for the effect of urbanization, industrialization, income, and education. If relationships between malapportionment and state policies which appear in simple correlation coefficients disappear when socio-economic variables are controlled, then we may conclude that there is no independent relationship between malapportionment and public policy. On the other hand, if the correlation coefficients between malapportionment and state policies remain significant, even after the effects of socio-economic variables are controlled, then we may more readily conclude that malapportionment does have an independent effect on public policy.

In interpreting correlation coefficients in this study, it was decided to dismiss as insignificant those coefficients which might easily have occurred by chance. An analysis of variance test for the significance of $r$ identifies those coefficients which could occur by chance more than 5 out of 100 times in the correlation of any set of random digits.[15] All calculations are made on the basis of observations about all 50 states (except with regard to party competition for which Nebraska and Minnesota are dropped from analysis because of their non-partisan character). Given a constant number of observations in all correlations, it is possible to state that only simple coefficients above .30 and partial coefficients above .35 are significant at the .05 level, and that all other coefficients can be dismissed as likely to be a product of chance.

## Malapportionment and Party Competition

Before turning to a discussion of malapportionment and public policy, let us briefly consider the impact of malapportionment on party competition in state legislatures. Party competition in state legislatures is measured here by the percentage of total seats in each house of the legislature between 1954 and 1964 which were held by the majority party. Percentages are then inverted so that the competition scores in the house and senate of Alabama, Arkansas, Louisiana, Mississippi, and South Carolina, where the minority party did not hold a single seat during those years, are set at 0 and all other scores range upward. If it is true that malapportionment adversely affects party competition, then malapportioned legislatures should be less competitive than well-apportioned legislatures, and these differences in competition should be attributable to malapportionment rather than some other social or economic condition.

TABLE 1. THE RELATIONSHIP BETWEEN MALAPPORTIONMENT AND PARTY COMPETITION IN STATE LEGISLATURES, CONTROLLING FOR THE EFFECT OF FOUR SOCIO-ECONOMIC VARIABLES

| Party Competition 1954–1964 | MALAPPORTIONMENT | | | | | |
|---|---|---|---|---|---|---|
| | Index of Representation | | Urban Under-Representation | | Apportionment Score | |
| | Simple | Partial | Simple | Partial | Simple | Partial |
| Lower Houses | .13 | .28 | .44 | .35 | .39 | .27 |
| Upper Houses | .06 | .30 | .50 | .38 | .43 | .29 |

Note: Figures at the left under each heading are simple correlation coefficients for 48 states; figures at the right are fourth-order partial coefficients which control for the effect of urbanization, industrialization, income, and education.

The simple correlation coefficients in Table 1 indicate a significant relationship between the index of urban under-representation and party competition in both upper and lower chambers. Discrimination against urban areas in representation is associated with decreases in party competition. However, this relationship noticeably weakens when the effects of urbanization, industrialization, income, and education are controlled. The apportionment score also appears related to party competition in simple correlations, but this relationship falls well below accepted significance levels once socio-economic variables are controlled.

Coefficients obtained with the index of urban under-representation are higher than those obtained with either the index of representativeness or the apportionment score. Both of these latter two indices measure malapportionment in an abstract sense and not its discrimination against a particular interest. We might conclude that malapportionment itself does not affect party competition except when it operates to discriminate against urban areas. However, none of the coefficients in Table 1 are very high. Urban under-representation at best can explain less than 25 per cent of the variation among the several states in party competition. Factors other than urban under-representation must be looked to in order to account for 75 per cent of the total variation in party competition among the states.

*Malapportionment and Public Policy*

Table 2 shows the relationship between malapportionment and 30 separate measures of education, welfare, and tax policies in the fifty states. Simple correlation coefficients are shown at the left under each measure of malapportionment, while partial coefficients—controlling for the combined effect of urbanization, industrialization, income, and education in the states—are shown at the right. Perhaps the most striking feature of Table 2 is that none of the coefficients are very high. For the most part, variations in public policy among the states can *not* be explained by malapportionment.

In the field of education, it might be hypothesized that malapportionment results in lower per pupil expenditures, lower teachers' salaries, and higher pupil-teacher ratios, which in turn produce lower teacher qualifications, higher drop-out rates, and more selective service mental failures. The signs of the coefficients in Table 2 tend to bear out these relationships, but few of the coefficients obtain at a level of

TABLE 2. THE RELATIONSHIP BETWEEN MALAPPORTIONMENT AND STATE EDUCATION, WELFARE AND TAX POLICIES CONTROLLING FOR THE EFFECT OF FOUR SOCIO-ECONOMIC VARIABLES

| State Policy Measures | MALAPPORTIONMENT | | | | | |
|---|---|---|---|---|---|---|
| | Index of Representation | | Urban Under-Representation | | Apportionment Score | |
| | Simple | Partial | Simple | Partial | Simple | Partial |
| *Education* | | | | | | |
| Per Pupil Expenditures | .12 | .06 | .36 | .12 | .09 | .01 |
| Average Teachers' Salaries | .28 | .20 | .30 | −.17 | .01 | .27 |
| Teachers With B.A. | .24 | .18 | .13 | .29 | .12 | .24 |
| Teachers With M.A. | .07 | .10 | .14 | .07 | .09 | .04 |
| Male Teachers | .22 | −.01 | .15 | .01 | .01 | −.10 |
| Pupil-Teacher Ratio | −.11 | −.23 | −.31 | −.40 | −.15 | −.21 |
| Drop-out Rate | .06 | .29 | .37 | .53 | .15 | .29 |
| Mental Failures | −.09 | −.27 | −.15 | −.26 | −.16 | −.14 |
| Size of School Districts | −.24 | −.31 | −.10 | −.20 | −.14 | −.15 |
| State Participation | −.25 | −.34 | −.32 | −.42 | −.23 | −.28 |
| Federal Participation | −.06 | −.13 | −.33 | −.38 | −.07 | −.18 |
| Higher Education Expenditures | −.07 | −.07 | −.15 | −.07 | −.16 | −.20 |
| *Welfare* | | | | | | |
| Unemployment Benefits | .17 | .20 | .29 | .09 | .13 | .03 |
| Old Age Benefits | −.01 | .07 | .37 | .04 | .01 | .06 |
| ADC Benefits | .12 | .11 | .49 | .06 | .14 | .09 |
| Blind Benefits | −.08 | .16 | .32 | .09 | .01 | .02 |
| Kerr-Mills Benefits | .13 | .18 | .34 | .27 | .05 | .05 |
| Welfare Expenditures, Per cap. | .04 | .05 | .09 | .01 | −.17 | .02 |
| Health Expenditures, Per cap. | −.21 | .03 | −.01 | .01 | −.08 | .05 |
| State Participation, Welfare | −.12 | −.17 | −.26 | −.11 | −.08 | −.05 |
| State Participation, Health | .10 | .06 | .34 | .31 | .17 | .18 |
| Federal Participation | .01 | −.08 | −.31 | −.18 | −.28 | −.29 |
| *Taxation* | | | | | | |
| Total Taxes Per capita | .15 | .05 | .26 | .17 | .01 | .09 |
| State Revenue Per capita | −.16 | −.07 | −.18 | −.17 | −.10 | −.09 |
| State Percent of Total Revenue | −.01 | −.06 | −.30 | −.20 | −.13 | −.10 |
| Federal Percent of Total Revenue | −.03 | −.09 | −.36 | −.23 | −.04 | −.08 |
| Income Taxes | .12 | .07 | .14 | .01 | .02 | .05 |
| Sales Taxes | −.14 | −.15 | −.20 | −.20 | −.14 | −.09 |
| Alcohol & Tobacco Taxes | .14 | .04 | .13 | −.01 | .02 | .07 |
| Motor Fuel Taxes | .22 | .08 | .01 | .04 | −.19 | .14 |

*Note:* Figures at the left under each heading are simple correlation coefficients for 50 states; figures at the right are forth-order partial coefficients which control for the effect of urbanization, industrialization, income, and education.

significance that would merit much confidence in these hypotheses. None of the coefficients under the index of representativeness or the apportionment score are statistically significant. This helps confirm our suspicion that malapportionment in its technical aspects has no policy relevance. Only six of the twelve simple co-efficients under the index of urban under-representation are above the level of significance and only four of these hold up well once socio-economic variables are controlled. Urban under-representation is slightly related to higher pupil-teacher ratios, higher drop-out rates, and increased state and federal participation in public school finance. Yet these relationships are not so close to warrant predictions about changes in these policies once urban areas are given better representation. Per-pupil school expenditures decline with increases in malapportionment, yet this rela-tionship is clearly a product of the fact that pupil expenditures are greater in the rural, less wealthy, agricultural states; once socio-economic variables are controlled, the relationship between pupil expenditures and malapportionment disappears. Likewise the relationship between low teachers' salaries and malapportionment also disappears once socio-economic variables are controlled.

Few policy variables in the welfare field appear related to malapportionment. The closest relationship is between urban under-representation and state participa-tion in the provision of health and hospital services. Yet urban under-representation accounts for only 11 percent of the total variation among the states in the extent of their participation in the health field. The level of payments to recipients of unemployment compensation, old age assistance, aid to dependent children, and aid to the medically indigent aged under Kerr-Mills laws, appears to be slightly related to urban under-representation on the basis of simple coefficients. Most of these coefficients disappear, however, once socio-economic variables are controlled. In short, the relationship between urban representation and welfare policies among the fifty states is a product of intervening socio-economic variables. There is no evidence that reapportionment will bring any noticeable liberalization of welfare policies.

Not one of the relationships between malapportionment and the eight selected tax policies is statistically significant. It is doubtful, for example, that reappor-tionment will bring higher tax levies. Neither total state and local taxes per capita nor total state revenues per capita are significantly related to apportionment. While federal grants constitute a larger share of the revenue of malapportioned states, this is merely a product of the fact that these states tend to be less wealthy; the relationship between federal support and malapportionment disappears when socio-economic variables are controlled. State revenues are a larger share of total revenues in malapportioned states, but this relationship also appears as a product of socio-economic variables rather than malapportionment itself. It was hypoth-esized that well-apportioned states would place greater reliance in their tax struc-ture on progressive income taxation, while malapportioned states would rely more on regressive sales taxation. The signs of the coefficients in Table 2 tend to confirm this hypothesis, but the coefficients are so low, the relationships so slight, that they might easily have occurred by chance. Certainly there is no evidence that reappor-tionment will bring about any substantial changes in state tax structures.

It is interesting to note that the few significant policy correlations obtained in this study, were obtained with David and Eisenburg's index of urban under-representation. This index measures the degree to which a particular political interest is affected by malapportionment rather than the existence of malapportionment in the technical sense. The failure to obtain any significant policy correlates with the index of representativeness suggests that the theoretical minimum population which *could* control a legislature is not a relevant political variable. Nor does the extent to which the populations of legislative districts approach a normal statistical curve, as measured by the Schubert and Press apportionment score, appear to be a politically relevant variable. Schubert and Press rebuked earlier scholars for their technically unsophisticated measures of malapportionment ("the difference in the costs for the computation of precise and crude indices is . . . minimal.").[16] Yet it turns out that David and Eisenburg with their less sophisticated measure came closer to identifying the relevant political aspect of malapportionment than Schubert and Press. For malapportionment becomes relevant when it operates to discriminate against specific political interests in a state.

## Conclusion

On the whole, the policy choices of malapportioned legislatures are not noticeably different from the policy choices of well-apportioned legislatures. Most of the policy differences which do occur turn out to be a product of socio-economic differences among the states rather than a direct product of apportionment practices. Relationships that appear between malapportionment and public policy are so slight that reapportionment is not likely to bring about any significant policy changes. Of course, these conclusions are predicted on results obtained from analyzing 30 selected measures of public policy in three seperate fields—education, welfare, and taxation. Conceivably malapportionment could have a more direct effect on some area of policy-making that was not investigated. However, expenditures for welfare and education, the liberality of welfare benefits, teachers' qualifications and salaries, the quality of public education, the tax burden, the revenue structure, and the extent of state participation in education, health, and welfare, are certainly among the most important issues in state politics. And apportionment practices seem to have little impact on the outcome of these issues.

At this point it seems appropriate to enter a caveat regarding the conclusions that can be drawn from these operations. All that has been shown is that reapportionment is not likely to have a direct impact on party competition or on certain policy outcomes. This is *not* to say that reapportionment will have no effect on state political systems or processes. Quantification necessitates a simplification of what may be a very complex question. The consequences of reapportionment may be so subtle and diverse that they defy quantitative measurement. Perhaps the consequences in each state will vary so much that direct interstate comparisons are inappropriate. Certainly we need more refined analyses of the impact of apportionment systems on state political processes and policy outcomes; we especially need more "before and after" studies of reapportionment. But these operations do succeed in challenging the easy assumptions and simple generalizations about the effects of malapportionment on public policy, and they caution us not to expect major policy changes in the wake of reapportionment.

How can we account for the bitter political battles fought over reapportionment in many states if malapportionment really has little effect on public policy? Perhaps the explanation lies in the distinction between the potential for power and the exercise of power. Certainly malapportionment overweights rural representation in legislatures. Malapportionment may give rural legislators a potential for power over their urban counterparts, *but* if they do not vote together with a high degree of unity to oppose urban interests on actual questions of public policy, their "power" may be more hypothetical than real. Legislative control can change hands and still leave policies unchanged if there are few policy differences between those placed in power and those dispossessed. Suburban voters, for example, may be just as conservative as the rural voters whose voice they may replace. In addition, divisions other than rural-versus-urban may characterize much of the legislative process: divisions between the parties, between a Governor's supporters and his opponents, between economic interests and organized groups, between liberals and conservatives, between labor and management, between regions of a state, and so forth. Reapportionment could change the distribution of power between rural and urban constituencies and yet have so subtle an effect on these other divisions that few policy changes would result. In short, even if rural-urban divisions are affected by reapportionment, these divisions are only one of many types of legislative divisions.

These conclusions need not moderate enthusiasm for reapportionment. The moral case for equality of representation is as compelling as it ever was. The impact on reapportionment of public policy, however, may be somewhat less sweeping than many expect.

## NOTES

1. See Charles Adrian, *State and Local Governments* (New York: McGraw-Hill, 1960), pp. 306–307; Daniel Grant and H. C. Nixon, *State and Local Government in America* (Boston: Allyn and Bacon, 1963), pp. 204–205; Richard Frost, "On Derge's Metropolitan and Outstate Legislative Delegations," *American Political Science Review,* Vol. 53 (September, 1959), pp. 792–795; Commission on Intergovernmental Relations, *A Report to the President for Transmittal to Congress* (Washington: U.S. Government Printing Office, 1955), p. 39; Malcolm Jewell, *The State Legislature* (New York: Random House, 1962), pp. 30–33; V. O. Key, Jr., *American State Politics: An Introduction* (New York: Knopf, 1956), pp. 76–77.

2. See "After Redistricting Decision—Where States May See Changes in Taxes, Welfare, Highways," *U.S. News and World Report,* July 6, 1964, pp. 34–36; and "A New Charter for State Legislatures," *Time,* June 26, 1964, pp. 22–23.

3. *Baker* v. *Carr,* 369 U.S. 186 (1962); *Reynolds* v. *Sims,* 84 S.Ct. 1362 (1964).

4. E.g., "The conception of political equality from the Declaration of Independence to Lincoln's Gettysburg Address, to the Fourteenth, Fifteenth, Seventeenth, and Nineteenth Amendments can mean only one thing—one person, one vote." *Gray* v. *Sanders,* 83 S.Ct. 801 (1963), p. 809.

5. *Wesberry* v. *Sanders,* 84 S.Ct. 526 (1964), p. 530.

6. David Derge, "Metropolitan and Outstate Alignments in the Illinois and Missouri Legislative Delegations," *American Political Science Review,* Vol. 53 (December, 1958), pp. 1051–1065.

7. Duane Lockard, *The Politics of State and Local Government* (New York: Macmillan, 1963), p. 319.

8. Herbert Jacob, "The Consequences of Malapportionment: A Note of Caution," *Social Forces,* Vol. 43 (December, 1964), pp. 256–261.

9. Manning J. Dauer and Robert G. Kelsay, "Unrepresentative States," *National Municipal Review,* Vol. 44 (December, 1955), pp. 571–575.

10. Paul T. David and Ralph Eisenberg, *Devaluation of the Urban and Sub-urban Vote,* Bureau of Public Administration, University of Virginia, 1961.

11. Glendon Schubert and Charles Press, "Measuring Malapportionment," *American Political Science Review,* Vol. 58 (June, 1964), pp. 302–327; and corrections published December, 1964, pp. 966–970.

12. The simple correlation coefficients between these three measures are as follows: index of representativeness and urban under-representation: .45; index of representativeness and apportionment score: .52; urban under-representation and apportionment score: .65.

13. Sources of data on education, welfare, and tax variables were: U.S. Office of Education, *Statistics of State School Systems 1961–62* (Washington: U.S. Government Printing Office, 1963); National Education Association, *Rankings of the States 1963* (Washington: National Education Association, 1963); U.S. Bureau of Census, *Statistical Abstract 1963* (Washington: U.S. Government Printing Office, 1963).

14. See, for example, Jerry Minar, *Social and Economic Factors in Spending for Public Education* (Syracuse: Syracuse University Press, 1963); Richard E. Dawson and James A. Robinson, "Inter-party Competition, Economic Variables and Welfare Policies in the American States," *Journal of Politics,* Vol. 25 (May, 1963), pp. 265–289.

15. The analysis of variance test determines the possibility that any coefficient might have been obtained by correlating sets of 50 random numbers from an imaginary infinite universe of states. It does not matter that the fifty states are a universe rather than a sample. The allusion to sampling in tests of significance is a hypothetical one. It helps us to determine whether the correlations which are obtained might have been obtained by correlating various columns of 50 digits found in a table of random numbers. See Hubert M. Blalock, *Social Statistics* (New York: McGraw-Hill, 1960), pp. 302–305.

16. Schubert and Press, *op. cit.,* p. 311.

# 4. Inter-Party Competition for Congressional Seats *

CHARLES O. JONES

One of the many dilemmas in a two-party democracy is that created by the conflicting requirements of competition and stability. We want our system of representation to be sensitive to competitive pressures and, at the same time, stable for continuity of leadership and program. We are apt to emphasize—at least in the rhetoric of our democratic myth—the need for competition. It may be fair to say that in the game of politics, as in football, we believe that the best results for all concerned, spectators and players alike, obtain when there is a rather high level of competition.

Commenting on the New York State congressional delegation, a recent editorial in the *New York Times* illustrates our professed beliefs about the effect of a lack of competition.

> The pedestrian character of most of the delegation is the product of *one-party domination* so unshakable that it makes the election of any Democratic nominee almost as certain in some districts as it would be in the deep South. The *corrosive effect of such monolithic control* is equally evident in many upstate areas, where ironclad Republican rule has similarly resulted in the fobbing off on the voters of *mediocre Congressmen*.[1]

The standard objections to a low degree of competition include: less public participation, sluggishness of the machinery of government, lack of responsiveness to group demands, and absence of criticism of policy. Many political sophisticates would not agree that all of the above are concomitants of a lack of competition or that they are necessarily dysfunctional for democracy. They would, however, list other deleterious effects. There is, they would assert, responsiveness to groups but only to certain groups. Conversely, there is differential access for a constituency's groups. There is criticism of policy but a congressman is virtually immune from some publics' criticism. James M. Burns, in his most recent book, *The Deadlock of Democracy*, states the case:

> . . . the congressman from a safe seat usually follows the easy alternative: he stays put. He placates the dominant social forces in the district; "protects" his district against hostile outside forces; does a great many individual favors; lobbies for benefits for the district; maintains a friends-and-neighbors political

* From *The Western Political Quarterly*, Vol. 17 (1964), pp. 461–476. Reprinted by permission of the University of Utah, copyright owners.

organization that scares would-be opponents out of the primary or trounces them if they come in; and comfortably overwhelms the opposition party's candidate . . . on election day. His main commitment politically is to the status quo.[2]

Thus, both the democratic ideologue and the careful student of democratic political processes find shortcomings in a low degree of inter-party competition.

On the other hand, we also believe that advantages accrue from stability in the political system. The principal advantage is that low turnover in leadership (an aspect of stability which is of importance here) results in continuity. A reasonable guarantee of continuity means that representatives may ignore the short-run protests of constituents for the long-term best interests of the public. Continuity also may result in expertise—a much admired attribute in the twentieth century. Too many leadership changes too often, can result in instability, with new and inexperienced leaders trading office every election. Lack of continuity may lead to chaos since there is little or no carry-through on policy proposals.

This article will concentrate on a major national and political institution that has frequent elections—the House of Representatives—and therefore, on the surface, might be expected to be more competitive than stable. Both national and regional data on the patterns of competition for congressional seats will be presented. More specifically, the article will describe the trends in competitive patterns for House seats and trends in party domination of House seats by examining four time periods—1914–26, 1932–40, 1942–50, and 1952–60.[3] What are the national trends in competition? What are the regional trends? How do they vary between regions? What are some of the factors which explain regional trend variations? How are the trend data related to the political parties?

Schattschneider states that there has been "a very great extension of the area of party competition."[4] Paul David is more precise: "Competition between the parties in presidential contests has spread into the gubernatorial, senatorial, and *congressional contests*. . . ."[5] The over-all conclusions that emerge from the data for House seats, however, are (1) competition is relatively low—the incumbent party candidate wins most of the time—and (2) the Democrats continue to be the dominant party in a majority of congressional districts.

### Method of Study

Competition is multi-dimensional. In their study of inter-party competition, Ranney and Kendall developed a calculus for classifying state party systems on the basis of the number of elections won and the percentage of victory for candidates.[6] Joseph Schlesinger introduced refinements by developing a "two-dimensional scheme" which included an over-all dimension measuring "the division in party control of a particular office over a period of time" and a cyclical dimension measuring "the rapidity with which parties alternate in their control of an office."[7] Both of these approaches emphasize important elements of competition. Schlesinger stresses that even though election percentages may be close over a period of time, one party may win every election. Thus, one should account for party change, or lack of it, within a constituency. Ranney and Kendall's dimensions suggest that even though a party may consistently win or lose a number of constituencies, the pattern of competition among them may differ significantly. The percentage of victory seems to be a crucial variable. If a party fails to win the seat, but continues to get a sizable percentage of the vote, that party will no doubt continue to compete strongly in the constituency.

Several other scholars have presented variations of these measures of inter-party competition.[8] The number of studies of congressional seats, however, is small. One of the most elaborate studies of House seats, that of Paul Hasbrouck, is now thirty-five years old.[9] Edward Cox questions the validity of studying congressional races apart from other election contests in a congressional district. He states that "inclusion of the results of more than one contest held simultaneously will yield a more reliable criterion of each party's election achievement than will the outcome of but the one contest." [10] Cox, however, is studying over-all party strengths. He wishes to show the utility of congressional districts as "comparative electoral units." The focus here is party control of House seats, not over-all party strength in congressional districts.

The method adopted here is principally that of Hasbrouck. For present purposes we are less interested in the percentage of victory (an important factor in the Ranney-Kendall procedure) than we are in the long-term results. Our questions relate to the relative stability of the House of Representatives—the ultimate focus is on that institution rather than on the elections in and of themselves. Schlesinger's procedure would be of value except that the cyclical dimension cannot really be measured. The decennial reapportionment followed by redistricting makes it virtually impossible to measure cycles except in districts which remain unchanged.[11]

Hasbrouck relied on two measures as indicators of party competition for congressional seats. The first measure is what Hasbrouck called "standpatism." [12] He simply counted the number of congressional districts which were won by the same party every election between 1914 and 1926. These will be referred to as "no change" districts here. The second measure is a "percntage of fluidity." [13] Hasbrouck calculated the potential change in congressional races by multiplying the number of districts by one less than the number of elections in the period measured. During the 1914–26 period there were seven elections in 435 constituencies. The potential number of changes (i.e., perfect competition by this measure) was 2,610 (435 × 6). He then counted the actual number of changes and divided by the potential change. There were 308 changes or a 12 per cent fluidity. If F indicates fluidity percentage, AC the number of actual changes, C the number of constituencies, and E the number of elections, then the formula for the percentage of fluidity can be stated as follows:

$$F = \frac{AC}{C(E-1)}$$

These two measures are related (and one would expect the high inverse correlation which actually exists between them—see Table III) but they measure different phenomena. The first is a straight measure of how many districts are always won by the same party. The second gives an indication of how many changes occur in the districts where there are changes.

### National and Regional Patterns of Competition

A sizable majority of congressional seats is won by the same party in every election. Table I presents the results for the nation as a whole. All figures indicate a rather low degree of competition and all but one show a trend toward less rather than more competition. The exception is the 1932–40 fluidity percentage. Though it is less than the 1914–26 figure, it is also less than the 1942–50 figure. This means that though there were more districts which had changes in 1932–40, most of these (68 per cent) were "one-change" districts (see Table II). In 1942–50, there were fewer districts which had party changes but most of the "change" districts (58 per cent) had more than one change.

TABLE I. INTER-PARTY COMPETITION FOR CONGRESSIONAL SEATS

| Time Period | Percentage of Fluidity | Percentage of No Change Districts | Actual Number of Changes |
|---|---|---|---|
| 1914–26 | 11.8 | 62.1 | 308 |
| 1932–40* | 10.6 | 69.9 | 184 |
| 1942–50† | 11.9 | 74.0 | 199 |
| 1952–60‡ | 7.8 | 78.2 | 135 |

*Minnesota, Missouri, and Kentucky did not redistrict until after the 1932 election. There were no party changes for Missouri and Kentucky so all five elections are included. There were several party changes in Minnesota so only four elections are included.

†New York and Pennsylvania did not redistrict until after the 1942 elections. Calculations for those states are based on four elections. Other redistricting in the period was minor and does not affect the study.

‡Redistricting in the period was minor and does not affect the study.

The greater length of the earlier period (1914–26) does affect the comparisons made throughout the paper, and the reader should bear this in mind. There is no simple way to resolve the difficulty, however, since the choice of five elections in this seven-election period would be based on a diffrent criterion than that used for the other periods (i.e., the decennial reapportionment).[14]

TABLE II. NUMBER OF PARTY CHANGES IN CONGRESSIONAL DISTRICTS

| | NUMBER OF CONGRESSIONAL DISTRICTS WITH | | | | | | |
|---|---|---|---|---|---|---|---|
| Time Period | No Changes | 1 | 2 | 3 | 4 | 5 | 6 |
| 1914–26 | 270 | 68 | 67 | 19 | 8 | 1 | 2 |
| 1932–40 | 304 | 89 | 32 | 9 | 1 | * | * |
| 1942–50 | 322 | 48 | 47 | 15 | 3 | * | * |
| 1952–60 | 340 | 60 | 31 | 3 | 1 | * | * |

*Only four changes possible in a five-election period

The mean number of changes per district for the four periods is quite low. In no case does it reach *one* change. The highest overage is for the longest period, 1914–26, where $\bar{x} = .71$. The mean drops to .42 for 1932–40, to .46 for 1942–50, and to .31 for 1952–60.

One cannot assume that where there is party change there automatically will be strong competition. Both the one- and two-change districts may be dominated by one party. In fact in the 1932–40, 1942–50, and 1952–60 time periods, a majority of these seats were won by one party in four out of five elections. Of 117 one- and two-change seats during the first period (subtracting 4 such seats in Minnesota where there were only four elections measurable), 56 were captured by one party 80 per cent of the time. In 1942–50, 40 of the 72 one- and two-change seats (subtracting 23 in New York and Pennsylvania where there were only four elections measurable) were won by one party 80 per cent of the time. And in 1952–60, 55 of 91 such seats were won by one party in four of the five elections. Of course, where there is so little competition the fact that there are changes at all is notable.

Even though we have no absolute standard by which to measure, the national data for House seats suggest a low degree of competition and that the trend is toward *less* rather than *more* competition. Schattschneider's observation that "the election of 1932 . . . greatly enlarged the scope of party competition," [15] has to be more carefully elucidated. His supporting data are principally taken from presidential elections. Data at the constituency level (i.e., between candidates) for House seats do not support his thesis.

If we examine the figures by geographical region we may note sectional trends and compare trend data. Table III presents the data for the four periods examined here.[16]

TABLE III. REGIONAL BREAKDOWN OF CONGRESSIONAL INTER-PARTY COMPETITION

| Region* | 1914–26[†] | | 1932–40[†] | | 1942–50[†] | | 1952–60[†] | |
|---|---|---|---|---|---|---|---|---|
| | F | NC | F | NC | F | NC | F | NC |
| New England | 7.8 | 71.9 | 19.0 | 55.2 | 12.5 | 78.6 | 15.2 | 60.7 |
| Middle Atlantic | 17.9 | 52.7 | 10.5 | 73.1 | 15.9 | 69.6 | 5.7 | 83.9 |
| Central | 14.2 | 52.0 | 17.8 | 45.0 | 16.9 | 64.9 | 9.1 | 74.0 |
| West Central | 10.9 | 57.7 | 20.4 | 47.7 | 9.1 | 80.5 | 17.1 | 56.1 |
| Border | 23.4 | 37.5 | 5.1 | 88.6 | 20.4 | 55.8 | 10.9 | 71.8 |
| South | 1.6 | 93.3 | .0 | 100.0 | .0 | 100.0 | .7 | 97.2 |
| Mountain | 18.3 | 50.0 | 14.3 | 57.1 | 20.3 | 56.3 | 12.5 | 62.5 |
| Pacific | 11.4 | 47.4 | 12.9 | 62.1 | 18.2 | 45.5 | 8.5 | 70.7 |

* The regions are those used by Hasbrouck, p. 176. The states included in each region are:

New England: Connecticut, Maine, Massachusetts, New Hampshire, Rhode Island, Vermont
Middle Atlantic: New Jersey, New York, Pennsylvania
Central: Illinois, Indiana, Michigan, Ohio
West Central: Iowa, Kansas, Minnesota, Nebraska, North Dakota, South Dakota, Wisconsin
Border: Delaware, Kentucky, Maryland, Missouri, Oklahoma, West Virginia
South: Alabama, Arkansas, Florida, Georgia, Louisiana, Mississippi, North Carolina, South Carolina, Tennessee, Texas, Virginia
Mountain: Arizona, Colorado, Idaho, Montana, Nevada, New Mexico, Utah, Wyoming
Pacific: California, Oregon, Washington

† The coefficients of correlation between the two measurements for the four periods are high, though inverse: 1914–26, r = –0.93; 1932–40, r = –0.98; 1942–50, r = –0.9] 1952–60, r = –0.98.

While Table III provides a clear indication of the trends, it is clumsy to use because of the need to trace two measures of competition which are inversely correlated. As noted above, the two percentages are necessary as complements to one another, but it is possible to develop a single index of competition which is descriptive of a region. Such an index number should account for both phenomena, fluidity and no change. Since there is such a high inverse correlation between the two measures, a reliable index of competition is arrived at by subtracting the fluidity percentage from the no change percentage and subtracting that figure from 100. The formula is: $I = 100 - (NC-F)$, where $I$ = index, $NC$ = no change percentage, and $F$ = fluidity percentage.[17] Table 4 presents the indexes of competition for the four periods. Also included is an indication of the change in competition between the periods.

There are important shifts in all sections of the country except the South.[18] As would be expected in view of national trends, the general pattern is toward less competition. If we disregard the 1932–40 period for the time being, we note that though they were highly competitive in the early period, the Middle Atlantic, Central, Border, Mountain, and Pacific states show rather sharp decreases in competition. The New England, West Central, and Southern regions have increased competition (1952–60 over 1914–26).

What happens when the 1932–50 period is included? This remarkable period in American politics not only cannot be permanently disregarded in these calcula-

TABLE IV. NATIONAL AND REGIONAL INDEXES OF COMPETITION *

| | 1914-26 | 1932-40 | | 1942-50 | | 1952-60 | |
|---|---|---|---|---|---|---|---|
| | Index | Index | Change† | Index | Change | Index | Change |
| National | 49.9 | 40.7 | — | 37.9 | — | 29.6 | — |
| Regional | | | | | | | |
| New England | 35.9 | 63.8 | + | 33.9 | — | 54.5 | + |
| Middle Atlantic | 65.2 | 37.4 | — | 46.3 | + | 21.8 | — |
| Central | 62.2 | 72.8 | + | 52.0 | — | 35.1 | — |
| West Central | 53.2 | 72.7 | + | 28.6 | — | 61.0 | + |
| Border | 85.9 | 16.5 | — | 64.6 | + | 39.1 | — |
| South | 8.3 | .0 | — | .0 | NC | 3.5 | + |
| Mountain | 68.3 | 57.2 | — | 64.0 | + | 50.0 | — |
| Pacific | 64.0 | 50.8 | — | 72.7 | + | 37.8 | — |

* Index calculated by subtracting the fluidity percentage (F) from the percentage of no change districts (NC) and that figure from 100. $I = 100-(NC-F)$.
† The minus sign indicates less competition; the plus sign indicates more.

tions, but it also provides clues to an explanation of the trend variations over the forty-four years covered by the study. Economic and social upheavals of the period found political expression in the elections of the 1930's. Professor Schattschneider notes this as a period in which there was a "displacement" of the old pattern of conflicts.[19] However it is described, the Republican party has never quite recovered.

The regional trends show interesting variations. During 1932–40 there was increased competition in traditionally Republican areas (New England, Central, and West Central states). Democrats won seats in these states in the early elections

(1932, 1934, 1936) and the Republicans recaptured them in 1938 and 1940. There was decreased competition in traditionally Democratic regions (Border states and the South) and in those regions which have traditionally been more two-party oriented (Middle Atlantic states) and/or where there is considerable sensitivity to trends (Mountain and Pacific states). There were, of course, variations among the states, which will be discussed.

The third period (1942–50) showed a general reversal of 1932–40. Republicans continued to recover earlier losses (particularly in 1942 and 1946). Competition was reduced in Republican regions (New England, Central, and West Central) and, with the exception of the South, it increased elsewhere. In no region, however, were Republicans able to return to levels of strength achieved prior to the Depression.

During the 1952–60 period, despite overwhelming victories for the presidential Republican party, there was a repetition of the 1932–40 pattern—though less devastating to congressional Republicans. There was a decline in the number of Republican House seats in 1954, 1956, and 1958. Increased competition in New England and the West Central states benefited Democrats, and in the South benefited Republicans. Decreased competition in the other regions generally indicates increased Democratic strength since it represents the gradual take-over of formerly competitive districts by that party.

### Shifts in Political Party Dominance

The several dimensions of competition have been noted—percentage of victory, number of elections won, party control of a constituency over time, etc. There is also more than one *level* of competition. The foregoing shows that inter-party competition within a constituency is rather low. There could be a complete absence of inter-party competition within constituencies, however, and the two parties could, theoretically, compete intensely in the national legislature if each maintained solid control of half of the congressional districts. That is, it is possible to have the Democrats and Republicans each winning 217 districts without opposition from the other party (a total *lack* of competition by the measures used here). Were such an unlikely circumstance to emerge there would, in theory, be perfect competition in the House (especially if the 435th seat were vacant or were held by a third party). Thus, another level of competition exists, more directly policy-oriented, which is an important factor in our competitive system. It is at this national level of competition that Professor Schattschneider's conclusions about the effect of the 1932 election on competitive patterns are more appropriate. Certainly, outside the South, there has been a trend toward increased competition at this level.

What is the precise nature of this national level of competition? The evidence overwhelmingly reflects the dominance of the Democratic party and suggests its continued majority control of the House of Representatives. Continued Democratic control of the South has been padded by important gains in other regions. This conclusion will not be startling to those who follow election returns, but the data collected here do provide a description of the precise patterns involved.

Table V shows the full impact of the 1932–40 period on the Republican party. There is a drop of 30.5 per cent in the number of no change districts dominated by Republicans between the first two periods despite the fact that there is an increase in the number of no change districts from 270 to 304. As was reflected in the competition indexes, the 1942–50 period shows a substantial recovery for Republicans but the final period shows another decline. Over-all the pattern is clear. There is a gradual increase in the total number of no change districts (see column 1, Table V), with the Democrats dominating the additional ones. After the collapse of Republican dominance in 1932–40, Republicans regained control of about the same

TABLE V. PARTY CONTROL OF NO CHANGE DISTRICTS

| Time Period | Total NC Districts | NC Districts Dominated by Republicans | NC Districts Dominated by Democrats |
|---|---|---|---|
| 1914–26 | 270 | 148 (54.8%) | 122 (45.2%) |
| 1932–40 | 304 | 74 (24.3%) | 230 (75.7%) |
| 1942–50 | 322 | 147 (45.7%) | 175 (54.3%) |
| 1952–60 | 340 | 136 (40.0%) | 204 (60.0%) |

number of seats they had in 1914–26 (147 and 136 compared with 148). The important over-all shifts are as much a result of Democratic gains as Republican losses. Though the Republicans lost control of only 12 seats between the first and last periods, the Democrats gained control of 82.[20]

A regional breakdown of these party control data is presented in Table VI. Republican fortunes declined in every region but the South, where they made extremely modest gains. The figures show in detail where the Republicans lost in 1932–40 and the degree to which they were able to recover in the next decade. Losses in the Middle Atlantic, Central, and Western regions were staggering: the recovery in 1942–50 was incomplete in every region except the West Central. Democrats again increased their no change districts during 1952–60 in all regions except the South.

One important factor in analyzing these data is the index of political competition. Where Republicans declined or gained, was the area more or less competitive? If, for example, Republicans control all the seats in an area when it has an index of zero (all seats won by Republicans in every election), the situation differs greatly from that where the Republicans control all the seats when the area has a higher index, e.g., 75 (indicating that there are fewer no change seats). In both cases the

TABLE VI. PERCENT OF NO CHANGE DISTRICTS DOMINATED BY REPUBLICANS

| Region | 1914–26 | 1932–40 | Change* | 1942–50 | Change | 1952–60 | Change |
|---|---|---|---|---|---|---|---|
| New England | 91.3 | 62.5 | – | 72.7 | + | 53.0 | – |
| Middle Atlantic | 85.4 | 48.5 | – | 64.1 | + | 57.5 | – |
| Central | 92.3 | 33.3 | – | 78.0 | + | 64.9 | – |
| West Central | 100.0 | 73.7 | – | 100.0 | + | 82.6 | – |
| Border | 27.8 | .0 | – | 12.5 | – | 10.7 | – |
| South | 2.1 | 2.9 | + | 1.9 | – | 4.9 | + |
| Mountain | 71.4 | .0 | – | 44.4 | + | 30.0 | – |
| Pacific | 100.0 | 22.2 | – | 66.7 | + | 62.1 | – |

* The plus sign indicates increase in the percent of no change districts dominated by Republicans; the minus sign indicates a decrease.

Republicans control 100 per cent of the no change seats but their relative position has changed.

A second factor of importance (though less significant) is reapportionment. Which regions receive increases or decreases in representation? Which party is dominant in the gaining and losing regions? These two factors are of value in explaining variations among the states.

## Variations by States

A state-by-state analysis reveals further variations within the patterns of competition for congressional seats. In the traditionally Republican regions (New England, Central, West Central) the Democrats, reapportionment, and the trends in competition have worked against the Republicans. New England has changed since 1914–26 from an area with a relatively low index of competition and a high percentage of Republican no change seats to increased competition and a greatly reduced Republican margin. Republicans controlled twenty-one of twenty-three no change districts in 1914–26. By 1952–60 there were seventeen such districts and Republicans controlled only nine of them (fewer even than in 1932–40). In addition, New England lost four seats by reapportionment in the period measured and continues to lose seats (three more in 1960).

The most important changes have occurred in Connecticut and Maine. The index of competition in Connecticut has risen from fifty-three in 1914–26 to one hundred thirty-seven and one-half in 1952–60! Connecticut congressional politics are among the most competitive of any in the nation. Connecticut's second district, for example, had three changes in 1932–40, four in 1942–50 (RDRDR) and two in 1952–60. The figures for Maine show an index of 29 in 1914–26, 133.3 in the Depression period, zero in 1942–50, and 100 in the last period. Vermont's situation is more novel than important. A Democrat was elected for the first time in over 100 years in 1958 to Vermont's only congressional seat. Massachusetts has the largest number of seats in New England and maintains the most consistent index of competition of any heavily populated state outside the South. Other industrial states show considerable fluctuation. There is one important shift in Massachusetts, however. The Democrats increased their no change districts from four in 1942–50 to six in 1952–60.

With the exception of the Depression years, competition and Republican dominance have steadily declined in the Central states. During the early period there were thirty-nine no change seats and the Republicans controlled thirty-six of them. In 1952–60, there were fifty-seven. While the Republicans controlled about the same number as before (thirty-seven), the Democrats were dominant in seventeen more than in the early period. Thus, competition in the Central states differs from that in New England. The latter had less because of Republican dominance and is moving toward increased competition as Democrats win Republican seats. The former had more competition and is moving toward less as Democrats win control of formerely competitive seats.

Individual states in this region vary considerably. Ohio had the largest and most consistent trend toward lessened competition with indexes of 73.2, 91.7, 57.6, and 28.2. Republicans have consolidated their position and the decrease in competition in this state was as much due to Republican gains as Democratic gains. With the inevitable exception of 1932–40, Michigan maintained low indexes throughout with the Democrats making modest gains. Indiana maintained high indexes in all periods (the lowest was 77.2), though the Republicans were clearly dominant in the state. Indiana congressional districts seem unusually sensitive to political shifts. For example, four of the eleven districts had RRRDR patterns in 1952–60, indicating that Republican districts fell to Democrats in 1958 and were recaptured in 1960. Illinois increased competition during the middle periods and decreased in 1952–60. The decrease in the latter period was the result of important Democratic gains, an increase from four to nine no change districts.

The West Central farm states have been and remain a Republican stronghold. Democrats have made inroads, however, particularly in those years of economic distress on the farms (1932–40, 1952–60). Competition has increased and even though Republicans still maintain a large percentage of no change districts, there are fewer such districts. Further, reapportionment has resulted in a loss of eleven seats since 1914–26 (and four more in 1960). This region illustrates the plight of the Republican party. It is the area where Republicans are able to maintain strength, but it is an area which finds its power (in the form of numbers of representatives) being siphoned off by "growth" states.

The West Central state-by-state figures show that there was complete recovery after 1932–40 but in 1952–60 Democrats controlled four no change seats and won seats at least once in twenty districts. Iowa, Kansas, and Wisconsin contributed most to the increase in competition in 1952–60. Competition in Iowa and Kansas rose from indexes of zero in 1942–50 to 68.8 and 91.7 respectively. Republicans won all fourteen seats every election in the two states during 1942–50 but only six of the fourteen in the last period. Wisconsin's index increased from 32.5 to 52.5 between the last two periods. In 1942–50 the Republicans won eight Wisconsin seats in every election; but in 1952–60 they won only five, the Democrats one.

Nebraska and South Dakota had surprisingly high indexes throughout but they have so few seats that any change results in a high index. Minnesota had consistently high indexes (67.0, 66.7, 77.8) during the first three periods and then dropped to 30.5 in 1952–60 as Democrats captured firm control of several districts, winning three seats in every election.

Traditionally Democratic regions (Border, South) have remained so. The Border states had high indexes in 1914–26 and 1942–50 but, as Table VI shows, the Republicans were competitive only—they did not control many seats. The trend in these states is toward less competition and increased Democratic control. Despite the fact that the area has lost nine seats in reapportionment, the Democrats have gained solid control of the region. They controlled thirteen no change seats 1914–26 and twenty-five in 1952–60. The West Central was an analogous Republican region. It lost eleven seats but instead of winning more, the Republicans controlled fewer no change seats in 1952–60 than at any time except 1932–40.

Maryland, Missouri, Oklahoma, and West Virginia have had the most significant index changes among Border states. Competition in Maryland was intense in all periods except 1932–40, when the Democrats won all the seats in every election. Republicans offered strong competition in the other periods. Missouri was highly competitive in 1914–26 (I = 104) and 1942–50 (I = 90.3) but markedly less so in 1952–60 (I = 36.4). In 1942–50 Republicans competed strongly in Missouri but their efforts in 1952–60 were considerably less impressive. They still controlled one no change district in 1952–60 but the Democrats increased from four to seven their no change seats. Oklahoma had relatively high indexes in the first and third periods (75.0 and 40.6 respectively) but dropped to zero in the Depression years (all Democratic seats) and 1952–60 (all but one were Democratic seats). West Virginia has reduced its competition markedly from 137.0 in 1914–26 to 50.0 in 1952–60 because of Democratic gains.

Other Border states show less significant shifts. In 1932–40 there was perfect competition in Delaware's at-large (and only) seat, which is one of the most competitive in the nation. Kentucky's indexes did not vary greatly between periods with the exception of 1932–40, when the Democrats won all the seats.

The South is the only bright spot for Republicans and the glare is somewhat less than blinding. Competitiveness has increased modestly in the last thirty years and Republicans have increased ever so slightly the number of no change districts they dominate (from two to five). There may be a future for the Republican party in the South but the evidence here does not indicate that a revolutionary change can be expected soon.[21]

The Middle Atlantic states have a large number of seats and are much coveted by both parties. The parties have strong organizations in this region and have traditionally competed intensely. The evidence shows, however, that competition is increasingly at the second level (i.e., in the number of seats each party dominates) rather than within the constituency. Competition has declined from 65.2 to 21.8 between the first and last periods (with a brief upsurge in 1942–50) and Republican fortunes have suffered proportionately. As the number of no change districts increases (from 48 of 91 in 1914–26 to 73 of 87 in 1952–60), Republicans are able to control about the same number but whereas Democrats controlled only seven such districts in the early period, they controlled thirty-one in the last period. Thus, a large number of seats which were competitive are now controlled by Democrats. Bear in mind the full significance of these data. We are not just discussing single Democratic victories—we are examining districts which Democrats have won for *five consecutive elections*.

Among the individual states, New York accounts for much of the decrease in competition with indexes of 69.2, 21.7, 37.7, and 17.5. Republicans have actually increased their strength in New York over the last three periods. They gained five no change districts between the last two periods and dominated five of the six one-change districts. New Jersey also shows a steady decline but there is a shift in party strength which has occurred between the last two periods. In 1942–50, Republicans controlled eight of the ten "no change" districts; in 1952–60 they controlled seven of eleven such districts. Pennsylvania increased competition during the middle periods but fell off to 24.2 in 1952–60. Much of the increase was due to a substantial increase in the number of no change districts (from twenty in 1942–50 to twenty-five in 1952–60). The Democrats controlled six additional no change seats and the Republicans lost one between the two periods. One Pennsylvania district, the nineteenth, had perfect competition in 1952–60 with an RDRDR pattern.

Finally, the western regions (Mountain and Pacific) show great sensitivity to national trends. They were highly competitive for the entire period measured (37.8 being the lowest index for either region). The Mountain states have few representatives (an average of two per state in 1960) and therefore are of less consequence to the analysis. Their orientation, once Republican, is now definitely Democratic.

The Pacific region is becoming the prize which both parties covet. This is the region of growth. It has gained twenty-two seats since 1914–26 and gained eight more in 1960. The Republicans are still dominant but it is only a question of time until increased Democratic strength is evidenced in the number of no change districts they control. It is likely that the next ten-year period will see a further reduction in the Republican percentage of no change seats.

Shifting within states in this region follows no set pattern. Over-all there is a decrease in competition and this is due principally to a drop in California indexes from 86.7, 65.0, and 86.9 during the first three periods to 34.2 in the last. The Republicans are still in a strong position in California—winning twelve of twenty-two no change seats in 1952–60. Washington Republicans have recovered fully from the 1932–40 debacle when Democrats won all six seats every election. In 1952–60, Republicans controlled five of the six no change districts in Washington. Oregon showed a reverse situation. After Republicans rebounded in 1942–50 to win all four seats in every election, they dominated only one during 1952–60. The Pacific area seems to be in a continued state of flux. The 1962 elections give further indications of Democratic growth in California and Oregon but a pattern is by no means set.

In general, the state variations illustrate the decline of the Republican party. Where there is less competition, it is usually due to Democrats dominating formerly competitive districts, although Republicans have made gains in some states. Where there is more competition, it is usually a result of traditionally Republican districts being won by Democrats in a "swing" year (e.g., 1958). Republicans have made slight gains in the South and scattered gains elsewhere, but these are either too small or are potential (i.e., still not resulting in actual winning of seats). The Democrats have been able to maintain their strength in traditionally Democratic areas and make impressive gains in traditionally Republican ones. The Schatt-schneider thesis of increased party competition was based in part on this fact of Democratic gain in the North. "The elections since 1932 have *substituted a national political alignment for an extreme sectional alignment everywhere in the county except the South.*" [22] A significant consequence of this national alignment, he adds, *"has been the increased likelihood of a relatively frequent alternation of the parties in power."* [23] It is apparent that, for House seats at any rate, such an adjustment as occurred in 1932 will result in Democratic dominance. The South has over 100 House seats. A pattern whereby Democrats continue to win all or nearly .all of them and to compete strongly in Republican areas (even dominating in some traditionally Republican areas) is one that guarantees their numerical control of the House of Representatives. There has not been "frequent alternation" of party control of the House (or the Senate) and these data fail to substantiate any such prediction for the immediate future.

## Summary and Conclusions

This study has presented gross data on inter-party competition for congressional seats. From the data it seems clear that the House of Representatives is more *stable* than *competitive*. Though it is difficult to say how much competition is necessary for "democratic" policy-making, the evidence here suggests that the House is weighted toward stability in its practical resolution of the competition-stability dilemma. These data lend greater support to the summary statement of Professor Burns on inter-party competition: "Parties need the stimulus of competition. But real two-party competition is precisely what is lacking in many states and localities," [24] than to that of Schattschneider: "We are, for the first time in American history, within striking distance of a competitive two-party system throughout the country. . . ." [25] In short, by the measures employed here, competition at the constituency level (i.e., between candidates) is low, and the trend is toward less rather than more competition. Increasingly, it seems, if the present trends continue, the incumbent will win. Based on the data here, a simple prediction that the incumbent party will win five consecutive elections will probably hold true for 70 to 80 per cent of all congressional districts.

The data on party affiliation of the incumbent demonstrate that the Republican party has been unable to "shake loose" from the crushing defeats of the early 1930's. The Democrats won 204 congressional seats *in every election* between 1952 and 1960 (the Eisenhower years). This is only 26 fewer seats than the number they won between 1932 and 1940, when Roosevelt was at his peak of popularity, and 29 *more* than were won between 1942 and 1950, when both Roosevelt and Truman were in the White House.

There are regional and intra-regional differences which are of note. Certain traditionally one-party areas (New England and the West Central States for the Republicans, and the South for the Democrats) are becoming increasingly competitive. Over-all, the Democrats have gained in total seats, because the increased competition in the South has as yet resulted in few actual Republican victories, whereas Democrats in the North are now winning formerly Republican seats five elections in a row. Other regions (Middle Atlantic, Central, Mountain, Pacific) were less competitive in 1952–60 than in any previous period measured. This decline is generally attributable to consecutive Democratic victories in formerly competitive districts.

What is the significance of these data for democratic policy-making? Though we have presented no evidence which directly relates to policy-making, we can speculate about policy effects of those data which we have developed. We have introduced considerable data which demonstrate that there are relatively few (with a trend toward fewer) party changes in the competition for House seats. If an important measure of stability for a representative body is continuity of personnel (or personnel from the same party), then the House of Representatives is indeed a stable body. And a stable representative body is not likely to shift its behavior from term to term.

Thus, when President Johnson presents his legislative program to Congress, it is a fact of some significance that nearly 80 per cent of the congressional districts represented in the House have been represented by the same party (if not the same man) for five consecutive elections. As Lewis A. Dexter points out in *American Business and Public Policy:* "Congress is not a temporary convocation. It is an ongoing social system which must preserve itself intact and which deals with problems on a long-run, rather than a one-shot, basis." [26] The data here lend further support to Dexter's analysis. There has been criticism of the House of Representatives for not supporting the late President Kennedy's program, but the criticism often fails to recognize the "permanent" nature of the House—that it is a continuing and highly stable body. It does not change and adapt quickly to a new administration or to new leadership.

It is historical fact that we don't often get major "displacements of conflict," to use Schattschneider's apt phrase. This same idea was expressed in my conversation with a flight engineer recently. His good-sense observation was: "It's the old story in democracy. We don't elect anybody—we just throw the other guy out." Unless there is good reason, voters don't "throw out" the incumbent. The "party change" dimension of competition is apparently not so important to the voters in a working democracy. They prefer stability in conflict patterns, and that, at present, means Democratic party dominance of the House of Representatives.

## NOTES

1. *New York Times,* October 24, 1962, p. 38 (emphasis added).

2. James M. Burns, *The Deadlock of Democracy: Four Party Politics in America* (New York: Prentice-Hall, 1963), pp. 243–44.

3. The following sources were used in compiling data for the four periods: *Biographical Directory of the American Congress, 1774–1961* (Washington, D.C.: Government Printing Office, 1961); Congressional Quarterly, Inc., *Complete Returns of the 1960 Elections by Congressional District,* Special Report, March 10, 1961; Paul Hasbrouck, *Party Government in the House of Representatives* (New York: Macmillan, 1927), chap. ix; Malcolm Moos, *Politics, Presidents and Coattails* (Baltimore: Johns Hopkins Press, 1952); Richard Scammon (ed.), *America Votes,* Vols. 1–3 (New York: Macmillan, 1956 and 1958, and Pittsburgh: University of Pittsburgh Press, 1959); and U.S. Department of Commerce, Bureau of the Census, *Congressional District Data Book* (Washington, D.C.: Government Printing Office, 1961).

4. E. E. Schattschneider, *The Semisovereign People* (New York: Holt, Rinehart and Winston, 1960), p. 90.

5. Paul David, "The Changing Party Pattern," *Antioch Review,* 16 (Fall 1956), 343 (emphasis added).

6. Austin Ranney and Willmore Kendall, *Democracy and the American Party System* (New York: Harcourt, Brace, 1956), chap. 7 and 8. The procedure used by Ranney and Kendall was as follows: all states where the second party won 25 per cent of the elections were classified "two-party" states; states where the second party won over 30 per cent of the vote in 70 per cent of the elections and 40 per cent of the vote in 30 per cent of the elections were "modified one-party" states; the rest of the states were "one-party" states.

7. Joseph Schlesinger, "A Two-Dimensional Scheme for Classifying the States According to Degree of Inter-Party Competition," *American Political Science Review,* 49 (December 1955), 1121–22. Schlesinger's categories were: competitive, cyclically competitive, one-party cyclical, one-party predominant, and one-party states.

8. Other studies of note are: Cortez A. M. Ewing, *Congressional Elections, 1896–1944* (Norman: University of Oklahoma Press, 1947), chap. iv; Arthur N. Holcombe, *The Political Parties of To-day* (New York: Harper, 1924), and *The New Party Politics* (New York: Norton, 1933); V. O. Key, Jr., *American State Politics* (New York: Knopf, 1956), chap. 4; Joseph Schlesinger, "The Structure of Competition for Office in the American States," *Behavioral Science,* 5 (July 1960), 197–210; William H. Standing and James A. Robinson, "Inter-Party Competition and Primary Contesting: The Case of Indiana," *American Political Science Review,* 52 (December 1958), 1066–77; Julius Turner, "Primary Elections as the Alternative to Party Competition in Safe Districts," *Journal of Politics,* 15 (May 1953), 197–210. There are also some studies of the relationship between intra-constituency competition and roll-call voting: Robert Becker *et al.,* "Correlates of Legislative Voting: Michigan House of Representatives," *Midwest Journal of Political Science,* 6 (November 1962), 384–96; Duncan MacRae, Jr., *Dimensions of Congressional*

*Voting* (Berkeley: University of California Press, 1958), pp. 284–89; Warren Miller, "Majority Rule and the Representative System" (Paper presented at the 1962 meeting of the American Political Science Association, Washington, D.C., September 5–8, 1962); David B. Truman, *The Congressional Party* (New York: Wiley, 1959) (less directly related). For a most interesting discussion of another aspect of competition, see: Donald E. Stokes, "Spatial Models of Party Competition" (Paper presented at the 1962 meeting of the American Political Science Association, Washington, D.C., September 5–8, 1962).

9. *Party Government in the House of Representatives* (New York: Macmillan, 1927), chap. ix. Malcolm Moos also has considerable data on House seats in *Politics, Presidents and Coattails.*

10. Edward F. Cox, "Congressional District Party Strengths and the 1960 Election," *Journal of Politics,* 24 (May 1962), 282.

11. I did examine the 210 congressional districts which had no boundary changes between 1942 and 1960. Sixty per cent of the 210 seats were won by the same party in all ten elections, and 76.2 per cent were won by the same party in nine of the ten. The fluidity percentage (see below for explanation) was 9.2 per cent for this period. I did not include this period in the sample because it is not strictly comparable, but the percentages are similar to the other findings.

The method relied on here is not perfect. It does not take into account the percentage of victory and, as Ranney and Kendall observe, this factor may be significant in both the policy behavior and campaign behavior of congressmen. We are not measuring those behaviors directly in this study, however. We are trying to establish the degree to which there are party changes in congressional districts. A second problem in the method adopted is that it does not reflect party change which occurs at the ten-year break—e.g., between 1940 and 1942. In 1932, the Republicans lost 101 seats—the greatest change of seats in this century. In 1942, the Republicans gained 47 seats, and in 1952, they gained 22 seats. In defense of the method employed, it can be said that a major shift, such as that occurring in 1932, will be reflected ultimately in the figures showing party dominance of congressional seats. Further, the decennial reapportionment makes it exceedingly difficult to measure reliably longer time periods.

12. Hasbrouck, *op. cit.,* chapter ix. It should be noted that Hasbrouck was able to examine seven elections (1914–26) because reapportionment was delayed in 1920 for partisan and personal reasons. Actually, eight elections took place under the 1911 apportionment arrangement, but Hasbrouck eliminated the 1912 election because it was "not typical of the two-party system" (p. 171).

13. *Ibid.*

14. NC for 1914–26 is markedly lower because seven elections are measured. One would expect fewer no change districts as more elections are added. F does not increase correspondingly, however, since the subtraction of a district which has one party change from the no change column has a greater percentage effect on NC than on F. An illustration will clarify. Assume Situation A where there are ten districts for a five-election period, and Situation B where there are ten districts for a seven-election period:

| *Situation A* | *Situation B* |
|---|---|
| 7 districts—no change | 6 districts—no change |
| 2 districts— 1 change | 2 districts— 1 change |
| 1 district — 2 changes | 2 districts— 2 changes |
| 10 districts— 4 changes | 10 districts— 6 changes |
| NC = 70 per cent | NC = 60 per cent |
| F = 10 per cent | F = 10 per cent |

Note that F stays the same for both situations even though NC drops 10 per cent. Further, in order for F to remain the same, there must be two changes in the district which is subtracted from the no change column. If there is only one change, F actually decreases (to 8.3 per cent).

15. Schattschneider, *op. cit.*, p. 89.

16. The regional breakdown used here is that relied on by Hasbrouck. The only regional alignment which is questionable is that of the Border states. A case can be made for so labeling them, but Delaware, Maryland, and Oklahoma can also be included in other regions.

17. Unless (NC−F) is subtracted from 100 there is confusion since a *low* index would mean *increased* competition and a *high* index would mean *decreased* competition.

18. Competition indexes for the nation as a whole would be increased if the South were excluded from the analysis. The South is included here because of its importance as a solid base of support for Democrats and as a potential source of strength for Republicans.

19. See Schattschneider, *op. cit.*, chap. v.

20. Republican percentages improve if we include all districts in this analysis. Thus, in a five-election period one party will dominate every constituency in the sense of winning a majority of elections (three of five or more). Republicans dominated a majority of the change districts in the last three periods. This might be expected since these were all periods of Democratic dominance over-all and, for the most part, Republican seats were changing hands, not Democratic seats. In 1932–40, Republicans were dominant in 27.7 per cent of *all* districts (contrasted with 24.3 per cent in Table V); in 1942–50, they were dominant in 48.0 per cent (45.7 per cent in Table V); in 1952–60, they were dominant in 46.4 per cent (40.0 per cent in Table V).

21. The 1962 congressional elections showed that there are prospects for increased Republican representation in the South. Three seats were won from Democrats (Tennessee, Texas, and North Carolina), and one seat was picked up in reapportionment (Florida). In addition, many Republican candidates garnered high percentages in normally safe Democratic seats.

22. Schattschneider, *op. cit.*, p. 89 (emphasis his).

23. *Ibid.*, p. 92 (emphasis his).

24. Burns, *op. cit.*, p. 238.

25. Schattschneider, *op. cit.*, p. 90.

26. Raymond Bauer, Ithiel de Sola Pool, and Lewis A. Dexter, *American Business and Public Policy* (New York: Atherton Press, 1963), p. 427.

# 5. Party Legislative Representation as a Function of Election Results[*]

JAMES G. MARCH [1]

The relationship between election results (i.e., the distribution of votes received by the several parties) and seats gained in the legislative body has long concerned normative theorists of political systems. Patently, one of the foundations of representative democracy is the relationship between votes and seats. Recently, the normative discussion appears to have focused primarily on the arguments for and against strict proportional representation and on the methods by which a strictly proportional allocation of seats can be made with minimum sacrifice to other goals.[2] More generally the object of a normative theorist is to define an optimum method for transforming voting results into a division of legislative seats, the optimality of any system being of course relative to a specified set of goals.

Despite the history of interest in the normative aspects of representation functions, the empirical study of such functions has been relatively neglected in the United States until very recently. Specifically, we can pose the question: What is the relationship between voting results and legislative representation in a two-party, single-member constituency, plurality election system? In his works on electoral prediction, Bean came close to studying this relationship. For example, he considered the relationship between party vote for President and seats gained by a party in the House of Representatives.[3] But, at least as far as could be determined, he never published any results relating the aggregate vote for Congress with the distribution of seats in the House. The various commercial organizations that engage in public opinion polling and the prediction of election results in the United States have made predictions regarding the outcome of congressional elections that may (or may not) have been based on calculations of the aggregate distribution of votes to be cast, but again no published treatment of the relationship could be found. Ewing made a detailed study of the results of Congressional elections over a period of twenty-five elections beginning in 1896 and reached a number of conclusions about the character of the relationship between votes and seats.[4] For the present it is enough to note that although he computed a substantial number of statistics which can be pieced together into an approximation, Ewing never focused his attention on an explicit statement of the relationship examined here. Moos in his study of voting for Congress did not consider this question.[5]

Schattschneider in his early work presented an approximate table for relating votes to seats. He stated that with less than 25 per cent of the vote a party would receive a negligible number of seats, that with 35 percent of the vote it would re-

[*] From *The Public Opinion Quarterly*, Vol. 21 (1957–1958), pp. 521–542. Reprinted by permission.

ceive about 15 per cent of the seats, and that 45 per cent of the vote would produce victories in 40 per cent of the seats.[6] Since Schattschneider does not distinguish one party from another, appropriate values above 50 per cent can be exhibited by symmetry.

Recently Dahl has examined the nature of the relationship between seats and votes in the United States.[7] He treated as variables the Democratic proportion of the total two-party vote for the House of Representatives and the Democratic proportion of the total two-party seats in the House and analyzed the data over the period 1928–1954. He found that the relationship between votes and seats was linear (the fit of a linear regression line was exceptionally good) in the range represented by the data. So long as the Democrats gained between .40 and .60 of the two-party vote, the Democratic proportion of seats in the House could be closely approximated by the linear equation

$$y = 2.5x - .7 \tag{1}$$

where $y$ is the proportion of seats won and $x$ is the proportion of votes. Thus, if the Democratic Party received 45 per cent of the total two-party vote for Congress, Democratic candidates would win in approximately 42.5 per cent of the constituencies; if the Democrats received 55 per cent of the vote, they would gain about 67.5 per cent of the seats.

From equation (1) it follows that the equation for the Republican proportion of seats as a function of proportion of votes was

$$y = 2.5x - .8. \tag{2}$$

It will be noted (a) that the equations differ (i.e., that in this sense the electoral system did not treat the parties identically) and (b) that gains or losses in a party's share of the vote were magnified by a factor of 2.5 when they were translated into a distribution of seats.

## Votes and Seats

With the exceptions of Schattschneider and Dahl, American students of elections have not attempted to explore in detail the relationship between aggregate votes and seats, although this problem has received considerable professional and popular attention in England. Stimulated by the resurrection in the *Economist* [8] of a "law" apparently first cited by J. P. Smith in testimony before a Royal Commission on Systems of Elections in 1909,[9] a number of British scholars have made studies of the votes-seats relationship. Specifically, the focus has been on testing the validity of the following proposition: if the ratio of aggregate votes gained in contested constituencies by the two parties be cubed, the resulting ratio will equal the ratio of contested seats won by the two parties. Strictly speaking, Smith made a less powerful proposition, but current interest has been turned to the equality specified above, which has come to be known as "the cube law."

Since election results are typically given in terms of percentages and the Dahl regression coefficients reflect a specification of a relationship between the proportion of seats and the proportion of votes, it is somewhat awkward to deal with the cube law in terms of ratios as is done in its statement by Smith and most of his discussants. Consequently, it will be transformed here [10] into an equation where, as before, $x$ is the proportion of aggregate votes cast for, and $y$ the proportion of seats won by a given party. The cube law becomes in those terms

$$y = \frac{x^3}{3x^2 - 3x + 1.} \tag{3}$$

The graph of the cube law is indicated in Figure 1. Note that the cube law, unlike Dahl's computed regression line, but like Schattschneider's proportions, is the same for both parties. Also unlike the linear regression line, equation (3) has the *a priori* reasonable feature that it passes through the points $(0,0)$ and $(1,1)$.

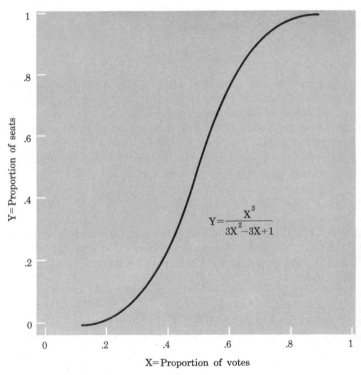

FIGURE 1. The Cube Law

A striking characteristic of the cubic relationship for present purposes is the fact that it is very nearly linear for a range of values of $x$ from .40 to .60. In that range the cube law can be closely approximated by the first-order equation

$$y = 2.808x - .904. \tag{4}$$

Table 1 shows values of $y$ for different values of $x$ (from .40 to .50) computed from the cube law and from the linear approximation. Since both (3) and (4) are symmetric around the point (.5, .5), the comparison for values of $x$ from .50 to .60 is unnecessary.

TABLE 1. COMPARISON OF CUBE LAW AND
LINEAR APPROXIMATION FOR $x$ VALUES
FROM .40 TO .50

| $x$ | $\dfrac{x^3}{3x^2 - 3x + 1}$ | $2.808x - .904$ |
|---|---|---|
| .40 | .229 | .219 |
| .41 | .251 | .247 |
| .42 | .275 | .275 |
| .43 | .300 | .303 |
| .44 | .326 | .332 |
| .45 | .354 | .360 |
| .46 | .382 | .388 |
| .47 | .412 | .416 |
| .48 | .440 | .444 |
| .49 | .471 | .472 |
| .50 | .500 | .500 |

Since the differences between the cubic and the linear approximation are so slight it will be legitimate to treat them as substantially interchangeable below where it is more convenient to make tests of hypotheses using the linear form rather than the cube law itself.

### The Fit of the Cube Law

Granted that the cube law has some admirable mathematical and/or aesthetic qualities, its significance lies not in such attributes but rather in the fact that it appears to conform to observed results in a number of countries once the results from uncontested constituencies are eliminated. Kendall and Stuart,[11] Butler,[12] and Cadart [13] have all explored in detail the extent to which British election results fit the model in the five elections since 1935 in which essentially a two-party system has prevailed. If one computes a least squares linear regression line from the British data, the equation (with respect to Conservative seats) is

$$y = 2.77x - .87. \qquad (5)$$

This is, of course, extraordinarily close to the linear approximation to the cube law. Although some restraint in interpretation is necessary in the light of the small number of elections involved (five), the evidence of the last five British elections is not consistent with rejecting the cube law as an empirical regularity. This fact has been partly obscured by the tendency of British writers to devote a substantial amount of time to explaining minor deviations from the law and implicitly to impose a goodness-of-fit criterion that seems to the present writer inordinately severe. Similarly, the *Economist* reports a close congruence between the law and the results in recent elections in New Zealand.[14]

Curiously, in the light of the relatively long period of British concern with the cube law, the fit of data from United States elections has not been tested against

TABLE 2. COMPARISON OF ACTUAL SEATS
WON BY THE DEMOCRATS IN THE HOUSE OF
REPRESENTATIVES, 1928–1954, AND OUT-
COME PREDICTED BY THE CUBE LAW

| Year | Cube Law | Actual Results |
|------|----------|----------------|
| 1928 | 156 | 166 |
| 1930 | 211 | 215 |
| 1932 | 298 | 313 |
| 1934 | 284 | 315 |
| 1936 | 305 | 325 |
| 1938 | 240 | 258 |
| 1940 | 251 | 261 |
| 1942 | 217 | 223 |
| 1944 | 240 | 243 |
| 1946 | 189 | 188 |
| 1948 | 263 | 263 |
| 1950 | 239 | 235 |
| 1952 | 212 | 213 |
| 1954 | 254 | 232 |

such predictions. Yet, it would appear from a casual comparison of equations (1) and (4) that the results of American elections may be quite consistent with the cube law. Moreover, both Schattschneider's formulation of the relationship cited above and Ewing's observations concerning the relationship in eastern states [15] bear a close resemblance to the cube law equation. To explore the American experience in detail the fourteen elections from 1928 to 1954 were considered, this being the same period covered by the Dahl analysis. If we apply the cube law to aggregate votes gained in contested constituencies to determine the number of contested seats won by the Democrats and add to the figure thus obtained the number of uncontested seats won by the Democrats, we have an estimate of the number of seats the Democrats would have gained if the cube law operated exactly. Table 2 compares such estimates with the actual results. The mean absolute difference between the cube law figure and the actual outcome is 10.4 seats in a legislative body of 435 seats. Whether one considers this error large or small depends somewhat on one's expectations, but it might be instructive to attempt to specify other non-obvious propositions concerning the American political system with as much apparent validity. (Since this paper was written, the 1956 election has provided another test of the cube law. In that election the cube law predicted the Democrats would win 231 seats. They actually won 234 seats.)

Using the data on contested seats only over the 1928–1954 period, one can make a more rigorous comparison of the actual results with the cube law by comparing their linear regression coefficients.[16] The regression line computed from the data is defined by

$$y = 3.331x - 1.143. \tag{6}$$

In Figure 2 the scatter diagram of the fourteen elections is shown along with the computed regression line and the linear approximation to the cubic.[17]

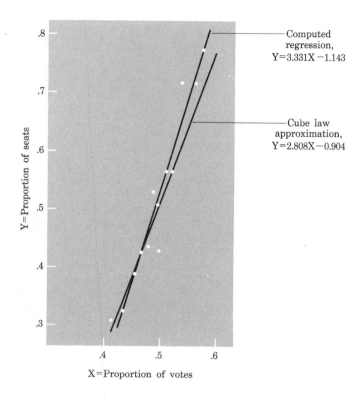

FIGURE 2. Observed Relationship Between Democratic Proportion of Aggregate Two-Party Vote and Democratic Proportion of Two-Party Seats in Contested Constituencies, U.S. Congressional Elections, 1928 to 1954

In Figure 3 the results of such an investigation are presented. The elipse represents a probability of .90 of not accepting the null hypothesis when it is false. For any pair of coefficients (a, b) outside the elipse the probability of accepting the cube law when a and b are the true coefficients is less than .10. The extraordinary power of the F-test indicated by this figure stems primarily from the extremely small standard error of the observations around the regression line.

We can conclude, therefore, that the cube law does not hold in a strict sense in the United States but that it is nonetheless a close approximation. Given the present state of knowledge concerning political behavior, it is difficult to imagine a theoretical explanation of why the cube law might hold that would not also serve as a reasonable explanation for most of the observed relationship between votes and seats in the United States. Here, as in the British case, it is probably unwise for some purposes to establish an extreme goodness-of-fit criterion since that tends to focus attention on the nuances of the relationship before the grosser attributes are suitably explained.

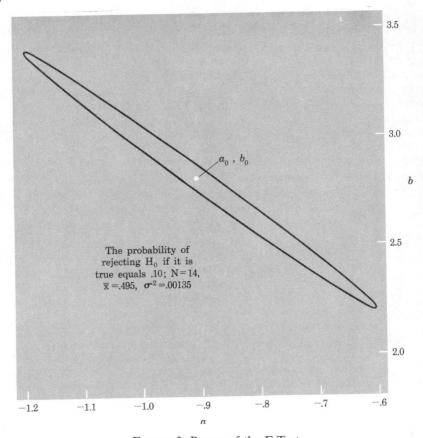

FIGURE 3. Power of the F-Test

Values of $a$ and $b$ in the Equation $Y = a + bx$ which if they are the true population parameters the probability of rejecting the null hypothesis ($H_0$: $a = -.904$,
$b = 2.808$) is equal to .90

There is another method for testing the goodness-of-fit of election data to the
cube law that has generally been used in the English treatments of the law. At
the cost of making one not unreasonable assumption, it permits a test for fit over
the entire range of possible vote outcomes rather than being restricted to the
range available in actual elections. Suppose we assume that shifts in popular support for a party will be approximately homogenous throughout the country,
specifically that they will be independent of the level of party support in a constituency.[18] Then, the cube law plotted in Figure 1 can be viewed as a distribution
function of constituencies according to party strength and the observed distribution
for any election can be compared with the distribution defined by the law. It would
appear the cube law was originally based on some such analysis since that is the
basis both for Edgeworth's pioneer paper [19] and for the work of Martin [20] on which
presumably Smith (and/or MacMahon) based their conclusions. As Kendall and
Stuart point out, the distribution function defined by the cube law is almost identical to the distribution function of a normal distribution with mean .5 and
variance .0187.[21] That is to say that if the homogeneity assumption is met and if

a/a+b (where a and b are the votes received by the two parties in a constituency) is distributed normally with the indicated mean and variance, the cube law follows. Moreover, so long as the election outcome is not extreme (say, that one party's total vote does not exceed 65 per cent of the total) balanced abnormality at the tails of the distribution or moderate shifts in the variance will still yield results consistent with the cube hypothesis. For a full discussion of the fit of the British data to the cube law, the extended literature on the subject should be consulted.[22]

Kendall and Stuart considered briefly, but indecisively, the fit of Congressional election data to this distribution function. We have considered the distributions in four elections, 1928, 1944, 1948, 1952. The frequency distributions are indicated in Table 3 for all constituencies in which each party received more than 10 per cent

TABLE 3. DISTRIBUTION OF DEMOCRATIC % OF THE TWO-PARTY VOTE, U.S. CONGRESSIONAL CONSTITUENCIES, 1928, 1944, 1948, 1952

| Democratic % of Two-Party Vote | 1928 | 1944 | 1948 | 1952 |
|---|---|---|---|---|
| 10–19 | 9 | 0 | 0 | 0 |
| 20–29 | 41 | 6 | 1 | 19 |
| 30–39 | 98 | 73 | 51 | 97 |
| 40–49 | 105 | 103 | 104 | 87 |
| 50–59 | 55 | 83 | 91 | 74 |
| 60–69 | 20 | 50 | 54 | 37 |
| 70–79 | 13 | 21 | 25 | 17 |
| 80–89 | 14 | 11 | 20 | 6 |

of the vote. In effect, we treat constituencies in which one party received more than 90 per cent of the vote as *de facto* uncontested. An inspection of the table will indicate that the American distribution is not normal. In fact, it appears to be more nearly a Poisson distribution.[23] In Figure 4, the observed frequencies are compared with theoretical frequencies derived from a Poisson distribution with mean and variance equal to 1.87 and class intervals equal to .1.[24] Some reasons why the United States distribution should approximate a Poisson rather than a normal distribution are indicated below. Here it may be enough to observe that a Poisson distribution with mean 1.87 has a distribution fairly close to that of the normal with variance .0187, as indicated in Table 4.[25] Consequently, results close to the cube law will be observed if the distribution is a Poisson with mean 1.87 and changes are substantially homogeneous.

In general, whether one uses the observed outcomes over the 1928–1954 period or the distribution of constituencies in a given election, the results in the United States are not as clearly consistent with the cube law hypothesis as are the recent elections in Britain; but they do not deviate much from the results that would obtain under the cube law. The fact that the cube law fits election results with this much accuracy both in Great Britain and the United States is enough to stimulate the interest of both laymen and professional students of political systems.

Perhaps partly because of this high curiosity value, professional interest in the relationship has been subjected to some criticism as being superficial.[26] Briefly,

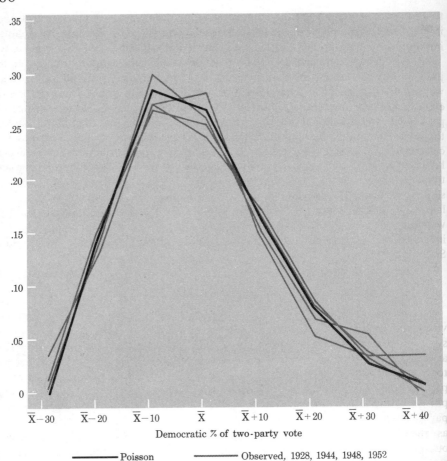

FIGURE 4. Theoretical (Poisson) Distribution and Actual Distribution of Constituencies in Four Elections

TABLE 4. A COMPARISON OF DISTRIBUTION FUNCTIONS FOR THE CUBE LAW, NORMAL DISTRIBUTION, AND THE POISSON DISTRIBUTION

| Democratic proportion of two-party vote | Democratic proportion of two-party seats under | | |
|---|---|---|---|
| | Cube Law | Normal | Poisson |
| 0 | 0 | .000 | .003 |
| .1 | .002 | .001 | .010 |
| .2 | .015 | .014 | .032 |
| .3 | .073 | .072 | .093 |
| .4 | .229 | .232 | .229 |
| .5 | .5 | .5 | .461 |
| .6 | .771 | .768 | .742 |
| .7 | .927 | .928 | .945 |
| .8 | .985 | .986 | 1. |
| .9 | .999 | .998 | 1. |
| 1. | 1. | 1.000 | 1. |

the import of the complaint is (a) that the cube law does not "fit" and (b) even if it did fit, it would be a freak with little predictive utility and less theoretical importance.

As in all cases of fitting empirical data to theoretical equations, the fit can be judged as "good" or "poor" only in terms of a set of expectations that presumably vary from one investigator to another. It is true that the cube law is not the best estimator of the outcome in the United States over the 1928–1954 period. A prediction based on the linear regression equation specified in (6) would predict the outcome in contested districts with somewhat greater accuracy than would the cube law, although the differences are not of very great magnitude. The point, however, is not that the cube law rather than some other quite similar law holds but that the relationship is quite regular and that the true parameters of the relationship, whatever they are, are not far from the parameters specified by the cube law. Once this is granted, it is reasonable to ask why the relationship holds and why one party's percentage of the two-party vote has the approximate distribution indicated above in political systems such as those of Great Britain and the United States.

### The Constituency Distribution Problem

One of the problems in providing an interpretation for the relationship between votes and seats in a two-party, single-member constituency, plurality election system is that of defining a frame of reference for comparison. If one starts from an implicit standard of proportional representation, the major problem appears to be that of explaining why the system provides a bias in favor of the majority party in the range around 50 per cent so that an increase of 1 per cent in the party's voting strength results in an increase of approximately 3 per cent in the party's strength in the house.[27] Looked at in another way, the problem is perceived as that of explaining why the variance is as small as .0187. As Rustow has pointed out, instituting anything approaching proportional representation in a single-member constituency, plurality election system is virtually impossible.[28] Consequently, although it has been the implicit approach of some students of the cube law, comparison of the observed results with a normative proportional representation model tends not to be particularly fruitful insofar as one is interested in empirically-grounded theory.

On the other hand, it is possible to approach the constituency distribution problem from the point of view of sampling theory. This is the method used originally by Edgeworth[29] and more recently by Kendall and Stuart.[30] Anyone using a sampling model is struck not by the smallness of the variance but rather by its largeness. If constituencies were samples drawn randomly from a parent population, the variance of the Democratic proportion of the two-party vote would be extremely small. In fact, under such conditions if the Democrats received 51 per cent of the vote, they would be expected to win all of the seats in the House of Representatives. It is true that under the central limit theorem random sampling would yield a normal distribution, but some other models are necessary to explain the magnitude of the variance in this case.

Kendall and Stuart suggest two different stochastic models that would explain the outcome. Their first suggestion is a Markoff process in which there exists a high correlation between successive trials or drawings. Thus, imagine that voters are assigned to constituencies under a scheme in which the probability of the next person assigned to a given constituency being a Democrat or a Republican depends only on whether the previous person assigned was a Democrat or a Republican. Then, if the probability of the voter being a Democrat given the previous voter was a Democrat is very high (nearly 1.0) and the probability of his being a Republican given the previous voter was a Republican is also very high (nearly 1.0), the observed variance can be explained. The level of correlation between successive drawings is, as Kendall and Stuart comment, improbably extreme under this model. In fact, the probability of the next drawing being the same as the previous one must be greater than .999 for both Democrats and Republicans.

Perhaps more important in view of the data presented in this paper is the fact that the parameters of the Markoff model estimated from the British data will not explain the United States data. This follows from the fact that although the variance in the United States case is approximately that found in Britain, constituency sizes are larger by a factor of about four. Moreover, the size of constituency in New Zealand, the other country in which a fit for the cube law has been reported, is less than one-third the size of the constituencies in Great Britain. The tendency for the variance among constituencies to be independent of constituency size suggests that perhaps the constituency *per se* is a meaningful unit and that sampling explanations (being typically dependent on sample size) must be at least partially modified in order to account for the observed result.

The second Kendall and Stuart suggestion suffers less from the sample size problem. Suppose that we conceive of a number of populations (perhaps conforming to more or less identifiable socio-economic groups) such that the probability of a voter chosen at random being a Democrat is different in different populations. And suppose that each of these populations contributes equally to the total number of voters and that each constituency is drawn from one and only one of the populations. Then the variance of constituencies will (given the sample sizes we are dealing with) be substantially independent of sample size. However, one of the assumptions of the scheme represents another form of the sample size problem. If we are to assume that each constituency is drawn from only one population, we need to offer some rationale for believing that the demography of a country and the size of its constituencies will be functionally related. This assumption seems unrealistic, but an approximation to it can be achieved. Suppose that we identify basic socio-economic groups in New Zealand, Great Britain, and the United States, considering them as our statistical populations. Suppose further that the variance of proportions among these populations is the same in the three countries. Finally suppose that we conceive of ourselves as drawing sub-constituencies of say 20,000 voters at a time from one population in each country. By this device we make the demography of the country and the sample size independent. In order to produce a result in which the variations due to sample size will be small, it is only necessary to impose the condition that in drawing successive sub-constituencies to complete a given constituency the probability of drawing from a given population decreases rapidly as the difference between the proportions in the previous population and the given one increases. This means that two successive drawings will ordinarily be from quite similar populations and thus the effect on the variance of increases in sample size will be restricted.

Patently, this scheme of sampling leaves something to be desired as an explanation of the result. Nevertheless, its assumptions are not so unlikely as to be rejected cavalierly. If the cube law can be explained in these terms, it is worth careful consideration. In fact, however, the second scheme suggested by Kendall and Stuart can at best provide only a partial explanation of the phenomenon. In particular, it does not provide explanations for why the distribution of proportions among the several populations is approximately normal in Great Britain and approximately a Poisson in the United States? Kendall and Stuart suggest that the scheme will explain the observed normality in the distribution of constituencies in Great Britain, but this does not appear to follow independently of the distribution of population proportions. In fact, under such a scheme and large sample sizes, the distribution of sample proportions will be almost exactly the same as the distribution of population proportions, and the scheme does not specify that distribution. Secondly, the Kendall-Stuart scheme depends, as do other sampling models, on an assumption of approximately equal constituencies. We would not expect results from elections to the United States Senate to follow the cube law since the sizes of senatorial constituencies are notoriously varied. Nevertheless, Dahl reports [31] an extremely good fit to the 1928–1954 data on Senate elections of a linear regression equation

$$y = 3.02x - .95. \tag{7}$$

As can be seen by comparing (7) with equation (4), the results in Senate elections are close to the cube law approximation. Finally, if the explanation of the result lies in the geographic distribution of voters (as is implied in a sampling explanation), there should be no difference between the distribution of constituencies according to the Democratic proportion of the two-party vote in the vote for President and the vote for Congress in the same year. However, in each of the four elections on which data are available on this point (1940, 1944, 1948, 1952),[32] the variance of the distribution for Congressional elections is significantly larger than is the comparable distribution for Presidential elections (the ratios ranging from 1.45 to 1.65). The vote for President is less dispersed than the vote for Congress.

In the light of the limitations of our present knowledge concerning political behavior, it is probably not realistic to expect a precise explanation of· these phenomena until further research is completed. The most that will be attempted here is an indication of some processes that, combined with a sampling procedure would give results approximating the observed outcomes. We will focus on two processes for which there is some empirical evidence and/or reasonable rationale. First, we will consider the entrepreneurial aspects of the behavior of political parties in organizing coalitions. Second, we will consider the intra-constituency processes of activation and persuasion and their effects respectively on the probability of a voter voting and the probability of his voting for a given party.

I am aware that there are more elegant ways of presenting the theoretical explanations I should like to make in the next sections. A model with equilibrium properties consistent with the cube law undoubtedly can be developed in a number of ways. I think such model construction would be extremely valuable. However, at the present stage of our knowledge, some discussion in general terms of the political processes by which distributions such as those described above might be generated seems to me a more pressing need.

## Inter-Party Negotiations

Can we imagine what the distribution of contested constituencies would be if we could eliminate all major effects except negotiations by political parties with interest groups to form coalitions? Although this could be formalized in terms of game theory, we will not attempt to do so here.[33] It will be enough to note that if the political parties are "rational," they will be willing to "pay" more for alliances that will give them control (i.e., over 50 per cent of the seats) than for other alliances. In general, they will not be willing to pay much for alliances that will give them additional seats once they have a majority.[34] This will be reinforced by the fact that the other party will be willing to pay more for such seats (and be in a position to do so). Thus, both parties want to have either 51 per cent of the vote or none of the vote in a given constituency. Since the major payments the parties can offer are in the form of public policy decisions, there are constraints placed (a) on the coalitions that are feasible (some demands are mutually exclusive) and (b) on the precision with which even a "rational" politician can achieve exactly 51 per cent of the vote in exactly 51 per cent of the constituencies and no vote anywhere else.[35]

Assuming roughly these pressures, it is reasonable to anticipate that inter-party negotiations will tend to produce a modal value for the distribution of .50 with monotonic decreases to zero on both sides of the mode. Moreover, it is reasonable to expect that the curve will be concave on both sides of the mode since the inter-connections among constituencies are likely to be such that the pressure toward .50 will keep most constituencies close to that figure. For the same reason, we expect the variance to be fairly small.

For the sake of an example, and without the intention of taking the actual numbers too seriously, suppose that the distributions resulting from this political negotiation pressure toward .50 are as indicated in Figure 5 for Britain. We will consider this as a very rough approximation to what would happen if there were no intra-constituency processes operating.

## Intra-Constituency Pressures

Now imagine what the distribution would be if only intra-constituency pressures were observed. We can note the following: (a) It is usually argued that the prime force tending to produce party equality in a constituency is something similar to what we have called political negotiation. Implicit in this characterization is the expectation that without such negotiation, there would be a divergent tendency (b) Variations in the turnout tend to be related to the extent to which there is a contest in the election, and at least at the extremes it is clear that both majority and minority voters tend to withdraw. (c) Such evidence as there is, however suggests that in the moderate ranges minority voters withdraw proportionately more than majority voters.[36]

The twin mechanisms of despair (by the minority) and confidence (by the majority) affect the motivation to work for a party. If we assume that the probability of an individual shifting from one party to another is a linear function of the pressure exerted on him by other individuals to do so (and the net shift a function of the differences between the two pressures) and that the pressure exerted equals the number of supporters of the party times their motivation to work for the party, we can construct a model that depends simply on the relationship between the size of the existing majority on the one hand and minority despair and majority confidence on the other. We will argue that it is reasonable to assume that the despair and confidence functions are identical and approximately logarithmic. Under such assumptions, the distribution will tend to be bimodal with virtually no constituencies at the .50 point, a substantial number in the moderate ranges (say about .40 and .60), and fewer and fewer constituencies at the more extreme points. Quite aside from the rationale for it provided here, such a distribution has (at least to the present writer) some intuitive appeal.

As in the case of the political negotiation factor, the actual frequencies indicated in Figure 5 are not particularly important. All that is argued is that the form of the curve might be expected to assume approximately this shape in elections in Britain and the United States.

## The Combined Distribution

Finally, if we combine these two pressures by assuming (arbitrarily) equality of weights, we generate the combined distribution indicated in Figure 5. This distribution is close to the normal form with variance .0187. To be sure, the precise outcome indicated in the figure is based on the arbitrarily chosen frequencies that have been used and those frequencies were chosen partly with an eye to the theoretical goal involved. However, the frequencies are not "unreasonable" on the basis of common sense and available data; they probably come fairly close to the true distributions.

Of much greater importance, however, is the fact that if we use the same basic parameters and apply them to the American situation, we obtain the observed distribution in the United States. In Great Britain, we have assumed that the mode and median of the distribution are the same and equal to .50. This is a reasonable approximation when the uncontested districts are equally shared by the two parties since we then expect the two parties to tend toward equality in contested seats. In the United States, one party has much the greater share of uncontested seats and, therefore, requires less than half of the contested seats to achieve a majority. Under such conditions, we expect the mode to be .50 as before since inter-party competition will still be concentrated at that point; but because one party (Republican) requires a greater number of victories in uncontested seats than the other, the distribution will not be symmetric around the mode. In Figure 6 distributions for the United States comparable to those in Figure 5 for Britain are indicated. It is assumed that one-fourth of the seats are won by the Democrats without contest. This exaggerates the true situation only slightly and is arithmetically convenient. Thus, the frequencies on one side of the mode are cut precisely in half. Note that otherwise the distributions (in frequency terms) are the same as in Figure 5. This results in a combined distribution that is very close to the observed distribution for United States constituencies. Compare the solid line in Figure 6 with the distributions in Figure 4.

With all appropriate qualifications stemming from imprecision in present knowledge, there is a certain plausibility to an explanation that follows the lines outlined

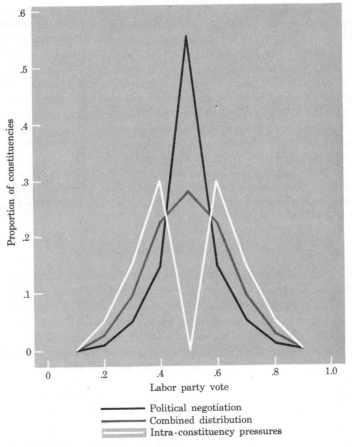

FIGURE 5. Hypothetical Distribution of Seats Resulting from
Processes of Political Negotiation and Intra-Constituency
Pressures (Great Britain)

here. We cannot claim anything more than that for it. It offers some reasons for a
normal distribution of constituencies in Great Britain and a Poisson distribution
in the United States. In addition, it makes reasonable the fact that the variance
among constituencies in the vote for President is significantly less than the variance
among the same constituencies at the same election in the vote for Congress and
that the data for elections to the United States Senate "fit" the cube law. In the case
of the vote for President, some of the internal constituency processes are damped
considerably because the constituency is not an electoral unit. Similarly, political
negotiation is based on statewide rather than simply congressional district considerations. Both of these factors operate to make the variance in the vote for
President less than that observed in the vote for Congress.

That the Senate elections fit the cube law follows from the above model. If we
consider politicians as bidding for support in order to achieve a majority in the
legislative body, the value of a voter is a function of his control over a winning
majority.[37] In a system of equal constituencies, each voter is formally equal in this

sense. In a system of unequal constituencies such as the United States Senate, we can specify blocs of voters that are equal, and a "rational" politician will offer no more to 100 voters in New York than he will to one voter in Nevada insofar as he is attempting to influence the election of a majority in the Senate. That this is approximately how the system operates is frequently alleged. Thus, the processes

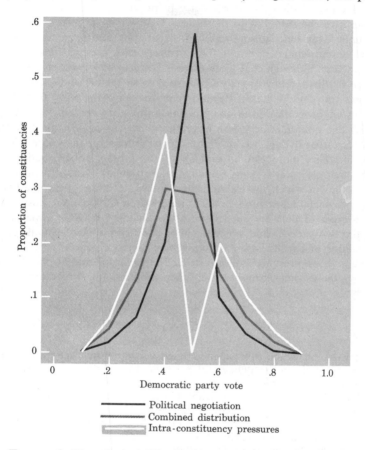

FIGURE 6. Hypothetical Distribution of Seats Resulting from Processes of Political Negotiation and Intra-Constituency Pressures (United States)

outlined above should operate in senatorial elections as well as in elections to the House of Representatives, and the distributions of electoral districts should be approximately the same. However, if one party were to specialize in gaining support of voters in states having small populations (a perfectly feasible strategy), the cube law would not follow. What deters a party from such specialization is, of course, the fact that elections to the Senate are only one of several elections to be contested for control of the national government; and there are (at best) only slight advantages of small state specialization to balance against the disadvantages stemming from the interdependence of voting preferences on the part of individual voters.

## Conclusion

We have attempted to provide an explanation for some of the similarities and differences between the distribution of party vote in constituencies in the United States and Great Britain and particularly to provide possible reasons for the approximate fit of the cube law to those data. Our model specifies rough parameters for two underlying mechanisms: political negotiation and intra-constituency interaction. These parameters appear to be consistent with present knowledge concerning such factors, although that knowledge is scarcely so precise as to permit great confidence in them. They are also consistent with the observed results in Great Britain and the United States. Beyond that we can claim only that the amount of freedom we have allowed in constructing a model to explain the data has been substantial but not unlimited. For example, once we specify the distributions in Figure 5 for Great Britain, we have also specified them for the United States.

Before anything more can be said about the present rough model, additional testing in other electoral systems is indicated. Particularly fruitful would be further tests in systems in which the electoral necessities are different for the two parties. State and provincial legislatures in the United States, Canada and Australia provide possible sources of data for such tests; although there may be some problems in meeting the two-party [38] and single-member constituency [39] prerequisites. Another possible source of data is voting in non-governmental organizations. The processes specified above are presumably not restricted to governmental institutions, and tests of the hypotheses suggested here in other representative institutions should be possible.[40]

## NOTES

1. The work on which this paper is based was done in large part at the Center for Advanced Study in the Behavioral Sciences. In addition to the usual published sources of election statistics, the writer has had the advantage of access to unpublished data collected by Robert A. Dahl, Cortez A. M. Ewing, and V. O. Key, Jr., for which grateful acknowledgement is made. He also wishes to acknowledge helpful comments on the manuscript by James S. Coleman and Herbert McClosky and the computational assistance of Susan F. March.

2. Two of the classics are G. H. Hallett, Jr., *Proportional Representation* (New York, 1926) and F. A. Hermens, *Democracy or Anarchy?* (Notre Dame, 1941). See also, Duncan Black, "Some Theoretical Schemes of Proportional Representation," *Canadian Journal of Economics and Political Science,* Vol. 15, pp. 334–343 (Aug., 1949).

3. Louis H. Bean, *How To Predict Elections* (New York, 1948), p. 67.

4. Cortez A. M. Ewing, *Congressional Elections, 1896–1944* (Norman, 1947).

5. Malcolm Moos, *Politics, Presidents and Coattails* (Baltimore, 1952).

6. E. E. Schattschneider, *Party Government* (New York, 1942), pp. 74–75.

7. Robert A. Dahl, *A Preface to Democratic Theory* (Chicago, 1956), p. 148.

8. "Electoral Facts," *Economist,* Vol. 158, pp. 5–7 (Jan. 7, 1950).

9. A verbatim report of the key testimony by Smith is quoted in M. G. Kendall and A. Stuart, "The Law of Cubic Proportions in Election Results," *British Journal of Sociology,* Vol. 1, pp. 183–197 (Sept., 1950), at pp. 183–184.

10. By solving the equation $\left(\dfrac{y}{1-y}\right) = \left(\dfrac{x}{1-x}\right)^3$ for $y$.

11. *Ibid.;* M. G. Kendall and A. Stuart, "La Loi du Cube dans les Elections Britanniques," *Revue Francaise de Science Politique,* Vol. 2, pp. 270–276 (April–June, 1952).

12. D. E. Butler, *The British General Election of 1951* (London, 1952); D. E. Butler, *The Electoral System in Britain, 1918–1951* (Oxford, 1953); D. E. Butler, "An Examination of the Results," in H. G. Nicholas, *The British General Election of 1950* (London, 1951), pp. 306–333. See also Appendices III and IV in R. B. McCallum and Alison Readman, *The British General Election of 1945* (London, 1947) for which the authors give major credit to Butler.

13. Jacques Cadart, "Les Elections Generales du 26 Mai 1955 en Grande-Bretagne, *"Revue Francaise de Science Politique,* Vol. 5, pp. 799–817 (Oct.–Dec., 1955).

14. "Electoral Facts," *op. cit.*

15. Ewing, *op. cit.,* pp. 85, 101.

16. Although the regression coefficients are reported in the general form $y = a + bx + \varepsilon$, the actual computations used estimated them for the form $y = a + \bar{b} (x - x) + \varepsilon$. This form has the advantage of making the estimates of the coefficients independent and thus facilitates analysis. The results have been translated back to the more common form simply for purposes of presentation.

17. The null hypothesis tested is that the data come from a population in which the linear approximation to the cubic (4) holds. The test is an F-test. Since we are somewhat more concerned about rejecting it when it is true than is typical in research, we set the significance level at .10. (Actually, we should like to make the significance level depend on both the power of the test and our evaluations of the "costs" of making the two types of errors, but the problems of statistical decision theory involved in such a procedure have not been sufficiently clarified to warrant its adoption here. As an alternative some data on the power of the test and its implications are presented below.) The computed value for F is not consistent with the null hypothesis. From this we conclude that the data on elections to the House of Representatives are not consistent with the cube law hypothesis. To explain why such apparently small differences yield a result of statistical significance, we examine the power of the F-test in this case. The power of a test specifies the probability of rejecting the null hypothesis when it is in fact false (i.e., the probability of not making a Type II error). In general, the power of a given test depends on the significance level chosen, the sample size, the population variance, and the magnitude of the error represented by the null hypothesis. In the present case, the significance level is fixed at .10, the sample size is 14, and the populations variance can be estimated from the data. Consequently, we can specify for any ordered pair of coefficients (a, b) the probability of our rejecting the null hypothesis ($a_o$, $b_o$) when in fact the true values are a and b. Estimation of the power of the test is based on charts provided in E. S. Pearson and H. O. Hartley, "Charts of the Power Function for Analysis of Variance Tests, Derived from the Non-central F-Distribution," *Biometrika,* Vol. 38, pp. 112–130 (June, 1951) and on computional forms in J. L. Hodges, Jr., "On the Non-central Beta Distribution," *Annals of Mathematical Statistics,* Vol. 26, pp. 648–653 (Dec., 1955). I am indebted to Professor I. Richard Savage for his help on this problem.

18. There is some empirical evidence that this is not always strictly true. See Cadart, *op. cit.;* Philip Williams, "Election Analysis," *Socialist Commentary,* pp. 210–211, 228 (July, 1955).

19. F. Y. Edgeworth, "Miscellaneous Applications of the Calculus of Probabilities," *Journal of the Royal Statistical Society,* Vol. 61, pp. 534–544 (Sept., 1898).

20. R. B. Martin, "The Electoral 'Swing of the Pendulum,'" *Journal of the Royal Statistical Society,* Vol. 69, pp. 655–707 (Dec., 1906).

21. Kendall and Stuart (1950), *op. cit.*

22. See footnotes 8–13, *supra*.

23. Discussions of the Poisson distribution can be found in almost any elementary statistics text. For example, G. Udny Yule and M. G. Kendall, *An Introduction to the Theory of Statistics,* 14th ed. (London, 1950), pp. 189–194.

24. This, of course, makes the standard deviation equivalent to that cited above for the normal distribution. The frequencies used for the figure are derived in the following way. In each observed distribution the observed mean is computed. Then by interpolation in Table 3 a new distribution is determined in which the class intervals are .1 as above but the boundaries are defined in terms of the mean rather than in absolute terms. This is equivalent to viewing the distribution as displaced on the scale without change in configuration. As is clear from the figure, the similarities between the theoretical and the observed distributions are striking despite the fact that the theoretical mean is determined without reference to the observed distribution. The differences between the three recent elections and the Poissons are not significant at the .05 level by Fisher's variance test. In the case of the 1928 election the error on the tail of the distribution makes it possible to reject the hypothesis of a Poisson, but again we are dealing with a very powerful test, and the differences are not great.

25. Linear interpolation is used to compute the distribution function for the Poisson.

26. For example, Samuel J. Eldersveld, "Polling Results and Prediction Techniques in the British Election of 1950," in *British Election Studies 1950,* ed. Pollock (Ann Arbor, 1950), pp. 54–78.

27. Butler tends to operate from this model, for example. See the works cited in footnote 11, *supra.*

28. Dankwart A. Rustow, "Some Observations on Proportional Representation," *Journal of Politics,* Vol. 12, pp. 107–127 (Feb. 1950).

29. Edgeworth, *op. cit.*

30. Kendall and Stuart (1950), *op. cit.*

31. Dahl, *op. cit.,* p. 149.

32. The data for 1940, 1944, and 1948 are taken from Moos, *op. cit.,* The 1952 data are from the *Congressional Quarterly.* In the analysis, only constituencies in which there was a contest in the congressional election were considered. For present purposes, Moos' data are incomplete in two respects. First, he did not include any southern states. Since many of the constituencies in the south are uncontested, this is not a serious disability. Second, he does not present a breakdown of the Presidential vote within metropolitan areas. In lieu of a reason for believing that this bias is systematically related to the comparison under analysis (and particularly in the light of the 1952 results which include the metropolitan and contested southern districts), it has seemed reasonable to believe that the relationships found in the 1940, 1944, and 1948 samples are characteristics of the whole population of districts for those elections.

33. For a formalization of a related question, see L. S. Shapley and Martin Shubik, "A Method for Evaluating the Distribution of Power in a Committee System," *American Political Science Review,* Vol. 48, pp. 787–792 (Sept., 1954).

34. This point has been made by Schattschneider. E. E. Schattschneider, *op. cit.,* pp. 95–96.

35. In addition, politicians don't behave entirely in the manner specified by the game theorist. Personal motivations complicate "party" motives. Subparty or inter-party coalitions may be of considerable importance. In the face of uncertainty regarding individual loyalties to the party, 51 per cent may not be considered a "safe" objective. All of these factors also tend to prevent a "perfectly rational" solution to the coalition problem.

36. See Seymour M. Lipset, Paul F. Lazarsfeld, Allen H. Barton, and Juan

Linz, "The Psychology of Voting: An Analysis of Political Behavior," in the *Handbook of Social Psychology,* ed. Lindzey (Cambridge: Addison and Wesley, 1954), Vol. 2, pp. 1124–1175, at pp. 1146–47.

37. See Shapley and Shubik, *op. cit.*

38. See Joseph A. Schlesinger, "A Two-Dimensional Scheme for Classifying the States According to Degree of Inter-Party Competition," *American Political Science Review,* Vol. 49, pp. 1120–1128 (Dec., 1955); Austin Ranney and Willmore Kendall, "The American Party Systems," *American Political Science Review,* Vol. 48, pp. 477–485 (June, 1954).

39. See Maurice Klain, "A New Look at the Constituencies; The Need for a Recount and a Reappraisal," *American Political Science Review,* Vol. 49, pp. 1105–1119 (Dec., 1955).

40. For example, James S. Coleman (Chicago) has recently been considering the distribution of votes in union locals in a labor union having a well-developed two-party system.

# Part II

# Actors

# Introduction

THE FIFTY-ONE discrete American legislative systems focus around the activities and interactions of 535 members of the United States Congress and about 7,700 state legislators. The legislative representatives who serve in American legislative institutions are members of organizations which have developed a very high degree of stability, complexity, autonomy, coherence, adaptibility, and uniformity. In a word, American legislative organizations are highly *institutionalized*. Although Congress is more highly institutionalized than are state legislatures, and some state legislatures are more highly institutionalized than others, in every case the person who becomes a representative enters an organization with well-established career lines. These paths of opportunities may, as in the case of the Congress, lead to lifetime careers within the institution. Or, as is the case in most state legislatures, service as a legislative representative may more often than not be a transient stage in a political career.

Those who pursue a legislative career find the work demanding and usually burdensome. They are required to cope with the demands, standards, and complexities of the legislative institution. The work load is great for most legislators, and the collective decision-making mechanisms of American legislatures do not facilitate efficiency in the office management, quality control, or time-in-motion senses. Learning the legislative way of life is essential for the effectiveness of a legislator, and this encomposses the capability of utilizing staff and service facilities as well as working with legislative leaders, committees, party groups, state delegations, and the like.

In addition to his very considerable legislative work, a representative ordinarily devotes substantial effort to providing services to his constituents and campaigning for re-election. The first selection in this anthology underscores the heavy involvement of congressmen in providing services. "In recent years," said former Representative Jerry Voorhis, "the congressman's job has become more and more that of an ambassador, attorney, and secretary for the people of his district in the national capital." [1] While, in general, the service-performing tasks of the American state legislator are probably less onerous, and certainly less organized, than those of a congressman, state representatives do frequently regard themselves as the "errand boys" of their constituents. As one state legislator put it:

> The legislator can be of help to his people in many ways. He is the go-between for the people and the officeholders. They need things done which the representative can do better for them. I'm able to help them in other ways also. I just came from a committee hearing where they are hearing a bill I'm putting up for the people of my county.

You're the contact between the people back home and the state government. They wouldn't come up here to speak for themselves but they will come to you. In a way we're sort of an errand boy for the people.[2]

In 1957 the legislators in four states were asked what were the most important aspects of their jobs as representatives; 27 per cent spontaneously mentioned services to constituents. When a sample of congressmen was asked directly about the importance of constituent services to a congressman's job, over three-fourths agreed that these were important, and about the same proportion indicated that constituent services were a major time-consuming aspect of their job.[3]

But if the American legislator is close to his constituents in the way in which he conceives of his job and consumes his energy, the American legislatures are not mirrors of the personal, social, or economic composition of the general public. Though American legislators tend to be "local boys," many of them long-time residents of the districts they are elected to represent, a very high proportion of them come from middle- and upper-middle-class family backgrounds. Furthermore, legislators are drawn from preponderantly business and professional occupations, as Table I illustrates.

TABLE I

| State | Per Cent of Legislators from Business and Professional Occupations |
|---|---|
| California (1957) | 83 |
| New Jersey (1957) | 83 |
| Ohio (1957) | 83 |
| Tennessee (1957) | 79 |
| Wisconsin (1957) | 63 |
| Minnesota (1951) | 33 |
| Indiana (1961) | 61 |
| Washington (1951) | 66 |
| Pennsylvania (1958) | 69 |
| U.S. Senate (1947–1957) | 93 |
| U.S. House (1949–1951) | 91 |

The most notable occupational category among American legislators is that of the lawyer. Although business and professional occupations generally are predominant in American legislatures, lawyers may be particularly heavily recruited for legislative roles because they are relatively more "dispensable" in the sense that they can more easily leave their work for extended periods of time to serve as legislators. Lawyers are not notably distinguishable from non-lawyer legislators in their voting cohesion or their liberalism-conservatism. Lawyer-legislators are, however, more actively participant than non-lawyers in the formulation stages of the legislative process; this fact is probably due to the higher incidence of general political involvement among those who become lawyers rather than to any attribute of the legal profession itself.[5]

## NOTES

1. Jerry Voorhis, *Confessions of a Congressman* (Garden City, N. Y., 1947), p. 299.
2. John C. Wahlke, Heinz Eulau, William Buchanan, and LeRoy C. Ferguson, *The Legislative System* (New York, 1962), p. 306.
3. U. S. Congress, Joint Committee on the Organization of the Congress, *Hearings Pursuant to S. Con. Res. 2,* 89th Congress, 1st Session (Washington, D. C., 1965), p. 775.
4. Malcolm E. Jewell and Samuel C. Patterson, *The Legislative Process in the United States* (New York, 1966), p. 108.
5. Heinz Eulau and John D. Sprague, *Lawyers in Politics* (Indianapolis, 1964), pp. 54–86.

# 6. The Congressman as a Legislator*

## CHARLES L. CLAPP

A frequently expressed comment of congressmen about their job is that they lack time to perform it, especially the legislative functions, which presumably should constitute their primary responsibility. The very volume of legislative proposals and the wide diversity of the subject matter are in themselves staggering. Mastery of the meaning and potential consequences of much proposed legislation requires not only intensive study but also technical competence that few but the specialist can hope to achieve. Ability aside, in terms of available time it is impossible for the legislator to comprehend these proposals, earnest as he may be in his desire to do so.

Though many veteran legislators have long since made their compromise with the system, for the conscientious beginner the responsibility and the task may seem nearly overwhelming. Two comments of freshman House members reflect their early impressions:

> Perhaps the most impressive thing here is that the operation is so vast. If one stops to think about it, one just has to wonder how it possibly could work. We have reasonably good men working in Congress; if they weren't reasonably good they wouldn't be here. Some of them are real technicians, many are lawyers trained by long experience. But in the overall congressional picture they are merely babes in the woods, called upon to pass technical legislation in a wide, wide variety of fields. We are supposed to be experts in banking and currency activities, space activities, public opinion, world affairs, pension problems, labor matters—all of these things and many more. Obviously this is impossible. The miracle is that the member of Congress knows so much, considering how difficult his job is. People are too prone to criticize the congressman when actually he faces an impossible task and probably does as well as could possibly be expected under the circumstances.

> *

> I am appalled at how much congressmen are expected to do for the nation. We have to know too much. We have to make too many decisions. There is a tremendous problem in international relations and congressmen are constantly involved in this. But in addition we are supposed to know all about domestic activities—about education, water pollution, small business problems, dams, etc. No matter how hardworking and conscientious a congressman is, no matter how much homework he does, he just can't master these problems. We just don't have the time to keep informed properly.

* From *The Congressman: His Work as He Sees It* (Washington, D. C., 1963), pp. 104–127, 144–161. By permission of The Brookings Institution.

### Time-Consuming Nonlegislative Work

As though the problem of grappling with the mass of variety of legislative proposals were not a sufficient burden, the situation is complicated by the public's disposition to request personal services in such quantity as legitimately to occupy all the time of a member. Many of these requests are not significant, though they often are time-consuming, but no elected public official can afford to ignore or give cursory attention to them. The consequences of such treatment, if pursued as a standard policy, could easily be the loss of his seat, or so the congressman fears. But the result of cultivating such requests, while comforting to the ego and to his humanitarian instincts, is to decrease appreciably the already inadequate time available for the pursuit of knowledge about legislation.

At some point, nearly every House member asks himself how he can shed some of these nonlegislative tasks in order to devote more attention to legislative responsibilities. For virtually all of them the inescapable conclusion is that expressed by a fourth-termer: "The legislative role certainly suffers. We spend far too much time on the errand boy activities, probably at a cost to government. But the real question is how we can help doing that. I think the answer is that we cannot."

There are, however, dissenters who believe legislators can and should drop some of their nonlegislative activities.

One of the hardest working Republican members comments:

Many members of Congress will tell you the legislative role simply has to suffer here. I don't think that this is true at all. I just don't let it suffer. Organization is part of the answer, I suppose, but a lot of my colleagues carry on many unnecessary activities. You'll never see me conducting a tour of the capitol for two or three constituents. They can do that themselves.

An important Democrat when asked whether activities associated with the legislative role were most likely to suffer in the face of the many demands on a member's time also replied in the negative. Said he:

I don't see why. A person who comes from a nearby district has a terrible problem, but one coming from a reasonably distant district has considerable choice. My own judgment is that outside of a limited [geographical] area you have a wide area of choice as to how much time you spend on legislation and how much you spend on the very legitimate services that a member should perform for his constituents. I think it is a question of organizing your office to do the one and yourself to do the other.

Most impartial observers of the congressional scene agree that congressmen unnecessarily devote excessive time to constituent requests, performing many tasks better left to staff or a department of the government. In their view, the belief of some legislators that they have no alternative but to continue to burden themselves with many menial tasks is erroneous. Sometimes, it is suspected, the decision to do this is deliberate: Some legislators do not like to legislate. Obviously, legislators differ markedly in their approach to their job and in what they find most interesting and rewarding about it. When asked to describe how his experience as a congressman had differed from what he had anticipated it would be, one House freshman responded:

> I didn't realize there was so much to learn nor did I realize a congressman's position and job entailed so much public relations and service as an employment agency or a court of last resort to so many people. But I am very happy about these aspects of the position because I wouldn't be entirely satisfied if it was just a legislative job. Naturally, legislation is our primary concern but frankly it is the other things that make it interesting. I am not a lawyer whereas most members of Congress are. Drafting and enacting legislation is much more interesting to them, I am sure, than it is to me.

According to an energetic and talented House member, activities in behalf of constituents possess therapeutic value: were it not for them, congressmen, prevented by House procedure from playing an influential role in the legislative process, would be even more frustrated. In his words:

> If it were not for these diversions, these administrative duties, there would be tremendous dissent on the floor of the House by many of the 435 congressmen who would thus be so frustrated under the one minute rule, the five minute rule, and the other very necessary clogs on debate, that St. Elizabeth's would be full of us. In the House this is a poultice which draws the excess energies of eager beavers. If there were no constituent pressures, it would be necessary to invent them.

There is much to be said for that view, although it was challenged by one of the most respected strategist in the House, who stated:

> I want to take issue with that because I don't believe there is any man in the House who can do a really effective legislative job on more than two bills in a year. If you do that you have a full-time job. This implies that you know reasonably well the position of each of the other members on the bill and the important amendments that may be proposed, and that is an incredibly time-consuming job. I am frustrated because I can only work on a couple of bills a year. The legislative process could absorb all our time and still cause no frustration.

### Little Time for Meditation

In determining allocation of their time, congressmen constantly weigh the priority of alternatives—in terms of such factors as personal desire, urgency, political survival, and advancement. Uninterrupted periods essential to careful study of many legislative proposals and to reflection on the broader goals and trends are rare indeed in the life of a congressman. No matter how much he desires isolation, no matter how protective his staff may be, a congressman at his desk is always vulnerable to intrusion. Urgently needing time for concentrated work, it is little wonder that many legislators (and their staffs) become adept at inventing barriers to those who would invade their privacy. At the same time, motivated by the desire to strengthen the bonds of constituent support, some except "home folks" from a general directive that they are not to be disturbed.

The home is little better as a place of refuge than the office, as congressional wives readily attest. Since they particularly resent the intrusion on the relatively brief time their husbands are able to spend with their families, they have vivid memories of unnecessary and inappropriate attempts to communicate with their husbands at all times of day and night. Because the congressman is home so seldom, it is understandable that his family should resent his efforts to seclude himself while there. If he has had a busy day at the capitol, it is even more difficult for him to engage in serious study. One conscientious representative who has heavy committee responsibilities discusses the dilemma:

> The pressures are so continuous and so great that they leave little time for meditation and for study. It is very difficult to be a conscientious congressman who feels he is on top of the issues. I cannot possibly study my serious committee work except in the evenings. There are far too many interruptions during the day. And yet when you have worked hard here all day, you don't feel much like working once you get home. Your family doesn't want you to work either and that causes problems. I take home a brief case every evening and I work every weekend, yet I can never seem to catch up.

### Does Legislative Work "Pay Off"?

Many kinds of temptation lead legislators away from concentration on purely legislative pursuits, among them the desire to assist constituents with personal problems, despair at the impossible nature of the task, and greater interest in other aspects of the job. Important, too, is the recognition that such concentration usually does not provide the best means of impressing the voter. Said one member, "The footwork of Congress may be important to people in Washington, but residents of communities in my state don't appreciate the footwork at all." The following discussion illustrates congressional views about voter reaction to some of their achievements:

> If there is one thing I have found my people care nothing about it is my attainments in Congress. I could say I was chairman of four standing committees. I think they relate that to being chairman of a PTA committee or a Lions committee. I defeated a good man who made much of the fact that he was chairman of a congressional committee, and people laughed about it. I had hundreds tell me, "Why you will be a committee chairman before you have been up there three months." Recently, I went home and began to talk about the _____ act. I was pleased to have sponsored that bill, but soon it dawned on me that the point wasn't getting through at all. What was getting through was that the act might be of help to people. I changed the emphasis: I didn't mention my role particularly, but stressed my support of the legislation.

\*

> Wouldn't you amend that to say that while the rank and file don't attach much importance to your committee assignment and your effectiveness, there

are a handful of people in almost every community who will attach importance to them, and they are the ones who have considerable influence on public opinion?

*

Wouldn't everyone agree that if you can get something done that you can't justify on merit, but which goes into your district, the so-called pork barrel project, that you find it is effective? I agree there are a sophisticated few very substantial opinion molders who get the implications of this, perhaps even before you bring home the bacon. And I think the sophisticated few are pretty important.

The necessity of building a favorable image in his district and the difficulty of accomplishing this merely by achieving distinction on the Hill as an effective, conscientious legislator creates special problems. There is little in the nature of performing diligently the day-to-day legislative chores that lends itself to dramatization by, or attention from, the news media. Colleagues may recognize and admire a member's hard work and general competence, and this respect may be shared by other close observers of Congress. But this is no indication that his constituents recognize these qualities—or care about them. The temptation may become strong, therefore, to avoid the tedious but important aspects of legislative work, since all but the most unusual efforts pass unrecognized by those in whose hands the political future of the member lies.

Even the member who successfully resists this temptation may find it expedient to resort to the window dressing type of project to get publicity in his district, although it constitutes no real measure of his effectiveness or interests. It may divert him temporarily from his primary function, but it pays off in publicity and good will. He must face re-election, and if the price of continued success at the polls is emphasizing the less substantial achievements at the expense of his real contributions, it is a price he is prepared to pay. As one straightforward, hard-working congressman puts it:

> I guess we all do whatever we can to stimulate interest in what we are doing here. The sad thing is that often you have to emphasize the less important things because sometimes it is easier to make a better story out of them. This whole public relations aspect of the job is a very significant one, and the effect it has on the members is also significant. You find you have to do certain things to impress the public while many of your more substantial contributions are very difficult to get across.

For many legislators this fact in no way diminishes their zeal, although they find it regrettable that their significant work is passed over so casually. For others, this realization leads to decreased interest in the hard, often boring, legislative work and concentration on the publicity-seeking accomplishments or devices. Congressmen tend to appreciate one another's problems, and while they reserve their greatest accolades for the top notch legislative experts and technicians among their colleagues, they also speak with envy and a kind of admiration of certain members who have been especially successful in keeping their names before their constituents. The inattention to legislation which characterizes certain of the showman-type congressmen, some of whom even take their committee responsibilities lightly, may irritate colleagues. At the same time, however, their mastery of the techniques of publicity (freely translated by colleagues into votes and victory) often arouses favorable comment.

### Specialization

From every quarter congressmen are pressed for action and decision. Though many of the matters brought to them should more appropriately have been taken elsewhere, they usually are reluctant to decline to accept jurisdiction, particularly if voters of their district are involved. At the same time, the serious substantive legislative problems with which they must concern themselves have become more numerous and more complex, making evaluation more necessary and decision more difficult. Further, the nature of the relationship between legislator and constituent has undergone many changes over the years. A congressman today has far more constituents than his predecessors, and they are much more likely to communicate with him on a wide variety of problems.

Faced with an impossible workload, congressmen have responded in different ways, most of them seeking refuge in specialization, a tendency which is encouraged by the committee system and other aspects of congressional procedure. They become expert, or at least facile, in a particular field, earn the respect of their colleagues for their diligence and command of the subject matter, and eventually come to be recognized as one of the congressional authorities in that area, a ready source of information and advice. Such recognition is accompanied by influence and has implications both within and without the Congress, though its impact, legislators complain, too seldom extends to the congressional district.

One member discusses the process by which many legislators begin to specialize:

> The nature of our set-up here in the House is such that our work on legislation suffers tremendously where matters outside the jurisdiction of our own committee are involved. We may have come here with deep interests in subjects unrelated to our committee, but we are so busy there that we never get around to thinking through or drafting legislation covering other matters. If we do draft it, and it is referred to another committee, we may not be able to get a hearing if we are in the minority and, anyway, a committee other than our own is handling it and is less interested in its success. So we begin to concentrate on the committee on which we serve, even though our interests may not lie there.

The emphasis on specialization simplifies significantly the task of the representative. Colleagues turn to him for aid in determining their own position on legislative matters which arise within his field of competence; he, in turn, settles on one or two trusted members on each committee to whom he can turn for clarification or advice regarding proposals falling within their committee's jurisdiction.

There are some legislative areas where congressmen consider themselves particularly dependent on the advice of their colleagues. Defense matters constitute an especially difficult problem since much of the information available to the appropriate committees in helping them assess defense requirements is not available to other congressmen. Though virtually no criticism is heard of the Defense Subcommittee of the Appropriations Committee, which is considered to be of unusually

high calibre, there is some uneasiness in the House because there is little opportunity for most representatives to reach an independent evaluation of defense
needs. This uneasiness and concern is expressed in the observations of three talented
House members—a conservative Republican, a liberal Republican, and a liberal
Democrat.

> I'd say that not one percent of the House knows anything about the work
> of the Defense Subcommittee, yet it involves crucial decisions. Only the
> written reports provide a clue to the real issues in much legislation, and they
> aren't particularly helpful in connection with the work of the Defense Sub-
> committee. In this business you've just got to trust your colleagues, especially
> when it comes to the committees on Ways and Means and Appropriations.
> The legislation with which those committees deal is so complicated and con-
> tains so many technical amendments that it is virtually impossible for the
> ordinary member to have any idea about what is going on. It is an unsatis-
> factory way to legislate, but unfortunately there is no alternative.

*

> It is pretty hard for the average member to know too much about some
> situations, other than those in which he is directly involved. The defense
> budget is beyond the comprehension and understanding of most congressmen.
> We have to take things pretty much on faith and on the word of those
> members who deal directly with the problem. Fortunately they are a pretty
> dedicated group, although even that just isn't enough sometimes.

*

> This matter of the budget, especially the defense budget, and the whole
> area of executive oversight is a very difficult one. The people in Congress who
> are concerned with defense matters are worked awfully hard. There is a
> tendency for the average member to throw up his hands in handling such
> matters. There is also a haunting fear that if we vote to cut certain phases of
> the program we may be hampering national defense. It takes a lot more
> courage to go against recommendations in this area than it does in other areas.

Dependence on colleagues for advice does not mean, of course, that the representative abdicates his responsibility to reach his own decision regarding legislation,
or to seek to ascertain the facts himself. It is but one method by which he meets
this responsibility.

### Becoming Informed

Although "the most important single source of information in evaluating legislation is the opinion of the trusted colleague," legislators may use many sources in
the course of their deliberations. The role of each varies significantly from issue to
issue and from member to member, depending on the type of legislation involved
(complexity, importance, and political implications are factors, for example), the
experience and philosophy of the legislator, the interest of various groups in society,
etc. Among the potential sources of information are individual colleagues, informal
organizations of congressmen to which a legislator belongs, committee and personal
staffs, the hearings and reports of committees, pressure groups, executive depart-

ments, the mail, and floor debate. Helpful, too, may be periodicals and professional journals (some congressmen are avid readers despite busy schedules), the academic community, the Library of Congress, research units of the various political party organizations, the news media, private research organizations, and staff arms such as the Office of the Legislative Counsel and legislative liaison groups. Travel constitutes another means of acquiring significant and relevant knowledge. The contributions of several of these are touched on in the pages which follow.

*The Library of Congress.* Created by and for Congress in 1800, the Library of Congress with a staff in excess of 2,700, 250 miles of bookshelves, and more than 42,000,000 items, constitutes a valuable source of information for congressional committees and harassed legislators and their staffs. Of particular help is the Legislative Reference Service organized in 1914 to meet the needs of Congress for specific reference assistance. In 1962 this division answered 99,430 congressional requests for information,[1] while other units of the Library handled 42,970 more. Requests ranged from those involving readily available information, such as furnishing a single fact from reference books, to detailed reports requiring weeks of intensive research and analysis of complex problems. The majority of requests were met by forwarding prepared materials.

The importance of the Legislative Reference Service to Congress is evident from the fact that in a typical year requests are received from all members of the Senate, virtually all members of the House, and from more than eighty committees and subcommittees. During one month alone the service was used by all but fourteen members of Congress and by sixty-two committees and subcommittees.

At the beginning of each Congress, the Library sponsors a luncheon for new members to acquaint them with the services available; the congressman who is aware of the kinds of help that can be obtained is in a position to benefit tremendously. One legislator, after emphasizing the importance of becoming recognized by one's colleagues as a specialist, commented that with the resources of the Library of Congress at his disposal, this was a goal not too difficult to achieve.

In addition to preparing speeches and analyses of legislative proposals, the Library provides such varied assistance to congressmen as briefings on important judicial decisions, background reports on legislation relating to important public problems, translations of foreign language materials, drafting committee prints, the preparation of charts and graphs, and assembling of packets of materials on certain subjects. Library personnel are also lent to congressional committees for special assignments.

Library officials complain that more than one third of congressional requests represent constituent rather than member inquiries, some of which require extensive research. The impact of these demands is to limit the time available for work on matters of direct interest to members of Congress, the *raison d'étre* of the Legislative Reference Service—with a direct effect on the quality and thoroughness of some of the work produced. Though performing research for the general public is in violation of the operating procedure of the Reference Service, Library officials are understandably reluctant to decline to handle requests that are received from congressional offices, regardless of their point of origin.[2]

Severe time limitations and the necessity of maintaining strict impartiality between philosophical viewpoints and political parties have led to mild congressional criticism of the Reference Service. The Service is considered very good for short, factual information but less satisfactory with respect to longer, more complicated materials. An often expressed congressional comment is that "LRS is good, but sterile." Another typical observation is that expressed by one Democrat: "They have been helpful to me, but they are a bit spotty. You cannot anticipate the level of the work. You never know whether it is going to be good or bad."

Because of the heavy and continuing demands on its staff (which is in excess of 200) LRS officials admit it sometimes is "hardpressed to maintain high standards . . . frequently unable to devote as much time to inquiries as they deserved." Often deadlines are met only by replying by telephone or by forwarding materials to offices rather than by submitting completed reports or memoranda. And, when the work is prepared in more organized form, the finished product often requires substantial reworking. Even so, Congress is grateful that the Service exists. In the words of one member, "It is the best single source I have found in Washington for getting information in a hurry." Another testifies, "I have had some wonderful experiences with Legislative Reference. They have been very fine and their work very adequate. Sometimes I have had to rewrite the stuff, but from the standpoint of the specific information I want, I have had good response."

There is general recognition that much material emanating from the Library needs the personal touch of the congressman or his staff. Some members accept this as inevitable; others regard it as a weakness that should be corrected. It should be clear that, to be most effective, products of a detached research arm such as the Legislative Reference Service ought to be recast in a congressional office to reflect the personal emphasis and style of the legislator, and in the light of the situation and interests of the constituency concerned. If this is kept in mind, the tremendous contribution of the Service to the work of a congressional office can be recognized and properly appreciated. Without the Service, many of the more active congressional offices unquestionably would be severely handicapped.

*The Executive Branch.* The executive branch is potentially a leading source of information for the legislator, although some of it is more readily available to the members of the President's party than to the opposition. It is necessary, however, to distinguish between official and unofficial sources of information within the executive. Official responses to congressional requests are normally sent out over the signature of a departmental officer; if the information has political implications and will be useful to members of both parties, congressmen allied with the President may receive it first. And the executive may take the initiative in supplying them with information judged to be helpful in encounters with the opposition. Sometimes, however, the opposition party retains close affiliations with members of the bureaucracy despite a change in administration and continues to benefit from "inside" information denied it by upper echelon political appointees. As one House Democrat said during the Eisenhower administration:

> In some parts of the executive, the bureaucracy can be separated from the administration. For example, there are sharp differences in Agriculture between the Benson [the Secretary of Agriculture] people and the career bureaucrats. The Corps of Army Engineers is another example. I have some pretty good contacts with them and with others in the bureaucracy and I know they often proceed independent of—and sometimes in opposition to—official policy.

Much the same point was made in a group discussion:

> As a practical matter, the executive branch is not readily available to us members of the opposition party. It undoubtedly is available to our Republican opposite numbers. I think that the remnants of what used to be the Democratic executive branch of seven years ago—which still exists in sort of shadow form in Washington—is of help to some of us. There are people who may have been in the State Department and who are now practicing law or who are around town.

*

> I disagree with what you say about the executive because I still have some excellent contacts in the administration.

*

> They are helpful, but not on an official basis. There are friends in the Bureau of the Budget, for example, who quietly—and you have to protect them—will give you help.

Yet even by working through formal channels, it is possible for the opposition to obtain information and assistance from the executive in the preparation of materials that are in conflict with the President's program. Related one congressman, not of the President's party:

> I have had much cooperation. For example, I had an agricultural bill drawn which dealt with marketing agreements and which certainly was not in accord with the Secretary of Agriculture's thinking. I contacted the Department of Agriculture and got their chief counsel in charge of marketing agreements to draw the bill for me. When he finished, of course, he said, "You understand this does not reflect the thinking of the department." But the fact is that they very willingly will lend their people to assist you in the preparation of legislation. I have had this same offer from a number of departments. They will even do research for you to back up your position.

For the administration official, however, cooperating with members of Congress not of the President's party may be dangerous. Partisans of the President in Congress complain frequently (and often loudly) that their opponents are given too much information and too soon—they find themselves "scooped" by the opposition on announcements from which they had expected to reap political benefits. When decisions have been reached to award contracts, build post offices or other federal buildings, establish new government installations, or increase ones presently in existence, it is standard procedure to inform the appropriate members of Congress of the President's party prior to passing on the information to those members of the opposition whose constituencies are also affected. One may receive the news by telephone shortly after the decision is made; the other may learn of the action by mail a day later; at the very least, the members of the opposition are informed several hours later than political allies of the President. Yet, no matter which party occupies the White House, there are occasional infractions of the general rule of giving preference to the President's party, much to the dismay of the Executive, which must bear the ire of the disappointed and angry legislator. Even when the situation relates to requests from congressional opponents for information rather than announcements of executive action, care must be taken to see that appropriate supporters of the President are provided the same information. Related one Democratic congressman who had once served in the executive branch:

> May I say from previous executive office experience that when Roosevelt and Truman were in power, there was fine liaison between Democratic members of Congress and the executive branch, both formally and informally. However, our agency once made the mistake of replying to a Republican query for more recent information than we have provided the Democratic leadership. No carbon copy was provided to the majority leadership. The Republican took the floor and used the more recent material to attack the official position being taken by the Democratic majority. The agency got thoroughly blistered for its failure to provide its own party in congress with the information they were providing the opposition. I suspect that if we succeed in getting any information in an official way from the Eisenhower administration, the Republican counterpart has a carbon copy of what we receive.

Though there were Republican complaints that Democrats sometimes got too much assistance from the executive branch when Eisenhower was President, there was general agreement that his administration was very helpful in providing both information and partisan materials to the Republicans in Congress. Said two congressmen:

> The departments are helpful. There are individuals who are very useful in discussing both the practical situation with which you may be faced—the political situation—and a comparison of different bills, the pros and cons of them. Certainly the executive branch is a potential source of great value to us, and to some extent they cooperate with the opposition too. It isn't a completely closed shop.
>
> *
>
> I think that when we were in the minority and the White House was held by the opposition we got relatively little help from the executive branch. Now at least I can go and get information there, but in the previous administration you got the barest minimum of assistance.

Members of the executive branch work especially closely with those supporters of the President who are responsible for guiding his program through the Congress. Thus key committees and legislators are provided with briefings, speeches, useful documents, and strategy suggestions. Sometimes representatives of the Executive are permitted to attend executive sessions of congressional committees in order to provide first-hand information on the Executive's position on proposed legislation and to indicate where compromise between that position and the stand taken by the committee is likely to be acceptable. This may be especially important when the President's party does not have a majority in the Congress.

The presence of individuals not members of the committee—or even of the Congress—is not unusual in executive sessions of some House units. In some committees, interest group representatives also may be present, though members of the

Congress not on the committee may be excluded. Participation of both executive and interest groups is pointed up in this discussion:

> The executive branch actively participated during the time our committee was in executive session on the education bill, to see if a compromise couldn't be worked out that would meet the basic principles and recommendations of President Eisenhower in this field and at the same time pay some sort of lip service to what the Democrats were agitating for.

> *

> Many times we have representatives of organizations like the Grange, Farmers Union or the Wheat Growers Association or Farm Bureau sitting in on our executive sessions of the Agriculture Committee. They are invited, the Grange more often than anyone else. I wondered whether other committees ever invited recognized lobbyists in to consider the final details of the bill.

*Intra-Congressional Groups.* An important source of information for many legislators are the various groups and organizations that have sprung up in the House in recent years. One small group that made extensive use of scholars was the Liberal Project, which in 1959 included eleven liberal Democratic House members. They invited forty-six natural, political, and social scientists to develop long-term national goals in defense and foreign policy. The essays that resulted were published as a book, *The Liberal Papers,* the purpose of which, according to a member of the House group, was to "reopen the political forum" through the contributions of "intellectuals whose ideas were uncommon and provocative." The book was criticized by Republicans who sought to make it a campaign issue. A GOP group hopes to publish its counterpart, *The Conservative Papers* in 1964. A larger, less doctrinaire, somewhat less issue-oriented organization of liberal Democrats is the Democratic Study Group mentioned in Chapter I. In the 1960 and 1962 elections, leaders of this group wrote nonincumbent Democratic congressional nominees offering campaign assistance in the form of making available hearings and reports likely to be of interest to the individual nominees. The Study Group is somewhat of a misnomer in that extensive study has not been undertaken; meetings are held to determine positions and to discuss strategy and occasionally subcommittees prepare surveys of legislative proposals.

The Republicans have no comparable organization—although efforts were made in 1961 and 1962 to develop counterparts—but various social groups, which initially grew up around classes of entering freshmen but which have modified their membership with the passing of time, have meetings devoted to issues and constitute valuable focal points for information about legislation.

Breakfast group sessions of legislators with common interests often deal with issues and feature experts outside of the congress as speakers. Several freshmen cited these breakfasts as among the most valuable sources of guidance on legislative problems. There are a few bipartisan groups that seek to obtain information that will help legislators meet their responsibilities more intelligently. In one such endeavor, a first term Republican member organized a group in 1959 to receive briefings from representatives of the State Department; this successful venture has been continued into the Kennedy administration.

*Academicians.* The influence of the academician on individual members of Congress both in the formation of decisions and in serving as a source of ideas and advice is generally regarded as negligible, both within the academic community and on Capitol Hill. His role is thought to be greater with committees than with individual legislators and stronger in the Senate than in the House. Yet it is clear to close observers of the House that the academician does exert a positive influence on the thinking of some of the more active and thoughtful members and that he enjoys their respect and is sought out by them. The Democratic Liberal Project is but one example of the attempt to use their knowledge; the Republican Policy Committee and the Republican Conference are also enlisting the assistance of scholars and "experts" in the formulation of action programs. Individual legislators are increasingly reaching out to them. During a discussion of important sources of information, an influential House Democrat confirmed this view:

> The group I find most useful in terms of information is the one I describe as the academic community, with particular emphasis on personal contacts within the group. They are either people who are academicians at present or who formerly held academic positions and are presently located in government or business or something of that nature. In that group are found the few people I really value highly and contact often. They don't have an axe to grind, or at least I am not sufficiently smart to observe it.

The comment was endorsed by another highly articulate and effective congressman. Said he, "I certainly find that group helpful too. They are, I think, much more useful than any of those mentioned."

*Travel.* In recent years travel, especially abroad, has become an important means by which legislators have sought to become better informed. Not until 1936 did a congressman inspect, at government expense, the United States foreign service and, according to a long-term member of the House Foreign Affairs Committee, prior to World War II, congressmen who went overseas did so as tourists or limited their travel to inspection of government-owned facilities in the territories of the United States. By 1959, however, about one-third of the House members and half of the senators were traveling abroad, nearly all in official capacities at a cost of more than $400,000 in counterpart funds alone. For 1962, more than $400,000 in foreign currency and dollar expenditures was reported by congressmen traveling overseas on committee or interparliamentary business.

The rapid increase in congressional travel abroad has been accompanied by criticism both within the congress and without, although there is much support for the practice, too. Defenders assert that the trend is a logical and necessary outgrowth of the increased role of this country in world affairs, and insist that it represents legitimate investigation by conscientious members of Congress whose legislative actions have world-wide impact. In order to legislate intelligently, it is argued, first-hand information about such matters as the effectiveness of our foreign aid program and the strength of our military bases is helpful, if not essential. Such travel has gone far to dilute the provincialism of some legislators. At the same time it has strengthened the position of the United States abroad by demonstrating to friendly nations its interest in their progress.

Critics concede that a large proportion of the authorized trips are desirable and necessary but suggest that many represent nonessential activities arranged for the convenience of members of Congress. In some instances, it is asserted, they constitute little more than a paid vacation for congressmen and their families. Trips for "lame duck" congressmen are particularly attacked. Even within the Congress there has been recognition that insufficient supervision by committee chairmen and those committees having jurisdiction for approving vouchers has resulted in abuses that serve to discredit the many worthy undertakings.

The secrecy in which authorization for committee travel was clothed until 1960 lent credence to rumors that the program was characterized by widespread misuse of funds. Revelations of certain excesses in 1960 brought about reform. An itemized public accounting of all expenditures (either appropriated dollars or foreign currencies) was required of members of Congress, congressional committees, and congressional employees, traveling either abroad or within this country. While this information was not always organized in a way designed to facilitate effective scrutiny, it represented an important step forward.

Criticism of certain trips in 1961 and 1962, however, led to further demands for control. Finally, early in 1963 the House adopted restrictions on the spending of its membership abroad. Some committees were restricted to activities within the United States. More detailed accounting procedures were also provided for. Members of congress and congressional staff authorized to travel abroad were required to use counterpart funds, if available, instead of appropriated dollars, and expenditures were limited to the maximum per diem allowed under standard government travel regulations. Only actual transportation costs could be paid, the government agency furnishing transportation had to be identified, and a report on the number of days spent in each country was required.

In May 1963 the House, with only two dissenting votes, passed and sent to the Senate a bill extending overseas travel restrictions to all House and Senate committees. Senate action was expected on the measure. To obtain more than the government's maximum per diem rate, a member would have to supply documents showing actual expenditures. Executive agencies would report any expenditures made in connection with congressional travel, and reports filed by them, members of Congress, and congressional staff would be published in the *Congressional Record* annually. Travel of "lame duck" congressmen would be curtailed.

*Floor Attendance and Activity.* Although the House spends less time in formal session than does the "other body" [3] and for much of it very few legislators are present, the average congressman does spend considerable time on the floor. Some members, it is true, shun the floor, asserting that their time can be spent more profitably elsewhere, except when they are required to vote or when a subject of importance to them or their friends is before the House. Others, however, veiw attendance as a valuable learning experience, which has its ultimate reward both within the House and within the constituency. And junior members are advised that the best way to catch the feel of the House and to master its procedures is to attend House sessions as often as possible.

The presence of a member does not ensure that his attention is directed to the speaker, of course. Some members sign mail or read should the discussion be uninteresting. Others talk with colleagues about legislative or political matters of mutual interest or merely strengthen personal relationships. This practice may be even more widespread when controversial measures are under consideration than when routine matters are before the House, since the expectation of controversy increases attendance and the likelihood that the colleagues with whom one wishes to confer will be present. Related one legislator:

> A two hour debate session provides a good opportunity for individual members to talk to their colleagues. Right now, for example, there are about six members I want to see, either to find out about legislation or to discuss legislation in which I'm particularly interested or which directly affects my district. While you are on the floor, you have an ideal opportunity to chat with colleagues and get business done which it proves impossible to accomplish in any other way. An opportunity is afforded to participate in a clearing house sort of operation in which valuable information can be forthcoming. It is similar to the way the London coffee houses used to be.

There is no doubt that many important decisions are reached and increased rapport developed in informal conversations held on the floor. The fact that there are no assigned seats (though some delegations or groups of members regularly sit in the same general area), promotes informality and visiting. Quite apart from the substantive work accomplished. House sessions have a socializing effect on the membership. In the words of one junior Democrat:

> It is very important to sit in [on House sessions]. That is the way you get to know members, to assess them. It is the way you get to know the rules. Many bills which are essentially the same come up year after year; House attendance helps you acquire the background of basic legislation.

Experienced legislators emphasize the importance of being on the floor when the House is meeting as the Committee of the Whole House on the State of the Union. Here much work is accomplished with smaller quorum requirements (100) and none of the disadvantages of recorded votes. Attendance is less crucial during the period of general debate but is definitely important when a bill is being read for amendment. Under the rules of procedure, if an amendment is defeated in the Committee of the Whole, it cannot be brought up again later in the House. If, on the other hand, an amendment is successful in the committee, it remains subject to review and a roll-call vote once the House has received the committee's recommendation.

Small attendance characterizes most sessions of the Committee of the Whole. A small, unified core of members of Congress can, by defeating proposed amendments there, prevent the full membership from working its will later. Regular participants in the Committee of the Whole therefore achieve greater voting power than their less available colleagues. Respected legislators and strategists of both parties stress the importance of the work done there and emphasize the difficulty of achieving a large attendance of party adherents, even on many major issues. Since the votes taken are teller, division, or voice votes rather than recorded ones, there is less incentive for many congressmen to be present. If, as often happens, a decision is reached on a Thursday not to have any roll calls until the following Tuesday, many congressmen return to their districts for that period; at such times frantic party whip calls are of no avail. There are complaints, too, that congressmen in their offices cannot get to the floor quickly enough to participate in a teller vote once the bells have rung to alert them to the event. Many legislators, having learned from experience that the effort would be futile, no longer attempt to get there. Thus, unlike the situation that exists when roll-call votes are held, members not already on the floor seldom are able to participate in the decisions. When there is a roll-call vote, legislators who are working in their offices can get to the House in time to be recorded provided they leave when the bells ring to alert them that a roll call is under way.

In discussing the situation, one group of legislators referred to a meeting of the House of Representatives when approximately 100 members wrote amendments into a Rivers and Harbors bill by a two or three vote margin each time. A member of the party whip organization related that two general whip calls had been made in an effort to get colleagues to the floor. These Friday afternoon efforts were unsuccessful because the congressmen could not be found. "A whole trend," he said in despair, "was being determined by a margin of about five votes. Once members began to break through with their special projects the process could not be stopped." Commented one legislator, "it was a very discouraging experience. It seemed as though the only ones there were people interested in their pet projects, including members [of two large state delegations]." Another congressman said that the session "was rather horrifying to me." But when a colleague observed that strict adherence to the rules would bring about better attendance for sessions of the Committee of the Whole, he was told his solution was not satisfactory. He stated that according to the rules if a quorum call recorded a member as being absent, he was subject to being docked a day's salary.[4] His colleagues reminded him that his party was in the minority; a full attendance would "result in our being trounced. This way we have a chance to slip something through."

### The Role of Debate

One factor contributing to attendance problems in the House is the general dissatisfaction that exists with respect to provisions for debate. The membership recognizes that the size and responsibilities of that body make some regulation inevitable. Widespread criticism of current procedures is heard, nonetheless. There is considerable disagreement with the much quoted view of the late Sam Rayburn that the rules "are pretty nearly perfect." One veteran Democrat referring to the curtailing of debate as the "greatest shortcoming of our system" went on to say. "It is most unfortunate that we cannot approximate real debate. Under the rules it is absolutely impossible to have a case argued in a manner approaching the way it should be argued, even on important issues.

Major legislation may be passed following debate of only two hours; seldom does a discussion extend beyond two days. Not only are the time limitations on debate unrealistic in terms of permitting a full discussion of the issue before the House, but they serve to limit participation to a few members. Frequently, general debate is consumed entirely by members of the committee studying the proposed legislation. The representative who has been unable to obtain a seat on the committee, but who has much interest in the proposal and possesses ideas about it, is thus denied the opportunity to present his views in the House. Efforts to extend debate time are usually defeated; only rarely are motions to close debate voted down. Complained one congressman, "Despite the difficulties members have in obtaining debate time you will find nearly everyone not actually participating in a bill on the floor willing to vote to curtail the time of others who want to participate."

Legislators disagree regarding the extent to which debate affects the fate of legislative proposals. The prevailing view is that speeches rarely influence many House votes. Their main effect, it is said, is to reinforce views already held, and their purpose is to make a record for the Speaker and a case for the position he supports. There is considerable support, however, for the position that debates are significant often enough in this regard to defy being dismissed as inconsequential and to question the accuracy of the description of the House as a dividing and voting body rather than a deliberative or debating one. Its deliberative nature is far more evident when powerful personalities and leaders take opposing stands. Observed one representative:

> Most House members will be more impressed by who is making a speech about a particular proposition than by what is said on the subject. I am not saying they would just judge by whether or not they like the individual. What is important is their evaluation of his knowledge and mastery of the subject and his experience in the field.

Legislators commonly believe that debate is more important in terms of public education than for member education, but there is recognition that considerable member education is involved also. And lawmakers cite specific instances when a determined and informed committee minority has upset the recommendations of the majority, once the bill has reached the House floor. Here, it is conceded, such action is more likely on bills about which the membership is unlikely to possess much knowledge or strong ideological predispositions. Even on important issues, however, debate on amendments may be determinative.

In connection with debate, there is considerable sentiment that because of the advent of television, increased restrictions on debate, and other factors, oratory has declined in the House over the years, although some congressmen deny the allegation. Not all legislators lament the passing of the art. Explained one:

> Frankly, I think it ought to be an obsolete art on the floor of the House. It is almost an insult to my intelligence to have a fellow get up and rant and rave and think he can influence my vote by tactics which should be reserved for the stump if used at all.

The advent of television is credited with having had an especially important effect on the speechmaking techniques of legislators. Members believe that "the kind of speeches which are effective on the floor of the House are not the most persuasive on television. Some of the orators don't do as well on TV."

> That is absolutely right. When _____ was speaking today I was struck by the fact that he was using a sort of "eating and meeting on the ground" style of oratory, the hell, fire, and damnation sort of thing.

*

> I make no bones about the fact that I consider myself about the least effective speaker in the House, but I will do as well as anybody on television.

That calls for a conversational approach and you can be very persuasive with it. You are putting yourself in the person's home. But standing on the House floor you are trying to get attention by the sheer weight of your voice, trying to break up those conversations.

Some congressmen are concerned about their failure to participate in floor debate often, and wonder whether their colleagues think less of them because of it. Others believe the wiser course is to avoid participation unless the subject is one about which there is little division in a member's district. One congressman reflected both these views when he told his colleagues:

I worried about debating on the floor and the fact that I had never had any experience in such matters. After a year or so in Congress I went to my committee chairman who was a very good speaker and told him I was concerned. I wondered what he thought about the fact I hadn't made any speeches on the floor. He said, "let me tell you something, son. No congressman has ever been defeated by a speech he didn't make on the floor of the House." I have thought about it many times because the man who told me was defeated after many years by speeches he did make on the floor. Words were thrown back to him that he had spoken twenty years before. . . .

### Voting

Voting is, of course, one of the most important responsibilities of members of Congress, and one which the vast majority of them take seriously, particularly when a controversial issue is involved. While some of the most important votes in the House are of the unrecorded type (teller or division votes in the Committee of the Whole, which affect the direction of important legislation, are often decided by very slim majorities), representatives are most diligent in attendance when roll-call votes are anticipated and demanded.

On some occasions a high sense of drama pervades the House as the voting on a closely contested issue gets underway and proceeds to its conclusion. A roll call may be preceded by division or teller votes that reveal that a surprise could be in store for the leadership or that a "cliff hanger" is in prospect. On the roll call, there may be things to watch—the vote switches that occur under the prodding of party leaders, the movement of latecomers to the well of the House to be recorded, the withholding of votes on the first call by certain legislators anxious to see the trend or to determine whether their votes are needed to bring victory to the party, the tallying of the vote by leaders on both sides of the issue to determine whether they will need to call up votes they are holding in reserve, or can release those who would prefer to vote on the other side but who have agreed to vote with them if such action will alter the outcome.

In campaigning for re-election members often point with pride to their high percentage of participation in these recorded votes; they are aware, too, that extensive absenteeism may be noted by an opponent and seized on as an election issue. During the Eighty-sixth Congress (1959–1960) the average member of the House cast "yea" or "nay" votes on 89 percent of the 180 roll calls; this percentage carried through the first session of the Eighty-seventh Congress, but dropped to 83 percent in the second session. If "pairs" were included, participation percentage would be even higher. Individual percentages varied markedly from 100 percent down to a low of 32 percent. The legislator with the poorest participation record in the 1960 session, had been present for only 17 percent of the roll calls, a figure far below that of any of his colleagues. Elected from a "safe" district where he controls the party organization, he is a chronic absentee, but his contituents do not seem to mind; he has been returned many times.

In more than half (97) of the 180 roll calls in the Eighty-sixth Congress a majority of the Democrats in the House were on one side of the issue, and the bulk of the Republicans on the other. There was no appreciable difference between the percentage of time the average Democrat and Republican voted with his party majority, in disagreement with that of the opposition party.

*Considerations in Voting.* Casting one's vote is not always an easy task. On some occasions the pressures on a congressman to vote a certain way are numerous and conflicting. Complicating the problem, especially where complex issues are involved, is the concern of some members that they do not possess all the facts on which to base a decision. Though there is evidence that even were additional information available, busy legislators would not have time to examine or assimilate it, there are some complaints that the Executive, to cite one source of dissatisfaction, requests the Congress to approve programs on the basis of incomplete information and is guilty of withholding data pertinent to the decision. Nor is it always easy to reconcile conflicting statements about legislative proposals. Lamented one legislator:

Another thing which disturbs me is the amazing lack of exact information which seems to be prevalent. I know it is a complex job and that we have to deal with many complicated problems. Yet it is disturbing to find people coming out with an opposite set of facts on the floor of Congress. . . . It is very difficult for a congressman to know what the truth is or where to find it when you hear such contradictory statements.

Advice regarding voting comes from many quarters. Sources and the extent of their influence on the final decision vary. Trusted colleagues, party leaders in Congress and without, the state delegation, committee chairmen, the executive, lobbyists, or interest groups, individual constituents or prevailing district sentiment, friends or family, the press—these are among the many contributors, at one time or another to voting decisions of members of Congress. Important, too, of course, is the personal predisposition of the legislator. His background, training, and fundamental social and economic philosophy play important roles in such judgments. The congressman may also be influenced heavily by the tug of party, of intra-House blocs or clubs with which he is associated, or a colleague to whom he is indebted. A representative who comes from a district in which the dominant political organization is particularly strong may enjoy special advantages over more hard-pressed colleagues whose districts are marginal politically, in that he may have greater flexibility in voting what he considers to be "the national interest" as opposed to the more parochial local interests, provided of course the organization permits him the flexibility. Said one congressman:

The stronger the party organization in your district the more independent and statesmanlike you can be, if the organization will permit it, naturally. Take

_____. He can do anything he pleases and know the voters won't turn him out next time. The unfortunate thing in that situation is that the other five from that city have to do whatever he wants them to do. They have no alternative. Sometimes the type of discretion which is permitted in certain strong party areas can be very good for the country.

The fact is that the number and range of issues are so great that no one can safely rely solely on his own information and vote intelligently. Commented one lawmaker: "You have to take so much faith on bills brought into the House; sometimes you get fooled." In that connection, deference to colleagues or to leadership opinion may be especially characteristic where the less important proposals are concerned.

One first term member, after expressing amazement at the "enormity of the workload" stressed that it was "impossible to keep up on legislation" and mentioned his heavy reliance on committee work and committee members with whom he had rapport. He explained:

> I turn to committee members in whom I have confidence for their integrity and ability and rely on them especially when the legislation is not of paramount importance. The best I can do is to devote my time to the major pieces of legislation which come before the House, and rely on others for advice in connection with less major legislation. I admit there are many drawbacks to such a system, but I want to impress upon you that there is no alternative.

It seems evident that the advice of trusted colleagues is all but determinative where minor legislation is concerned and is heavily weighed, at the very least, where the legislation is major. Where the issue has political overtones and the congressman finds his personal views in conflict with those of his district or the party leadership, he finds himself in a dilemma, particularly if he is convinced his position is the correct one. On this point one forthright veteran legislator had this to say:

> We have much leeway in voting, but we can't go against the district too often, I think. On *really* important issues I always vote my conviction regardless of the pressures which are put upon me. On less important votes politics may be followed on an expedient basis. I think members have to decide where they are going to make their stand and at what point the issue isn't too important. Sometimes it is easier to follow what your district wants you to do.

Consider this only semi-facetious exchange:

> I think very definitely that when your own personal convictions on an issue are at variance with the majority opinion of your constituents you should vote your convictions even when you know you are displeasing your constituents.
>
> *
>
> And what district did you represent?

*Little Knowledge of Minor Bills.* As noted, bills that are regarded as noncontroversial usually do not gain much attention from the heavily burdened legislators. This is especially true of measures on which there is not likely to be a roll-call vote. The typical representative is virtually uninformed with respect to bills reaching the House floor via the private or consent calendars, but in such cases his conscience is eased, for specific responsibility for ensuring that such bills are meritorious is delegated by party leadership to official party objectors whose job it is to screen the bills carefully. Democrats and Republicans have objector committees for both private and consent calendar items; [5] these representatives are on the floor when the calendars are called up. Since the majority of the bills passed are taken up by the private or consent calendar route, these committees have important responsibilities.

When a group of congressmen were asked how frequently they found themselves without strong views or even a position on matters coming before the House, they readily replied that this often happened ("all the time," "frequently," "except on very important legislation," "all the bills on the private calendar and half the others"). Because of the safeguards that existed, they were not disturbed by this.

Not ten people in Congress know the content of the bills on the consent calendar. Bills get there through request of the committee which has originally considered them, which is an indication of no opposition.

*

So that our failure to know about all bills will not be considered negligence on our part, we can point out that there are about ten thousand bills introduced each session, and about one thousand of fairly general nature reach the floor.

*

I think the problem of being adequately informed goes beyond the consent calendar items. Even with respect to bills on which there is a roll call I often have a hard time finding out what the issue is.

*

Lest we leave the impression legislation is too haphazard, we should remember that every piece of legislation which gets on the consent calendar has cleared the committee and has been cleared with the leadership. In addition, it must get past official objectors designated by each party. All of these hurdles have to be passed before you get it on the floor. There are other basic rules for the consent calendar, too. For example, an expenditure of less than $1 million must be involved, and the measure cannot have had an adverse report from the executive department concerned.

Occasionally, of course, errors occur. In 1960, for example, while trying to aid certain rural businessmen, the House voted to take minimum wage protection away from 14 million covered workers. The faulty proposal was offered as an amendment to a measure raising the minimum wage to $1.15. With only about twenty minutes debate remaining on the bill when the amendment came up, it slipped by on a voice vote, without opposition and with little discussion. It was intended to bar some farm processing workers from the coverage of the law, but as worded it actually removed all workers except those in cities of 250,000 or more. Remedial action followed quickly.

*Primary Dependence on Self and Colleagues.* Members of Congress indicate a heavy reliance on two main sources in arriving at a final decision regarding a vote: (1) their own personal judgment and (2) the views of trusted colleagues, usually those sitting on the committee having jurisdiction over the proposal under discussion. Most emphasize that the ultimate decision is their own, but the trusted colleague is mentioned nearly as frequently, particularly by representatives who have served more than one term. Since the colleagues consulted are nearly always of the same party as the member seeking advice, one could cite the practice as an indirect reinforcement of the influence of party in voting. Freshmen seem more anxious than their more senior associates to mention their independence of their districts when their own views conflict with those of their districts, though some are not anxious to publicize this independence. Said one freshman: "I came with the intention of voting my own convictions and not necessarily the will of the district. I consider that to be the proper view, although I don't think I would have wanted my constituents to know that while I was running for office."

*Sources of Advice for Freshmen.* When a group of freshmen members of Congress, interviewed separately, were asked to whom they turned in forming their judgments, they indicated in their responses that they placed great value on their own judgment. Beyond that, there was much divergence—colleagues, family, and friends, business associates, constituents, personal and committee staffs, party leadership, and state delegation deans being among the groups cited.

> I cannot say I lean on any particular individual. I am likely to trust my own judgment first. I study the issues as best I can, then I contact key pepole in our district in whom I have confidence.

*

> I listen to my fellow freshmen and I tend to turn more to junior congressmen in whom I have confidence, than to senior men. A Wednesday morning breakfast group which contains many new members and junior members has been very helpful.

*

> Frankly the give-and-take between junior and senior congressmen is quite limited. I'm the sort of person who likes to make up his own mind. I do consult with my administrative assistant and talk with my law partner at home whenever I have a serious problem. Another source of assistance are my former associates in the state legislature. I talk occasionally to the dean of our state delegation. If the matter relates to my committee work, I often consult the committee counsel.

*

> I am trying to become an expert in my committee assignment, and I rely on people of other committees to help me on other legislative matters, if I feel I don't have the information. Inversely, there are people on other committees I watch just because I expect to be on the opposite side from them.

*

> When I was first elected I asked a friend, whose judgment I value very much, which member of the state delegation could be most helpful to me, was

most likely to be informed on legislation, and could give me some idea of what a good congressman should do. I followed his advice, got acquainted with the member he suggested, and have never regretted it. I don't always agree with him, but I know I can go to him for honest advice.

*

I believe in party responsibility and I follow the President's lead wherever possible. Certainly there should be no criticism within the party for that action.

*

Primarily I depend on myself for decisions. I also turn often to my administrative assistant, and to my wife—she occasionally feels strongly I am doing the wrong thing. I also try to take advice from businessmen in my state. I turn also to senior members from my region regarding procedure and discuss issues with many of the new members, particularly those on my committee.

*Relatively Little Leadership Pressure.* Many new members of the House express surprise that so little pressure is exerted by the party leadership regarding voting. Clearly they had anticipated more frequent guidance or instruction. Their more senior colleagues also indicate that leadership intervention is minimal. Activities of the party whips prior to a vote generally consist of little more than perfunctory requests to be on the floor or occasional checks regarding the intended vote of the member. Seldom is advice given or a party position urged.

As long as the veteran Democratic and Republican leaders, Sam Rayburn and Joseph W. Martin, retained power, it was likely that leadership would be moved by pleas that, on certain issues, prevailing constituency opinion required individual congressmen to deviate from the official party position. It was also likely that relatively few demands would be made on members of the House, although adherents of both parties indicated their belief that "pressure" was more understandable when exerted by the party in control of the White House. Member consensus is that one should support one's party whenever it is possible to do so, and one or two veteran members caution that where a party position is known and one intends, for whatever reason, to vote contrary to it, it is wise to inform the leadership of that intention as early as possible.

As might be expected, constant deviation from the party position is likely to affect adversely the career and influence of a member of Congress. One of the most promising members to appear in the House in many years discovered early in his congressional career that his frequent votes in opposition to the stand taken by a majority of his party colleagues was the subject of much discussion and seemed destined to limit severely his influence within party councils. After a careful assessment of the situation, he set about to remedy it, with extraordinary results. On very important issues about which he has strong convictions, he stands firm despite his divergence from his fellows; on less crucial issues, he goes along wherever possible with the majority of his party. Conversations with some of his early critics reveal an almost complete reversal in their assessment of him. Though he is still regarded as somewhat atypical within his party (and has been denied the committee assignment he wants), respect for him has increased sharply, and there is no doubt that he is more effective than he would have been had he pursued his initial voting pattern.

In discussing the problem of casting intelligent votes in the House, one congressman declared that occasionally when members are called to the floor and arrive in the midst of a roll call, they may have difficulty in discovering what issues are involved in the vote or even the subject of the vote. In such instances, he complained, an inquiry at the party leader's table may result in advice on how to vote without an explanation of why that position should be supported. In illustration of his point he said:

> Usually we have the bills and reports before us prior to voting, and ordinarily I take a look at those and make up my mind before going over to vote. Once in a while you get there and are not prepared to cast a good vote or have not anticipated the vote. Usually, you ask some of the party leaders what the bill is all about. Sometimes it is difficult to get any information. For example, today we were voting on a not too important item because one of our people had demanded a roll call. I went over to the leader's table and said, "What is this all about? What are we voting on?" Do you know what I was told? "The vote is no." I said, "Okay, the vote is no. Why should it be no? What is the issue?" The answer was, "Someone is trying to give away a couple of hundred thousand dollars, and we are against it." They don't seem to like it when you ask why you should vote a certain way. I had to wander around to find someone who could explain the issue to me. Then I voted.

Representatives, like most politicians, speak often of their independence, especially when voting is discussed. They resent actions which might be construed as efforts to tell them how to vote. Yet, while emphasizing their determination to arrive at their own decisions, the legislators may express irritation with the party leadership because of its failure to state vigorously, and campaign aggressively for, its position on certain proposals. Irritation of this kind is not infrequent and is almost always expressed when the party position coincides with that of the outraged member. Failure of the party to achieve success with respect to measures in which congressional interviewees were especially interested, for example, was commonly attributed, in part at least, to weak, half-hearted leadership. "We could have defeated that bill," grumbled one Democrat, "if Sam Rayburn had just applied the pressure instead of letting the word get out that while he hoped people would vote against it, he realized we had to bear in mind the views of our districts." Liberal junior Democrats, in the last days of the Eighty-sixth Congress, were especially distressed by what they regarded as lack of effective leadership.[6] Many of them were equally dissatisfied in the Eighty-seventh Congress, though the leadership had changed.

*Executive Leadership or Executive Pressure?* Congressional members of a political party that controls the presidency but has minority status within the Congress find themselves under special psychological pressure to support the administration's program, especially if the issue involved is one on which the opposition can be expected to take the contrary position. Passage of the President's program will normally be difficult enough when his party is in the minority, and defections are regarded as somewhat more serious than would be true if he possessed a working majority.

During most of the Eisenhower administration, Congress was controlled by the

Democrats, but the President's problem was further complicated by the tendency for the congressional Republicans to be more conservative—some of them inflexibly so—than the President. Unity was essential, but in the face of widespread hostility or unenthusiastic support for certain aspects of the program, how far could the President go in marshaling congressional Republicans behind his proposals? In view of the situation, it was not surprising to find within the ranks of the Republicans expressions of dissatisfaction with the efforts made to unite the party on legislation. Criticism of this sort, understandably, came largely from people who, favoring the administration's position, believed that its position was not clearly stated or that insufficient efforts were being made to ensure party support for it. The frustration of one member of this group is evident in the following discussion:

There have been some instances when I have felt the Executive should have taken a more positive position. Take a bill like Jenkins-Keogh, which the administration was against,[7] yet completely ignored for a while. I felt if they wanted us to vote against the bill they should start calling us up and sending arguments and making statements out of the White House. Yet nothing happened. The day we were to vote on the bill the Secretary of the Treasury came out with a statement against it.

*

One reason they didn't make a fight is that they figured the bill was going to be killed in the Senate. You must remember, too, that they can lose face if they make an all-out fight for a lost cause.

*

One problem I had was that accountants and lawyers from my district were badgering me to vote for the thing. I would say that the administration was against it, and they didn't know that. I called Treasury and said, "If you expect us to vote with you on this you'd better start publicizing your position." If the administration feels it is important to vote against or for something they have to build towards that end. They may not get their congressmen to go with them but they sure ought to try.

*

I have never seen the unconscionable pressure that was applied to me on the Reciprocal Trade Act which I opposed. Carrots were offered to one of my industries and then the whip was offered to me. I had some of the very high people in our government calling me personally and trying to persuade me.

There were attempts in the course of the same discussion to distinguish between executive leadership and executive pressure with respect to legislation.

There is a fine line between pressure and leadership. I would say that in the last four years I have heard more gripes among Republicans because they didn't know what the administration's position was than gripes about having too much pressure put on them. We occasionally have been embarrassed in our committee work because we haven't known the administration's position.

*

I think we all expect that on an important issue we should hear, directly or indirectly, from the administration as to its position. I wouldn't consider it pressure to be informed by them, directly or indirectly, of their position. I consider that to be leadership and if I choose not to vote with them that is my own decision.

Republicans generally agreed that the replacement as minority leader of Joe Martin by Charlie Halleck resulted in stronger party cohesion in the House and more effective leadership, in the Eighty-sixth Congress. However, there was some criticism that failure of the Republican administration to pursue its position energetically on legislation had provided an opportunity for the more conservative party leadership in the House to drag its feet occasionally. An excerpt from one discussion of Republican members illustrates this point. The group was talking about an action of the House in approving an appropriation for construction of a prison. Most of the members present had opposed the appropriation, but two who had supported it commented:

What irritated me was the fact that the story being spread was not factually true. It was said the administration was half-hearted in support of the legislation, which isn't true. The Attorney General testified for it. Those members of our party from the state concerned who opposed the legislation did so for political reasons. They felt passage might help the sponsor in his district, and he had defeated a Republican who was popular here.

\*

The Attorney General was very clear that the prison was needed, that he wanted it, and that it was part of the President's program. Then on the floor I heard one influential Democrat argue the amendment was ridiculous because $10 million was needed for the prison and only $2 million was requested. I called the head of the Bureau of Prisons. He said that was absurd, $2 million was enough to get the thing started, the prison was needed and he was for it. I ran into the minority leader right before the vote and asked, "What is your position on this prison?" He said, "I hope to God we kill it." I asked, "What is the administration's position?" He said, "I don't think they really want it."

The experience of members of Congress with respect to receiving pressure from the party leadership—either that within the Congress or the administration—differs significantly. A partial explanation for the divergent testimony on this matter, it may be assumed, rests with differing interpretations of what constitutes pressure and what should be regarded as an expression of leadership. None of the Republicans attending the Brookings sessions had ever received a personal phone call from the President requesting their support for or against a measure, and the majority stated that no direct pressure had ever been applied to them. Although in many instances this might be attributable to the fact that on the important votes their preferences were known to be consistent with the party position anyway, in other cases their stand was in opposition to that of the leadership. While no one had been subjected to pressure often, several legislators identified specific measures on which they and colleagues had received strong overtures from the executive branch. Some participants often not sympathetic to the administration reacted to their testimony with genuine expressions of surprise.

The experiences and reactions of some members of Congress with respect to executive pressure are revealed in the exchange presented below, which also identifies several ways in which the executive attempts to influence votes.

I haven't been requested by anybody in the House or in the executive departments to vote a particular way on any measure. I have had representatives of the leadership say, "If you feel you can, we would like to have you go along on this bill." But as far as saying or intimating it might influence my future, that has never happened.

*

I have never had pressure but once and I am shocked to hear anyone say pressure is put on Republicans to vote a certain way.

*

Pressure *is* put on and I know about some of it. For example, one of the first problems I ran into was when the administration decided they wanted to extend the excess profits tax. I received calls from people in my district that were the result of calls to them from the administration. I made it very clear I though the tactics were pretty lousy.

*

The use of the carrot is much more effective than the use of the stick. Placement of installations, judgeships, postmasterships, selection of appraisers by the Veterans Administration, jobs in the executive—these are made with votes in mind.

*

Last year the President listed three measures as criteria for determining support of the administration and even suggested he might go out and fight you if you voted against them—foreign aid, reciprocal trade, and defense reorganization. Several of you were, like myself, in the position of having to oppose him on at least two of the three. Were you subjected to any pressures? I wasn't even asked to support them.

*

An Assistant Secretary of Commerce, knowing my antagonism to the Reciprocal Trade Act, approached me with a booklet showing the amount of business being brought in to my district by the measure and the number of jobs involved: he did that for every congressional district in the country. I don't think that is pressure. The executive did a better job selling members of Congress on this legislation than any other legislation I know of. It was a demonstration of leadership.

*

I don't mean to contribute to your disillusionment, but as far as I can see it was a case of executive pressure. Until just before the vote I felt the proposed amendments [weakening the act, in the opinion of its supporters] would carry. Then things happened. Cabinet officials were calling congressmen with whom they had the most influence, the bait was held out of direct subsidies on lead and zinc, and things just went "a-scooting." Also it was an election year and many Republicans wanted to be with the administration.

*

Don't you think it might have been a combination of pressure plus presentation?

\*

I'd say that westerners were pretty much inclined to vote against the bill until the Mineral Stabilization program was announced with the blessing of the administration. I am not going to say they didn't buy a lot of votes with that program. I have always been for reciprocal trade and probably would vote for it again, but I know a few boys who voted for it for that reason.

\*

There is another, indirect pressure on us Republicans, too. I know I feel it frequently because of the fact that I often find myself in disagreement with the administration position. When it comes right down to party responsibility and you know your vote may make the difference between passage or defeat of a measure, it is much more difficult to vote against it than it is when you can say, "Oh well, it is going to pass anyway and I can vote as I see it."

\*

This is all sort of amazing to me. I guess I have the poorest record of any Republican in support of the administration, except for one or two members. But no one has tried to put pressure on me. When I was going to vote against the administration position on reciprocal trade, a cabinet member spoke to me about it and asked whether I couldn't go along on it. I said no. On a couple of other bills, people have called me, but they didn't try pressure. They didn't offer to do anything for my district, or promise to campaign for me, or offer me any bribes. It was the sort of action I would call leadership, executive effort to get their position across.

One device used by the executive to strengthen the base of its support in Congress is to encourage important community leaders and organization officials to write their congressmen urging them to back or oppose certain proposals. Although there is widespread agreement that the Chief Executive has a right—and perhaps a responsibility—to seek passage of measures in which he believes, some legislators are not enthusiastic about his resorting to that particular technique, especially when more direct approaches are not fully used. Congressmen clearly believe that Congress should be consulted in advance by the Executive. While risks are involved in such consultations, many a worthwhile proposal has foundered because of a failure to adhere to this policy. The following discussion took place in the Republican group:

The President made no bones about the fact he had written to about fifty top executives saying, "Do what you can for my military organization plan."

\*

He didn't write and ask them to get in touch with you and try to persuade you, did he?

\*

Yes. Don't you think he did? It was reported he had done so. The men who wrote me were all loyal Republicans and large contributors to the party. They were of such a calibre that they wouldn't have accepted a suggestion from anybody who wasn't pretty important. I don't see why the President shouldn't do that. I think a Chief Executive has the right to write anybody he wants to.

*

I am not condemning him for his action. I think I would have done the same thing under the circumstances if I felt strongly about that bill. You use any tool that comes to your hand. You want to change minds.

*

As you will recall, he had a love feast with the Republican House members this spring and said that his support would go to members who supported three bills—foreign aid, reciprocal trade, and defense reorganization. And a good batting average was 33⅓ percent—we all tried to get at least that.

*

I heard that speech and I didn't think there was anything wrong with it. That is my idea of leadership. I think a Chief Executive is entitled to do that. I have a feeling that over his shoulder might come the thought that all Republicans are valuable to him at this particular time because when they are getting scarcer and scarcer people might be allowed latitude to express their own feelings.

*

Well, *I* object to it until the reasons and facts are presented to the people involved. I don't object to the Executive taking a strong position if he is doing so with knowledge of the issues and after consultation with members of his own party in the Congress who have some knowledge of the subject.

*Influence of the District.* Those legislators who decide that the best way to ensure continued success at the polls is to adhere closely to district sentiment on issues often discover that ascertaining the preferences of the constituency is not always an easy task. And, some solons declare, the public is fickle: legislators may be held accountable for judgments which, though consistent with prevailing district views at the time they were made, eventually prove to have been unsound. As one conference participant stated, "You must be as smart in prospect as they [the voters] are in retrospect."

To gauge the thinking of district residents with respect to important issues, members of Congress rely heavily on their own conversations with friends and acquaintances, party leaders, and newsmen back home to provide them with information as to local reaction. Congressional mail may be an important factor, although it should be clear that the form letter and the mass mailing ordinarily have little impact. District newspapers are generally read by the congressman and/or his staff, but they tend to be considered a somewhat less accurate index of district opinion. Another rough guide is the questionnaire "poll" which a majority of the House members distribute annually within their constituencies. In recent years, an increasing number of legislators are turning to scientific samplings of district sentiment undertaken by professional polling organizations.

Some representatives believe efforts to stay attuned to district sentiment are doomed to disappointment since the citizens themselves are subjected to so many cross-pressures by the mass media that they cannot reach very firm judgments on public issues; nearly every legislator agrees that constituents do not give or withhold electoral support solely, or even primarily, on the basis of recorded votes. Said one congressman:

> The huge bombardment of our citizens means they have little time to concentrate on what congressmen are doing. Things are so complex now and there are so many media providing information to individuals that I don't think they know which way to turn. There are millions of stimuli and it is difficult to know how they arrive at a decision.

Uncertainty regarding the preferences of constituents distresses many congressmen. True, discretion in voting becomes more permissible or acceptable if it is concluded that no strong mandate is evident, but the danger exists that a serious misinterpretation of local views or ignorance of firmly held opinions may prove fatal to the elected official. Thus, as one able congressman put it, how far you go beyond your interpretation of district preference depends primarily on whether you think the proposed deviation is "viable." The following discussion of Democratic congressmen includes many points commonly raised with respect to the issue.

> The key is that we members of Congress behave as one would normally expect us to. We represent our districts.

> \*

> We go beyond the district. You left the party's farm program, for example, and I have stayed with it, for reasons that relate to our districts. TVA is still viable as an idea in your district, but the farm program no longer is. It is in my city which has 67 percent of its income based on agriculture and the remainder based on manufacturing.

> \*

> Who knows what is viable? That is the big question I have. I think it is almost, if not completely, impossible—at least in city districts—for a representative to know what a majority of the people think. I don't think there is any way of finding out.

> \*

> All I am saying is that we decide we are able to stick with our ideologies, our views, our judgments, with relation to the effective opposition in our district.

> \*

> I think in terms of pressures being imposed and I don't think the majority of the people put pressures on you. Your pressures come from organizations and you respond to the organizations. For example, take the bill which came to the floor yesterday. The doctors and lawyers were for it, and many congressmen voted for the bill because of them. Yet I think if it were explained fully, a majority of the people wouldn't be for it.

*Votes May Not Be What They Seem.* It is true, too, that recorded votes do not always mean what they seem to mean. Measures may be passed by one body by large margins after assurances that the other body will scuttle them; the purpose may be to permit congressmen to be recorded so as to enhance their stature back home. Sometimes understanding colleagues rally behind an associate who needs support in his district, secure in the knowledge that a House-Senate conference will eliminate the not-too-meritorious measure he is sponsoring. The following discussion concerns a bill passed by the House:

His friends certainly rallied around and showed up today. Yesterday afternoon when [the bill] was first discussed no one was on the floor, but today everyone was out backing him. The Appropriations Committee had stricken a $10 million budget item and he moved to put back $2 million believing his district would get the construction.

\*

Rumor has it that _____ [an important committee chairman] wants the project in his own district. I heard that he got the subcommittee to keep the item out of the bill until he got an agreement from the administration to have it built in his district.

\*

It was amazing. Of all congressmen except _____, the sponsor could be expected to have the smallest following in the House. Yet he got out the vote.

\*

There were other things involved, I assume. The money was included in the President's budget and that made it easier than pushing for something not in the budget. He made an excellent presentation, and he did an excellent job of contacting people in advance to get them on the floor to help him.

\*

I talked to a Democrat from my state who wasn't around today when we voted, but who was working hard in opposition to the amendment yesterday. When I asked him why he was missing he said the leadership had agreed to give a favorable vote because they had gotten agreement from the Senate that they would knock it out of the appropriations bill and then in conference nobody would push for it. The House sponsor wouldn't be put on the conference committee. What harm had been done? He had made his pitch and was successful, would be regarded as a big hero back home, and yet the bill could be killed.

*Logic Not the Sole Determinant.* Congressional voting is a complex process which involves many considerations not always readily observed or understood by the outsider. Perhaps the best explanation of why its mysteries sometimes escape many observers is that offered by one freshman member of Congress. Said he:

You've got to realize that not only are we sitting there trying to analyze legislation, trying to do the best job we can, but that factors other than absolute reason are always entering the situation. We are not participating in this process in an academic environment, secluded from pressures and other factors which may not be completely relevant to the situation at hand. We are operating in a political environment, surrounded by lobbyists, constituents, the leadership, and jangling telephones and we virtually have no time alone to think and reflect upon the problems before us. The big miracle is that somehow all of this works. On paper, looking at the situation, you'd say it couldn't possibly work and yet the fact is that it does.

The legislative process is, as it should be, the central interest of most representatives. The congressman is both attracted and humbled by the difficulty of making wise decisions. He is frustrated by his inability to master all subjects of legislation, but he finds ways of informing himself, or of getting cues from trusted prompters in voting, and so evolves his own scheme of decision making. Yet he sometimes worries lest some inadvertent slip or unpredictable circumstance turn his constituents against him. His knowledge of the House grows with experience, but he never ceases to be amazed by the nuances of the legislative process itself.

## NOTES

1. An increase of 18 percent over 1961. Congressional inquiries have increased every year in the past ten years and have about doubled since 1954.

2. Commented one legislator familiar with Library of Congress procedure: "One of the problems of LRS and the Library is that they are too scared of everybody. Recently the House Committee on Administration had to pass a resolution making it unnecessary for them to translate a couple of Japanese books. I don't know why they couldn't have declined on their own initiative. One congressman got eight state newspapers, three Washington papers, and thirty-odd magazines delivered to his office as they came out and the Library asked our committee to stop that too."

3. In 1959, for example, the House was in session for 527 hours and the Senate for 1,009 hours (spread over 141 and 140 days respectively); in 1960, the House sat for 512 hours, the Senate for 1,188 hours, spread over 124 and 140 days respectively. In 1961, the House total was 569 hours compared with 1,005 for the Senate (spread over 147 and 146 days respectively); in 1962, the House total was 656 hours and the Senate 1,159 hours (spread over 159 and 177 days respectively).

4. An 1872 law, never revoked, directs House and Senate officials to deduct from a member's salary a day's pay for each day's absence except in cases of illness. Periodically, individual congressmen urge the House to invoke the provision.

5. According to a statement submitted in the opening days of the 88th Congress by the majority and minority objectors for the consent calendar, the following requirements should be met before a bill is passed by unanimous consent in the House: (1) It must involve aggregate expenditures of less than $1 million. (2) It should not change national or international policy. (3) It should not affect a majority of the congressional districts. If it does, and meets other requirements, it will be "passed over without prejudice" one or more times to permit congressmen to become informed as to its content. (4) It must not run counter to the President's program and should be the subject of reports from the Bureau of the Budget and the executive departments affected by such legislation.

6. A major cause of this dissatisfaction was the passage of the Landrum-Griffin labor bill, which most liberals in the House opposed.

7. But which was supported by a majority of House Republicans.

# 7. United States Senators—
# A Collective Portrait*

DONALD R. MATTHEWS [1]

"Ever since Webster and Calhoun," one perceptive observer of the American scene has recently observed, "the style in senators has been as rigid, classic and widely recognized as the Washington Monument. Everybody knew what a proper senator was supposed to look like; the mane of white hair sweeping down over his collar, the dignified paunch, the black string tie knotted like a Mississippi gambler's, the frock coat, the broadbrimmed Stetson, the mottled jowls, the countenance of a slightly apprehensive Roman emperor. He had been born in a log cabin; his voice sounded like a church organ with the *vox humana* pulled out; he walked as if he were leading a parade." [2] There is one trouble with this mental image—the classic senator is "gone, wind and all."

The aim of this article is to present a more accurate and revealing picture of today's United States senators. Data on the social backgrounds and political careers of the 180 men and women who served in the Senate between January 1947 and January 1957 has been collected from biographical directories, newspaper and magazine stories, personal correspondence and interviews.[3] This data makes it possible for us to present a group portrait of the postwar senators, to compare this picture with the characteristics of the American people as a whole, and to examine the differences in backgrounds and careers found among the members of the upper house of the American National Congress.

The potential rewards of such an analysis are substantial. If we are to understand the behaviour of United States senators we must know who they are, the kinds of experiences they have had, the skills, group loyalties and prejudices they bring with them into the chamber. A collective biography of United States senators is an essential first step to an understanding of senatorial behaviour.

## Age and Sex

Originally, a Senate was an assembly of old men. The description is less apt but not too inappropriate when applied to the upper house of the American Congress today. Article I, Section 3 of the Constitution requires that United States senators be at least thirty years of age. On the whole, during the postwar period, the senators met this age requirement with quite a few years to spare. The "average" senator is in his mid-fifties, and was in his late forties or early fifties when first elected or appointed to the chamber (Table 1). True, a handful became

* From *The International Social Science Journal*, Vol. 13 (1961), pp. 620–634. Reprinted by permission.

TABLE 1. AGE DISTRIBUTION OF SENATORS AND OF POPULATION OVER 30 YEARS OF AGE (1950)

| Age Group | Distribution of Senators By Age Group (%) | Senators' Average Age Distribution 1947–57 (%) | Population over 30 Years (%) | Index of Over Representation* |
|---|---|---|---|---|
| 30–34 | 1 | 1 | 15 | 0.1 |
| 35–39 | 9 | 3 | 15 | 0.2 |
| 40–44 | 12 | 8 | 13 | 0.5 |
| 45–49 | 22 | 12 | 12 | 1.0 |
| 50–54 | 24 | 20 | 11 | 1.8 |
| 55–59 | 15 | 20 | 10 | 2.0 |
| 60–64 | 10 | 15 | 8 | 1.9 |
| 65–69 | 5 | 8 | 7 | 1.1 |
| 70–74 | 2 | 8 | 5 | 1,6 |
| 75 and over | 0 | 5 | 5 | 1.0 |
| Total | 100 | 100 | 100 | |
| | (n = 180) | (n = 180) | | |

* The 'index of over-representation' is a way of expressing numerically the relationship between an actual and an expected proportion. If the senators' age distribution had been the same as that of the eligible population, the index for each group would be 1.0. Where the index is greater than 1.0, the age group is over-represented; where less than 1.0, under-represented. In this table, the index was computed using the average age distribution of the chamber, 1947–1957. (In this table, and some others, columns do not add up to 100% because of rounding.)

senators while still in their thirties, a few were over seventy-five before they were elected. We shall try to explain these differences later. For now it is enough to note that a far smaller proportion of the senators are in their thirties than is true for the population, and about the same proportion of senators as ordinary citizens are over sixty-five. It is the late forties and fifties that are "over-represented" [4] in the "most exclusive gentlemen's club in Washington."

And the Senate is indeed a gentlemen's organization: of the 180 persons who served in the United States Senate between January 1947, and January 1957, only three were women. Two of these served for only a few weeks each. Only Margaret Chase Smith of Maine served in the Senate for a significant period during the postwar years. Her success in the Senate constitutes a major exception to the hoary rule that politics is a man's game. But in another sense, her career underlines the past and present male domination of the Senate. She, like almost all the other women who have served in the Congress, is a widow of a congressman. Few others have been able or willing—as has Mrs. Smith—to launch what amounts to an independent career.

### Mainstreet, Middletown, USA

America was a rural country when most of the postwar senators were born. It is not surprising, then, that a majority of them were born in rural areas. But while the rural-born are in a clear majority, there are fewer of them than might reasonably be expected. In 1900, which is the census year closest to the median birthdate of the senators, 60 per cent of the American people lived in rural areas, yet only 52 per cent of the senators were rural born. While in a minority, the urban-born actually won more than their statistical share of the Senate seats in the period from 1947 to 1957. But there are many varieties of urban places. Table 2 shows that the most consistently over-represented birthplaces ranged in size from 2,500 to 5,000 inhabitants. These small towns produced twice as many Democrats and four times as many Republicans as one might expect on the basis of chance.

TABLE 2. SIZE OF SENATORS' BIRTHPLACES AND RESIDENCES COMPARED WITH POPULATION DISTRIBUTION

| Size of Place | Birthplaces (%) | Population Distribution 1900 (%) | Senators' Residences (%) | Population Distribution 1950 (%) |
|---|---|---|---|---|
| Rural | 52 | 60 | 15 | 41 |
| 2 500–5 000 | 12 | 4 | 8 | 4 |
| 5 000–10 000 | 7 | 4 | 13 | 5 |
| 10 000–25 000 | 8 | 5 | 15 | 8 |
| 25 000–50 000 | 6 | 4 | 15 | 6 |
| 50 000–100 000 | 3 | 4 | 7 | 6 |
| 100 000 + | 12 | 19 | 27 | 30 |
| Total | 100 | 100 | 100 | 100 |
| | (n = 177) | | (n = 180) | |

The same over-representation of the nation's smaller towns and cities is true for the senators' present-day residences. By 1950, 64 per cent of the American people lived in urban areas and 56 per cent in metropolitan areas. The present-day residences of the senators reflect this shift: 86 per cent of the senators have their official residences in urban areas, 41 per cent in metropolitan areas. But most of the urban senators live in the small and medium-sized cities of the United States (see Table 2). The rural areas and large cities remain under-represented.

*Class Origins*

Despite a widespread preference not to talk about such matters, few observant Americans would deny that individuals in the United States are ranked or "stratified" on generally accepted scales of social inferiority and superiority. Moreover, most would agree that individuals sharing roughly equal positions in this system of invidious distinctions tend to group into "classes." [5]

The most important single criterion of ranking in the United States seems to be occupation. While it is by no means a certain index to social standing, it is the closest approach to such an infallible guide. Thus information on the occupations of the senators' fathers should provide a reasonably accurate picture of the senators' class origins. Table 3 shows that, with only a handful of exceptions, the senators were sons of men possessing upper and middle-class occupations. The children of low-salaried workers, wage-earners, servants, and farm labourers, which together comprised 66 per cent of the gainfully employed in 1900, contributed only 7 per cent of the postwar senators.[6] Moreover, the differences in occupational-class origins of Democrats and Republicans are small. Fifty-eight per cent of each party were the sons of either professionals, proprietors, or officials; the remainder were sons of farmers, low-salaried workers or wage-earners.

TABLE 3. OCCUPATIONAL CLASS DISTRIBUTION OF SENATORS' FATHERS COMPARED WITH OCCUPATIONAL DISTRIBUTION OF LABOUR FORCE IN 1900

| Occupational Class | Fathers of Senators (%) | Labour Force in 1900 (%) | Index of Over-Representation |
|---|---|---|---|
| Professional | 24 | 6 | 4.0 |
| Proprietors and officials | 35 | 7 | 5.0 |
| Farmers | 32 | 22 | 1.5 |
| Low-salaried workers | 2 | 5 | 0.4 |
| Industrial wage-earners | 5 | 39 | 0.1 |
| Servants | 0 | 5 | 0.0 |
| Farm labourers | 0 | 17 | 0.0 |
| Unknown | 2 | – | – |
| Total | 100 | 100 | |

(n = 180)

## Race, Nationality, Creed

The happy diversity of the American peoples is only dimly reflected in the racial, national and religious backgrounds of the senators. One out of every ten Americans is a Negro. They may have been amply represented in the Senate in other ways but not, during the post World War II period, by a member of their own race. Immigrants and second-generation whites suffer from a milder discrimination. A smaller proportion of the senators than of the white population were first- or second-generation Americans (Table 4). Moreover, this preference for Anglo-Saxon origins is also demonstrated by the fact that the three immigrants who served in the postwar Senate came from Great Britain, Canada and Germany. Furthermore, virtually all the second-generation Americans in the Senate were from northwestern and central Europe, while the many new Americans from other parts of the world were almost unrepresented in the chamber (Table 5).

This preference for senators with "Yankee" backgrounds—or, failing that, for those with origins that approach as closely as possible the Anglo-Saxon ideal—is

TABLE 4. PERCENTAGE OF SENATORS WHO WERE FIRST- AND SECOND-GENERATION AMERICANS COMPARED WITH THAT OF WHITE POPULATION IN 1950

| | Democrats (%) | Republicans (%) | All (%) | White Population 1950 (%) | Index of Over-Representation |
|---|---|---|---|---|---|
| Immigrants | 2 | 1 | 2 | 7 | 0.3 |
| Second-generation | 15 | 11 | 13 | 16 | 0.8 |

TABLE 5. ORIGINS OF SECOND-GENERATION SENATORS, BY REGIONS, COMPARED WITH THOSE OF ALL SECOND-GENERATION AMERICANS IN 1950

| Region | Senators (%) | All second-generation Americans, 1950 (%) | Index of Over-Representation |
|---|---|---|---|
| North-western Europe | 75 | 28 | 3.7 |
| Central Europe | 17 | 32 | 1.9 |
| Eastern Europe | 0 | 11 | 0.0 |
| Southern Europe | 6 | 14 | 0.4 |
| Other Europe | 0 | 1 | 0.0 |
| Asia | 0 | 1 | 0.0 |
| America | 0 | 12 | 0.0 |
| All other | 0 | 1 | |
| Total | 100 | 100 | |

also reflected in the religious affiliations of the senators. Protestants are substantially over-represented, Roman Catholics and Jews under-represented in the Senate (Table 6). The same preference for those with high-prestige religious affiliations is found among the Protestants. There are about three times the number of Episcopalians and twice the number of Presbyterians among the Protestant senators as would be found in a randomly selected group of Protestants. The Methodists and Congregationalists have about their fair share of the Senate seats, while the Baptists and Lutherans are considerably under-represented.[7]

The seriousness of this bias against members of America's minority groups is mitigated, however, by several factors. First of all, the Democratic party is more open to minority group political talent than is the Republican party (see Tables 4 and 6). Moreover, a minority group member's chances of becoming a senator depended upon the constituency he sought to represent. Generally speaking, the heavier the concentration of minority group members in his state, the better were his chances. But this tendency holds true *only* when the senators are Democrats.

## Education

Senators are among the most educated—in the formal sense of the word—of all occupational groups in the United States. Almost 85 per cent of them attended college, a level of education achieved by only 14 per cent of the adult population in 1950 (Table 7). The educational gap between the people and the members of the Senate is actually much wider than these figures indicate: 45 per cent of the senators attended both undergraduate college and law school, 8 per cent of them engaged in some other form of postgraduate work.

This high level of education can be accounted for, in part, by the senators' relatively high class origins. Numerous studies show that, while the American educational system is one of the most equalitarian in the world, substantial differences in educational opportunities exist between social classes. Financial pressure, lack of motivation for academic success, the unconscious preference of middle-class teachers for middle-class children, and so on, place the child from working- or lower-class families at a distinct disadvantage even when his intelligence is the same

TABLE 6. RELIGIOUS AFFILIATION OF SENATORS COMPARED WITH THAT OF POPULATION

|  | Democratic (%) | Republican (%) | All (%) | Population Self-Identification (%) | Claimed Church Membership (%) | Index of Over-Representation |
|---|---|---|---|---|---|---|
| Protestant | 81 | 95 | 88 | 72 | 59 | 1.2 |
| Roman Catholic | 15 | 5 | 11 | 21 | 34 | 0.5 |
| Jewish | 4 | 0 | 1 | 3 | 6 | 0.3 |
| Other | 0 | 0 | 0 | 3 | 1 | – |
| Total | 100 | 100 | 100 | 100 | 100 | |

Note: Religious self-identification was computed from a sample of the national electorate in A. Campbell, G. Gurin and W. Miller, The Voter Decides, (Evanston, Ill., 1954), p. 214. The figures on claimed church membership are from The World Almanac, 1951, p. 481. The index of over-representation was computed using self-identification as the criterion of church membership.

TABLE 7. SENATORS' EDUCATIONAL ATTAINMENT COMPARED TO THAT OF WHITE POPULATION, 25 YEARS OLD OR OVER IN 1950

| Highest level of Schooling | Democrats (%) | Republicans (%) | All Senators (%) | White population over 25 (1950) (%) | Index of over-Representation |
|---|---|---|---|---|---|
| Grade school | 1 | 1 | 1 | 48 * | 0.2 |
| High school | 7 | 22 | 14 | 38 | 0.4 |
| College | 91 | 77 | 84 | 14 | 6.0 |
| Law school | (10) | ( 7) | ( 8) | | |
| College | (22) | (25) | (23) | | |
| College & law | (45) | (41) | (45) | | |
| Postgraduate | (11) | ( 5) | ( 8) | | |
| Unknown | 1 | 0 | 1 | 0 | |
| | 100 | 100 | 100 | 100 | |

* Includes those with no formal education.

as the middle-class child's.[8] But this is far from a total explanation of the superior educational attainments of the senators for, *regardless of their class origins,* more senators attended college than other members of the white adult population (Table 8). Thus the high educational level of senators is not just the result of their greater opportunities but also reflects exceptional academic interest, ability and achievement.

There are interesting party-line differences in educational levels, too. The Democrats are more educated than the Republicans (see Table 7). Again, this is not the result of different class origins, for, when the levels of education of Democratic and Republican senators with roughly the same class origins are compared (see Table 8), the Democrats come out well ahead, especially among the senators with lower-class origins.

What kinds of schools did the senators attend? As undergraduates, the senators studied in 104 different educational institutions. State universities were the most

TABLE 8. PERCENTAGE OF SENATORS ATTENDING COLLEGE, BY OCCUPATIONAL
CLASS LEVELS OF THEIR FATHERS

| Occupational Class of Father | Democrats (%) | Republicans (%) | All Senators (%) |
|---|---|---|---|
| Professional | 93 | 100 | 96 (n = 43) |
| Proprietors and officials | 96 | 82 | 84 (n = 61) |
| Farmers | 87 | 74 | 81 (n = 51) |
| All lower occupations | 75 | 24 | 53 (n = 15) |

popular type of undergraduate institution—about half of the senators attending undergraduate schools went to a state university at one time or another. But a very large share of all college graduates in the United States attended these uniquely American institutions. What type of college graduated the largest share of senators, taking into account the size of its alumni body? The answer—as clearly as we are able to supply one—is to be found in Table 9. Harvard, Yale, Princeton, and the smaller but well-known Eastern colleges graduated more than their share of the senators, especially Republicans.

TABLE 9. TYPES OF COLLEGES ATTENDED BY COLLEGE-GRADUATE SENATORS
COMPARED WITH COLLEGES ATTENDED BY WORKING MALE COLLEGE GRADUATES
IN 1940

| Type of Undergraduage College | Democrats (%) | Republicans (%) | All Senators (%) | All College Graduates 1940 (%) | Index of Over- Representation |
|---|---|---|---|---|---|
| Harvard, Yale & Princeton | 5 | 19 | 10 | 5 | 2.0 |
| Other Ivy League* | 2 | 2 | 2 | 6 | 0.3 |
| 20 Outstanding eastern schools† | 9 | 14 | 11 | 5 | 2.2 |
| Big ten ‡ | 4 | 12 | 6 | 12 | 0.5 |
| All other | 81 | 52 | 69 | 72 | 1.0 |
| Total | 100 | 100 | 100 | 100 | |
| | (n = 54) | (n = 42) | (n = 96) | | |

* Dartmouth, Cornell, Pennsylvania, Columbia.
† Amherst, Bates, Bowdoin, Brown, Clark, Colby, (Maine), Franklin and Marshall, Hamilton, Haverford, Hobart, Lafayette, Lehigh, Middlebury, Rutgers, Swarthmore, Trinity (Conn.), Tufts, Union (NY), Wesleyan, Williams.
‡ Chicago, Illinois, Indiana, Iowa, Michigan, Minnesota, Northwestern, Ohio State, Purdue, Wisconsin.
Source: F.C. Babcock, The US College Graduate, (New York, 1941), p. 42 (Table DD).

A similar picture emerges from a close look at the 51 law schools the senators attended. On the basis of a thorough survey of legal education in 1920 (about the time most senators went to law school), A. Z. Reed found four levels of excellence in the nation's law schools.[9] Almost half the law schools attended by the senators were of the highest quality (at a time when only one-fifth of all American law schools belonged to that category) and another 30 per cent of the senators attended schools of the second-ranking type (Table 10). Again, a considerably greater percentage of Republicans than Democrats attended the first-ranking schools.

TABLE 10. TYPES OF LAW SCHOOL ATTENDED BY SENATORS (IN PERCENTAGE OF ALL SCHOOLS ATTENDED)

| Type of School | Democrats (%) | Republicans (%) | All Legally Trained Senators (%) | Proportion of all Law Schools in Category, 1920 (%) | Index of Over-Representation |
|---|---|---|---|---|---|
| High entrance, full-time | 31 | 68 | 47 | 21 | 2.2 |
| Low entrance, full-time standard length | 38 | 20 | 30 | 29 | 1.0 |
| Part-time | 23 | 12 | 18 | 39 | 0.5 |
| Short course | 8 | 0 | 5 | 11 | 1.5 |
| Total | 100 | 100 | 100 | 100 | |
| | (n = 61) | (n = 49) | (n = 110) | (n = 142) | |

*Occupation*

As might be expected from a group of highly educated men, most of the senators started work near the top of America's occupational hierarchy: 88—almost exactly one-half—of the senators began working as lawyers, 13 as teachers, 12 as journalists, 6 as professors, 6 as merchants, 5 as executives in manufacturing concerns. On the other hand, a few of the senators began work in less desirable jobs, for example, 8 senators started out as farmers, another 8 as clerks, 4 as salesmen, 2 as common labourers, 3 as printers, 1 each as an electrician, machinist, pipe-fitter, factory worker, and farm labourer. But when all the senators' first occupations are lumped into occupational classes, it is clear that the "log-cabin-to-Capitol-Hill" myth of American politics needs considerable revision—81 per cent of the senators *started work* in the two highest classes.

By the time the senators settled into their main non-political occupations, a good deal of job shifting had occurred (Table 11). By this stage of their careers, *all* the senators are to be found in the top quarter of the labour force.

Almost 60 per cent of the senators were serving in political office at the time of their election or appointment to the Senate. Of those elected to the upper house from "civilian" occupations, the lawyers were most numerous (38), followed at a considerable distance by merchants (6), publishers (3), and manufacturing executives (3). All told, 82 per cent of the prospective senators were professionals (including public officials) and 15 per cent proprietors and officials at the time of their election. Only four of the 180 men were full-time farmers and one was a factory worker when elected to the Senate. Senators, quite obviously, are elected from, at, or near the top of the nation's occupational class system.

TABLE 11. OCCUPATIONAL HISTORY OF SENATORS

| Occupational Class | Fathers' Principal Occupation (%) | Senators' 1st Occupation after Schooling (%) | Senators' Principal Occupation (%) | Senators' Occupation at time of 1st Entry into Senate (%) | Occupation of labour force (1940)(%) |
|---|---|---|---|---|---|
| Professional | 24 | 68 | 64 | 82 | 7 |
| Proprietors, officials | 35 | 13 | 29 | 15 | 8 |
| Farmers (owners, tenants) | 32 | 4 | 7 | 2 | 11 |
| Low salaried workers | 2 | 8 | 0 | 0 | 17 |
| Industrial wage-earners | 5 | 6 | 0 | 1 | 40 |
| Servants | 0 | 0 | 0 | 0 | 11 |
| Farm labourers | 0 | 1 | 0 | 0 | 7 |
| Unknown | 2 | 0 | 0 | 0 | 0 |
|  | 100 | 100 | 100 | 100 | 100 |
|  | (n = 180) | (n = 180) | (n = 180) | (n = 180) | |

## The Lawyers

The legal profession comprises about one-tenth of 1 per cent of the American labour force, and yet about half of the senators were lawyers. No other occupational group even approaches the lawyers' record. Why this predominance of lawyers? They meet what seems to be one test of top level leadership—they are a high prestige profession. But why are not other equally prestigeful occupations equally represented among the senators?

A partial answer to these questions can be found in the skills of the lawyer and in the nature of the legal profession in America. The lawyer, in his everyday occupational role, develops ability in interpersonal mediation and conciliation and skill in verbal manipulation. Lasswell and McDougal do not exaggerate when they say: ". . . the lawyer is today . . . the one indispensable adviser of every responsible policy-maker of our society—whether we speak of the head of a government department or agency, of the executive of a corporation or labour union, of the secretary of a trade or private association, or even of the humble independent enterpriser or professional man. As such an adviser the lawyer, when informing his policy-maker of what he can or cannot legally do, is in an unassailably strategic position to influence, if not create, policy. . . . For better or worse our decision-makers and our lawyers are bound together in a relation of dependence or identity." [10] With the development of these skills in the normal course of a legal career, the lawyer has a substantial advantage over the average layman who decides to enter politics.

The professional skills developed by lawyers do not alone explain their dominance in the political leadership groups of America. Unlike many European countries, the United States has never had a landed aristocracy with a tradition of political participation. Relatively few senators are the possessors of *inherited* wealth. In a highly competitive society, where occupational success is the most highly valued goal for the ambitious, who can, with the least danger, leave their job for the tremendous risks of a political career? Among the high-prestige occupations it seems to be the lawyers. Certainly, other professional men find the neglect of their careers for political activity extremely hazardous. To those in professions where the subject matter is rapidly changing, a few years of neglect of their vocations and their skills would be either lost or outmoded. The active businessman, be he an individual entrepreneur or a member of a corporate bureaucracy, would find the neglect of his vocation for politics no asset to his primary occupational interest. These barriers to political participation either do not exist or are decreased in significance for the lawyer. The law changes relatively slowly. The lawyer, as Max Weber argued, is "dispensable," he can most easily combine his occupation, on a part-time basis, with political activity. Moreover, this activity can be a positive advantage to his occupational advancement—free and professionally legitimate advertising, contacts, opportunities to meet important lawyers of his region result from his political activities. Finally, lawyers possess a monopoly of public offices relating to the administration of law and the court system.[11] Since in America "every political question tends to become a legal question," the offices of judge and prosecuting attorney provide lawyers (and lawyers alone) relatively easy entry into the political world and important springboards to higher offices.

### Political Careers

Most of the post-World War II senators began their political careers early in life. Almost half of them held their first public office before their thirtieth birthday; a full three-quarters of them were public officials before they were forty years old. Of course, these figures exaggerate the age at which the senators became politically active, for few persons achieve public office without prior years of political activity. Thus the "average" senator probably became immersed in politics shortly after the completion of his education.

The senators' first public offices varied widely in their character and importance (Table 12). Almost exactly half of the senators began either as law-enforcement officers (prosecuting attorneys, judges, or marshals) or by serving in their state legislatures. No other offices were nearly so popular at this stage in their careers.

TABLE 12. FIRST PUBLIC OFFICE ACHIEVED, AND LAST PUBLIC OFFICE BEFORE BECOMING SENATORS

| Type of Office | First Public Office (%) | Last Public Office (%) |
|---|---|---|
| US senator | 9 | — |
| State governor | 2 | 22 |
| United States representative | 4 | 28 |
| State legislator | 21 | 10 |
| State-wide elective official | 4 | 2 |
| Local elective official | 14 | 6 |
| Law enforcement | 28 | 15 |
| Administrative | 14 | 17 |
| Congressional staff | 3 | 1 |
| *Total* | 100 | 100 |
| | (n = 180) | (n = 164) |

Those who entered politics as relatively young men usually began by serving as state legislators, in law-enforcement or state-wide or local elective offices, or as congressional staff members. The older men tended to begin as senators, governors, United States representatives, or as some kind of administrator. The senators' occupations were also related to their first public offices. Half of the lawyers began as law-enforcement officers, a quarter of them as state legislators. The businessmen most frequently began as local elective officials; the farmers, as state legislators; the professors, most often in appointive administrative positions.

Once started, most senators stayed in politics. By the time they were elected to the Senate, they had held no fewer than 495 public offices, not counting re-elections to the same office. The mythical "average senator" had held about three public offices and had devoted about ten years or approximately half his adult life to office holding *before* arriving at the upper chamber. Again we find vast departures from these norms. Some of the senators had served seven, eight, or nine offices for more than twenty-five years, and virtually their entire adulthood. Others were completely without office-holding experience before their election or appointment to the Senate.

What kind of men tended to be most politically active before their election to the Senate? What kind of men were elected or appointed to the Senate with little previous experience? There appear to be two major differences between the most and the least politically experienced senators. The first of these is occupational: the farmers and lawyers were the most politically active and experienced before their election to the Senate; the businessmen and professors were far less so (Table 13). The second difference is partisan: the Democrats, especially those from the Southern and Border States, were more active than the Republicans.

TABLE 13. PERCENTAGE OF THE SENATORS' ADULT LIFE IN PUBLIC OFFICE, BY OCCUPATION

| Senators' Principal Occupation | 0–19% | 20–39% | 40–59% | 60–79% | 80% plus |
|---|---|---|---|---|---|
| Lawyers | 19* | 26 | 25 | 23 | 7 (n = 96) |
| Businessmen | 42 | 25 | 25 | 8 | 0 (n = 53) |
| Farmers | 15 | 15 | 46 | 8 | 15 (n = 13) |
| Professors | 50 | 50 | 0 | 0 | 0 (n = 8) |

* These figures represent percentages of the samples under consideration.

By the time they became senators, our 180 subjects had held almost every conceivable kind of public office. From this it might be inferred that almost any public office can serve as a likely stepping-stone to the power and prestige of the Senate chamber. Such, however, is not the case. About 30 per cent of the senators were elected from the House of Representatives; 20 per cent after serving as state governors; 17 per cent, as administrators; 15 per cent, as law-enforcement officers; and 10 per cent, as state legislators. Very few senators were elected from any other kind of office (see Table 12). When one stops to think that there are only 50 state governorships and 437 seats in the House of Representatives, while there are many thousands of these other positions, it is clear that a far larger *proportion* of governors and congressmen are "promoted" to the Senate than is true of other officeholders. In this sense, the governorships and the House of Representatives are the two major channels to the Senate.

## Summary and Conclusions

The new look in United States senators now can be quickly summarized. The "typical" senator during the postwar years was a late-middle-aged or elderly, white, Protestant, native-born man with small town and upper middle-class origins. He began his political career shortly after graduating from law school and spent about ten years in public office—including service either as a state governor or United States representative—before his election to the Senate.

*Recruitment and the Class System.* This collective portrait has considerable utility. For one thing, it shows how different the "typical" senator is from the "typical" American. While the constitutional requirements for Senate membership have something to do with this distortion, the principal causal factor appears to be the structure of American society.

The senators were selected, with few exceptions, from near the top of the society's class system. This study and others like it suggest that governmental offices are class ranked in America—the more important the office, the higher the social status of its normal incumbent.[12] While this conclusion rings harsh in many an American democrat's ear, it should not be a particularly surprising conclusion. So long as the system of stratification in a society is generally accepted, one must expect people to look for political leadership toward those who have met the current definition of success and hence are considered worthy individuals. American voters seem to prefer candidates who are not like themselves but are what they would like to be.[13]

Of course, the existence of this class bias in the recruitment of senators may not be solely the result of popular consent. Those with high status positions in American society have more money (and easier access to still more) than the ordinary American and it takes money to become a senator. They have more leisure and more flexible work schedules, too. Members of the upper and upper-middle classes in America are more politically aware than the average American and thus may be more prone to entering politics. And, as a general rule, they are more likely to possess the requisite skills for successful political careers.

*Recruitment and Differential Access.* This class bias in the recruitment of senators is no doubt related to the conservatism of the Senate. "You've got to approach them within the context of their own experience," one Washington lobbyist, himself a former senator, has said. "A man doesn't change a whole lot just because he has been elected to the Senate. If he's been a small-town lawyer, or a banker, or a businessman, he is going to think and act like one when he gets to the Senate." Actually things are not that simple. Not all small-town lawyers, or bankers, or businessmen think or act the same way, either in or out of the chamber. And one cannot assume that senators necessarily share the dominant political attitudes of the social strata from which they are selected, or that—even if they do—these attitudes invariably control their official behaviour. But the class bias in the recruitment of senators does give high status groups in American society an advantage in establishing "access."[14] They "speak the same language," share much the same style of life, have had many of the same experiences and training as the senators. This gives high-status groups political advantages above and beyond those which may flow from a similarity of political attitude with the high-status senators.

*Types of Careers.* At the same time that our group portrait furnishes insight into these matters it is an abstraction which deliberately blurs over much diversity in favour of the central tendency. It is not likely to be of much assistance in understanding the wide differences in behaviour found *among* senators. What might help in this endeavour is a typology of senatorial careers based on the very differences in their backgrounds which a collective picture ignores.

For example, the senators *as a group* possess unusually high social status. *As a group* they were extremely active in politics before their election to the Senate. But not all senators possess both of these attributes. Logically, therefore, there should be senators who have relatively high social status and unusually substantial records of political accomplishment, those who rank relatively low in both, and those who rank high in one but not the other. When the senators are classified according to this scheme, four distinct types of senatorial careers emerge.

*Patrician politicians* came from America's relatively few "old families," with the assured wealth and prestige which this position provides. At the same time, they are highly experienced politicians before they become senators. Usually, they begin their political careers by running for a relatively minor elective office while still in their twenties, and rise to the Senate while still in their thirties or forties. About 7 per cent of the postwar senators, about equally divided between Democrats and Republicans, might be classified as Patricians. Almost all of them were from New England and the South, portions of the country which most clearly possess "old family" strata.

*Amateur politicians* are sharply differentiated from the Patricians by their far lower level of pre-Senate political activity and accomplishment. Usually successful businessmen, lawyers, or professors, they tend to start a political career relatively late in life—usually when appointed to an important executive position—and are elected to (or frequently appointed to a vacancy in) the Senate in their fifties. A third of the postwar senators might be called Amateurs, and they were Republicans almost two to one. Paradoxically, the politically inexperienced Amateurs are most apt to become senators from the two-party states, where politics is most competitive and the risks of a political career most severe.

*Professional politicians* are as politically involved and experienced as the Patricians, but do not possess "old family" origins. Most often lawyers, the Professionals enter politics early in life, rise to the Senate through the House of Representatives or state governorships, and arrive at the Senate considerably later in life than the Patricians but earlier than the Amateurs. About 55 per cent of the postwar senators might be classified as Professionals. The Democrats were far more likely to be Professionals than the Republicans.

*Agitators* are the men elected to the Senate without the inherited prestige of the Patricians, the solid record of business and professional accomplishment of the Amateurs, or the political accomplishments of the Professionals. Normally, becoming a senator is a time-consuming and difficult task. The merits of those who aspire to the office are tested, in a rough and ready way, by the necessity for a fairly distinguished career either in or out of politics. Agitators have "beaten the game." Sometimes this may have been because of fantastic good luck, but more often it would seem to have been the result of a willingness to resort to demagoguery and unscrupulous methods, to ignore "the rules of the game."

Four per cent of the postwar senators possessed this type of pre-Senate career. These Agitators were elected primarily from the western states. The reason for this is not at all clear. But perhaps this is because the social structure of the west is more "open," less stratified, than in the east and south. Moreover, in the western states, the party leadership is relatively powerless to influence nominations, and Agitators are not the kind of candidates likely to appeal to responsible party leaders. In the southern one-party states, where party leaders have even less influence on the nomination process than in the west, the social structure is more highly stratified. The combination of a relatively fluid social structure with almost leaderless political parties seems to provide the conditions from which Agitators are most likely to emerge.

NOTES

1. In writing this article I have drawn heavily upon my book *U.S. Senators and Their World,* Chapel Hill, University of North Carolina Press, 1960 (Chapters 2–3). Readers wishing more detail than can be presented here are referred to this work.

2. "Personal and otherwise," *Harper's,* CCX, February 1955, p. 18.

3. For additional details see Matthews, op. cit. (Appendix B).

4. The term "over-representation" is used here in a statistical sense to mean merely that there is a larger proportion of senators possessing a given attribute than of the American people as a whole. The term should not be taken to imply that members of the Senate *ought* to be exactly like the people they represent.

5. For a good survey see R. M. Williams, Jr., *American Society,* New York, Alfred A. Knopf, 1951 (Chapter 5).

6. E. Sibley, "Some Demographic Clues to Stratification," in: L. Wilson and W. Kolb (eds.), *Sociological Analysis,* New York, Harcourt, Brace and Co., 1949, p. 642–50; W. L. Warner, R. J. Havighurst and M. B. Loeb, *Who Shall Be Educated?,* New York, Harper and Brothers, 1940; C. A. Anderson, "Social Class Differentials in the Schooling of Youth Within the Region and Community Sized Groups of the United States," in: K. Davis, M. Levy and H. C. Bredemeier, *Modern American Society,* New York, Rinehart and Company, 1949, p. 421–31; R. A. Mulligan, "Socio-economic Background and College Enrollment," *American Sociological Review,* XVI, 1951, p. 188–196; A. B. Hollingshead, *Elmtown's Youth,* New York, Wiley, 1949.

7. For prestige rating of Protestant denominations, see W. and B. Allinsmith, "Religious Affiliation and Politico-economic Attitude: A Study of Eight Major US Religious Groups," *Public Opinion Quarterly,* XII, 1948, p. 377–89.

8. See note 6.

9. A. Z. Reed, *Training for the Public Profession of Law,* New York, Carnegie Foundation for the Advancement of Teaching, 1921 (Bulletin no. 15).

10. H. D. Lasswell and M. S. McDougal, "Legal education and public policy," in Lasswell, *Analysis of Political Behaviour,* London, Routledge and Paul, 1948, p. 27.

11. J. A. Schlesinger, "Lawyers and Politics: A Clarified View," *Midwest Journal of Political Science,* I, 1957, p. 26–39.

12. See D. R. Matthews, *The Social Background of Political Decision-Makers,* Garden City, Doubleday and Company Inc., 1954.

13. Ironically enough, in a society with a relatively rigid class system the class

bias in the recruitment of top level public officials seems less than in the United States. In class systems with substantial mobility, such as America's, individuals tend to identify with higher strata and accept it as their standard of value. In a less open society, this identification does not exist and there is a tendency to look to one's own class for political leadership.

14. This concept was developed into a powerful tool of political analysis by D. B. Truman, *The Governmental Process,* New York, Alfred A. Knopf, 1951.

# 8. The Lawyer as Decision-Maker in the American State Legislature [*]

DAVID R. DERGE

> The government of democracy is favorable to the political power of lawyers; for when the wealthy, the noble, and the prince are excluded from the government, the lawyers take possession of it, in their own right, as it were, since they are the only men of information and sagacity, beyond the sphere of the people, who can be the object of the popular choice.
>
> —DeTocqueville [1]

DeTocqueville's thesis regarding the political power of American lawyers has long been a concern of both the legal profession and political scientists. This concern over the lawyer in American politics stems from several considerations. First, the lawyers are demonstrably "overrepresented" as an occupational group among American decision-makers.[2] Second, it is generally assumed that the lawyer, through training, aptitudes, and skills peculiar to his profession, is better fitted to become a powerful political figure than the person without these benefits. Third, the long association of legal practitioners with the wealthy economic interests in the society has created an image of the lawyer as a conservative spokesman standing in the way of social progress, and it is thus felt that the policy end-product of the lawyer as decision-maker will differ considerably from that of the non-lawyer. Finally, there is the public image of the legal profession as the legitimate source of public leadership. Both the public and the legal profession wonder whether the lawyer is fulfilling this high calling with the nobility and devotion to the public interest associated with the "golden age" of public leadership by the bar in the late eighteenth and early nineteenth centuries.[3]

Recent studies in political science have supplied data on the social background of lawyers,[4] the lawyer as governor of states,[5] and a very promising group effort to study the lawyer in politics is now in progress.[6]

This paper attempts to examine the characteristics, role, and behavior of the lawyer as a decision-maker in the American state legislature, and to test some propositions found in the literature on state legislatures. Data are drawn from two states, Illinois and Missouri, and in particular from the experiences of the lower chambers in these states. Both Illinois and Missouri are two-party states.[7] During the past decade, the Illinois Assembly has been predominantly Republican-controlled, and the Missouri Assembly predominantly Democratic-controlled.[8] In the

[*] From *The Journal of Politics*, Vol. 21 (1959), pp. 408–433. Reprinted by permission.

sessions of 1955 and 1957, to which much of the data in this paper relate, the Assembly and Governor were Republican in Illinois and Democratic in Missouri.[9]

## A Profile of the Lawyer-Legislator

Lawyers clearly contribute a disproportionate share of the total membership of American state legislatures. Hyneman reported that 28% of the 12,689 legislators serving in thirteen lower chambers and twelve Senates between 1925 and 1935 were lawyers,[10] and according to Zeller 22% of the members of the forty-eight state legislatures in 1949 were lawyers.[11] Both studies show that Senates contain a higher proportion of lawyers than lower chambers. Another source estimates that the legal profession "has provided about one-fourth of the total number of state legislators since 1900." [12]

During the period 1937 through 1957 Illinois and Missouri corresponded closely to the above patterns. In Illinois 27% of the House and 42% of the Senate were lawyers, and in Missouri 23% of the House and 49% of the Senate were lawyers. Data in the 1950 U. S. Census on the proportion of lawyers in the experienced, employed civilian labor force of these states underscore the "overrepresentation" of this profession in the Assemblies: lawyers made up only four-tenths of one per cent of the labor force in Missouri, and five-tenths of one per cent in Illinois.

Personal characteristics of state legislators have received some attention from political scientists, and some have concluded that these characteristics will affect the nature and content of the decision-making process in the legislatures.[13] While there is no conclusive evidence that a change in these characteristics would produce a given change in legislative behavior, it seems reasonable to assume that they may set certain bounds and suggest certain biases in the decision-making process. Thus a study of the lawyer-legislator must include an examination of his characteristics as a decision-maker.

1. *Experience and Quality of Lawyer-Legislators.* Beliefs regarding experience and quality of lawyer-legislators vary widely and are often contradictory. One often hears that "young" lawyers predominate in the legislature because this experience provides both income and advertisement during the lean years of establishing a practice, but that as the lawyer becomes successful, hence busy, he will leave legislative service to devote full time to the law. On the other hand, the explanation for large numbers of lawyer-legislators is said to be the flexible nature of legal practice which allows a man to be away for extended periods of time without abandoning his livelihood, and that continued public service encourages a growing, lucrative practice.[14]

Table 1 contains findings on the average number of years in practice for lawyer-legislators serving in the 1955 and 1957 sessions of the Missouri and Illinois legislatures, and for a three per cent random sample of the total law population in each state.[15]

These data indicate that with the exception of the Missouri House lawyers, the average number of years in practice of the lawyer-legislator group corresponds closely to the average of the random sample. In this sense, then, legislatures were not populated by "young" or "inexperienced" lawyers to a much greater degree than the whole law population.

TABLE 1. AVERAGE NUMBER OF YEARS IN THE PRACTICE OF THE LAW OF
LAWYERS IN THE 1955 AND 1957 MISSOURI AND ILLINOIS LEGISLATURES, AND A
THREE PER CENT RANDOM SAMPLE OF THE LAW POPULATION OF EACH STATE

| | MISSOURI | | ILLINOIS | |
|---|---|---|---|---|
| | N | Average Number of Years in Practice | N | Average Number of Years in Practice |
| Random Sample | 190 | 23.7 | 463 | 22.4 |
| 1957 House | 27 | 10.2 | 55 | 20.9 |
| 1957 Senate | 19 | 23.6 | 28 | 23.8 |
| 1955 House | 30 | 14.6 | 42 | 19.2 |
| 1955 Senate | 19 | 24.0 | 24 | 22.6 |

The problem of determining the "quality" of legislators is extremely difficult
because of the wide variation in belief about what constitutes a "good" or "bad"
legislator. However, political scientists and journalists, to say nothing of the general public, have not hesitated to make judgments on the question, and on the
whole have concluded that the quality is low. There are apparently as many tests
of quality as there are critics of the legislature. No attempt is made here to define
what makes a good legislator, but since it is often heard around statehouses that
on the whole lawyer-legislators are below par as lawyers go, some attempt will be
made to compare the legal ability of the two groups.

The legal profession has not yet found formal tests for quality of a lawyer
beyond the qualifying examination for admission to the bar, standards for practice
before the several courts, and criteria for disbarment, although the cumulative
opinion of the profession may create or destroy an attorney's reputation. The only
attempt to rate the ability of attorneys through the use of opinions of professional
colleagues is contained in the annual Martindale-Hubbell listings. The ratings of
lawyers are made by field representatives of the Martindale-Hubbell service who
consult with members of the local bench and prominent attorneys. The Martindale-
Hubbell statement of standards explains that "No arbitrary rule for determining
legal ability can be formulated. Ratings are based upon the standard of ability for
the place where the lawyer practices. Age, practical experience, nature and length
of practice, and other relevant qualifications are considered. Reports are obtained
through various channels and we endeavor to reflect the consensus of reliable opinion." Thus, the ratings may reflect at least two dimensions: 1) the legal ability
of the lawyers, and 2) the perceptions of the lawyer's peer group. While these
ratings are not as rigorous as the social scientist might wish them to be, they
nevertheless provide the only ready basis for comparing the quality of lawyer-
legislators with the quality of the law population of the whole state. They provide
a starting point for testing the quality of state legislators.

Attorneys rated by Martindale-Hubbell are given A, B, or C ratings depending
on legal ability and number of years practiced. The highest rating, "A," is reserved
for lawyers with at least ten years of practice who are rated "very high." The "B"
rating goes to lawyers with more than ten years practice who are rated "high," and
to lawyers with more than five, but less than ten years practice who are rated
"very high." The "C" ratings is given to lawyers with at least five years practice

who are rated "fair." Attorneys with less than five years practice are not eligible to be rated.

The majority of lawyers listed are not rated. Martindale-Hubbell explains this selectivity by stating that "absence of rating characters must not be construed in any case as derogatory to anyone, as we do not undertake to publish complete ratings of all lawyers." There are two obvious categories of lawyers who would not be rated: 1) those who would be rated "poor" or "very poor," since no categories exist for these, and 2) those whose professional activities were not well known or recognized by the legal community. Conversely, we might expect that these who are rated possess legal ability held in some esteem by their professional colleagues who contribute to the ratings, and have a professional "visibility" sufficient to be known in the legal community.[16]

The Martindale-Hubbell ratings of all lawyers serving in the 1955 and 1957 Missouri and Illinois legislatures were examined, and three per cent random samples of all listed lawyers in each state were selected as control groups. Table 2 contains these findings.

TABLE 2. MARTINDALE-HUBBELL LEGAL ABILITY RATINGS OF LAWYERS SERVING IN THE 1955 AND 1957 ILLINOIS AND MISSOURI LEGISLATURES, AND OF A THREE PER CENT RANDOM SAMPLE OF LAWYERS IN EACH STATE

| | | PER CENT RATED | | | PER CENT NOT RATED | | |
|---|---|---|---|---|---|---|---|
| | N | Very High | High | Fair | Eligible | Not Eligible | Total |
| ILLINOIS | | | | | | | |
| Random Sample | 463 | 15 | 7 | 5 | 65 | 8 | 100 |
| House | 97 | 7 | 23 | 8 | 60 | 2 | 100 |
| Senate | 52 | 23 | 29 | 8 | 38 | 2 | 100 |
| MISSOURI | | | | | | | |
| Random Sample | 190 | 13 | 11 | 3 | 69 | 4 | 100 |
| House | 57 | 5 | 33 | 19 | 25 | 18 | 100 |
| Senate | 38 | 18 | 47 | 8 | 29 | 3 | 100 |

Nearly three-fourths of the lawyers in the random samples were not rated, while the lawyer-legislator group in each case had a higher percentage rated than did the sample. It is notable that of lawyers eligible for rating in Missouri, more than twice as many lawyer-legislators are rated as lawyers not in the legislature. More frequent rating of lawyer legislators in Illinois also occurred, but not to such a marked extent. The qualities necessary for rating are evidently possessed more by lawyers in the legislature than by their colleagues in private life. If the significance of rating suggested above is valid, the conclusion must be that the lawyer-legislator possesses higher legal ability or is better known in the community or both.

Lawyers in the two Senates received higher "legal ability" ratings than lawyer in the random sample. Senators did better in the "very high" legal ability ratings and four times as many lawyer-Senators received "high" legal ability rating as did non-legislators in the random sample. Lawyers in the lower chambers did not fare as well on the "very high" ratings. A higher percentage of the random sample received this rating in both states.

A clue to the higher incidence of "A" ratings in Senate and random sample groups than in House groups may be the fact that House lawyers on the average have been in practice for a shorter period of time, hence some are not eligible for "very high" ratings. Since a "high" rating is the most a lawyer with less than ten years in practice is eligible to receive, a correction for number of years in practice may be made by combining the "very high" ratings of lawyers with more than ten years practice and "high" ratings of lawyers who have less than ten years in practice. The group with "high" ratings, but less than ten years in practice, undoubtedly contains the potential "very high" ratings.

This revision brings the Missouri House lawyer groups above the random sample (on which the above correction was also made), but while the position of the Illinois House group is improved, it still lags behind both the random sample and Senate groups. Thus, when the four House and four Senate groups are compared with the random sample groups to determine the percentage of lawyers who received the highest legal ability rating for which they were eligible, it is found that all Senate groups and the Missouri House groups were superior to the sample but that the Illinois House groups fell below the sample standard by about five percentage points.

It is significant that in all legislative groups the proportion of lawyer-legislators holding "high" legal ability ratings was two or three times as great as among lawyers in the random samples. The "fair" legal ability ratings did not differ significantly between lawyer-legislator and the random samples except in the case of the Missouri House groups. Here most of these ratings were held by young lawyers with five to eight years in practice. An examination of the distribution of "fair" ratings in the random sample led the writer to conclude that this rating is reserved largely for younger lawyers with less than ten years practice. It is likely that these "fair" ratings change to "high" ratings as the young lawyer gains more experience.

If the Martindale-Hubbell ratings of legal ability are useful tests for the comparison of lawyers in the legislature with lawyers in the state legal population, one must conclude that the lawyers in the 1955 and 1957 Illinois and Missouri legislatures were on the whole at least as good as, and sometimes superior to, their professional colleagues outside the assembly halls.[17]

2. *The Political Background of Lawyers and Non-Lawyers.* It is often stated that training in the law and legal practice fit an individual for public office, and that individuals interested in public service often seek an avenue through the law. If one or both of these assumptions is true, one would expect to find that lawyers in the legislature have had considerable prior political experience. Table 3 contains findings on the prior party experience and public office-holding of 144 (70%) of 205 Missouri House members in the 1955 and 1957 sessions, and the political experience of their parents.[18] Since the number of respondents fell short of the desired 100%, conclusions should be treated as tentative.

While less than one out of every four lawyers came to the legislature without some prior elective political experience, three out of every five non-lawyers listed election to the legislature as their first political experience.[19] The lawyers were clearly more politically experienced as measured by election to party and public office. It is difficult to state conclusively that experience gained in public or party office in local government provides an advantage in the decision-making process

TABLE 3. POLITICAL EXPERIENCE OF 144 MISSOURI HOUSE MEMBERS AND PO-
LITICAL EXPERIENCE OF THEIR PARENTS

| | | TYPE OF POLITICAL EXPERIENCE PRIOR TO ELECTION TO THE LEGISLATURE | | | | | Parent Elected to Party or Public Office | |
| | | No Prior Political Experience | Election Party Office Only | Election Public Office Only | Election Party and Public Office | Total | Yes | No |
| Occupation | N | % | % | % | % | % | % | % |
| --- | --- | --- | --- | --- | --- | --- | --- | --- |
| Lawyer | 35 | 23 | 23 | 31 | 23 | 100 | 46 | 54 |
| All others | 109 | 60 | 17 | 13 | 10 | 100 | 22 | 78 |
| All members | 144 | 51 | 19 | 17 | 13 | 100 | 28 | 72 |

at the state level. However, to the extent that this experience involved dealing with public demands, organizing the public and groups within it into majorities, and gaining acceptance of policies from other decision-makers, the person with such experience would probably be in a better position to act effectively in a legislative body than the person without such experience. In this sense, and to the extent that such activities have their parallel in the practice of the law, the lawyer may be expected to have a head start on the non-lawyer.

The data also show that lawyers came more frequently from politically motivated families. Family backgrounds which included a father or mother who had held an elective party or public office were more than twice as frequent among lawyers as among non-lawyers. This might be expected since the questionnaire also revealed that on the whole parents of lawyers had obtained more formal education and enjoyed a higher socio-economic status than parents of non-lawyers. Children from these families with a commitment to politics or public service might well have been encouraged to use the law as an avenue to the satisfaction of such ambitions, in keeping with the widely held belief that a law degree eases the passage into public life.

The examination of post-legislative political careers was beyond the scope of the questionnaire, but on the basis of the above data an hypothesis that lawyer-legislators do not retire from politics when they retire from the legislature would probably prove valid.

3. *Social Background of the Lawyer.* Matthews states that "probably the most important single criterion for social ranking in the United States is occupation. Although it is by no means a certain index to an individual's social standing in the community, occupation is perhaps the closest approach to an infallible guide." [20] Table 4 shows the occupational class of fathers of 1955 and 1957 Missouri House members.[21]

Assuming that the categories of professional, proprietors, managers, and officials represent the high social status occupations, these data support the proposition that legislators come more often from high social status families than do non-legislators and that lawyer-legislators come more often from high social status families than do non-lawyer legislators.

One-fourth of the fathers of all legislators were in occupations of high socio-

TABLE 4. OCCUPATIONAL CLASS OF FATHERS OF MISSOURI HOUSE
MEMBERS SERVING IN THE 1955 AND/OR 1957 SESSION (N-142)

| Father's Occupation | MISSOURI LEGISLATORS | | | U.S. Labor Force of 1890 |
| | Lawyers | Non-Lawyers | Total | |
| | % | % | % | % |
|---|---|---|---|---|
| Professional | 14 | 9 | 11 | 5 |
| Proprietors, managers, officials | 21 | 12 | 14 | 6 |
| Farmers, farm managers | 21 | 31 | 28 | 26 |
| Other occupations | 44 | 48 | 47 | 63 |
| *Total* | 100 | 100 | 100 | 100 |
| | (N=34) | (N=108) | (N=142) | |

economic status in contrast to about one-tenth of the labor force of 1890 in which
we assume these fathers would be found. In this sense, the families of legislators
were in a more important position in the society than were the families of non-
legislators. It can also be seen that fathers of lawyers appeared in the high status
occupations about three times more frequently than would be expected if they
represented a cross-section of the labor force of their day, and about 50% more
often than the fathers of non-lawyer legislators. Conclusions drawn from these
data must, of course, remain tentative until further investigations are made.

In his study of the occupational class of fathers of U. S. Senators in the 81st
Congress (1949) and the U. S. Representatives of the 77th Congress (1941),
Matthews reports that more than 90% of these fathers were professionals, proprietors, officials, or famers,[22] with the first three groups accounting for 58% of the
fathers of Senators and 62% of the fathers of Representatives. Thus, U. S. Congressmen came more often from high social status families than did Missouri
Representatives.

4. *Other Demographic Characteristics of Lawyer-Legislators.* In this section the
factors of age, education, and urban-rural constituency will be considered.

On the basis of experience in the lower chambers of Illinois and Missouri, it
might be said that the lawyers bring youth to the legislature. Each time these
chambers have met since 1937 the lawyer's mean age has been lower than that of
the non-lawyers. Lawyers enter and leave the legislature at a younger age than do
their non-lawyer colleagues. Over the twenty year period, about half of the lawyers
entered before they had reached forty, while less than a quarter of the non-lawyers
entered by this age. About 50% more non-lawyers began legislative service between
the ages of forty and fifty-nine.[23] The pattern of age at retirement reflects the
same bias toward youth in the lawyer group. More than twice as many lawyers
retired from legislative services before they had reached age forty, and more than
twice as many non-lawyers continued legislative service beyond age sixty.

These data support the assumption that the career pattern of lawyers allows
an early entry into the legislature while other occupational groups find their ways
to the state capitol at more advanced ages. In view of the prevalence of lawyers
in the state senates and other elective offices in state and local government, it is

likely that many of the lawyers do not cease to be office-seekers when they terminate legislative service at a relatively young age. It is possible that the lawyer perceives his legislative experience as an important but transitory phase of political development while other occupational groups treat legislative service as the beginning and end of office-holding.

It is not surprising to find that lawyers have a level of educational achievement considerably above that of any other occupational group in the legislature. About 95% of the lawyers serving in the Illinois and Missouri Houses since 1937 completed a baccalaureate degree, while only one in six of the non-lawyers went this far. About 40% of the non-lawyers either completed a degree or obtained some college education. Thus more than half of the non-lawyers earned a high school diploma or less.[24] If it can be said that formal education is an important preparation for public service and policy-making then it is clear that the lawyer group is superior on this count.

Metropolitan areas in both Illinois and Missouri have contributed more than their share of lawyers to the lower chambers of the legislatures. Lawyers constituted 27% of the legislators serving in the Illinois House between 1937 and 1957, and 23% of the legislators serving in the Missouri House during the same period. But 34% of the legislators from Chicago, and from St. Louis and Kansas City, were lawyers during the twenty year period. In these states the legislators from out-state metropolitan constituencies, defined as districts where more than half of the population resided in cities of 30,000–125,000 population, were 31% lawyers in Illinois, and 34 lawyers in Missouri. In Illinois 22% of the more rural legislators were lawyers, and in Missouri 20% were lawyers. These data are in keeping with the distribution of lawyers in the random sample compiled from Martindale-Hubbell listing which showed a preponderance of lawyers listed as practicing in urbanized areas.

If it is true that lawyers represent an important influence on policy-making, the relatively greater frequency of lawyers in metropolitan delegations may be a factor in the success of these delegations in the legislature. While metropolitan areas have been numerically under-represented in the Illinois and Missouri Houses the success of metropolitan delegations has been greater than their numbers might suggest.[25]

5. *Two Characteristics of Legislative Service: Length of Service and Cause of Retirement.* Students of the legislative process appear to agree unanimously that legislatures are strengthened as the length of service of legislators increases. One writer states that "certainly the ordinary legislator is more than twice as valuable during his second term."[26] Such propositions about length of service seem to make good sense, although no empirical evidence has been adduced to establish the relationship between length of service and quality of the legislator. Table 5 presents data on length of service of all members serving at least one session between 1936 and 1956 in the Illinois or Missouri House and finally retiring from legislative service prior to 1956. "Final retirement" means that the legislator was not at a later time again elected to the House.

The length of service patterns differ significantly between Illinois and Missouri. While only one out of ten Missouri House members served as many as five sessions, over one-third of the Illinois House members served five or more sessions. During this period less than one out of a hundred Missouri House members served nine

TABLE 5. LENGTH OF SERVICE AT FINAL RETIREMENT OF
MEMBERS WHO RETIRED FROM ILLINOIS OR MISSOURI HOUSE
BETWEEN 1938 AND 1956

| Sessions Served | ILLINOIS | | MISSOURI | |
|---|---|---|---|---|
| | Lawyers | Others | Lawyers | Others |
| | % | % | % | % |
| 1 – 2 | 45 | 40 | 68 | 65 |
| 3 – 4 | 17 | 21 | 23 | 25 |
| 5 – 6 | 16 | 14 | 8 | 8 |
| 7 – 8 | 5 | 11 | 1 | 1 |
| 9 or more | 17 | 14 | 0 | 1 |
| Total | 100 | 100 | 100 | 100 |
| | (N=88) | (N=261) | (N=154) | (N=464) |

sessions or more, while more than one of seven Illinois legislators acquired such a record.[27]

Length of service patterns do not differ significantly between lawyers and non-lawyers. There is no evidence that lawyers as a group are noted for their short legislative service, while seasoned legislators come from outside the ranks of lawyers. If a "seasoned legislator" were defined as one who has served five sessions or more, there would be an almost equal distribution of such legislators between lawyers and non-lawyers over a twenty-year period in the Illinois and Missouri House.

What causes legislators to retire from legislative service? Table 6 shows the distribution of lawyers and non-lawyers by cause of retirement for all legislators who left the Illinois or Missouri House between 1936 and 1958.

TABLE 6. CAUSE OF RETIREMENT FROM LEGISLATIVE SERVICE OF LAWYERS AND
NON-LAWYERS: ILLINOIS AND MISSOURI HOUSE, 1936–1958 *

| | ILLINOIS | | | MISSOURI | | |
|---|---|---|---|---|---|---|
| | Lawyers | Others | All | Lawyers | Others | All |
| | % | % | % | % | % | % |
| Defeated in attempt to return to House | 24 | 38 | 35 | 25 | 46 | 41 |
| Ran for seat in state Senate | 18 | 13 | 14 | 13 | 6 | 7 |
| Died | 6 | 13 | 11 | 1 | 6 | 5 |
| Voluntary retirement or cause unknown | 52 | 36 | 40 | 61 | 42 | 47 |
| Total | 100 | 100 | 100 | 100 | 100 | 100 |
| | (N=102) | (N=305) | (N=407) | (N=167) | (N=510) | (N=677) |

* This includes all multiple retirements of legislators who had broken service in the House.

While length of service patterns mentioned above may be disheartening to those interested in experienced legislatures, it should be comforting to observe that more than half of the House retirements in both states resulted from defeat in attempt to return to the House, attempt to move to the Senate, and death.

Lawyers and non-lawyers differed significantly in cause of retirement. Only one-fourth of the lawyers in Illinois and Missouri were defeated in attempts to return to the House, but 46% of the non-lawyers in Missouri and 38% in Illinois left legislative service for this reason.

6. *The Lawyer as Legislative Leader.* Both Illinois and Missouri legislatures have drawn heavily on lawyers to fill their key leadership positions. In the period of 1937 through 1951, each legislature elected eleven Speakers of the House and eleven Presidents Pro Tempore of the Senate. In Missouri eight Speakers and eight Pro Tems were lawyers, and in Illinois five Speakers and seven Pro Tems were lawyers.[28] It is thus clear that lawyers as an occupational group dominated leadership billets.

On the other hand, the number of committee chairmanships held by lawyers was not out of proportion to the seats they held. If anything, lawyers lagged a few percentage points behind in chairmanships held.[29] It should be noted, however, that lawyers were given preference in certain committee assignments. Committees dealing with legislation relating to the state judicial system, civil and criminal procedures, and technical legal problems were almost exclusively the province of the lawyer-legislator. The powerful Judiciary Committees of the two legislatures were made up wholly of lawyers. The Illinois House practice of assigning all lawyers in the chamber to the Judiciary Committee twice took precedence over the traditional system of majority control in committees being the same as majority control in the chamber. The Democratic House in 1949 had a Judiciary Committee with a clear Republican majority, and the Republican House in 1955 had a Judiciary Committee with a narrow Democratic majority. In these cases the occupational characteristics of the committee members apparently loomed greater than their party affiliation. This in itself is a tribute to the image of the lawyer-legislator as subject-matter expert. It should also be noted that lawyer representation on the powerful Rules Committee was heavier than might have been expected. Lawyers dominated a majority of these committees in both states over the twenty year period.

## The Lawyer and Legislation

Beliefs regarding the impact of the lawyer on policy-making in the state legislature must necessarily be based on the effect he has on the end-product of the process—law. Data in preceding sections of this paper suggest that the lawyer is potentially a great force in the legislature by virtue of his background, training, and ability. It remains to be discovered whether lawyers are an important sponsor of legislation, whether lawyers stand as a solid group in decision-making, and whether lawyers take clear-cut positions which can be called "conservative" or "liberal." These questions will be examined below.

1. *The Lawyer as Sponsor of Legislation.* The volume of legislative business generated by lawyers may be considered a rough test of the extent of their participation

in proposing and formulating public policy. Such a test may not adequately reveal the pervasiveness of lawyer influence on law-making as a skilled job, but should serve as an indicator of lawyer leadership in structuring legislative activity. Table 7 contains data on sponsorship of bills by lawyers and non-lawyers in the Illinois and Missouri House sessions of 1955 and 1957.

TABLE 7. SPONSORSHIP OF LEGISLATION BY LAWYERS AND NON-LAWYERS: ILLI-
NOIS AND MISSOURI HOUSE SESSIONS OF 1955 AND 1957

| | MISSOURI | | | | ILLINOIS | | | |
| | 1955 | | 1957 | | 1955 | | 1957 | |
| | N | % | N | % | N | % | N | % |
| --- | --- | --- | --- | --- | --- | --- | --- | --- |
| Seats held by lawyers | 30 | 19 | 27 | 17 | 42 | 28 | 55 | 31 |
| Total bills introduced | 612 | 100 | 637 | 100 | 1279 | 100 | 1415 | 100 |
| Bills sponsored by lawyers | 257 | 42 | 172 | 27 | 537 | 42 | 566 | 40 |
| Average number of bills sponsored: Lawyers | 9 | | 7 | | 13 | | 10 | |
| Average number of bills sponsored: Non-lawyers | 2 | | 4 | | 7 | | 7 | |
| Median number of bills sponsored: Lawyers | 8 | | 6 | | 6 | | 6 | |
| Median number of bills sponsored: Non-lawyers | 1 | | 1 | | 3 | | 3 | |

In each case the lawyers sponsored considerably more than their share of bills. For example, in the 1955 Missouri House lawyers held 19% of the seats but sponsored 42% of the bills considered by the chamber. Except for the 1957 Missouri House session, at least two-fifths of all bills were lawyer-sponsored. Findings on the median numbers of bills sponsored indicate lawyers were more consistently sponsors of several bills, while in the non-lawyer groups relatively fewer persons sponsored several bills.[30] The ratio between the average number of bills sponsored by lawyers and the number sponsored by non-lawyers ran from 9:2 in Missouri to 10:7 in Illinois.

Mere sponsorship of bills is not a final test of the impact of the lawyer on the total output of the legislative session. A further examination to determine whether lawyer-sponsored bills have as good a chance of passage and approval by the governor as those sponsored by non-lawyers is necessary. The percentage of all bills sponsored was about equal to the percentage of all bills passed and approved by the Governor for both lawyer and non-lawyer groups in both states. Thus, lawyers led non-lawyers in bills passed and approved by about the same proportion as they led on bills sponsored.[31]

These data support the proposition that the lawyer is an important figure in the proposal and formulation of legislative policy.[32] It should be noted that sponsorship of legislation in these two states usually goes beyond the simple act of attaching the legislator's name to the measure. Sponsorship includes the job of defending the bill in committee hearings, acting as leading proponent in floor debate and chief critic of amendments proposed from the floor, serving as co-ordinator between House and Senate during Senate action on the bill, and sometimes advising the governor prior to his decision on the bill. Thus a high level of activity in sponsorship implies a high level of activity at other stages of the legislative process. This high level of legislative activity seems to be characteristic of the lawyer-legislator.

2. *Cohesion of Lawyers on Legislative Roll-Calls.* Much of the concern about "overrepresentation" of the lawyer in the legislature and the potential lawyer-domination of the legislative process must proceed from the assumption that lawyers will stand together as a group when decisions are made.[33] A member of the New York legislature has stated that "bankers, lawyers, farmers and other occupational groups organize influential 'cells' which wield great influence . . ." [34] and Governor Herbert Lehman complained of "the conspiracy of lawyer-legislators to perpetuate for their profession the obstructions to justice by which it prospers." [35] In view of what has been said in the foregoing sections about lawyers in the Illinois and Missouri legislatures, one must suppose that if the lawyers present a solid front on public policy they will be a formidable, if not the determining, factor in writing the state's laws.

An examination of the cohesion of the lawyer group on legislative roll-calls will give some indication of the tendency of this group to act together in law-making. A total of 5,555 roll-calls were taken in the 1955 and 1957 sessions of the Illinois and Missouri Houses. From these was selected a group of 1,642 roll-calls on which at least 10% of the chamber's membership was on the losing side. Each of these "contested" roll-calls was analyzed to determine the voting cohesions of lawyers, farmers, and a control group of legislators selected without regard to occupation. The control group included the same proportion of Democrats and Republicans as the lawyer group, and its members were chosen on a random basis. Since the purpose of this test is to determine whether a substantial majority of group members act together on contested public policy questions, the minimum voting cohesion considered will be 67% of the elected membership of the group, or two out of every three members voting together. Table 8 contains the findings on frequency of high voting cohesion among lawyers, farmers, and the control group.

These data reveal that the lawyers did not regularly vote together with high cohesion. As the level of cohesion increased the frequency of lawyer solidarity decreased until in no instance did lawyers vote with a cohesion of 90% or more on

TABLE 8. GROUP VOTING COHESION ON CONTESTED ROLL-CALLS IN THE ILLINOIS AND MISSOURI HOUSE SESSIONS OF 1955 AND 1957

| State | Contested roll-calls | | Percentage of contested roll-calls on which group voted with cohesion of: | | | | | | | | |
|---|---|---|---|---|---|---|---|---|---|---|---|
| | | | 67—79% | | | 80—89% | | | 90—100% | | |
| | N | % | Law | Farm | Control | Law | Farm | Control | Law | Farm | Control |
| MISSOURI | | | | | | | | | | | |
| 1955 | 551 | 100 | 5 | 9 | 6 | * | 2 | * | 0 | 0 | * |
| 1957 | 402 | 100 | 6 | 12 | 6 | 1 | 2 | 1 | * | * | 0 |
| ILLINOIS | | | | | | | | | | | |
| 1955 | 308 | 100 | 12 | 16 | 15 | 4 | 2 | 4 | 0 | * | 0 |
| 1957 | 381 | 100 | 12 | 28 | 16 | 1 | 8 | 4 | 0 | 2 | 0 |

*less than 1%

at least 1% of the session's roll-calls. Frequency of high farmer cohesion was consistently greater than that of lawyers. Perhaps the most telling commentary on lawyer solidarity is that the cohesion patterns of the control groups closely resemble those of the lawyers. On the whole lawyers voted less often with high cohesion than did the control group, which suggests that there is no more reason to expect lawyers to act with unity than to expect a group of legislators chosen at random to vote together. If there were a solid lawyer "bloc" or "cell" in decision-making the frequency of high cohesion would be much greater.

When the frequency of high voting cohesion among lawyers is related to the degree of conflict on roll-calls, it is found that this group does not stand together when a substantial part of the chamber is on the losing side of the roll-calls. Lawyers voted with high cohesion on less than 2% of the roll-calls where at least 20% of the chamber membership was on the losing side. Lawyers voted with a cohesion of 67% or more on one roll-call in Missouri and one roll-call in Illinois where at least 30% of the chamber was on the losing side of the vote. Thus as the degree of controversy on policy increases, high lawyer cohesion, which is infrequent at best, decreases until it disappears when the chamber is fairly evenly divided.[36]

It might be supposed that the infrequent high cohesion among lawyers was in each case the result of a lawyer "caucus," and that their high degree of success in being on the winning side of these roll-calls was a product of the ability of the lawyers to persuade the non-lawyers. A much more reasonable interpretation of the data leads one to conclude that most high lawyer cohesion was the result of chance and that lawyers do not vote together self-consciously.

If all cases of high voting cohesion among lawyers occurred on matters closely related to the general practice of law there would be some basis for concluding that lawyers were acting as a professional interest group in the legislature. An analysis of subject matter was made for those bills on which lawyers voted together with a cohesion of 67% or more. The findings are contained in Table 9.

It is evident that high lawyer cohesion was not peculiar to any particular type of bills. In view of this, and the conclusion that most lawyer solidarity was probably

TABLE 9. SUBJECT MATTER OF BILLS ON WHICH LAWYERS VOTED WITH A COHESION OF 67% OR MORE

| | NUMBER OF BILLS | | | |
|---|---|---|---|---|
| | MISSOURI HOUSE | | ILLINOIS HOUSE | |
| Subject-Matter of Bills | 1955 | 1957 | 1955 | 1957 |
| Regulation of transportation | — | 7 | 11 | 6 |
| Local government | 2 | 3 | 11 | 7 |
| Education | 3 | — | 6 | 13 |
| Court organization and operation | 4 | 8 | 2 | 5 |
| 18 year old vote | 2 | — | 4 | 5 |
| State government organization and operation | 7 | 2 | 2 | — |
| Regulation of occupations | 1 | 4 | 2 | 4 |
| Personal damages | 3 | — | 2 | 1 |
| Labor relations | — | — | 3 | 1 |
| Taxation and appropriations | 5 | 2 | 4 | 2 |
| Miscellaneous | 3 | 3 | 1 | 7 |
| Total | 30 | 29 | 48 | 51 |

attributable to chance, we must conclude that lawyers reacted to public policy decisions on some other basis than professional identification. A good example is provided by the long-awaited attempt to submit to referendum a constitutional amendment modernizing the Illinois court system. In 1957 two joint resolutions were introduced, each of which contained a different proposal. Together these resolutions caused thirty contested roll-calls in the House. Lawyers voted with a cohesion of 67% or more on only three of these roll-calls, while high farmer cohesion occurred on six of the thirty roll-calls. On the three roll-calls showing high lawyer cohesion, lawyers were on the prevailing side which represented a substantial majority of the whole chamber.

3. *Conservatism of Lawyers on Social and Economic Issues.* One of the most widely discussed aspects of the lawyer in policy-making is his reaction to social and economic problems. It has been suggested that the lawyer is an essentially conservative person because of his training, skepticism, and case-by-case approach to conflict, and that his close relationship to powerful economic interests in the society causes him to react slowly and unfavorably to social change.[37] Extreme proponents of this position have claimed that the lawyer may be the major deterrent to progressive legislation, but typically such speculations have been unsupported by data. Recently this assumption has been questioned, but again largely on grounds of reason and logic.[38] Agger poses the problem in this way:

> The phenomenon of conservatism among lawyers, to the extent it exists, is not disturbing *per se,* but when political mechanisms for orderly social change are monopolized by lawyers and become mechanisms for personal power and reward—whether harnessed to social change or to status quo—the great number and influence of lawyers in politics deserves to be questioned.[39]

Two tests were devised to assess the position of 1957 Missouri House members on political, social and economic problems. The first is based on the voting behavior of these legislators on nine bills which invited a liberal or conservative stand on a social or economic issue. These bills provided for liberalizing retirement provisions for public school teachers, expansion of rehabilitation efforts for injured workmen, establishment of a retirement program for state employees, exemption of prescription drugs from sales tax, requirement of added safety protections for construction workers, repeal of the state's "Little Taft-Hartley" law, prohibition of certain child labor, a state minimum wage of 75¢ per hour, and the requirement that workers be paid prevailing local wages when employed on public works contracts.[40] Each legislator was assigned a support score arrived at by subtracting the number of bills he voted against from the number of bills he voted for. Scores ranged from −9 to +9. The mean score for lawyers was +1.77 and for non-lawyers +1.96, while the median score for both groups was +3.[41] Thus there is no significant difference in the behavior of lawyers and non-lawyers on bills liberalizing retirement systems, easing tax burdens on middle and lower classes, and improving the lot of the working man.[42]

The second test is based on responses to fifteen items on attitudes regarding political and economic issues.[43] The legislator's score is obtained by subtracting the number of conservative responses from the number of liberal responses. Scores range from −15 to +15. The mean score was −1.5 for lawyers and 0 for non-lawyers.[44] Lawyer median score was −2 and non-lawyer median score was 0. As in the results of the roll-call behavior test we find no striking difference between lawyers and non-lawyers on conservative and liberal positions.[45]

The results of these two tests do not support the familiar conclusion that lawyers are the bastion of conservatism in the state legislatures. On the contrary, a tentative conclusion is that the political attitudes and behavior of lawyers are quite similar to those of non-lawyers, and that the more significant difference is between political parties. It is thus reasonable to assume that lawyers will be found on both liberal and conservative sides of political, social, and economic issues, and that the considerable influence of the lawyer group in the legislature will not be concentrated in support of, or opposition to, progressive legislation.

4. *The Lawyer as "Intellectual Jobber and Contractor."* In summarizing the public status of the legal profession, A. A. Berle stated that "intellectually the profession commanded and still commands respect, but it is the respect for an intellectual jobber and contractor rather than for a moral force." [46] One explanation for the high level of legislative activity among lawyers, the lack of lawyer solidarity in decision-making, and the probability that lawyers reacted to legislation on some other basis than professional self-consciousness, may lie in Berle's characterization and in the nature of the group process in legislation. The "intellectual jobber and contractor" role of the lawyer in advocating and representing the interest of his client commits the lawyer, within bounds of ethical canons, to devote himself to those who hire the use of his time and talents. This corresponds nicely to the theory of representation which obligates the legislator to pursue the perceived interests of his constituency regardless of his personal beliefs in the matter. It is a common assumption of the office-holder, both before and after his behavior is tested in the crucible of popular elections, that constituents will judge him on how vigorously and successfully he worked for them in office. Indeed, one of the consummate skills of the successful American politician is the fabrication of a clientele which will assure him success at the polls. It is reasonable, then, to suppose that lawyers will behave as "client-caretakers" of constituencies and intra-constituency groups first, and as an internal legislative bloc second, if at all.

If the lawyer does have peculiar skills or experience in the advocacy of client-interests, he may be perceived by groups interested in passage or defeat of legislation as the preferred sponsor of bills and legislative spokesman.[47] Weber's examination of the "university-trained jurist" as one major type of professional politician led him to conclude that "the modern lawyer and modern democracy absolutely belong together." He reasoned that "the management of politics through parties simply means management through interest groups. The craft of the trained lawyer is to plead effectively the cause of interested clients." [48] This thesis is in keeping with the findings that lawyers are particularly active in sponsorship of bills and all of the advocacy, mediation, and negotiation which follows from sponsorship.

The lawyer may also stand out in another, yet correlative, legislative role. According to the group process analysis of legislative behavior, the role of the decision-makers must be to receive demands from groups in the society who seek fulfillment of perceived needs, and to consider these demands in relation to one another and to the fabric of public policy as it exists at the time. The attempts to satisfy as many of these demands as possible, and to as complete a degree as possible, may require the same skills which the lawyer exercises in the practice of his profession as he advocates, arbitrates, mediates, and negotiates the wide range of interests-in-conflict which are destined at one time or another to find their way into the legislative arena.

## Notes

1. Alexis de Tocqueville, *Democracy in America* (New York, 1954), I, 285.

2. See footnote 30 *infra*.

3. For a discussion of the historical role of the bar in public leadership see James W. Hurst, *The Growth of American Law* (Boston, 1950), part V. Legal periodicals abound with articles on the social responsibilities of the lawyer. See the *Index to Legal Periodicals* under the headings of "Attorneys," "The Legal Profession," "Legislatures," and "Politics."

4. Donald R. Matthews, *The Social Background of Political Decision-Makers* (New York, 1954).

5. J. A. Schlesinger, "Lawyers and American Politics: A Clarified View," *Midwest Journal of Political Science*, II (May, 1957), 26.

6. R. E. Agger, "The Lawyer in Politics," *Temple Law Quarterly*, XXIX (Summer, 1956), 434 describes the research design. For an earlier study see M. Louis Rutherford, "Lawyers as Legislators," *Annals of The American Academy of Political and Social Science*, CXCV (January, 1938), 53. Also see Rutherford's *The Influence of the American Bar Association on Public Opinion and Legislation* (Philadelphia, 1937).

7. See Austin Ranney and Willmore Kendall, *Democracy and the American Party System* (New York, 1956), p. 162. *Cf.,* Joseph A. Schlesinger, "A Two-Dimensional Scheme for Classifying the States According to the Degree of Inter-Party Competition," *American Political Science Review*, XLIX (December, 1955), 1125, for the classification of Illinois and Missouri as "one-party predominant" states.

8. Robert F. Karch, in *Essentials of Missouri Government* (Columbia, 1955), p. 14, classifies 47 Missouri counties as "normally safe Democratic," 42 as "normally safe Republican," and 26 as "normally doubtful," on the basis of elections held between 1934 and 1954. George S. Blair, in "Cumulative Voting: Patterns of Party Allegiance and Rational Choice in Illinois State Legislative Contexts," *American Political Science Review*, LII (March, 1958), 125, reports that between 1944 and 1954 Democrats were predominant in 11 of the 51 Assembly districts, Republicans were predominant in 23 districts, and party control shifted between the parties in 17 districts.

9. Party divisions within the House and the lawyer groups during these two sessions were as follows:

|  |  | 1955 Session |  |  | 1957 Session |  |
|---|---|---|---|---|---|---|
|  |  |  | Non- |  |  | Non- |
| Illinois | N | Lawyers | Lawyers | N | Lawyers | Lawyers |
| Democrat | 74 | 22 | 52 | 83 | 30 | 53 |
| Republican | 78 | 20 | 58 | 94 | 25 | 69 |
| Missouri |  |  |  |  |  |  |
| Democrat | 97 | 19 | 78 | 93 | 16 | 77 |
| Republican | 60 | 11 | 49 | 64 | 11 | 53 |

10. C. S. Hyneman, "Who Makes Our Laws?," *Political Science Quarterly,* LV (December, 1940), 556.

11. Belle Zeller (ed.), *American State Legislatures* (New York, 1954), p. 71.

12. A. P. Blaustein and C. O. Porter, *The American Lawyer: A Summary of the Survey of the Legal Profession* (Chicago, 1954), p. 97.

13. For example, Zeller states that because few laboring men are legislators "state legislatures are likely to reflect a conservative economic point of view: few legislators can be counted upon to voice the views of organized labor." Zeller, *op. cit.*, p. 72. See also P. Beckett and C. Sunderland, "Washington State's Lawmakers: Some Personnel Factors in the Washington Legislature," *Western Political Quarterly*, X (March, 1957), 198.

14. Blaustein and Porter, *op. cit.*, p. 98, quote a veteran lawyer-legislator: "A seat in our state senate is worth $10,000 a year to a practicing lawyer, even if he is a man of absolute professional integrity."

15. These data are drawn from the *Martindale-Hubbell Law Directory* (Martindale-Hubbell, Inc., Summit, New Jersey). Data used in this study appear in the 87th Annual Edition (1955) and the 89th Annual Edition (1957). The random samples were drawn by assigning each lawyer listed a number and selecting 3% of the numbers through the use of a table of random digits. The *Directory* attempts to list all lawyers in practice in the United States and some foreign areas. The listing is apparently fairly complete. For example, Martindale-Hubbell lists 6,437 lawyers in Missouri (1957 Edition). The Missouri Bar, Integrated, states that there were 6,839 persons licensed to practice law in Missouri in 1956, the year in which the 1957 Edition was being compiled. Undoubtedly some of these were either retired or not in active practice, hence not listed in Martindale-Hubbell. I acknowledge the assistance of Mr. Chong-Do Hah in the compilation of these data.

16. It is not unlikely that legislative office creates a feedback in the rating system. Lawyers attain visibility from their legislative service, which in turn enhances their practice and their chance for re-election. It is doubtful, however, that mere visibility guarantees a rating.

17. C. S. Hyneman compared the Martindale-Hubbell ratings of 214 lawyer-legislators serving in the 1934–1935 sessions of eleven state legislatures with the ratings of 200 Syracuse, New York and 20 Iowa attorneys and concluded that the lawyer in the legislatures was "a shade better" than the members of the profession at large. Hyneman, *op. cit.*, p. 573.

18. Eighty-five per cent of the lawyers, and sixty-seven per cent of the non-lawyers are included in the sample. These data are drawn from a questionnaire administered by George D. Young to members of the 1955 and 1957 sessions of the Missouri House. Young, a member of the House since 1954, has made a study of party behavior which includes some analyses of the questionnaire. *Political Parties in the Missouri House* (unpublished Ph.D. dissertation, University of Missouri, 1958). I am indebted to Dr. Young for making these data available to me.

19. Epstein found that 51% of the 1957 Wisconsin legislators had been elected to public office prior to their election to the legislature. Leon D. Epstein, *Politics in Wisconsin* (Madison, 1958), p. 191.

20. Matthews, *op. cit.*, p. 23.

21. Totals in this table vary from those in Table 3 because no data were available for two legislators.

22. Matthews, *op. cit.*, p. 23.

23. It is interesting to note that a substantial number of non-lawyers (22%) "retire" to legislative service in Missouri after they have reached age 60. About 5% of the Missouri lawyer-legislators enter after 60.

24. It should be noted that educational achievement of the legislators was substantially above mean school years completed for persons 25 years old and over. The figure is 8.8 years for Missouri and 9.3 years for Illinois. About six times as

many legislators finished college as did the general population, and about five times as many attended college but did not finish.

25. For an analysis of metropolitan and non-metropolitan relationships see David R. Derge, "Metropolitan and Non-Metropolitan Alignments in Illinois and Missouri Legislative Delegations," *American Political Science Review*, LII (December, 1958), 1051–1066.

26. Robert S. Babcock, *State and Local Government and Politics* (New York, 1957), p. 175. Supporting evidence for this assumption appears in C. S. Hyneman and E. F. Ricketts, "Tenure and Turnover of the Iowa Legislature," *Iowa Law Review*, XXIV (May, 1939), 674, and C. S. Hyneman, "Tenure and Turnover of the Indiana General Assembly, I," *American Political Science Review*, XXXII (February, 1938), 53.

27. The two factors which were probably most important in this difference were legislative pay and political security. Illinois House members received substantially more than their Missouri colleagues in salary. For example, the present legislative salary in Illinois is $12,000 per biennium, while in Missouri legislators receive only $3,000 per biennium plus $10 for each legislative day, which provides a maximum salary of $4,000 per biennium. The unique system of cumulative voting in Illinois has provided House members with greater assurance of re-election than the single-member district plan of Missouri makes possible. For an analysis of the cumulative voting system see C. S. Hyneman and J. D. Morgan, "Cumulative Voting in Illinois," *Illinois Law Review*, XXXII (May, 1937), 12–31. A later study on this subject is G. S. Blair, "Cumulative Voting: An Effective Electoral Device in Illinois Politics," *Southwestern Social Science Quarterly*, XXXIV (March, 1954), 3–18.

28. In the case of two of the seven Illinois Pro Tems, the legislator had an LL.B. degree, but did not list his major occupation as lawyer.

29. In his study of thirteen lower chambers and twelve Senates during the period 1925–1935, Hyneman found that lawyers held more chairmanships than any other occupational group in twenty of the twenty-five chambers, while they were the largest single occupational group in only seventeen. He concluded that chairmanships were divided among the occupational groups in approximately the same proportions as were all memberships. Hyneman, "Who Makes Our Laws?," *op. cit.*, p. 562.

30. A careful examination of the sponsorship patterns in the 1957 Missouri House and a cursory examination of these patterns in the 1955 Missouri House and both sessions of the Illinois House led me to conclude: 1) lawyers and non-lawyers do not differ significantly in the tendency to be lone sponsors of bills; 2) there is no reason to believe that lawyer-sponsors seek out non-lawyer co-sponsors for their bills, or vice versa. However, the practice of multiple-sponsorship in these two states makes such analyses difficult.

31. Illinois lawyers ran about two percentage points behind non-lawyers. This is probably explained by the fact that Democrats were in majority in the lawyer group but in a minority in the chamber. In Missouri, Democrats were in a majority both in the lawyer group and in the chamber.

32. For an earlier study which includes data on sponsorship of bills by lawyers, see Howard Lang, "They Legislate for Missouri," *Annals of the American Academy of Political and Social Science*, CXCV (January, 1938), 40. Lang's findings confirm conclusions presented in this study.

33. After examining the literature on state legislatures, I have concluded that writers who charge that a particular occupational group is "over-represented" do not really mean that the occupational group is being "represented" in the same sense that a legislative district constituency is represented. Their concern is really about the over-population of the legislative body by people who have the same

occupation. They then proceed from the empirical fact of numerical over-population to speculations that the occupational group will receive more favorable treatment in the legislative process than occupational groups who have fewer members in the body. For examples of these speculations see studies cited in footnote 11 *supra.*

34. Thomas S. Desmond, "Those Dinosaurs—The State Legislatures," *New York Times Magazine* (January 16, 1955), p. 15.

35. Quoted in Robert S. Allen, *Our Sovereign State* (New York, 1949), p. xxxvi.

36. When lawyers voted with high cohesion they should have almost always been on the winning side of the roll-call. Lawyers lost on four contested roll-calls in the Missouri House sessions, and on one contested roll-call in the Illinois House sessions. This should also lay to rest any fear that lawyers attempt to ram through special interest legislation over the protests of their lay colleagues. The possibility that they were successful in passing unpopular measures by cleverly constructing overwhelming majorities among non-lawyer legislators is very unlikely.

37. Hurst, *op. cit.,* p. 374, remarks that the "basic economic fact of the legal profession in mid-twentieth century United States" is that it gets "the bulk of its clients and business from about the top 13% of the population, measured by income."

38. Blaustein and Porter, *op. cit.,* p. 100, argue that "there is no evidence that lawyers in Congress and the state legislatures are, as a group, any more conservative than other members on general social and economic questions." See also Zeller, *op. cit.,* p. 72.

39. Agger, *op. cit.,* p. 439.

40. Three of these bills were sponsored by lawyers.

41. Divisions within the lawyer and non-lawyer groups on these nine roll-calls were fairly similar. In none of these roll-calls were a majority of the lawyers opposed to a majority of the non-lawyers. A chi-square test of these distributions on each roll-call produced no value significant at the $P$-.02 level, and four at the $P$-.05 level.

42. Democratic mean score was $+4.6$ and Republican mean score was $-1.9$. There was no significant difference between mean scores of lawyers and non-lawyers within the political parties.

43. One hundred and six (68%) of the 156 members responded, with party division within the respondent group deviating from the chamber party division by less than 3%. Party division within the lawyer group deviated less than 1% from the chamber party division and less than 3% from the party division within the non-lawyer respondent group. "Liberal" items were: The government ought to guarantee adequate medical care for people who can't provide it for themselves; Radicals and extremists strengthen society because they challenge existing beliefs; Federal aid to education is the best way to alleviate the present situation in our schools; A public housing program is the best way to insure that our people get the kind of homes they ought to have; If private enterprise had its way about everything the average person would be worse off than he is today; One of the primary jobs of government should be to see that every man, woman, and child enjoys a good standard of living; One of the big struggles in America today is between the ordinary citizens and the privileged few; There is too much concern about protecting private enterprise and not enough concern about assuring a decent living for everyone. "Conservative" items were: Private charity is a better way to help unfortunate people than government social welfare programs; Most people who have felt hardships in depressions have only themselves to blame for their hard times; Human nature being what it is, we're usually better off letting ourselves be guided by traditional ways than experimenting with new and untried ideas; Big unions are as great a threat to the American system as big business; If we Ameri-

cans paid more attention to the old nautral laws of economics, there wouldn't be the problem of inflation facing us now; One of the surest ways to ruin our prosperity is to place more restrictions and regulations on private enterprise system. Coefficient of reliability on all items exceeds .85. Although these items have not been scaled, it is felt that data presented here are adequate to suggest tentative conclusions regarding conservatism of lawyers.

44. Democratic mean score was +1.9 and Republican mean score was −3.4. As in the test based on roll-call behavior, there was little difference between lawyer and non-lawyer groups within each party.

45. A rank-order correlation between the legislators ranked according to the roll-call test and according to the attitude test yields r = .432, which gives a $t$ value significant at the .01 level, indicating a significant relationship between the two rankings.

46. Quoted in Hurst, *op. cit.,* p. 355.

47. In this regard Epstein reports that an impressive percentage of ex-legislators-lawyers became lobbyists before the Wisconsin legislature. Epstein, *op. cit.,* p. 119.

48. H. H. Gerth and C. W. Mills, *From Max Weber: Essays in Sociology* (New York, 1946), 94.

# Part III

# Structure

# Introduction

THE AMERICAN legislature is a multi-hierarchical formal organization. These legislatures differ in many ways in their organizational structures. They vary in size from the 35 members of the Delaware House of Representatives to the 435 members of the U.S. House of Representatives, and from the 17 members of the Nevada Senate to the 100 U.S. Senators. While all states but Nebraska have two legislative houses, the organizational status of the houses differs considerably among the legislatures. In some states the lower house dominates the organization, in others the senate is dominant, and in still others both houses vie for co-equal status. The scope and structure of intercameral contact and coordination varies widely. Some, like Congress or the Massachusetts General Court, are in session almost all of the time; others meet for as little as sixty days or less every two years. The committee organization of the legislatures varies in number of committees, jurisdictions, appointment, legislative powers, and intra-legislative prestige and influence. The internal organization of some legislative bodies, like those of Connecticut or New Jersey, is hallmarked by party caucus and leadership control. In the Congress, parties play a less dominant and more complex role, and in many state legislatures the internal party structure is weak or insignificant. To these structural differences in legislative organization could be added a multitude of other variations in constitutional powers, procedures and practices, leadership structure, executive influence, and organizational ethos.

Legislative behavior research has by no means fully accounted for the causes or consequences of the manifold organizational variations in American legislatures. The selections in this section simply illustrate in a variety of contexts the structural characteristics and consequences of legislative committees, party organizations, and informal influence structures.

Legislative organizations require some mechanisms for division of labor and specialization in order to convert the multiplicity of demands upon them into effective public policy. The committee structure is the major vehicle for the division of labor in legislative organizations. Every American legislature is organized into permanent substantive committees which provide for subject-matter specialization. Legislators with extended experience on subject-matter committees provide the expertise referents for other legislators whose own specializations fall in different substantive areas. Since in a modern legislature no individual member can become expert in all areas of policy deliberation, the legislature becomes a reciprocal expertise reference structure based upon its committee organization. This, of course, does not mean that committee structures have the same importance in every legislative organization. The place of committees in legislative decision-making, or in oversight of the administrative agencies of government, varies greatly among legislatures in terms of their institutionalization, organizational context, and legal powers and prerogatives.

A committee structure makes other contributions to a legislative organization, as well as to the more inclusive legislative system with components from the bureaucracy, constituencies, interest groups, and political parties. Conflicts over issues, values, or status which arise in or are transferred to legislatures create organizational stress or tension. Committees provide ways to facilitate tension release by structuring cathartic opportunities for conflicting groups or individuals, as well as by making policy decisions which, at least temporarily, resolve conflicts. For example, committees typically hold hearings on issues, and the committee hearing is quite often mainly a safety-valve device for the expression of individual or group dissatisfactions, complaints, concerns, or viewpoints. Again, a legislative committee structure is important to individual legislators. Where committees are strong, relatively independent and autonomous, and stable, they are powerful forces in the socialization of new members of the legislature, and their norms of behavior contribute greatly to the integration of the organization. Furthermore, committees give members of the legislature a secure place in the organizational structure, and because committees commonly vary in status and prestige, they confer status and prestige on individual legislators. Also, the specialization afforded by committees, along with whatever prestige they confer on their members, may contribute to the effectiveness with which individual legislators relate themselves to their constituencies, and perhaps help members to get re-elected. Finally, legislative committees are themselves human groups with their own norms—standards based on custom and tradition, goal or task related expectations, or requirements of personal conduct and ethics. The policy-making role of a legislative committee is greatly influenced by the nature of its internal group life.

If committees provide the most prominent feature of the organizational structure of American legislatures, party organization and leadership play a part perhaps largely underestimated in literate discussions of legislative institutions. Legislative committee and legislative party organization may be contradictory. Where party leadership is compelling and powerful, committee organization is likely to be weak or to be simply a reflection of party control. Similarly, whenever party organization is weak, insignificant, or nonexistent, decentralized committee control can be very important in the legislative process.

As Huitt has amply demonstrated for committees of the U.S. Senate, congressional committees are very independent and powerful. The congressional party organization is not strongly reflected in the work of the major committees of the Congress, where committee-related rather than party norms predominate. To use the words of Dean Truman, the congressional party is a "mediate group" in the sense that "its members' fortunes are not identical with those of the legislative party, but at the same time they are not completely independent of it." The mediate, or distant, character of congressional parties, along with the immediate, or proximate, character of congressional committees has meant that the problems of party leadership in the Congress are very considerable ones. The nature of the congressional party is clearly illustrated by the ambiguities of strategy and influence available to the party leader, further complicated by potentially conflicting role expectations coming from the legislative house and the executive branch.

State legislative committees are, on the other hand, rarely free from control by party or factional leaders. This does not mean that they are unimportant. Expertise and influence, as Francis' study of the Indiana Senate shows, may be attributed by legislators to members of both political parties. In addition, general influence across legislative policy areas, including party leadership, is highly related to the acquisition by legislators of recognized expertise in a specialized area identifiable with the legislative committee structure.

# 9. The Little Governments of the Standing Senate Committees[*]

### RALPH K. HUITT

The ultimate check on party government in the United States is the system of standing commitees in Congress. This is another way to say that the ultimate check is the coordinate status of the legislature and the executive branches, so long as Congress is able roughly to hold its own. Because a coordinate legislature must have some way to gather and assess information on its own, if it is not to be a ward of the bureaucracy, the most efficient, practical way is to divide up in committees which specialize and develop a measure of expertise. Committees which specialize and have exclusive jurisdiction over certain kinds of legislation become little legislatures themselves, with power largely independent of the elected leadership of the parent body. Centralized power and dispersed power are contradictions; to the degree that the latter exists the former is limited.

It is necessary, therefore, to see the committees both as organs of investigation and deliberation, indispensable to Congress, and as subsystems of power, crucial both to the interests which seek access to government and to the work satisfactions and career aspirations of their members.

### Internal Life of the Committees

The chairman of a major standing committee in the Senate is an influential and important man indeed. He usually is in virtual control of his committee. He calls committee meetings, decides what bills will be considered, appoints subcommittee chairmen, controls the selection of witnesses, and, excepting bills of overriding importance, determines which bills favorably reported by his committee really will be pressed for floor consideration. He probably will lead the floor fight for it or designate the man who will. In practice, he chooses committee members who will go to conference with the House on committee bills and may choose to lead the group himself. The chairman decides whether the staff will be as large and expert as money will buy or funds will be returned to the Treasury; whether the staff will be encouraged to be aggressive or passive; and whether a real fight will be made to carry the bill through floor and conference as the committee wrote it or the effort will be half-hearted.

That is why the mode of selection of the chairman is so important. Certainly

* From Ralph K. Huitt, "The Internal Distribution of Influence: The Senate," from David B. Truman, Editor, *The Congress and America's Future,* © 1965 by The American Assembly, Columbia University, New York, New York. Reprinted by permission of Prentice-Hall, Inc., Englewood Cliffs, New Jersey.

the seniority system, which moves the ranking member of the majority on the committee automatically to the chairmanship, provokes hot debate. The principal points are clear. Seniority is good because it settles out-of-hand the most disruptive organizational problem Congress ever faced, which sometimes took months to settle. Seniority is bad because it gives a margin of influence to those states and sections which regularly return the same men—if one happens not to like their point of view. These obvious aspects of seniority obscure others as important, on which not much is known. What is the effect on committee operations and policy when a new chairman drastically different in style or ideology takes over—such as happened to the Senate Judiciary Committee when liberals Kilgore and Langer served as chairmen between conservatives McCarran and Eastland? Are there institutional devices for cushioning the change? What can committees do when the chairman becomes incompetent, perhaps from senility or especially if he has enough wit and obstinacy to hold on to the committee reins? Occasionally the leadership is forced to intervene, as the Democrats had to do with the Foreign Relations Committee chairmanship in Johnson's tenure as a leader, but there must be cases which have not been pushed that far. When a seniority chairman is out of step with a majority of his committee, what happens? Can he tyrannize over them and does he, or are reasonable accommodations made? These are questions to be answered if an intelligent assessment of the seniority system is to be made.

These questions lead to more basic ones. What are the patterns of relationships between chairmen and their committees? Or put somewhat differently, how do individual incumbents perceive the chairman's role? It should be obvious that elements discussed earlier which affect the floor leader's performance should be equally pertinent here. A chairman assumes a job that is fairly narrowly defined by the institutional history of his house. He confronts certain situational aspects: the size of his majority and its temper, the urgency at the moment of his committee's business, the attitudes and demeanor of his party's congressional and executive leaders. But within the limits of this institutional and situational frame he surely is as free as the floor leader to try to behave as he pleases.

Unfortunately, the behavior of chairmen has not been subjected to much scholarly or even journalistic scrutiny. It is not safe or fair, therefore, to try to offer examples. Even so, some "ideal types" of chairmen can be suggested. There is the chairman who successfully dominates his committee. He may use his dominion to make an empire, grasping all the legislative business he can claim title to, or he may suppress committee activity because he is out of sympathy with the majority; either way, he is the boss. A different kind of chairman may not be especially interested in his committee's subject matter, but may see his job as a facilitator of whatever its members want to do. He is a genuine chairman, the servant of the group's goals. Still another may be unsympathetic with what the majority wants but conscientiously helps them; he is a "service" chairman, reinforcing the majority sentiment with assistance only a chairman can give. Still another may regard his committee as a stage for his own performance, an extension of his own personality. He is not so much concerned with what it does as he is with the setting it provides for him. Undoubtedly the list could be extended. What matters, of course, is to discover through comparative studies the *range* of behavior open to chairmen, the patterns it commonly falls into.

The chairman's notion of his own role will probably determine how he reacts to that grievous problem, the need for subcommittees. The Legislative Reorganization Act of 1946 reduced the number of Senate committees from thirty-three to fifteen. What it did not and could not do was reduce the volume of committee business. The result was a steady proliferation of subcommittees, each of which tends to carve out for itself some specialized part of the full committee's jurisdiction. The subcommittee chairmen thus parcel out to a degree the chairman's power, as he and his colleagues have parceled out the power of the leadership. Some chairmen we have described do not care; at least one has given a subcommittee to every majority member of his committee (although he *did* later abolish one because he did not like what its chairman did with it). But to the man who hoards the power he has waited so long to get there must be other alternatives. He may eschew subcommittees entirely, putting the whole burden on the full committee. He may make himself chairman of every subcommittee. He may try to prevent specialization by the subcommittees, numbering instead of naming them and referring bills of all kinds to each of them. Needless to say, the subcommittee chairmen understand the game; they trade bills around until they have established *de facto* jurisdictions.

A problem faced by every member is what to do about transferring from one committee to another. Not many senators can at once get the committee they most want, and there definitely is a status system among committees. Donald Matthews studied gains and losses of membership on Senate committees over a period of a decade (1947–57) and found a discernible pecking order, with committees tending to lose members to committees above them and to gain from those below.[1] Foreign Relations, Appropriations, Finance, and Armed Services headed the list; the District of Columbia Committee was a predictable last. A transfer, regardless of his *Senate* seniority, is last in *committee* seniority; the agonizing question then is: better junior on a good committee or senior on a less prestigious one? The problem is complicated by the impossibility of calculating the rate at which senior members will die or retire.

Like other institutionalized human groups, committees tend to become small social systems in their own right, reflecting the norms of the larger system but developing nevertheless a group life of their own. Richard Fenno's study of the House Committee on Appropriations is a brilliant pioneering effort to explore the life of one such small system.[2] He found the principal norms to be a dedication to work and a passion for protecting the Treasury. Junior members were socialized to respect these norms, and those who conformed best gained committee status earliest. It is probable that committees with great turnover do not develop a highly integrated group life, but the stable groups with great prestige surely must. If so, the character of that internal life, the norms that shape it, should be of great concern to bureaucrats, interest groups, and party leaders whose success may turn on their ability to placate and influence the committee.

But the balance must be kept: a committee is an institution of Congress; it exists to serve the purposes of congressmen. These are individual purposes as often as they are institutional or partisan. No one who has ever looked seriously at the committee's public activity, the hearing, can doubt that. David Truman has said that there are three functions or purposes of public hearings.[3] The first is to provide "a means of transmitting information, both technical and political, from various actual and potential interest groups to the committee." The second function "is as a propaganda channel through which a public may be extended and its segments partially consolidated or reinforced." The third is "to provide a quasi-ritualistic means of adjusting group conflicts and relieving disturbances through a safety valve." These purposes or functions relate to the performance of the committee as a working unit of the legislature, carrying its share of the work load, representing groups and reconciling their conflicts, reinforcing the authority of the political system. But the committee also affords the member a chance to get *his* job done. He may wish to make himself a national leader, build a reputation as a subject-matter expert, advertise himself to the constituency, do a favor for a supporter, discharge some of his own aggressions—the list could be a long one.[4] What is important is to see that in every aspect of congressional life it is necessary to satisfy both the system needs and the largely personal needs of the member who must keep himself solvent in a free-enterprise politics.

### External Relations of Committees

Like every other human group, the Senate committee lives in an environment which affects and is affected by it, with which it must somehow get along. Its environment is both congressional and noncongressional—and the latter may extend around the globe. In the congressional environment there are the other committees. The relationship seems to be largely live and let live, which the party leadership, overlapping memberships, frequent transfers, the smallness of the body and the frequent testimony of members before committees not their own, all make easier. Some tension between the legislative committees and the Appropriations Committee seems to exist beneath the surface, because what the former authorizes the latter may reduce or even deny, but this seems less sharp in the Senate than in the House. Undoubtedly friction is lessened by the Senate Committee's practice of inviting senior members of the legislative committee to participate when appropriations for their programs are discussed. Apparently little attempt is made generally for committees with the same jurisdictions in the two houses to work together; sometimes their staffs collaborate a bit, but the committees seem to work independently and meet in conference. The two taxing committees are an exception. Their senior members belong to the Joint Committee on Internal Revenue Taxation, through which they share an expert staff and collaborate effectively.[5] The separateness of the parallel committees reflects the separateness of the two houses, whose majority leaders probably meet only at the White House unless they are personal friends, as Johnson and Rayburn were. It is indeed true that "two houses do not make a home."

In the non-congressional environment, the most frequent and immediate relations of senatorial committees are with the administrative agencies. This usually is called "legislative oversight of administration," a term which is more misleading than not because it suggests a clear legislative mandate to the agency which the committee is determined to see carried out. Undoubtedly there is some of this in the relationship, and committees are directed in the Legislative Reorganization Act of 1946 to supervise the work of the agencies which fall within their jurisdiction. But unfortunately the mandate often is left unclear, sometimes deliberately so, and problems come up not dreamed of when the legislation was passed. Again, the relationship between committee and agency sometimes more nearly resembles a partnership than master and servant.

If oversight is the relationship the committee *does* want, there are traditional tools available to it. The appropriations committees in either house can guide and direct, under the threat of reduced funds. The committee may investigate the stewardship of the agency. The principal agency officers have to come before the committee before confirmation by the Senate. Congress can legislate in detail, telling the agency precisely what is desired. These formidable-seeming tools should be enough, but in practice they raise questions. Can the spending committees actually get to the heart of the matter in the enormous budgets they report, or are they limited to granting an increment, more or less, over last year? After the committee has terrorized the agency, does anything change or do the bureaucrats go back to business as usual? Is confirmation before assumption of office much of a check? How much effect on actual agency operations does the political officer have anyway? How can Congress effectively legislate in detail when the last century of administrative history has been that of increasingly large delegations of legislative power because of the legislature's inability to cope with the bewildering details of modern industrial life?

Moreover, despite a dearth of analysis of the oversight exercised by individual committees, there is enough to show that it varies widely from committee to committee. One may interfere with administrative detail outrageously, another may simply try to keep informed through its professional staff, and a third may decline to supervise at all. A single committee may bear down hard on one agency and be indifferent to another, and its militancy may wax and wane over time. Some variables might be suggested. The first, obviously, is the chairman: one aggressively suspicious of bureaucrats may be succeeded by another who thinks they should be let alone. A second is the character of the agency: a senator who would be horrified at the thought of congressional interference with the Federal Reserve Board may attempt to retry a National Labor Relations Board case in committee. Still another is the character of the program: one with wide interest and visibility will get more attention than one requiring expertise and secrecy. Again there is the closeness to the constituency: the State Department obviously does not affect as many people directly as the Department of Agriculture does. Finally, there is the quality and size of the professional staff: this may in fact be an *index* to the intentions of the chairman. What matters once again are *patterns* of recurring relationships, the *range* of behavior open to committee and staff.

These considerations are not unrelated to the question of power structure within the Senate; far from it. When committee and agency can work out something resembling a partnership, there is advantage in it for both sides. The committee adopts the agency; it protects the agency from other agencies and from executive control to the limit of its (perhaps considerable) ability. On the other hand, if the agency controls what senators (and their constituents) want, the senator with preferred access to the agency has far less need to get legislation. As a man with access to scarce services, he is in a bargaining position with legislator and bureaucrat alike. He can perform services which may make him unbeatable. These are power relationships—perhaps the most important of all and the least understood by outsiders.

## NOTES

1. Donald R. Matthews, *U. S. Senators and Their World* (Chapel Hill, 1960), pp. 148-152.
2. Richard F. Fenno, Jr., "The House Appropriations Committee as a Political

System: The Problem of Integration," *American Political Science Review,* 56 (June 1962), 372.

3. David B. Truman, *The Governmental Process* (New York, 1953), p. 372.

4. Ralph K. Huitt, "The Congressional Committee: A Case Study," *American Political Science Review,* 48 (June 1954), 340–365.

5. Ralph K. Huitt, "Congressional Operations in the Field of Money and Credit," in W. Fellner, *et al., Fiscal and Debt Management Policies* (Englewood Cliffs, N.J., 1963), pp. 446–457.

# 10. The Congressional Party[*]

## DAVID B. TRUMAN

One of the implications of the mediate character of the Congressional party is that the risks to which its members are subject are not fully integrated into the shared attitudes and goals of the group, as they would be in an immediate group such as a militant labor union, a military combat group, or even a well-managed business firm. Its members' fortunes are not identical with those of the legislative party, but at the same time they are not completely independent of it. The degree of independence . . . is probably less in the House than in the Senate. In addition, the degree of independence is not a fixed quantity but is subject to fluctuation with various circumstances—the nature of emergent issues, the timing and imminence of the re-election contest, the vigor and popular standing of the President, and the like. These fluctuations usually are not highly predictable or subject to precise ranking. Hence the distribution of risks as between those produced by the performance and fortunes of the legislative party and those more closely related to "outside" groups is often decidedly unclear and ambiguous.

This ambiguity of risk and the mediate function of the legislative party seem to be the keys to the roles of the principal elective leaders. Ambiguity may help to support the demands of the Floor Leader if he is able, unconsciously or by design, so to define the context in which the party's members make their choices that the apparent risks involved in opposing the leadership are emphasized. The ambiguity of risk also places a premium on being close to the centers of communication within the legislative party, for to be "in the know" concerning impending events in and outside the Congress is to be better prepared to minimize the risks they may imply. In consequence, the influence of one who, like the Floor Leader, occupies a position at the center of such communication can hardly fail to be enhanced.[1]

Given the mediate function of the Congressional party, the powers of its leaders, especially its principal elective leaders, cannot be expected, except in very small measure, to be formalized, codified, and at all times fully adequate for meeting the vicissitudes of their roles. Rather they are for the most part informal, personal, interstitial, and—somewhat like those of the President—often less extensive than the range of expectations they must meet. . . . There appear to be differences in this respect between the House and Senate party leaders, but in both chambers the influence of the principal leaders depends heavily upon their recurrently improvising effective combinations among fragments of power of the most varied sorts.

A former leader, commenting upon this aspect of the role, reported that he had

* From *The Congressional Party: A Case Study* (New York, 1959), pp. 293–308. Reprinted by permission of John Wiley & Sons, Inc.

on occasion persuaded a "lobbyist" whom he knew to be close to a wavering member of his party to influence the latter to vote with the party and its leadership. This testimony illustrates both the mediate character of the party and the kinds of fragments of power on which the elective leader must often rely. The fragment in this instance was formally outside the party group. It thus resembled the kind of leverage with which a President's initiatives may provide a Majority Leader, for clearly the leader of a mediate group, who almost by definition ranks little above his colleagues, must, if he chooses to perform his role with maximum effectiveness, avail himself of any outside resources that may be converted into influence within the legislative party.

. . . The imperatives of the Presidency and the peculiarities of leadership in a Congressional party with the characteristics of a mediate group make collaborative relations between the President and the principal elective leaders of his legislative party functionally useful for both participants.

Illustrations of this utility are not hard to find. A key leader in the House, who has been Majority Leader both when the President was of his party and when he was not, described his efforts under the latter circumstances to negotiate with the standing committee chairmen, individually, in order to develop an agreed program for a Congressional session. When asked whether the President's being of his party made any difference in the performance of this task, the immediate reply was, "Much easier, much easier." [2] A respected and experienced member of the Senate's staff, commenting on his own observation of the relations of Floor Leader and President, noted their tendency toward collaboration and emphasized particularly the inclination of Senate elective leaders not only to acquiesce in but to encourage presidential initiatives. He cited the case of a Floor Leader, not publicly known for his dependence on his party's President, who increasingly during his tenure solicited White House intervention with wavering senators in aid of agreed legislative projects.

The utility of the collaborative relation between the President and the leaders of his legislative party is further suggested by the fact that the regular White House meetings of the President and the "Big Four" or "Big Six" of the Congressional parties, meetings which in the past two decades have become a normal feature of governmental operation, provide the most regular contact between President and Congress and the only institutionalized point of meeting for the leaders of the parties in the Senate and House. Other communications between them takes place, of course, but apparently more casually and in a more restricted context. The White House meetings are not highly formalized, their results normally are not recorded except in the limited replies to inquiries from the press or in accounts of later discussions in the policy committees, and there is in the public domain little information concerning precisely how they operate. Some former participants have stated in interviews that at least occasionally the meetings involve considerable give and take and some effort to achieve common ground.

From the standpoint of their value for the performance of the elective leader's role, however, the precise character of the meetings is probably less important than their regular occurrence and the comparative privacy surrounding them. Some reporting of the discussions is usually made in the meetings of the policy committees and other sessions of the legislative party leaders, but if all that occurred in them immediately transpired, their utility would be considerably reduced, both as a locus of genuine negotiation and as a source of leverage for the Congressional party's leaders. The mere fact of the meetings, uniquely composed as they are and normally conducted without even the presence of staff, presumptively gives the Congressional participants "inside" intelligence concerning both the President and the other chamber that, whether communicated subsequently or not, in the context of the mediate group can be a source of influence. [3]

These comments should not be interpreted as suggesting that the elective leaders of the Congressional party do or can have a monopoly of information, especially concerning the President's intentions. Individual seniority leaders, perhaps especially in areas where the President's prerogatives and responsibilities are large, such as foreign policy, may enjoy a high degree of intimacy. But these are inevitably single areas, however important, and the data on the seniority leaders and the principal elective leaders would support the inference that they probably do not extend very far over the interconnections among all the parts of the legislative program. Moreover, the suspicion is strong that if these relations with the committee chairmen do not supplement but steadily bypass the elective leaders, they may reduce rather than augment the President's influence. Given the tremendous range of demands on his time and energies, to say nothing of the obstacles inherent in the Congressional institution, the President probably cannot successfully attempt to become regularly the direct leader of the Congressional party, working exclusively through the committee chairmen or directly with the rank and file. If this interpretation is correct, Franklin Roosevelt's reliance upon the leaders of the Congressional party and his refusal to bypass them by creating an alternative structure of communication with the Congress showed more wisdom than some of his critics are willing to grant. [4] He could and did attempt to influence the legislative party's choice of elective leaders, but had he not relied upon them, once they were chosen and regardless of whether they were his favored candidates, his effectiveness almost certainly would have been reduced.

Experienced members of both parties testify to the desirability of being "in on things," of knowing what is going on, and the importance of such information is suggested by the regular, but frequently unsatisfied, demands of the more junior members of the rank and file on both sides of the aisle for more meetings of party members. . . . Those who stand at major junction points in an important communication network may acquire power from that fact alone. Even the appearance of being on the inside, however little it corresponds to reality, may have value for the leadership of a mediate group.

Other things being equal, therefore, the elective leaders of the President's legislative party have a stake in their regular meetings at the White House and a corollary interest in the President's political standing. As leaders, they lose if he loses. Other things, of course, may not be equal. Attachment to the role of elective leader may be less than that to other opportunities and aspirations. Personal and political animosities may be too strong to be submerged in even the semblance of a collaborative effort. Participants on either side may be insensitive to the subtleties of the relation. Or a President's missteps and misfortunes may make association with him an embarrassment rather than a reliance. Proximity to the White House is not the only fragment of power available to the leaders of the Congressional party, and circumstances may reduce it to unimportance despite a general tendency in the other direction.

The benefits of a fruitful collaboration, however, are not all on one side. They accrue also to the President's account. In the thundering crises that are the normal lot of Presidents in times when "normalcy" exists only in the past, the clock provides no hours for the cultivation of rank-and-file legislators which direct leadership of the Congress would require. But in addition the President is dependent upon the principal elective leaders of the Congressional party in much the same way, if not to the same degree, as are their colleagues on the Hill. If the agenda he sets is to emerge in a product he favors, he must have the information and the means for day-to-day assessment, if not actual guidance, of Congressional activity. The elective leaders wield no monopoly here, but, standing at strategic communication points, they are, for the President much as for their legislative associates, an important source of intelligence, entirely aside from their capabilities as facilitators or obstructors of his program. And on the score of obstruction, the lengths to which as adroit a tactician as Franklin Roosevelt went in 1937 to forestall the selection of an uncongenial Senate Majority Leader are illustrative enough of this aspect of the mutually dependent relation.[5] But the President, save in exceptional instances, must rely on the leaders of the Congressional party. If means exist by which he can do without them on a continuous, day-by-day basis, the record does not reveal what they are. Relations with the leaders of the Congressional party can be supplemented, as they often have been, but no substitutes have appeared on which he can rely with equal confidence. To the degree that the mechanism of the Congressional party is relied upon, however, it must be taken as it is, with the leaders it has produced. For a President to attempt to act directly as the leader of the Congressional party almost certainly would be to destroy, for the time being, this valuable, if variable, governing instrument.

To call the relations between the President and the leaders of his Congressional party collaborative and mutually useful is to raise the problem of whether occupants of these legislative positions are to be viewed primarily as "his" or as the leaders of their respective houses and Congressional parties. The formal answer, that their principal loyalties must be toward those whose suffrage they hold, their colleagues in the Congressional party, is not very helpful since it avoids the underlying realities. The question itself would lack point, in fact, if an answer were given categorically either way.

The fundamental complexity and subtlety of the role lies in the fact that the elective leaders are, and probably must be, both the President's leaders and the party's leaders. However, if the analysis developed in these pages is valid, it follows that, in order to be fully effective as leaders of the Congressional parties, they must above all be effective spokesmen for the President; or at least, excepting the most unusual circumstances, they must appear to be his spokesmen. The data on the Floor Leaders in the Eighty-first Congress clearly point in this direction. Senator Lucas . . . appeared somewhat to the "left" of the center of his party largely because of his position on the Administration support votes, and Representative McCormack apparently went to considerable lengths to avoid being recorded in opposition to the President, even when the overwhelming majority of the House Democrats were opposing the White House. Open opposition to the President—as distinguished, perhaps, from covert failure to press his programs aggressively—apparently was something to be avoided.

The position that support for the President is a pivotal element in the roles of the principal elective leaders of the President's Congressional party is not accepted by some observers, especially as it applies to the Senate. William S. White, whose discerning observations on the upper chamber cannot be dismissed lightly, places chief emphasis on the requirement of loyalty to the views of legislative colleagues. Noting that in the Senate there is little agreement on what a Floor Leader ought to do but a broad consensus on what he ought not to do, White argues that "in all but those rare and comparatively brief periods when it is thrust into the background by extraordinary circumstances" the Senate "expects" that the Floor Leader of the party holding the White House "will not so much represent the President as the Senate itself." At the height of Franklin Roosevelt's prestige, White observes, "there arose a highly oversimplified public notion of the duties of Senate leadership based on the assumption that a leader of Democrats in the Senate *necessarily* owed obedience to a Democratic President. The compulsive actions of the Senate itself . . . for a time had the effect of promoting what the Senate felt to be a profound heresy." [6]

In these comments White correctly calls attention to the element of variability in the role of the Senate leader. The broad discretionary range implied in the expectations composing it, inevitably reflecting changes in the external setting of the legislative party, is unquestionable. The data (for the 81st Congress) amply demonstrates that in attempting to reach an understanding of leadership in the Congressional party one must beware of beguiling absolutes. One must seek central tendencies, not constants. Nor can one quarrel with the proposition that a Leader not in sympathetic communion with his legislative colleagues will in most circumstances fail to perform his functions effectively.

One must acknowledge also a reality of structure and of attitude in the separation of Senate from House and especially of both from the President. [7] The patterns of risk are not the same. They do converge, but convergence does not produce identity. Nevertheless, if the findings (for the 81st Congress) are in any degree representative, the imperatives of presidential politics produce more than an echo in the Congressional party, and the partisan responses at either end of Pennsylvania Avenue have a detectable mutual resemblance.

Within the Congress the contrasts between the Senate and the House, rooted in differences of risk and in the related factor of the size of the two bodies, are real and perceptible. They supply additional reason for the elective leaders to avoid too open emphasis upon their ties to the President. These contrasts are reflected in the rules of the two chambers, in the relative "visibility" of senators and representatives, in the attitudes of the members and even of the professional staff in one house toward the other, and in a variety of other ways. The two chambers are not totally unlike, but they are quite different groups. In consequence, the legislative parties within them do not impose the same requirements on their leaders, and preservation of the leaders' base of influence assumes sensitivity to these difference in demand.

The disposition of the elective leaders to play down their spokesmanship for the President also follows from the fact that the Congressional party as a mediate group affords its leaders little opportunity for command, in the strict sense. Their influence in either house is only slightly the product of hierarchy and, because the limits of their influence are ambiguous, their power may in fact be more extensive than any of their followers would be willing to grant in a formal delegation of authority. Actions propose definitions, and in a loosely integrated structure—perhaps in any structure—action that explicitly proposes to invoke the outer limits of implied power is likely to fail, and the resulting definition to fall short of what had previously received *de facto* acknowledgment.[8] If the elective leaders only rarely can command, they also can publicly commit their followers to a given action only after elaborate preparation.

An instance that can be interpreted as illustrating the caution imposed on the leaders of the legislative party by the requirements of their roles was provided by the events surrounding the creation of a Democratic advisory committee following the election of 1956. Meeting shortly after the election, in which the Democrats retained control of the Congress despite a landslide victory for President Eisenhower that included marked gains in most of the large metropolitan areas, the executive committee of the Democratic National Committee decided to create an advisory committee to develop a legislative program for the party. Early in December Chairman Paul Butler named twenty members to the group, including the seven principal elective leaders in both houses: from the Senate, Majority Leader Lyndon Johnson, Whip Mike Mansfield, and Chairman of the Campaign Committee George Smathers; from the House, Speaker Sam Rayburn, Majority Leader John McCormack, Whip Carl Albert, and Campaign Committee Chairman Michael Kirwan. Despite some press reports that Butler's invitations were merely a formality and that acceptance had been assured before the list was announced, within ten days all seven of these leaders declined to serve. Since the movement for the committee was known to have been sponsored by the national committeemen from California, Pennsylvania, and Illinois, and since some of its proponents presented it as an effort to produce a "liberal" legislative program and, at least by implication, to bypass the Congressional leadership, interpretations of Mr. Butler's somewhat comic embarrassment almost inevitably talked about "liberals" against "conservatives" in the party and about challenges to the Congressional leaders.

Although party factions and the status of the Congressional leaders obviously were relevant, the debacle can be interpreted in quite different terms. Even if the seven leaders of the Congressional party were in sympathy with the substantive objectives of the movement, which is well within the realm of the possible, and even if the preliminary arrangements had been made more adroitly so that the announcement could have come as the result of negotiations between the National Committee and the Congressional leaders rather than as a proposal from the Committee to the legislative leaders, Messrs. Johnson and Rayburn and their associates would have been ill advised to enter the group.

For if its decisions were made public, as the proposals of the subsequently reconstituted committee have been, the leaders of the Congressional party would have assumed a position of command that they may have by implication and after maneuver and negotiation but that they can rarely announce in open forum. Even after conferences with the President the leaders of his legislative party, though they may head a majority, normally avoid specific public commitments about what the Congressional party will do. Rather they report what the President wants and indicate an intent to help get it for him if they can. What they do not do as spokesmen for the White House they clearly cannot appear to do as members of a group created by the National Committee.

Matters would not be much different if the decisions of such an advisory committee were not made public. In their negotiations within the Capitol the principal elective leaders would not seem to be speaking in the comfortably ambiguous name of an unspecified "party" majority composed of colleagues similarly situated and with equivalent political risks, nor would they be speaking for a President with at least contingent claims upon their support. Rather they would appear to be acting for an "outside" agency without status or legitimacy.[9]

In either case, with or without publicity, the party leaders recurrently would be placed in a position, whether justifiably or not, of asking or commanding without success. Given the mediate character of the legislative party and its attendant factionalism, commitment of the party by the elective leaders normally must follow internal negotiation, not precede it, and, if negotiation fails, the leaders will be better off in most cases if they are not too frequently and openly identified with the losing side. In his dealings with the Congress, a President may be able without net loss to make public demands that are repeatedly denied by the legislature, if he makes compensating gains within the electorate. The leaders of the Congressional party are not situated in the same way. Repeated failure of their public initiatives, even if enunciated in the name of the President, is more likely to destroy them entirely. They can, as Senator Johnson did in declining membership on the advisory committee, invite the views of an "outside" group, but if these views commit the leaders, the implied initiatives are likely to produce a restricted rather than a broadened definition of their power.[10]

The two requirements, that the principal elective leaders of the Congressional party support a President of their own party and that they function as the spokesmen for their colleagues in the Congress, are not always clearly compatible. At the same time it seems clear that they are generally interdependent, in the sense that representing the President provides a focus and part of the leverage for leadership of the Congressional party, and sympathetic reflection of the problems of legislative colleagues is an essential in advancing the President's program. One or the other element may be more conspicuous from time to time. Apparently, moreover, the Congressional base is generally nearer the surface; it is more openly expressed. But the element of support for the Administration is normally present, if only implicitly and though often reflected in ambivalent terms.

The implicitly acknowledged interdependence of these two features of the role and the resulting ambivalence concerning them, especially in the case of the Floor Leader, can be easily illustrated. They are evident, for example, in estimates of the special hazards associated with the position. When a number of senators, representatives, and staff people were asked whether they felt a Floor Leader ran any special risks, the almost unanimous response was in the affirmative, the normal explanation being that as Leader he was obliged to act and to vote as he would not act and would not vote if he were an ordinary member of the Congress.

The typical illustrations for this reply were the cases of Majority Leader Lucas and Majority Whip Myers, both of whom failed to be re-elected in 1950, and the case of Majority Leader McFarland, who was defeated in the election of 1952. There may well be doubt whether holding these positions and being identified with the Administration in fact contributed significantly to the defeat of these men. The important point is that in and around the Congress a strong belief persists that this was the case. There is evidence that Senator Lister Hill for just this reason was persuaded, after the departure of Lucas, not to become Majority Leader, as he might easily have done. The choice of McFarland, although undoubtedly it owed much to the sponsorship of Senator Russell, can be traced in part to the reluctance of more vigorous members of the party to accept a post that would inevitably involve representation of an Administration increasingly regarded as a political liability.

The criticism of McFarland as Senate Majority Leader in the Eighty-second Congress and even some of the explanations of his shortcomings illustrate the ambivalence concerning the dual aspects of the role.[11] The Arizona Senator, though personally popular, was regarded as insufficiently aggressive, as unable to be "tough" with his colleagues. But in extenuation it is said that, even had he chosen to be less complacent, McFarland could not have been much more effective because of the declining prestige of President Truman. In other words, he was expected to be aggressive, and the basis for such behavior normally would be the White House program.

The conflicts, ambiguities, and ambivalences in the role of the Senate Majority Leader are particularly well illustrated by the case of Senator Knowland in the Eighty-third Congress and especially in 1954. In February, 1954, Knowland spoke and voted against President Eisenhower's position on the so-called Bricker amendment to the Constitution, which proposed to place restrictions on the treaty power. During the summer he advocated a declaration that the United States would withdraw from the United Nations if the Communist government of China were admitted to membership and also called for breaking diplomatic relations with the Soviet Union. Finally, in November he called for a Congressional review of the Administration's entire policy in the "cold war." [12]

These actions provoked a good deal of comment. The press carried reports of intense resentment in the White House, of suggestions that Knowland should resign as the Republican Leader, and even of rumors that he would resign.[13] Commenting on these responses, White says that ". . . men very high in the Eisenhower Administration honestly felt that Senator Knowland of California simply had no *right* as the Republican leader to denounce Administration policy on China. The Senate itself has been wholly unimpressed; . . . Knowland, . . . far from overextending his credit in the Institution as Republican leader, became in a way even more acceptable to it during the Eisenhower years." [14]

Criticisms of Knowland were not confined to "outsiders," however. In an interview some time later a former Senate Majority Leader, albeit a Democrat, stated flatly that he would have resigned as Floor Leader if he felt that he could not go along with a President of his own party, especially on a matter of foreign policy. Knowland himself, moreover, said that he would resign his post if the Administration ever granted diplomatic recognition to the Communist government of China. By this statement, as Arthur Krock noted in the *New York Times,* the Republican Senate Floor Leader conceded implicitly "that there are limits to the usefulness of a party leader in Congress who opposes a major policy of a President of that party." [15]

More significant than this implied acknowledgment by Knowland of the dual character of his role was the dramatically explicit gesture that the Republican Leader made early in this series of events. This came after the Bricker amendment had been altered by the Senate's adopting changes proposed by Senator Ferguson and acceptable to the President and by its passage of alterations sponsored by Senator George that were not approved by the White House. Just as the final roll call was about to be taken on the modified Bricker resolution, when, after five weeks of debate, senators were calling for a vote, Mr. Knowland exchanged desks with Senator Saltonstall, the Republican Whip, and addressed the chair:

> Mr. President, I know the hour is growing late, and I do not wish to detain the Senate. . . .

I have left the desk of the majority leader because I wish to make it very clear that what I say is not said as majority leader, but is said in my capacity as an individual Senator of the United States. . . .

So far as I know, the President of the United States has not changed his view that the only amendments acceptable to the administration were those which were presented by the distinguished Senator from Michigan [Mr. Ferguson]. . . . I say that in order that there may be a clear understanding that there has been no change in the situation, and in order that no Senator may vote under a misapprehension.

I have left the desk of the majority leader because I feel that I have an obligation, while speaking in my individual capacity, to make that very clear.[16]

He then went on to an account of his prolonged efforts at reaching a compromise satisfactory to the President and to the sponsors of the measure, explained his concern over the issue, and announced that he would vote for the resolution.

Although Senator Knowland did not repeat this gesture in his later estrangements from the President—when no votes were involved—he here clearly demonstrated the point that, subject to some variations in the conceptions of individual incumbents, the role required him to be also the President's leader if he was to be the Senate party's leader.[17]

These are requirements of the Leader's role, but the precise definition of those requirements lies within the discretion of the man performing it at the time. His background, his skills, his energy level, and his own policy preferences will determine his conception of the role and, in general, his effectiveness in performing it. He may easily be satisfied with exploiting the potentialities of the role at a minimal level, especially if the President's own skills in this realm are not an inducement to vigorous activity.

It is also possible that practice, resting on convention alone rather than on a full appreciation of possibilities, encourages performance at levels well below the full potential. Thus the data on the importance of the state delegations in the House, which were examined in Chapter 7, raise the question whether the influence of these intradelegation relations reflects a sort of power vacuum within the party or rather an inevitable restriction on the influence of the leaders. The data of the present study will not permit an adequate answer to this question, but, to the extent that the unity of the delegations is a response to ambiguity in the House rather than to claims from the constituency—and some of the evidence points in the former direction—it may indicate a failure of the leaders to realize the full potential of their roles.[18]

Some circumstantial evidence carries the same implication. Interviews with representatives in both parties indicate that communication of the policy preferences of the party leaders is frequently badly timed, inadequate, and ambiguous. Representatives on one side of the aisle, moreover, many of whom have served several terms in the House, support this point implicitly by exaggerating the quality of performance on the other. Though an adequate sample has not been taken, scattered testimony indicates that many Republican legislators regard the Democrats as better organized and more aware of their leaders' policy views than are those on their own side, and many Democratic legislators have a similar view of the Republicans. These symptoms are hardly conclusive, but, if they are reliable, they suggest the possibility that the roles of the elective leaders may one day, as a result of the skill and imagination of a single incumbent, break with existing practice and move to a new level of effectiveness. Such a level, once achieved, would likely remain the norm, even for less talented successors, as long as the underlying conditions remained unchanged. A Lyndon Johnson, under whom the office of Floor Leader apparently became a clearance point for the whole Senate party to an unprecedented degree, might, after long occupancy of the position, bequeath to his successor a role whose dimensions had been materially altered.

Whatever the extent of the gap between performance and potentiality, it is important to emphasize that these inferences concerning the role of the principal elective leaders, especially in their relations with the White House, do not and almost certainly could not span the whole range of the legislative agenda. Inevitably they refer to major items and to leading proposals. Most of what is routine, uncontested, or only narrowly controversial—probably the bulk of Congressional business —and some of what is highly explosive is left to the committees, their chairmen, the executive departments and agencies, and the relevant interest groups, except as one of the elective leaders may have a personal stake in them. Within these circles, of course, commitments and prerogatives become established, and, as in almost any complex organization, intervention from unaccustomed quarters in matters that have suddenly been projected from the obscurity of custom into the center of controversy may provoke resistance that places restrictions on any leadership, even if it has the prestige of presidential endorsement.

The Congressional party, in the form of the President's majority, is a governing instrument of great, possibly growing, value, but it is important to remember that it is not the only mechanism for determining legislative action. . . . Coalitions and alliances, operating *ad hoc* or more or less continuously through the leadership of particular committee chairmen, along lines of sectional and interest-group affiliation, are a normal feature of the Washington scene, and they may provide patterns of action entirely outside those of the legislative party on matters of grave importance. The Congressional party, however, is a system of relations at least as important as these and probably more lasting than any of them.

## NOTES

1. Presumably much the same inference is to be drawn from the apparent value of belonging to what William S. White calls "the Inner Club" in the Senate (*Citadel*, New York: Harper, 1957, chap. 7). Voorhis makes the same point in discussing the "select circle" in the House. "I confess," he says, "to having had a deep desire to have the friendship and understanding—if not the agreement—of certain of these men." (Jerry Voorhis, *Confessions of a Congressman*, pp. 31–32.)

2. Programming is not equivalent to implementation, as Neustadt has pointed out, but in this context the two may be regarded as closely related. See Richard E. Neustadt, "Presidency and Legislation: Planning the President's Program," *American Political Science Review*, Vol. 49, no. 4 (December 1955), p. 1016.

3. Informants report a more formalized arrangement during most of the Eisenhower Administration, with attendance at the meetings by the Assistant to the President and the Deputy Assistant to the President, and apparently with minutes taken at least concerning the agreements reached. The effect of this formalization, especially the presence of presidential staff, may be to reduce the utility of the meetings for participants on both sides. One suspects that such alterations would not be acceptable to some Democratic leaders, such as Speaker Sam Rayburn.

4. See James M. Burns, *Roosevelt: The Lion and the Fox,* New York: Harcourt, Brace, 1956, pp. 348-350 and *passim.*

5. *Ibid.,* pp. 309, 361-362.

6. White, *Citadel,* pp. 96-98. Italics in the original.

7. The restraining impact of this reality is suggested by President Truman in a comment on relations between a President, on the one hand, and the Speaker and Vice President, on the other. "The President cannot afford to have his confidential matters discussed in Senate cloakrooms. A leak from the White House to the Senators and Representatives is always worth a headline, and that compels a President always to be on guard when he is being interviewed by members of Congress. That is also one of the reasons why it is very difficult for a President to take the Vice President completely into his confidence." (Harry S. Truman, *Memoirs,* Vol. I, *Year of Decisions,* New York: Doubleday, 1955, p. 54.)

8. This appears to be the real significance of the "overthrow" of Speaker Joseph Cannon in 1910-1911.

9. Even when acting on behalf of the President, a Congressional leader cannot afford to appear to be speaking exclusively to rather than from his colleagues. Thus after the Eighty-third Congress (1953-1954) the view was common on Capitol Hill that Representative Martin was stronger in the House than Representative Hallock, who, as Majority Leader, had become so completely and so dogmatically a spokesman for the Administration that he had lost some of his effectiveness in the House.

10. This account is based on the reports and interpretations published in the *New York Times* for November 28, December 6, 13, 14, 19, and 23, 1956, and January 16, 1957. It should not be construed as a negative assessment of the utility of the reconstituted committee, but only of the original plan to include the Congressional party leaders.

11. Compare White, *Citadel,* p. 106.

12. A good summary of these events and the text of Senator Knowland's speech demanding a review of foreign policy appeared in the *New York Times,* November 16, 1954.

13. *New York Times,* July 1, November 17 and 21, and December 2 and 3, 1954.

14. White, *Citadel,* p. 98.

15. *New York Times,* May 3, 1955. Krock added that the chief difference between Knowland and his critics was that they thought these limits had already been passed.

16. *Congressional Record,* 83rd Cong., 2nd Sess., 100:2 (February 26, 1954), 2371.

17. The Knowland example sharpens the implications of Senator Barkley's resignation as Majority Leader following Franklin Roosevelt's veto of the 1944 tax bill, for the implied relations were not clear on the face of that incident. Barkley's vigorous speech of denunciation was in response to what he regarded as a gratuitous insult to the Congress, yet in discussing the case later he referred to himself as "the Administration's floor leader" and expressed his conviction that he was obliged to resign in the event of a "fundamental and irreconcilable disagreement with the President." (Alben W. Barkley, *That Reminds Me,* New York: Doubleday, 1954, p. 173.) Roosevelt's action undermined Barkley's value as the Administration's leader by treating him, implicitly, as exclusively that. Barkley's resignation and immediate re-election as Majority Leader restored the emphasis on his ties to his colleagues and re-established the dual relationship, though not, apparently, in identical form. Illustrations such as these occur more readily in the Senate than in the House in part because of the circumstances that make the Leader's behavior in the upper chamber more conspicuous. Since in the House the Speaker does not vote and neither he nor the Majority Leader takes as open and prominent a part on the

floor as does the Senate Leader, their positions are less obvious and their apparent commitments more ambiguous. There is every reason to assume, however, that duality is as central to a definition of their roles as it is in the Senate.

18. H. Bradford Westerfield, *Foreign Policy and Party Politics: Pearl Harbor to Korea,* New Haven: Yale University Press, 1955, pp. 92 and *passim,* offers the opinion that House Democratic leaders did not utilize the full resources of their positions.

# 11. Legislative Leadership and Political Ideology *

### Samuel C. Patterson

In recent years there has been a growing interest in the extent to which legislative leaders represent rank-and-file members of legislative bodies, and in characterization of the kinds of representative relationships uniformly observable in legislative situations.[1] This analysis seeks to explore further the "ideological" representativeness of legislative leaders in a variety of legislative situations. It seeks to investigate the leader-follower relationship on issues in an interparty context in both state and national legislative bodies. What ideological positions do legislative leaders hold? Are there uniform relationships between leadership status and "ideological" position? Here the term "leader" refers exclusively to the holders of formal positions of leadership in legislative bodies, and the term "ideology" is operationally defined in terms of cumulative scales derived from roll-call votes on specific legislative issues.[2] We are thus focusing upon only one sort of legislative leader, the one who is officially selected to a leadership position by election, co-option, or seniority. And we are viewing "ideology" in the very narrow sense of relative position on certain scales derived from a limited number of legislative issues that appear logically to involve liberal-conservative differentiation.

The limited research bearing on the ideological position of legislative leaders suggests two hypotheses about the representative character of the leadership role in the legislative situation. One can be denominated the "middleman" hypothesis, the other, the "extremity" hypothesis. The first has been advanced principally in connection with studies of the Congress, and the latter is associated with at least one analysis of state legislative leadership.

### The "Middleman" Hypothesis

The principal statement of the "middleman" hypothesis is to be found in the recent analysis of congressional party structures by Truman. He adopts as a working assumption the notion that congressional parties perform a "mediating" function, integrating the disparities in ideological position within both parties. The hypothesis follows, he argues, that legislative leaders are likely to be "middlemen." With respect to House floor leaders, Truman writes:

> Given the cleavages within both parties and the admissibility of the assumption that the legislative parties in the House, like those of the Senate, are mediate

* From *The Public Opinion Quarterly,* Vol. 2 (1963), pp. 399–410. Reprinted by permission.

groups, one would expect to find the Floor Leaders located toward the center of their respective parties.[3]

In his discussion of the Senate floor leaders, Truman suggests that the leader

> who accepted any degree of responsibility for the substantive actions of the party would almost certainly be a middleman, not only in the sense of a negotiator but also in the literal structural sense. One would not expect that he could attract the support necessary for election unless his voting record placed him somewhere near the center of an evenly divided party, and one would not expect him to be effective in his role unless he continued to avoid identification with one of the extreme groups within his nominal following.[4]

Matthews' data, based upon a cardinal index of liberalism-conservatism for Senators from the 80th to the 84th Congress, appear to show that Senate leaders (elective leaders and committee chairmen) tend to occupy middle-of-the-road ideological positions. Commenting upon his findings, Matthews observes that

> the recruitment of party leaders favored "moderates" in both parties. . . . The extreme ends of the ideological spectrum were under-represented among the leaders of both parties; moderate Democrats and Republicans were favored as leaders . . . the party leaders' ideological positions tended, after their election, to shift slightly away from the political center toward the centers of gravity of their respective parties.[5]

MacRae's highly sophisticated and penetrating analysis of roll-call voting in the House of Representatives during the 81st Congress contains data relevant to the ideological position of House leaders. Comparing Democrats on a Fair Deal scale and Republicans on a Welfare State scale, MacRae found floor leaders in both parties tended to occupy positions nearer the median scores on both scales. He also found, however, that Democratic committee chairmen tended to be found at the more liberal extreme of the Fair Deal scale, and ranking Republican committee members tended to be found at the more conservative extreme of the Welfare State scale.[6]

The "middleman" hypothesis is an attractive one to many political scientists. The virtues of the congressional leadership role on the Lyndon Johnson model have been widely extolled, and notions about the mediating, negotiator, or broker role of the legislative leader in American politics are widely held.[7] But, as MacRae has pointed out, hypotheses about the central position of congressional leaders need to be explored more extensively.[8] It is not difficult to demonstrate, for instance, that along some dimensions of liberal-conservative voting behavior congressional leaders do not fall into median scale scores. This can be shown by comparing Senate leaders' positions on two recently derived cumulative scales related to liberalism-conservatism: Belknap's scale of seven Senate roll calls on Taft-Hartley issues during the 80th Congress, and a scale of eight issues involving the role of the Federal government in domestic policy constructed for Senators during the 87th Congress.[9]

Belknap's scale of issues associated with the Senate passage of the Taft-Hartley Act in 1947 identifies one dimension of liberalism-conservatism among Senators.

It does not do violence to the term "liberal" to assume that one of its components is pro-labor sentiment, or to the term "conservative" to assume that one of its components is hostility toward union "monopoly." Similarly, on the Federal Role scale we will assume that Senators indicating strong support for legislative proposals that involve an increase in the role of the Federal government in domestic policy can be identified as "liberals," and those who oppose expanded Federal functions can be identified as "conservatives."

In assessing the ideological position of Senate leaders on these two dimensions of liberalism-conservatism, we will include as "primary" leaders the president pro tempore, the floor leaders, and the whips. The category of "secondary" leaders will include all Senate committee chairmen or ranking minority members not included as primary leaders. The relative "representation" of Senate leaders in the range of cumulative scale types for each of these scales will be assessed by means of an "index of overrepresentation," a device utilized both by MacRae, and Matthews.[10] This index simply "measures the ratio of the proportion of congressmen in a given scale type who have gained positions of leadership, to the over-all proportion of such positions." [11] An index of 1.0 means that leaders in a given scale type neither under- nor over-represent all Senators in that scale type; an index of 2.0 indicates that a given scale type has twice the over-all proportion of individuals in the leadership category; and so on.

In Table 1 are shown comparisons of Democratic and Republican leaders' indices of overrepresentation on the Taft-Hartley, or Labor Relations, scale.[12] Note that Lucas and Barkley appear at the "liberal" end of the scale, and Vandenberg, White, and Wherry occupy "conservative" scale positions. Insofar as this particular dimension of liberalism-conservatism is concerned, Senate primary leaders do not appear to have been "middlemen." In the case of both Democratic and Republican committee, or secondary, leaders the median scale position is underrepresented, as is the "liberal" extreme, although scale position 2 contains almost twice the proportion of Democratic seniority leaders and more than three times the proportion of Republican chairmen. Since scale position 2 is the most overrepresented ideological position for both Democratic and Republican committee leaders, it appears that, at the secondary leadership level, more moderate individuals acquire leadership positions *with reference to this specific dimension.*

TABLE 1. COMPARISON OF SENATE DEMOCRATIC AND REPUBLICAN LEADERS AND POSITION ON THE LABOR RELATIONS SCALE, 80TH CONGRESS

| | INDEX OF OVERREPRESENTATION | | | |
|---|---|---|---|---|
| | DEMOCRATS | | REPUBLICANS | |
| Labor Relations Scale Score | Primary Leaders | Secondary Leaders (N = 16) | Primary Leaders | Secondary Leaders (N = 15) |
| 9 ("liberal") | Lucas | 0.8 | | 0.0 |
| 1 | Barkley | 1.7 | | 1.7 |
| 2 | | 1.9 | | 3.4 |
| 3 | | 0.0 | | 0.6 |
| 4 | | 0.9 | | 0.0 |
| 5 | | 0.6 | Vanderberg | 1.4 |
| 6 ("conservative") | | 1.0 | White Wherry | 0.9 |

A similar analysis on the basis of the Federal Role scale is shown in Table 2. This scale was constructed from Senate roll calls during the 87th Congress that related to the expansion of Federal functions. The scale included votes on area redevelopment, minimum wages, aid to education, electric power generation, manpower retraining, aid to migratory farm workers, and election reform. Each involved an increase in Federal functions, power, or responsibility. While this scale is obviously not independent of administration loyalty, it seems clearly to involve a dimension of liberalism-conservatism. As Table 2 indicates, Humphrey, Mansfield, and Hayden occupy the "liberal" scale positions, and Dirksen occupies the extreme "conservative" scale position. Kuchel's scale position is more "liberal" than the median position. In the case of the Federal Role scale, Republican secondary leaders tend to be overrepresented in the more "conservative" scale positions, but Democratic committee chairmen tend to be more overrepresented in the scale positions around the median.

Significant departures from the "middleman" hypothesis are evident in the data presented in Tables 1 and 2. If anything, these data seem to suggest that primary Senate leaders are more likely to occupy extreme scale positions along liberal-con-

TABLE 2. COMPARISON OF SENATE DEMOCRATIC AND REPUBLICAN LEADERS AND POSITION ON THE FEDERAL ROLE SCALE, 87TH CONGRESS

| | INDEX OF OVERREPRESENTATION | | | |
|---|---|---|---|---|
| | DEMOCRATS | | REPUBLICANS | |
| Federal Role Scale Score | Primary Leaders | Secondary Leaders (N = 15) | Primary Leaders | Secondary Leaders (N = 16) |
| 8 ("liberal") | Humphrey | 0.7 | | 0.0 |
| 7 | Mansfield | 0.5 | | 0.0 |
| 6 | Hayden | 0.0 | | 0.9 |
| 5 | | 1.1 | Kuchel | 0.0 |
| 4 | | 4.3 | | 0.0 |
| 3 | | 4.3 | | 0.0 |
| 2 | | 0.0 | | 1.4 |
| 1 | | 0.0 | | 2.2 |
| 0 ("conservative") | | 2.6 | Dirksen | 0.5 |

servative differentia, while secondary leaders appear to be more "moderate" along some dimensions than others.[13]

## The "Extremity" Hypothesis

The "extremity" hypothesis is suggested by data presented by MacRae for members of the Massachusetts House of Representatives for sessions in the early 1950's. This hypothesis asserts that legislative leaders will tend to occupy the extreme ends of the ideological continuum, with Democratic leaders more "liberal" than rank-and-file Democrats, and Republican leaders more "conservative" than rank-and-file Republicans. MacRae hypothesized "an overall association between legislative status and liberalism (for the Democrats) or conservatism (for the Republicans)."[14] He found that the primary leaders of both parties in the Massachusetts House tended to assume the most extreme positions on a scale of liberalism-conservatism. But he found that secondary leaders (committee chairmen) tended to be less extreme. His findings are tantalizing, and encourage a similar kind of investigation for other state legislative bodies. We can present roughly comparable data for two other legislatures: for both Democrats and Republicans in the 1957 Wisconsin Assembly, and for Democrats in the 1959 Oklahoma House of Representatives.

Data for members of the 1957 Wisconsin Assembly are presented in Tables 3 and 4 for Republicans and Democrats respectively. In this case a liberalism-conservatism cumulative scale was derived from ten issues voted on by Assemblymen during the 1957 session.[15] The roll calls selected for inclusion in the scale involved issues concerning censorship, lobbying, railroad employment, political contributions by unions, maximum hours of work, racial and religious discrimination, unemployment compensation, corrupt practices, Federal aid to education (a memorial resolution), and reapportionment.

It will be noted from Table 3 that Republican leaders in the 1957 Wisconsin Assembly tended to occupy scale positions at the conservative extreme of the scale, scale positions 8 and 9 being overrepresented by primary Republican leaders. On the other hand, secondary Republican leaders as a group tended to be less extreme. Both Speaker Marotz and Majority Floor Leader Grady are located in the most "conservative" scale position.

In the case of Democratic leaders in the Assembly, the most extremely liberal scale position is overrepresented, although Minority Floor Leader Huber occupied scale position 1, and was thus not at the most extreme end of the continuum. But this analysis of Democrats has limited utility because of the large proportion of Democratic members clustered in one scale position.

The 1957 Wisconsin Assembly was highly partisan, and the two parties were relatively cohesive, a situation not unlike that to be found in the Massachusetts House of Representatives earlier in the decade. The data for the Assembly tend to be consistent with MacRae's findings in terms of the associations between leadership status and ideological position.

TABLE 3. COMPARISON OF REPUBLICAN SCORES ON THE LIBERALISM-CONSERVATISM SCALE AND POSITIONS OF LEADERSHIP, 1957 WISCONSIN ASSEMBLY

| Liberalism-Convervatism Scale Score | NUMBER OF | | | | INDEX OF OVER-REPRESENTATION | |
| | Primary Leaders | Secondary Leaders | Rank-and-file Members | Total | Primary Leaders | Secondary Leaders |
| --- | --- | --- | --- | --- | --- | --- |
| 10 ("conservative") | 3 | 8 | 9 | 30 | 0.7 | 1.6 |
| 9 | 8 | 2 | 5 | 15 | 2.4 | 0.5 |
| 8 | 2 | 1 | 4 | 7 | 1.3 | 0.5 |
| 7 | | 1 | 3 | 4 | 0.0 | 1.0 |
| 6 | 1 | 3 | 6 | 10 | 0.5 | 1.2 |
| 5 | | 1 | 2 | 3 | 0.0 | 1.3 |
| 4 | | | 5 | 5 | 0.0 | 0.0 |
| 0–3 ("liberal") | | | 1 | 1 | 0.0 | 0.0 |
| Total classified | 14 | 16 | 35 | 65 | | |

Primary leaders = members of the Steering Committee, the Joint Finance Commitee, and the Rules Committee.
Secondary leaders = all other committee chairmen.

TABLE 4. COMPARISON OF DEMOCRATIC SCORES ON THE LIBERALISM-CONSERVA-
TISM SCALE AND POSITIONS OF LEADERSHIP, 1957 WISCONSIN ASSEMBLY

| Liberalism-Conservatism Scale Score | NUMBER OF | | | Index of Overrepresentation |
| | Leaders | Rank-and-file Members | Total | |
| --- | --- | --- | --- | --- |
| 3 ("conservative") | | 1 | 1 | 0.0 |
| 2 | | 1 | 1 | 0.0 |
| 1 | 3 | 21 | 24 | 1.0 |
| 0 ("liberal") | 1 | 6 | 7 | 1.2 |
| Total classified | 4 | 29 | 33 | |

What would be our expectations in a legislature of the one-party type? The 1959 session of the Oklahoma House of Representatives provides an interesting contrast, and roughly comparable data are presented in Table 5. In the Oklahoma House the Democrats had an overwhelming majority, and the Republican contingent was both minute and subdued. What is more, while there were pro-Governor and anti-Governor cleavages in the House on some issues, these factions were not persistent and the cleavages were not notable.[16] A scale was constructed for Oklahoma House members derived from six roll calls involving labor and welfare issues.[17] These issues concerned public assistance, industrial health and safety, workmen's compensation, and unemployment compensation. In this case the liberal position involved support for labor and welfare proposals, and the conservative position involved opposition to them.

It is interesting to note, in the case of the Oklahoma House, the extent to which primary leaders tend to be more "moderate" and secondary leaders more extremely "liberal." Both Speaker Livingston and Majority Floor Leader Ogden were assigned to scale position 4. Obviously, a direct relation between leadership status and liberalism or conservatism does not hold for Oklahoma legislators.

## Discussion

It is pretty clear that neither the middleman nor the extremity hypothesis serves very well in predicting the ideological positions of legislative leaders. One can show that, on liberal-conservative dimensions, congressional and state legislative leaders are sometimes middlemen and sometimes occupy the ideological extremes. Hypothetical development with respect to the ideological positions of legislative leaders must be more highly refined.

It is quite possible that, on over-all indices of liberalism-conservatism such as that employed by Matthews, leaders might appear to cluster toward the median because the over-all index is a kind of average of extreme positions occupied by leaders on several, possibly unrelated, dimensions of ideology. Other attitudinal research suggests that liberalism-conservatism is a multidimensional variable. One investigator found, for instance, that liberalism-conservatism was not a unitary dimension but rather "a complex group of relatively independent continua." [18] The relative ideological positions of legislative leaders may well vary depending upon which dimension is measured; whether it relates to issues involving the welfare state, freedom of speech, the rights of racial minorities, or international issues. It may be necessary to design research so as to identify these dimensions in such a

TABLE 5. COMPARISON OF DEMOCRATIC SCORES ON THE LABOR AND WELFARE SCALE AND POSITIONS OF LEADERSHIP, 1959 OKLAHOMA HOUSE OF REPRESENTATIVES

| Labor and Welfare Scale Score | NUMBER OF | | | | INDEX OF OVER-REPRESENTATION | |
|---|---|---|---|---|---|---|
| | Primary Leaders | Secondary Leaders | Rank-and-file Members | Total | Primary Leaders | Secondary Leaders |
| 6 ("liberal") | 1 | 9 | 16 | 26 | 0.7 | 1.5 |
| 5 | 5 | 6 | 12 | 23 | 1.0 | 1.1 |
| 4 | 7 | 6 | 13 | 26 | 1.3 | 1.0 |
| 3 | 3 | 1 | 5 | 9 | 1.6 | 0.5 |
| 2 | 3 | 0 | 3 | 6 | 2.4 | 0.0 |
| 1 | 1 | 0 | 2 | 3 | 1.6 | 0.0 |
| 0 ("conservative") | 1 | 1 | 3 | 5 | 1.0 | 0.9 |
| Total classified | 21 | 23 | 54 | 98 | | |

Primary leaders = Speaker, Speaker Pro Tempore, Majority Floor Leader, three Assistant Majority Floor Leaders, Democratic Caucus Chairman, and the Democratic members of the General Conference Committee on Appropriations.

Secondary leaders = all committee chairmen not included as "primary" leaders except the chairmen of the Committees on Engrossed and Enrolled Bills and House Administration.

way that we can more accurately predict the conditions for relationships between leadership status and ideological position.

Insofar as our assessments of the ideological positions of legislative leaders continue to be based on "issue preferences" derived from legislative roll-call votes, situational factors are likely to be important intervening variables. Obviously, legislative leaders are also constituency representatives, and their voting behavior is apt to be affected by constituency pressures. Differences from legislature to legislature in terms of legislative-executive relationships clearly can have an effect upon the leadership recruitment process, as well as on the behavior of leaders. To suggest an illustration, the Congress ordinarily selects its own leaders independently of executive interference, but in Oklahoma selection of legislative leaders by the Governor is the more common occurrence.

In addition, ideological militancy on the part of legislative leaders may be, in part, a function of partisanship. "Liberal" and "conservative" ideological positions do not appear to be uniformly associated with leadership status, but such relationships may depend upon the extent to which there are highly homogeneous and cohesive parties in the legislature. Of the legislatures referred to here, those in Massachusetts and Wisconsin were characterized by the highest degree of party cohesion. The Congress and the Oklahoma House were less cohesive. In nonpartisan, one-party, or split-party legislatures, leaders may, along certain ideological dimensions (say, the welfare-state dimension), tend more to be recruited from among the "moderates," at least for some leadership positions. Variation in the ideological position of leaders may occur depending upon whether the leader's party is in the majority or in the minority. The data presented above suggest the possibility that this may be true, at least for secondary leaders. Majority-party secondary leaders may well take more moderate ideological positions on roll-call votes, while minority-party secondary leaders may tend to take more extreme positions. No similarly uniform difference is indicated by this limited data for primary legislative leaders.

Finally, personality factors clearly must be taken into account in comprehending the effects of ideological position on the behavior of legislative leaders, and the effects of leadership roles on ideological orientation.[19] It is reasonable to suppose that legislative leaders are recruited or selected to a considerable extent because they display desired personality characteristics, and some personality traits may be more significant in the recruitment process than a known ideological orientation. The interaction of personality and attitudinal factors for legislative leaders and rank-and-file members needs to be understood a great deal better than it is presently.

## Conclusion

Two essentially contradictory hypotheses concerning the relationship between leadership status and ideological position in legislative voting have been examined. One, the middleman hypothesis, predicts that legislative leaders will be ideological moderates; the other, the extremity hypothesis, predicts that legislative leaders will tend to be more extreme ideologically than rank-and-file legislators. Data bearing on these hypotheses, fragmentary to be sure, have been presented for the 80th and 87th Congress, the Wisconsin Assembly, and the Oklahoma House of Representatives. Significant divergences from these hypotheses characterize the data, and no generally uniform relationship between leadership status and idological position has been found. This result seems to warrant a refinement of hypotheses, taking into account the probable multidimensionality of liberalism-conservatism, situational factors, and personality characteristics.

## NOTES

1. See Lester G. Seligman, "The Study of Political Leadership," *American Political Science Review,* Vol. 44, 1950, pp. 904–915.

2. The term "ideology" has been discussed in its broadest sense in Vladimir C. Nahirny, "Some Observations on Ideological Groups," *American Journal of Sociology,* Vol. 47, 1962, pp. 397–405. Here the "content" of thought is used as the criterion of ideology, and the liberal-conservative dimensions are identified on "issue preference" grounds. For a variety of definitions and a most useful discussion, see David W. Minar, "Ideology and Political Behavior," *Midwest Journal of Political Science,* Vol. 5, 1961, pp. 317–331. See also Charles Farris, "A Method of Determining Ideological Groups in Congress," *Journal of Politics,* Vol. 20, 1958, pp. 308–338.

3. David B. Truman, *The Congressional Party: A Case Study,* New York, Wiley, 1959, p. 205.

4. *Ibid.,* p. 106.

5. Donald R. Matthews, *U.S. Senators and Their World,* Chapel Hill, University of North Carolina Press, 1960, pp. 131–132.

6. Duncan MacRae, Jr., *Dimensions of Congressional Voting,* Berkeley, University of California Press, 1958, pp. 293–295.

7. Huitt has carefully described Senator Johnson's leadership tactics. See Ralph K. Huitt, "Democratic Party Leadership in the Senate," *American Political Science Review,* Vol. 55, 1961, pp. 333–344.

8. MacRae, *op. cit.*, p. 295.

9. Belknap's Taft-Hartley scale will be found in George M. Belknap, "A Method for Analyzing Legislative Behavior," *Midwest Journal of Political Science,* Vol. 2, 1958, pp. 377–402. Its coefficient of reproducibility was .98. The Federal Role scale for Senators in the 87th Congress was developed by Mark Schantz in a Seminar on Legislative Parties at The University of Iowa. It produced a coefficient of reproducibility of .94.

10. See MacRae, *loc. cit.*, and Matthews, *op. cit.*, pp. 273–274. This index appears to have been first used by students of social mobility. See Natalie Rogoff, *Recent Trends in Occupational Mobility,* Glencoe, Ill., Free Press, 1953, pp. 31–32. The index is computed as follows:

$$\text{Index of overrepresentation} = \frac{x_{ij}}{R_i C_j / N}$$

where $x_{ij}$ = members in scale type $i$ occupying leadership position $j$
$R_i$ = number of members in scale type $i$
$C_j$ = number of members in leadership position $j$
$N$ = total number of members

11. MacRae, *op. cit.*, p. 293.

12. Derived from Belknap, *op. cit.*, pp. 394–396.

13. It is interesting to note that MacRae found the reverse to be true with respect to House floor leaders and committee chairmen for the 81st Congress. He found committee chairmen were more overrepresented in the extreme scale positions, while Democratic Leader McCormick and Republican Leader Martin tended to occupy more "central" positions. See MacRae, *op. cit.*, pp. 292–295.

14. Duncan MacRae, Jr., "Roll Call Votes and Leadership," *Public Opinion Quarterly,* Vol. 20, 1956, p. 552.

15. The scale produced a coefficient of reproducibility of .95.

16. See my "Dimensions of Voting Behavior in a One-party State Legislature," *Public Opinion Quarterly,* Vol. 26, 1962, pp. 185–200.

17. This scale produced a coefficient of reproducibility of .95.

18. See Willard A. Kerr, "Untangling the Liberalism-Conservatism Continuum," *Journal of Social Psychology,* Vol. 35, 1952, pp. 111–125; Leonard W. Ferguson, "A Revision of the Primary Social Attitudes Scales," *Journal of Psychology,* Vol. 17, 1944, pp. 229–241; Marvin E. Olsen, "Liberal-Conservative Attitude Crystallization," *Sociological Quarterly,* Vol. 3, 1962, pp. 17–26; and Gerhard Lenski, *The Religious Factor,* New York, Doubleday, 1961, pp. 187–191.

19. See Herbert McClosky, "Conservatism and Personality," *American Political Science Review,* Vol. 52, 1958, pp. 27–45, where McClosky demonstrates that "support for conservative doctrines is highly correlated with certain distinct personality patterns" (p. 38); and John B. McConaughy, "Certain Personality Factors of State Legislators in South Carolina," *American Political Science Review,* Vol. 44 1950, pp. 897–903. It is unfortunate that McConaughy's investigation has not stimulated more expansive work of this sort.

# 12. Influence and Interaction in a State Legislative Body[*]

WAYNE L. FRANCIS

The purpose of this article is to investigate distributions of influence in a legislative body, to spell out the resulting hypotheses, to introduce a method for estimating the degree of interaction between legislators, and to demonstrate the relevance of specific indicators to the study of legislative behavior. The methodological task falls somewhere between the small group laboratory situation and the more complex arena of community decision-making. Intense observation, control, and precision are sacrificed in favor of a real and vital situation. The analysis of a relatively self-sufficient political entity is lost in favor of maintaining some of the advantages of laboratory research. The universe selected for this study consists of fifty people who must directly or indirectly, but not remotely, rely upon each other in order to satisfy their official purposes.

## I. Distribution of Influence

Data classified here under the term "influence" are accumulated from responses to nine items included in a structured interview form. The items were administered to 47 of 50 members of the 1961 Indiana Senate while the 1961 session was in progress. The responses represent "attributed" influence; that is, each response is treated as a reflection of the degree of influence one senator attributes to another.

*Influence Data.* The reliability of attribution data is a function of experimental conditions. The writer judged that the conditions of this experiment were favorable. The respondents were members of a face-to-face group where knowledge about other members is likely to be relatively great, especially in view of the fact that the continuity of membership from session to session has been high. The respondents were encouraged to make only those choices about which they had information. The sample approached the total universe about which conclusions are drawn. And finally, pre-session interviewing contacts and the usual assurance of anonymity aided in establishing the proper *rapport*. For reasons of convenience the term "attributed" will not be reiterated in the presentation of data. It should suffice to keep in mind that interview responses are classified under "influence" because the key word in the questions asked of legislators is the word "influential." The first question asked was read as follows:

[*] From *The American Political Science Review,* Vol. 56 (1962), pp. 953–960. Reprinted by permission.

Generally speaking and regardless of the legislator's formal position, who would you say are the most influential members of your chamber when it comes to determining policy?

The second question was stated in the following way:

Regardless of the legislator's formal position, who would you say are the most influential members of your chamber in each of the following areas when it comes to determining policy?

Eight areas were then considered:

1. Local Government
2. Agriculture
3. Education
4. Appropriations
5. Labor
6. Business
7. Taxation
8. Benevolent Institutions

Legislators were invited to supply as many names as they wished for each item. Of the 25 Democrats and 22 Republicans interviewed for these items, no respondent named only his own party associates.[1] Approximately five names per respondent were obtained from the general influence question; the substantive area question elicited approximately two names per respondent for each item. Some respondents made no choice for certain items. Four of the substantive areas utilized reflect the names of Senate Committees (Agriculture, Education, Labor, Benevolent Institutions); the others do not. The distinction in design was made in order to avoid a group of responses that might adhere strictly to the formal structure of the legislature.

Senators were grouped and ranked according to the following distinctions:

1. *General Influence*—the number of times they were named in response to the question on general influence.
2. *Specific Area Influence*—the total number of times they were named in all substantive areas taken together.
3. The number of times they were named in each substantive area.
4. The number of substantive areas in which they were mentioned.

The distribution of responses for (1), (2) and (3) consistently characterizes a large majority of senators as having relatively little or no influence. The number of mentions tends to accelerate when moving from the least to the most frequently mentioned senator, in a graphic approximation of the "J" curve. In the substantive areas with designations that do not coincide with the names of Senate Committees, the responses tend to be spread among more members and are not so concentrated upon one or two members. The data reveal the same distributions for each political party, when political party is held constant.

*General Influence and Specific Area Influence.* The ten senators most frequently mentioned in the responses to the general influence question are named in a large number of substantive areas as well (Table I). Eight of the senators ranking highest in general influence make up eight of the top nine ranked by the number of areas in which senators were mentioned. Four of the top ten in general influence—numbers one, four, five, and ten—held Senate offices (excluding committee positions), and five of the ten were members of the minority party. Only two of the top ten general influencers were mentioned in relatively few substantive areas. Both exceptions held the office of Conference Chairman, but in opposite parties.

TABLE I. RELATIONSHIP BETWEEN GENERAL INFLUENCE AND THE NUMBER OF SUBSTANTIVE AREAS IN WHICH GENERAL INFLUENCERS ARE MENTIONED

| (Question #1) Rank of Senators by General Influence | (Question #2, Items 1–8) Number of Areas Mentioned | | | | | | | | |
|---|---|---|---|---|---|---|---|---|---|
| | 8 | 7 | 6 | 5 | 4 | 3 | 2 | 1 | 0 |
| 1 | 1 | | | | | | | | |
| 2 | | | 1 | | | | | | |
| 3 | | 1 | | | | | | | |
| 4 | | 1 | | | | | | | |
| 5 | | | | | | 1 | | | |
| 6 | | 1 | | | | | | | |
| 7 | | 1 | | | | | | | |
| 8 | | | 1 | | | | | | |
| 9 | | | 1 | | | | | | |
| 10 | | | | | | 1 | | | |
| 11–50 | | | 1 | 3 | 7 | 9 | 11 | 6 | 3 |
| Totals | 1 | 4 | 4 | 3 | 7 | 11 | 11 | 6 | 3 |

TABLE II. RELATIONSHIP BETWEEN GENERAL INFLUENCE AND SPECIFIC AREA INFLUENCE

| | High Specific Area Influencers | Low Specific Area Influencers |
|---|---|---|
| High general influencers | 21 | 4 |
| Low general influencers | 4 | 21 |

$x^2 = 23.12$, $p < .001$.

The number of substantive areas in which legislators were named as influential, however, does not reveal the degree of influence they had in each substantive area. A handy way to gauge roughly the amount and scope of a legislator's influence is to total the number of times he is named in a variety of policy-making areas. The resulting total is described as the legislator's *specific area* influence score. In the

Indiana Senate, senators who scored high in specific area influence tended also to score high in general influence. To illustrate, in Table II the median serves to distinguish between high influencers and low influencers. High general influencers tend to be high specific area influencers, and low general influencers low specific area influencers. General influence appears to be related to several sub-structures of influence which are based upon policy determination within certain substantive areas.

## II. Emergence of Influence

If influence or power relationships are vital to an understanding of political phenomena, then the emergence of influence or power is of special significance. Insight into the emergence of influence can be acquired by examining attribution data. While the data and categories are derived from responses to interview questions, the resulting generalizations need not be untenable if they are otherwise consistent with our present knowledge of human behavior.

Observers of legislative activity don't need to be told there is a direct relationship between length of service and degree of influence, *ceteris paribus*. The Indiana Senate conforms to that expectation. Both general influence and specific area influence are strongly associated with length of service. In the full spread of the data for general influence rankings, there is a clear break between senators serving in at least their fourth session and those still in their first, second or third session. The former tend to be high general influencers, and the latter low.[2]

Specific area influence and length of service present a slightly different relationship. Of the six senators in their third session of service five rank high and one low in specific area influence; yet only two of these senators rank high in general influence. Senators in their first or second session of service tend to be low specific area influencers.[3] Although the number of senators involved in these correlations is fairly small, the evidence does suggest that specific area influence tends to precede general influence.

One cannot simply assume, however, that legislators always will first become influential in rather specific substantive areas and then broaden their scope of influence with time. Recall that the Conference Chairmen were named a large number of times in response to the question on general influence; yet they were named relatively few times for the more specific influence items. It is possible that their policy specialties were not included among the influence items; however, it was the writer's observation that they seldom attempted to argue the specific content of important legislation. Their roles were more attuned to the maintenance of party organization and discipline. One would need to search their earlier records to see if they once possessed an influence now lost in specific areas.

The evidence also indicates that some legislators become highly specialized without the reward of becoming generally influential in the legislature. Of the top ten specific area influencers, four do not fall among the top ten general influencers. The four exceptions have a fairly similar influence description (Table III). Their recognized influence fell primarily into one substantive area. They received respectively 93, 92, 93, and 57 per cent of their mentions in that single area. Among the top ten general influencers, only the minority party Conference Chairman received more than 60 per cent of his mentions in one substantive area, and only one other received more than 50 per cent in one area. Furthermore, the substantive areas listed in Table III are highly significant areas from the legislators' standpoint. When senators were asked to rate their preferences among committee assignments, Education ranked first, Finance fourth, Labor fifth, and Benevolent and Penal Institutions tenth in a listing of 29 committees.

TABLE III. SENATORS IDENTIFIED WITH ONE SUBSTANTIVE AREA

| Total No. of Mentions | No. of Mentions in One Area | Name of Area | No. of Areas Mentioned | Specific Area Influence Ranking |
|---|---|---|---|---|
| 1 | 44 | 41 | Benevolent Institutions | 3 | 5 |
| 2 | 39 | 36 | Labor | 3 | 6 |
| 3 | 30 | 28 | Education | 3 | 8 |
| 4 | 30 | 17 | Appropriations | 5 | 9 |

*Tentative Hypotheses.* The terms utilized to specify substantive areas of policy (taxation, labor, education, etc.) may perhaps more realistically be described as interviewing stimuli which represented different contexts of ideas; then legislators responded to these terms by naming those they regarded as influential within the context of ideas represented by each term. Alternatively, legislators responded by naming those they had heard of as influential within the same contexts.

The foregoing data then suggest that: (1) legislators generally become recognized as influential within certain policy-making areas before they achieve general influence; (2) organizational skills, falling outside the context of ideas relating to specific policy-making areas, give legislators recognition as having general influence; (3) in the terms utilized in the interviews, legislators become recognized as competent or influential in more than one context of ideas before becoming recognized as generally influential (*i.e.,* among the top ten general influencers).

Specialization in the Indiana Senate is not as complete as one might find in other legislative bodies, such as Congress. Members of the 1961 Indiana Senate served on a minimum of three and a maximum of eight committees. When the tasks are more complex, when the stakes are higher, and when the institutional arrangements enforce a greater division of work, the emergence of influence may change accordingly. A legislator may then find that the path of least resistance calls for a demonstration of competence in a single context of ideas relating to policy and a greater emphasis upon organizational skills.

### III. Exercise of Influence

Influence is exercised through interaction, along patterns related to the proximity of issues, ideas and people, and via certain styles. These facets of influence are the concern of this section. More specifically, I have devised and applied an interaction scale, an index to influence transferability, and indices to bill success and formal position success, to analyze them.

*Influence and Interaction.* Influence is exercised through interaction in one form or another. Like "influence," "interaction" is an elusive concept. Ambiguity is reduced, it may be hoped, when such concepts are applied to specific sets of data. In this article "interaction" is described in a scale administered to 48 of 50 members of the Indiana Senate while the 1961 session was in progress. Every senator was asked to rate every other senator according to the following items and scale of weights:

0—Do not connect the name with the face
1—Recognize him, but have only a greeting acquaintance
2—Stop and talk with him regularly
3—Aid each other in common activities through actual personal contact
4—Visit or entertain in each other's house, apartment, or rooms, or eat meals together frequently, as well as aid each other in common activities

The total of scores that each senator received was calculated and utilized as a rough measure of this degree of interaction. For this immediate research senators were then grouped into quartiles by ranking their interaction scores.[4]

Both influence and interaction scores are calculated from responses to interview items; however, the judgments necessitated by the two types of questions are quite different. The interaction scale called for a judgment applying only to the respondent when paired with each colleague in turn. The influence questions called for a judgment of each colleague's impact on the entire chamber. From these very different judgments comes the relationship between interaction scores and influence totals.

TABLE IV. RELATIONSHIP BETWEEN GENERAL INFLUENCE AND
LEGISLATIVE INTERACTION

| | INTERACTORS | | | |
|---|---|---|---|---|
| | Very High | High | Low | Very Low |
| High general influencers | 11 | 10 | 3 | 1 |
| Low general influencers | 1 | 3 | 9 | 12 |

$x^2 = 23.12$, $p < .001$, when $df = 1$.

High legislative interactors (those falling above the median) tend to be high general influencers, and low legislative interactors tend to be low general influencers (Table IV). High legislative interactors also tend to be high specific area influencers and low legislative interactors tend to be low specific area influencers.[5] The distribution of Democrats and Republicans into high and low on these variables approximates the distribution in the chamber as a whole and can be ruled out as an explanatory factor.

In order to exert influence, senators must communicate either directly or indirectly with other senators. Those who are recognized as most influential interact at a higher rate than others; furthermore, the items of the scale indicate that the interaction is direct and face-to-face. Influence tends to be exerted or exercised through that type of interaction.

*Index of Influence Transferability.* The exercise of influence follows patterns partly determined by the nature of the tasks a group must perform. A task-diversified organization requires a number of skills, many of which the members of the organization can recognize. Over time skills build up priorities in relation to specific tasks. In a legislature the skills are not always easily identified, and their priorities in relation to policy-making follow no rigid standard. However, certain patterns are distinguishable through the use of attribution data. Substantive areas of policy can be identified. The top influencers in each area can be compared with the top influencers in every other area. Legislators with recognized skills in one area can influence other areas with varying degrees of difficulty. Certain types of influence, that is, are more transferable than others. For instance, influence in the area of taxation may be more transferable than influence in the area of agriculture.

The term "transferable" is employed in place of a lengthy explanation of assumptions concerning the reasons why legislators with influence in certain areas tend to have influence in certain other areas. The patterns along which influence is exercised are the major concern here. The immediate and central questions are: (1) from which substantive areas is a legislator most likely to transfer his influence to what other substantive areas; and (2) which areas appear to be characterized by high general influence? Rough answers to these questions can be calculated through a percentage matrix (Table V).

TABLE V. MATRIX OF AN INDEX OF INFLUENCE TRANSFERABILITY

| | Gen. Infl. | Tax. | Appr. | Bus. | Educ. | Agr. | Ben. | Lab. | Loc. | Area $\tilde{x}$ | Area Rank | Gen. Infl. Rank |
|---|---|---|---|---|---|---|---|---|---|---|---|---|
| Gen. Infl. | X | .7 | .6 | .7 | .4 | .3 | .3 | .3 | .5 | | | |
| Tax. | .7 | X | .7 | .6 | .4 | .4 | .3 | .2 | .2 | .40 | 1 | 1.5 |
| Appr. | .6 | .7 | X | .4 | .5 | .4 | .2 | .3 | .2 | .39 | 2 | 3 |
| Bus. | .7 | .6 | .4 | X | .3 | .2 | .1 | .4 | .4 | .34 | 3 | 1.5 |
| Educ. | .4 | .4 | .5 | .3 | X | .2 | .3 | .2 | .2 | .30 | 4 | 5 |
| Agr. | .3 | .4 | .4 | .2 | .2 | X | .1 | .2 | .1 | .23 | 7 | 7 |
| Ben. | .3 | .3 | .2 | .1 | .3 | .1 | X | .1 | .1 | .19 | 8 | 7 |
| Lab. | .3 | .2 | .3 | .4 | .2 | .2 | .1 | X | .5 | .27 | 5 | 7 |
| Loc. | .5 | .2 | .2 | .4 | .2 | .1 | .1 | .5 | X | .26 | 6 | 4 |

$r' = .84*$

*Rank correlation coefficient computed from formula (10.19) appearing in Allen L. Edwards, *Statistical Methods for the Behavioral Sciences* (New York, 1960) p. 195.

The top ten influencers from each influence category are compared with the top ten influencers of every other category.[6] In those substantive areas in which a greater percentage of top influencers overlap into other influence categories there is also a tendency to overlap more frequently into the general influence category. For example, of the ten members rated as having the highest influence in the area of taxation, seven fall into the top ten in the general influence category, an overlap which is as high as, or higher than, the overlap between general influence and any other substantive area. Correspondingly, members of the taxation influence area also fall more frequently into other substantive areas ($\bar{x}$ = .40). The rank correlation coefficient of .84 demonstrates the more general nature of this tendency.

Several hypotheses can be drawn from the matrix analysis of the index of influence transferability, bearing in mind again that the matrix is composed from attribution data, while the discussion runs in terms of "influence." One underlying assumption concerning the matrix should be made clear. It is assumed that the substantive areas in the matrix do overlap, but that they nevertheless connote different meanings to respondents. No two substantive areas follow entirely consistent patterns when compared against other substantive areas and general influence, and no two substantive areas demonstrate a one-to-one correspondence when compared against each other. This assumption allows one to make tentative statements concerning the nature of influence transferability:

1. The higher the index of influence transferability between any two substantive areas, the easier it is for a legislator to transfer his influence from one area to the other area.

2. Conversely, the lower the index of influence transferability between any two substantive areas, the more difficult it is for a legislator to transfer his influence from one area to the other area.

EXAMPLE: It is easier for a legislator with high influence in the area of taxation to transfer his influence to the area of appropriations than to the area of labor.

3. At any given level of influence transferability between two substantive areas, a legislator with high influence in the area more closely associated with general influence can more easily transfer his influence to the other area than a legislator with high influence in the area less closely associated with general influence.

EXAMPLE: It is easier for a legislator with high influence in the area of taxation to transfer his influence to the area of benevolent institutions than it is for a legislator with high influence in the area of benevolent institutions to transfer his influence to the area of taxation.

4. If two substantive areas A and B have the same index value in relation to area C, and if area A is more closely associated with general influence than area B, a legislator who is identified with area A will find it easier to transfer his influence to area C than will a legislator identified with area B.

EXAMPLE: It is easier for a legislator with high influence in the area of taxation to transfer his influence to the area of labor than it is for a legislator with high influence in the area of agriculture, even though both taxation and agriculture demonstrate an index value of .2 in relation to the area of labor.

Certainly there are factors not fully taken into account when applying the index and stating the consequent hypotheses. For example, the index does not account for differences resulting from the influence rank of legislators within a given substantive area. Will a legislator with the highest rank in the area of taxation find it easier to transfer his influence to the area of education than the fifth ranking legislator in the area of taxation, assuming their ranks are equal in the area of education? Or if the answer is self-evident, then how much easier is it for him to transfer his influence to the area of education? The latter question opens up the old problem of how to measure the relative influence of individuals in a problem-solving situation, an answer for which this research will lay no claim to provide.

The index of influence transferability is further limited in the sense that it does not pinpoint the substantive and environmental complexities encountered in any specific piece of legislation, nor does it account for personality differences which might have an effect upon the influence structure.[7] Such limitations, however, do not prevent more general probability statements. Although the index may not apply to a specific legislator in regard to a specific piece of legislation, it is not so unreasonable to apply it to a group of legislators in regard to a large number of bills that fall more or less within a certain substantive area. Or it might be reasonable to advise a legislator to become recognized as competent in the areas of taxation and appropriations rather than in the areas of agriculture, benevolent institutions, or labor if he wishes to have the best chance of influencing all areas of legislation at some date in the future. Finally, the index lends itself to a more precise way of stating common sense judgments concerning the associations between substantive areas of legislative activity as they relate to the influence structure.

*Styles of Influence.* The previous analysis, as explained, rests upon attribution data acquired through interviews. The data so gathered can be supported and supplemented by specific legislative facts, and, in turn, the arrangement of specific legislative facts can be supported by the judgments of qualified interview respondents. In this section two sets of facts are analyzed, bill sponsorship and passage data, and formal or official position data. The data are arranged into two indices: (1) the index to bill success; and (2) the index to formal position success.

The index to bill success *for each legislator* is defined as:

$$\frac{\text{Number of his sponsored bills passing chamber}}{\text{Number of bills he sponsored}}$$

The index is the ratio of bills passed to bills sponsored, the numerator squared because of a J-distribution of bill sponsorship among senators.

The index to formal position success for the *minority party* member is defined as:

$$\frac{\text{Committee assignment total}}{\text{Number of assigned committees}}$$

The committee assignment total is calculated by assigning group weights to a list of all committees ranked on the basis of the questionnaire previously mentioned, and then determining the committees to which each minority party member belongs. The same calculation is made for the majority party members, except that an allowance is made for those senators with official chamber positions by totaling the *official position weight* of each (President Protem = 10; Conference Chairman = 5; Committee Chairman = 3; Ranking Majority Member = 1). Thus the index to formal position success for these *majority party* senators is defined as:

$$\text{Official Position Weight} \times \frac{\text{Committee assignment total}}{\text{Number of assigned committees}}$$

Minority and majority party members are then ranked separately and distributed proportionally into four Senate quartiles.

Six classifications of legislators are relevant at this point. Legislators have been classified according to general influence, specific area influence, degree of interaction, the index to bill success, and the index to formal position success. The latter two are treated as indices to *styles* of influence. Some legislators exercise influence by actively and personally sponsoring legislation. Others seek and obtain strategic committee assignments and positions of authority, and exercise the sorts of influence that flow from these positions. Some legislators practice both styles effectively. To accommodate the third group, a sixth classification will be based upon a combination of the bill and formal position indices.[8]

Since the number of legislators involved in each classification is constant ($N = 50$), though small, it is practical to employ the phi coefficient ($r\phi$) to measure the observed degree of association between the various classifications.[9] Three relationships were considered earlier: (1) the significant relationship between general influence and specific area influence ($r\phi = .68$); (2) the significant relationship between general influence and degree of interaction ($r\phi = .68$); and (3) the significant relationship between specific area influence and degree of interaction ($r\phi = .60$). These strongly related variables can be given greater meaning when they are compared with the remaining classifications.

TABLE VI. DEGREE OF ASSOCIATION BETWEEN VARIABLES

| | General Influence | Specific Area Influence | Interaction |
|---|---|---|---|
| Bill success | .20 | .36 | .44 |
| Formal position success | .20 | .44 | .28 |
| Bill and formal position success | .32 | .64 | .48 |

Phi Coefficients, $N = 50$

The index to bill success is significantly related to specific area influence and degree of interaction, but not significantly related to general influence (Table VI). Senators who sponsor a substantial number of bills which pass the chamber tend to be senators who are high interactors. In the Indiana Senate sponsors are generally responsible for their own bills.[10] That they should of necessity interact with other senators at a high rate in order to have high bill success seems quite reasonable; however, there are certainly off-setting factors such as the aid of lobbyists or the governor's support, either of which might diminish the need for interaction by the sponsor.

Senators who have high bill success also tend to have high specific area influence. Their influence is felt within vital substantive areas of legislation. However, they are not necessarily recognized as *generally* influential in the chamber. The bills they sponsor may be narrow in scope, falling predominantly in to one area of legislation. To be recognized as generally influential may require activities in addition to those required by bill sponsorship.

The index to bill success does not relate significantly to the index to formal position success.[11] Senators who sponsor a relatively large number of bills which pass the chamber do not necessarily achieve formal positions of authority or serve on the most sought-after committees. One type of activity neither precludes nor necessitates the other; yet, like senators with high bill success, senators with high formal position success tend to be high specific area influencers, high interactors, but not necessarily recognized as high general influencers. High formal position success (as defined above) is not sufficient for high general influence.

Senators who have high bill and formal position success tend to be high interactors, high specific area influencers, and high general influencers. When the bill and formal position indices are combined the phi values rise in each case (Table VI). Bill and formal position success is most closely related to specific area influence ($r\phi = .64$). Senators who serve on the most preferred committees, who hold such positions as committee chairman, and who sponsor a large number of bills which pass the chamber, are mentioned frequently as the most influential within substantive areas of legislation. Senators who practice both styles of influence effectively also tend to be recognized as generally influential ($r\phi \cong .32$).

## IV. Analysis of Exceptions

The brief analysis below attempts to explain exceptions to observed relationships, through the use of variables and relationships already considered, and with a minimum of recourse to other related variables.

In Table IV eight legislators did not fit the predominant pattern. Four were high general influencers but low interactors, and four were low general influencers and high interactors. Of the former, three were serving in at least their seventh session of the legislature and were members of the middle age group (born between 1900 and 1919) for members serving in the 1961 Senate. Experienced senators tend to be high general influencers, as previously noted. Senators born between 1900 and 1919 also tend to be high general influencers (Table VII). But why do a few highly experienced senators approaching the age norm of the chamber have a tendency to interact at a low rate?

TABLE VII. RELATIONSHIP BETWEEN AGE AND GENERAL INFLUENCE

| Date of Birth | High General Influencers | Low General Influencers |
|---|---|---|
| 1900–1919 | 17 | 9 |
| Before 1900 or After 1919 | 8 | 16 |

$x^2 = 5.12$, $p < .05$.

Perhaps they have learned to communicate efficiently in order to fulfill their policy desires, or possibly the mere fact that they do approach the age norm has an effect which reduces the need for high interaction. It should be stressed, however, that the interaction questionnaire was designed to test interaction for only the 1961 session. Past interaction in previous sessions may very well carry over into the influence structure of the session under study, yet this past interaction would not necessarily register for certain items on the questionnaire. Finally, there is the possibility that the senators had outside sources of influence which minimized the need for high interaction with other senators. All but the last of these suggestions prove too much: they are as applicable to the normal as to the deviant cases.

The fourth senator who was characterized as having high general influence and low interaction was a freshman senator who interacted at a higher rate, at least, than any other freshman senator—a borderline case.

Of the four senators who were characterized as having low general influence but high interaction rates, one fell into the oldest age group and was serving in his sixth session, one was a female legislator, and the remaining two were in their second and third sessions of service. The latter two were rated high in specific area influence and would conform to the previous hypothesis on the emergence of influence if they should become recognized as general influencers in future sessions of the legislature. The other two evidently were content to talk without action.

The exceptions to the direct relationship between specific area influence and degree of interaction can to a large extent be accounted for by the same reasoning, partly because many of the same legislators are involved. Four of the ten exceptions to this second relationship appear to be of a different character; however, all four were in either their second or third session of service which appears to be a transitional phase of interaction and influence in the Indiana Senate.

There are eight exceptions to the direct relationship between general influence and specific area influence. All but one were in their first, second, or third session of service, and six of them were in their second or third session. These exceptions did not support the hypothesis that specific area influence precedes general influence, nor did they support the contrary. On the other hand, the evidence did suggest that those classified as high specific area influencers but low general influencers were named significantly more frequently in one single substantive area than were those classified as low specific area influencers but high general influencers.

## NOTES

1. The Democrats held 26 seats and the Republicans 24. The Democratic majority was the first in the Indiana Senate since 1939.

2. $\chi^2 = 15.7$, $df = 1$, $p < .001$.

3. $\chi^2 = 16.34$, $df = 1$, $p < .001$.

4. The interaction scale is an adaptation from a scale presented by Theodore Caplow and Robert Forman, "Neighborhood Inter-action in a Homogeneous Community," *American Sociological Review*, Vol. 40 (June, 1950), p. 358. An elaborate description of its reliability and usefulness can be found in a work by Theodore Caplow, Sheldon Stryker, and Samuel E. Wallace, *The Urban Microcosm: Neighborhood Structure in a Changing Metropolis*, manuscript in preparation. Establishing the reliability of the neighborhood interaction scale, of course, only indirectly supports the use of a similar scale in a legislative situation. In the adaptation of the scale it was feared that the seasonal nature of legislative activity would raise the interaction ratings during the latter part of the interviewing period. Consequently, three weeks were allowed to elapse before beginning the interviews, in the hope that the social patterns would stabilize by that time. The evidence indicates that this was the case. The first ten interviews were compared with

the last ten and no rise occurred in the average scale value for the ratings made by the latter ten. By necessity, no interviews were conducted during the last week of the session; however, for each group of ten interviews the party distribution and experienced-inexperienced distribution reasonably approximated the distributions in the entire Senate and for all those interviewed.

5. $\chi^2 = 17.8$, $df = 1$, $< .001$.

6. Ties occurring at the lowest boundary of categories were broken randomly. For more precise purposes the index would not require equal groups of ten or any other number, but for the sake of clarity it is helpful to think of a .7 index value as an overlap of seven senators out of ten for two separate sets of data.

7. Carl I. Hovland, Irving L. Janis, and Harold H. Kelley, *Communication and Persuasion* (New Haven, 1953). The authors emphasize the importance of personality in determining influence patterns.

8. This classification is based upon an accumulative quartile ranking. Let Q1 be the highest ranking and Q4 the lowest for both bill success and formal position success. A legislator's accumulative ranking can then range from the sum of 2 to the sum of 8. The line between high and low was drawn at that class boundary which most closely approaches the median (between the sums of 4 and 5).

9. $r\phi = \sqrt{\chi^2/N}$. The phi coefficient has more meaning when it is considered in conjunction with chi-square ($\chi^2$). When $N$ is constant $r\phi$ varies directly with $\chi^2$; therefore, certain values of $r\phi$ reflect significant values of $\chi^2$. When $N = 50$, the probability of a distribution occurring by chance less than five times out of a hundred reflects a phi coefficient of at least .277. Thus when $p < .05$, $r\phi > .277$; when $p < .02$, $r\phi > .329$; when $p < .01$, $r\phi > .365$; when $p < .001$, $r\phi > .466$.

10. In the Indiana Senate no bill may have more than two named sponsors. The sponsors generally explain their own bills on the floor and quite often in committee.

11. $\chi^2 = 2.00$, $df = 1$, $p > .05$.

# Part IV

# Expectations and Perceptions

# Introduction

THE AMERICAN legislator plays a very complex *role* because he is faced with many, and potentially conflicting, expectations about how he should perform his job. A fairly wide variety of the salient aspects of legislative role definition are explored by the authors of the contributions in this section. Miller and Stokes focus upon legislative role behavior in terms of the causal paths from constituency attitudes on three legislative issues to the roll-call voting behavior of congressmen. Their research indicates that congressmen's policy-related attitudes, constituents' attitudes, and representatives' perceptions of constituents' attitudes are differently related to roll-call voting behavior in different policy domains. Their analysis supports the notion that varying conceptions of the legislative role may be invoked under different kinds of policy circumstances.

Additional analysis of the Miller-Stokes data by Cnudde and McCrone has made it possible to remove one connection in the chain of relationships between constituents' attitudes, congressmen's attitudes, congressmen's perceptions, and roll-call behavior in the issue area of civil rights.[1] It can be shown statistically that the appropriate causal model for the civil rights inter-correlations (see p. 224) looks like Figure 1.

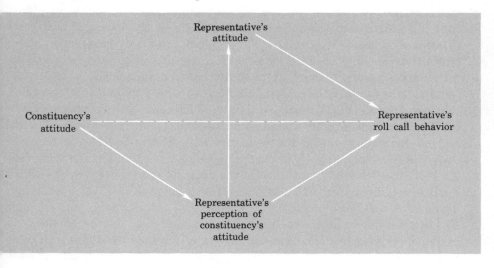

FIGURE 1

In other words, it is possible with the Miller-Stokes data to demonstrate that the attitudes of constituents and congressmen are not directly related on civil rights issues. Rather, congressmen's attitudes toward civil rights legislation tend to be formulated *through their perceptions of constituents' attitudes.* Nearly 88 per cent of the linkage between constituents' attitudes toward civil rights and legislators' roll-call voting can be accounted for in the Miller-Stokes data by a causal path from constituents' attitudes to representative's perceptions to representative's attitude to roll-call votes. Thus, it would seem that the close proximity of congressional voting to constituency attitudes on civil rights legislation results not so much from the recruitment process, where members might be selected who simply share the views of their constituents, but from a cognitive process in which congressmen vote constituents' attitudes through a fairly accurate perception of them. Civil rights provides an issue domain in which legislators tend to play an instructed delegate role, but other issue areas like those of social welfare or foreign policy exhibit different tendencies in the links between constituency attitudes and congressional voting behavior.

Wahlke, Eulau, Buchanan, and Ferguson approach the analysis of expectations about legislative behavior from the point of view of legislators' own orientations. By conceptually clarifying important elements of Edmund Burke's classic commentary on representation, and by systematically interviewing legislators in four states, these investigators show empirically the differences in representational styles and area foci. This four-state study suggests that the so-called "trustee" orientation to the legislative role is predominant; combining the data for the four states, 63 per cent of the state legislators were characterized as trustees. But much of the research stimulated by the seminal work of Wahlke, Eulau, Buchanan, and Ferguson has shown that in other states delegate-oriented legislative roles are more common, and sample data for United States representatives suggests a relatively low incidence of trustee-oriented roles there. We can now add legislators in Pennsylvania, Wisconsin, North Carolina, and the U.S. House of Representatives to the Wahlke-Eulau presentation (see p. 243).[2] In terms of representational role orientations, representatives in these legislatures are proportionately more delegate-oriented than are legislators in Ohio, New Jersey, California, and Tennessee. These comparative data indicate considerable variations among legislative bodies, and no one has accounted for them very well. The explanation in terms of "governmental complexity," or even perceived complexity, does not seem very adequate for Tennessee, and it certainly does not help to explain the differences between Ohio and Wisconsin or between Pennsylvania and New Jersey. These data, and those presented by Wahlke and his associates, raise two sets of questions for students of legislative behavior. One set of questions is explanatory: what variables are causing these interstate variations in legislative role orientations? The other set of questions is methodological: to what extent can we be sure that coding standards for legislator interviews have been rigorous and comparable? We simply do not yet have answers to these questions.

Since the connection between representational style and focus is such that we would expect delegate-oriented legislators to focus on their own districts

TABLE I

| | Pennsylvania (N = 106) | North Carolina (N = 100) | Wisconsin (N = 89) | U.S. House (N = 116) |
|---|---|---|---|---|
| Trustee | 33 | 38 | 21 | 28 |
| Politico | 27 | 5 | 4 | 50 |
| Delegate | 39 | 57 | 66 | 20 |
| Not classified | 1 | — | 9 | 3 |
| Total | 100 | 100 | 100 | 101 |

(as opposed to the state as a whole), and since the legislators we have added to the Wahlke-Eulau analysis are largely delegate- or delegate-politico-oriented, we would expect to find legislators in Pennsylvania, North Carolina, Wisconsin, and in the U.S. House to be heavily district-oriented. This expectation is verified by the figures in Table II.[3]

TABLE II

| | % District-Oriented |
|---|---|
| California | 35 |
| New Jersey | 27 |
| Ohio | 28 |
| Tennessee | 21 |
| Pennsylvania | 45 |
| North Carolina | 65 |
| Wisconsin | 70 |
| U.S. House of Representatives | 35 |

These findings cast some doubt on the generalizations of Wahlke, Eulau, Buchanan, and Ferguson regarding representational focus and political competitiveness, at least as it applies across states. As in the case of interstate variations in representational style, no clear explanation of the variations in district-orientation is now available. All the attempts at explaining these variations do suggest, however, that adequate explanation will require research about the political cultures of the states and the actual expectancy patterns to which legislators respond, as well as the legislators' own orientations.

Huitt provides us with an analysis, in one case, of conformity to patterns of expectations within legislatures vis-à-vis the behavior of legislators. He shows that, for the United States Senate, a wide latitude of role-playing is permitted and may contribute to organizational and personal goals, and he suggests that severe sanctions are not applied to "outsiders."

Finally, by systematically setting forth the principal conditions for legislative control, Scher provides an interesting exposition of the expectations congressmen have about legislative oversight of executive agencies.

## NOTES

1. Charles F. Cnudde and Donald J. McCrone, "The Linkage Between Constituency Attitudes and Congressional Voting Behavior: A Causal Model," *American Political Science Review,* Vol. 60 (1966), pp. 66–72.

2. The data on representational styles are taken from the following sources: Frank J. Sorauf, *Party and Representation* (New York, 1963), p. 124; Malcolm E. Jewell and Samuel C. Patterson, *The Legislative Process in the United States* (New York, 1966), p. 398; Donald P. Sprengel, *Legislative Perceptions of Gubernatorial Power in North Carolina* (Unpublished Ph. D. dissertation, University of North Carolina, Chapel Hill, 1966), p. 55; and Roger H. Davidson, "Congress and the Executive: The Race for Representation," in Alfred de Grazia (ed.), *Congress: The First Branch of Government* (Washington, D. C., 1966), p. 394.

3. These data are from Sorauf, *op. cit.,* p. 124; Jewell and Patterson, *op. cit.,* pp. 388–89; Sprengel, *op. cit.,* p. 53; and Davidson, *op. cit.,* p. 394.

# 13. Constituency Influence in Congress [*]

Warren E. Miller and Donald E. Stokes

Substantial constituency influence over the lower house of Congress is commonly thought to be both a normative principle and a factual truth of American government. From their draft constitution we may assume the Founding Fathers expected it, and many political scientists feel, regretfully, that the Framers' wish has come all too true.[1] Nevertheless, much of the evidence of constituency control rests on inference. The fact that our House of Representatives, especially by comparison with the House of Commons, has irregular party voting does not of itself indicate that Congressmen deviate from party in response to local pressure. And even more, the fact that many Congressmen *feel* pressure from home does not of itself establish that the local constituency is performing any of the acts that a reasonable definition of control would imply.

## I. Constituency Control in the Normative Theory of Representation

Control by the local constituency is at one pole of *both* the great normative controversies about representation that have arisen in modern times. It is generally recognized that constituency control is opposite to the conception of representation associated with Edmund Burke. Burke wanted the representative to serve the constituency's *interest* but not its *will,* and the extent to which the representative should be compelled by electoral sanctions to follow the "mandate" of his constituents has been at the heart of the ensuing controversy as it has continued for a century and a half.[2]

Constituency control also is opposite to the conception of government by responsible national parties. This is widely seen, yet the point is rarely connected with normative discussions of representation. Indeed, it is remarkable how little attention has been given to the model of representation implicit in the doctrine of a "responsible two-party system." When the subject of representation is broached among political scientists the classical argument between Burke and his opponents is likely to come at once to mind. So great is Burke's influence that the antithesis he proposed still provides the categories of thought used in contemporary treatments of representation despite the fact that many students of politics today would advocate a relationship between representative and constituency that fits *neither* position of the mandate-independence controversy.

[*] From *The American Political Science Review*, Vol. 57 (1963), pp. 45–56. Reprinted by permission.

The conception of representation implicit in the doctrine of responsible parties shares the idea of popular control with the instructed-delegate model. Both are versions of popular sovereignty. But "the people" of the responsible two-party system are conceived in terms of a national rather than a local constituency. Candidates for legislative office appeal to the electorate in terms of a *national* party program and leadership, to which, if elected, they will be committed. Expressions of policy preference by the local district are reduced to endorsements of one or another of these programs, and the local district retains only the arithmetical significance that whichever party can rally to its program the greater number of supporters in the district will control its legislative seat.

No one tradition of representation has entirely dominated American practice. Elements of the Burkean, instructed-delegate, and responsible party models can all be found in our political life. Yet if the American system has elements of all three, a good deal depends on how they are combined. Especially critical is the question whether different models of representation apply to different public issues. Is the saliency of legislative action to the public so different in quality and degree on different issues that the legislator is subject to very different constraints from his constituency? Does the legislator have a single generalized mode of response to his constituency that is rooted in a normative belief about the representative's role or does the same legislator respond to his constituency differently on different issues? More evidence is needed on matters so fundamental to our system.

## II. An Empirical Study of Representation

To extend what we know of representation in the American Congress the Survey Research Center of The University of Michigan interviewed the incumbent Congressman, his non-incumbent opponent (if any), and a sample of constituents in each of 116 congressional districts, which were themselves a probability sample of all districts.[3] These interviews, conducted immediately after the congressional election of 1958, explored a wide range of attitudes and perceptions held by the individuals who play the reciprocal roles of the representative relation in national government. The distinguishing feature of this research is, of course, that it sought direct information from both constituent and legislator (actual and aspiring). To this fund of comparative interview data has been added information about the roll call votes of our sample of Congressmen and the political and social characteristics of the districts they represent.

Many students of politics, with excellent reason, have been sensitive to possible ties between representative and constituent that have little to do with issues of public policy. For example, ethnic identifications may cement a legislator in the affections of his district, whatever (within limits) his stands on issues. And many Congressmen keep their tenure of office secure by skillful provision of district benefits ranging from free literature to major federal projects. In the full study of which this analysis is part we have explored several bases of constituency support that have little to do with policy issues. Nevertheless, the question how the representative should make up his mind on legislative issues is what the classical arguments over representation are all about, and we have given a central place to a comparison of the policy preferences of constituents and Representatives and to a causal analysis of the relation between the two.

In view of the electorate's scanty information about government it was not at all clear in advance that such a comparison could be made. Some of the more buoyant advocates of popular sovereignty have regarded the citizen as a kind of kibitzer who looks over the shoulder of his representative at the legislative game. Kibitzer and player may disagree as to which card should be played, but they were at least thought to share a common understanding of what the alternatives are.

No one familiar with the findings of research on mass electorates could accept this view of the citizen. Far from looking over the shoulder of their Congressmen at the legislative game, most Americans are almost totally uninformed about legislative issues in Washington. At best the average citizen may be said to have some general ideas about how the country should be run, which he is able to use in responding to particular questions about what the government ought to do. For example, survey studies have shown that most people have a general (though differing) conception of how far government should go to achieve social and economic welfare objectives and that these convictions fix their response to various particular questions about actions government might take.[4]

What makes it possible to compare the policy preferences of constituents and Representatives despite the public's low awareness of legislative affairs is the fact that Congressmen themselves respond to many issues in terms of fairly broad evaluative dimensions. Undoubtedly policy alternatives are judged in the executive agencies and the specialized committees of the Congress by criteria that are relatively complex and specific to the policies at issue. But a good deal of evidence goes to show that when proposals come before the House as a whole they are judged on the basis of more general evaluative dimensions.[5] For example, most Congressmen, too, seem to have a general conception of how far government should go in the area of domestic social and economic welfare, and these general positions apparently orient their roll call votes on a number of particular social welfare issues.

It follows that such a broad evaluative dimension can be used to compare the policy preferences of constituents and Representatives despite the low state of the public's information about politics. In this study three such dimensions have been drawn from our voter interviews and from congressional interviews and roll call records. As suggested above, one of these has to do with approval of government action in the social welfare field, the primary domestic issue of the New Deal-Fair Deal (and New Frontier) eras. A second dimension has to do with support for American involvement in foreign affairs, a latter-day version of the isolationist-international continuum. A third dimension has to do with approval of federal action to protect the civil rights of Negroes.[6]

Because our research focused on these three dimensions, our analysis of constituency influence is limited to these areas of policy. No point has been more energetically or usefully made by those who have sought to clarify the concepts of power and influence than the necessity of specifying the acts *with respect to which* one actor has power of influence or control over another.[7] Therefore, the scope or range of influence for our analysis is the collection of legislative issues falling within our three policy domains. We are not able to say how much control the local constituency may or may not have over *all* actions of its Representative, and there may well be pork-barrel issues or other matters of peculiar relevance to the district on which the relation of Congressman to constituency is quite distinctive. However, few observers of contemporary polititcs would regard the issues of government provision of social and economic welfare, of American involvement in world affairs, and of federal action in behalf of the Negro as constituting a trivial range of action. Indeed, these domains together include most of the great issues that have come before Congress in recent years.

In each policy domain we have used the procedures of cumulative scaling, as developed by Louis Guttman and others, to order our samples of Congressmen, of opposing candidates, and of voters. In each domain Congressmen were ranked once according to their roll call votes in the House and again according to the attitudes they revealed in our confidential interviews. These two orderings are by no means identical, nor are the discrepancies due simply to uncertainties of measurement.[8] Opposing candidates also were ranked in each policy domain according to the attitudes they revealed in our interviews. The nationwide sample of constituents was ordered in each domain, and by averaging the attitude scores of all constituents living in the same districts, whole constituencies were ranked on each dimension so that the views of Congressmen could be compared with those of their constituencies.[9] Finally, by considering only the constituents in each district who share some characteristic (voting for the incumbent, say) we were able to order these fractions of districts so that the opinions of Congressmen could be compared with those, for example, of the dominant electoral elements of their districts.

In each policy domain, crossing the rankings of Congressmen and their constituencies gives an empirical measure of the extent of policy agreement between legislator and district.[10] In the period of our research this procedure reveals very different degrees of policy congruence across the three issue domains. On questions of social and economic welfare there is considerable agreement between Representative and district, expressed by a correlation of approximately 0.3. This coefficient is, of course, very much less than the limiting value of 1.0, indicating that a number of Congressmen are, relatively speaking, more or less "liberal" than their districts. However, on the question of foreign involvement there is no discernible agreement between legislator and district whatever. Indeed, as if to emphasize the point, the coefficient expressing this relation is slightly negative (—0.09), although not significantly so in a statistical sense. It is in the domain of civil rights that the rankings of Congressmen and constituencies most nearly agree. When we took our measurements in the late 1950s the correlation of congressional roll call behavior with constituency opinion on questions affecting the Negro was nearly 0.6.

The description of policy agreement that these three simple correlations give can be a starting-point for a wide range of analyses. For example, the significance of party competition in the district for policy representation can be explored by comparing the agreement between district and Congressman with the agreement between the district and the Congressman's non-incumbent opponent. Alternatively, the significance of choosing Representatives from single-member districts by popular majority can be explored by comparing the agreement between the Congressman and his own supporters with the agreement between the Congressman and the supporters of his opponent. Taking *both* party competition and majority rule into account magnifies rather spectacularly some of the coefficients reported here. This is most true in the domain of social welfare, where attitudes both of candidates and of voters are most polarized along party lines. Whereas the correlation between the constituency majority and congressional roll call votes is nearly +0.4 on social welfare policy, the correlation of the district majority with the non-incumbent candidate is —0.4. This difference, amounting to almost 0.8,

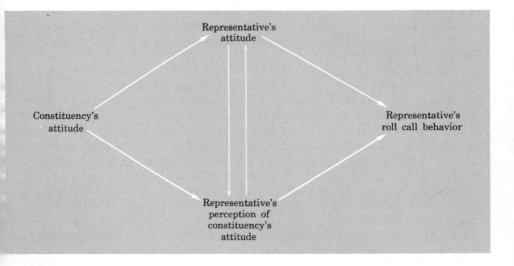

FIGURE 1. Connections Between a Constituency's Attitude and Its Representative's Roll Call Behavior

between these two coefficients is an indicator of what the dominant electoral element of the constituency gets on the average by choosing the Congressman it has and excluding his opponent from office.[11]

These three coefficients are also the starting-point for a causal analysis of the relation of constituency to representative, the main problem of this paper. At least on social welfare and Negro rights a measurable degree of congruence is found between district and legislator. Is this agreement due to constituency influence in Congress, or is it to be attributed to other causes? If this question is to have a satisfactory answer the conditions that are necessary and sufficient to assure constituency control must be stated and compared with the available empirical evidence.

### III. The Conditions of Constituency Influence

Broadly speaking, the constituency can control the policy actions of the Representative in two alternative ways. The first of these is for the district to choose a Representative who so shares its views that in following his own convictions he does his constituents' will. In this case district opinion and the Congressman's actions are connected through the Representative's own policy attitudes. The second means of constituency control is for the Congressman to follow his (at least tolerably accurate) perceptions of district attitude in order to win re-election. In this case constituency opinion and the Congressman's actions are connected through his perception of what the district wants.[12]

These two paths of constituency control are presented schematically in Figure 1. As the figure suggests, each path has two steps, one connecting the constituency's attitude with an "intervening" attitude or perception, the other connecting this attitude or perception with the Representative's roll call behavior. Out of respect for the processes by which the human actor achieves cognitive congruence we have also drawn arrows between the two intervening factors, since the Congressman probably tends to see his district as having the same opinion as his own and also tends, over time, to bring his own opinion into line with the district's. The inclusion of these arrows calls attention to two other possible influence paths, each consisting of *three* steps, although these additional paths will turn out to be of relatively slight importance empirically.

Neither of the main influence paths of Figure 1 will connect the final roll call vote to the constituency's views if either of its steps is blocked. From this, two necessary conditions of constituency influence can be stated: *first,* the Representative's votes in the House must agree substantially with his own policy views or his perceptions of the district's views, and not be determined entirely by other influences to which the Congressman is exposed; and, *second,* the attitudes or perceptions governing the Representative's acts must correspond, at least imperfectly, to the district's actual opinions. It would be difficult to describe the relation of constituency to Representative as one of control unless these conditions are met.[13]

Yet these two requirements are not sufficient to assure control. A *third* condition must also be satisfied: the constituency must in some measure take the policy views of candidates into account in choosing a Representative. If it does not, agreement between district and Congressman may arise for reasons that cannot rationally be brought within the idea of control. For example, such agreement may simply reflect the fact that a Representative drawn from a given area is likely, by pure statistical probability, to share its dominant values, without his acceptance or rejection of these ever having been a matter of consequence to his electors.

### IV. Evidence of Control: Congressional Attitudes and Perceptions

How well are these conditions met in the relation of American Congressmen to their constituents? There is little question that the first is substantially satisfied; the evidence of our research indicates that members of the House do in fact vote both their own policy views and their perceptions of their constituents' views, at least on issues of social welfare, foreign involvement, and civil rights. If these two intervening factors are used to predict roll call votes, the prediction is quite successful. Their multiple correlation with roll call position is 0.7 for social welfare, 0.6 for foreign involvement, and 0.9 for civil rights; the last figure is especially persuasive. What is more, both the Congressman's own convictions and his perceptions of district opinion make a distinct contribution to his roll call behavior. In each of the three domains the prediction of roll call votes is surer if it is made from both factors rather than from either alone.

Lest the strong influence that the Congressman's views and his perception of district views have on roll call behavior appear somehow foreordained—and, consequently, this finding seems a trivial one—it is worth taking a sidewise glance at the potency of possible other forces on the Representative's vote. In the area of foreign policy, for example, a number of Congressmen are disposed to follow the administration's advice, whatever they or their districts think. For those who are, the multiple correlation of roll call behavior with the Representative's own foreign policy views and his perception of district views is a mere 0.2. Other findings could be cited to support the point that the influence of the Congressman's own preferences and those he attributes to the district is extremely variable. Yet in the

House as a whole over the three policy domains the influence of these forces is quite strong.

The connections of congressional attitudes and perceptions with actual constituency opinion are weaker. If policy agreement between district and Representative is moderate and variable across the policy domains, as it is, this is to be explained much more in terms of the second condition of constituency control than the first. The Representative's attitudes and perceptions most nearly match true opinion in his district on the issue of Negro rights. Reflecting the charged and polarized nature of this area, the correlation of actual district opinion with perceived opinion is greater than 0.6, and the correlation of district attitude with the Representative's own attitude is nearly 0.4, as shown by Table I. But the comparable correlations for foreign involvement are much smaller—indeed almost negligible. And the coefficients for social welfare are also smaller, although a

TABLE I. CORRELATIONS OF CONSTITUENCY ATTITUDES

| | CORRELATION OF CONSTITUENCY ATTITUDE WITH | |
| --- | --- | --- |
| *Policy Domain* | *Representative's Perception of Constituency Attitude* | *Representative's Own Attitude* |
| Social welfare | .17 | .21 |
| Foreign involvement | .19 | .06 |
| Civil rights | .63 | .39 |

detailed presentation of findings in this area would show that the Representative's perceptions and attitudes are more strongly associated with the attitude of his electoral *majority* than they are with the attitudes of the constituency as a whole.

Knowing this much about the various paths that may lead, directly or indirectly, from constituency attitude to roll call vote, we can assess their relative importance. Since the alternative influence chains have links of unequal strength, the full chains will not in general be equally strong, and these differences are of great importance in the relation of Representative to constituency. For the domain of civil rights Figure 2 assembles all the intercorrelations of the variables of our system. As the figure shows, the root correlation of constituency attitude with roll call behavior in this domain is 0.57. How much of this policy congruence can be accounted for by the influence path involving the Representative's attitude? And how much by the path involving his perception of constituency opinion? When the intercorrelations of the system are interpreted in the light of what we assume its causal structure to be, it is influence passing through the Congressman's perception of the district's views that is found to be preeminently important.[14] Under the least favorable assumption as to its importance, this path is found to account for more than twice as much of the variance of roll call behavior as the paths involving the Representative's own attitude.[15] However, when this same procedure is applied to our social welfare data, the results suggest that the direct connection of constituency and roll call through the Congressman's own attitude is the most important of the alternative paths.[16] The reversal of the relative importance of the

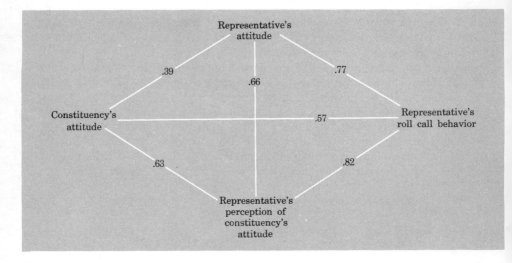

FIGURE 2. Intercorrelations of Variables Pertaining to Civil Rights

two paths as we move from civil rights to social welfare is one of the most striking findings of this analysis.

## V. Evidence of Control: Electoral Behavior

Of the three conditions of constituency influence, the requirement that the electorate take account of the policy positions of the candidates is the hardest to match with empirical evidence. Indeed, given the limited information the average voter carries to the polls, the public might be thought incompetent to perform any task of appraisal. Of constituents living in congressional districts where there was a contest between a Republican and a Democrat in 1958, less than one in five said they had read or heard something about both candidates, and well over half conceded they had read or heard nothing about either. And these proportions are not much better when they are based only on the part of the sample, not much more than half, that reported voting for Congress in 1958. The extent of awareness of the candidates among voters is indicated in Table II. As the table shows, even of the portion of the public that was sufficiently interested to vote, almost half had read or heard nothing about either candidate.

Just how low a hurdle our respondents had to clear in saying they had read or heard something about a candidate is indicated by detailed qualitative analysis of the information constituents *were* able to associate with congressional candidates. Except in rare cases, what the voters "knew" was confined to diffuse evaluative judgments about the candidate: "he's a good man," "he understands the problems," and so forth. Of detailed information about policy stands not more than a chemical trace was found. Among the comments about the candidates given in response to an extended series of free-answer questions, less than two percent had to do with stands in our three policy domains; indeed, only about three comments in every hundred had to do with legislative issues of *any* description.[17]

This evidence that the behavior of the electorate is largely unaffected by knowl-

TABLE II. AWARENESS OF CONGRESSIONAL CANDIDATES
AMONG VOTERS, 1958

| | | Read or Heard Something About Incumbent[a] | | |
|---|---|---|---|---|
| | | Yes | No | |
| Read or Heard Something About Non-Incumbent | Yes | 24 | 5 | 29 |
| | No | 25 | 46 | 71 |
| | | 49 | 51 | 100% |

[a]In order to include all districts where the House seat was contested in 1958 this table retains ten constituencies in which the incumbent Congressman did not seek re-election. Candidates of the retiring incumbent's party in these districts are treated here as if they were incumbents. Were these figures to be calculated only for constituencies in which an incumbent sought re-election, no entry in this four-fold table would differ from that given by more than two percent.

edge of the policy positions of the candidates is complemented by evidence about the forces that do shape the voters' choices among congressional candidates. The primary basis of voting in American congressional elections is identification with party. In 1958 only one vote in twenty was cast by persons without any sort of party loyalty. And among those who did have a party identification, only one in ten voted against their party. As a result, something like 84 percent of the vote that year was cast by party identifiers voting their usual party line. What is more, traditional party voting is seldom connected with current legislative issues. As the party loyalists in a nationwide sample of voters told us what they liked and disliked about the parties in 1958, only a small fraction of the comments (about 15 per cent) dealt with current issues of public policy.[18]

Yet the idea of reward or punishment at the polls for legislative stands is familiar to members of Congress, who feel that they and their records are quite visible to their constituents. Of our sample of Congressmen who were opposed for re-election in 1958, more than four-fifths said the outcome in their districts had been strongly influenced by the electorate's response to their records and personal standing. Indeed, this belief is clear enough to present a notable contradiction: Congressmen feel that their individual legislative actions may have considerable impact on the electorate, yet some simple facts about the Representative's salience to his constituents imply that this could hardly be true.

In some measure this contradiction is to be explained by the tendency of Congressmen to overestimate their visibility to the local public, a tendency that reflects the difficulties of the Representative in forming a correct judgment of constituent opinion. The communication most Congressmen have with their districts inevitably puts them in touch with organized groups and with individuals who are relatively well informed about politics. The Representative knows his constituents mostly from dealing with people who *do* write letters, who *will* attend meetings, who *have* an interest in his legislative stands. As a result, his sample of contacts with a constituency of several hundred thousand people is heavily biased: even the contacts he apparently makes at random are likely to be with people who grossly over-represent the degree of political information and interest in the constituency as a whole.

But the contradiction is also to be explained by several aspects of the Representative's electoral situation that are of great importance to the quesion of constituency influence. The first of these is implicit in what has already been said. Because of the pervasive efforts of party loyalties, no candidate for Congress starts from scratch in putting together an electoral majority. The Congressman is a dealer in increments and margins. He starts with a stratum of hardened party voters, and if the stratum is broad enough he can have a measurable influence on his chance of survival simply by attracting a small additional element of the electorate—or by not losing a larger one. Therefore, his record may have a very real bearing on his electoral success or failure without most of his constituents ever knowing what that record is.

Second, the relation of Congressman to voter is not a simple bilateral one but is complicated by the presence of all manner of intermediaries: the local party, economic interests, the news media, racial and nationality organizations, and so forth. Such is the lore of American politics, as it is known to any political scientist. Very often the Representative reaches the mass public through these mediating agencies, and the information about himself and his record may be considerably transformed as it diffuses out to the electorate in two or more stages. As a result, the public—or parts of it—may get simple positive or negative cues about the Congressman which were provoked by his legislative actions but which no longer have a recognizable issue content.

Third, for most Congressmen most of the time the electorate's sanctions are potential rather than actual. Particularly the Representative from a safe district may feel his proper legislative strategy is to avoid giving opponents in his own party or outside of it material they can use against him. As the Congressman pursues this strategy he may write a legislative record that never becomes very well known to his constituents; if it doesn't win votes, neither will it lose any. This is clearly the situation of most southern Congressmen in dealing with the issue of Negro rights. By voting correctly on this issue they are unlikely to increase their visibility to constituents. Nevertheless, the fact of constituency influence, backed by potential sanctions at the polls, is real enough.

That these potential sanctions are all too real is best illustrated in the election of 1958 by the reprisal against Representative Brooks Hays in Arkansas' Fifth District.[19] Although the perception of Congressman Hays as too moderate on civil rights resulted more from his service as intermediary between the White House

TABLE III. AWARENESS OF CONGRESSIONAL CANDIDATES
AMONG VOTERS IN ARKANSAS FIFTH DISTRICT, 1958

| | | Read or Heard Something About Hays | | |
|---|---|---|---|---|
| | | Yes | No | |
| Read or Heard Something About Alford | Yes | 100 | 0 | 100 |
| | No | 0 | 0 | 0 |
| | | 100 | 0 | 100% |

and Governor Faubus in the Little Rock school crisis than from his record in the House, the victory of Dale Alford as a write-in candidate was a striking reminder of what can happen to a Congressman who gives his foes a powerful issue to use against him. The extraordinary involvement of the public in this race can be seen by comparing how well the candidates were known in this constituency with the awareness of the candidates shown by Table II above for the country as a whole. As Table III indicates, not a single voter in our sample of Arkansas' Fifth District was unaware of either candidate.[20] What is more, these interviews show that Hays was regarded both by his supporters and his opponents as more moderate than Alford on civil rights and that this perception brought his defeat. In some measure, what happened in Little Rock in 1958 can happen anywhere, and our Congressmen ought not to be entirely disbelieved in what they say about their impact at the polls. Indeed, they may be under genuine pressure from the voters even while they are the forgotten men of national elections.[21]

## V. Conclusion

Therefore, although the conditions of constituency influence are not equally satisfied, they are met well enough to give the local constituency a measure of control over the actions of its Representatives. Best satisfied is the requirement about motivational influences on the Congressman: our evidence shows that the Representative's roll call behavior is strongly influenced by his own policy preferences and by his perception of preferences held by the constituency. However, the conditions of influence that presuppose effective communication between Congressman and district are much less well met. The Representative has very imperfect information about the issue preferences of his constituency, and the constituency's awareness of the policy stands of the Representative ordinarily is slight.

The findings of this analysis heavily underscore the fact that no single tradition of representation fully accords with the realities of American legislative politics. The American system *is* a mixture, to which the Burkean, instructed-delegate, and responsible-party models all can be said to have contributed elements. Moreover, variations in the representative relation are most likely to occur as we move from one policy domain to another. No single, generalized configuration of attitudes pat-perceptions links Representative with constituency but rather several distinct patterns, and which of them is invoked depends very much on the issue involved.

The issue domain in which the relation of Congressman to constituency most nearly conforms to the instructed-delegate model is that of civil rights. His conclusion is supported by the importance of the influence-path passing through the Representative's perception of district opinion, although even in this domain the sense in which the constituency may be said to take the position of the candidate into account in reaching its electoral judgment should be carefully qualified.

The representative relation conforms most closely to the responsible-party model in the domain of social welfare. In this issue area, the arena of partisan conflict for a generation, the party symbol helps both constituency and Representative in the difficult process of communication between them. On the one hand, because Republican and Democratic voters tend to differ in what they would have government do, the Representative has some guide to district opinion simply by looking at the partisan division of the vote. On the other hand, because the two parties tend to recruit candidates who differ on the social welfare role of government, the constituency can infer the candidates' position with more than random accuracy from their party affiliation, even though what the constituency has learned directly about these stands is almost nothing. How faithful the representation of social welfare views is to the responsible-party model should not be exaggerated. Even in this policy domain, American practice departs widely from an ideal conception of party government.[22] But in this domain, more than any other, political conflict has become a conflict of national parties in which constituency and Representative are known to each other primarily by their party association.

It would be too pat to say that the domain of foreign involvement conforms to the third model of representation, the conception promoted by Edmund Burke. Clearly it does in the sense that the Congressman looks elsewhere than to his district in making up his mind on foreign issues. However, the reliance he puts on the President and the Administration suggests that the calculation of where the public interest lies is often passed to the Executive on matters of foreign policy. Ironically, legislative initiative in foreign affairs has fallen victim to the very difficulties of gathering and appraising information that led Burke to argue that Parliament rather than the public ought to hold the power of decision. The background information and predictive skills that Burke thought the people lacked are held primarily by the modern Executive. As a result, the present role of the legislature in foreign affairs bears some resemblance to the role that Burke had in mind for the elitist, highly restricted *electorate* of his own day.

## NOTES

1. To be sure, the work of the Federal Convention has been supplemented in two critical respects. The first of these is the practice, virtually universal since the mid-19th Century, of choosing Representatives from single-member districts of limited geographic area. The second is the practice, which has also become virtually universal in our own century, of selecting party nominees for the House by direct primary election.

2. In the language of Eulau, Wahlke, *et al.*, we speak here of the "style," not the "focus," of representation. See their "The Role of the Representative: Some Empirical Observations on the Theory of Edmund Burke," *American Political Science Review,* Vol. 53 (September, 1959), pp. 742–756. An excellent review of the mandate-independence controversy is given by Hanna Fenichel Pitkin, "The Theory of Representation" (unpublished doctoral dissertation, University of California, Berkeley, 1961). For other contemporary discussions of representation, see Alfred de Grazia, *Public and Republic* (New York, 1951), and John A. Fairlie, "The Nature of Political Representation," *American Political Science Review,* Vol. 34 (April-June, 1940), pp. 236–48, 456–66.

3. The sampling aspects of this research were complicated by the fact that the study of representation was a rider midway on a four-year panel study of the electorate whose primary sampling units were not congressional districts (although there is no technical reason why they could not have been if the needs of the representation analysis had been foreseen when the design of the sample was fixed two years before). As a result, the districts in our sample had unequal probabilities of selection and unequal weights in the analysis, making the sample somewhat less efficient than an equal-probability sample of equivalent size.

It will be apparent in the discussion that follows that we have estimated characteristics of whole constituencies from our samples of constituents living in particular districts. In view of the fact that a sample of less than two thousand constituents has been divided among 116 districts, the reader may wonder about the reliability of these estimates. After considerable investigation we have concluded that their sampling error is not so severe a problem for the analysis as we had thought it would be. Several comments may indicate why it is not.

To begin with, the weighting of our sample of districts has increased the reliability of the constituency estimates. The correct theoretical weight to be assigned each district in the analysis is the inverse of the probability of the district's selection, and it can be shown that this weight is approximately proportional to the number of interviews taken in the district. The result of this is that the greatest weight is assigned the districts with the largest number of interviews and, hence, the most reliable constituency estimates. Indeed, these weights increase by half again the (weighted) mean number of interviews taken per district. To put the matter another way: the introduction of differential weights trades some of our sample of congressional districts for more reliable constituency estimates.

How much of a problem the unreliability of these estimates is depends very much on the analytic uses to which the estimates are put. If our goal were case analyses of particular districts, the constituency samples would have to be much larger. Indeed, for most case analyses we would want several hundred interviews per district (at a cost, over 116 districts, of several small nuclear reactors). However, most of the findings reported here are based not on single districts but on many or all of the districts in our sample. For analyses of this sort the number of interviews per district can be much smaller.

Our investigation of the effect of the sampling variance of the constituency estimates is quite reassuring. When statistics computed from our constituency samples are compared with corresponding parameter values for the constituencies, the agreement of the two sets of figures is quite close. For example, when the proportions voting Democratic in the 116 constituencies in 1958, as computed from our sample data, are compared with the actual proportions voting Democratic, as recorded in official election statistics, a product moment correlation of 0.93 is obtained, and this figure is the more impressive since this test throws away non-voters, almost one-half of our total sample. We interpret the Pearsonian correlation as an appropriate measure of agreement in this case, since the associated regression equations are almost exactly the identity function. The alternative intraclass correlation coefficient has almost as high a value.

Although we believe that this analysis provides a textbook illustration of how misleading intuitive ideas (including our own) about the effects of sampling error can be, these figures ought not to be too beguiling. It is clear that how close such a correlation is to 1.0 for any given variable will depend on the ratio. of the between-district variance to the total variance. When this ratio is as high as it is for Republican and Democratic voting, the effect of the unreliability of our constituency estimates is fairly trivial. Although the content of the study is quite different, this sampling problem has much in common with the problem of attenuation of correlation as it has been treated in psychological testing. See, for example, J. P. Guilford, *Fundamental Statistics in Psychology and Education* (New York, 1956), pp. 475–78.

4. See Angus Campbell, Philip E. Converse, Warren E. Miller, and Donald E. Stokes, *The American Voter* (New York, 1960), pp. 194–209.

5. This conclusion, fully supported by our own work for later Congresses, is one of the main findings to be drawn from the work of Duncan MacRae on roll call voting in the House of Representatives. See his *Dimensions of Congressional Voting: A Statistical Study of the House of Representatives in the Eighty-First Congress* (Berkeley and Los Angeles: University of California Press, 1958). For additional evidence of the existence of scale dimensions in legislative behavior, see N. L. Gage and Ben Shimberg, "Measuring Senatorial Progressivism," *Journal of Abnormal and Social Psychology,* Vol. 44 (January, 1949), pp.

112–117; George M. Belknap, "A Study of Senatorial Voting by Scale Analysis" (unpublished doctoral dissertation, University of Chicago, 1951), and "A Method for Analyzing Legislative Behavior," *Midwest Journal of Political Science,* Vol. 2 (1958), pp. 377–402; two other articles by MacRae, "The Role of the State Legislator in Massachusetts," *American Sociological Review,* Vol. 19 (April 1954), pp. 185–194, and "Roll Call Votes and Leadership," *Public Opinion Quarterly,* Vol. 20 (1956), pp. 543–558; Charles D. Farris, "A Method of Determining Ideological Groups in Congress," *Journal of Politics,* Vol. 20 (1958), pp. 308–338; and Leroy N. Rieselbach, "Quantitative Techniques for Studying Voting Behavior in the U. N. General Assembly," *International Organization,* Vol. 14 (1960), pp. 291–306.

6. The content of the three issue domains may be suggested by some of the roll call and interview items used. In the area of social welfare these included the issues of public housing, public power, aid to education, and government's role in maintaining full employment. In the area of foreign involvement the items included the issues of foreign economic aid, military aid, sending troops abroad, and aid to neutrals. In the area of civil rights the items included the issues of school desegregation, fair employment, and the protection of Negro voting rights.

7. Because this point has been so widely discussed it has inevitably attracted a variety of terms. Dahl denotes the acts of *a* whose performance *A* is able to influence as the *scope* of *A*'s power. See Robert A. Dahl, "The Concept of Power," *Behavioral Science,* Vol. 2 (July 1957), pp. 201–215. This usage is similar to that of Harold D. Lasswell and Abraham Kaplan, *Power and Society* (New Haven: Yale University Press, 1950), pp. 71–73. Dorwin Cartwright, however, denotes the behaviorial or psychological changes in *P* which *O* is able to induce as the *range* of *O*'s power: "A Field Theoretical Conception of Power," *Studies in Social Power* (Ann Arbor: Research Center for Group Dynamics, Institute for Social Research, The University of Michigan, 1959), pp. 183–220.

8. That the Representative's roll call votes can diverge from his true opinion is borne out by a number of findings of the study (some of which are reported here) as to the conditions under which agreement between the Congressman's roll call position and his private attitude will be high or low. However, a direct confirmation that these two sets of measurements are not simply getting at the same thing is given by differences in attitude-roll call agreement according to the Congressman's sense of how well his roll call votes have expressed his real views. In the domain of foreign involvement, for example, the correlation of our attitudinal and roll call measurements was .75 among Representatives who said that their roll call votes had expressed their real views fairly well. But this correlation was only .04 among those who said that their roll call votes had expressed their views poorly. In the other policy domains, too, attitude-roll call agreement is higher among Congressmen who are well satisfied with their roll call votes than it is among Congressmen who are not.

9. During the analysis we have formed constituency scores out of the scores of constituents living in the same district by several devices other than calculating average constituent scores. In particular, in view of the ordinal character of our scales we have frequently used the *median* constituent score as a central value for the constituency as a whole. However, the ordering of constituencies differs very little according to which of several reasonable alternatives for obtaining constituency scores is chosen. As a result, we have preferred mean scores for the greater number of ranks they give.

10. The meaning of this procedure can be suggested by two percentage tables standing for hypothetical extreme cases, the first that of full agreement, the second that of no agreement whatever. For convenience, these illustrative tables categorize both Congressmen and their districts in terms of only three degrees of favor and assume for both a nearly uniform distribution across the three categories. The

terms "pro," "neutral," and "con" indicate a relative rather than an absolute opinion. In Case I, full agreement, all districts relatively favorable to social welfare action have Congressmen who are so too, etc.; whereas in Case II, or that of no agreement, the ordering of constituencies is independent in a statistical sense of the ranking of Congressmen: knowing the policy orientation of a district gives no clue at all to the orientation of its Congressman. Of course, it is possible for the orders of legislators and districts to be *inversely* related, and this possibility is of some importance, as indicated below, when the policy position of non-incumbent candidates as well as incumbents is taken into account. To summarize the degree of congruence between legislators and voters, a measure of correlation is introduced. Although we have used a variety of measures of association in our analysis, the values reported in this article all refer to product moment correlation coefficients. For our hypothetical Case I a measure of correlation would have the value 1.0; for Case II, the value 0.0. When it is applied to actual data this convenient indicator is likely to have a value somewhere in between. The question is where.

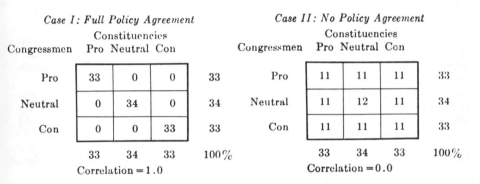

| *Case I: Full Policy Agreement* | | | | | *Case II: No Policy Agreement* | | | |
|---|---|---|---|---|---|---|---|---|
| | Constituencies | | | | | Constituencies | | |
| Congressmen | Pro | Neutral | Con | | Congressmen | Pro | Neutral | Con |
| Pro | 33 | 0 | 0 | 33 | Pro | 11 | 11 | 11 | 33 |
| Neutral | 0 | 34 | 0 | 34 | Neutral | 11 | 12 | 11 | 34 |
| Con | 0 | 0 | 33 | 33 | Con | 11 | 11 | 11 | 33 |
| | 33 | 34 | 33 | 100% | | 33 | 34 | 33 | 100% |
| | Correlation = 1.0 | | | | | Correlation = 0.0 | | | |

11. A word of caution is in order, lest we compare things that are not strictly comparable. For obvious reasons, most non-incumbent candidates have no roll call record, and we have had to measure their policy agreement with the district entirely in terms of the attitudes they have revealed in interviews. However, the difference of coefficients given here is almost as great when the policy agreement between the incumbent Congressman and his district is also measured in terms of the attitudes conveyed in confidential interviews.

12. A third type of connection, excluded here, might obtain between district and Congressman if the Representative accedes to what he thinks the district wants because he believes that to be what a representative *ought* to do, whether or not it is necessary for re-election. We leave this type of connection out of our account here because we conceive an influence relation as one in which control is not voluntarily accepted or rejected by someone subject to it. Of course, this possible connection between district and Representative is not any the less interesting because it falls outside our definition of influence or control, and we have given a good deal of attention to it in the broader study of which this analysis is part.

13. It scarcely needs to be said that demonstrating *some* constituency influence would not imply that the Representative's behavior is *wholly* determined by constituency pressures. The legislator acts in a complex institutional setting in which he is subject to a wide variety of influences. The constituency can exercise a genuine measure of control without driving all other influences from the Representative's life space.

14. We have done this by a variance-component technique similar to several others proposed for dealing with problems of this type. See especially Herbert A.

Simon, "Spurious Correlation: A Causal Interpretation," *Journal of the American Statistical Association,* Vol. 49 (1954), pp. 467–479; Hubert M. Blalock, Jr., "The Relative Importance of Variables," *American Sociological Review,* Vol. 26 (1961), pp. 866–874; and the almost forgotten work of Sewall Wright, "Correlation and Causation," *Journal of Agricultural Research,* Vol. 20 (1920), pp. 557–585. Under this technique a "path coefficient" (to use Wright's terminology, although not his theory) is assigned to each of the causal arrows by solving a set of equations involving the correlations of the variables of the model. The weight assigned to a full path is then the product of its several path coefficients, and this product may be interpreted as the proportion of the variance of the dependent variable (roll call behavior, here) that is explained by a given path.

A special problem arises because influence may flow in either direction between the Congressman's attitude and his perception of district attitude (as noted above, the Representative may tend both to perceive his constituency's view selectively, as consistent with his own, and to change his own view to be consistent with the perceived constituency view). Hence, we have not a single causal model but a whole family of models, varying according to the relative importance of influence from attitude to perception and from perception to attitude. Our solution to this problem has been to calculate influence coefficients for the two extreme models in order to see how much our results could vary according to which model is chosen from our family of models. Since the systems of equations in this analysis are linear it can be shown that the coefficients we seek have their maximum and minimum values under one or the other of the limiting models. Therefore, computing any given coefficient for each of these limiting cases defines an interval in which the true value of the coefficient must lie. In fact these intervals turn out to be fairly small; our findings as to the relative importance of alternative influence paths would change little according to which model is selected.

The two limiting models with their associated systems of equations and the formulas for computing the relative importance of the three possible influence paths under each model are given below.

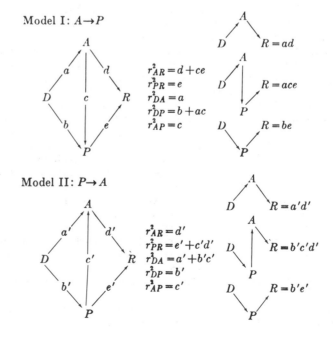

Model I: $A \rightarrow P$

$$r_{AR}^2 = d + ce$$
$$r_{PR}^2 = e$$
$$r_{DA}^2 = a$$
$$r_{DP}^2 = b + ac$$
$$r_{AP}^2 = c$$

$R = ad$

$R = ace$

$R = be$

Model II: $P \rightarrow A$

$$r_{AR}^2 = d'$$
$$r_{PR}^2 = e' + c'd'$$
$$r_{DA}^2 = a' + b'c'$$
$$r_{DP}^2 = b'$$
$$r_{AP}^2 = c'$$

$R = a'd'$

$R = b'c'd'$

$R = b'e'$

15. By "least favorable" we mean the assumption that influence goes only from the Congressman's attitude to his perception of district attitude (Model I) and not the other way round. Under this assumption, the proportions of the variance of roll call behavior accounted for by the three alternative paths, expressed as proportions of the part of the variance of roll call votes that is explained by district attitude, are these:

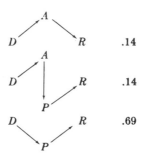

Inverting the assumed direction of influence between the Congressman's own attitude and district attitude (Model II) eliminates altogether the effect that the Representative's attitude can have had on his votes, independently of his perception of district attitude.

16. Under both Models I and II the proportion of the variance of roll call voting explained by the influence path involving the Representative's own attitude is twice as great as the proportion explained by influence passing through his perception of district attitude.

17. What is more, the electorate's awareness of Congress as a whole appears quite limited. A majority of the public was unable to say in 1958 which of the two parties had controlled the Congress during the preceding two years. Some people were confused by the coexistence of a Republican President and a Democratic Congress. But for most people this was simply an elementary fact about congressional affairs to which they were not privy.

18. For a more extended analysis of forces on the congressional vote, see Donald E. Stokes and Warren E. Miller, "Party Government and the Saliency of Congress," *Public Opinion Quarterly,* Vol. 26 (Winter 1962), pp. 531–546.

19. For an account of this episode see Corinne Silverman, "The Little Rock Story," Inter-University Case Program series, reprinted in Edwin A. Bock and Alan K. Campbell, eds., *Case Studies in American Government* (Englewood Cliffs, 1962), pp. 1–46.

20. The sample of this constituency was limited to twenty-three persons of whom thirteen voted. However, despite the small number of cases the probability that the difference in awareness between this constituency and the country generally as the result only of sampling variations is much less than one in a thousand.

21. In view of the potential nature of the constituency's sanctions, it is relevant to characterize its influence over the Representative in terms of several distinctions drawn by recent theorists of power, especially the difference between actual and potential power, between influence and coercive power, and between influence and purposive control. Observing these distinctions, we might say that the constituency's influence is *actual* and not merely *potential* since it is the sanction behavior rather than the conforming behavior that is infrequent (Dahl). That is, the Congressman is influenced by his calculus of potential sanctions, following the "rule of anticipated reactions" (Friedrich), however oblivious of his behavior the constituency ordinarily may be. We might also say that the constituency has *power*

since its influence depends partly on sanctions (Lasswell and Kaplan), although it rarely exercises *control* since its influence is rarely conscious or intended (Cartwright). In the discussion above we have of course used the terms "influence" and "control" interchangeably.

22. The factors in American electoral behavior that encourage such a departure are discussed in Stokes and Miller, *loc cit*.

# 14. The Role of the Representative*

HEINZ EULAU, JOHN C. WAHLKE, WILLIAM BUCHANAN,
and LEROY C. FERGUSON

The problem of representation is central to all discussions of the functions of legislatures or the behavior of legislators. For it is commonly taken for granted that, in democratic political systems, legislatures are both legitimate and authoritative decision-making institutions, and that it is their representative character which makes them authoritative and legitimate. Through the process of representation, presumably, legislatures are empowered to act for the whole body politic and are legitimized. And because, by virtue of representation, they participate in legislation, the represented accept legislative decisions as authoritative. But agreement about the meaning of the term "representation" hardly goes beyond a general consensus regarding the context within which it is appropriately used. The history of political theory is studded with definitions of representation,[1] usually embedded in ideological assumptions and postulates which cannot serve the uses of empirical research without conceptual clarification.[2]

*I*

Many familiar formulations treat representation in a non-functional fashion, viewing it as something valuable in itself, as an ultimate end, and seek to discover or specify its "nature" or "essence." Functional theory, on the other hand, deals with representation from the point of view of the political system as a whole or its component units. Herman Finer, for instance, has suggested that "responsibility is the chief and wider aim, and representativeness merely a convenient means to attain this. . . . The desire for responsible government is paramount; people not merely wish to represent their views, but actually to make and unmake governments."[3] But while functional formulations treat representation as a means for the attainment of some other political objective, failure to test functional propositions by way of empirical research leaves the problems raised by theory in the realm of hypothesis rather than reliable knowledge. In connection with Finer's proposition, for example, there has been little, if any, empirical analysis of the extent to which the represented do, in fact, want to enforce political responsibility, and how capable they are, under modern conditions, of exercising the necessary control. Nevertheless, once relevant concepts are clarified, a functional formulation of representation can open up areas of research which, in turn, may contribute to theoretical cumulation.

The relationship between the representative and the represented is at the core

* From *The American Political Science Review*, Vol. 53 (1959), pp. 742–756. Reprinted by permission.

of representational thory. The term "representational" directs attention, first of all, to the attitudes, expectations and behaviors of the represented—to their acceptance of representatives' decisions as legitimate and authoritative for themselves. More particularly, representation concerns not the mere fact that they do accept such decisions, but rather the reasons they have for doing so, their rationalization of the legitimacy and authority of the decisions made by their representatives.

Sometimes the adjective "representative" denotes nothing more than the publicly approved process by which representatives are to be chosen—as when a distinction is made between a "representative body" (meaning a group of men elected by specific modes of popular election) and a "non-representative body" (meaning a group of men selected by royal or executive appointment, entailed inheritance, or some other non-electoral process). Such usage implies that citizens' attitudes and expectations include, and may extend no farther than, the belief that representatives' decisions must be accepted as legitimate and authoritative *if* the representatives have been selected in the approved manner. In other words, elected officials are called "representatives" primarily because of the way they have been chosen. Even in a looser usage an appointed commission may be approvingly called a body of "representative" citizens, or may be attacked as "unrepresentative," depending on whether its members might conceivably have been chosen had they been subject to election rather than appointment; and their views will correspondingly be accorded or denied a measure of authority and legitimacy.

But the appropriate process of selecting public decision-makers has never been the really fundamental question for theories of representation. Behind every proposal for altering the method of selecting officials is some assumption, at least, about the effect of such changes on what decision-makers or decision-making institutions do, and how they do it. Proposals for reform must assume or show that the proposed change will bring it about that *what* representatives decide and *the way* they reach decisions is more nearly in accord with expectations and demands of the represented than has been in the case under the system to be reformed. The various defenses of existing systems of selection which postulate "virtual representation" have in common some shading of the belief that the process of selection is not of major significance in determining what representatives do or how they do it, or that decisions made by representatives can be brought in harmony with public expectations, without altering whatever process of selection is being defended by the advocacy of virtual representation.

The relationship between the process of selection of legislators and the modes and consequences of legislative behavior, or the relationship between public expectations and legislative decisions, offer wide and fertile fields for empirical research. Our purpose here, however, is less ambitious than a full-scale investigation of such relationships. It is to eliminate those particular ambiguities in the concept of representation which concern the actions or behavior of representatives, by use of the concept of "role," and to demonstrate the utility of this approach for further research relevant to the theory of representation.

*II*

A convenient and useful starting point in theoretical clarification is Edmund Burke's theory of representation. For, in following his classic argument, later theorists have literally accepted Burke's formulation and ignored its contextual basis and polemical bias. Burke ingeniously combined two notions which, for analytical purposes, should be kept distinct. In effect, he combined a conception of the *focus* of representation with a conception of the *style* of representation. Parliament, Burke said in a famous passage,

> is not a *congress* of ambassadors from different and hostile interests; which interests each must maintain, as an agent and advocate, against other agents and advocates; but parliament is a *deliberative* assembly of *one* nation, with *one* interest, that of the whole; where, not local purposes, not local prejudices ought to guide but the general good, resulting from the general reason of the whole.

The sentence indicates that Burke postulated two possible foci of representation: local, necessarily hostile interests, on the one hand; and a national interest, on the other hand. He rejected the former as an improper and advocated the latter as the proper focus of the representative's role. But in doing so, he also linked these foci of representation with particular representational styles. If the legislature is concerned with only one interest, that of the whole, and not with compromise among diverse interests, it follows that the representative cannot and must not be bound by instructions, from whatever source, but must be guided by what Burke called "his unbiased opinion, his mature judgment, his enlightened conscience." Moreover, Burke buttressed his argument by emphasizing the deliberative function of the legislature—presumably in contrast to its representational function. Yet if one rejects his notion of the legislature as only a deliberative body whose representational focus is the whole rather than its constituent parts, the logic of Burke's formulation is no longer necessary or relevant.

Today, many "publics" constitute significant foci of orientation for the representative as he approaches his legislative task. Under the conditions of a plural political and social order, these foci of representation may be other than geographical interests, be they electoral districts or the larger commonwealth. The modern representative faces similar choices concerning the style of his representational role not only *vis-à-vis* his constituency or state. and nation, but *vis-à-vis* other clienteles, notably political parties, pressure groups and administrative agencies. From an analytical point of view—though not, of course, from an empirical standpoint—the style of the representative's role is neutral as far as these different foci of representation are concerned. Regardless of his focus of representation—a geographical unit, a party, a pressure group, or an administrative organization—he is not committed to take either the role of free agent, following his own convictions, or the role of delegate, bound by instructions. In other words, Burke's linkage of a particular areal focus of representation with a particular representational style constitutes only a special case in a generic series of empirically viable relationships between possible and different foci of representation and appropriate styles of representation.

Of course, different foci of representation need not be mutually exclusive. They may occur simultaneously, and appropriate role orientations may be held simultaneously. For instance, a party may be so strong in a district that, in the representative's mind, the interests of district and party are identical. Or a pressure group may have such pervasive influence—as, for example, the Farm Bureau in a predominantly agricultural constituency, or the AFL-CIO in a predominantly working class district—that, again, the interests of district and pressure group become identified. Moreover, it is possible that different focal role orientations are activated *seriatim* as circumstances require. In particular, one may assume that on matters of no relevance to the representative's district, roles oriented towards party or lobby as foci of representation may serve as major premises of choice.

The generic extension of Burke's special case, broken down into analytic components, suggests that the focal and stylistic dimensions of representation must be kept separate in empirical research. Burke combined them for polemical reasons: he was writing in opposition to the idea of mandatory representation which had much popular support in the middle of the eighteenth century.[5] The result of this polemical commitment was that the problem of *how* the representative should behave *vis-à-vis* his clienteles became a substantive problem—*what* he should do for the clienteles. But the fact that a representative sees himself as reaching a decision by following his own convictions or judgment does not mean that the content of his decisions is necessarily oriented towards a general rather than a particular interest, just as his acceptance of instructions from a clientele group does not necessarily mean that he is oriented towards a special rather than the public interest. A representative may base his decisions on his own conscience or judgment, but the cause he promotes may be parochial. Or he may follow instructions, but the mandate may be directed towards the realization of the general welfare.

The distinction between the focal and stylistic dimensions of the representative's role allows us to suggest that representation is not concerned with what decisions should be made, but with how decisions are to be made. Now, it is axiomatic that decisions made in institutional contexts, such as legislatures provide, are made in terms of a set of premises which guide the behavior of decision-makers. The notion —explicit in Burke and other traditional formulations—that legislative decisions can be purely rational is not tenable in view of the fact that rationality, while not altogether absent, is invariably bounded by the legislature's institutional environment.[6] One of these boundaries is the representational fabric of the legislature. The representative system provides the representative with some of the assumptions in terms of which he defines his role. The roles he takes, in turn, whether in the focal or stylistic dimensions of representation, provide the premises for decision.

Premises underlying decisions made by legislatures, then, may be of two kinds: (1) they may be premises relevant to the focus of representation; and (2) they may be relevant to the style of representation. With regard to the first kind, for instance, a representative may be guided by premises such as that legislation should benefit either his district or the state, that it should be "liberal" or "conservative," that it should or should not favor special interests, that it should or should not be in performance of his party's campaign pledges, and so on. With regard to the second kind of premises, the representative's choices may be circumscribed by his stylistic role orientation, whether he sees himself following his own conscience or instructions. In this dimension the premises involved in his decisional behavior refer not to the focus but to the style of his role as representative.

*III*

The issue of styles of representation—free agency versus mandate—has been confounded by the fact that the enabling source of a representative's power is the electorate of a geographical district. Representation of geographical areas introduces a certain amount of ambiguity into the relationship between representative and represented which is likely to be absent under schemes of proportional or vocational representation.[7] Part of this ambiguity is the widely held expectation, contested by Burke but shared by many citizens and politicians alike, that the representative is a spokesman of the presumed "interests" of the area from which he has been elected. Of course, implicit in this expectation is the assumption that a geographical unit has interests which are distinct and different from those of other units, and which should be represented in public decision-making. This assumption has been challenged on a variety of grounds: that the geographical area as such, as an electoral unit, is artificial; that it cannot and does not generate interests shared by its residents; that it has no unique interests; and so on. Schemes of proportional or vocational representation have been advanced to make possible the representation of allegedly more "natural" interest groupings, such as minority groups, skill groups or economic groups.[8]

The assumption that geographical districts have particular characteristics—such as population attributes and industrial, agricultural or commercial properties—and, hence, unique interests which are, or ought to be, factors influencing the direction of public decisions continues to be shared not only by voters, politicians and others involved in policy-making, but also by scientific students of the political process. It underlies many studies which seek to relate legislative roll-call votes to the socio-economic characteristics of electoral districts,[9] as well as those studies which analyze the socio-economic composition of legislatures.[10]

It is a further assumption of these studies that legislators, having lived in their districts for all or substantial parts of their lives, share the values, beliefs, habits and concerns of the people who elected them and whom they presumably represent. Indeed, a literal interpretation of "represent" is to make something present that is not actually present. But this interpretation is most tenuous under modern conditions. Electoral districts tend to be so heterogeneous in population attributes, so pluralistic in the character of their group life, so diverse in the kinds of values and beliefs held, that whatever measures of central tendency are used to classify a district are more likely to conceal than to reveal its real character. The notion that elections are held as a method to discover persons whose attributes and attitudes mirror these most widely shared by people in their district appears to be of dubious validity.

This does not mean, of course, that the geographical district is dysfunctional from the point of view of maintaining the political system. The very circumstance of heterogeneity in the district tends to free the representative from being readily bound by a mandate, to make for discretion and political responsibility, and to enable him to integrate conflicting demands. The function of representation in modern political systems is not to make the legislature a mathematically exact copy of the electorate.

But the difficulty of finding an identity between representative and represented does not also mean that a representative's point of reference in making decisions cannot be his district. It may or may not be, and whether it is or not is a matter of empirical inquiry. We merely doubt that what orients a representative towards his district rather than some other focus of attention is the similarity between his district's characteristics and his own. We cannot assume, therefore, that even if a representative incorporates in himself the characteristics of his district—which, for argument's sake, may be admitted when he comes from a relatively homogeneous area—he will be more oriented towards the district than a representative who, from the point of view of district characteristics, is a deviant. In fact, the latter may be more concerned with his district and seek to discover its "interests," if they are discoverable, than the former. And if a district interest, so-called, can be specifically singled out, it is more likely to be the interest of a politically salient group in the district than of the district as an undifferentiated entity.

In so far as the district rather than some other unit, such as the entire commonwealth, is at the representative's focus of attention, it is more likely to be a function of political than of demographic or socio-economic variables. The problem is one of discovering under what conditions the representative can afford to disregard the district and still hope to maintain the confidence of his constituents. We might speculate, for instance, that in so far as he cherishes the position of power he holds, he is unlikely to ignore his district. We should expect, therefore, that representatives from districts where competition between the parties is keen are more district-oriented than representatives from one-party districts. Yet, we also know that competitive districts are more likely to be found in the heterogeneous metropolitan areas where district "interests" are difficult to ascertain.[11] In other words, what tends to orient the representative towards his district is likely to be the mechanism of political responsibility effectuated by political competition. District-oriented representatives from metropolitan areas where party competition is strong are, therefore, likely to rely on their own judgment, for a mandate must yield here to discretion to satisfy the demands of political responsibility. Discretion, of course, does not mean that the representative is wholly free to act as he pleases. On the contrary, it means that he will have due regard for all the considerations relevant in the making of legislative decisions. And among these considerations, certainly, the "interests" of his electorate or segments of the electorate, as well as his own estimate of the limits which these interests set to his actions, are important. As Burke admitted,

> it ought to be the happiness and glory of a representative to live in the strictest union, the closest correspondence, and the most unreserved communication with his constituents. Their wishes ought to have great weight with him; their opinion high respect, their business unremitted attention. . . .

Though analytically the foci and the style of the representative's role are distinct, they can be expected to be related empirically in a system of mutually interpenetrating orientations. In other words, just as we need not assume that a commitment to district invariably involves the representative's following instructions from his district (the role orientation of Delegate), or that a commonweal-oriented representative is invariably a free agent (the role orientation of Trustee), so also we need not assume that the foci of a representative's role are invariably unrelated to his representational style. In fact, it is the functionally related network of roles which makes for a representational *system*. We can assume, for instance, that a representative who is highly sensitive to the conflict of pressure groups, but not committed to any one, is more likely to be a Trustee in his representational role than the representative who feels close to a particular group and, consequently, is more likely to be a Delegate. Similarly, we might expect that a representative not strongly attached to a party, but not independent of it, is likely to shift between his own judgment and instructions (the role orientation of Politico).

## IV

An opportunity to test the validity of the theoretical distinction here made, between the focus and style of representation, as well as of the representative's role, was afforded in connection with a comparative research project undertaken by the authors during the 1957 sessions of the state legislatures in California, New Jersey, Ohio and Tennessee.[12] State legislators in these four states were asked the following question, among others: "How would you describe the job of being a legislator —what are the most important things you should do here?" Of the 474 respondents, 295 gave answers relevant to the stylistic dimension of the representative's role, and 197 of these gave additional answers referring to the areal focus of their role.[13]

Responses concerning the stylistic dimension yielded three major representational role types: Trustee, Delegate, and Politico.[14] These types may be described as follows:

1. *Trustee:* This role finds expression in two major conceptions which may occur separately or jointly. First, a moralistic interpretation: the representative is a free agent, he follows what he considers right or just—his convictions or principles, the dictates of his conscience. Second, a rational conception: he follows his own judgments based on an assessment of the facts in each case, his understanding of the problems involved, his thoughtful appraisal of the sides at issue.

The orientation of Trustee derives not only from a purely normative definition, but is often grounded in conditions which make it functionally necessary. The represented may not have the information to give intelligent instructions; the representative is unable to discover what his clienteles want; preferences remain unexpressed; there is no need for instructions because of a presumed harmony of interests between representative and represented—all of these circumstances may be cited as sources of the role orientation of Trustee.

2. *Delegate:* Just as the Trustee is by no means an empirically pure type, the orientation of Delegate allows for a number of conceptions. All Delegates are, of course, agreed that they should *not* use their independent judgment or convictions as criteria of decision-making. But this does not mean that they feel equally committed to follow instructions, from whatever clientele. Some merely speak of consulting their constituents, though implying that such consultation will have a mandatory effect on their behavior. Others frankly acknowledge their direct dependence on instructions and accept them as a necessary or desirable premise for their decisions. Some may even follow instructions counter to their own judgment or principles. In other words, the possibility of conflict in role orientations is clearly envisaged and resolved in favor of subordinating one's independence to what is considered a superior authority.

3. *Politico:* The classical dichotomization of the concept of representation in terms of free agency and mandate was unlikely to exhaust the possibilities of representational styles. Depending on circumstances, a representative may hold the Trustee orientation at one time, and the Delegate orientation at

another time. Or he might seek to reconcile both in terms of a third. One can think of representation as a continuum, with the Trustee and Delegate orientations as poles, and a midpoint where the orientations tend to overlap and, within a range, give rise to a third role. Within this middle range the roles may be taken simultaneously, possibly making for conflict, or they may be taken serially, one after another as conditions call for.

Because the data do not permit sharp discrimination between the two possibilities, we shall speak of representatives who express both orientations, either simultaneously or serially, as Politicos. In general, then, the Politico as a representational role type differs from both the Trustee and the Delegate in that he is more sensitive to conflicting alternatives in role assumption, more flexible in the way he resolves the conflict of alternatives, and less dogmatic in his representational style as it is relevant to his decision-making behavior.

The spell of the Burkean formulation on the interpretation of representation tended to create reactions which, it seems, are almost as arbitrary as Burke's formula itself. In particular, the functional notion, itself quite realistic under modern conditions, that the legislature is an agency for the coordination and integration of diverse social, economic and political interests makes apparent the simple-mindedness of Burke's theory, now as then. Carl J. Friedrich, for instance, has pointed out that "the pious formula that representatives are not bound by mandate, that they are subject only to their conscience and are supposed to serve the common weal, which is repeated in so many European constitutions, while significant as a norm, may lead to differentiating as well as to integrating results." [15] Yet, in concentrating on the multiplicity of potential representational foci, Friedrich went too far in his rejection of Burke. For, once the distinction is made between the style of the representative's role and its focus, Burke's "pious formula" is still relevant. Both the focus and the style are likely to be influencd by the character of politics at a given time and by the demands of contemporary political circumstances on the representative as a decision-maker. Functional analysis cannot limit itself to the foci of representation alone, but must also pay attention to those political requirements which may be relevant to the representative's style.

Our hypothesis may be stated as follows: the exigencies of modern government, even on the relatively low level of state government, are exceedingly complex. Taxation and finance, education and public welfare, legal reform, licensing and regulatory problems, transportation, and so on, are topics more often than not, beyond the comprehension of the average citizen. Unable to understand their problems and helpless to cope with them, people are likely to entrust the affairs of government to the elected representatives who, presumably, are better informed than their constituents. People may pay lip service to the notion that a representative should *not* use his independent judgment,[16] but in fact they are unable, or do not care, to give him instructions as may once have been possible when the tasks of government were comparatively simpler. It is likely, therefore, that the representative has become less and less a Delegate and more and more a Trustee as the business of government has become more and more intricate and technical. Rather than being a "pious formula," the role orientation of Trustee may be a functional necessity, and one should expect it to be held by state legislators more frequently than that of Politico, and the latter more frequently than that of Delegate.

TABLE I. DISTRIBUTION OF REPRESENTATIONAL ROLE ORIENTATIONS IN FOUR STATES

| Representational Role Orientation | Calif. (N = 49) | N.J. (N = 54) | Ohio (N = 114) | Tenn. (N = 78) | Total (N = 295) |
|---|---|---|---|---|---|
| Trustee | 55% | 61% | 56% | 81% | 63% |
| Politico | 25 | 22 | 29 | 13 | 23 |
| Delegate | 20 | 17 | 15 | 6 | 14 |
| Total | 100% | 100% | 100% | 100% | 100% |

A test of this general proposition is possible by way of comparative analysis of the distribution of representational role styles in the four states. As Table I indicates, the role orientation of Trustee is held by a greater number of legislators than that of either Politico or Delegate. In all four states it appears more frequently, and significantly more frequently, than the other two. Moreover, the Politico appears somewhat more frequently in all states than the Delegate.

The Trustee orientation appears significantly more frequently in Tennessee than in the other three states, a fact that seems to contradict the proposition that the orientation of Trustee varies with the complexity of governmental affairs. As Tennessee is less urbanized and industrialized than the other states, one should expect Tennessee legislators to be less often Trustees and more often Delegates than legislators in California, New Jersey or Ohio. But it may also be that "complexity" is a function of perceptions, regardless of the real situation. If so, then to Tennesseans the relatively less complex character of socio-economic life may appear more complex than it actually is, compared with the other states. The more frequent appearance of the Trustee orientation there may only be symptomatic of an even greater feeling of helplessness and inefficacy on the part of people *vis-à-vis* governmental problems, as it is perceived by state representatives. Such perceptions may be a reflection of the lower educational level in Tennesse; but to demonstrate this is beyond the limits of this analysis.[17]

## V

If, as suggested earlier, a representative's areal-focal orientation does not automatically derive from ascertainable district interests or from personal characteristics he may share with his constituents, the question arises where such orientations do come from, and how they intrude on the representative's conception of his role. For the purposes of this study, it was possible to delineate three areal-focal orientations which may be described as follows:

1. *District-orientation:* District-oriented representatives had essentially two alternatives: either they could simply mention their districts or counties as being relevant in their conception of their jobs, or they could explicitly place their districts as being above .the state as an important factor in their legislative behavior. Among the former, the most frequent responses suggested that it is the representative's job to take care of his district's needs and pass legislation

which will benefit his district or county. Others emphasized the policy problems involved in legislation and the necessity to protect what they considered district interests from the policy point of view. Or the emphasis was on the services which these representatives think they are expected to render for their district. Another group of district-oriented representatives specifically pointed to the importance of placing the interests of their district above those of the state, though they usually admitted that state concerns should also be given consideration.

2. *State-orientation:* As in the case of the district-oriented respondents, state-oriented representatives may either mention the state alone as the salient focus, or they may also mention the district, but clearly tend to place state above district. Some emphasized the need of state policy or state programs as an overriding consideration. A second group pointed to both state and district as relevant foci, but tended to give the benefit of doubt to the state. Finally, some state-oriented representatives explicitly emphasized the desirability of overcoming parochial considerations in favor of the state.

3. *District-and-state-orientation:* A third major group of respondents who spontaneously concerned themselves with the areal focus of their role mentioned both district and state, but, apparently, did not envisage a possibility of conflict and thought that they could attend to both foci without undue difficulty. Yet, the generality of the responses given in this connection may be deceptive, and coding them under this rubric may have been somewhat arbitrary in a number of cases. Though the actual language used tended in the direction of the state as the focus of role orientation, the tone often appeared to be more indicative of a latent district orientation. One should expect these hyphenated representatives to resemble district- more than state-oriented representatives.

Areal role orientations may be assumed to be a function of the dynamics of the democratic political system with its emphasis on the responsibility of the representatives to the represented. Political responsibility—a set of relationships in which the elected are sensitive to the power of the electors over them, and in which the elected are aware of the sanctions which make responsibility a reality—is predicated on the existence of a competitive political system where constituents have a genuine choice, *i.e.,* where the representatives are periodically confronted with the real possibility of removal from office. The sanction of removal inherent in a competitive party system serves to focus representatives' attention on their district rather than the state as the crucial point of reference. Represenatives from competitive areas are more likely to be district-oriented than representatives from one-party areas, while representatives from one-party areas are more likely to be state-oriented than those from competitive areas.

An initial, though crude, test of this hypothesis is possible by examining the distribution of areal role orientations in the four states. Tennessee representatives might be expected to be less district-oriented than representatives in the other states, in view of the predominant one-party character of Tennessee politics. As Table II indicates, the data support this hypothesis. Though the percentage differences are small and statistically not significant, except in the California-Tennessee contrast, only 21 per cent of the Tennessee representatives are district-oriented as against 35 per cent in California, 27 per cent in New Jersey, and 28 per cent in

TABLE II. DISTRIBUTION OF AREAL ROLE ORIENTATIONS IN FOUR STATES

| Areal Role Orientation | Calif. (N = 113) | N.J. (N = 79) | Ohio (N = 162) | Tenn. (N = 120) | Total (N = 474) |
|---|---|---|---|---|---|
| District | 35% | 27% | 28% | 21% | 27% |
| District-and-State | 14 | 28 | 25 | 8 | 19 |
| State | 20 | 14 | 16 | 9 | 15 |
| No mention | 31 | 31 | 31 | 62 | 39 |
| Total | 100% | 100% | 100% | 100% | 100% |

Ohio. But the most noticeable aspect of Table II is the fact that Tennessee representatives in significantly greater proportion failed to express themselves spontaneously in this connection. Why this is so can, at this point, be only a matter of speculation. Tennessee representatives may take whatever areal foci they have so much for granted that they feel no need to mention them, or they may simply be less articulate than representatives elsewhere. Finally, while there is a somewhat sharper differentiation between district and state role orientations in California than in New Jersey and Ohio (where the combined category figures more prominently), relatively few representatives in all states mentioned the state alone as the focus of their areal orientation.

A more severe test of the hypothesis is possible by relating areal role orientations to the political character of representatives' home districts. Because party competition as an independent variable has no room for operation in predominantly one-party Tennessee,[18] Table III presents the combined data for California, New

TABLE III. POLITICAL CHARACTER OF ELECTORAL DISTRICTS AND AREAL ROLE ORIENTATIONS IN THREE STATES *

| Areal Role Orientation | POLITICAL CHARACTER OF DISTRICT | | |
|---|---|---|---|
| | Competitive (N = 72) | Semi-competitive (N = 77) | One-party (N = 96) |
| District | 53% | 48% | 33% |
| District-and-State | 28 | 34 | 33 |
| State | 19 | 18 | 34 |
| Total | 100% | 100% | 100% |

* California, New Jersey and Ohio. "Non-respondents" on the areal dimension have been ommitted.

Jersey and Ohio alone.[19] As Table III shows, 53 per cent of the representatives from competitive districts were district-oriented, while only 33 per cent of those from one-party districts were so classified. On the other hand, one-party district representatives held in significantly greater proportion a state orientation than those from competitive districts.[20] The data support the hypothesis that areal orientation varies with the political character of the district in which representatives are elected.[21]

*VI*

The analytical distinction between the foci and the style of representation is helpful in dissecting the representative's role. Actual behavior is not a function of discrete role orientations, however, but of a system of such orientations. It is the network of interpenetrating roles which gives pattern and coherence to the representational process. It is essential, therefore, to relate areal and stylistic role orientations to each other in terms of significant hypotheses about conditions of their co-variation in the representational system.

It has been suggested earlier that, analytically, stylistic role orientations are neutral. What correlation may be found empirically, therefore, should depend on some crucial attribute in the independent variable—in this connection the areal role orientation. It may be suggested that this crucial attribute is the condition of effective political responsibility. In so far as they differ, district-oriented representatives are ultimately responsible to their constituents, while state-oriented representatives are not responsible to an equivalent state-wide constituency. The state-oriented representative cannot point to a state-wide clientele from which he could possibly receive a mandate.[22] Hence the hypothesis may be advanced that state-oriented representatives are more likely to be Trustees than district-oriented representatives, whereas the latter are more likely to be Delegates than the former. As Table IV demonstrates, this is in fact the case. While 84 per cent of the state-oriented representatives are Trustees, only 37 per cent of the district-oriented and 55 per cent of the district-and-state-oriented representatives are so. And while 36 per cent of the district-oriented representatives are Delegates, only 8 per cent of the district-and-state-oriented and none of the state-oriented hold a mandatory view of their representational role.

Moreover, Table IV supports some corollary hypotheses. In the first place, because a representative is district-oriented, he need not be a Delegate any more frequently than a Trustee. This simply means that though a representative may clearly have his district at his focus of attention, he may nevertheless act on behalf of the district, in his own conception, as a free agent. Such a representative will say that he knows and understands what the district needs and wants, and he rejects the notion that anybody in the district can tell him what to do. As Table IV shows, among the district-oriented representatives, almost equal proportions, 37

TABLE IV. AREAL-FOCAL AND REPRESENTATIONAL ROLE ORIENTATIONS IN FOUR STATES *

| Representational Role Orientation | District-oriented (N = 89) | State-District-oriented (N = 64) | State-oriented (N = 44) |
|---|---|---|---|
| Trustee | 37% | 55% | 84% |
| Delegate | 36 | 8 | — |
| Politico | 27 | 37 | 16 |
| Total | 100% | 100% | 100% |

* $x^2$ for the entire array = 37.759; d.f. = 4; $p < .001$.

per cent and 36 per cent respectively, are Trustees and Delegates. On the other hand, state-oriented representatives are more likely to be Trustees than anything else. This hypothesis is based on the assumption that the state-oriented representatives do not and cannot recognize a state-wide areal clientele which could give them instructions. As Table IV indicates, none of the state-oriented representatives is a Delegate, and only 16 per cent are Politicos.

Finally, if the representative's areal focus is both his district and the state, one should expect that he will take the role of Politico more frequently than either the district- or the state-oriented representative. For, because he stresses both foci, he is likely to be subject to cross-pressures: as a district-oriented representative he will take the role of Delegate at least as frequently as that of Trustee; as a state-oriented representative he will take the role of Trustee more frequently than any other. We should expect, therefore, that this representative will not only be a Politico more frequently than the other two areal-orientational types, but also that he will take the Trustee role more frequently than the Delegate role. Both hypotheses find support in the data reported in Table IV. While the differences are small, 37 per cent of the district-and-state-oriented representatives are Politicos, while only 16 per cent and 27 per cent of the other two groups admit to this representational style. Moreover, a majority are also Trustees, while only 8 per cent are Delegates—evidence of the differential effect of areal role orientations on the particular stylistic roles which seem most appropriate.

This analysis supports the notion that the areal-focal and stylistic dimensions of representation give rise to role orientations which, though analytically distinct, constitute a role system, and that this system gives the process of representation both its structure and its function.

## NOTES

1. For a convenient and comprehensive summary of definitions, see John A. Fairlie, "The Nature of Political Representation," *American Political Science Review,* Vol. 34 (April–June, 1940), pp. 236–48; 456–66.

2. An effort at conceptual clarification is made by Alfred De Grazia, *Public and Republic—Political Representation in America* (New York, 1951).

3. Herman Finer, *The Theory and Practice of Modern Government* (New York, rev. ed., 1949), p. 219.

4. In his "Speech to the Electors of Bristol" (1774), *Works,* Vol. II, p. 12.

5. *Cf.* Samuel H. Beer, "The Representation of Interests in British Government," *American Political Science Review,* Vol. 51 (Sept. 1957), p. 613, who points out how little general legislation was proposed or enacted in those days.

6. For the conception of "bounded rationality" as well as the notion that roles constitute some of the premises of decision-making behavior, we are indebted to Herbert A. Simon's writings, notably *Models of Man* (New York, 1957). Our own formulations of the concept of role are developed in John C. Wahlke and Heinz Eulau, *Legislative Behavior: A Reader in Theory and Research* (Glencoe, 1959).

7. For a perspicacious discussion of ambiguities in representation, see Harold F. Gosnell, *Democracy—The Threshold of Freedom* (New York, 1948), pp. 124–42.

8. Most theories of functional or proportional representation are motivated or supported by tacit and untested assumptions about the relationship of legislators' behavior to the process by which they are selected. This is merely a special case of the general democratic assumption that political responsibility is the mechanism

*par excellence* for bringing legislators' actions in line with the expectations of the represented.

9. See, for instance, Julius Turner, *Party and Constituency: Pressures on Congress* (Baltimore, 1951); or Duncan MacRae, Jr., *Dimensions of Congressional Voting* (Berkeley, 1958).

10. See, for instance, Donald R. Matthews, *The Social Background of Political Decision-Makers* (Garden City, 1954); or Charles S. Hyneman, "Who Makes Our Laws?" *Political Science Quarterly,* Vol. 55 (December, 1940), pp. 556–81.

11. See Heinz Eulau, "The Ecological Basis of Party Systems: The Case of Ohio," *Midwest Journal of Political Science,* Vol. 1 (August, 1957), pp. 125–35.

12. The samples for the four legislatures are 91 per cent in Tennessee, 94 per cent in California and Ohio, and 100 per cent in New Jersey. The four states composing the total sample represent different regions of the country, different ratios of metropolitan and non-metropolitan population, and different degrees of party competition. The interviews, using fixed schedules, uniform in all four states and including both open-ended, focussed-type questions as well as closed, or fixed-answer type questions, averaged about two hours.

13. The reduction in the number of respondents from the total samples is, of course, due to the open-endedness of the question. Hence not all respondents could be used in the construction of the role types as they emerged from representatives' own definitions, and in the analysis.

14. In constructing stylistic and areal-focal role orientation types, the responses to the question were coded in terms of (a) characterization of job; (b) objectives of job; and (c) criteria of decision. Each total answer was broken up into individual statements and coded in terms of manifest content rather than latent meanings, though meaning was taken into consideration in locating manifest statements. Role orientation types were constructed by combining relevant manifest statements which seemed to make for a major orientational dimension. In general, data concerning criteria of decision yielded the stylistic orientation, and data concerning the objectives of the job yielded the areal orientation.

15. *Constitutional Government and Democracy* (Boston, rev. ed., 1950), p. 297.

16. In the years before the second World War, public opinion polls several times sampled expectations in this regard. Relevant poll questions were: (1) Do you believe that a Congressman should vote on any question as the majority of his constituents desire or vote according to his own judgment? (2) Should members of Congress vote according to their own best judgment or according to the way the people in their district feel? (3) In cases when a Congressman's opinion is different from that of the majority of the people in his district, do you think he should usually vote according to his own best judgment, or according to the way the majority of his district feels? In three of four polls, 61, 63 and 66 per cent, respectively, of the respondents said the Congressman should vote the way people feel. In the fourth poll, only 37 per cent gave this answer. See Hadley Cantril, ed., *Public Opinion, 1935–1946* (Princeton, 1951), p. 133.

17. As the Trustee orientation includes responses stressing traditional moral values, it might be assumed that these virtues—such as following one's conscience or what one feels to be "right"—are more valued in rural Tennessee than in the three more urbanized states. But inspection of the frequency with which this attitude appears in Tennessee as against the other states does not reveal significantly different distributions of relevant responses: California—18%; New Jersey—8%; Ohio—28%; and Tennessee—23%.

18. Of the 46 Tennessee respondents who mentioned an areal orientation, only four came from competitive and five from semi-competitive districts.

19. Competition in district was severally defined in the four states on the basis

of past election returns. Space limitations prevent us from specifying the criteria here. They may be obtained from the authors.

20. $\chi^2 = 9.238$ for the entire array, where d.f. $= 4$, p $\geqslant$ .05. If the middle categories are omitted and only competitive and one-party districts are compared with respect to state and district orientation alone, $\chi^2 = 7.12$; d.f. $= 1$; p $<$ .01.

21. However, this finding may be spurious. It might be less a function of the political character of the district than of its ecological character. Competitive districts are, more often than not, located in metropolitan areas, while one-party districts are more frequent in non-metropolitan areas. It seemed advisable, therefore, to control the districts' political character by their ecological character. For this purpose, the districts were divided on the basis of the 1950 Census specifications. The hypothesis concerning the relationship between political character of district and areal orientation was clearly maintained in both metropolitan and non-metropolitan districts. However, while the pattern proved similar in both ecological categories, a greater proportion of district-and-state-oriented representatives appeared in the non-metropolitan than in the metropolitan areas, suggesting a pull towards greater dichotomization of areal orientations in the metropolitan environment. In view of the intimate connection in industrialized states between metropolitan and state-wide problems, this result is not surprising. It seems that the state is more salient as a focus of attention for representatives from metropolitan districts (no matter what their political character) than from non-metropolitan districts.

22. He might, of course, receive instructions from a state-wide clientele such as a pressure group or political party, but these constitute other dimensions of his attention foci.

# 15. The Outsider in the Senate—An Alternative Role[*]

RALPH K. HUITT

The growing concern of students of politics with the social structure of official bodies and the behavior expected of their members promises to make the Senate of the United States a prime target of research. Two recent books make notable contributions and suggest the trend. One is William S. White's *Citadel: The Story of the U.S. Senate*,[1] an "insider's" impressions based on years of close observation; and the other is Donald R. Matthews' *U.S. Senators and Their World*,[2] the work of a political scientist. One (though not the only) concern of both books is the system of norms for behavior of members of the Senate.[3] Although reached through different routes (White's largely inferred from observed behavior, Matthews' principally from interviews) their statements of Senate norms and the way they work have much in common. The norms (or "folkways," as Matthews calls them) are viewed as cultural "oughts" upon which there is a high degree of consensus. The members who conform most closely to the norms are, generally speaking, the most influential and effective members. This general view is almost certainly correct, as it would be for any stable human group; in this the Senate is not unique (as White sometimes seems to suggest it is) but typical.[4]

But what about the senator who does not conform? What is his place in the Senate and what happens to him there? This study will explore these questions through a case study of such a senator. But first it may be useful to try to restate the relevant parts of the analysis of White and Matthews (without holding them in any way responsible for the restatement) in terms of role theory, which will provide the conceptual framework for the analysis of the senator's experience.[5] In this the senators will be seen as actors in a political sub-system called the Senate, vested with an official position (or status) called "senator." The analyst's problem then is to describe the "senator" role—the dynamic, behavioral aspect of the official position. The new senator, with different motivations, faces much the same problem: he must learn or be taught the norms which define the rights and obligations of his position in order to take the actions which will validate, poorly or well, his occupancy of the position. White and Matthews, in effect, describe the senator role by stating the norms which prescribe how persons who occupy the senator position are expected to behave. Needless to say, it is essential to identify *whose* expectations are meant—who, that is, prescribes the appropriate behavior. For White the expectations apparently emanate from a powerful elite he calls the "Inner Club" whose members, appropriately referred to as the "Senate type," most nearly fulfill

[*] From *The American Political Science Review*, Vol. 55 (1961), pp. 566–575. Reprinted by permission.

the requirements of the role, and who wield the internal sanctions. Matthews suggests that the expectations are widely shared by the membership as a whole.

What is the "senator" role (White's "Senate type" or "Senate man," Matthews' effective senator) which emerges from these two books? It is one of a prudent man, who serves a long apprenticeship before trying to assert himself, and talks infrequently even then. He is courteous to a fault in his relations with his colleagues, not allowing political disagreements to affect his personal feelings. He is always ready to help another senator when he can, and he expects to be repaid in kind. More than anything else, he is a Senate man, proud of the institution and ready to defend its traditions and perquisites against all outsiders. He is a legislative workhorse who specializes in one or two policy areas, says Matthews. He has a deep respect for the rights of others, says White, making his institution the last citadel of individualism. In this composite, the senator as an ideal type is a man of accommodation who knows that "you have to go along to get along"; he is a conservative, institutional man, slow to change what he has mastered at the expense of so much time and patience.

But what of the man who does not play by the rules? What sanctions, if any, does the system impose? White suggests small inconveniences: the formal rules, for instance, may be closely applied to him.[6] But the Senate is disinclined to proceed against *any* senator; the "great ones" do about as they please and the others, except for a few who are not acceptable at all, can get away with almost anything so long as it is not directed against a member of the Inner Club.[7] The whole thrust of his book nevertheless suggests that the non-Senate type who does not make the Inner Club never amounts to much in the Senate. This is essentially Matthews' point, too, which he arrives at through some ingenious measurements showing on their face, that the senator who violates the folkways is less effective in getting his bills passed.[8] Neither is bothered much by the cases of spectacularly successful senators who do not altogether fit the type—the talkative Humphrey, whom White firmly locates in the Inner Club; the domineering Taft and Johnson, who leapt immediately to leadership. White explains them simply as "authentic geniuses among Senate types," [9] which indeed is consistent with his emphasis on sentiment and feeling rather than overt behavior. In Matthews' collective profile they cause hardly a wrinkle.

This study is a participant-observer analysis of a single case of presumptively deviant senatorial behavior, that of William Proxmire, Democrat of Wisconsin, in his first year in the Senate. The observer was legislative assistant to Senator Proxmire that year. The observer's assumption was that one way to gain insights into the structure and working rules of a social system is to learn what the neophyte has to learn during his "initiation" period. Senator Proxmire was an ideal subject. He went to the Senate keenly aware of the importance of learning its norms and constructing with care the role he should play there. His interest was theoretical as well as practical; as a person trained in the social sciences he was self-conscious about his learning experiences and determined to rationalize them in order to develop a consistent view of the Senate and his place in it.[10] More than that, he was willing to share his experiences and discuss them regularly with the observer.

Because this is a study of an individual in his relations with an institution, an attempt will be made first to suggest some of the relevant personality factors. Then Proxmire's choice of role will be recounted. After that some inferences will be drawn and hypotheses suggested about the role systems of the Senate.

*I*

A complex human being like William Proxmire cannot be psychologically categorized by a layman. Nevertheless, analysis begins with simplication; from the whole man must be abstracted some elements which shape him as a political personality, which identify him as a political type. In Proxmire's case, the first would seem to be a driving ambition to succeed, to which almost everything else in his life is subordinated, coupled with a puritan's belief in the sanctity of unremittent work.

Only a man with Proxmire's bottomless ambition and faith in the efficacy of effort would have believed he had any prospects at all in Wisconsin politics. His disabilities were perhaps best summed up in an apocryphal story given wide currency in the state in 1952, when he first ran for governor. It relates a conversation between his opponent, Governor Walter Kohler, and, say, Driscoll of New Jersey, at the governors' conference that year.

"Have you an opponent, Walter?" asks Driscoll.

"Yes," replies Kohler. "He's the son of an Illinois Republican. He graduated from Yale and Harvard, worked for J. P. Morgan and married a Rockefeller, and just moved into Wisconsin three years ago."

"My God, Walter," explodes Driscoll. "Did you pick him yourself?"

The presumed liabilities bear closer inspection.[11] The Illinois Republican father was a physician who worked long hours seven days a week until his death at 79, who taught his son that it is morally wrong as well as inefficient to be awake and not at work. At Yale Proxmire learned the rewards of perseverance: too light for football, he nevertheless made every practice, spring and fall, for four years and finally got his letter by participating in one play in a "letter" game. His experience at the Harvard graduate school confirmed what Proxmire had suspected while working for Morgan, that the financiers no longer made the decisions that mattered; the politicians did. The public life therefore offered the largest opportunities for a man who would make his mark. There also his political values crystallized. ("I didn't raise my son to be a Democrat," said Dr. Proxmire. "Harvard did it to Bill.")[12] To decide to be governor of his newly adopted state did not seem preposterous to Proxmire; experience had taught him that he could reach his goals because he wanted to more than most people and would pay a higher price.

Another lesson of experience, reenforced by temperament, was that he did better alone. The second personality trait—and I think the decisive one—which affected Proxmire's choice of role in the Senate is his compulsive independence. No group can contain him long; he does not trust it to take care of him nor make his decisions, and he cannot abide the restrictions on his actions which would go with truly belonging. Claims upon him which would limit his freedom of action, even those of friends and supporters, are onerous. His position in the Democratic Party of Wisconsin is a case in point.

The value of Proxmire's winning a Senate seat in 1957 to a party which had won only one other statewide race in 25 years can hardly be overstated.[13] Nevertheless, before the election an astute political reporter said in his syndicated column that it was no secret that there were "some pretty substantial Democrats who would not mind Proxmire's defeat in the senatorial election, considering their personal feelings alone and not the welfare of the party to which they owe their allegiance."[14]

Some understanding of this estrangement is crucial to an explanation of Proxmire's political personality.

After World War II a group of Wisconsin Democrats, many of them Madison intellectuals, undertook the seemingly impossible task of rejuvenating their moribund and reactionary party. Their success, after a decade of effort, was spectacular; in 1958 the Democrats captured the state Assembly, all statewide offices but one, and half the congressional seats. These organization people naturally would like a dominant voice in party affairs, and at the minimum they expect to be consulted. Proxmire has not done much consulting, the plain fact being that if he had he almost surely would never have gone to the Senate. He had barely qualified to vote in the state when he won his first office—from a Democratic assemblyman who had lived all his 65 years in one Wisconsin county. After that Proxmire ran as he pleased (three times for governor before going to the Senate) without heeding pointed suggestions that he had "had his chance."

His indefatigable campaigning undoubtedly did much to rebuild the party, but as usual he made his own calculations along the way. He discovered very early that time spent hunting up a county chairman is, on the average, enough to shake two hundred hands downtown. Whether the chairman would get him any votes was problematical; not so with the handshaking. With Democratic politicians at that time virtually ignored by communication media in large areas of this Republican state, direct personal contact through continuous campaigning seemed the one sure way to make himself known. This piece of practical wisdom, acted upon, did not endear him to the organization but it made him unbeatable in a primary.

More important, a strong hold on the electorate, which can control him only in the most general sense, enables him to resist any group (including his staunch supporters) which might seek to exercise specific influence. Two incidents will illustrate. The morning after his first election to the Senate Proxmire stood with his wife before daybreak in the rain at a plant gate in Milwaukee, thanking the workers for their help. A couple of weeks later, when a labor leader dared to suggest that he was the union's man, Proxmire chose a state CIO convention as the place to declare his independence of labor. One act was as significant as the other and they were not unrelated.

## II

Throughout the spring of 1958, for roughly half his first session in the Senate, Proxmire strove earnestly to be a model freshman senator. He worked hard on his committees and took care of his constituents. He accepted cheerfully a mammoth portion of the burden of freshmen of the majority party, presiding over the Senate. He did much more than his share; an unofficial tabulation midway in the session showed that he had sat in the chair longer than anyone else and about sixteen times as long as Vice President Nixon. The club apparently approved of him. No senator can ask his colleagues how he is doing, but his staff members can and do check with *their* peers. The reports at first were always the same: He's doing fine; he hasn't made a single mistake.

But Proxmire had not satisfactorily answered the question that mattered most to him: How much could he talk on the floor? Ordinary prudence, as well as Senate practice, counsel a neophyte to bide his time before exercising very freely his undoubted right to speak at any time. But to a man like Proxmire the life of the

Senate is the debate on the floor. Not to be there and participate is to deny himself equal membership in the Senate. Proxmire said of a freshman colleague who seldom spoke: "He might as well not be a senator!"

Nevertheless he forbore, trying to find socially acceptable ways to take some part. The "morning hour," that period at the beginning of each day when senators introduce bills and insert material in the *Congressional Record,* seemed safe enough so he quickly became a regular contributor to the *Record.* He entered colloquies on the floor only when specifically invited to do so by senior members. He cautiously scheduled his first major speech for the day before the Easter recess when most members would be gone, having been assured that this was an appropriate time for a freshman to talk. Only two members heard him through, the presiding officer and Senator Douglas (who canceled an appointment in order to give Proxmire an audience).[15]

But almost as if he could not help himself, Proxmire became steadily more active in debate until he was one of the busiest men on the floor. Then came the first warnings that he was "talking too much." The warnings were characteristic of the operations of the Senate. None of them was direct. They came in friendly tips: someone heard an unnamed person say it; the report was passed on to a Proxmire staff man for what it was worth. Or a very senior senator in the chair would pointedly overlook Proxmire standing at his desk, to recognize other members ahead of him out of turn.

Proxmire retired, brooding, to his office. He was puzzled and frustrated. He believed that he *had* exercised great restraint. He had kept his speeches short, except when asked by a party floor man to help kill time. So he sat mute. Not even a debate on unemployment compensation, in which he was deeply interested, could make him speak.

Then the dam broke. In the first week of June Proxmire offered six amendments to the Mutual Security Act and pressed them to a vote.[16] Inasmuch as Proxmire was not a member of the Foreign Relations Committee, and four of his amendments were first introduced on the floor so the committee had no chance to consider them, the performance was hardly a demonstration of modesty and withdrawal. Criticism was sharp and immediate (though indirect, as always), and it spurred Proxmire to a decision: he would "be a senator like Wayne [Morse] and Paul [Douglas]"; he would talk when he pleased on whatever he chose and would not worry about his influence in the Senate. He had found his role.

The Senate soon learned what that meant. In mid-July, for instance, Proxmire served notice that "I intend to rise every day, from now on until social security improvement is adopted, to plead for it," [17] which he did, on 27 consecutive occasions. But if the club was unused to being lectured by a freshman member, it must have been wholly unprepared for his threat to hold them beyond adjournment by the very antithesis of freshmanlike behavior, a filibuster.

The provocation was a bill to allow the Metropolitan Sanitary District of Chicago to increase the amount of water it may withdraw from Lake Michigan by a thousand cubic feet per second for a three-year test period.[18] Similar bills had been passed by both houses twice before (by the Senate in the closing hours of a session with scant debate) only to be vetoed by the President because of objections raised by Canada. Once more it appeared that the bill would come up in the flood of last-minute legislation, and with committee and leadership support it seemed sure to slide through the tired Senate. Moreover, because the Canadian position was now ambiguous the President might sign the bill.

But the pressure for adjournment which was the greatest factor in favor of the bill's passage could also be its doom—if its opponents had sufficient nerve. Their hope was to stall consideration as long as possible, then make it clear that the cost of passage was extended debate. It was a simple, time-proven strategy, but not one designed to make friends.

Proxmire was by no means the only man fighting the bill—there was a militant bipartisan coalition on each side—but he was probably the most determined and certainly the most conspicuous. It was he who blocked unanimous consent to allow any deviation from the rules in handling the bill. Thus he objected to a meeting of the Public Works committee while the Senate sat, and to the bill's being reported to the Senate after the expiration of the morning hour—tactics which brought sharp rebukes from two senior members but delayed the bill a day.[19] And it was he who held the floor from nine till midnight the last night of the session, until the water-diversion bill was put aside for other business; [20] and he who sat through the early morning hours, armed with a score of amendments and great piles of materials, ready to resume the debate. When the session ended at 4:11 A.M. the unfinished business of the Senate was a Proxmire amendment to the bill. It is not likely that anyone on the floor that night doubted that Proxmire was ready to talk on through Sunday if need be, but probably few present realized how eager he was to do just that.

### III

What may be suggested about the "senator" role from this summary statement of the first stage of Proxmire's socialization in the Senate?

First, at a certain point in his first session, Proxmire selected the role he would play. He did not play badly the role associated with the member of the Inner Club; he rejected it. He did not fail in an effort to make himself acceptable to the Inner Club; he decided he did not want to try to be one of them. The role he chose was one suited to his personality and temperament, one he had played before.[21] In his opinion it offered him the best opportunities to attain his goals in the Senate. Conformity with the folkways would not have allowed him, for instance, to associate himself so persistently with expansion of social security nor to make his Horatio-like stand against the water-diversion bill. Moreover, the independent role clearly was congenial to his constituency—Proxmire's seat had been held successively by "Old Bob" LaFollette and his son and by Joe McCarthy—and Proxmire was up for reelection. But it is important that his performance was not simply a bid for votes; it was rather a deliberately adopted legislative style which he has followed consistently since reelection.[22]

Second, he had a model to go by. He mentioned two senators and could have named others. The norms for his behavior were furnished by a small group within the Senate, just as the norms of the "Senate type" are likewise furnished by another, perhaps much larger, group within the Senate. The model, moreover, is rooted in Senate history. There have always been members of the Senate labelled variously as "independents," "mavericks," and the like. They have come from all sections of the country, although the midwest seems to have produced more than its share. It is not necessary to try to establish a roster of such senators; a voluminous popular literature and common knowledge support the contention that the "loner," the man who conspicuously walks his own way, is a familiar figure in the Senate.[23] What is more important is to try to sharpen the description of the role and to distinguish it from its opposite, the "Senate type" which makes up the membership of the Inner Club.

Because the most significant characteristic of the role is its conscious rejection of the behavior associated with belonging to the Inner Club, we might tentatively label it the "Outsider." The term is not meant, however, to apply indiscriminately to all members of what White calls the Outer Club (*i.e.,* all senators not in the Inner Club), who may simply have failed somehow to be taken into the inner communion, but to the man who does not *want* to be in.

If the "Senate type" who belongs to the Inner Club is distinguished by his sensitiveness to Senate moods, his regard for Senate traditions and norms, and his spirit of accommodation, the Outsider is notable for his determination to speak out whenever he pleases on whatever subject he chooses without regard to whether he can get any vote but his own. And if the "Senate type" cares more for the esteem of like-minded colleagues than any other kind of approval, the Outsider typically looks elsewhere—to his constituents and to his ideological allies across the nation, perhaps more than to those other members of the Senate whose norms he shares.

The difference between the Outsider and the Senate type is not so much in ideology or issue orientation (although the Outsider is more likely to be liberal, as his opposite number is apt to be conservative) as in legislative style. The popular literature of forty years has drawn a sharp picture of that style. The Outsider feels impelled to stand for principle absolutely, preferring defeat on those terms to half-a-loaf. He likes to tell people what they should and frequently do not want to hear. He is never so confident of the soundness of his opinions as when he holds them alone. He is as comfortable alone against the crowd as the Senate type is in the bosom of the club; indeed he is probably happiest when he stands by himself against powerful and wrong-headed foes. As a consequence few people, in the body or outside, are lukewarm toward him; they tend to like or dislike him strongly. He is like the "sons of the wild jackasses" who came out of the midwest thirty years ago, of whom it was said that "theirs is not a compromising spirit, and this lack of the give-and-take philosophy may, with their want of a sense of humor, be their greatest weakness but it has often proved to be their strength." [24]

The characterization is not really adequate. For one thing, it is undoubtedly too harsh. Many who helped shape it were deeply unsympathetic with the goals and tactics of the men they described, among whom there were, then and now, attractive as well as powerful personalities. Nevertheless there is more than a suggestion that unpopularity was not unknown to them and they were not dismayed by it. Even if it were wholly fair, the description obviously would not apply in all its details to any individual. What we have sketched here is an "ideal type"; real people are only more or less like it.[25] Its relevance is that it suggests what I shall argue here, that the Outsider is not a deviant at all but a person playing a recognizable and recognized role, a legitimate alternative to some others which he might select.

Deviant behavior has been defined as "behavior which violates institutionalized expectations—that is, expectations which are shared and recognized as legitimate in a social system." [26] My argument is that the Outsider role has been accepted and esteemed by a considerable part, at least, of the general public and by the specialized publics of close students of the Senate and that within the Senate itself it is recognized as legitimate whether it is popular with a majority or not. Most theories of deviant behavior postulate an effort (even if ineffective) by the social system to eliminate or at least control the offending behavior. The Senate has proved that it can and will take telling measures against what it considers deviant behavior, but the kind of behavior associated with the Outsider role is remarkably free of institutional inhibitions.

One piece of evidence supporting the assertion of widespread public acceptance of the role is the long tenure in office usually enjoyed by the established maverick. Approval by the special publics is suggested by the frequency with which close observers rank men noted for their independence at or close to the top of lists of outstanding senators. Thus a group of political scientists who specialized in legislation (presumed to be able to make informed judgments largely free from provincial, partisan or emotional bias) were asked in 1950 to "grade" all members of the Senate; they consistently put Douglas first, and the next three in order were Kefauver, Morse and Lehman.[27] The same year *Time* included Douglas among the "Senate's most valuable ten," calling him, among other things, a "maverick liberal." [28] *Collier's* congressional award for 1946 went to Robert LaFollette, Jr., "as notable an independent as the Senate has known since his fiery father, Wisconsin's famous Old Bob . . ." who always "has been free to do his stuff as he thought it should be done." [29] One of two awards made by the American Political Science Association in 1959 to outstanding members of the Senate went to John J. Williams of Delaware, who is noted for his lone-wolf assaults on wasteful spending, subsidies, and tax privileges.[30]

More than that, the Senate itself has in a sense put its *imprimatur* on the role. In 1955 the Senate set about selecting "five outstanding persons, but not a living person, who have served as members of the Senate" whose portraits would be painted in oval spaces left blank for that purpose when the Reception Room was decorated a century earlier.[31] A committee of five senators chaired by John F. Kennedy considered nominations for two years with advice from many people.[32] The senators finally selected were Webster, Calhoun, Clay, Taft, and the senior LaFollette. The names fall almost automatically into slots—the nationalist, the sectionalist, the compromiser, the arch Republican, the maverick liberal.[33] Was the committee—perhaps consciously—filling historic roles? The choice of LaFollette is striking. It is doubtful that any man ever aroused more bitter antagonisms in the Senate or was ever more reviled by his colleagues than he.[34] That LaFollette was selected as a prototype seems more likely from the fact that his closest competitor was George W. Norris, a man not like any of the other "outstanding persons" but the most like LaFollette.[35]

What happens inside the Senate to the Outsider? Not much; as White observed, the Senate is not a body disposed to impose sanctions on any behavior but the most outrageous. The point is important. A group may be expected to punish deviant behavior, and the Senate has proved that it can and will do so with dreadful finality.[36] Calculated and continued flouting of the dignity and good order of the Senate, easier to recognize than define, is deviance which compels sanctions. It will be punished finally, as Huey Long and Joe McCarthy learned, by a spiritual banishment more conclusive than formal censure and more galling, in its daily erosion of ego, than physical expulsion. But the Senate is of all official bodies (again, as White remarked) perhaps the most tolerant of individualistic, even eccentric, behavior.

Institutional arrangements, both formal and informal, encourage tolerance. An external system determines who shall be members and confers upon them an equal official status, and the seniority system softens the contest for status and preference internally. The Senate is a relatively large group (though its smallness has always been emphasized); it *does* have a hundred members, and the staff people who share intimately in the work of the body multiply that number several times. Differences in style, temperament and goals therefore may be softened by simple avoidance if not by the sharing of committee tasks, or by the temporary alliances of mutual interest which account for much legislation. And because the Senate agenda is managed largely by unanimous consent a majority judiciously refrains from employing against irksome behavior the small sanctions which serve merely to irritate the offending member. The imposition of censure or ostracism is a rare and traumatic action reserved for really deviant behavior usually borne a long time.

The evidence is strong that the Senate accepts as legitimate a wide range of behavior. Its members advance without hindrance to the perquisites of seniority, and some of the most powerful committees have had rather odd chairmen. Relations among subgroups appear to be easy; an Outsider who fights with only a handful of friends on one issue may, because of personal expertness on the subject, be chosen by the leadership to lead the party on a crucial measure the next week. Proxmire has said that no sanctions have been imposed on him; on the contrary, the leadership gave him substantial help in 1960 in the passage of a dairy price support bill which was helpful to his constituents.[37] Proxmire, like other Outsiders, readily joins subgroups in support of common interests and frequently votes with the majority. The behavior associated with the Outsider role seems to fall well within the bounds of what most members of the Senate regard as tolerable.

If this analysis is correct, an assumption of role consensus in the Senate is incorrect; there is variability not only in the behavior of occupants of the senator position but in the expectations—the "ideal patterns"—of behavior to which members may conform.[38] The Outsider therefore is not a deviant but an alternative role. It would be a mistake also to assume, without empirical justification, a bimodal distribution of acceptable behaviors—the Inner Club member and the Outsider. What is more probable is the existence of several legitimate "senator" roles. One thinks, for instance, of the persistence of the pure service type, the "Errand Boy," who eschews controversy and distinguishes himself neither in committee nor on the floor, but renders himself unbeatable by causing his beneficence to fall like gentle rain on all but constituents, Democrats and Republicans alike. The identification and conceptualization of alternative roles will in turn provide important clues to strains and conflicts, or to the existence of subsystems, within the body.[39]

It should be emphasized, however, that the successful performance of this task would by no means exhaust the sets of role orientations in the Senate which are worth analysis.[40] What we are dealing with here—the way the senator relates himself generally to his colleagues and the obligations of his office, or better, the *style* of his performance in chamber, committee room and office—is concerned with only one set, albeit an important one. Externally it is the image of himself as senator which he projects to his publics. Within the Senate it is the cluster of attitudes and modes of behavior toward other members which identify him to them and stimulate and shape their attitudes and behavior toward him. The choice of this role among available alternatives is therefore crucial to the successful performance of his other roles and to his self-esteem, and its importance is heightened by the fact that, once adopted, it is not easy to change.

## IV

The disability usually supposed to be associated with the Outsider role is that the senator who chooses it is thereby doomed to be less effective in the Senate. White puts it indirectly: the Inner Club runs the Senate; [41] the Outsider would be then, by definition, not of much consequence. Matthews goes further, attempting to test the proposition that the more effective member abides by the folkways. He constructs an index of "Legislative Effectiveness" by calculating the proportion of all public bills and resolutions introduced by each senator in two successive congresses that were passed by the Senate, arguing that "to the extent that the concept as used on Capitol Hill has any distinct meaning, 'effectiveness' seems to mean the ability to get one's bills passed." He then plots the effectiveness index against indexes measuring conformity with two Senate folkways and concludes: "The less a senator talks on the Senate floor, and the narrower a senator's area of legislative interest and activity, the greater is his 'effectiveness.' " [42]

It should be said at once that Matthews is as modest in his claims for his statistical test as he is resourceful in constructing it. Nevertheless the effectiveness index raises questions too important to ignore. To the individual senator, to whom being a senator is part of a professional career, the ability to get reelected might be considered a fair test of effectiveness and any behavior judicious which helps him pass the test. From the point of view of society, the conception of the Senate as a bill-and-resolution factory where the individual members are paid on a piece-work basis seems both too narrow and contrary to fact. To take the last point first, the passage of a bill is a collective process in which the introducer may have played a very small part, if indeed his bill was not changed beyond recognition. [43] Conversely, bill introduction may be no more than a form of advocacy, or a way to state a personal platform, or simply a bid for publicity. Or again, a senator may persistently sponsor legislation he knows can pass only well in the future, if at all, as George Norris did the TVA. [44] But more important, the enactment of legislation is but one and perhaps not the most important function of either house of Congress, let alone of all members individually. An adequate assessment of the effectiveness of alternative Senate roles or individual role-takers must await an analysis of the political functions performed by the Senate. [45]

Suppose, for instance, that one function of the legislature should prove to be "the institutionalization, crystallization and resolution of conflicts." [46] Might not then the Outsider's outspoken championship of minority, perhaps unpopular, views contribute to the process? The analysis would have to take account of the latent functions—the unintended and unrecognized consequences—as well as the manifest functions. [47] A latent function of the legislature might be to provide catharsis for fringe views which never will prevail. [48] If so, what better agent than the lone fighter against hopeless odds (regardless of his motivations or what he fights for) who, as he afflicts the mighty, may serve as the psychological representative of all the Outsiders in the great society? [49] To turn the questions around, is it likely that certain modes of legislative behavior should persist over long periods of time *without* having relevance for the political functions the legislature is called upon to perform?

It may be that Senate role and Senate function are directly linked and either may be approached through the other. The "ideal pattern" of behavior which we have called "role" may embrace one or more basic functions of the Senate, performed in greater or less degree by all the members, writ large and personified in the "ideal" role-taker. Thus the Errand Boy, if we may assume there is such a role, simply is performing to the virtual exclusion of everything else a function which by all accounts has always consumed a great deal of energy and time of senators and (especially since the Legislative Reorganization Act) their staff. In any event, what is important is that a functional analysis be made, and that it take into account what the legislators actually do and not just putative functions ascribed to them. Not until such an analysis has been satisfactorily performed can anyone say what senatorial role is "effective" and what is not.

Any sophisticated assessment of Senate roles, moreover, must recognize that any role, or even a single item of behavior, may have "diverse consequences, functional and dysfunctional, for individuals, for sub-groups, and for the more inclusive social structure and culture." [50] Thus the behavior of the Senate type who is in the Inner Club may be functional for groups which benefit from preserving the status quo, dysfunctional for those seeking change; functional for the preservation of harmony within the body, dysfunctional for conflict resolution in the larger society. The behavior associated with the Outsider may be functional for protest groups seeking a spokesman, dysfunctional for groups needing leverage inside the legislative body. It may even be functional for the leadership, to the degree that it makes more persuasive the middle position usually taken by the leaders. A given role may be functional in some respects for the role-taker, dysfunctional in others. Proxmire, for example, unquestionably has paid a price for choosing the Outsider role (as he would if he had chosen another) which he believes to be justified by the increased freedom of action it gives him. The important thing would seem to be not what role is chosen but what the role-taker uses it for, what goals are served by it. The Inner Club member may get little more than the personal satisfaction of belonging, the Outsider no more than personal publicity. Either may, on the other hand, choose his role self-consciously with the probable consequences clearly in mind, in order to maximize the advantages to be gained toward legislative goals he has set himself.

## NOTES

1. New York, 1956.
2. Chapel Hill, 1960.
3. See especially White, chs. 5–10, and Matthews, ch. 5.
4. George Homans, *The Human Group* (New York, 1950), pp. 147, 169–170, 426–28.
5. "Role" and related concepts are defined in a great variety of ways by social scientists, depending upon the discipline of the definer and the special problems which engage his interest. For an excellent clarification of the definitional problem see Neal Gross, Ward S. Mason and Alexander W. McEachern, *Explorations in Role Analysis: Studies of the School Superintendency Role* (New York, 1958), ch. 2. Because the purpose of the present study is not to refine role theory but to

employ it rather crudely to gain some insights into the behavior of senators, concepts are stated with as little elaboration as possible. For the theoretical formulation principally relied on see Theodore Sarbin, "Role Theory," in Gardner Lindzey (ed.), *Handbook of Social Psychology* (Cambridge, Mass., 1954), Vol. I, pp. 223–58.

6. *Op. cit.*, p. 82.

7. *Ibid.*, pp. 122–126.

8. *Op. cit.*, pp. 114–17. More will be said about this later.

9. *Op. cit.*, p. 82.

10. Proxmire has a B.A. degree from Yale, an M.B.A. from the Harvard Graduate School of Business Administration, and he carried his doctoral program in government at Harvard to the dissertation-writing stage.

11. See the sketch of Proxmire's life and personality by Godfrey Sperling, Jr., in *The Christian Scientist Monitor,* August 31, 1957; or the Chicago *Sun-Times,* August 25, 1957.

12. Chicago *Daily News,* August 8, 1957, p. 22.

13. Proxmire was elected in August, 1957 to the unexpired term of Senator McCarthy, and to his first full term in 1958.

14. John Wyngaard, August 17, 1957.

15. *Congressional Record,* Vol. 104 (April 3, 1958), pp. 6200–14.

16. *Ibid.* (May 26, 1958), pp. 9424–25; (May 28), p. 9655; (June 4–5), pp. 9868–69, 10157–63, 10260–62, 10266–70.

17. *Ibid.* (July 18), p. 14187.

18. H. R. 2, 85th Cong. See S. Rept. 2482, *Congressional Record,* Vol. 104 (August 20, 1958), p. 18606.

19. *Ibid.* (August 19), p. 18457.

20. *Ibid.* (August 23), pp. 19464–66, 19469–78, 19522–39, 19554–55.

21. In his first press conference after winning the special election in 1957, Proxmire shunned labels such as "liberal" and "Douglas Democrat," but mentioned approvingly that some labor leaders had described him as a "maverick." Chicago *Daily News,* August 29, 1957.

22. Representative actions are not hard to find. In 1959 Proxmire made three speeches criticizing the Democratic party leadership in the Senate, with support from four other senators. *Congressional Record,* Vol. 105 (February 23), pp. 2814–20. (March 9), pp. 3559–78, (April 15), pp. 5956–59. In 1960 he opposed the judicial nomination of a Wisconsin man who had massive support from within and outside the state, with no one else from Wisconsin in opposition. (Proxmire said: "I have had more visits and phone calls in connection with this nomination than with any other matter I have dealt with since I came to the Senate.") Hearings, Senate Judiciary Subcommittee, 86th Cong., 2d sess., *Nomination of James R. Durfee; Congressional Record,* Vol. 106 (January 25), pp. 1027–1033, (April 19), pp. 7577–78, (April 20), p. 7750. In 1961 he was the first to make a fight against a Kennedy nominee. *Ibid.* (daily edition, January 23, 1961), pp. 1086–1100.

23. "Borah and Johnson, Disturbers of the Senatorial Peace," *The Literary Digest* (August 23, 1919), pp. 52, 55; Austin Haines, "Smith W. Brookhart, Dissenter," *Nation* (November 1, 1922), pp. 465–7; Richard Barry, "A Radical in Power: A Study of La Follette," *Outlook* (November 29, 1922), pp. 564–7; Chester H. Rowell, "LaFollette, Shipstead, and the Embattled Farmers," *World's Work* (August, 1923), pp. 408–20; F. E. Haynes, "LaFollette and LaFollettism," *Atlantic Monthly* (October, 1924), pp. 536–44; Bruce Bliven, "Robert M. LaFollette's Place in Our History," *Current History* (August, 1925), pp. 716–22; Charles Merz, "Androcles and the Lion: The Silent President and the Roaring Borah," *Century* (April, 1926), pp. 698–703; Richard Washburn Child, "He Rides Alone," *Saturday Evening Post* (May 21, 1927), pp. 6–7, 187, 189; Dixon Merritt, "Four Senators,"

*Outlook* (December 28, 1927), pp. 531, 534; Ray T. Tucker, "Those Sons of Wild Jackasses," *North American Review* (February, 1930), pp. 225–33; Frederick R. Barkley, "The Voice of the Corn Belt: Senator Norris—Square Peg in the G.O.P.," *Outlook* (January 14, 1931), pp. 52–4, 74–5; Louis H. Cook, "Brookhart, Insurgent," *North American Review* (February, 1931), pp. 178–84; Oswald Garrison Villard, "Borah Goes on the War Path," *Nation* (July 25, 1934), p. 91; "Borah: Political History-Maker," *Literary Digest* (February 1, 1936), p. 9; Richard L. Neuberger, "Wayne Morse: Republican Gadfly," *American Mercury* (July, 1947), pp. 16–24; Robert L. Riggs, "Wayne Morse: The Peril of Independence," *The New Republic* (March 2, 1953), pp. 10–12; Robert L. Riggs, "That Maverick Morse," *Nation* (May 5, 1956), pp. 380–2.

24. Tucker, *op. cit.,* pp. 226–27.

25. This should be emphasized. No classification of individuals is intended. Where individuals are mentioned it is only to illustrate a characteristic in the construction of a type.

26. Albert K. Cohen, "The Study of Social Disorganization and Deviant Behavior," in Robert K. Merton et al. (eds.), *Sociology Today* (New York, 1959), pp. 461–84, 462. Robert A. Dentler and Kai T. Erickson argue that deviants are functional to the group, testing and tracing its boundaries, as opposed to the notion of deviance as a dysfunctional aspect of group or society; but they accept Cohen's definition and it is clear that they are talking about behavior which is regarded as illegitimate by the group. "The Function of Deviance in Groups," *Social Problems,* Vol. 7 (Fall, 1960), pp. 98–107.

27. Byron L. Johnson and W. E. Butt. "Rating the Senators," *New Republic* (March 3, 1952), pp. 10–11.

28. "Senate's Most Valuable Ten," *Time* (April 3, 1950), p. 20.

29. James C. Derieux, "For Distinguished Congressional Service," *Collier's* (April 26, 1947), pp. 78–79. The awards, made each year for four years to one member of each house, consisted of a $10,000 cash prize and a gold medal presented by the President of the United States. Other senators chosen were Arthur H. Vandenberg (1945), Alben W. Barkley (1947), and Vandenberg again (1948). Young Bob's style in the Senate was not his father's; indeed, by the time the *Collier's* award was made he probably was a valued member of the Inner Club. But the point is that his independence was' stressed in the article announcing the award.

30. *Congressional Record,* Vol. 105 (September 11, 1959), pp. 19085–86. See also William Benton, "For Distinguished Service in Congress," *New York Times Magazine* (July 24, 1955), pp. 14 ff.

31. New York *Times,* May 5, 1957, IV, p. 2.

32. The original committee was made up of Lyndon B. Johnson, chairman; Richard B. Russell, Styles Bridges, Mike Mansfield, and Eugene D. Millikin. *Congressional Record,* Vol. 101 (August 2, 1955), p. 12967. Johnson later was replaced by Kennedy and Millikin by John W. Bricker. For a description of the selection process, see John F. Kennedy, "Search for the Five Greatest Senators," *New York Times Magazine* (April 14, 1957), pp. 14–18.

33. See S. Rept. No. 279, 85th Cong., 1st sess., *Congressional Record,* Vol. 103 (May 1, 1957), pp. 6206–08.

34. This was frankly acknowledged in the committee report, *ibid.,* p. 6205, which says of LaFollette, in part: "Ceaseless battler for the underprivileged in an age of special privilege, courageous independent in an age of partisan conformity, he fought memorably against tremendous odds and stifling inertia for social and economic reforms which ultimately proved essential to American progress in the 20th century. . . . The bitter antagonisms stirred by his unyielding opposition to international commitments and conflict were ultimately submerged by widespread

admiration for his dedicated life-long fight against political corruption and corporate greed." An editorial criticism of the selections characterizes LaFollette as "the champion of lost causes." "What Makes These Senators Great?" *Christian Century* (May 15, 1957), p. 612.

35. *Congressional Record, ibid.,* pp. 6212–13.

36. White, *op. cit.,* pp. 121–35.

37. S. 2917, S. Rept. 1592, 86th Cong., 2d sess.; P.L. 86–799. See *Congressional Record* (daily edition, August 19, 1960), pp. 15594–600.

38. See the discussion of "the postulate of role consensus" in Neal, et al., *op. cit.,* ch. 2.

39. *Ibid.,* pp. 25–26.

40. The most perceptive and elaborate statement of the interrelated sets of roles within a legislative sub-system is found in the comparative study of four state legislatures by Heinz Eulau, John C. Wahlke, LeRoy C. Ferguson and William Buchanan, "The Role of the Representative: Some Empirical Observations on the Theory of Edmund Burke," *American Political Science Review,* Vol. 53 (September, 1959), pp. 742–56; "The Legislator as Specialist," *Western Political Quarterly,* Vol. 13 (September, 1960), pp. 636–51; and especially their mimeographed working paper, "The Role Concept in the Comparative Study of State Legislatures," pp. 3–17. See also my "The Congressional Committee: A Case Study," *American Political Science Review,* Vol. 48 (June, 1954), pp. 340–365.

41. *Op. cit.,* pp. 86–87.

42. *Op. cit.,* pp. 114–17.

43. In determining standards for the selection of the five outstanding senators, Kennedy rejected the notion of choosing those whose names are prominently associated with legislation. He pointed out that the senator whose name a bill bears may not be for the bill and may not even have read it, while a senator whose legislative efforts fail may find that later on someone else will take up his bill and succeed. John F. Kennedy, *op. cit.*

44. Stephen K. Bailey and Howard D. Samuel, *Congress at Work* (New York, 1952), ch. 8; Henry C. Hart, "Legislative Abdication in Regional Development," *Journal of Politics,* Vol. 13 (1951), pp. 393–417.

45. Robert K. Merton, *Social Theory and Social Structure* (Glencoe, Ill., 1957), pp. 19–84.

46. In their forthcoming comparative study of four state legislatures, Eulau, Wahlke, Ferguson and Buchanan use this phrase to define the legislative process.

47. *Op. cit.,* pp. 60–84. Merton makes "the distinction between manifest functions and latent functions; the first referring to those objective consequences for a specified unit (person, sub-group, social or cultural system) which contribute to its adjustment or adaptation and were so intended; the second referring to unintended and unrecognized consequences of the same order."

48. David B. Truman suggests this as one of the functions of the public hearing of the congressional committee. *The Governmental Process* (New York, 1953), pp. 372–77.

49. This is suggested by Proxmire's mail from all over the country when, for instance, he criticized his party's leadership in the Senate.

50. Merton, *op. cit.,* p. 30.

# 16. Conditions for Legislative Control[*]

SEYMOUR SCHER

Democratic ideology requires control of administrative action by elected representatives of the people. As the scope of public in relation to private decisions expands, the tendency is to expand the area of administrative in relation to legislative policy. With this tendency the control of administrative agencies becomes a pressing issue.[1] A good deal has been said about the merits of control centered in legislatures as compared with elected executives.[2] The antagonists typically argue not for control located in one elective institution to the exclusion of any other but about the amount and kind of oversight that is appropriate for legislatures in relation to executives.[3] Legislators, understandably, see themselves as the community's primary agents for the job of reviewing administrative performance. In 1946 this conviction was formalized by the Congress of the United States when it charged its standing committees and their staffs with responsibility for continuous oversight of the federal agencies. Relatively little has been said, however, about the way in which this responsibility is managed.[4]

This paper is an attempt at identifying the conditions under which committee review is likely to occur and, conversely, the factors which explain why frequently it does not occur at all. The character of agency review, when it is undertaken, is not of primary concern. What is offered are some propositions that emerge from a review of hearings and reports for the period 1938 to 1961 of two House committees and one Senate committee within whose oversight jurisdiction fall seven of the regulatory commissions [5] and from interviews with members of these House and Senate committees and with members of the committee staffs.[6] Since these propositions are derived from data that apply to one kind of committee—the substantive legislative committee—as it deals with a particular variety of agency—the independent regulatory commission—they must be considered hypotheses. Because of space limitations, only some of the pertinent data is included here. These findings invite further investigation to determine what may be of more general applicability. Without pursuing the similarities and differences here, it is supposed that oversight through the appropriations committees, for example, is subject in some ways to influences other than those stated in this paper. Similarly the conditions for and the character of committee review of the executive service-type agency as compared with the independent regulatory agency are presumed to offer some contrasts. But this is a matter for investigation.[7]

[*] From The Journal of Politics, Vol. 25 (1963), pp. 526–551. Reprinted by permission.

## I

It is useful to consider the conditions under which committees become involved in agency oversight [8] as ones in which Congressmen make rational decisions about the allocation of their scarce personal resources (energy, time, etc.) so as to maximize gains to themselves in things which they value and minimize losses in those things.[9] Some prime legislator values are support, influence, and prestige. In a setting in which there are innumerable claims upon his time, both from those within his immediate group environment (his Congressional and committee colleagues) and those outside (his local party, the President, groups in and outside of his constituency),[10] the Congressman must early choose those that will occupy him. He realizes that how he accommodates these demands is likely to be crucial to the success of his efforts to maintain and if possible improve his legislative and electoral position. Although each Congressman necessarily makes his own appraisal of his situation and the manner in which he must deal with it, common to all is the necessity for such an appraisal. In making this estimate, which is subjected to continuing review, he will allocate his scarce time and energies on something very much like a cost and return basis. Considering what is expected of him within his immediate Congressional-committee setting and in the parts of his external environment which can affect his survival, he arranges his priorities. What will be the likely cost to him in support, influence, and prestige measured against the likely gain in these same valued things of pursuing one course of action rather than another? What profit and what loss can be anticipated from satisfying committee and party leadership expectations if this means rejecting, even though momentarily, constituent or interest group demands which he considers important? What price will he have to pay in order to reap the psychic rewards of following his own ideological predispositions—or in his language "his conscience"—when these run counter to the position expected of him by committee or party colleagues whose good will and support he values? This is not to suggest that he typically confronts a stark either-or situation in deciding what he will do, but his earliest experience with conflicting demands is likely to stimulate a determination of priorities which will prepare him for the times when he is forced to choose a course where gains can be had only at a price.

## II

These theoretical observations have an empirical basis in attitudes expressed by Congressmen. Among twenty-three interviewed for this purpose,[11] a recurrent theme was the concern with spending scarce time "well." All did not agree on what this required but each agreed that he established some kind of priority system which indicated his estimate of things that were important. And the standard of importance tended to be a highly personal one—"what would do *me* the most good." The concept of costs and gains was always implicit, at least, in the descriptions of their choice-making processes.[12]

The Congressman formally recognizes and guards his obligation not only to participate in the legislative process but to "keep an eye" on how legislative policy fares after it is turned over to an administrative agency to interpret and apply.

Particularly among members whose committee responsibility involves review of regulatory agency performance, the ideology of the maintenance of Congressional prerogatives is forcefully asserted. Whatever the situation with Executive departments and bureaus, the regulatory commissions are considered "arms of Congress" and how those agencies read legislative policy is seen as primarily the business of Congress. But the Congressional norm requiring oversight from the legislature is of limited use in explaining the frequency of the oversight. In practice committee review is a spasmodic affair marked by years in which the agencies are virtually ignored followed by spurts of committee interest in agency activity.[13] The committee member who has an opportunity to choose between devoting his own and committee time to a review of agency procedures and policies or to new legislative activity can be expected to ask himself "what's in it for me?" Although typically it is the chairman who decides what his committee will do, all members may propose committee action to him albeit with varying results. And once action is initiated, members tend to make their own determinations of the extent of their participation in the committee's work. For the committee leader as well as the member the allocation of time and energy is determined in terms of expected pay-offs—to party, constituent, group, and through these, to the Congressman himself.

The years during which the agencies, except for the yearly defense of appropriations and occasional confirmation of appointments, escape Congressional notice are probably explained by the decision of committee leaders or individual committee members that their energies are likely to be better spent elsewhere. This decision, in turn, might be explained by the presence of any or a combination of the following circumstances.

1) *Congressmen tend to see opportunities for greater rewards in the things they value from involvement in legislative and constituent-service activity than from participation in oversight activity.* Of course, this estimate is likely to change if the legislator believes that important constituent and group purposes can be served by committee rather than exclusively personal contact with an agency. But without this incentive, the committee man would rather be associated with popular, district-serving legislation and individual constituent services than with what he sees as typically unnoticed hearings on agency performance. This is made clear when Congressmen explain the amount of time and work they devote to each of their committee assignments. In cases where they attend committee hearings at which regulatory agency officials are being examined on agency policies or procedures the members frequently view their participation with a "somebody has to do it" attitude. If he can choose between attendance at such meetings and others dealing with proposed legislation which the legislator believes is important for his district, he chooses the latter. One committee chairman put it this way: "There is always so much the committee has to do with important legislation, we just can't take the time to worry about what an agency is doing with something we drafted five or ten years ago. The agency's going to be on its own for the most part because nobody wants to do the job of checking on it." According to another Congressman on the same committee: "There's always an election around the corner and what we do between times has to have something in it that we can sell back home." But this same standard explains the successful pressure by a member of one committee for the creation of a special subcommittee to review the performance of a regulatory agency. A barrage of complaints from powerful groups in his district about ill-treatment at the hands of the agency convinced him that an investigation, par-

ticularly one which he headed, was necessary. This subcommittee chairman then insisted, somewhat formally, that "it is the responsibility of Congress through its committees to police these agencies. The 1946 Reorganization Act requires it." From among twenty-three Congressmen interviewed on this issue all but three indicated they considered committee review of agency activity a time-expensive, low priority concern except when there was likely to be something "big" in it.

2) *Committee members tend to view the agencies as impenetrable mazes and to believe that any serious effort at penetrating them poses hazards for the inexpert Congressman which outweigh any conceivable gain to him.* New committee members are more likely to admit this than their senior colleagues but it is a common committee attitude to see agency procedures and decisions as snarled in unnecessary complexities, with many Congressmen believing that this situation exists as part of a bureaucratic design to conceal agency activity from Congressional and public view. In spite of this, the committee member is likely to avoid heavy involvement with these agencies in public hearings believing, first, that they are immovable objects and second, that attempts at moving them might show to disadvantage the Congressman who typically has only a superficial familiarity with the statute or the agency's policies and procedures. This was put well by one Senator as follows:

Even when we [on the committee] suspect something's not right [in the agencies] what can we do about it? It would take forever to really get into the thing. First we'd get a long run-around in and out of the statute. There's always some little provision that nobody knew was there, except the bureaucrat who pulls it out of the hat—"but, Senator, the law does require that we do such and such." Before we finish they have us thinking it's all because of the terrible law we wrote and nothing at all to do with how they treated it.

A member of a House committee put it more simply: "The [regulatory] agencies' work is pretty technical. Most of us just don't know enough about it to even begin to ask intelligent questions."

This reluctance to engage in committee review of agency activity is mitigated to a limited extent by the availability of sometimes expert committee staff upon whom would fall the bulk of the detailed work of examining the agencies. The role of the committee staff man in the committee's work is itself a subject for much needed investigation. In the committees dealing with the seven regulatory agencies the staffmen tend to be involved in the many things other than agency oversight that occupy their Congressmen employers. In recent years, however, the Senate Labor and Public Welfare Committee has assigned a majority and a minority staff person to concentrate on NLRB and Labor Department activity for the information of the committee members. However, in a situation in which the committee, as a committee, only rarely examines agency behavior these staff men find themselves well supplied with expertise on agency affairs but with little demand from the committee members for their information. This condition seemed to prevail even in the House Subcommittee on Regulatory Agencies, a subcommittee intended especially for agency oversight. The relative quiescence of the subcommittee after the busy investigative years from 1958 to 1960 left a few staff men digesting agency decisions and reports and then sharing their information primarily with other staff men rather than with the subcommittee leadership.

3) *Congressmen who have established mutually rewarding relationships with agency people tend to be reluctant to initiate or become actively engaged in a close review of that agency's affairs.* In spite of the common legislators' suspicion of the bureaucracy, this feeling does not keep the Congressman from forming close ties with agency people in order to serve group or constituent needs or for other reasons. Even without friendly personal links to the agencies, the committee member's concern for promoting and protecting interests that are subject to agency regulation will incline him to leave the agency alone if those interests are not faring badly. As one Congressman put it: "Unless I get a lot of noise from people back home, I hardly give a thought to what they're [the regulatory agencies] doing. There are just too many other things to do." In committees that deal with regulatory policy the committee chairman and senior members who have worked in the area over a long period of time tend to develop personal associations with both regulatory commissioners and parts of the agency clientele. Whether based on personal regard or on shared ideological or group sympathies, these ties serve to prolong the periods in which the agencies escape careful Congressional scrutiny. This, naturally, is difficult to document but it is at least unlikely that a committee leader who counts as friends leaders in the natural gas industry or in radio and television broadcasting or in labor unions will be much inclined to put the agencies regulating in these areas under a committee light if the regulated themselves are not unhappy. And it is of some interest that Congressmen have this impression of one another: "You can't really expect a Congressman—to push the FCC into tougher regulation of broadcasters considering his own interests in a television channel back home." Or, "When you consider how much we [in Congress] depend on our local [radio and television] stations for free time to report to our constituents and for air time during the campaigns, we're going to do what we can to help them [station owners], too." Or, "Everybody knows [Congressman] Z is a natural gas man. As a matter of fact, he helped get [FPC commissioner] A his job. He won't go upsetting any apple carts." Congressmen who are friends of an agency or of group interests that are promoted rather than regulated by an agency do not normally make aggressive overseers.

4) *Congressmen tend to view their personal contacts with the agencies as more efficient than committee investigations for serving constituent and group needs.* From the perspective of the Congressman the characteristic legislator-to-regulatory commissioner telephone calls, which range from inquiries on the scheduling of constituents' cases to overt efforts at influencing an agency's determination in a particular case, afford generally satisfactory communication between the two. This is not to say that Congressmen invariably get what they want through this procedure, but it works well enough so that they normally prefer their own direct dealings with agency people to committee activity over which individual Congressmen obviously have less control. In interviews with twenty-three members of committees with jurisdiction over regulatory agencies fourteen indicated that their personal efforts with agencies in behalf of constituents involved in adjudicatory or licensing proceedings consumed "some" amount of their own or their staff's time. Of these, eight stated they would inquire only about the status of cases, while six indicated an "I do what I can" approach in their agency communications. Of this group of fourteen, eleven believed that direct personal contacts with the agency generally were adequate for their local needs. Three indicated that committee hearings were necessary when they believed "nothing else would do any good." Of the twenty-

three respondents, three said they did not personally ask anything of regulatory agency officials in behalf of groups in or out of their districts—that instead, their committee was the place for the regulated to bring their grievances. Six indicated that "a lot" of their own or their staff's time was occupied with inquiries to the agencies in response to outside requests for help. Of these, all indicated a belief that the route of individual Congressman-to-agency official generally told them what they needed to know about the agencies' activities. Thus, a total of seventeen of twenty-three members seemed to be satisfied that their individual relations with the agencies were adequate to deal with their requests for help from "outside." And committee oversight might very well make the useful personal communications between Congressman and agency official more difficult and thus less rewarding. As stated by one member of a committee with jurisdiction over regulatory agencies: "Why should [Congressman] Y bite the hand that feeds him—they [agency officials] 'cooperate' with him now. What hearings might do is just dry up his [agency] channels." Although *ex parte* contacts between Congressman and regulatory agency are not often subjects for Congressional scrutiny, investigations, once begun, often take unpredicted courses with sometimes unintended consequences. It is probably true, for example, that the publicity resulting from disclosures by the House Legislative Oversight Subcommittee of off-the-record contacts between agency adjudicators and their regulated clientele made similar contacts initiated thereafter by Congressmen more self-conscious and less frequent. But at least one Senator publicly declared that these disclosures would have little effect on his unrestricted communications with agency officials in behalf of constituents. Witness this statement by Illinois Senator Everett Dirksen:

Ever since 1933, when I came here as a freshman Congressman, I have been calling every agency in Government in the interest of my constituents. I expect I am going to continue to do it whether this becomes law or not, and I am afraid this bill [to bar *ex parte* communications by "any person" in adjudicatory proceedings] is not going to become law with my sanction, because I don't go that far.

I make the case just as clear as crystal, so the whole world may know. But now let's get the specific examples. There is an airline, let us say X, based in Chicago. I know the president and all the personnel and a good many of the pilots. There is another airline based in Missouri, my neighboring State. I don't know very much about it. But there is a petition or an application pending before CAB, and they both want to be certified for a stop in Iowa, so I call up this Chairman of the CAB and I say: "Look, Mr. ———, X Airlines has an application pending. I know these people, they are good, reliable operators; they are good, solid citizens. I just want to know what the status of the matter is."

*

These people get lost down here in this baffling, bewildering labyrinthine Government. Even we Senators get lost in it. I sometimes wonder what the average citizen would do if he didn't have the opportunity to come down here and talk with us and see what his rights are, and where he has to go, and whether we can't do a little something for him.

*

I went way beyond the trial examiner; I didn't even bother with him; he is just an intermediary, I went where the decision is to be made. The Commissioner I talked to would have a vote. If it is a five-man commission and I get three votes on that commission for my constituent, everything is hunky-dory. So I went right to the point where the decision is made.[14]

5) *Committee members will tend to avoid agency review if they expect it will provoke costly reprisals from powerful economic interests regulated by the agencies.* There is ample testimony from Congressmen of the political hazards they had incurred as a result of participating too vigorously in investigations which, for example, betrayed improper relations between an agency and its regulated clientele. A primary fight for renomination, financial support for an opponent, clandestine organized campaign activity against his reelection remind the aggressive Congressman-investigator of the far-reaching implications of his oversight vigor. The Congressman is likely, therefore, to take careful stock of his reserves of support from other sources before becoming too deeply involved with groups subject to agency regulation, particularly if they are strongly represented in his own district. In more cases than not, this estimate is likely to convince him that engaging in committee activity which antagonizes these groups is not economical. It obviously is difficult for public officials to admit to anyone (sometimes including themselves) that they fear retaliation for their public acts. But in talks with committee members whose legislative and oversight responsibilities involved the sensitive areas handled by the regulatory agencies, frequent references were made by them to the "influence" of particular regulated industries or groups which they thought inhibited *their colleagues* from vigorous committee action! One member of the House Legislative Oversight Subcommittee who was noted for his vigor in pressing for disclosures of links between some regulatory agencies and their clientele told of his conviction that political retribution had been visited upon him as a result. As he described it, there occurred a procession of people from his district in the industries involved who suggested to him that the regulatory commissioners were, after all, "good fellows" and there was thus no reason to cause them any embarrassment. But the Congressman's persistence thereafter led, he believed, to campaign support of an opponent which otherwise would not have developed. That this kind of pressure can be effective was suggested when this Congressman later indicated his belief that the oversight subcommittee had probably done its job—he at least, wouldn't press for its continuance.

6) *Congressmen who perceive that gains to themselves can be had by loyalty to the President can be expected to avoid close examination of the performance of agency officials appointed by the Executive.* For example, whatever inclination the Democratic members of the House commerce committee had from 1957 to 1960 to examine the performance of Eisenhower-appointed regulatory commissioners had been largely exhausted by 1961 as the Democratic leadership in Congress confronted appointees of President Kennedy in the agencies. In interviews held in 1961 and 1962 members of both parties on the committee were agreed that the prospect was remote of a Democratic majority continuing its inquiry into agency relations with their regulated clientele once the new administration's appointees began to appear in the agencies' top positions. Similarly, Democratic Congressman Roman Pucinski who, for primarily local reasons, chaired an investigation of the National Labor Relations Board in 1961 by a House labor subcommittee, was

urged by fellow partisans in and out of Congress not to prolong his inquiry unnecessarily. The agency by then was being populated by Kennedy appointees and the Congressman was reminded that any criticism of the pre-1961 NLRB would probably make more difficult the work of the new agency officials. According to a variety of informants who were intimately concerned with the NLRB investigation, the subcommittee chairman was directly and indirectly advised by spokesmen for the AFL-CIO, the President, the agency itself, and by many administration supporters among his colleagues in the House that his critical study of the "Eisenhower" NLRB could easily be misinterpreted by many as an attack on the "new Kennedy" Board members. The Congressman, according to these reports, was further advised that the "new" Board ought to be given a chance to function without the distractions of a Congressional investigation led by members of the administration's own party in Congress.

In spite of the typical Congressional insistence that the regulatory agencies are "arms of Congress" and thus not part of the President's administration, in a more realistic mood the legislator is likely to admit that the successes or failures of the "independent" as well as of the executive agencies will be publicly credited to or blamed on the President. Thus, the President's allies in Congress tend to assume a posture of support and protectiveness toward his appointees in whatever agency. Witness, for example, the attitude of minority (Republican) members of the 1957-60 House Oversight Subcommittee toward the majority report. The Republican members argued that the Harris Committee Democrats unfairly emphasized improper conduct between Eisenhower officials (Sherman Adams) and Eisenhower agency appointees, but ignored or treated gingerly efforts by prominent Democrats (Thomas Corcoran) to get off-the-record favors from the agencies.[15] Only the most unusual circumstances in agency conduct will justify violating that elementary rule of party politics which requires that the opposition be denied any good targets at which to shoot. Such circumstances apparently did confront Republican members of the House Legislative Oversight Subcommittee and, indeed, President Eisenhower himself in 1958. The disclosures by subcommittee counsel Bernard Schwartz of off-the-record influence directed at FCC Commissioner Richard A. Mack, and Eisenhower appointee, in allocating the Miami Television Channel 10 caused Republican committee members as well as the Eisenhower Administration some embarrassment. Considering the subcommittee staff's case against Mack, the Congressmen apparently had little choice but to join belatedly in the criticism of the Commissioner. The President eventually called for and received his resignation from the FCC.[16]

7) *As committee routines become fixed, for all of the foregoing reasons, in ways that make no regular provision for agency oversight,[17] in the absence of powerful external stimuli they tend to resist change.* Unless there are compelling reasons, such as those that are considered below, to alter normal committee life by "taking on" the agencies, committee members are likely to consider it easier and less costly not to. One Senate and three House chairmen whose committees are concerned with regulatory policy were in agreement, in interviews, on the low priority which they gave to committee reviews of agency performance. All considered such reviews to be outside of their committees' routines. "The pressure of current legislative business" and the absence for long periods of time of what they considered any urgent need to lay aside that business for the sake of an examination of agency activity were cited as explanations. But several other members of these committees

expressed the belief that while legislative oversight is likely to be occasional and irregular, they were satisfied nonetheless that agency people are kept "on their toes" for not knowing "where and when lightning will strike." According to this view, uncertainty over when a committee will focus its attention on any agency is sufficient to keep the agency "honest" in much the same way as would regular and frequent surveillance.[18]

## III

The typical pattern of committee review of the regulatory agencies is, then, one of no review at all for long periods of time. But these occasionally are interrupted. The years between 1958 and 1961, for example, saw a progression of committees —standing, special and *ad hoc*—deal with the agencies. The House Legislative Oversight Subcommittee, an *ad hoc* subcommittee on the National Labor Relations Board, Senate subcommittees on agency organization and procedure, plus standing committees of the two houses that considered Presidential reorganization plans for half a dozen independent commissions suggests a mass of oversight activity in apparent contradiction of the propositions stated above. What all this seems to represent, however, is a series of oversight bursts.[19] When and why do they occur? Again a profit-cost kind of analysis is relevant. *Committee leaders can be expected to involve committee resources in studies of agency performance if and when the likely gain in things valued by Congressmen is gauged as greater than any prospective loss in those things.* This situation may prevail under these possible conditions.

1) *When the leadership of the majority party in Congress believes it can cause sufficient embarrassment, with accompanying profit for itself, to a past or current opposition President who is held responsible for the performance of his agency appointees, committee oversight tends to be used for this purpose.* This accounts in part at least for the probe by the Democratic (Pucinski) subcommittee, immediately following the 1960 Kennedy election victory, of the NLRB's performance in the Eisenhower years. In another situation a Democratic Congressman who in 1958 pressed for a close look at the six other regulatory agencies by the House Legislative Oversight Subcommittee summed up the basis for his enthusiasm in what he saw as Republican President Eisenhower's "holier than thou" attitude. "We [Democrats] knew damn well that there were things [improper influence] going on between people in the White House and agency officials that shouldn't have gone on. We might not have bothered with it if it hadn't been for that pious business of Eisenhower's before he was elected about keeping his administration 'as clean as a hound's tooth'." Other Democrats on the subcommittee admitted that the communications between Eisenhower assistant Sherman Adams and regulatory agency officials normally would have aroused no more than a mild flurry in Congress. What helped mobilize at least these Congressmen to expose this influence situation was the irresistible urge to tarnish a popular Republican's administration plus an opportunity to topple his disliked and resented assistant from his position of power.

The estimate of the prospects for party gain to be had from oversight activity is made in light of several limiting circumstances. First, among all the possible ways of embarrassing an administration, there must be enough of sufficient dramatic quality that can emerge from probing the regulatory agencies to justify utilizing that procedure rather than other politically profitable techniques, assuming a choice among techniques needs to be made. The possibility is always present that a committee investigation of these agencies will get lost in the morass of agency decisions and procedures so that the moral of presidential failure cannot be strongly driven home. According to one senior committee member: "Getting involved with those agencies can be a trap. We start out with what is a good case of hanky-panky and by the time we finish clearing away the smoke-screen they [the agency] send up, the point's lost." And from another member: "Before our hearings [on agency performance in an opposition President's administration] we sent a couple of our staff people over to the agency to go through their files of decisions and intra-agency memoranda. They were snowed under. It would have taken an army of staff men a year to begin to make sense out of what's going on over there. We just did what we could." Secondly, the fixing of responsibility for agency action or inaction is likely to be difficult in circumstances where appointees carried over from an earlier friendly administration concurred in the very agency decisions and practices which are considered ripe for partisan committee attack. Unless there is good reason to believe that investigation of an agency will produce vivid easily grasped conclusions it is more likely that other routes to partisan advantage will be exploited instead.

2) *When the committee leadership or powerful committee members believe that constituent or group interests important to them cannot be satisfied by the routine personal intercessions between Congressman and agency, committee review tends to be used as a substitute.* When a Congressman perceives a pattern of unfriendly agency decisions or the thwarting of friendly decisions because of an agency's strangulation in its own procedures, or both, the mobilization of committee in place of individual Congressman's weapons may be considered necessary. The committee member becomes aware of these agency tendencies as a result of incessant and anxious communications over a period of time from economic groups in or out of his district whose interests he shares. In the NLRB's history, for example, the 1940 House special investigation resulted from both AFL and employer pressure for an exposure of what each viewed as discriminatory agency action. Similarly, the 1947 and 1953 labor committee hearings, especially those in the House, gave primarily disgruntled employers an opportunity to air grievances against the agency. And in 1961 another House special investigative subcommittee was organized in response to urgings from particular unions which suffered injury that was attributed to agency action or inaction. In each case some segment of the agency's clientele had communicated for years to friendly Congressmen its dissatisfaction with agency performance and had urged committee exposure and remedy. The employer pressure that preceded the 1940 and 1947 hearings originated immediately after the agency began to function effectively in 1937. The 1961 investigation was the culmination of union discontent that had simmered all through the Eisenhower years until ultimately a committee leader was persuaded to undertake the investigative job.

Those whose dissatisfaction initially brought the agency's activities to the Congressman's attention will need to be convinced that the committee's efforts were worthwhile. When committee review of agency performance occurs under these circumstances, it is likely to be directed at those features of agency conduct that are expected to produce maximum returns in favorable publicity to the committee members.

Congressmen are prone to admit that a primary source of the ailment plaguing the regulatory agencies is their intricate, delay-serving-procedures. Yet these Congressmen also agree that legislative studies of agency procedure are seriously lacking in political appeal and are usually embarked upon by committee members with great reluctance and a sense of self sacrifice.[20] Clearly preferable in terms of potential constituent and group payoffs is a committee inquiry which might substantiate group allegations of agency bias or of improper links between agency officials and some of their clientele. A 1961 House investigation with some of these characteristics was directed, under liberal Democratic auspices, at the National Labor Relations Board. House labor committee chairman Adam Clayton Powell designated Congressman Roman C. Pucinski of Illinois to direct a special subcommittee's investigation of the Board's performance in the Eisenhower years. Considerable attention was given to the organizing difficulties of the Textile Workers' Union in the South, difficulties attributed, in part, to alleged appeals by employers, without challenge by the NLRB, to employees' racial feelings. A Chicago Democratic Congressman, such as Pucinski, concerned with the status of minorities and with the movement of industry from northern unionized cities to non-unionized low-wage areas in the South, could be expected to seek and work hard at an agency investigation in which such issues were raised.[21] In short, the Congressman tends to become interested, and will try to interest committee and house colleagues, in a committee probe of agency activity when he believes that his own intervention with the agency in behalf of groups with whom he identifies is not enough and that the heavier weapon of committee action is required. He will press for this commitee action with the conviction that the support it will generate from these groups is more important to him than is the loss of support from others who may be disadvantaged by a close committee look at the agency. Among seventeen Congressmen interviewed who participated actively in two sets of committee hearings involving agency review, in all but three cases there appeared a clear orientation to one or another of the private group interests which were subject to agency regulation. In each of these fourteen cases, the respondent was not only willing to associate himself with the regulated but also judged the need for and the results of the committee's work in part, at least, in terms of its effects on them.

3) *When Congressmen perceive a threat, particularly from the President, to their traditional prerogatives of primacy in relation to the regulatory agencies, committee interest in the agencies is a likely response.* The concern for guarding these prerogatives is based only in part on an abstract attchment to a Constitutionally prescribed separation of Executive and Legislature. The designation of the regulatory agencies as "arms of Congress" originates basically in a determination by Congressmen that the policy areas administered by these agencies should be subject to direct and primary influence by the Congress. Despite the fact that long periods of time elapse during which Congress as a body takes no notice of the agencies, and that when interest in them occurs it tends to be expressed through individual legislators or committees largely uncontrolled by the parent body, the defense by Congressmen of legislative supremacy in relation to these agencies is no less vigorous. The Congressman's recognition that the regulatory commissions affect private interests whose fate is or may be important to him contributes to his commitment to preserve the agencies' status within Congress' primary sphere of influence. As one member of a committee that deals with the regulatory agencies put it:

With [President] Kennedy and his boy Landis [James Landis, special assistant for regulatory agencies to President Kennedy] calling signals at the FCC the [broadcasting] industry is in for a hard time. We [in Congress] have to constantly remind them [the regulatory agencies] that they're arms of the Congress and not of the President. If somebody needs to tell them what to do, we'll do it.

Or, from a Democratic committee chairman from a gas-producing state:

The President [Eisenhower] left them [the FPC] pretty much alone and everybody got along just fine. Once he appointed a group of honest people to the commission there was no need for him to keep looking over their shoulders. People like ————— [a Congressman from a Northern natural gas-consuming area] will always be screaming that the agency's working for the gas producers but there's no call for any of that. They're [agency officials] hardworking folk doing their best. And our committee has been a pretty good watchdog.

Moves, real or imagined, to expand Presidential direction over the agencies can be expected to be met by Congressmen, regardless of party, with a burst of interest in what these "arms of Congress" are doing. The 1961 Presidential reorganization plans, for example, preceded as they were by a Kennedy assistant's indictment of what he saw as the agencies' ineffectiveness and by suggestions for expanding Presidential direction over them, prompted committee examination of agency procedures which probably would not have occurred otherwise.[22] A vivid illustration of Congressmen's feelings about Presidential "interference" with these agencies is found in the following colloquy between James Landis, President Kennedy's special assistant for regulatory agencies, and members of a House Commerce subcommittee to consider Presidential reorganization plans:

MR. YOUNGER. Were the reports in the newspaper correct when they said that you had recommended a czar to be established in the executive department overseeing the regulatory agencies?

MR. LANDIS. No, they were not correct. They were far from correct.

MR. YOUNGER. To what extent were they not correct?

MR. LANDIS. They were not correct because my recommendations were simply a recommendation to establish in the Office of the President an individual, an office, which would oversee—I think the word was chosen wrongly on my part—which would oversee the operations of these administrative agencies and bring to their attention or to the attention of the appropriate authorities, Congress or otherwise, lags in the process, the logjams that were occurring, and suggestions as to how to deal with these.

\*

MR. YOUNGER . . . but as I understand in your answer before to questions by Mr. Springer, you held that these regulatory agencies were arms of Congress.

MR. LANDIS. That is right.

MR. YOUNGER. Then if they are arms of Congress, how can you put somebody in the executive branch to oversee them?

*

MR. YOUNGER. Well, it seems to me, just as a layman, that what you are trying to get is a control of the regulatory agencies and you were not able to get in your plan of having somebody in the executive office. Apparently that idea died or was abandoned for some reason and the reorganization plan was substituted. But I am rather convinced by your testimony and the reorganization act that you are attempting to accomplish exactly the same thing by putting all the power in the Chairman of these Commissions with the Chairman designated by the President and the executive would accomplish exactly the same thing as you originally had in mind by putting a so-called czar in the executive branch. I cannot get away from that idea, Dean. I am not a lawyer and I cannot see through all of these ramifications, but I think I can see and follow a line of direct authority, and I am sure in my own mind that you still have that idea of a czar in mind and this reorganization plan has that same thought, but in a much more subtle and roundabout way.

MR. LANDIS. I will deny that . . .

*

CHAIRMAN [Oren Harris]. . . . The concern that we have, and it has always been my concern during the entire time, is the independence of these agencies. I do not think that there is any great area of disagreement that these are agencies that were established by the Congress and they are independent branches of our Government, set up to act for and instead of the Congress and in some way to legislate on behalf of the Congress.

It is our feeling, and certainly mine, and I think it is the feeling generally of this subcommittee, that that independence shall not in any way be interfered with. There is grave concern on behalf of the committee that there might be an unwarranted interference on behalf of the Executive and not necessarily because this administration happens to be in office now, but with reference to any administration. I am very glad, as has been expressed by others here, that with all deference to you, that your recommendation of the so-called czar, which you said you did not intend, and you did not claim that characterization of it, but an overseer just the same—I am very glad that that recommendation has not been carried out, and I think that that would probably be an unwarranted invasion of authority and inffuence and interference of these agencies as an independent branch of the Government, designed to perform a particular purpose.[23]

4) *When, periodically, interest builds in Congress for revising regulatory policy, committee attention to the regulatory agency tends to occur as a by-product.* Agency oversight, when it occurs, is frequently incidental to the primary committee purpose of considering and drafting substantive legislation. Group demands for the revision of regulatory statutes are likely to include demands for a review of agency administration of existing law. In fact, proposals in Congress for new

legislation are often stimulated by regulated groups conveying to Congress their dissatisfaction with agency handling of legislative policy. In the 79th and 80th Congresses, for example, the irritation with what was considered overly aggressive and irresponsible labor union activity transferred naturally to the Wagner Act, which was written to protect union organization, and the National Labor Relations Board which, in applying the legislative policy, was viewed as a union captive. In the course of proposing new legislative restraints on unions, the Republican-controlled House labor committee directed vigorous criticism at the agency's performance and wrote into the amended labor-management statute a major organizational overhaul designed in large part to prevent agency scuttling of the new policy.

The process by which private groups and committee members build their case for new legislation often includes critical examination of the performance of the agency which applied the old (bad legislation, administered with necessarily bad effects, justifies new legislation). Sometimes support for an old policy is circumvented by a committee determination that while there is nothing wrong with that policy, its vagueness gives the administering agency an opportunity to distort its original good purpose; therefore, to prevent agency sabotage, more precise (typically meaning *new*) legislative standards need to be enacted.[24] An examination of agency conduct frequently is used, in such cases, as a screen behind which new legislation is built.

5) *When the committee leadership becomes convinced that interests to which it is opposed can be substantially advanced by the exposure of dramatic evidence of agency failure, it can be expected to move first to neutralize or minimize these gains by initiating its own inquiry.* Those leader identifications which prompt such "preventive oversight" often are those of the individual leader rather than those of a cohesive legislative party for whom he acts. A review of agency activity in these circumstances is undertaken with an expectation that it can be kept under careful leadership control. Only selected aspects of agency performance are likely to be examined and with only such intensity as will satisfy interested observers of the honesty of the investigation. Witness, for example, the perfunctory hearings in 1939 by Democratic Congresswoman Mary Norton's House labor committee in grudging response to the pressure from an unusual alliance of employer associations, the American Federation of Labor, and their respective Congressional supporters for drastic revision of the Wagner Act and for judicializing its administering agency. The Chairman and a committee majority, supported by the Congress of Industrial Organizations, had little intention of disturbing the status quo and managed only to stimulate bipartisan moves to bypass that committee. A year later a still Democratic House with Republican help and over Chairman Norton's bitter objections created a special committee under Democrat Howard W. Smith of Virginia that produced a devastating indictment of the NDRB and the Wagner Act.[25]

The importance of group orientations as compared with loyalty to a Congressional party as a determinant of committee behavior has been suggested, too, in the performance of the House Legislative Oversight Subcommittee from 1958 to 1960. Since these hearings were conducted by a Democratic committee during a Republican President's administration, one might have expected, assuming a cohesive legislative party, vigorous committee action for partisan advantage. Yet, according to the subcommittee's first counsel [26] and some dissident Democratic subcommittee members,[27] such was not the case. According to this minority Democratic view the committee leadership and some Democratic committee members behaved in a fashion that would have been expected of a Republican committee doing its best under opposition party pressure to protect a Republican administration. It was suggested that the ties of Congressmen in both parties to personnel in some of the agencies and to parts of the agencies' clienteles led to a "minimum" inquiry that could not be avoided rather than to a partisan no-holds-barred examination of agency-clientele-White House relations.[28] As one Democrat on the subcommittee phrased this:

> This [special oversight subcommittee] was a good case of a shotgun marriage. The [Democratic commerce committee] leadership didn't want much of an investigation of the agencies and the [Eisenhower] administration certainly didn't want one. But once the staff started turning up all those interesting things the leadership either had to slam the lid down tight and risk getting clobbered for it, or lift it just a little to let out some of the steam. As far as I'm concerned, a real job still needs to be done—it certainly can't hurt me any. But I suppose it's not likely to happen very soon.[29]

There is much to suggest that the decision of committee leaders and members to initiate and participate in a review of agency policies and practices often results from an unenthusiastic determination that a limited examination of an agency by its friends may cost less than an uncontrolled one by its enemies.[30]

## Summary

What has been proposed here are statements of general tendencies. They are offered as hypotheses that are supported by some evidence but which invite further testing. They are not intended to be exclusive. No doubt there are other explanations for committee oversight of administrative agencies or the absence of it. From the documents produced by a limited number and a particular kind of Congressional committee and from interviews with committee members and staff, these propositions appear to be major ones. As suggestions of tendencies they might be useful in alerting us to the contrasts between prescribed Congressional conduct— the "continuous watchfulness" called for in the 1946 Reorganization Act—and real attitudes and behavior. But these propositions are offered also to suggest some theoretical unity which links them to one another. Congressional committee leaders and members are viewed as people who act on the basis of rational estimates of their situation. The decision to initiate, participate actively in or avoid committee inquiry into agency performance is understood by the Congressman as one involving costs and gains. The political environment in which he lives—one requiring that he decide which among multiple and often conflicting demands he will try to satisfy in exchange for rewards he can expect in return—explains his frequent preference for leaving the agencies alone as well as his periodic willingness to examine them closely. In a decentralized party system in which his loyalty to Congressional and Presidential parties is sporadic, the Congressman's decision tends to result most often from his generally closer identification with constituent, local-party, and interest-group needs.

NOTES

1. See, for example, L. D. White, "Congressional Control of the Public Service," *American Political Science Review* 39 (1945), 1–11; Herman Finer, "Administrative Responsibility in Democratic Government," *Public Administration Review* 1 (1941), 335–50; Charles S. Hyneman, *Bureaucracy in a Democracy* (New York, 1950), espec. ch. i–iii. For a somewhat different view of the adequacy of political control of administration see Carl J. Friedrich, "Public Policy and the Nature of Administrative Responsibility," in C. J. Friedrich and E. S. Mason (eds.), *Public Policy, 1940* (Cambridge, 1940), pp. 3–24.

2. For the best recent examples see Charles S. Hyneman, *op. cit.;* also Emmette S. Redford, *Administration of National Economic Control* (New York, 1952); Marver Bernstein, *Regulating Business by Independent Commission* (Princeton, 1955), pp. 150–54. But according to Hyneman, "writers about public administration differ sharply as to what the President can do best and what Congress can do best in the direction and control of administration, and their differences stem largely out of states of mind that are not derived from objective examination and evaluation of evidence." Hyneman, p. 66.

3. Emmette Redford, for example, calls for an effort to provide "more effective congressional oversight of administration." But, "irrespective . . . of success in this effort, it appears that congressional control is too remote, divisive and sporadic to compensate for the absence of a clearly recognized executive authority of coordination and direction. The tendencies in modern congressional control strongly confirm the judgment of the framers of the Constitution on the need for unity in the executive branch of the government." Redford, *op. cit.,* p. 306; see also, pp. 354 ff; and in the same vein see Pendleton Herring, "Executive-Legislative Responsibilities" *American Political Science Review* 38 (1944), 1153–65; but *cf.* Hyneman, *op. cit.,* espec. pp. 168–72.

4. But see V. O. Key, "Legislative Control" in F. Morstein-Marx (ed.), *Elements of Public Administration* (Englewood Cliffs, N. J., 1949), pp. 312–33; Arthur W. Macmahon, "Congressional Oversight of Administration: The Power of the Purse," *Political Science Quarterly* 58 (1943), 161–90, 380–414; Hyneman, *op. cit.,* chap. ix; Bernard Schwartz, *The Professor and the Commissions* (New York, 1959); Seymour Scher, "Congressional Committee Members as Independent Agency Overseas: A Case Study," *American Political Science Review* 54 (1960), 911–20; George B. Galloway, "The Operation of the Legislative Reorganization Act of 1946," *American Political Science Review* 45 (1951), 59–62.

5. The House Committee on Interstate and Foreign Commerce has oversight jurisdiction over the Civil Aeronautics Board, the Federal Communications Commission, the Federal Power Commission, the Federal Trade Commission, the Interstate Commerce Commission, the Securities and Exchange Commission. The House Committee on Education and Labor and the Senate Committee on Labor and Public Welfare deal with the National Labor Relations Board. For the purposes of this paper, it is these seven agencies that are meant by the term "independent regulatory commission."

6. Interviews were conducted in 1954, 1955, 1961 and 1962 with, among others, 58 Senators, Representatives, and committee staffmen. These interviews contributed to a larger study by the writer on legislative control to be published shortly. The interviews were semi-structured and ranged in duration from fifteen minutes to six hours, in one, two, and three installments. Although the bulk of the data relates to House attitudes and performance the evidence, documentary and interview, that related to Senate committee behavior suggests few differences in the two houses in the conditions under which agency review occurs.

7. *Cf.* Arthur W. Macmahon, *op. cit.;* Lucius Wilmerding, *The Spending Power,* (New Haven, 1943); J. Leiper Freeman, *The Political Process: Executive Bureau-Legislative Committee Relations* (New York, 1955); James A. Robinson, *Congress and Foreign Policy-Making* (Homewood, Ill., 1962); Robert R. Wallace, *Congressional Control of Federal Spending* (Detroit, 1960).

8. The terms "oversight," "control," and "review" are all used here with the meaning of the 1946 Reorganization Act which gave to the standing committee the responsibility of maintaining "continuous watchfulness of the execution by the administrative agencies concerned of any laws the subject matter of which falls within the jurisdiction of such committee." This "watchfulness" may take the form of special committee investigations of agency activity or of inquiry into agency policies and procedures which occurs in the course of a committee's performance of its legislative function.

9. This framework of the rational (in the sense of efficient) estimate of loss and gain in political decision-making is a crude application of concepts familiar in economic theory, and employed particularly in game theory. This kind of analysis is used with interesting results by Anthony Downs in the analysis of democratic voting and government decision-making. See his "An Economic Theory of Political Action in a Democracy," *Journal of Political Economy* 65 (1957), 135–50; also his *An Economic Theory of Democracy* (New York, 1957). See also the collection of articles on game theory in Martin Shubik, *Readings in Game Theory and Political Behavior,* (New York, 1954), and particularly the foreword by Richard C. Snyder, v–x. For an application by political scientists of a decision-making analysis using concepts of costs and gains in national values which result from the choice among a range of alternatives, but choice in which rationality is not assumed, see Richard C. Snyder and Glenn D. Paige "The United States Decision to Resist Aggression in Korea: The Application of an Analytical Scheme," *Administrative Science Quarterly* 3 (1958), 341–78.

10. See J. Leiper Freeman, *op. cit.;* David Easton, "An Approach to the Analysis of Political Systems" *World Politics* 9 (April 1957), 383–400; David Truman, *The Congressional Party* (New York), pp. 279 ff.

11. All of these were members of subject matter committees with oversight jurisdiction over the regulatory agencies.

12. These were some of the phrases used to suggest this concept: "I know what I need to do, and if I can, I do it;" "we always keep an ear out for reaction at home"; "most of us don't want any part of that—it's too hot"; "I want to know where this will leave me with the [committee, house] leadership"; "that isn't as pressing as ———; it can wait," "something has to be done about ———, and the people expect us to do it," "there just isn't time for everything"; "if I only had a larger staff . . ." "you can easily spend lots of time chasing up a blind alley and get nowhere"; "nobody really wants to get involved in ———; there's just not enough in it"; "maybe some people here don't have to worry about it but I have an election this year"; "we all know why Congressman X got on to that: there was good mileage in it"; "normally none of us would touch it, but if we thought it would make a big bang. . . ." The rational estimate of costs and gains is an abstraction from what is an everyday reality to legislators.

13. See Robert E. Cushman, *The Independent Regulatory Commission* (New York, 1951), p. 678 ff., Bernstein, *op. cit.,* p. 83; Hyneman, *op. cit.,* p. 166; also the report by James M. Landis on regulatory agencies in U. S. Senate, *Report on the Regulatory Agencies to the President-Elect* [Committee Print] Committee on the Judiciary, 85th Cong. 2nd Sess. (Washington, 1960), p. 35. In the case, for example, of the NLRB, which was established in 1935, the agency's policies or procedures were the object of a substantial amount of attention from the House and Senate labor committees in 1939, 1946, 1947, 1949, 1953, 1959 and 1961.

Except for 1961, notice of the agency by these committees was coincidental with committee consideration of proposals for legislative revision. The 1961 House (Pucinski) Subcommittee on the NLRB was intended and functioned primarily for agency review. Of course the NLRB's performance figured prominently in the activity of committees other than labor: for example, the 1941 House Special (Smith) Committee to Investigate the NLRB, which was designed to by-pass the House labor committee; the 1948–1949 Joint "Watchdog" Committee to observe the Board's implementation of the new Taft-Hartley Act; and House and Senate committees in 1950 and 1961 that considered Presidential reorganization plans for the agency. What the bulk of this committee activity represents is not regular or routine committee review of agency performance but responses by committees to periodic demands from dissatisfied private groups for an opportunity to air grievances against the agency, revision of the regulatory statute or both.

14. In U. S. Senate, *Administrative Procedure Legislation,* Hearings before the Subcommittee on Administrative Practice and Procedure of the Committee on the Judiciary, 86th Cong., 1st Sess. (Washington, 1959), pp. 92 ff.

15. In U. S. House of Representatives, *Independent Regulatory Commissions,* Report of the Special Subcommittee on Legislative Oversight of the Committee on Interstate and Foreign Commerce, 86th Cong., 2nd Sess. (Washington 1961), p. 85 ff.; on the other hand there obviously are occasions when even administration supporters in Congress break with the White House; see, *e.g.,* the alignment in the Senate in 1961 on President Kennedy's nomination of Lawrence J. O'Connor to the F.P.C. After a lengthy criticism of the nomination by Democratic Senator Proxmire, the nomination was confirmed. But nay votes came in this case not primarily from the Republican opposition but from such regular Kennedy supporters in addition to Proxmire as Senators Church, Douglas, Gruening, Hart, Kefauver, McNamara, Morse, and Young of Ohio. 107 *Daily Congressional Record* (1961), 14183. These people apparently found in O'Connor's prior ties to the natural gas industry justification for opposing his nomination to a position which involved regulating that industry.

16. See Report of the Special Subcommittee on Legislative Oversight, 1959 *op. cit.,* pp. 24–26, 93–98; Bernard Schwartz, *op. cit.,* pp. 101 ff., 110 ff.

17. This, of course, does not apply to a committee like the House Oversight Subcommittee which was created especially for agency surveillance, although, as a special committee, with a limited life. It was succeeded in the 87th Congress by a Subcommittee on Regulatory Agencies of the House Commerce Committee. At this writing, it is too early to determine the extent and character of agency review by this new committee.

18. These Congressmen appeared sensitive to the apparent gap between their expressions of support for the norm of continuous legislative watchfulness and their own unwillingness to act according to the norm.

19. Some striking evidence of these alternating periods of committee oversight activity and inactivity can be found in the sharp reduction of staff between 1960 and 1961 when the House Commerce Committee's oversight subcommittee went out of existence and was replaced by the Subcommittee on Regulatory Agencies. A professional staff of eighteen dwindled to a staff of three with responsibility for maintaining surveillance over six commissions.

20. According to Senator John Carroll who chaired a 1959 Senate Judiciary Subcommittee on Administrative Practice and Procedure which considered proposed legislation directed at curbing *ex parte* contacts, including those by Congressmen, with the regulatory agencies:

"Now by the same token, as I understand this legislation, or my purpose in being here as a chairman, or I wouldn't have taken on this difficult task—it is a task on which we will be here for a long time [*sic*]. I was not sent here by the people of Colorado to come into this jungle that has grown up here for 25 years. I have other important work to do. But I see the tremendous importance of this issue . . ." In U. S. Senate, *Administrative Procedure Legislation*, Hearings before the Subcommittee on Administrative Practice and Procedure of the Committee on the Judiciary, 86th Cong., 1st Sess. (Washington, 1959), p. 96.

21. The following statements made at the subcommittee hearings by Congressman Pucinski and an aggrieved union witness are suggestive:

MR. PUCINSKI. It rather disturbs me to see a great deal of industry leaving northern industrial centers, including Chicago, going down to these areas where the atmosphere of hostility to any efforts of organizing the workers is so pronounced, and then apparently if your testimony stands unrefuted, getting the blessing of the National Labor Relations Board to conduct this kind of tactics and condone such situations.

I think this is extremely disturbing to someone like myself who does represent an area where the workers are highly organized and do get a reasonably decent standard of living.

✻    ✻    ✻    ✻    ✻

MR. PUCINSKI. I must say myself I am very surprised to hear testimony today to know that the Board would condone this almost barbaric appeal to racial prejudice to frustrate the efforts of organizing these people in the South.

UNION WITNESS. Mr. Chairman, the only difference between you and me is that you are apparently learning about it today and we have been suffering it now for many, many years.

MR. PUCINSKI. This is one purpose for these hearings.

See U. S. House of Representatives, *Administration of the Labor Management Relations Act of the NLRB*, Hearings of the Subcommittee on National Labor Relations Board of the Committee on Education and Labor, 87th Cong., 1st Sess. (Washington, 1961), p. 576 ff., also pp. 147–349. An NLRB investigation with some similar characteristics occurred in 1953 as Republican and conservative Democratic members of the House labor committee conducted a review of the allegedly anti-employer tendencies in the Truman-appointed agency. See Seymour Scher, *op. cit.*, espec. pp. 913 ff.

22. See the Landis report on the regulatory agencies in U. S. Senate, Committee on the Judiciary, *Report of the Regulatory Agencies to the President-Elect*, [Committee Print] 86th Cong., 2nd Sess. (Washington, 1960); and see the committee hearings on FCC organization following the defeat in the House of the Presidential reorganization plan for that agency, in U. S. House of Representatives, *Federal Communications Commission Reorganization*, Hearings before a Subcommittee of the Committee on Interstate and Foreign Commerce, 87th Cong., 1st Sess. (Washington, 1961).

23. In U. S. *House Reorganization Plans 1 and 2 of 1961*, Hearings before a Subcommittee of the Committee on Interstate and Foreign Commerce, 87th Cong., 1st Sess. (Washington, 1961) pp. 37 ff., 49.

24. This argument, among others, was used with some success in 1947 by the Republican leadership of the labor committees in order to win bipartisan committee and floor support for the Taft-Hartley amendments to the Wagner Act.

25. See U. S. House of Representatives, *Proposed Amendments to the National Labor Relations Act*, Hearings before the Committee on Labor, 76th Cong., 1st Sess. (Washington, 1939); and U. S. House of Representatives, *To Investigate the National Labor Relations Board*, Hearings before the Special Committee to Investigate the National Labor Relations Board, 76th Cong., 3rd Sess. (Washington, 1940).

26. See Bernard Schwartz, *op. cit.,* espec. pp. 82–90.

27. In interviews.

28. This tends to be a somewhat different picture of the relevance to a Congressman's behavior of his legislative party, particularly for members of the majority party, than that presented by David Truman in his examination of roll call votes in the 81st Congress. See his *The Congressional Party,* espec. pp. 280 ff. This contrary evidence is inconclusive, however, since there are occasions in which the inclinations of majority as well as minority members to engage in agency review are closely related to their loyalty to a President of their party. See, *e.g.,* hypothesis 6 above, section II.

29. The new situation which in 1961 made even less likely than before such an intensive examination of agency performance by a Democratic committee was the filling of top agency positions with appointees of a new Democratic President. See hypothesis 6 above.

30. This language—"better by friends than by enemies"—was in fact used by several committee members to explain their willingness in a given case to review agency programs.

# Part V

# Communication

# Introduction

THE LEGISLATIVE system can be conceived of as a complex communication network with a multiplicity of messages, senders, channels, gatekeepers, receivers, and feedback loops. Political theories of representation imply communications relationships when they deal with legislator-constituent relations. Legislators' perceptions of constituency attitudes are presumably influenced by constituent communication, and constituency attitudes are to some extent affected by legislators' communications to them. Legislators attempt to communicate to their constituents through newspapers, newsletters, radio and television broadcasts, and personal contact. The political campaign—an intensification of these communication activities—is a recurring ingredient of legislative politics. Legislators seek to get constituency opinions through the communication channels of personal contact, letter-writing, and opinion polls.

However, incongruities in legislator-constituency communication are very great. In communication terms, it may be said that there is a substantial amount of *noise* or *static* in the legislator-constituency channels. As Stokes and Miller make clear, in the general population the salience of legislators is very low. Although constituents pay rather little attention to legislative issues, many congressmen regard their stands on issues as important factors in their re-election. Perhaps the lowest threshold to be crossed in order for constituents to communicate with legislators is possession of some basic information about legislators. Yet, there is abundant evidence that large majorities of Americans have very little such information. For the congressional level, public ignorance is underscored by a nationwide survey conducted by the Gallup Poll (AIPO) in 1965 (see Table I). The survey shows that well over half of the people polled did not know their congressman's name, nearly three-fourths did not know when he would come up for re-election, and more than 80 per cent were unaware of their representative's votes or efforts for his district. Educational levels produce differences in legislative awareness, but even for college graduates the salience levels are not high. While we lack systematic evidence for many of the states, the available data suggest that cognitive levels *vis-à-vis* state legislators are much lower than those for congressmen. In Washington State only 23 per cent of a state-wide sample could name a legislator from the respondent's district, only a third knew when the legislature met, and only 40 per cent knew which political party controlled the lower house.[1] Data from a Missouri survey support the finding of low salience for state legislators, and indicate further the effects of place of residence upon legislator recognition. In Missouri, only 6 per cent of the respondents in large cities could identify their representative, while about four-fifths of the small-town and -city resi-

TABLE I

| | PER CENT RESPONDING "NO" BY EDUCATIONAL LEVEL | | | |
| --- | --- | --- | --- | --- |
| | College | High School | Grade School | Total |
| "Do you happen to know the name of the present Representative in Congress from your district?" | 38 | 57 | 68 | 57 |
| "Do you happen to know when he comes up for election next?" | 55 | 69 | 79 | 70 |
| "Do you know how he voted on any major bills this year?" | 62 | 82 | 90 | 81 |
| "Has he done anything for this district that you definitely know about?" | 80 | 85 | 91 | 86 |

Source: Gallup Political Index, Report No. 5 (October, 1965), p. 18.

dents could do so.[2] Interpersonal communications channels appear to be more open in less densely populated legislative districts in the sense that legislators in such districts are more visible to their constituents.

Opinion polling provides one means available to legislators for getting communications from constituents. Apparently, about one-fourth of the members of Congress utilize opinion polling of some kind, though the technical adequacy of congressional polls is open to serious question.[3] Letters from constituents are widely relied upon by legislators as reflections of constituency opinions, and the extent of legislative mail has expanded greatly since the New Deal.[4] Legislators obviously receive constituency communications from a non-random sample of the people in their districts, and in all probability, representatives most directly respond to the attentive public in the constituency. The legislator's attentive constituency is an elite group composed of the more highly educated, politically active upper-middle- and middle-class people in his district. They know who he is, what he is doing, and what his issue positions have been.

Of course, in addition to their constituents, legislators communicate with a variety of other political actors. One group of communicants for legislators is the lobbyists. Milbrath describes the various communications channels utilized by Washington lobbyists, and finds that communications which national legislators receive from lobbyists are largely directed through intermediaries. Legislator-lobbyist communication at the state level usually is more direct. Because the state legislatures are smaller in size, less heavily supported by professional staffs, more informal and unstructured, state legislators generally are more accessible to direct contact by lobbyists; thus, personal contact is a more widely available form of communication in the states than in the national capital.[5]

Legislators also communicate regularly with executive and administrative agents. Such communications are patently exhibited in the formal settings of legislative hearings, where exchanges between legislators and administrators may be preserved in a written record. But innumerable informal contacts take place between legislators and executives, and approval of administration policy may, as Robinson shows in the case of foreign policy, be related to legislator satisfaction with the communications process.

Communications between constituents, legislators, lobbyists, and administrators are quintessential in maintaining a supportive environment for the legislative system. Communication networks between these sets of political actors provide linkages between public opinion and elite activity. The selections which follow only begin to show the importance and complexity of these linkages.

## NOTES

1. Morris Showell, "Political Consciousness and Attitudes in the State of Washington," *Public Opinion Quarterly,* Vol. 17 (1953), p. 395.

2. David A. Leuthold, "Missouri Attitudes Toward the Legislature and Its Reapportionment," paper presented to the Missouri Political Science Association Convention, October, 1966, p. 7.

3. Leonard A. Marascuilo and Harriett Amster, "Survey of 1961–1962 Congressional Polls," *Public Opinion Quarterly,* Vol. 28 (1964), pp. 497–506.

4. See Leila A. Sussmann, *Dear FDR: A Study of Political Letter-Writing* (Totowa, N. J., 1963); and Raymond A. Bauer, Ithiel de Sola Pool, and Lewis A. Dexter, *American Business and Public Policy* (New York, 1963).

5. See Harmon Zeigler, "Interest Groups in the States," in Herbert Jacob and Kenneth N. Vines (eds.), *Politics in the American States* (Boston, 1965), pp. 135–141; and Samuel C. Patterson, "The Role of the Lobbyist: The Case of Oklahoma," *Journal of Politics,* Vol. 25 (1963), pp. 72–92.

# 17. Party Government and the Saliency of Congress *

DONALD E. STOKES and WARREN E. MILLER

Any mid-term congressional election raises pointed questions about party government in America. With the personality of the President removed from the ballot by at least a coattail, the public is free to pass judgment on the legislative record of the parties. So the civics texts would have us believe. In fact, however, an off-year election can be regarded as an assessment of the parties' record in Congress only if the electorate possesses certain minimal information about what that record is. The fact of possession needs to be demonstrated, not assumed, and the low visibility of congressional affairs to many citizens suggests that the electorate's actual information should be examined with care.

How much the people know is an important, if somewhat hidden, problem of the normative theory of representation. Implicitly at least, the information the public is thought to have is one of the points on which various classical conceptions of representation divide. Edmund Burke and the liberal philosophers, for example —to say nothing of Hamilton and Jefferson—had very different views about the information the public could get or use in assessing its government. And the periods of flood tide in American democracy, especially the Jacksonian and Progressive eras, have been marked by the most optimistic assumptions as to what the people could or did know about their government. To put the matter another way: any set of representative institutions will work very differently according to the amount and quality of information the electorate has. This is certainly true of the institutional forms we associate with government by responsible parties. A necessary condition of party responsibility to the people is that the public have basic information about the parties and their legislative record. Without it, no institutional devices can make responsibility a fact.

To explore the information possessed by those who play the legislative and constituent roles in American government, the Survey Research Center of the University of Michigan undertook an interview study of Congressmen and their districts during the mid-term election of Eisenhower's second term. Immediately after the 1958 campaign the Center interviewed a nationwide sample of the electorate, clustered in 116 congressional districts, as well as the incumbent Congressmen and other major-party candidates for the House from the same collection of districts.[1] Through these direct interviews with the persons playing the reciprocal roles of representative government, this research has sought careful evidence about the perceptual ties that bind, or fail to bind, the Congressman to his party and

* From *The Public Opinion Quarterly,* Vol. 26 (1962), pp. 531–546. Reprinted by permission.

district. We will review some of this evidence here for the light that it throws on the problem of party cohesion and responsibility in Congress.

## The Responsible-Party Model and the American Case

What the conception of government by responsible parties requires of the general public has received much less attention than what it requires of the legislative and electoral parties.[2] The notion of responsibility generally is understood to mean that the parties play a mediating role between the public and its government, making popular control effective by developing rival programs of government action that are presented to the electorate for its choice. The party whose program gains the greater support takes possession of the government and is held accountable to the public in later elections for its success in giving its program effect.

Two assumptions about the role of the public can be extracted from these ideas. *First,* in a system of party government the electorate's attitude toward the parties is based on what the party programs are and how well the parties have delivered on them. The public, in a word, gives the parties *programmatic* support. And, in view of the importance that legislative action is likely to have in any party program, such support is formed largely out of public reaction to the legislative performance of the parties, especially the party in power.

*Second,* under a system of party government the voters' response to the local legislative candidates is based on the candidates' identification with party programs. These programs are the substance of their appeals to the constituency, which will act on the basis of its information about the proposals and legislative record of the parties. Since the party programs are of dominant importance, the candidates are deprived of any independent basis of support. They will not be able to build in their home districts an electoral redoubt from which to challenge the leadership of their parties.[3]

How well do these assumptions fit the behavior of the American public as it reaches a choice in the off-year congressional elections? A first glance at the relation of partisan identification to the vote might give the impression that the mid-term election is a triumph of party government. Popular allegiance to the parties is of immense importance in all our national elections, including those in which a President is chosen, but its potency in the mid-term congressional election is especially pronounced. This fact is plain—even stark—in the entries of Table 1, which break down the vote for Congress in 1958 into its component party elements. The table makes clear, first of all, how astonishingly small a proportion of the mid-term vote is cast by political independents. Repeated electoral studies in the United States have indicated that somewhat fewer than 1 American in 10 thinks of himself as altogether independent of the two parties.[4] But in the off-year race for Congress only about a twentieth part of the vote is cast by independents, owing to their greater drop-out rate when the drama and stakes of the presidential contest are missing.

Table 1 also makes clear how little deviation from party there is among Republicans and Democrats voting in a mid-term year. The role of party identification in the congressional election might still be slight, whatever the size of the party followings, if partisan allegiance sat more lightly on the voting act. But almost 9 out of every 10 partisans voting in the off-year race support their parties. Indeed, something like 84 per cent of *all* the votes for the House in 1958 were cast by

TABLE 1. 1958 VOTE FOR HOUSE CANDIDATES, BY PARTY
IDENTIFICATION (IN PER CENT)

| | PARTY IDENTIFICATION° | | | |
| --- | --- | --- | --- | --- |
| | Democratic | Independent | Republican | Total |
| Voted Democratic | 53† | 2 | 6 | 61 |
| Voted Republican | 5 | 3 | 31 | 39 |
| Total | 58 | 5 | 37 | 100 |

°The Democratic and Republican party identification groups include
all persons who classify themselves as having some degree of party
loyalty.
† Each entry of the table gives the per cent of the total sample of
voters having the specified combination of party identification and vote
for the House in 1958.

party identifiers supporting their parties. The remaining 16 per cent is not a trivial
fraction of the whole—standing, as it did in this case, for 8 million people, quite
enough to make and unmake a good many legislative careers. Nevertheless, the low
frequency of deviation from party, together with the low frequency of independent
voting, indicates that the meaning of the mid-term vote depends in large part on
the nature of party voting.

## The Saliency of the Parties' Legislative Records

If American party voting were to fit the responsible-party model it would be
*programmatic* voting, that is, the giving of electoral support according to the
parties' past or prospective action on programs that consist (mainly) of legislative
measures. There is little question that partisan voting is one of the very few things
at the bottom of our two-party system; every serious third-party movement in a
hundred years has foundered on the reef of traditional Republican and Democratic
loyalties. But there is also little question that this voting is largely nonprogram-
matic in nature. A growing body of evidence indicates that party loyalties are
typically learned early in life, free of ideological or issue content, with the family
as the main socializing agency. Certainly the findings of adult interview studies
show that such loyalties are extremely long-lived and, summed across the population, give rise to extraordinarily stable distributions.[5] The very persistence of party
identification raises suspicion as to whether the country is responding to the parties'
current legislative actions when it votes its party loyalties.

That this suspicion is fully warranted in the mid-term election is indicated by
several kinds of evidence from this research. To begin with, the electorate's perceptions of the parties betray very little information about current policy issues.
For the past ten years the Survey Research Center has opened its electoral interviews with a series of free-answer questions designed to gather in the positive and
negative ideas that the public has about the parties. The answers, requiring on the
average nearly ten minutes of conversation, are only very secondarily couched in
terms of policy issues. In 1958, for example, more than six thousand distinct

positive or negative comments about the parties were made by a sample of 1,700 persons. Of these, less than 12 per cent by the most generous count had to do with contemporary legislative issues. As this sample of Americans pictured the reasons it liked and disliked the parties, the modern battlefields of the legislative wars—aid-to-education, farm policy, foreign aid, housing, aid to the unemployed, tariff and trade policy, social security, medical care, labor laws, civil rights, and other issues—rarely came to mind. The main themes in the public's image of the parties are not totally cut off from current legislative events; the political activist could take the group-benefit and prosperity-depression ideas that saturate the party images and connect them fairly easily with issues before Congress. The point is that the public itself rarely does so.

How little awareness of current issues is embodied in the congressional vote also is attested by the reasons people give for voting Republican or Democratic for the House. In view of the capacity of survey respondents to rationalize their acts, direct explanations of behavior should be treated with some reserve. However, rationalization is likely to increase, rather than decrease, the policy content of reasons for voting. It is therefore especially noteworthy how few of the reasons our respondents gave for their House votes in 1958 had any discernible issue content. The proportion that had—about 7 per cent—was less even than the proportion of party-image references touching current issues.

Perhaps the most compelling demonstration of how hazardous it is to interpret party voting as a judgment of the parties' legislative records is furnished by the evidence about the public's knowledge of party control of Congress. When our 1958 sample was asked whether the Democrats or the Republicans had had more Congressmen in Washington during the two preceding years, a third confessed they had no idea, and an additional fifth gave control of the eighty-fifth Congress to the Republicans. Only 47 per cent correctly attributed control to the Democrats. These figures improve somewhat when nonvoters are excluded. Of those who voted in 1958, a fifth did not know which party had controlled Congress, another fifth thought the Republicans had, and the remainder (61 per cent) correctly gave control to the Democrats. However, when a discount is made for guessing, the proportion of voters who really *knew* which party had controlled the eighty-fifth Congress probably is still not more than half.[6]

It would be difficult to overstate the significance of these figures for the problem of party government. The information at issue here is not a sophisticated judgment as to what sort of coalition had *effective* control of Congress. It is simply the question of whether the country had a Democratic or a Republican Congress from 1956 to 1958. This elementary fact of political life, which any pundit would take completely for granted as he interpreted the popular vote in terms of party accountability, was unknown to something like half the people who went to the polls in 1958.

It is of equal significance to note that the parties' legislative record was no more salient to those who *deviated* from party than it was to those who voted their traditional party loyalty. It might be plausible to suppose that a floating portion of the electorate gives the parties programmatic support, even though most voters follow their traditional allegiances. If true, this difference would give the responsible-party model some factual basis, whether or not the greater part of the electorate lived in darkness. But such a theory finds very little support in these data. In 1958 neither the issue reasons given for the congressional vote nor the awareness of party control of the Eighty-fifth Congress was any higher among those who voted *against* their party identification than it was among those who voted *for* their party, as the entries of Table 2 demonstrate. If anything, correcting perceived party control for guessing suggests that voters who deviated from their party in 1958 had poorer information about the course of political events over the preceding two years.

TABLE 2. ISSUE RESPONSES AND AWARENESS OF WHICH PARTY CONTROLLED 85TH CONGRESS AMONG PARTY SUPPORTERS AND VOTERS WHO DEVIATED FROM PARTY

| | OF PARTY IDENTIFERS WHO | |
| --- | --- | --- |
| | *Voted for Own Party* | *Voted for Other Party* |
| Per cent aware of party control: | | |
| Uncorrected | 61 | 60 |
| Corrected for guessing° | 44 | 35 |
| Per cent giving issue reasons for House vote | 6 | 7 |

°This correction deducts from the proportion attributing control to the Democrats a percentage equal to the proportion attributing control to the Republicans. See footnote 6.

Nor do the perceptions of party control of Congress that *are* found supply a key to understanding the congressional vote. Whatever awareness of control the electorate had in 1958 was remarkably unrelated to its support of candidates for the House. To make this point, Table 3 analyzes deviations from party according to three perceptions held by party identifiers voting in 1958: *first,* whether they thought the country's recent domestic affairs had gone well or badly; *second* (to allow for the complication of divided government), whether they thought Congress or President had the greater influence over what the government did; and, *third,* whether they thought the Democrats or Republicans had controlled Congress. To

TABLE 3. PERCENTAGE OF PARTY IDENTIFIERS VOTING AGAINST PARTY IN 1958, BY PERCEPTION OF PARTY CONTROL OF GOVERNMENT AND COURSE OF DOMESTIC AFFAIRS

| *Thought That Domestic Affairs* | *Thought that More Effective Branch of Government was controlled by* | |
| --- | --- | --- |
| | *Own Party* | *Other Party* |
| | I | II |
| Had gone well | 16 (N = 43) | 22 (N = 46) |
| | III | IV |
| Had gone badly | 14 (N = 152) | 13 (N = 122) |

recreate the basis on which the voter might assign credit or blame to the parties, the second and third of these perceptions may be combined; that is, partisans may be classified according to whether they thought their own party or the opposite party had controlled the more effective branch of government. Crossing this classification with perceptions of whether domestic affairs had gone well yields four groups for analysis, two of which (I and IV) might be expected to show little deviation from party, the other two (II and III) substantially more. In fact, however, the differences between these groups are almost trifling. According to the familiar lore, the groups that thought affairs had gone badly (III and IV) are the ones that should provide the clearest test of whether perceptions of party control are relevant to voting for the House. Moreover, with a recession in the immediate background, most people who could be classified into this table in 1958 fell into one of these two groups, as the frequencies indicate. But when the two groups that felt there had been domestic difficulties are compared, it seems not to make a particle of difference whether the Democrats or Republicans were thought to have controlled the actions of government. And when the two groups (I and II) that felt things had gone well are compared, only a slight (and statistically insignificant) difference appears. Interestingly, even this small rise in the rate of deviation from party (in cell II) is contributed mainly by Democratic identifiers who wrongly supposed that the Congress had been in Republican hands.

The conclusion to be drawn from all this certainly is not that national political forces are without *any* influence on deviations from party in the mid-term year. Clearly these forces do have an influence. Although the fluctuations of the mid-term party vote, charted over half a century or more, are very much smaller than fluctuations in the presidential vote or of the congressional vote in presidential years, there is *some* variation, and these moderate swings must be attributed to forces that have their focus at the national level.[7] Even in 1958 one party received a larger share of deviating votes than the other. Our main point is rather that the deviations that *do* result from national forces are not in the main produced by the parties' legislative records and that, in any case, the proportion of deviating votes that can be attributed to national politics is likely to be a small part of the total votes cast by persons deviating from party in a mid-term year. This was specifically true in 1958.

If the motives for deviations from party are not to be found primarily at the national level, the search moves naturally to the local congressional campaign. A third possibility—that deviations are by-products of state-wide races—can be discounted with some confidence. Despite the popular lore on the subject, evidence both from interview studies and from aggregate election statistics can be used to show that the influence of contests for Governor and Senator on the outcome of House races is slight in mid-term elections, although these contests can have an immense influence on turnout for the House.[8] In our 1958 sample, a majority of those who deviated from party in voting for the House *failed* to deviate also at the state level; more often than not, what had moved them into the other party's column at the House level was dissociated from the contests for Governor or Senator in which they voted. Moreover, the fact that an elector deviates from his party in voting both for the House and some office contested on a state-wide basis is not conclusive evidence that the state race has influenced his choice for the House, rather than the other way round. When the possibility of *reverse* coat-tail effects is allowed for, the reasons for believing that the state-wide race is a potent force on the House vote seem faint indeed.[9] As we search for the motives for deviation from party, analysis of the local congressional race pays greater dividdends.

### The Saliency of Congressional Candidates

By the standards of the civics text, what the public knows about the candidates for Congress is as meager as what it knows about the parties' legislative records. Of the people who lived in districts where the House seat was contested in 1958, 59 per cent—well over half—said that they had neither read nor heard anything about either candidate for Congress, and less than 1 in 5 felt that they knew something about both candidates. What is more, these remarkable proportions are only marginally improved by excluding nonvoters from the calculations. Of people who went to the polls and cast a vote between rival House candidates in 1958, fully 46 per cent conceded that they did so without having read or heard anything about either man. What the other half *had* read or heard is illuminating; we will deal with its policy content presently. Many of our respondents said they knew something about the people contesting the House seat on the basis of very slender information indeed.

The incumbent candidate is by far the better known. In districts where an incumbent was opposed for re-election in 1958, 39 per cent of our respondents knew something about the Congressman, whereas only 20 per cent said they knew anything at all about his nonincumbent opponent. The incumbent's advantage of repeated exposure to the electorate is plain enough. In fact, owing to the greater seniority and longer exposure of Congressmen from safe districts, the public's awareness of incumbents who were unopposed for re-election in 1958 was as great as its awareness of incumbents who had had to conduct an election campaign that year.

The saliency of a candidate is of critical importance if he is to attract support from the opposite party. However little the public may know of those seeking office, any information at all about the rival party's candidate creates the possibility of a choice deviating from party. That such a choice occurs with some frequency is shown by the entries of Table 4, whose columns separate party identifiers in

TABLE 4. PERCENTAGE VOTING FOR OWN PARTY CANDIDATE AND OTHER PARTY CANDIDATE FOR HOUSE IN 1958, BY SALIENCY OF CANDIDATES IN CONTESTED DISTRICTS

| Voted for Candidate | VOTER WAS AWARE OF | | | |
|---|---|---|---|---|
| | Both Candidates (N = 196) | Own Party Candidate Only (N = 166) | Other Party Candidate Only (N = 68) | Neither Candidate (N = 368) |
| Of own party | 83 | 98 | 60 | 92 |
| Of other party | 17 | 2 | 40 | 8 |
| Total | 100 | 100 | 100 | 100 |

contested districts in 1958 according to whether they were aware of both candidates, the candidate of their own party or the other party only, or neither candidate. The condition of no information leads to fairly unrelieved party-line voting, and so to an even greater degree does the condition of information only about the candidate of the voter's own party. But if partisan voters know something about the opposition's man, substantial deviations from party appear. In fact, if such voters know *only* the opposition candidate, almost half can be induced to cast a vote contrary to their party identification. In the main, recognition carries a positive valence; to be perceived at all is to be perceived favorably. However, some *negative* perceptions are found in our interviews, and when these are taken into account the explanation of deviation from party becomes surer still. For example, if we return to Table 4 and select from the third column only the voters who perceived the candidate of the other party *favorably,* a clear majority is found to have deviated from party allegiance in casting their votes. And if we select from the first column only the handful of voters who perceived the candidate of their own party *negatively* and of the opposite party *positively,* almost three-quarters are found to have deviated from their party loyalty in voting for the House.

What our constituent interviews show about the increment of support that accrues to the salient candidate is closely aligned to what the candidates themselves see as the roots of their electoral strength. Our interviews with incumbent and non-incumbent candidates seeking election to the House explored at length their understanding of factors aiding—or damaging—their electoral appeal. In particular, these interviews probed the candidates' assessment of four possible influences on the result: traditional party loyalties, national issues, state and local contests, and the candidates' own record and personal standing in the district. Caution is in order in dealing with answers to questions that touch the respondent's self-image as closely as these. Specifically, we may expect some overstatement of the candidate's own importance, particularly from the victors, and we may expect, too, that too large a discount will be applied to party allegiance, since this "inert" factor, having little to do with increments of strength, is so easily taken for granted.

After these allowances are made, it is still impressive how heavy a weight the incumbent assigns his personal record and standing. The Congressman's ranking of this and the other factors in the election is shown in Table 5. As the entries of the table indicate, more than four-fifths of the incumbents re-elected in 1958 felt that the niche they had carved out in the awareness of their constituents had

TABLE 5. RELATIVE IMPORTANCE OF FACTORS IN RE-ELECTION AS SEEN BY INCUMBENT CANDIDATES IN 1958 (IN PER CENT)

| Perceived As | Personal Record and Standing | National Issues | Traditional Party Loyalties | State and and Races |
|---|---|---|---|---|
| Very important | 57 | 26 | 25 | 14 |
| Quite important | 28 | 20 | 21 | 19 |
| Somewhat important | 9 | 20 | 24 | 27 |
| Not very important | 3 | 27 | 18 | 19 |
| Not important at all | 3 | 7 | 12 | 21 |
| | 100 | 100 | 100 | 100 |

substantial impact on the race, a proportion that exceeds by half the percentage who gave as much weight to any of the three other factors. This difference is more than sheer puffing in the interview situation, and the perceptual facts it reveals deserve close attention. Among the forces the Representative feels may enhance his strength at the polls, he gives his personal standing with the district front rank.

In view of the way the saliency of candidates can move the electorate across party lines, great stress should be laid on the fact that the public sees individual candidates for Congress in terms of party programs scarcely at all. Our constituent interviews indicate that the popular image of the Congressman is almost barren of policy content. A long series of open-ended questions asked of those who said they had any information about the Representative produced mainly a collection of diffuse evaluative judgments: he is a good man, he is experienced, he knows the problems, he has done a good job, and the like. Beyond this, the Congressman's image consisted of a mixed bag of impressions, some of them wildly improbable, about ethnicity, the attractiveness of family, specific services to the district, and other facts in the candidate's background. By the most reasonable count, references to current legislative issues comprised not more than a thirtieth part of what the constituents had to say about their Congressmen.

The irrelevance of legislative issues to the public's knowledge of Representatives is underscored by the nature of some primary *determinants* of saliency. A full analysis of the causes of constituent awareness of candidates goes beyond the scope of this paper. Although our investigation has given a good deal of attention to communication factors and to characteristics of Congressmen and constituents themselves that determine the probability a given Congressman will be known to a given constituent, this interplay of causes cannot be explored very deeply here. However, it *is* noteworthy in the present discussion that many factors increasing the saliency of candidates are unlikely to enhance what the public knows about their stands on issues. An excellent example is sex. Both for incumbents and non-incumbents, a candidate property that is related to saliency is gender; one of the best ways for a Representative to be known is to be a Congress*woman*. How irrelevant to policy issues this property is depends on what we make of the causal relation between sex and salience. The fact of being a woman may make a candidate more visible, but a woman may have to be unusually visible (like a Congressman's widow, say) before she can be elected to the House, or even become a serious candidate. If the first of these inferences is even partially right, the salience of the candidate is not likely to be in terms of positions taken on legislative issues.

Given the number of women who run for Congress, the role of sex may seem a trivial example to demonstrate the irrelevance of issue stands to saliency. However, the same point can be made for a much wider set of districts by the greater saliency of candidates who live in the constituent's home community. Just as there is enormous variety in the communities that make up the American nation, so there is the widest possible variation in how well a congressional district coincides with a natural community, and the goodness of this fit is a fundamental way of typing districts. At one extreme is the constituency whose area is lost within one of the country's great metropolitan centers, comprising at best a small fraction of the whole community. At the middle of the range is the district that is itself a natural community, consisting of a single medium-sized city and its environs. At the other extreme is the district whose territory includes a great number of small communities, as well as surrounding open country that goes on, in some cases, for hundreds of miles. In all but the metropolitan districts the salience of the candidate for the voter differs markedly according to whether candidate and voter live in the same community. The fact of common residence—of being "friends and neighbors" —stands for important facts of communication and community identification. Candidates will be joined by formal and informal communication networks to many of the voters living in the same community, and they may also be objects of considerable community pride.

The reality of this local effect is demonstrated by Table 6. As the entries of the table show, dividing a nationwide sample of constituents according to whether they

TABLE 6. INFLUENCE OF "FRIENDS AND NEIGHBORS" FACTOR ON SALIENCY OF CANDIDATES FOR VOTERS   (IN PER CENT)

| Voter Is | INCUMBENT CANDIDATE LIVES IN | | NON-INCUMBENT CANDIDATE LIVES IN | |
|---|---|---|---|---|
| | Same Community As Voter (N = 269) | Other Community than Voter (N = 414) | Same Community As Voter (N = 304) | Other Community than Voter (N = 447) |
| Aware of candidate | 67 | 45 | 47 | 22 |
| Not aware of candidate | 33 | 55 | 53 | 78 |
| Total | 100 | 100 | 100 | 100 |

live in the same community as their Congressman or his opponent produces marked differences of saliency. The "friends and neighbors" effect made familiar by studies of primary voting in one-party areas has a counterpart in voting for Representatives throughout the country, apart from the large metropolitan areas.[10] And despite the fact that localism is found here in the context of as tightly party-determined an election as any in American politics, the irrelevance of local appeal to legislative issues is probably as great as it is in the wide-open, one-party primary.

## Conclusion

What the public knows about the legislative records of the parties and of individual congressional candidates is a principal reason for the departure of American practice from an idealized conception of party government. On the surface the legislative elections occurring in the middle of the President's term appear to be dominated by two national parties asking public support for their alternative programs. Certainly the electorate whose votes they seek responds to individual legislative candidates overwhelmingly on the basis of their party labels. Despite our kaleidoscopic electoral law, the candidate's party is the one piece of information every voter is guaranteed. For many, it is the only information they ever get.

However, the legislative events that follow these elections diverge widely from the responsible-party model. The candidates who have presented themselves to the country under two party symbols immediately break ranks. The legislative parties speak not as two voices but as a cacophony of blocs and individuals fulfilling their own definitions of the public good. Party cohesion by no means vanishes, but it is deeply eroded by the pressures external to party to which the Congressman is subject.

The public's information about the legislative record of the parties and of Members of Congress goes far toward reconciling these seemingly contradictory facts. In the congressional election, to be sure, the country votes overwhelmingly for party symbols, but the symbols have limited meaning in terms of legislative policy. The eddies and cross-currents in Congress do not interrupt a flow of legislation that the public expects but fails to see. The electorate sees very little altogether of what goes on in the national legislature. Few judgments of legislative performance are associated with the parties, and much of the public is unaware even of which party has control of Congress. As a result, the absence of party discipline or legislative results is unlikely to bring down electoral sanctions on the ineffective party or the errant Congressman.

What the public's response to the parties lacks in programmatic support is not made up by its response to local congressional candidates. Although perceptions of individual candidates account for most of the votes cast by partisans against their parties, these perceptions are almost untouched by information about the policy stands of the men contesting the House seat. The increment of strength that some candidates, especially incumbents, acquire by being known to their constituents is almost entirely free of policy content. Were such content present, the Congressman's solidarity with his legislative party would by no means be assured. If the local constituency possessed far greater resources of information than it has, it might use the ballot to pry the Congressman away from his party quite as well as to unite him with it. Yet the fact is that, by plying his campaigning and servicing arts over the years, the Congressman is able to develop electoral strength that is almost totally dissociated from what his party wants in Congress and what he himself has done about it. The relevance of all this to the problem of cohesion and responsibility in the legislative party can scarcely be doubted.

The description of party irresponsibility in America should not be overdrawn. The American system *has* elements of party accountability to the public, although the issues on which an accounting is given are relatively few and the accounting is more often rendered by those who hold or seek the Presidency than by the parties' congressional delegations. Especially on the broad problem of government action to secure social and economic welfare it can be argued that the parties have real differences and that these have penetrated the party images to which the electorate responds at the polls.

Nevertheless, American practice does diverge widely from the model of party government, and the factors underlying the departure deserve close analysis. An implication of the analysis reported here is that the public's contribution to party irregularity in Congress is not so much a matter of encouraging or requiring its Representatives to deviate from their parties as it is of the public having so little information that the irregularity of Congressmen and the ineffectiveness of the congressional parties have scant impact at the polls. Many of those who have commented on the lack of party discipline in Congress have assumed that the Congressmen votes against his party because he is forced to by the demands of one of several hundred constituencies of a superlatively heterogeneous nation. In some cases, the Representative may subvert the proposals of his party because his constituency demands it. But a more reasonable interpretation over a broader range of issues is that the Congressman fails to see these proposals as part of a program on which the party—and he himself—will be judged at the polls, because he knows the constituency isn't looking.

## NOTES

1. The 116 districts are a probability sample of all constituencies, although the fact that the study was piggy-backed onto a four-year panel study of the electorate extending over the elections of 1956, 1958, and 1960 made the design of the 1958 representation sample unusually complex. In particular, since metropolitan areas and non-metropolitan counties or groups of counties, rather than congressional districts, were used as primary sampling units when the panel sample was originated in 1956, the districts represented in our 1958 sample did not have equal probability of selection and the efficiency of the sample of districts was somewhat less than that of a simple random sample of equal size. Descriptions of the sample design may be obtained from the Survey Research Center.

2. For example, the 1950 report of the American Political Science Association's Committee on Political Parties, the closest approach to an official statement of the responsible-party view as applied to American politics, concentrates on the organization of Congress and the national parties and deals only very obliquely with the role of the public. See *Toward a More Responsible Two-party System,* New York, Rinehart, 1950. In general, theoretical and empirical treatments of party government have focused more on the nature of party *appeals*—especially the question of whether the parties present a real "choice"—than on the cognitive and motivational elements that should be found in the *response* of an electorate that is playing its correct role in a system of responsible-party government. For example, see the excellent discussion in Austin Ranney and Wilmoore Kendall, *Democracy and the American Party System,* New York, Harcourt, Brace, 1956, pp. 151–152, 384–385, 525–527.

It should be clear that the data of this report are taken from a particular election of a particular electoral era. We would expect our principal findings to apply to most recent off-year elections, but they are of course subject to modification for earlier or later periods.

3. This assumption does not imply that pressures toward party cohesion come *only* from the mass public. Other sanctions against party irregularity are of equal or greater importance, especially those available in the nominating process and within the legislative parties themselves. To cite the most celebrated empirical case, the cohesiveness of the British parliamentary parties is not enforced primarily, if at all, by the British electorate. Nevertheless, the public ought not to give aid and comfort to the legislative party irregular; the idea of the candidate building a local bastion of strength from which he can challenge the party leadership is clearly contradictory to the party-government model.

4. See Angus Campbell, Philip E. Converse, Warren E. Miller, and Donald E. Stokes, *The American Voter,* New York, Wiley, 1960, p. 124.

5. For evidence on this point, see *ibid.,* pp. 120–167.

6. Plainly, some deduction has to be made for guessing. One model of the situation would be to think of the sample as composed of three types of people: those who knew, those who didn't know and said so, and those who didn't know but guessed. Assuming that for those who guessed $p = q = \frac{1}{2}$, where $p$ is the probability of guessing Republican, we would deduct from the Democratic answers a percentage equal to the 18 per cent who guessed Republican incorrectly, hence reducing the proportion of voters who really knew which party controlled Congress

to 43 per cent. This model may be too severe, however, in view of the presence of the Republican President. It may be more reasonable to admit a fourth type of person, those who did not guess but were misled by Republican control of the White House. Or we might think of the guessers as following a probability law in which $p > \frac{1}{2} > q$. In either of these cases something less than 18 per cent would be deducted from the Democratic answers; hence, the proportion of voters who *knew* which party controlled Congress would lie somewhere between 43 and 61 per cent.

7. A simple but persuasive comparison is this: from 1892 to 1960 the standard deviation of the two-party division of the mid-term congressional vote was 3.9 per cent; of the presidential-year congressional vote, 5.5 per cent; of the presidential vote, 8.2 per cent. Moreover, if the realignment of party loyalties that occurred in the early 1930's is taken into account by computing deviations from pre- and post-1932 means, rather than from a grand mean for the whole period, the standard deviation of the mid-term congressional vote is found to have been 2.4 per cent, compared with a standard deviation of 7.5 per cent for the presidential vote. Some of the remaining variability of the mid-term vote may be due to fluctuations of turnout that do not involve deviations from party. Yet, even ignoring this possibility, the bounds within which national political forces can have influenced the off-year vote by inducing deviations from party appear narrow indeed.

8. A remarkable fact is that while the total vote for the House increased by 3 million between 1954 and 1958, more than 2 million of this increase was contributed by New York, where Rockefeller sought the governorship; by Ohio, where a fierce referendum battle was fought over the issue of "right-to-work"; and by California, where the fantastic Knight-Knowland-Brown free-for-all was held.

9. This conclusion is fully supported by an analysis of the variance of turnout and party vote in the mid-term congressional elections of the 1950's. If state-wide races have a major influence on local House races, the election results for the several congressional districts of a state should vary together; similar changes of turnout and party division should be seen in the districts that are influenced by the same state-wide contests. An analysis of the variance of the differences between the 1954 and 1958 turnout level and partisan division for all congressional districts in states having at least two districts indicates that state races have a large effect on turnout; the intraclass correlation expressing the ratio of the between-state variance to the total variance of turnout was more than .45. But this analysis shows, too, that state-wide races have almost no effect whatever on the party division of the House vote; the intraclass correlation expressing the ratio of the between-state variance to the total variance of the party division was not more than .02.

10. See V. O. Key, Jr., *Southern Politics,* New York, Knopf, 1949, pp. 37 ff. We have demonstrated the "friends and neighbors" effect in terms of candidate salience because of our interest in the policy content of candidate perceptions. However, owing to the impact of salience on the vote, living in the same community with the candidate has a clear effect on voting as well.

# 18. Lobbying as a Communication Process *

## LESTER W. MILBRATH

Lobbyists and their activities have traditionally been of interest to political scientists because they play a role in the governmental decision process. But just what is that role? Or, to put the question in a more researchable fashion, what kind of model can the analyst apply to their activities which will provide the most accurate perspective on their role? The answer to this question must be derived from the larger frame of reference of the over-all governmental decision process.

Social scientists have approached the analysis of governmental decision making from several different perspectives. For example, some analysts have approached it from the perspective of the role of groups in the process.[1] Others have done research which seemed to indicate that governmental decisions are made by a select power elite,[2] although the elite theory has been challenged by other scholars.[3] One could catalog additional perspectives on the process, some of which are very provocative,[4] but that is not the purpose of this paper. The purpose, rather, is to present an alternative perspective on the process which may provide some new insights and also lead to a communication model for analyzing the lobbying aspects of the process.

The perspective on the lobbying process reported here is gained from a sample survey of Washington lobbyists. The study focused primarily on lobbyists as individuals who comprise a political skill group rather than on the nature and power of the groups which they represent, as most other studies of lobbying have done. The universe from which the sample was selected included all the individuals with Washington addresses who registered as lobbyists with the Clerk of the House and Secretary of the Senate during the first two quarters of 1956 (the most recent period prior to the field-work phase of the study). One hundred and fourteen names were randomly selected from the total universe of 614; I succeeded in interviewing 101 of these individuals. These interviews were supplemented by interviews with 38 people in Congress, in order to get the perspective of the recipient of lobbying.

The confidential interviews averaged about two hours in length and covered such topics as the occupational history of the respondent; how he happened to get into lobbying; how well he likes the role he plays; what his political background was; what his socio-economic background was; how he relates to his employer; what role he plays in relation to the government; what tactics and techniques he uses and prefers for communicating with government decision makers; and how

* From *The Public Opinion Quarterly,* Vol. 24 (1960), pp. 32–53. Reprinted by permission.

he evaluates the lobbying process and the role he plays in it. Finally, each respondent was asked to fill out a short personality test.[5]

Under the American system of government, certain individuals, occupying certain governmental offices, are charged by the Constitution with making decisions which in effect lay down the policies for the country and which have the force of governmental authority and finality behind them. I am thinking mainly here of the President, the members of the Supreme Court, and the members of Congress. The charge has been made that the decisions pronouncd by these persons essentially are not their own, but rather they are merely parroting the decisions made by individuals and groups upon whom they are dependent for support. In one sense, close attention to the desires of supporters is considered laudable in a representative democracy. On the other hand, we are distressed if it seems that the decision maker is following the desires of some special interest and ignoring the general welfare.

Although students of politics have been making educated guesses for some time about the propensity for decision makers to follow either the general welfare or someone's special welfare, a clear-cut discernment of the influence of such factors as pressure-group activity or political money upon governmental decision makers can come only from detailed examination of the decision processes of these individuals. Unhappily, it is an extraordinarily difficult research problem to ascertain the bases for judgment made by these decision makers. Even if the researcher had free access to decision makers within a context of mutual trust and thirst for truth, it is highly unlikely that these persons could plumb their unconscious and dredge up all the factors that entered into any given decision. Detailed examination of the psychological processes of a decision maker concerning a given decision would probably, at least at this stage of social science, get bogged down in a mass of unanalyzable detail. Thus, it is not my purpose to present an analytical scheme for assessing the influence of lobbying on the governmental decision process.

My purpose, rather, is to build upon our general knowledge of decision making to construct a framework showing how lobbying fits into, or plays a role in, the over-all governmental decision process. In decision-making theory, an almost universally accepted concept is that a decision maker must have access to ideas, arguments, information, and so forth, before these factors can figure in his decision. Another concept of decision making suggests, however, that mere accessibility is not enough. Every person has a set of predispositions that derive from a variety of sources, such as conditioned learning experiences, which includes the whole of a person's background as well as the internalized role constraints of his present situation, physiological needs, and inherited physical characteristics and capabilities. These personal predispositions are enduring rather than transitory and condition the behavior of people on a long-term basis, so that we say everyone has a personality. We recognize this when we apply to people such adjectives as liberal, conservative, manipulative, submissive, sociable, cynical, and so forth.

The important thing about predispositions, for our analysis, is that they provide a perceptual screen for each individual. Some stimuli are allowed to pass through the screen, while others are stopped. It is a well-known phenomenon that different people viewing the same event may perceive it quite differently. The chairmen of our respective political parties almost invariably arrive at a different interpretation of the factors creating the outcome of an election. Anyone reading Congressional hearings extensively must arrive at the conclusion that most members of Congress hear what they want to hear from a witness. The process by which selected stimuli are allowed to pass through the perceptual screen can be referred to as "receptivity."

Anyone wishing to influence the decision of a governmental official, then, must be concerned not only with getting the information to him but also with the problem of presenting it so that the decision maker will be receptive. The only effective communications are those which get through the perceptual screen. In fact, there is no other way to influence governmental decisions short of remaking the personalities of decision makers or replacing them with other persons. The lobbying process, then, is essentially a communication process, and the task of the lobbyist is to figure out how he can handle communications most effectively in order to get through to decision makers.

Although many lobbyists did not use communication terminology, it was clear that most conceived of their job as one of communication. As the interviews progressed, it seemed that lobbyist communications tended to fall in three categories: facts, arguments, and power. As merchants of information, lobbyists generally have a factual base for their message; especially they provide facts about how a contemplated action will affect the group represented. Because of the constraints of the relationship between lobbyist and decision maker (to be discussed later), most lobbyists take particular pains never to present anything but accurate facts.

Lobbyists do not depend on facts alone; almost invariably the facts are accompanied by a set of arguments concerning the rightness, wisdom, or justice of the proposed action. Most lobbyists readily admit that these arguments usually present only one side of an issue, but they justify this on the ground that the decision maker knows the source and is likely to get arguments on the other side from opposing groups. Some lobbyists try to take a posture of objectivity by presenting arguments on both sides of the question, although generally they are also careful that the balance lie in their favor.

Much more difficult and subtle is the task of communicating power. While we recognize that for some officials re-election is not paramount, the majority of elective officials show great respect for power at the polls. In its rawest form, this power can be communicated by defeating an incumbent and substituting a new official who, persumably, will act favorably toward the concerns of the group which put him over. Most lobby groups do not have this much power to throw around and, furthermore, it is a rather crude and expensive way to communicate, especially since some competing group or coalition is likely to press vigorously in opposition.

Most lobbyists try to comunicate power without going to the trouble and expense of defeating someone at the polls. The accent is on subtlety, because an overt threat to defeat an official at the next election unless he "goes along" may serve only to stiffen his resistance. A forthright offer of campaign money to a cooperating decision maker might be used to smear the donor rather than accomplish its intended purpose. The much-publicized contribution to Senator Case of South Dakota from a natural gas lobbyist in early 1956 is an example. Even such a tactic as publicizing the voting records of incumbent members of Congress is looked upon as foolhardy by many lobbyists and resented by many members. Lobbyists prefer to approach officials through constituents, stimulate letter writing, put on a public relations campaign, and collaborate with other groups, as more subtle devices for communicating power.

In addition to its threatening aspects, power can be used in a supportive or positive way. A legislator may be assured of enthusiastic support at the next election by a large membership group as a reward for promotion of a policy that the group wanted. Power has another facet too: it is not only a relationship about which information can be communicated, but it is also a strong factor influencing decision makers to keep open channels of communication to groups which hold power. Officials keep open channels of communication for other affective reasons also, such as good will, rapport, rewards for service or favors, and so forth, but political power is a factor they may ignore only at considerable peril.

The lobbyists in this sample were asked to evaluate a series of tactics and techniques for communicating with decision makers. These tactics can be divided into three broad categories for analytical purposes: (1) techniques for direct personal communication between the lobbyist and decision maker, (2) techniques for communication through intermediaries, and (3) techniques for keeping channels of communication open. Although these materials have not yet been exhaustively analyzed, the analysis is far enough along to make possible some general comparisons.

### Direct Personal Communication

One assumption behind the practice of sending to the capital personal envoys of groups is that direct personal communication is more effective than written communication in gaining access and is more likely to reach the decision maker when he is in a receptive frame of mind.[6] The presence of a personal envoy at the capital normally tends to give one group a competitive advantage over another without an envoy. As a result, an ever-increasing number of groups have sent such envoys. Now, however, there are such a great number and variety of lobbyists competing for the limited time and attention of the decision makers that the Washington atmosphere has been characterized by some observers as filled with hustle and noise. One result of this competition is that lobbying resources are being diverted from direct communication toward communication through intermediaries who are believed to have better access. Indeed, there are many instances of successful lobbyists who have little or no direct contact with governmental decision makers. Seventy-five per cent of the lobbyists spent less than 10 per cent of their time calling on members of Congress and no more than another 10 per cent calling on staff assistants to decision makers.

*Personal Presentation of Arguments.* Despite this shift toward communication through intermediaries, lobbyists tend to believe that their most effective tactic is the personal presentation of their case to the officerholder, provided they can get in to see him or get him on the phone.[7] Out of the 101 lobbyists interviewed, 65 chose this technique as the one they prefer and generally follow. It is curious that lobbyists spend such a small part of their time calling on members of Congress or their staffs if this tactic is considered so effective. There are several reasons for this. Preparations for these presentations must be careful and thus consume some time in addition to all the other tasks of lobbyists. (About three-fourths of the lobbyists spend more than 40 per cent of their time in the office.) Another factor is that lobbying is only one of the responsibilities of most people who register. In addition to lobbying, they may be executives of their organization; act as a liaison between their organization and the executive department of government; carry on a law practice with a variety of clients, many of whom do not have legislative problems; and so forth. But perhaps the most important reason is that lobbyists must be careful not to "carry their pitcher to the well too often," as one Congressman put it. Most lobbyists perceive that they must save up their good will and access for a time when they want to see the decision maker about something really important. One lobbyist expressed it this way: "I figure I am doing them a favor by not inviting them out to dinner and by not calling on them until I really need something."

All the lobbyists were asked to rate the fourteen communication tactics discussed in this paper on a general scale running from 0 not effective at all to 10 for very effective. These tactics were evaluated primarily as devices for communicating with legislators; however, several are also applicable to communications with decision makers in the executive branch. The scale was presented visually in this form: 0__1__2__3__4__5__6__7__8__9__10, and the techniques to be rated were listed underneath it. Fifty-eight of the lobbyists rated personal presentation of arguments at 10 (or very effective), and the mean score for the entire group was 8.43 (see Table 1).[8] This technique rated higher than any other. When mean ratings

TABLE 1. RATINGS OF DIRECT PERSONAL COMMUNICATION: NUMBER IN EACH CATEGORY

| Rating | Personal Presentation of Arguments | Presentation of Research Results | Testifying at Hearings |
|---|---|---|---|
| 0 | 2 | 5 | 3 |
| 1 | 1 | 2 | 3 |
| 2 | 3 | 1 | 3 |
| 3 | 1 | 7 | 6 |
| 4 | 2 | 2 | 3 |
| 5 | 7 | 9 | 24 |
| 6 | 2 | 5 | 9 |
| 7 | 1 | 3 | 3 |
| 8 | 15 | 17 | 15 |
| 9 | 7 | 13 | 6 |
| 10 | 58 | 35 | 24 |
| Median | 9.15 | 7.91 | 5.83 |
| Mean | 8.43 | 7.40 | 6.55 |
| No response[a] | 15 | 15 | 15 |

[a] Includes 13 in the total sample of 114 who were not interviewed at all.

are broken down by the type of organization the lobbyist represents, and then ranked (see Table 2), we discover that personal presentation of arguments is given first rank by all except the representatives of farm groups, church and humanitarian groups, and foreign governments or firms, and even here arguments usually ranked very high.

The personal presentations discussed here are generally oral and incorporate both facts and arguments. Most members of Congress prefer that this statement be very brief and merely summarize the main points. Many lobbyists follow the practice of leaving a short written summary behind for future reference and thus

TABLE 2. RANK ORDER OF MEAN RATINGS OF DIRECT PERSONAL COMMUNICATION, BY GROUP REPRESENTED

| | Personal Presentation of Arguments | | Presentation of Research Results | | Testifying at Hearings | |
|---|---|---|---|---|---|---|
| Group | Rank | Mean Rating | Rank | Mean Rating | Rank | Mean Rating |
| Big labor (N=9) | 1 | 8.3 | 7 | 6.1 | 6 | 6.4 |
| Small labor (N=7) | 1 | 9.3 | 2 | 9.0 | 4 | 7.4 |
| Big farm (N=2) | 7 | 5.0 | 3ᵃ | 7.5 | 3ᵃ | 7.5 |
| Small farm (N=3) | 5 | 7.3 | 1 | 8.7 | 6 | 6.7 |
| Big trade assoc. (N=8) | 1 | 9.5 | 2 | 7.1 | 3 | 4.7 |
| Small trade assoc. (N=40) | 1 | 9.8 | 2 | 7.4 | 3 | 7.2 |
| Corporations (N=14) | 3 | 7.0 | 5 | 6.3 | 4 | 6.7 |
| Citizens' organizations (N=5) | 3 | 6.5 | 4 | 6.0 | 1 | 8.0 |
| Church and humanitarian (N=2) | 3 | 6.5 | 4 | 6.0 | 1 | 8.0 |
| More than one type (N=5) | 1 | 8.6 | 2 | 7.4 | 4 | 6.4 |

ᵃPresentation of research results and testifying at hearings were tied.

save the decision maker, or his staff, the trouble of taking notes. Most people in Congress report that they prefer that personal presentations be informative, unbiased, clear, short, sincere, and unaccompanied by pressure. The threat implied in pressure is painful, and persons who use it will be shunned when they try to gain access in the future. Members of Congress are also skeptical of lobbyists who play the role of advocate without personal conviction about the arguments they present. Members frequently probe for personal conviction and drastically discount the presentations of those who are mere advocates. Lobby groups guard against this by "sidelining" a lobbyist who does not share a particular policy position with the group he represents.

*Presenting Research Results.* The lobbyists were also asked to rate the presentation of research results. Most of them conceived of this as an integral part of arguments and had difficulty evaluating it separately. On the other hand, some lobbyists made little effort to bolster their arguments with research, either because they felt that their problem was not amenable to research or because they felt the research would not be respected. The representatives of large labor organizations and large trade associations ranked research considerably below arguments. Farm representatives, on the other hand, ranked research above arguments. *Post hoc* reasoning suggests that large labor and trade have sufficient membership to rate tactics related to politics (collaboration with other groups, constituent contact, letters, etc.) above research. Farm representatives with large memberships also rate these tactics highly, but they still place research above arguments. There is a deep-seated respect for research in the farming industry, and it may be that this colored their response to this tactic.

If one breaks down these mean ratings by the relation of the lobbyist to his employer (Table 3), one sees, interestingly, that legislative relations staff persons, who are generally in closer contact with Congress than those in other roles, place

TABLE 3. RANK ORDER OF MEAN RATINGS OF DIRECT PERSONAL COMMUNICATION, BY RELATION OF LOBBYIST TO HIS EMPLOYER

| Role of Lobbyist | Presentation of Arguments | | Presentation of Research Results | | Testifying at Hearings | |
|---|---|---|---|---|---|---|
| | Rank | Mean Rating | Rank | Mean Rating | Rank | Mean Rating |
| Trade association executive (N=19) | 1 | 8.2 | 2[a] | 6.9 | 5 | 6.0 |
| Officer of organization (N=6) | 1[b] | 9.0 | 1[b] | 9.0 | 6 | 6.5 |
| Legislative relations staff (N=12) | 2 | 7.8 | 7 | 6.2 | 4 | 7.0 |
| Legislative and executive relations staff (N=17) | 1 | 9.1 | 4 | 7.2 | 2 | 7.4 |
| Washington representative (N=16) | 1 | 9.1 | 2 | 7.9 | 3[c] | 6.3 |
| Lawyer, legal firm (N=8) | 2 | 7.5 | 3 | 7.0 | 1 | 7.6 |
| Lawyer, free-lance (N=13) | 1 | 8.1 | 2 | 7.5 | 3 | 5.7 |
| General counsel in organization (N=3) | 1 | 9.7 | 2 | 8.3 | 6 | 6.3 |
| Public relations counsel (N=2) | 4[d] | 5.0 | 2 | 6.5 | 2[e] | 6.5 |
| Lobbyist entrepreneur (N=3) | 1 | 10.0 | 2 | 9.3 | 3 | 6.0 |

[a] Tied with collaboration with other groups

[b] Personal presentation of arguments and representation of research results were tied.

[c] Tied with contact by constituent.

[d] Tied with public relations campaigns.

[e] Presentation of research results and testifying at hearings were tied.

less than average emphasis on research. They place greater emphasis on collaboration, constituent contact, hearings, letters, and so forth (see Tables 6 and 9). The generally close relationship between research and arguments, however, is shown in Table 1. Research has an over-all mean rating of 7.4, slightly lower than for arguments, but still higher than the rating for other techniques.

*Testifying at Hearings.* In contrast with presentation of one's case to a single person, most lobbyists rated testifying at hearings somewhat lower. Only 24 gave it a rating of 10, and the mean for the entire group was 6.55. The rank orders shown in Tables 2 and 3 disclose that hearings are ranked up close to arguments and research by most groups. They are about on a par with collaboration and constituent contact (Tables 5 and 6). Interestingly, the mean rating of hearings by corporations was only 4.7, lower than that of any other group; yet the rank order was 3 (above all other techniques except arguments and research), so one might surmise that corporation representatives have a generally more pessimistic view of most of the remaining techniques than do the people representing other kinds of organization.

Since hearings are formal procedures available to nearly anyone wanting to get his point of view before Congress and require only a single presentation, why is it that they are not the clearly preferred technique? Most lobbyists perceive that members of Congress give sporadic attention, at best, to hearing testimony. Furthermore, they are aware that many members of committees have already made up their minds before the hearings begin and there is little the lobbyist can say that will influence them. Another factor is that many hearings are held when only one member of the committee is present, to say nothing of the absence from hearings of all the other members of the House who are not on the committee. Although printed hearing records are available to members of Congress (also to the public), the average member does not have the time to read them. Despite the limitations of this means of communication, most lobbyists dare not forego an invitation to go on record favoring or opposing a particular course of action. There is always the possibility that some decision maker will read their testimony; it is an opportunity for some free publicity; and it is a useful way for the lobbyist to demonstrate to the membership that he is earning his salary. In other words, most lobbyists feel they are expected to testify, or have someone from their group testify, and therefore they nearly always do.

### Communication Through Intermediaries

Although lobbying connotes personal representation before government, a far-reaching effort to influence policy making must include communication with decision makers through intermediaries. The intermediaries chosen almost invariably have some special relationship to the decision maker, either a constituent relationship or a close personal relationship. Constituents can be urged to communicate with government in two basic ways. Voting is an indirect but very effective medium of communication. Even if an endorsed candidate does not win, a strong showing of votes indicates the desires and power potential of a large bloc of the incumbent's constituents. The second type of communication is the conventional written or oral message transmitted from the citizen ot people in government. Communications through intermediaries are, like the personal presentations of the lobbyist, also designed to communicate facts, arguments, and power. They are especially instrumental in communicating power.

*Contact by Constituent and Friend.* If the lobbyist believes that he will have difficulty getting an appointment with an elected official, or that the official will listen with a closed ear, he may attempt to communicate through a constituent whom he thinks the official respects. The constituent may be asked to phone the officeholder and set up an appointment for the lobbyist or he may be asked to present the case himself. Sometimes the constituent hastens to Washington and spends a few days calling on his representatives.[9]

The constituent is generally preferred over other intermediaries such as close friends of the decision maker. This is because many lobbyists feel the power relationship between constituent and officeholder more adequately ensures receptiveness to the communication. This is reflected in the tactic rankings shown in Table 5. The representatives of large membership groups with potential political power (big labor, farm, big trade, church and humanitarian) give constituent contact a much higher rating than friend contact; whereas the representatives of other groups give them more equal ratings. It is also reflected in Table 6, where the highest ratings for constituent contact are given by legislative relations people whose jobs take them into closest contact with Congress. The over-all picture is reported in Table 4, where we see that 24 lobbyists gave a rating of 10 to contact

TABLE 4. RATINGS OF COMMUNICATION THROUGH INTERMEDIARIES: NUMBER IN EACH CATEGORY

| Rating | Contact by Constituents | Contact by Close Freind | Letter and Telegram Campaigns | Public Relations Campaigns | Publicizing Voting Records |
|---|---|---|---|---|---|
| 0 | 14 | 26 | 20 | 21 | 49 |
| 1 | 3 | 5 | 6 | 2 | 8 |
| 2 | 6 | 8 | 6 | 2 | 12 |
| 3 | 8 | 13 | 5 | 3 | 5 |
| 4 | 2 | 3 | 7 | 2 | 4 |
| 5 | 11 | 15 | 19 | 15 | 8 |
| 6 | 7 | 6 | 1 | 2 | 2 |
| 7 | 4 | 6 | 7 | 11 | 4 |
| 8 | 8 | 6 | 17 | 17 | 2 |
| 9 | 12 | 5 | 4 | 5 | 2 |
| 10 | 24 | 5 | 7 | 17 | 2 |
| Median | 5.79 | 2.77 | 4.29 | 6.14 | 1.00 |
| Mean | 5.90 | 3.76 | 4.55 | 5.55 | 2.05 |
| No response[a] | 15 | 16 | 15 | 17 | 16 |

[a] Includes 13 in the total sample of 114 who were not interviewed at all.

by a constituent, whereas only 5 rated contact by a friend that highly. The mean rating for contact by a constituent was 5.9, and for a friend it was only 3.76. The difference in evaluation introduced by the political-power variable is also reflected in the greater variance shown for the constituent contact rating than for the friend contact rating.

*Letter and Telegram Campaigns.* A time-honored lobbying technique is the stimulation of a mass letter-writing and telegram campaign from constituents to their representatives. Most people in Congress are skilled at spotting form letters or telegrams which are inspired by some organization. They are likely to ignore or discount such a campaign on the ground that it does not accurately represent sentiment in the constituency; on the other hand, if the letters come in a deluge, they must pay attention because of the political weight they represent. Some members may move to counteract the campaign by sending out a mailing to the constituents in an attempt to inform them about the member's position, or they may request an opposing organization to turn out an equal or greater number of letters on the other side, leaving the representative free to vote as he chooses. Lobbyists are aware of these barriers to letters, and the mass campaign is not as widely used as it once was. Those who do use a letter or telegram campaign are generally careful to instruct their people to write each communication individually, speaking their personal thoughts on the subject. The lobbyist's calculation is that the representative will heed such a communication as a true reflection of sentiment.

There was a good deal of variation in the way lobbyists evaluated letter campaigns (Table 4): 20 gave it a 0 and 7 gave it a 10. Big labor and big farm lobbyists gave it higher rankings than other lobbyists did (Table 5). This suggests that organizations with a mass membership enabling them to turn out thousands of letters are more likely to believe that the tactic is effective. Corporation repre-

TABLE 5. RANK ORDER OF MEAN RATINGS OF COMMUNICATION THROUGH INTERMEDIARIES, BY TYPE OF GROUP REPRESENTED

| Group | Contact by Constituents | | Contact by Close Friend | | Letter and Telegram Campaigns | | Public Relations Campaigns | | Publicizing Voting Records | |
|---|---|---|---|---|---|---|---|---|---|---|
| | Rank | Mean Rating | Rank | Mean Rating | Rank | Mean Rating | Rank | Mean Rating | Rank | Mean Rating |
| Big labor (N=9) | 3 | 7.6 | 8 | 5.1 | 4 | 7.2 | 5 | 6.8 | 9 | 4.6 |
| Small labor (N=7) | 9 | 3.0 | 8 | 3.9 | 10 | 2.0 | 3 | 7.9 | 6a | 5.0 |
| Big farm (N=2) | 6 | 6.0 | 11b | 0 | 1 | 8.5 | 2 | 8.0 | 8c | 4.0 |
| Small farm (N=3) | 2d | 7.7 | 9 | 4.7 | 8 | 5.7 | 2d | 7.7 | 7 | 6.3 |
| Big trade association (N=8) | 2 | 7.9 | 7 | 5.0 | 8 | 3.9 | 4 | 6.8 | 13 | 1.4 |
| Small trade association (N=40) | 5 | 6.5 | 8 | 3.4 | 7 | 5.3 | 6 | 5.9 | 12 | 1.3 |
| Corporations (N=14) | 5 | 3.4 | 7 | 2.6 | 10 | 1.7 | 6 | 2.7 | 13 | .9 |
| Citizens' organizations (N=5) | 7 | 3.8 | 5 | 5.8 | 9 | 3.0 | 4 | 6.2 | 8 | 3.4 |
| Church and humanitarian (N=3) | 1 | 8.7 | 8 | 5.0 | 6 | 5.7 | 7 | 5.3 | 11 | 1.5 |
| Foreign government or firm (N=2) | 7 | 3.0 | 6 | 4.0 | 11e | .5 | 9f | 1.5 | 11e | .5 |
| More than one type (N=5) | 3 | 7.0 | 6 | 4.0 | 8 | 3.0 | 7 | 3.2 | 13g | 0 |

[a] Tied with campaign work.
[b] Contact with close friend, entertaining, giving a party, and bribery were all rated 0.
[c] Tied with contributing political money and campaign work.
[d] Contact by constituents, public relations campaigns, and collaboration with other groups were tied.
[e] Letters and telegram campaigns, publicizing voting records and contributing political money were tied.
[f] Tied with campaign work.
[g] Publicizing voting records and bribery were both rated 0.

sentatives and lobbyists for foreign governments or firms, with no mass membership behind them, ranked letters below the average. In Table 6 we see that those more intimately associated with a given organization (officers and staff) tended to rank letters higher than those in a more peripheral relationship (lawyers, "PR" men, etc.).

*Public Relations Campaigns.* A very expensive and indirect method of communication is the public relations campaign. The supposition is that if enough people favor the viewpoint of the organization sponsoring the campaign, this viewpoint, and the power behind it, will be communicated in various ways to Congress and the Administration. It is also hoped that the campaign will have long-range effects

TABLE 6. RANK ORDER OF MEAN RATINGS OF COMMUNICATION THROUGH INTER-
MEDIARIES, BY RELATION OF LOBBYIST TO HIS EMPLOYER

| Role of Lobbyist | Contact by Constituents | | Contact by Close Friend | | Letter and Telegrams Campaigns | | Public Relations Campaigns | | Publicizing Voting Records | |
|---|---|---|---|---|---|---|---|---|---|---|
| | Rank | Mean Rating | Rank | Mean Rating | Rank | Mean Rating | Rank | Mean Rating | Rank | Mean Rating |
| Trade association executive (N=19) | 7 | 4.3 | 8 | 3.2 | 6 | 5.5 | 4 | 6.1 | 12 | 1.2 |
| Officer of organization (N=16) | 7 | 6.2 | 8 | 4.2 | 5 | 7.5 | 3 | 7.8 | 9[a] | 2.8 |
| Legislative relations staff (N=12) | 3 | 7.5 | 8 | 4.5 | 5 | 6.8 | 6 | 6.7 | 9 | 4.2 |
| Legislative and executive relations staff (N=17) | 3 | 7.3 | 7 | 4.8 | 8 | 3.7 | 6 | 6.3 | 10 | 2.2 |
| Washington representative (N=16) | 3[b] | 6.3 | 8 | 4.4 | 6 | 5.4 | 5 | 5.8 | 9 | 2.8 |
| Lawyer, legal firm (N=8) | 4 | 5.4 | 9[c] | 1.6 | 9[c] | 1.6 | 6 | 3.1 | 11 | .6 |
| Lawyer, free-lance (N=13) | 5 | 5.4 | 9 | 2.3 | 7 | 2.9 | 6 | 3.9 | 13 | 1.1 |
| General counsel in organization (N=3) | 4 | 7.0 | 3 | 8.0 | 7[d] | 3.0 | 7[d] | 3.0 | 11 | 1.3 |
| Public relations counsel (N=2) | 1 | 7.0 | 9[e] | 2.5 | 12 | .5 | 4[f] | 5.0 | 13[g] | 0 |
| Lobbyist entrepreneur (N=3) | 11 | 1.3 | 9 | 2.0 | 6[h] | 3.0 | 5 | 3.3 | 10 | 1.7 |

[a] Tied with entertaining.
[b] Tied with testifying at hearings.
[c] Contact with close friend and letter and telegram campaigns were tied.
[d] Letters and public relations campaigns were tied.
[e] Tied with giving a party.
[f] Tied with personal presentation of arguments.
[g] Publicizing voting records and bribery were both rated 0.
[h] Tied with contributing political money.

on the voting behavior of the public and thus find policy expression through the selection of governmental decision makers. Since the effects of a PR campaign are so diffuse and delayed, they are extraordinarily difficult to measure. This is reflected in the wide variance in the lobbyists' ratings: 17 gave it a rating of 10 and 21 gave it a rating of 0 (Table 4).

The over-all mean rating for PR campaigns was 5.55, slightly higher than for letter campaigns, yet the pattern of response was very similar to that for letter campaigns. Mass-membership farm and labor lobbyists gave it the highest ratings, while church and humanitarian and foreign government or firm lobbyists gave it the lowest. Lawyers gave it a lower rating than did those closely tied into an organization, while officers of organizations gave it the highest rating. It is interesting that some lobbyists felt that the tactic had utility even though they were not sure their message was getting through to the public, not to mention getting from the public back to the decision makers. They reasoned that the decision makers are quite likely to conclude that the campaign is very persuasive and convincing many people how they should vote. Therefore, the decision maker may possibly alter his behavior in the desired way in anticipation of the reaction from his constituents, without receiving direct communication from many of them.

*Publicizing Voting Records.* Like the public relations campaign, the publicizing of voting records is a device for stimulating communications from the people to their representatives. (Both tactics are also used to generate political power, which has utility for keeping open channels of communication to decision makers.) Organizations which have considerable power at the polls (labor, farm, and large citizens' organizations) believe that the method is moderately efficacious (Table 5), while lobbyists from nearly all the other groups rate the method as almost worthless. In fact, many lobbyists actually view the method as dangerous, since a member of Congress whose voting record has been reported unfavorably is likely to resent it and may close the door to them in the future. Many lobbyists and members of Congress felt that voting records are misleading, because they do not accurately assess the over-all performance of a member.

### Opening Communication Channels

We noted above that it was just as important to the lobbyist to keep his channels of communication to decision makers open as it was to transmit the communications themselves. Lobbyists give a lot of attention to this problem and guide their behavior so as to create and maintain the open channel. There is a recognized *quid pro quo* relationship between lobbyist and decision maker. The lobbyist can provide information and perform certain chores that the decision maker desires. Several of the people in Congress that I interviewed reported that they lined up lobby groups as reinforcements to strengthen their side in policy battles. This practice is so prevalent that it is difficult to discover who is using whom in most instances. The *quid pro quo* for providing services that the decision maker wants is that he will lend a sympathetic ear when the lobbyist has a problem he wants to present. Mutual confidence is the lubrication which ensures the smooth working of this relationship. The official decision maker has the upper hand, however, in that he alone has the power to pass out the policy rewards that the lobbyist wants and can turn to many alternative sources for the services he wants. Access and a confidential relationship with officials are so crucial to the task of the lobbyist that most astute lobbyists would not consider jeopardizing them in any way. Many decision makers use their superior position to guide their relationships with lobbyists and will specify the conditions under which lobbyists are welcome. If the lobbyist does not conform to these expectations, the decision maker will discard him and turn to someone on whom he can depend. Interestingly, many lobbyists welcome these prescriptions for access because they give structure to a highly unstructured role and give them security in job performance.

One specific result of this relationship is that very little inaccurate information is presented by lobbyists to public officials. The harried decision maker frequently utilizes information provided by lobbyists, sometimes without double-checking, in speeches or other public communications. If the information should later prove to be false, or biased to the point of serious distortions, the decision maker is publicly embarrassed and is likely to retaliate by cutting off further access sought by the delinquent lobbyist. Another facet of this relationship is that lobbyists generally are scrupulously careful not to disclose things which are told to them in confidence by a decision maker; the cost of disclosure would be the cutting off of access.

*Entertaining and Parties.* One of the popular conceptions of the lobbying process is that most lobbyists depend on entertainment and parties to keep open the channels of communication to decision makers. The assumption here is that the official will be grateful for the favor and, therefore, will be receptive to the communications of the lobbyist. Almost the reverse is true. Officials feel they must attend a certain number of "required" social events and this, coupled with other responsibilities, places them under such time pressure that an evening spent at home with the family seems like a gift. Under such conditions, an invitation by a lobbyist to "do the town" is anything but welcome. Lobbyists are aware that entertainment is an imposition, and it is used very little as a device to keep the channels of communication open.

Nearly all the lobbyists rated both techniques very low (Table 7). Forty-seven

TABLE 7. RATINGS OF METHODS OF OPENING COMMUNICATION CHANNELS: NUMBER IN EACH CATEGORY

| Rating | Entertaining | Giving a Party | Bribery | Contributing Money | Campaign Work | Collaboration with Other Groups |
|---|---|---|---|---|---|---|
| 0 | 47 | 56 | 98 | 58 | 54 | 12 |
| 1 | 15 | 14 | 0 | 5 | 6 | 5 |
| 2 | 14 | 11 | 0 | 5 | 7 | 0 |
| 3 | 7 | 3 | 0 | 8 | 6 | 6 |
| 4 | 4 | 5 | 0 | 7 | 3 | 3 |
| 5 | 4 | 7 | 0 | 4 | 5 | 13 |
| 6 | 1 | 0 | 0 | 2 | 1 | 4 |
| 7 | 5 | 1 | 0 | 1 | 5 | 13 |
| 8 | 2 | 2 | 0 | 3 | 5 | 12 |
| 9 | 0 | 0 | 0 | 4 | 1 | 11 |
| 10 | 0 | 0 | 1 | 2 | 6 | 20 |
| Median | 1.17 | .88 | .51 | .85 | .92 | 6.50 |
| Mean | 1.59 | 1.24 | .10 | 1.88 | 2.28 | 6.16 |
| No response[a] | 15 | 15 | 15 | 15 | 15 | 15 |

[a]Includes 13 in the total sample of 114 who were not interviewed at all.

gave a rating of 0 to entertainment, and the mean for the group was 1.59. Interestingly, officers of organizations, who generally have more prestige than the average lobbyist and a less restricted expense account, gave entertainment a higher rating than did those in other roles, but even here the mean was only 2.8 (Table 9). Giving a party was felt to have even less utility; 56 rated it 0 and the mean was only 1.24. Only foreign governments or firms and church and humanitarian representatives ranked it much above next to the last place (Table 8).

TABLE 8. RANK ORDER OF MEAN RATINGS OF OPENING COMMUNICATION CHANNELS, BY GROUP REPRESENTED

| Group | Entertaining | | Giving a Party | | Bribery | | Contributing Money | | Campaign Work | | Collaboration with Other Groups | |
|---|---|---|---|---|---|---|---|---|---|---|---|---|
| | Rank | Mean Rating | Rank | Mean Rating | Rank | Mean Rating | Rank | Mean Rating | Rank | Mean Rating | Rank | Mean Rating |
| Big labor (N=9) | 11 | 2.4 | 13 | 1.2 | 14 | 0 | 12 | 2.3 | 10 | 2.6 | 2 | 7.7 |
| Small labor (N=7) | 12 | 1.3 | 13 | .4 | 14 | 0 | 11 | 1.7 | 6 | 5.0 | 5 | 6.6 |
| Big farm (N=2) | 11[b] | 0 | 11[b] | 0 | 11[b] | 0 | 8[c] | 4.0 | 8[c] | 4.0 | 5 | 7.0 |
| Small farm (N=3) | 10[d] | 1.7 | 10[d] | 1.7 | 12[e] | 0 | 12[e] | 0 | 12[e] | 0 | 2[f] | 7.7 |
| Big trade association (N=8) | 9 | 2.1 | 10[g] | 1.8 | 14 | 0 | 10[g] | 1.8 | 10[g] | 1.8 | 3 | 6.9 |
| Small trade association (N=40) | 11 | 1.4 | 13 | 1.2 | 14 | 0 | 10 | 2.0 | 9 | 2.3 | 4 | 6.6 |
| Corporations (N=14) | 11 | 1.3 | 12 | 1.2 | 14 | .7 | 8 | 2.0 | 9 | 1.9 | 4 | 3.6 |
| Citizens' organizations (N=15) | 11[h] | 2.5 | 13 | 1.8 | 14 | 0 | 11[h] | 2.5 | 10 | 2.6 | 6 | 5.4 |
| Church and humanitarian (N=3) | 10 | 2.3 | 9 | 3.3 | 14 | 0 | 12 | 1.0 | 13 | .7 | 2 | 7.7 |
| Foreign government or firm (N=2) | 5 | 5.0 | 8 | 2.5 | 14 | 0 | 11[i] | .5 | 9[j] | 1.5 | 2 | 7.0 |
| More than one type (N=5) | 11 | .4 | 12 | .2 | 13[k] | 0 | 10 | 1.0 | 9 | 1.4 | 5 | 5.0 |

[a] Tied with publicizing voting records.
[b] Contact by a friend, entertaining, giving a party, and bribery were all rated 0.
[c] Publicizing voting records, contributing money, and campaign work were tied.
[d] Entertaining and giving a party were tied.
[e] Bribery, contributing money, and campaign work were all rated 0.
[f] Tied with contact by a constituent and public relations campaigns.
[g] Giving a party, contributing money, and campaign work were tied.
[h] Entertaining and contributing money were tied.
[i] Tied with letter and telegram campaigns and publicizing voting records.
[j] Tied with public relations campaigns.
[k] Publicizing voting records and bribery both rated 0.

*Direct Bribery.* Contrary to another popular conception, lobbyists have no faith whatsoever in bribery as a device for keeping channels open. Only one lobbyist rated bribery any higher than 0 and he did so with the comment, "If this assumes that the member of Congress is bribable, in that case I'd say 10. There is no surer way to get him to come along with your point of view." But even he was aware that nearly all members of Congress are not open to bribes. A few lobbyists claimed to know of bribes that had been passed, but in every instance their knowledge was second- or third-hand. One Congressman reported that a bribe had been offered him in the guise of a campaign contribution, but, as a result, he reported it to the Justice Department and voted against the lobbyist.

Most lobbyists recognize that the method is not effective and will not have anything to do with it.[10] Most believed that nearly all members of Congress are unbribable. Also, most viewed it as a dangerous gamble, since it could well turn a member of Congress against the donor instead of producing the desired good

TABLE 9. RANK ORDER OF MEAN RATINGS OF OPENING COMMUNICATION CHANNELS, BY RELATION OF LOBBYIST TO HIS EMPLOYER

| Group | Entertaining Rank | Mean Rating | Giving a Party Rank | Mean Rating | Bribery Rank | Mean Rating | Contributing Money Rank | Mean Rating | Campaign Work Rank | Mean Rating | Collaboration with Other Groups Rank | Mean Rating |
|---|---|---|---|---|---|---|---|---|---|---|---|---|
| Trade assoc. executive (N=19) | 11 | 1.3 | 13 | 1.0 | 14 | 0 | 9 | 1.9 | 9[a] | 1.9 | 2[b] | 6.9 |
| Officer of organization (N=6) | 9[c] | 2.8 | 12 | 1.7 | 14 | 0 | 13 | 1.5 | 11 | 1.8 | 4 | 7.7 |
| Legislative relations staff (N=12) | 12 | 1.9 | 13 | 1.0 | 14 | .83 | 10 | 3.3 | 11 | 2.8 | 1 | 7.9 |
| Legislative and executive relations staff (N=17) | 11 | 1.8 | 13 | 1.4 | 14 | 0 | 12 | 1.6 | 9 | 2.3 | 5 | 6.4 |
| Washington representative (N=16) | 10[d] | 1.9 | 12 | 1.3 | 14 | 0 | 13 | .9 | 10[d] | 1.9 | 7 | 5.3 |
| Lawyer, legal firm (N=8) | 13 | .3 | 12 | .4 | 14 | 0 | 7[a] | 2.3 | 7[a] | 2.3 | 5 | 5.0 |
| Lawyer, free-lance (N=13) | 10 | 1.9 | 12 | 1.5 | 14 | 0 | 11 | 1.8 | 8 | 2.4 | 4 | 5.5 |
| General counsel in organization (N=3) | 12 | .7 | 9[e] | 1.7 | 14 | 0 | 9[e] | 1.7 | 13 | .3 | 5 | 6.7 |
| Public relations counsel (N=2) | 11 | 1.0 | 9[f] | 2.5 | 13[g] | 0 | 6[h] | 3.0 | 6[h] | 3.0 | 6[h] | 3.0 |
| Lobbyist entrepreneur (N=3) | 13 | .3 | 12 | .7 | 14 | 0 | 6[i] | 3.0 | 8 | 2.7 | 4 | 4.7 |

[a] Contributing money and campaign work were tied.
[b] Tied with presentation of research results.
[c] Tied with publicizing voting records.
[d] Entertaining and campaign work were tied.
[e] Giving a party and contributing money were tied.
[f] Tied with contact by friend.
[g] Publicizing voting records and bribery were both rated 0.
[h] Contributing money, campaign work, and collaboration with other groups were tied.
[i] Tied with letter and telegram campaigns.

will. An official whose ideological rudder is so vacillating that he can be bribed can also be bribed by the other side and does not constitute a very safe investment. Another controlling factor here, according to respondents, is that keeping a bribe secret is an exceedingly difficult task in a "rumor factory" like Washington.

*Contributing Political Money and Campaign Work.* Since nearly all elected officials have a profound respect for political power, the lobbyist who represents a group with power at the polls finds there is a distinct advantage in keeping channels of communication open to these officials. The tactics of publicizing voting records and conducting public relations campaigns, discussed above, have some utility in producing political power. But what do lobbyists think of direct political actions, such as having members of their groups contribute political money or do volunteer work in the campaign? Both tactics were generally rated quite low, but campaign work, with a mean of 2.28, usually was ranked higher than political money (mean 1.88). The higher mean for campaign work can be traced, in part, to the higher rating given to this tactic than to money by the representatives of small labor organizations (Table 8).

*Collaboration with Other Groups.* The tactic of collaborating with other groups in planning strategy and making presentations is difficult to categorize, since it has aspects of direct communication, communication through intermediaries, and keeping communication channels open. The tactic is generally highly prized (over-all mean of 6.16), although there was considerable variance in the ratings (see Table 7). We see in Table 9 that those whose lobbyist roles are closest to a given organization (executive, officer, staff) rate it higher than do lawyers and Washington representatives who generally represent more than one group. In fact, full-time legislative relations persons give it the highest ranking, even above presentation of arguments.

Several factors enter into an evaluation of collaboration. From the lobbyist point of view, it distributes the work load so that it is possible to communicate with more people on more issues. This is especially helpful for those groups with a wide range of policy interests. Lobbyists with common interests meet regularly to discuss strategy and exchange information. Not only does collaboration increase the volume and skill of communication, but it also communicates the enhanced power, in terms of numbers of committed persons, that lies behind a policy position. The member of Congress also welcomes joint presentations, because it means a saving of work and tension for him. Congress spends endless hours resolving controversies, and it is a welcome relief to have a controversy settled before it reaches that body.[11] Legislators are so relieved not to have to take a position favoring one group over another that any proposal which carries the backing of most potentially antagonistic groups will almost always be approved.

### Summary

The most adequate explanation of the impact of the lobbying process on governmental decision making would come from a detailed examination of all the influences or pressures producing the behavior of decision makers. The social scientist is not equipped conceptually or methodologically at this stage to handle such a research problem. On the other hand, he can make some headway in analyzing the lobbying process by viewing it as a communication process. Communication is not necessarily complete when stimuli have been presented by a lobbyist; he must also attempt to gauge the receptivity of the decision maker and, hopefully, get the message through to him. A communication model does not explain all the variables involved in any given decision, but it does include all the variables involved in the lobbying process. The lobbyist has finished his job when he has communicated in the most effective way possible. He cannot control the workings of the decision maker's mind unless he can remake his personality or, alternatively, get him thrown out of office and replaced by another person. Not only does a communication model encompass the lobby process, but it is also the simplest explanation which accounts for the known evidence.

In general, lobbyists favor face-to-face conversations for the communication of facts and the arguments which support them. However, competition for the limited attention of decision makers in recent years has forced lobbyists more and more to seek access through intermediaries, especially the constituents of elected officials who have a power relationship to the decision maker. In order to ensure receptivity, lobbyists also attempt in other ways to communicate subtly the political power behind their groups. Preservation of open communication channels to decision makers is of such prime importance to lobbyists that the possible cutting off of access can be used as a sanction forcing lobbyists to behave in ways that the decision makers find desirable.

## NOTES

1. The two outstanding examples probably are: Arthur F. Bentley, *The Process of Government*, Chicago, University of Chicago Press, 1908, and David B. Truman, *The Governmental Process*, New York, Knopf, 1951.

2. Some leading examples here are: Floyd Hunter, *Community Power Structure*, Chapel Hill, University of North Carolina Press, 1953, and his recent *Top Leadership U.S.A.*, Chapel Hill, University of North Carolina Press, 1959, C. Wright Mills, *The Power Elite*, New York, Oxford, 1956, and Ferdinand Lundberg, *America's Sixty Families*, New York, Vanguard, 1937.

3. See Robert A. Dahl, "A Critique of the Ruling Elite Model," *American Political Science Review*, Vol. 52, 1958, pp. 463–469.

4. As a result of some recent studies of community politics, Norton Long has suggested that community decision making can be analyzed with a game theory model. His concept is that political decision making results from the interactive forces of a variety of games being played in any given community. The players in one game may be the pawns in another game or may use players in other games as pawns in their own game. The remarkable thing is that community decisions result from the diverging activities and purposes of the games being played. See his "The Local Community as an Ecology of Games," *American Journal of Sociology*, Vol. 64, 1958, pp. 251–261. Although extensive research would be required for verification, the evidence suggests that national decision making may also be the result of an ecology of games.

5. The purposes of the study were broader than the analytical scheme presented in this paper; thus data were gathered on several topics that do not fit into a communication model.

6. Groups also send personal envoys to perform liaison functions. Many groups are worried that they will be taken advantage of unless they have someone on the scene to check on governmental activities.

7. Because of heavy time pressures on officials, it is often necessary for the lobbyist to present his case to the staff assistant of the decision maker rather than to the decision maker himself. This is technically communication through an intermediary rather than direct communication; however, most assistants are very close to their bosses and, therefore, for the analytical purposes of this paper, no distinction will be made between communications to staff and communications to the decision maker personally.

8. Both the median and the mean ratings for each technique are reported in Tables 1, 4, and 7. Both are less than perfect summary statistics. It is debatable whether the lobbyists were using identical subjective scales or were able to ensure equal distance between intervals as they rated; yet both are assumptions in calculating a mean. On the other hand, the median takes no account of the distance of extreme judgments from the center of the distribution and thus may distort as much as the mean. The full frequency distributions are the reader's best guide to the over-all evalution of each tactic.

9. It should also be recognized that constituents are speaking on their own behalves as well as acting as intermediaries between lobbyist and decision maker; thus the designation of communications from constituents as communications through an intermediary is true only from the perspective of the professional lobbyist. In practice, lobbyist and constituent frequently make joint calls on decision makers.

10. It should be noted that some use is made of small gifts and favors by lobbyists; these are given more to the staffs of decision makers than to decision makers themselves, because staff members also have considerable control over access. It is very difficult conceptually to draw firm lines between bribes, campaign contributions, gifts, and favors. Rather than explore such a conceptual tangle in this paper, suffice it to say that the remarks in this section refer primarily to direct bribery.

11. Corroborating evidence from Vermont is reported in Oliver Garceau and Corrine Silverman, "A Pressure Group and the Pressured," *American Political Science Review,* Vol. 48, 1954, pp. 672–691.

# 19. Process Satisfaction and Policy Approval in State Department– Congressional Relations *

James A. Robinson

Experimental and field studies have reported relationships between decision-makers' satisfaction with the process by which decisions are made and the content of the decisions.[1] It is not clear under what conditions satisfaction with process determines satisfaction with decisions or under what conditions there is a reverse relation. It is not improbable that a reciprocal relation exists between these two factors. The purpose of this essay is not to establish which is the dependent and which is the independent variable, but simply to determine whether a correlation between them may be found among a sample of members of Congress and among particular subsamples. This is part of a larger study of the effects of the legislative process on the attitudes and behavior of members of Congress with respect to foreign-policy decisions.

This article reports data from interviews with re-elected members of the Eighty-fifth Congress (1957–58). The 434 returning members were divided into those who occupied foreign-policy roles in the Eighty-fifth Congress and those who did not. A "foreign-policy role" was defined as membership in House committees: the Committee on Foreign Affairs, the subcommittees on foreign economic policy and the Department of State budget within the Committee on Appropriations, the subcommittee on international government operations within the Commitee on Government Operations, the House leadership (speaker, floor leaders, and whips); and membership in Senate committees: the Committee on Foreign Relations, Committee on Appropriations, and the Senate leadership (each of whom was on one of these committees). There were eighty who occupied such roles. We drew a random sample of fifty of these and a random sample of fifty from the 354 who did not have foreign-policy assignments.

During interviews, which were obtained with ninety-five of the hundred (in nine cases we were forced to gather data from administrative assistants rather than the members),[2] we asked four questions concerning the satisfaction the respondent's office has with the information process between Congress and the Department of State. The four questions were:

Now, I would like to ask you some questions about your evaluation of Congressional–State Department relations.

* From *The American Journal of Sociology,* Vol. 67 (1961), pp. 278–283. Reprinted by permission of The University of Chicago Press.

First, take the handling of constituents' problems which you refer to the Department. Are you well satisfied, moderately satisfied, or dissatisfied with the way these are handled?

How about the way the Department responds to your requests for information about foreign policy? Are you well satisfied, moderately satisfied, or dissatisfied?

What about the Department's record for voluntarily keeping Congress informed about foreign policy? Are you well satisfied, moderately satisfied, or dissatisfied?

When the Department is formulating foreign policy decisions, do you think Congressional opinion carries considerable weight, some weight, or no weight?

At the end of the interview each respondent was asked:

I would like your general evaluation of American foreign policy during the last two years. Do you, in general, strongly approve, moderately approve, or disapprove our foreign policy in the past couple of years?

We have examined the responses to these questions to see whether there is a correlation between satisfaction with information process and approval of policies.

### Satisfaction With Handling Constituents' Requests and Satisfaction With Policy

For a majority of members of Congress the most frequent occasion for contact with the Department of State is a request from a constituent. This may be an inquiry about some departmental action, a plea for help in acquiring a passport or obtaining a visa, or about any of a wide range of matters within the jurisdiction of the Department. Among respondents in our sample 78 per cent said they have more frequent contacts of this kind than contacts about foreign-policy legislation. While approximately 70 per cent of the members reported weekly contacts with the Department of State on behalf of constituents, approximately 30 per cent have such frequent communications about policy matters. The services which the Department's Office of Congressional Relations (headed by a political appointee with the rank of assistant secretary) provides to representatives and senators usually are not directly related to policy. This is almost as true for members of the principal foreign-policy committees as for other members.

The Department operates on the assumption that the more satisfactorily it handles requests initiated by constituents, the more likely it is to obtain the support of members on policy matters. The Department assumes that non-policy good will is transferred to and reinforces policy relations and, regardless of the content of a member's request, the Department is anxious to oblige. As one veteran liaison officer said when asked how the Department can most effectively promote agreement with Congress: "The most favorable way of getting results is to do something for a member." [3]

That the Department has performed these non-policy or "service" functions in a way to win congressional approbation seems clear from interviews with members from whom we heard few criticisms and many favorable comments about the liaison activities. For example, a Senate Republican supporter of the administration said: "The liaison office under Assistant Secretary William B. Macomber is available at all times. They do a good job of this function (handling constituents' matters)." A Senate Democratic critic said: "As to constituents' matters, I am very well satisfied. They have a wonderful office and furnish wonderful service to us." A sometimes critical House Republican said: "The most effective office in the executive branch is the Passport Office in the State Department. The others in the Department seem to handle your problems as well as they can." And a House Democratic supporter of administration foreign policies said, "The Department of State is a fine agency to do business with. There is none better. They're co-operative and attentive."

The high regard which congressmen have for the manner in which the Department handles their constituent matters extends to Democrats and Republicans alike, senators as well as representatives, and to those who do not occupy foreign-policy committee assignments as much as to those who do. But is there any relation between satisfaction with this aspect of the liaison function and support of policy? Regardless of the state of a member's approval of the Department's foreign policy during the previous two years, he was very likely to be highly pleased with departmental treatment of his constituents' problems. One who disapproved recent United States foreign policy was about as likely to give a favorable evaluation of the Department's performance on this count as one who approved. For example, although eighteen disapproved recent American foreign policy, fifteen of them nevertheless were well satisfied with the Department's liaison activities in behalf of their constituents. Although seventy-seven were moderately or well satisfied with the handling of constituents' requests, seventeen disapproved of the Department's recent policies. Thus, if one is given a member's evaluation of the Department's concern for his constituents, one cannot predict whether that member will approve a departmental policy.

That there is no statistical relation between these two variables is not the same as saying that the Department's attention to congressional "service" requests does not affect the Department's position with Congress. Our data certainly will not allow us to say that, all other things being equal, the Department's policies would receive the same support if it discontinued this function. Indeed, one would expect quite the opposite. If the Department were inefficient, unresponsive, or tardy in meeting congressmen's requests for assistance, Congress would have another ground on which to criticize the Department. While satisfactory performance of "service" functions may facilitate agreement on policy questions, it will not assure policy approval. Perhaps this is a necessary, but clearly not a sufficient, condition for establishing congressional support for departmental policies.

### Index of Satisfaction With Information Process and Policy Approval

We observe a different relationship between policy approval and satisfaction with other aspects of the information process than between policy approval and satisfaction with handling constituents' requests. The product moment correlation between satisfaction with responses to requests for foreign-policy information and policy approval is .37 (for $N = 75$, this is significant at the .01 level); between satisfaction with the Department's record for voluntarily furnishing foreign-affairs information and policy support is .33 (for $N = 77$, this is significant at the .01 level); between perception of weight given congressional opinion in departmental decision-making and policy approval is .31 (for $N = 77$, this is significant at the .01 level).

By combining responses to these three questions one can construct an index of satisfaction with the information process which has slightly more predictive power than any one of the items separately. The coefficient of correlation between this index and policy approval is .41 (for $N = 70$, this is significant at the .01 level).

Although the relationship is not one to one, members of the Eighty-fifth Congress who were satisfied with information parts of the process were also likely to be satisfied with the policy outcomes of the process. Members whose requests for foreign-policy information were satisfactorily answered, who were voluntarily supplied with information about international affairs, and who believed that congressional views were important to the Department of State were more likely to give their approval to departmental proposals than their colleagues who were not satisfied on any of these matters. Thus, speaking of the whole sample one may say that there is statistically significant correlation between satisfaction with the information process and policy approval. But does this relation hold for various subsamples of the whole sample? The data are in such a form that we can see whether similar correlations obtain when one controls for role assignment and political party.

### Differences Between Roles

As we noted earlier, we drew samples of equal size from among those who occupied foreign-policy assignments and those who did not. We defined foreign-policy role quite broadly in order to include members who sit on committees considering appropriations for foreign aid and on "oversight" committees which follow the expenditure and the administration of programs. In the House the mutual security appropriation bill is assigned to a subcommittee; in the Senate the full committee considers the same bill. In the sample from the House we also included several members from the Government Operations Subcommittee on International Government Operations which investigates the administration of the program.

Members with foreign-policy roles ($N = 38$) had a correlation of .44 (significant at the .01 level) between satisfaction with information process and policy approval. For occupants of non-foreign-policy roles ($N = 32$) the correlation between the same two variables was .26 (not significant).

### Differences Between Parties

Political party affiliation is obviously an outstanding empirical characteristic of executive-legislative relations in the United States national government, but the consequences of party for public policy, including foreign policy, seem to vary from study to study. One stream of thought holds that Democrats and Republicans per se are as Tweedledum and Tweedledee and that what makes the difference in legislative output is whether a coalition of southern Democrats and midwestern Republicans prevails over an alliance of northern Democrats and eastern Republicans.[4] Another line of research indicates that partly affiliation explains more congressional voting than any other single variable.[5] This dispute over the relative weight of party in accounting for congressional-executive relations is not likely to be settled with a clear-cut verdict in favor of, or opposed to, the proposition that party is crucial. Rather, what we might more likely expect is that under some conditions (say, on certain issues or on parliamentary questions) party will be crucial; while on others it will not be.

How are satisfaction with communication process, party affiliation, and policy preferences related with respect to attitudes on foreign affairs? When all responses are subdivided according to political party, one notes considerable differences between Democratic and Republican congressmen. Table 1 lists the correlations

TABLE 1. PROCESS SATISFACTION, POLICY APPROVAL, AND PARTY AFFILIATION

|  | All Respondents (N=70) | Democrats (N=40) | Republicans (N=30) |
|---|---|---|---|
| Correlation between satisfaction with handling of requests for policy information and policy approval | .33** | .60** | .11 |
| Correlation between satisfaction with the Department of State's record for volunteering information and policy approval | .32** | .57** | .25 |
| Correlation between perception of weight of congressional opinion in departmental decisions and policy approval | .30** | .33* | .44* |
| Correlation between index of satisfaction with information process and policy approval | .41** | .56** | .13 |

*Significant at .05 level.
**Significant at .01 level.

on each of the three information items and the index for all respondents and for Democrats and Republicans separately.[6] Except for the item on perception of weight given congressional opinion within the Department of State, evaluations by Democrats of the process are much more highly correlated with their evaluations of policies than are evaluations by Republicans. For Republican members of the Eighty-fifth Congress, satisfaction with the information process is not significantly related to policy approval; for Democratic representatives and senators, policy approval varies significantly with satisfaction with the information process.

What is the explanation for this difference? Why should satisfaction with information be relevant to Democrats but not to Republicans? Notice in Table 2

TABLE 2. COMPARISON OF CONGRESSIONAL PARTIES' SUPPORT FOR DEPARTMENT OF STATE POLICIES

|  | DEMOCRATS | | REPUBLICANS | |
|---|---|---|---|---|
|  | No. | Per Cent | No. | Per Cent |
| Disapprove | 21 | 52.5 | 2 | 6.6 |
| Moderately approve | 16 | 40.0 | 14 | 46.6 |
| Strongly approve | 3 | 7.5 | 14 | 46.6 |
| Total | 40 | 100.0 | 30 | 99.8 |

that congressional Republicans gave greater support to Department of State policies than Democrats. While approximately the same number and same percentage of Democrats as Republicans moderately approved of departmental policies, many more Democrats disapproved and many more Republicans approved. Whatever the explanation, party loyalty, as shown, for example, by Republican support for the Department, was high and satisfaction with the communications process did not seem to be related to this support. Inasmuch as most Republicans (all but two) at least moderately approved, there may not be much that more satisfactory information could do to improve Republican support.

For Democrats, however, satisfaction with policy did vary with satisfaction with the information process. In other words, it appears that the information process may be more important for the "out of executive" party than for the "executive" party. Republican legislators, by identifying with the Republican administration, may have reached policy conclusions irrespective of the information, or they received their facts and evaluations from other sources, such as the President's weekly conference with his party's congressional leaders. Democrats, on the other hand, who did not identify with the Department and who did not have similarly ready access to the President, may have depended more heavily on the communications channels to the Department.

### Generalizability of Findings

We have reported data on a special subset, the re-elected members of the Eighty-fifth Congress. One is entitled to inquire whether the relation between satisfaction with information process and policy approval may be generalized to other Congresses. An outstanding empirical characteristic of the Eighty-fifth Congress was that the majority party in Congress did not control the executive. Democrats organized both the House and Senate, re-elected Speaker Rayburn, and secured all committee chairmanships. However, the Department of State was headed by a Republican secretary, and the President's regular Tuesday morning "legislative conference" was attended by Republican congressional leaders only. This division of control of the two branches between parties was not peculiar to the Eighty-fifth Congress, but was also characteristic of the Eighty-fourth (1955–56) and the Eighty-sixth (1959–60). For six of the eight years of Dwight Eisenhower's presidency, the Congress was organized by the opposite party. Although this condition had occurred before (most recently during Herbert Hoover's second term in 1931–32, and Harry Truman's first in 1947–48), it has been unusual for the division to persist for such a long period. Analysis of the Eighty-fifth Congress, in addition to helping explain that particular Congress, may be relevant to other instances of "divided government." We are confronted not merely with a "single case" but with a special case of a type of "checks and balance" government.

Might this analysis apply more generally? Why should not these relations between information and policy also hold for the opposition party when the congressional majority corresponds to the presidential majority? A government without programmatic parties, with little formal party discipline, and with a consensus in favor of bipartisan foreign policies, will have need for alliances across party lines, regardless of whether the same party controls both branches.[7] Thus, one might expect similar findings in any Congress: the policy preferences of the executive-oriented legislators will not vary according to satisfaction with the information process, while the policy choices of the "out of executive party" legislators will be significantly related to satisfaction with information. If this theory is correct, we have additional evidence that the mechanism for what Westerfield calls "extra-partisanship" [8] lies in the character of the information process linking the executive and congressmen of the non-Executive party.

## Summary

Statistically significant relations do not exist between congressmen's satisfaction with the way the Department of State handles requests from constituents and satisfaction with foreign policy. However, significant relations are observed between satisfaction with other aspects of the communications network linking Congress and the Department and foreign policy. These include the Department's record for answering requests for policy information, volunteering information to Congress, and perception of the weight of congressional opinion in the Department's formulation of policy. These relations hold for congressmen who occupy foreign-policy roles but not for others. When members are divided according to their party affiliations, these relationships are found to hold for the "out of executive" party but not for the "executive" party. Such findings suggest that information processes and satisfaction with them may be an important element in establishing and maintaining bipartisan foreign policies.

### NOTES

1. The experimental literature is reviewed critically in Mauk Mulder, "Power and Satisfaction in Task-oriented Groups," *Acta Psychologica*, XVI (1959), 178–225 (also see D. G. Marquis, H. Guetzkow, and R. W. Heyns, "A Social Psychological Study of the Decision-making Conference," in Harold Guetzkow [ed.], *Groups, Leadership, and Men* [Pittsburgh: Carnegie Press, 1951], pp. 55–67; and Uno Remitz, *Professional Satisfaction among Swedish Bank Employees* [Copenhagen: Ejnar Munksgaard Ltd., 1960]).

2. For a discussion of our field problems, see James A. Robinson, "Survey Interviewing among Members of Congress," *Public Opinion Quarterly*, XXIV (Spring, 1960), 127–38.

3. The Department's liaison with Congress is discussed more thoroughly in my book, *Congress and Foreign Policy-making* (Homewood, Ill.: Dorsey Press, 1962).

4. The Brookings Institution, *The Formulation and Administration of United States Foreign Policy* (Study prepared at the request of the Committee on Foreign Relations, United States Senate [Washington: Government Printing Office, January 13, 1960]), p. 26.

5. Julius Turner, *Party and Constituency: Pressures on Congress* (Baltimore: Johns Hopkins Press, 1951); and H. Bradford Westerfield, *Foreign Policy and Party Politics* (New Haven, Conn.: Yale University Press, 1955).

6. Hereinafter we shall use only data from the seventy respondents who replied to each of the three items.

7. Westerfield, *op. cit.*, and Cecil V. Crabb, Jr., *Bipartisan Foreign Policy, Myth or Reality* (Evanston, Ill.: Row, Peterson Co., 1957).

8. Westerfield, *op. cit.*, p. 16. "Extra-partisanship" refers to an administration's practice of "working outside party lines while maintaining a base of support in its own party."

# Part VI

# Action

# Introduction

THE LEGISLATIVE process may be viewed as a series of incremental decision points, and thus legislative action may occur at many places in the process. In the Congress it is clear that action in committee is very often crucial. Committees play a less significant role in the legislative processes in most states, but even there decisions at the committee stage may constitute the crucial legislative action. Legislative committees are gatekeepers for legislative alternatives, only some of which go to the entire legislative membership for decision. The final decision, typically rendered by public voting, provides the data for the selections in this section. The following four research reports focus upon collective legislative decisions reached by public roll-call voting.

Roll-call data are easy to gather because they are a permanent part of the legislative record. Carefully used, they do reflect the public position of legislators in the final stages of the legislative process. Analysis of roll-call voting has developed to a fairly high state of sophistication. While roll-call voting is only one form of legislative action, and it may not be the crucial one for sorting out alternative policies or deciding in what policy areas to act or not, these data do yield fruitful indicators of legislators' general policy preferences.

The voting behavior of elected representatives is, in general, very consistent and clearly patterned. So regular are legislative voting patterns that they quite often fit the cumulative requirements of Guttman scaling, the measurement technique used in the following reports by Rieselbach, Andrain, and Patterson. Nothing is clearer from research on legislative voting than the fact that the responses of legislators at the roll-call vote stage are not chaotic or random; rather, they tend to follow a consistent pattern.

These regular voting patterns have been shown to possess varying correlates. Rieselbach and Andrain show, for foreign aid and civil rights legislation, that both party and constituency attributes can help to explain variations in legislative voting. In the case of foreign aid, where an analysis of voting patterns over a period of time is available, party differences seem to have been most compelling in some contexts, and constituency factors predominated in others. Various correlates are suggested with regard to civil rights, but party and regional differences seem to be the major determinants of voting behavior in this area. The civil rights case indicates the powerful intervening effect of regional differences on the behavior of Democrats: Northern Democrats are more different from Southern Democrats than from Republicans.

Where party is not available to legislators as a meaningful referent for voting behavior, they tend to respond to different kinds of behavioral factors in

331

different issue domains. In one-party or non-partisan legislatures the voting behavior of legislators is quite consistent, or patterned. However, if Patterson's Oklahoma study suggests the general case, voting is more multi-dimensional, issues areas are more compartmentalized, and the correlates of voting in one area differ from those of other areas.

# 20. The Demography of the Congressional Vote on Foreign Aid, 1939–1958[*]

Leroy N. Rieselbach

Recent applications of more elaborate quantitative methods (*e.g.,* bloc cluster analysis and Guttman scale procedures) to legislative politics have sharply improved the ability of political scientists to specify significant dimensions of voting behavior.[1] Party affiliation, constituency characteristics and cohesion within state delegations have been correlated with the congressional vote in a number of subject matter areas. Because of the masses of data to be handled, however, even the best of these studies have been limited in scope to a single year or to one Congress.[2] This restriction has not prevented the authors of these works from demonstrating clearly the utility of their methodology, but it has limited correspondingly either the generality or the reliability of their conclusions.[3] The present study, limited to the single issue of congressional voting on foreign aid, is an attempt to discover, by the application of quantitative methods to votes over longer time periods, how far the relationships previously suggested persist over time or are peculiar to the individual sessions in which they occur.

## I. The Study Design

To introduce a longer time perspective, four Congresses—the 76th (1939–40), the 80th (1947–48), the 83rd (1953–54), and the 85th (1957–58)—were examined originally. Since the issue posed for the 76th Congress, the repeal of the arms embargo provisions of the Neutrality Act, differs to a degree from the Mutual Security Act (or its successors) which confronted the three subsequent Congresses, the 77th Congress (1941–42), which saw the Lend-Lease Act passed, was also analyzed. Lend-Lease is more like the postwar foreign aid programs in that it directly committed American economic resources, at public expense, to the defense of the "free" world. Thus, a major "foreign aid" decision was taken in each of the Congresses selected for study.[4]

The second criterion for the selection of these particular Congresses was the relation of the presidency and Congress. A number of studies have suggested that the voting configurations in Congress are influenced by the status that a party

* From *The American Political Science Review,* Vol. 58 (1964), pp. 577–588. Reprinted by permission.

enjoys as majority or minority there, with or without a President in the White House.[5] The Congresses enumerated above were chosen to take this factor into account; they exemplify the major alternatives among the possible relationships between White House and Congress. Thus the 76th and 77th Congresses faced a Democratic President with a Democratic majority on the Hill; in the 80th Congress, a Democratic President confronted a Republican congressional majority; and the 83rd and 85th Congresses found a GOP Chief Executive with his party first in the majority and then reduced to minority status. This sample should permit greater confidence in findings that withstand changes in the party balance and control of the presidency.

The foreign aid roll calls in the House of Representatives have been analyzed through the use of Guttman scale procedures. The House was chosen in preference to the Senate because the congressional districts, being demographically more homogeneous than entire states, seemed better suited to test the association between constituency characteristics and voting behavior. The Guttman techniques of cumulative scaling were employed because of their proven capacity to specify general evaluative dimensions upon which the representatives judge proposals as they come before the House.[6] On the basis of scale scores, the members of the House were classified as "isolationists" (e.g., those whose votes indicate a reluctance to expand the size or scope of the American foreign aid program), "moderates," and "internationalists" (e.g., those who, by their votes, supported the maintenance of the program at the most extensive possible levels).[7] The natural breaks in the frequency distribution of scale scores determined the cutting points between classes; in each case the distribution was tri-modal.

The three groups of legislators were analyzed in terms of party affiliation and three types of demographic variables. First, the association of certain personal characteristics of the individual congressmen with their voting on foreign aid was examined. These attributes included educational attainment, occupation prior to election, religious affiliation, and prior service in the armed forces. Then, a set of "political" characteristics, including length of service in the House, committee service, and electoral margin, were related to votes on foreign aid. Finally, a number of constituency characteristics—region, ethnicity, ruralism, socio-economic status, and educational level—were correlated with positions on the foreign aid issue.[8] This paper will attempt to describe the isolationists and internationalists in terms of these types of variables.

## II. The Findings

Since political party has been, in the words of Turner, "more closely associated with congressional voting behavior than any other discernible factor," [9] it may be worth while at the outset to examine the relationship of party affiliation to the vote on foreign aid. The data in Table I indicate that the party factor is less constant than the observation just quoted suggests; in fact, over the period under consideration here, a striking change took place. In the 76th Congress, the parties were ranged with near unanimity on opposite sides of the question; in the 77th and 80th Congresses, a few members of each party broke ranks; and by 1958 no statistically significant difference (by the Chi Square test at the .05 level of confidence) between the parties remained. The Republicans in the 85th Congress provided a proportionately greater share of their votes to the internationalist cause.

TABLE I. DISTRIBUTION OF REPRESENTATIVES ON FOREIGN AID, BY
PARTY AND CONGRESS

| Party and voting position* | CONGRESS | | | | |
|---|---|---|---|---|---|
| | 76th | 77th | 80th | 83rd | 85th |
| Republicans | % | % | % | % | % |
| Isolationists | 81.9 | 84.0 | 24.4 | 36.7 | 36.8 |
| Internationalists | 0.0 | 6.2 | 14.4 | 55.2 | 54.9 |
| Democrats | | | | | |
| Isolationists | 0.0 | 4.1 | 3.1 | 13.4 | 20.8 |
| Internationalists | 79.8 | 89.1 | 65.6 | 72.2 | 47.1 |

*For the sake of simplicity, the moderate groups, and those who were not scalable, are omitted from the table. Thus the percentages for each party do not add to 100%. The percentage of moderates for each Congress is as follows: Republicans, 1.7, 8.6, 52.4, 4.5, 5.4; Democrats, 8.4, 0.0, 20.6. The percentages for the not scalable groups are: Republicans, 16.4, 1.2, 8.8, 3.6, 2.9; Democrats, 11.8, 6.7, 11.7, 3.2, 2.5. The latter category combines the non-scale types with those who could not be assigned because they were "on the record" too infrequently.

This finding is of interest for at least two reasons. First, it shows that the collapse of party solidarity began before, rather than after, World War II. Immediately after the 1940 election, a few Republicans crossed party lines to vote for an internationalist program while at the same time a handful of Democrats bolted and opposed Lend-Lease. Thus, while the war and the end of the Roosevelt era may have accelerated the change, the break-down of party unanimity cannot be attributed solely to these factors. Second, while the long-run development can be explained in terms of a number of factors—for example, the election of a Republican President, of an internationalist bent, which increased the pressures on G.O.P. legislators to back the foreign aid program; the simultaneous decline in the effectiveness of pulls from the executive on the Democrats; and the changing character of the American South which in turn led to increased fiscal conservatism and isolationism among representatives of that region [10]— the important point here is that with the passage of time the importance of single variables as correlates of voting behavior may ebb and flow. Specifically in this case, party was of considerably less importance as a determinant of foreign aid voting in the 85th Congress than it had been 20 years earlier.

Turning to the personal characteristics of individual legislators we find that only one of these, religious affiliation, was associated with the foreign aid voting patterns. The literature provides mixed counsel on this relationship,[11] but our data (Table II) show that in 16 of 18 possible comparisons congressmen of the Catholic faith were less isolationist or more internationalist than Protestants. This relationship does not appear to be an artifact of urban-rural or regional factors, for when controls were added for these variables, the association remained unaltered.[12] Thus, within urban areas and in the North, Catholics, controlled for party, consistently provided greater support for the foreign aid program than did non-Catholics.[13]

TABLE II. DISTRIBUTION OF REPRESENTATIVES ON FOREIGN AID, BY PARTY AND RELIGION *

| Party and Religious Affiliation | 76TH CONGRESS | | | 77TH CONGRESS | | |
|---|---|---|---|---|---|---|
| | % Isol. | % Int. | N | % Isol. | % Int. | N |
| Republicans | | | | | | |
| Catholic | (50.0)† | ( 0.0) | 2 | (66.7) | (33.3) | 3 |
| Protestant | 86.8 | 0.0 | 68 | 90.0 | 2.9 | 70 |
| Democrats | | | | | | |
| Catholic | 0.0 | 68.6 | 35 | 4.9 | 92.7 | 41 |
| Protestant | 0.0 | 89.5 | 76 | 5.4 | 90.5 | 74 |
| | 80TH CONGRESS | | | 83RD CONGRESS | | |
| Republicans | | | | | | |
| Catholics | 28.6 | 21.4 | 14 | 17.4 | 78.3 | 23 |
| Protestants | 23.4 | 15.6 | 128 | 36.8 | 56.4 | 163 |
| Democrats | | | | | | |
| Catholic | 2.8 | 86.1 | 36 | 3.9 | 94.1 | 51 |
| Protestant | 4.1 | 61.2 | 98 | 15.7 | 66.4 | 134 |
| | 85TH CONGRESS | | | | | |
| Republicans | | | | | | |
| Catholic | 19.2 | 69.2 | 26 | | | |
| Protestant | 39.2 | 52.9 | 176 | | | |
| Democrats | | | | | | |
| Catholic | 6.6 | 80.3 | 61 | | | |
| Protestant | 39.8 | 31.9 | 166 | | | |

* The table includes only those congressmen for whom information on religious affiliation was obtainable. The data were obtained from the biographies in the Congressional Directory and from listings from the more recent period supplied by the Legislative Reference Service of the Library of Congress.

† Percentages based on fewer than 10 cases are enclosed in parentheses in this and subsequent tables.

A number of possible explanations of this finding may be advanced. The position of the Catholic hierarchy may have been important, though it is difficult to assess the Church's influence because of its reluctance to announce positions on issues before Congress and because of inadequate knowledge of the degree to which the individual communicant follows the lead of the hierarchy. The support for foreign aid among Catholic representatives may have stemmed from the Church's position; it may have come in spite of the views of the Church as an institution. In the latter case, it may be that other factors—class, status, party affiliation, etc.—outweighed the counsel of Church elders. Then, congressmen may not have been typical of all church members; institutional factors peculiar to the House, or the responsibilities of public life, may have created a different set of pressures to which the legislator felt compelled to respond. Finally, since foreign aid went in large amounts to countries from which many Catholics emigrated to the United States, such programs may have appeared to Catholics as a means to assist their homelands in time of economic crisis. In any case, of the personal characteristics of the congressmen considered here only religious affiliation seems to have been associated with foreign aid voting alignments.

In addition to the personal attributes of the lawmakers, it seems likely that their "political" characteristics may have an impact on their vote decisions. A number of such variables were examined. Of these, only one, service on the Foreign Affairs Committee, survived controls for party and the passage of time, and appears to have been associated with voting alignments on foreign aid legislation.[14] The data in Table III show that in 15 of 18 instances members of the Committee were more internationalist or less isolationist than the remainder of their House colleagues.

TABLE III. COMPARISON OF FOREIGN AFFAIRS COMMITTEE AND REST OF HOUSE ON FOREIGN AID, BY PARTY AND CONGRESS

| Party and Assignment | 76TH CONGRESS | | | 77TH CONGRESS | | |
|---|---|---|---|---|---|---|
| | % Isol. | % Int. | N | % Isol. | % Int. | N |
| Republicans | | | | | | |
| Foreign Affairs | 80.0 | 0.0 | 10 | 90.0 | 10.0 | 10 |
| Rest of House | 80.5 | 0.0 | 149 | 84.7 | 6.1 | 131 |
| Democrats | | | | | | |
| Foreign Affairs | 0.0 | 80.0 | 15 | 6.7 | 93.3 | 15 |
| Rest of House | 0.0 | 81.2 | 218 | 4.5 | 88.6 | 220 |
| | 80TH CONGRESS | | | 83RD CONGRESS | | |
| Republicans | | | | | | |
| Foreign Affairs | 7.7 | 46.1 | 13 | 26.7 | 73.3 | 15 |
| Rest of House | 25.7 | 11.5 | 218 | 36.9 | 53.5 | 187 |
| Democrats | | | | | | |
| Foreign Affairs | 0.0 | 81.8 | 11 | 0.0 | 84.6 | 13 |
| Rest of House | 3.5 | 64.9 | 171 | 13.4 | 71.5 | 186 |
| | 85TH CONGRESS | | | | | |
| Republicans | | | | | | |
| Foreign Affairs | 33.3 | 66.7 | 15 | | | |
| Rest of House | 38.4 | 51.7 | 172 | | | |
| Democrats | | | | | | |
| Foreign Affairs | 17.6 | 76.4 | 17 | | | |
| Rest of House | 30.8 | 44.8 | 201 | | | |

One can argue, on the basis of this finding, that contact with foreign policy questions and officials in committee led members of Foreign Affairs to give an increased amount of support to international activity. If Carroll's conclusion is accurate, that "chance, modified occasionally by purposeful intrusions by the formal party leaders" determines the composition of House committees,[15] then it seems that the internationalism of Foreign Affairs members stemmed from something more than a self-selection process by which internationalists asked for and got seats on the Committee.

It is possible that the Committee, as it has legislative jurisdiction over foreign aid bills, was the focus of additional forces which inclined the members in the direction of internationalism. These forces include briefings, formal and informal, of legislators by the relevant executive agencies, direct contacts with the President or the Secretary of State, the exposures incident to foreign travel, and service as delegates to international conferences.[16]

This combination of specialization in the area of foreign policy and being subjected to the kinds of pressures suggested above may have led the Committee to develop a characteristics set of behavioral norms which persisted over time and by which new members of the Committee were "socialized." [17] Thus the internationalism of the Committee survived changes in the political situation. And the fact that membership on the Committee on Armed Services, also involved with matters of foreign policy though not with foreign aid legislation, was not related to foreign aid voting suggests that these sets of norms may be peculiar to individual committees.

The third category of variable examined, constituency characteristics, includes five factors—region, the urban-rural division, ethnicity, educational level, and socio-economic status—which appear to have been related to the vote patterns in the House on foreign aid. Consideration of constituency characteristics of course is predicated on the assumption that the individual legislator will be responsive to the wishes and desires of his constituents. However, some recent evidence has challenged the assumption.[18] Deferring for the moment any attempts to resolve the issue, we will look at the extent to which representatives from similar districts displayed similar voting records.

Region has perhaps been given most attention as a determinant of congressional voting. The literature suggests that the Midwest provided the greatest share of the isolationists and that the degree of Southern opposition to the aid program increased with the passage of time.[19] The data (Table IV) suggest that, while there is much to be said for these views, the true significance of region can be seen only with the introduction of controls for party. Midwestern [20] isolationism, to the extent it did exist, was peculiar to the Republican Party; G.O.P. congressmen from the central regions were more isolationist than those from the East and Pacific coasts in each Congress. On the other side of the aisle, however, Democrats from the Midwest were consistently more internationalist than those from the Southern and Mountain states, particularly after the 77th Congress.

With respect to the South, the data in Table IV again demonstrate the need to qualify regional generalizations by considering the parties separately. The decline in Southern internationalism was confined to the Democratic Party; Southern Republicans were, from the 77th Congress on, more isolationist than legislators from the East and Pacific coasts. Again, it is clear that regional groups within the two parties have behaved quite differently on foreign aid bills.

In truth, it may be that a region gets its political reputation from its dominant party. Thus the Midwest, the traditional center of Republican strength, became known as the isolationist capital of America because the G.O.P. lawmakers from the region were leading opponents of foreign aid. The regional label did not fit Midwestern Democrats. Southern Republicans also basked in reflected glory; they were consistently more isolationist than Republicans from the coastal regions. The upshot of all this is that explanations based on geography must be advanced with caution; we cannot simply assert that the Midwest because of its physical isolation was less conscious of the connections between the United States and foreign nations

TABLE IV. DISTRIBUTION OF REPRESENTATIVES ON FOREIGN AID, BY REGION AND PARTY

| Party and Region | 76TH CONGRESS | | | 77TH CONGRESS | | |
|---|---|---|---|---|---|---|
| | % Isol. | % Int. | N | % Isol. | % Int. | N |
| Republicans | | | | | | |
| East | 76.7 | 0.0 | 73 | 64.4 | 16.9 | 59 |
| South | (60.0) | (0.0) | 5 | (100.0) | (0.0) | 4 |
| Midwest | 88.4 | 0.0 | 86 | 96.4 | 0.0 | 84 |
| Mountain | (100.0) | (0.0) | 3 | (100.0) | (0.0) | 4 |
| Pacific | (77.8) | (0.0) | 9 | 81.8 | 0.0 | 11 |
| Democrats | | | | | | |
| East | 0.0 | 70.0 | 50 | 6.5 | 88.7 | 62 |
| South | 0.0 | 90.0 | 130 | 0.8 | 96.1 | 128 |
| Midwest | 0.0 | 68.5 | 54 | 10.2 | 81.6 | 49 |
| Mountain | 0.0 | 72.7 | 11 | 10.0 | 80.0 | 10 |
| Pacific | 0.0 | 73.7 | 19 | 0.0 | 64.7 | 17 |
| | 80TH CONGRESS | | | 83RD CONGRESS | | |
| Republicans | | | | | | |
| East | 5.5 | 31.9 | 91 | 12.0 | 84.0 | 75 |
| South | 28.6 | 7.1 | 14 | 21.4 | 71.4 | 14 |
| Midwest | 45.1 | 4.4 | 113 | 69.4 | 25.5 | 94 |
| Mountain | (11.1) | (0.0) | 9 | (44.4) | (44.4) | 9 |
| Pacific | 0.0 | 4.3 | 23 | 13.8 | 75.9 | 29 |
| Democrats | | | | | | |
| East | 6.7 | 86.7 | 30 | 0.0 | 97.6 | 42 |
| South | 3.2 | 58.7 | 126 | 21.7 | 55.0 | 120 |
| Midwest | 0.0 | 86.4 | 22 | 5.7 | 91.4 | 35 |
| Mountain | (0.0) | (28.6) | 7 | (14.3) | (71.4) | 7 |
| Pacific | 0.0 | 70.0 | 10 | 0.0 | 91.8 | 12 |
| | 85TH CONGRESS | | | | | |
| Republicans | | | | | | |
| East | 10.8 | 85.1 | 74 | | | |
| South | 40.0 | 46.7 | 15 | | | |
| Midwest | 60.7 | 29.8 | 84 | | | |
| Mountain | (28.6) | (14.3) | 7 | | | |
| Pacific | 33.3 | 66.7 | 24 | | | |
| Democrats | | | | | | |
| East | 0.0 | 93.5 | 46 | | | |
| South | 53.3 | 18.3 | 120 | | | |
| Midwest | 10.9 | 67.4 | 46 | | | |
| Mountain | 20.0 | 20.0 | 10 | | | |
| Pacific | 0.0 | 75.0 | 16 | | | |

and thus less able to conceive of American interests as including an active role in world affairs.

The fact is that if any part of the country can be given a regional tag, it is the Mountain states area. Though the numbers involved are small, the data show that in 15 of 17 possible comparisons, Mountain congressmen of both parties were more isolationalist than those lawmakers representing the two coasts. On the Democratic side, when the break in party cohesion came, it was the Mountain representatives who emerged as the leading isolationists.

One other relationship in Table IV transcends party lines, though it is of shorter duration than the 20-year period which has been our concern. In the two most recent (83d and 85th) of our five Congresses, Eastern and Pacific coast legislators of both parties were the most internationalist groups. The emergence of this association coincided with the decline in party cohesion on foreign aid noted above. This was particularly clear among Republicans; beginning in the 77th Congress, Eastern Republicans were party leaders in internationalism. As the discipline of the parties loosened, it seems that constituency factors, like region, came to exert influence. Thus it appears that coastal representatives, perhaps inclined toward internationalism by the greater social, economic, and political contacts with the overseas world, responded to the relaxation of party pressures by giving greater support to the foreign aid program. In any case, it should be clear that the voting patterns of the House reflect a complex interplay of party and regional factors.

Examination of other constituency characteristics underscores these same points. As party unity disintegrated on the foreign aid issue, a set of constituency variables came to be associated with vote choice. For example, urban [21] representatives of both parties, in the three most recent Congresses, provided more support for, and less opposition to, the aid program than those from rural areas (Table V). This

TABLE V. DISTRIBUTION OF REPRESENTATIVES ON FOREIGN AID, BY PARTY AND RURALISM

| Party and Constituency Type | 80TH CONGRESS | | | 83RD CONGRESS | | |
|---|---|---|---|---|---|---|
| | % Isol. | % Int. | N | % Isol. | % Int. | N |
| Republicans | | | | | | |
| Urban | 10.0 | 27.8 | 90 | 14.7 | 78.7 | 75 |
| Rural | 42.4 | 0.0 | 59 | 70.2 | 23.4 | 47 |
| Democrats | | | | | | |
| Urban | 2.9 | 82.6 | 69 | 2.4 | 92.9 | 85 |
| Rural | 4.8 | 52.4 | 84 | 23.3 | 59.3 | 86 |

| | 85TH CONGRESS | | |
|---|---|---|---|
| | % Isol. | % Int. | N |
| Republicans | | | |
| Urban | 26.4 | 70.8 | 72 |
| Rural | 65.7 | 25.7 | 35 |
| Democrats | | | |
| Urban | 3.3 | 80.2 | 91 |
| Rural | 52.5 | 24.2 | 97 |

finding survived the introduction of controls for region.[22] In addition, the correlation coefficients relating ruralism to foreign aid scale scores, displayed in Table VI, buttress this argument. Only in the 80th Congress, after the pure partisan cleavage had ended, did a statistically significant relationship appear between ruralism and the vote on foreign aid. The negative correlations suggest that the representatives

TABLE VI. CORRELATION COEFFICIENTS: CONSTITUENCY CHARACTERISTICS AND FOREIGN AID SCALE SCORES

| Constituency characteristics | CONGRESS | | | | |
|---|---|---|---|---|---|
| | 76th | 77th | 80th | 83rd | 85th |
| Ruralism | −0.5 | .01 | −.23* | −.43* | −.45* |
| Ethnicity | −.09 | −.16* | .25* | .21* | .19* |
| Educational Level | −.16* | −.17* | .08 | .15† | .16† |
| Socio-Economic Status | −.24 | −.24* | .11† | .26* | .27* |

* Significantly greater than zero at .01 level.
† Significantly greater than zero at 0.5 level.
Note: The correlations are product-moment correlations and the test of significance is an F test; see Hubert M. Blalock, Jr., *Social Statistics* (New York, 1960), pp. 285-305.

of rural areas tended to fall at the low (isolationist) end of the foreign aid scale. By way of explanation, it may be that in the absence of party unity, greater contacts with, and information about, foreign nations led to this greater receptivity of urban congressmen to appeals to back the aid program. In any case, the evidence suggests that the decline in the importance of party as a determinant of the congressional vote was accompanied by an increase in the importance of district characteristics.

Ethnicity is an additional factor which has received a good deal of attention, the thesis being that Americans of German and Irish background have been opposed to United States involvement in world affairs, lest this country come into conflict with Germany or alliance with Great Britain.[23] We have tested this notion by relating congressional voting records to the ethnic composition of the congressional districts. The data (Table VII) show that the negative association between high [24] ethnicity and internationalism existed only in the pre-World War II period, *i.e.,* in the 76th and 77th Congresses. In each Congress thereafter, the reverse was true; representatives of high ethnic districts gave greater support to the aid program than those from low ethnic areas. Nor did the addition of the available controls, in this case for ruralism, alter the relationship. The correlations between ethnicity and foreign aid scale score lend further support to these notions, for as Table VI shows, in each Congress since the 80th there was a significant, though small, positive correlation between ethnicity and internationalism.

The reason for the reversal of the association of ethnicity and the congressional vote after World War II may lie in the altered international situation which characterized the period. In contrast to the pre-War era, the challenge of world communism and the alliance between Germany and the United States greatly reduced the potential for German-American conflict and, at the same time, the emotional conflicts of Americans of German ancestry. The Soviet threat and other factors may also have been sufficient to diminish Anglo-Irish hostility or to subordinate it to more immediate concerns, thus allowing Irish-Americans to see benefit in support of Great Britain by the United States. Further, both Germany and Ireland were recipients of American aid during the postwar years and this may

TABLE VII. DISTRIBUTION OF REPRESENTATIVES ON FOREIGN AID, BY ETHNICITY AND PARTY

| Party and Constituency Characteristic | 76TH CONGRESS | | | 77TH CONGRESS | | |
|---|---|---|---|---|---|---|
| | % Isol. | % Int. | N | % Isol. | % Int. | N |
| Republicans | | | | | | |
| Low Ethnicity | 77.8 | 0.0 | 18 | 81.8 | 9.1 | 22 |
| High Ethnicity | 83.8 | 0.0 | 111 | 84.2 | 6.9 | 101 |
| Democrats | | | | | | |
| Low Ethnicity | 0.0 | 88.8 | 80 | 1.6 | 96.0 | 126 |
| High Ethnicity | 0.0 | 63.8 | 94 | 8.0 | 80.0 | 100 |
| | 80TH CONGRESS | | | 83RD CONGRESS | | |
| Republicans | | | | | | |
| Low Ethnicity | 46.3 | 1.9 | 54 | 64.5 | 39.5 | 43 |
| High Ethnicity | 18.3 | 23.1 | 104 | 34.5 | 62.2 | 19 |
| Democrats | | | | | | |
| Low Ethnicity | 8.3 | 41.7 | 12 | 18.8 | 68.8 | 16 |
| High Ethnicity | 2.6 | 86.8 | 38 | 0.0 | 100.0 | 54 |
| | 85TH CONGRESS | | | | | |
| Republicans | | | | | | |
| Low Ethnicity | 52.9 | 29.4 | 34 | | | |
| High Ethnicity | 33.0 | 61.4 | 88 | | | |
| Democrats | | | | | | |
| Low Ethnicity | 28.0 | 44.0 | 25 | | | |
| High Ethnicity | 0.0 | 95.0 | 60 | | | |

have led citizens with attachments to these countries to see value in the aid program. In sum, the "cold war" may have created a world in which isolationist views were no longer functional for the German and Irish ethnic groups.[25]

Finally, we may briefly note a set of similar developments with respect to the educational level and the socio-economic status of congressional districts. Both education and status seem to impel individuals in the direction of internationalism,[26] and this raises the question whether the legislators who represent them are similarly inclined. The data (Tables VIII and IX) suggest that this came to be true, but only after a substantial decline in party unity on the foreign aid issue. The representatives of highly educated and high status [27] districts were, in the 83d and 85th Congresses, the strongest backers of the aid program. No consistent pattern appeared in the three earlier Congresses.

The addition of controls for region and ruralism sustain the findings. Correlating the measures of education and status with internationalism (see Table VI) provides additional evidence in support of these relationships; significant, positive coefficients appeared in the two most recent Congresses.

From this we may conclude that education and status led to more information on, and concern about foreign policy, which, coupled with greater analytical powers, led to a greater receptivity to the arguments in behalf of enlarged interna-

TABLE VIII. DISTRIBUTION OF REPRESENTATIVES ON FOREIGN AID, BY EDUCATIONAL LEVEL AND PARTY

| Party and Constituency Characteristic | 83RD CONGRESS | | | 85TH CONGRESS | | |
|---|---|---|---|---|---|---|
| | % Isol. | % Int. | N | % Isol. | % Int. | N |
| Republicans | | | | | | |
| Low Education | 52.5 | 37.5 | 40 | 54.3 | 34.3 | 35 |
| High Education | 20.3 | 72.2 | 79 | 28.9 | 65.8 | 76 |
| Democrats | | | | | | |
| Low Education | 16.5 | 69.9 | 103 | 33.6 | 46.3 | 110 |
| High Education | 8.1 | 75.7 | 37 | 17.5 | 50.0 | 40 |

TABLE IX. DISTRIBUTION OF REPRESENTATIVES ON FOREIGN AID, BY SOCIO-ECONOMIC STATUS AND PARTY

| Party and Constituency Characteristic | 83RD CONGRESS | | | 85TH CONGRESS | | |
|---|---|---|---|---|---|---|
| | % Isol. | % Int. | N | % Isol. | % Int. | N |
| Republicans | | | | | | |
| Low SES | 66.0 | 24.5 | 53 | 68.9 | 24.4 | 45 |
| High SES | 13.8 | 80.0 | 80 | 26.0 | 68.8 | 77 |
| Democrats | | | | | | |
| Low SES | 19.1 | 64.8 | 105 | 40.5 | 37.7 | 116 |
| High SES | 2.2 | 86.7 | 45 | 8.3 | 66.7 | 48 |

tional political activity. When released from the obligation to back his political party, the representative of such people may have tended to vote in keeping with the views of his constituents. Such a tendency may have been reinforced by the fact that those with education and status probably had high visibility in the community and may have constituted a substantial pool of interested and articulate citizens who held internationalist attitudes on American foreign policy.

In sum, the discussion of the relationship of constituency characteristics to voting alignments on foreign aid in the House has suggested that the importance of district attributes is inversely associated with the significance of political party as a determinant of the congressional vote. As the cleavage between the parties vanished, a number of constituency factors took on value as a means for distinguishing between the proponents and foes of foreign aid legislation.

In addition, whatever the relationship between the individual legislator and his constituents, the fact remains that in certain periods of history the representatives of like districts display similar voting records in Congress. If such behavior is not the result of communication or pressure from constituency to congressman—and there is some evidence that it is not [28] then some other explanation for the meaningfulness of constituency must be found. It may be that the lawmakers tended to overestimate the degree to which the "folks back home" scrutinized legislative activity, and thus voted in accordance with their perceptions of voters' wishes, however accurate or inaccurate these may have been. Or legislators, and particularly those from relatively homogeneous constituencies, may have shared (have "internalized") the basic outlook of those they represented, and thus received cues from the district in the absence of any direct communication. In some such mechanism as these lies the explanation of the relevance of constituency in the consideration of the forces impinging on the congressional vote.

## III. Conclusion

The foregoing analysis permits a few general conclusions to be drawn:

(1) On the methodological side, the value of longitudinal studies should be apparent. The evidence presented here shows pretty conclusively that the voting patterns shift with the passage of time. While there are a few constants (*e.g.,* religious affiliation and Committee assignment), it is also true that in one era one factor may be of crucial importance as a determinant of vote (*e.g.,* party affiliation) while later a different set of variables (*e.g.,* constituency characteristics) may take on explanatory value. Such alterations obviously would be difficult to discover in studies limited to a single Congress or legislative session.

(2) Substantively, it is clear that the isolationist-internationalist scale is complex. At any point in time a cluster of variables appears to be related to the vote patterns within the House of Representatives. Specifically, in the 76th Congress, when the issue was the arms embargo repeal, political party seemed to be the crucial factor in vote decisions. Two years later, when the question posed was the Lend-Lease Act, party discipline cracked and regional factors became relevant. Mountain states Democrats emerged as the chief isolationists and Eastern Republicans became the leading internationalists within their respective parties. After the war, in the 80th Congress, urban-rural and ethnic variables took on importance, and in the 1950s, after a more marked decline in party cohesion, coastal, high ethnic, high education, highly urban, and high socio-economic status districts tended to send to Washington men of both parties more likely to support foreign aid legislation while Southern, low ethnic, low education, rural, and low SES constituencies supplied the greatest share of the opposition to the program. And the available controls suggest that each of these variables exerted an influence independent of the others.

These shifts occurred simultaneously with changes in the political context within which the legislative process operates. The control of the presidency passed from the Democrats to the Republicans in 1953, and with the change came alterations in the kinds of pressures brought to bear on individual representatives. For example, Southern Democrats, representing a rapidly industrializing area and without an obligation to support an incumbent President, began to oppose the aid program in larger numbers while Republicans began to rally around their internationalist President. Thus, a new set of political forces produced a situation in which factors other than party came to contribute to the pattern of congressional voting, and the alignment which emerged was, in a sense, the resultant of the intersection of these two sets of variables.

We should note, also, that different types of demographic variables appear to be associated with foreign affairs behavior. This study has singled out three types— personal, political, and constituency—and each has pointed to elements which, at one time or another, were related to the vote on foreign aid. In sum, a large number of variables of different types interacting with the political situation of the moment produce a vote configuration which alters with the passage of time. And an examination of other variables would undoubtedly introduce additional complexities.

## NOTES

1. See David B. Truman, *The Congressional Party* (New York, 1959) and Duncan MacRae, Jr., *Dimensions of Congressional Voting* (Berkeley, University of California Press, 1958).

2. The Truman and MacRae studies both examined the 81st Congress (1949–50); in addition, each treated the parties separately.

3. As Truman recognizes, *op. cit.*, pp. viii, 10–12.

4. The 76th Congress will be retained in the analysis both because the arms embargo repeal is related in content to the issues of the other sessions and because the near unanimity of party positions during the 76th Congress permits utilization of the arms embargo repeal vote as a base against which to note the subsequent breakdown of party solidarity on foreign aid.

5. See for example Julius Turner, *Party and Constituency: Pressures on Congress* (Baltimore, Johns Hopkins University Press, 1951), pp. 54–58; and Mark Kesselman, "Presidential Leadership in Congress on Foreign Policy," *Midwest Journal of Political Science*, Vol. 5 (1961), pp. 284–289.

6. My "Quantitative Techniques for Studying Voting Behavior in the UN General Assembly," *International Organization*, Vol. 14 (1960), pp. 291–306, discusses the relative advantages of scaling and other quantitative methods.

7. The terms "isolationist" and "internationalist" are labels of convenience, not intended to carry normative baggage here.

8. For a full discussion of the study design, including the items comprising the foreign aid scales and the methods of calculation of the measures of the demographic variables, see my *Congressional Isolationist Behavior* (unpublished Ph.D. dissertation, Yale University, 1963), ch. 2 and appendices I, II, and III.

9. *Op. cit.*, p. 34.

10. See Malcolm E. Jewell, "Evaluating the Decline of Southern Internationalism Through Senatorial Roll Call Votes," *Journal of Politics*, Vol. 21 (1959), pp. 624–646.

11. For instance, Bernard Fensterwald, Jr., "The Anatomy of American 'Isolationism' and Expansionism," *Journal of Conflict Resolution*, Vol. 2 (June and December, 1958), pp. 111–138 and 280–309, finds Catholics in "the front ranks of the 'isolationists'" (at p. 136), while John H. Fenton, *The Catholic Vote* (New Orleans, Hauser Press, 1960) finds that in 1959 Catholic representatives were more likely to support foreign aid than non-Catholics (pp. 87–108).

12. We applied controls only where there were a minimum of 10 congressmen in a party-religious category (*e.g.*, there had to be at least 10 Republicans of each religious conviction before we used controls). In this instance, there were too few Catholic representatives from rural areas and from the South for additional controls to be used.

13. This corroborates and strengthens Fenton's assertion (see note 11, supra), for it indicates that urban-rural controls, which Fenton omits, do not destroy the relationships. See *op. cit.*, pp. 105–108.

14. For evidence of a similar relationship in the Senate, see David N. Farnsworth, "A Comparison of the Senate and Its Foreign Relations Committee on Selected Roll Call Votes," *Western Political Quarterly*, Vol. 14 (1961), pp. 168–175.

15. Holbert N. Carroll, *The House of Representatives and Foreign Affairs* (Pittsburgh, University of Pittsburgh Press, 1958), pp. 29–30.

16. For a detailed discussion of the executive-legislative relationships, see *ibid.*, pp. 320–350.

17. Farnsworth, *op. cit.*, states this view clearly with regard to the Senate Foreign Relations Committee: "The most effective way to destroy the Anti-Internationalist sentiment in the Senate, other than defeat at the polls, is to make those Senators holding such attitudes members of the Committee." (p. 175) For an example of a similar mechanism on the House Appropriations Committee, see Richard F. Fenno, "The House Appropriations Committee," *American Political Science Review*, Vol. 56 (1962), pp. 310–324.

18. For evidence and discussion in support of the assumption, see MacRae, *op. cit.*, p. 278; George B. Galloway, *The Legislative Process in Congress* (New York, 1955), pp. 198–215; and Stephen K. Bailey and Howard D. Samuel, *Congress at Work* (New York, 1952), pp. 112–126. For evidence of the concern of state legislators for the views of their constituents, see Duncan MacRae, Jr., "The Relation Between Roll Call Votes and Constituencies in the Massachusetts House of Representatives," *American Political Science Review*, Vol. 46 (1952), pp. 1046–1055 and Wilder Crane, Jr., "Do Representatives Represent?" *Journal of Politics*, Vol. 22 (1960), pp. 295–299. On the other side, see Donald E. Stokes and Warren E. Miller, "Party Government and the Saliency of Congress," *Public Opinion Quarterly*, Vol. 26 (1962), pp. 531–546 and Miller and Stokes, "Constituency Influence in Congress," *American Political Science Review*, Vol. 57 (1963), pp. 45–56.

19. Turner, *op. cit.*, pp. 144–163; George L. Grassmuck, *Sectional Biases in Congress on Foreign Policy* (Baltimore, Johns Hopkins Press, 1951), pp. 141–174; MacRae, *Dimensions . . ., op. cit.*, pp. 276–278; Ralph H. Smuckler, "The Region of Isolationism," *American Political Science Review*, Vol. 47 (1953), pp. 386–401; Jewell, *op. cit.*

20. We have used the following regional breakdowns:

EAST: Conn., Del., Me., Mass., N. H., N. J., N. Y., Pa., R. I., Vt. (10 states).

SOUTH: Ala., Ark., Fla., Ga., Ky., La., Md., Miss., N. C., Okla., S. C., Tenn., Tex., Va., W. Va. (15 states).

MIDWEST: Ill., Ind., Iowa, Kan., Mich., Minn., Mo., Neb., N. D., Ohio, S. D., Wis. (12 states).

MOUNTAIN: Ariz., Colo., Idaho, Mont., Nev., N. M., Utah, Wyo. (8 states).

PACIFIC: Calif., Ore., Wash. (3 states).

21 Following MacRae, *Dimensions . . . , op. cit.*, we have used the per cent of the male working force employed in farm occupations as a measure of ruralism. The following breakdowns were used: 24.0% or more—rural district; 6.0–23.9% —mixed district; 5.9% or less—urban districts. The present writer is indebted to Professor MacRae for supplying occupational distributions for the period after the 1950 census. Since our purpose is to focus on the "pure" types, the data for the mixed districts have been omitted.

22. A word is in order about the limitations on the controls used. In order to differentiate the extreme cases from the moderates, the variables were trichotomized. Given the skewed distributions of the constituency attributes, there were too few cases in some cells to permit meaningful controls. For example, with respect to ruralism, only in the Midwestern region were there sufficient numbers of representatives of both urban and rural districts to allow controls.

23. Samuel Lubell is a major proponent of this argument. See his *The Future of American Politics* (New York, 1952), pp. 121–132, and *The Revolt of the Moderates* (New York, 1956), pp. 52–74.

24. By ethnicity, we mean the proportion of the population of German and Irish ancestry. Using census data the districts have been categorized as follows: Low Ethnic: 0.0–0.4% of the population; Moderate Ethnic: 0.5–0.9% of the pop-

ulation; High Ethnic: 1.0% or more of the population born in Germany or Ireland. Though the numbers of foreign born are small, we have used them as an index of ethnicity on the assumption that those who emigrate to the U. S. tend to settle in parts of the nation where others from the "old country" have settled. Since the census omits the data for the Southern states, only those Southern districts composed entirely of census tracts are included in the analysis. Also, as with other variables, the moderate ethnic districts are omitted from Table VII.

25. Lubell, *op. cit.*, relies mainly on pre-World War II data, specifically the behavior of the German-Americans in the 1940 presidential election, to support the ethnic-emotional argument. This may help account for the contrast between his view and that presented here.

26. On education, see Fensterwald, *op. cit.*, p. 137 and Smuckler, *op. cit.*, p. 399. On status, see Alfred O. Hero, *Americans in World Affairs* (Boston, World Peace Foundation, 1959), pp. 43–68.

27. The measure of education, compiled from the census, is the per cent of the district population who had attended college *at some time*. The following categories were used: Low Education: 0.0–9.9% of the population college trained; Moderate Education: 10.0–14.9% of the population college trained; High Education: 15.0% or more of the population college trained. For a measure of SES, we have used MacRae's occupational distributions, specifically the per cent of employed males engaged in managerial, technical, and professional occupations. Education is usually a concomitant of such activities; they are often rewarded by high income. The districts were categorized as follows: Low Status: 0.0–14.9% of population in managerial, technical and professional occupations; Moderate Status: 15.0–19.9% of population so engaged; High Status: 20.0% or more of population so engaged.

28. See the works of Miller and Stokes, cited above, footnote 18.

# 21. Senators' Attitudes Toward Civil Rights[*]

CHARLES F. ANDRAIN

Since the end of World War II, the struggle to secure civil rights for Negroes has assumed increasing importance on the American political scene. The movement of southern Negroes to the North means that integration has become less of a sectional and more of a national issue. In terms used by Donald E. Stokes, civil rights represents an example of a "position issue," i.e., an issue which involves "advocacy of government actions from a set of alternatives over which a distribution of voter preferences is defined." [1] On the basis of national sample survey data, V. O. Key reports that, of all contemporary problems, the issue of federal action to further school integration generates a bipolarized opinion of highest intensity.[2] With the decline of conflict over New Deal policies after World War II, the issue of civil rights has become the dominant position issue of American politics.

In view of this widespread disagreement on the value of integration, Guttman scale analysis represents an appropriate technique for assessing, in a relatively precise way, attitudes toward civil rights. Scale analysis assigns an individual a score somewhere between the two extremes of consistently favoring an issue and always opposing the issue. In a perfect Guttman scale, the items, or statements measuring an attitude, are cumulative. A person who responds favorably to an item also responds favorably to all items of higher rank. Likewise, anyone responding negatively to an item makes an unfavorable response to all items of lower rank. Statements forming a Guttman scale measure only one attitude. If the items fall into a fairly perfect cumulative scale pattern, they comprise a single core of meaning.[3]

Of all branches of government, the United States Congress has moved most slowly to secure the enforcement of integration. In 1960, however, Congress did approve a fairly comprehensive Civil Rights Act. By employing Guttman scaling procedures, we have measured senators' attitudes toward integration during the 1960 session. In this study, the issue of civil rights refers to federal government action to enforce political, economic, and social rights for Negroes, e.g., the right to vote, equal job opportunity, and desegregation of schools. Since we cannot directly measure senators' attitudes toward civil rights, we must infer their attitudes from the roll-call votes cast in 1960. Responses to these roll calls form the equivalent of "yes" and "no" answers to items on an attitude questionnaire.

* From *The Western Political Quarterly,* Vol. 17 (1964), pp. 488–503. Reprinted by permission of the University of Utah, copyright owners.

## Procedures

Although the Guttman techniques reveal which items form a common content, they offer little guidance in choosing the initial set of items to scale. I used two criteria for selecting roll calls. First, I rejected all those roll calls on which fewer than eighty senators voted. Theoretically, the larger the number of senators voting on a motion or amendment, the greater the importance they attach to that vote. Second, I selected only those roll calls on which more than fifteen senators voted on the losing side. Unanimous votes do not discriminate attitudes.[4]

In no scalogram do all responses of every individual fall into a perfect, cumulative pattern. We must thus decide what score to give a senator whose votes lie outside a cumulative pattern. I placed such senators in the scale score group with whom they could be assigned with the least number of changes in their votes. When an equal number of changes could put a senator in two or more groups, then he was placed in the scale score group that most nearly approaches the mean score of the total number of senators voting consistently.[5]

## Findings

The scalogram reproduced in Table I shows how one hundred senators voted on civil rights issues during 1960. The senators are divided into eleven groups, ranging from strongly pro-integration (scale score of 10) to strongly anti-integration (score of 0). The ten roll calls are ranked from most to least discriminating. The vote on the final passage of the amended civil rights bill was least discriminating; on this roll call, all but the eighteen senators from the deep South voted "yea."

The roll calls include amendments calling for registration of Negro voters, federal aid to desegregated schools, and a permanent Commission of Equal Job Opportunity. The items form a cumulative scale. The coefficient of reproducability is .96. The scalogram does not show too extreme marginal distribution of items. Eighteen per cent of the senators voted consistently against civil rights, whereas 30 per cent made a pro-integration response to every roll call.[6]

The thirty senators who voted pro-integration on all ten roll calls include mainly Northern Democrats, except Republicans Case of New Jersey, Javits and Keating of New York, Kuchel of California, and Scott of Pennsylvania. Representing mostly urbanized, industrialized states where Negroes comprise more than 2 per cent of the population, these thirty senators tend to favor political innovation and positive government intervention in American socioeconomic life. Scale scores of 8, 7, 6, 5, and 4 mark off few senators, twenty-three in all, including thirteen Republicans and ten Democrats. Of these twenty-three, all but three have inconsistent, non-cumulative scale patterns. The sixteen senators with scores of 3 include eleven Republicans, mainly from the Midwest, and five Democrats from the Southwest. Senators Johnson of Texas and Dirksen of Illinois, majority and minority floor leaders, are in this group. Senators scoring 2 and 1 comprise five conservative Republicans (Bridges of New Hampshire, Butler of Maryland, Goldwater of Arizona, Williams of Delaware, and Young of North Dakota) and five Democrats from border and southern states (Byrd of West Virginia, Frear of Delaware, Gore and Kefauver of Tennessee, and Kerr of Oklahoma). The eighteen Democrats from the deep South voted against civil rights on all ten roll calls.

TABLE I. SCALOGRAM OF 1960 VOTING PATTERNS ON CIVIL RIGHTS ISSUES

| Senator | Score | Non-Scale Responses | A | B | C | D | E | F | G | H | I | J |
|---|---|---|---|---|---|---|---|---|---|---|---|---|---|
| Carroll | 10 | | X | X | X | X | X | X | X | X | X | X |
| Case (N.J.) | 10 | | X | X | X | X | X | X | X | X | X | X |
| Douglas | 10 | | X | X | X | X | X | X | X | X | X | X |
| Engle | 10 | | X | X | X | X | X | X | X | X | X | X |
| Hart | 10 | | X | X | X | X | X | X | X | X | X | X |
| Hartke | 10 | | X | X | X | X | X | X | X | X | X | X |
| Humphrey | 10 | | X | X | X | X | X | X | X | X | X | X |
| Jackson | 10 | | X | X | X | X | X | X | X | X | X | X |
| Javits | 10 | | X | X | X | X | X | X | X | X | X | X |
| Keating | 10 | | X | X | X | X | X | X | X | X | X | X |
| Kennedy | 10 | | X | X | X | X | X | X | X | X | X | X |
| Kuchel | 10 | | X | X | X | X | X | X | X | X | X | X |
| Magnuson | 10 | | X | X | X | X | X | X | X | X | X | X |
| McCarthy | 10 | | X | X | X | X | X | X | X | X | X | X |
| McNamara | 10 | | X | X | X | X | X | X | X | X | X | X |
| Morse | 10 | | X | X | X | X | X | X | X | X | X | X |
| Moss | 10 | | X | X | X | X | X | X | X | X | X | X |
| Muskie | 10 | | X | X | X | X | X | X | X | X | X | X |
| Pastore | 10 | | X | X | X | X | X | X | X | X | X | X |
| Proxmire | 10 | | X | X | X | X | X | X | X | X | X | X |
| Randolph | 10 | | X | X | X | X | X | X | X | X | X | X |
| Scott | 10 | | X | X | X | X | X | X | X | X | X | X |
| Symington | 10 | | X | X | X | X | X | X | X | X | X | X |
| Williams (N.J.) | 10 | | X | X | X | X | X | X | X | X | X | X |
| Clark | 10 | 1 | X | X | X | X | X | Y | X | X | X | X |
| Dodd | 10 | 1 | X | X | X | X | X | Y | X | X | X | X |
| Gruening | 10 | 1 | X | X | X | X | X | Y | X | X | X | X |
| Hennings | 10 | 1 | X | X | X | X | X | Y | X | X | X | X |
| Lusk | 10 | 1 | X | X | Y | X | X | O | X | O | X | X |
| Young (Ohio) | 10 | 1 | X | X | X | X | X | X | X | X | Y | X |
| Bartlett | 9 | | Y | X | X | X | X | X | X | X | X | X |
| Beall | 9 | | Y | X | X | X | X | X | X | X | X | X |
| Long (Hawaii) | 9 | 1 | Y | X | X | X | X | X | X | X | Y | X |
| Bush | 8 | 1 | Y | Y | X | X | X | X | Y | X | X | X |
| Fong | 8 | 1 | Y | Y | X | X | Y | X | X | X | X | X |
| Lausche | 7 | 1 | Y | X | Y | X | X | X | X | X | X | X |
| Church | 7 | 2 | X | Y | Y | X | X | Y | X | X | X | X |
| Allott | 7 | 1 | Y | Y | Y | X | X | X | Y | X | X | X |
| Cannon | 7 | 2 | Y | Y | Y | X | X | Y | X | X | Y | X |
| Cooper | 7 | 2 | Y | Y | Y | X | X | X | Y | X | Y | X |
| Murray | 6 | 1 | Y | X | Y | Y | X | O | X | X | X | X |
| Morton | 6 | | Y | Y | Y | Y | X | X | X | X | X | X |
| Prouty | 6 | 1 | Y | Y | Y | Y | X | Y | X | X | X | X |
| Mansfield | 6 | 1 | Y | Y | Y | Y | X | O | Y | X | X | X |
| Anderson | 5 | 2 | X | Y | X | Y | Y | X | X | X | X | X |
| Monroney | 5 | 2 | X | Y | Y | Y | Y | X | X | Y | X | X |
| Aiken | 5 | | Y | Y | Y | Y | Y | X | X | X | X | X |
| Cotton | 5 | 1 | Y | Y | Y | Y | X | Y | X | X | X | X |
| Bennett | 5 | 1 | Y | Y | Y | Y | Y | X | Y | X | X | X |
| Brunsdale | 5 | 1 | Y | Y | Y | Y | Y | X | Y | X | X | X |
| Wiley | 5 | 1 | Y | Y | Y | Y | Y | X | Y | X | X | X |

TABLE I (continued)

| Senator | Score | Non-Scale Responses | ROLL CALLS | | | | | | | | | |
|---|---|---|---|---|---|---|---|---|---|---|---|---|
| | | | A | B | C | D | E | F | G | H | I | J |
| Smith | 4 | 1 | X | Y | X | X | Y | Y | X | X | X | X |
| Chavez | 4 | 1 | Y | X | O | Y | Y | Y | X | X | X | X |
| Yarborough | 4 | 1 | X | Y | Y | Y | Y | Y | X | X | X | X |
| Case (S.D.) | 4 | | Y | Y | Y | Y | Y | Y | X | X | X | X |
| Green | 4 | 2 | Y | Y | Y | X | Y | Y | X | X | Y | X |
| Saltonstall | 3 | 1 | Y | Y | X | Y | Y | Y | Y | X | X | X |
| Carlson | 3 | | Y | Y | Y | Y | Y | Y | Y | X | X | X |
| Curtis | 3 | | Y | Y | Y | Y | Y | Y | Y | X | X | X |
| Dirksen | 3 | | Y | Y | Y | Y | Y | Y | Y | X | X | X |
| Hayden | 3 | | Y | Y | Y | Y | Y | Y | Y | X | X | X |
| Hickenlooper | 3 | | Y | Y | Y | Y | Y | Y | Y | X | X | X |
| Hruska | 3 | | Y | Y | Y | Y | Y | Y | Y | X | X | X |
| Johnson | 3 | | Y | Y | Y | Y | Y | Y | Y | X | X | X |
| Martin | 3 | | Y | Y | Y | Y | Y | Y | Y | X | X | X |
| McGee | 3 | | Y | Y | Y | Y | Y | Y | Y | X | X | X |
| Mundt | 3 | | Y | Y | Y | Y | Y | Y | Y | X | X | X |
| O'Mahoney | 3 | | Y | Y | Y | Y | Y | O | Y | X | X | X |
| Schoeppel | 3 | | Y | Y | Y | Y | Y | Y | Y | X | X | X |
| Capehart | 3 | | Y | Y | Y | Y | Y | O | Y | O | X | X |
| Dworshak | 3 | | Y | Y | Y | Y | Y | Y | Y | O | X | X |
| Bible | 3 | 2 | Y | Y | Y | Y | X | Y | Y | X | Y | X |
| Byrd (W. Va.) | 2 | 1 | X | Y | Y | Y | X | Y | Y | Y | Y | X |
| Bridges | 2 | | Y | Y | Y | Y | Y | Y | Y | Y | X | X |
| Goldwater | 2 | | Y | O | Y | Y | Y | Y | Y | Y | X | X |
| Kerr | 2 | | Y | Y | Y | Y | Y | Y | Y | Y | X | X |
| Young (N.D.) | 2 | | Y | Y | Y | Y | Y | Y | Y | Y | X | X |
| Gore | 1 | 1 | X | Y | Y | Y | Y | Y | Y | Y | Y | X |
| Butler | 1 | | Y | Y | Y | Y | Y | Y | Y | Y | Y | X |
| Frear | 1 | | Y | Y | Y | Y | Y | Y | Y | Y | Y | X |
| Kefauver | 1 | | Y | Y | Y | Y | Y | Y | Y | Y | Y | X |
| Williams (Del.) | 1 | | Y | Y | Y | Y | Y | Y | Y | Y | Y | X |
| Byrd (Va.) | 0 | | Y | Y | Y | Y | Y | Y | Y | Y | Y | Y |
| Eastland | 0 | | Y | Y | Y | Y | Y | Y | Y | Y | Y | Y |
| Ellender | 0 | | Y | Y | Y | Y | Y | Y | Y | Y | Y | Y |
| Ervin | 0 | | Y | Y | Y | Y | Y | Y | Y | Y | Y | Y |
| Fulbright | 0 | | Y | Y | Y | Y | Y | Y | Y | Y | Y | Y |
| Hill | 0 | | Y | Y | Y | Y | Y | Y | Y | Y | Y | Y |
| Holland | 0 | | Y | Y | Y | Y | Y | Y | Y | Y | Y | Y |
| Johnston | 0 | | Y | Y | Y | Y | Y | Y | Y | Y | Y | Y |
| Jordan | 0 | | Y | Y | Y | Y | Y | Y | Y | Y | Y | Y |
| Long (La.) | 0 | | Y | Y | Y | Y | Y | Y | Y | Y | Y | Y |
| McClellan | 0 | | Y | Y | Y | Y | Y | Y | Y | Y | Y | Y |
| Robertson | 0 | | Y | Y | Y | Y | Y | Y | Y | Y | Y | Y |
| Russell | 0 | | Y | Y | Y | Y | Y | Y | Y | Y | Y | Y |
| Smathers | 0 | | Y | Y | Y | Y | Y | Y | Y | Y | Y | Y |
| Sparkman | 0 | | Y | Y | Y | Y | Y | Y | Y | Y | Y | Y |
| Stennis | 0 | | Y | Y | Y | Y | Y | Y | Y | Y | Y | Y |
| Talmadge | 0 | | Y | Y | Y | Y | Y | Y | Y | Y | Y | Y |
| Thurmond | 0 | | Y | Y | Y | Y | Y | Y | Y | Y | Y | Y |

TABLE I (continued)

LEGEND

*Symbols:*

    X—actual pro-integration vote.

    X—paired or announced pro-integration vote

    Y—actual anti-integration vote

    Y—pared or announced anti-integration vote

    O—absent or unannounced on roll call

*1960 Roll Calls:*

| Item | Pro-Integration Vote | Amendment or Motion |
|---|---|---|
| A | No | Table amendment to permit courts to waive requirements that a Negro seeking court certificate to vote must prove he tried to register with state authorities and was rejected after pattern of discrimination was found by courts. |
| B | No | Table amendment to add a plan for Presidentially appointed enrollment officers to register Negroes. |
| C | No | Table amendment (1) providing technical assistance to areas desegregating schools and (2) endorsing Supreme Court 1954 desegregation decision. |
| D | No | Table two amendments: (1) one to allow Attorney General to enter private suits for school desegregation, and (2) the other to add Part III, empowering Attorney General to seek injunctions to protect any civil right. |
| E | No | Table amendment to establish permament Commission on Equal Job Opportunity. |
| F | No | Table amendment to prohibit use of poll tax or property requirements as qualifications for voting in federal elections through statute rather than through constitutional amendment. |
| G | No | Table amendment requiring that a Negro must prove to referee only that he is qualified to vote. |
| H | No | Postpone further consideration of civil rights for one week. |
| I | No | Amend referres' plan to require that judges, when hearing Negroes' applications for voting certificates, must (1) call in opponents to applications and (2) hold advisory proceedings before deciding each case. |
| J | Yes | Pass amended civil rights bill (HR 8601), providing for court registration of Negroes and other matters. |

    The data on senators' votes appeared in *Congressional Quarterly Almanac*, 86th Cong., 2d Sess., 1960, pp. 473, 486–88. I have considered pairs and announced votes as votes actually cast. Absent and unannounced replies were regarded as scalar responses.

By the use of mean scores, we have related senatorial attitudes toward civil rights to other variables, such as the influence of political party affiliation, the personal background of the senators, and the type of state a senator represents. Within the Senate, principal influences on voting behavior include party affiliation, cues from the party leadership, and committee decisions. Table II reveals the

TABLE II. RELATIONSHIP BETWEEN SCALE SCORES AND INFLUENCE OF POLITICAL PARTY

| A. Party Affiliation | Number | Mean | Standard Deviation |
|---|---|---|---|
| All Senators | 100 | 5.2 | 3.9 |
| Republicans | 35 | 5.0 | 2.9 |
| Democrats | 65 | 5.3 | 4.3 |
| Northern Democrats | 43 | 7.8 | 3.0 |
| Southern Democrats | 22 | 0.4 | 1.1 |

| B. Senate Committees | Number | Mean |
|---|---|---|
| Policy Committee | | |
| Democrats | 9 | 3.8 |
| Republicans | 14 | 4.4 |
| Steering Committee | | |
| Democrats | 15 | 3.3 |
| Republicans | 12 | 5.5 |
| Chairmen of Senate Committees or Ranking Minority Members | | |
| Democrats | 16 | 2.8 |
| Republicans | 16 | 3.5 |
| Judiciary Committee | 15 | 4.7 |
| Democrats | 10 | 4.5 |
| Republicans | 5 | 5.2 |

| C. Number of Years in Senate | Number | Mean | DEMOCRATS No. | DEMOCRATS Mean | REPUBLICANS No. | REPUBLICANS Mean |
|---|---|---|---|---|---|---|
| 1– 5 | 31 | 8.4 | 23 | 8.6 | 8 | 7.8 |
| 6–10 | 24 | 5.9 | 10 | 6.8 | 14 | 5.2 |
| 11–15 | 14 | 4.2 | 8 | 5.2 | 6 | 2.8 |
| 16–20 | 7 | 5.1 | 2 | 10.0 | 5 | 3.2 |
| 21 and more | 6 | 4.0 | 4 | 4.2 | 2 | 3.5 |

The data on party affiliation, Senate leadership committees, and length of seniority were compiled from information in the *Congressional Quarterly Almanac, 86th Cong., 2d Sess., 1960.* Data on length of seniority omit scores of those senators voting against all civil rights roll calls. Number of years in Senate indicates years served through 1960.

relationship between a senator's scale score and his political party affiliation. Democrats and Republicans in 1960 have almost identical mean scores. The Republicans occupy an intermediate position between Northern and Southern Democrats. Moreover, there is greater variance in scores among Democrats than among Republicans. Northern Democrats show about the same variability as Republicans.[7]

While Democrats as a whole are not united in their attitudes toward integration, the Southern Democrats show intense solidarity on this issue. Only senators from Texas and Tennessee receive scale scores above 0. Of all the thirteen states in the old Confederacy, Texas and Tennessee have the lowest percentage of Negro residents. Furthermore, Tennessee has the highest rate of Negro voter registration, and Texas has the third highest rate. Since attitudes toward the Negro are related to percentage of Negro population in an area, these factors partly account for the greater support for integration shown by Senators Kefauver, Gore, Johnson, and Yarborough.[8]

Table II also demonstrates the difficulty in securing the passage of civil rights legislation through the Senate. Democratic leaders have lower mean scores than rank-and-file Democrats. The Policy and Steering committees are dominated by Southern Democrats and Northern Democrats unsympathetic to civil rights measures. On the Policy Committee, only Senator Hennings of Missouri has a score of 10. Two-fifths of the members of the Steering Committee, which makes Senate committee assignments, are Southern Democrats. Because senators from one-party states achieve greater seniority, the chairmanships of the Senate committees go most often to Southern Democrats; they chair nine committees. Senators Magnuson, Hennings, and Murray are the only committee chairmen with scores of 5 and above. Likewise, the Judiciary Committee, which handles civil rights legislation, is dominated by southern senators, namely, Eastland, the chairman, Kefauver, Johnston, McClellan, and Ervin. Three of the four Democrats scoring 10 rank lowest in seniority on this committee. Except for Senator Keating, Republican members of the Judiciary Committee have scores of 5 and below.

Republican leaders also have lower mean scores than rank-and-file Republicans in the Senate, although Republican leaders tend to vote more consistently to support integration than do Democratic leaders. In particular, the GOP Committee on Committees, the equivalent of the Democratic Steering Committee, includes Senators Case (N.J.), Javits, and Scott, who all have scores of 10. Moreover, the ranking Republican members of the Senate committees are more disposed to vote for civil rights measures than Democratic chairmen of these committees.[9]

In general, the number of years a senator has spent in the Senate is negatively related to scale scores. Those with least seniority demonstrate the greatest support for enforcement of integration. This relationship holds particularly true for Democrats, except those two senators—Morse and Magnuson—serving from 16 to 20 years in the Senate. Republican senators with greatest seniority have slightly higher means than those with medium seniority—11 to 15 years. The relationship between increasing seniority and decreasing scale scores may indicate the greater conservatism of older senators, as Table III demonstrates. Moreover, those serving longer in the Senate may become more influenced by the conservative norms of the leaders of the Senate "Establishment."

The personal background of a senator also has some influence on how he responds to civil rights issues. As shown in Table III, a senator's age is inversely related to mean scores. Young senators, those under fifty-five years of age, vote more in favor of civil rights bills than those over fifty-five. We can assume that younger members of the Senate grew up during an era in which the federal govern-

TABLE III. RELATIONSHIP BETWEEN SCALE SCORES AND PERSONAL BACKGROUND
OF SENATOR

| A. Age in Years | Number | Mean |
|---|---|---|
| 35–44 | 8 | 7.9 |
| 45–54 | 20 | 7.0 |
| 55–64 | 34 | 6.0 |
| 65–74 | 14 | 6.2 |
| 75 and above | 6 | 5.2 |

| B. Occupation | Number | Mean |
|---|---|---|
| Law | 47 | 6.7 |
| Journalism | 11 | 6.6 |
| Teaching | 15 | 6.1 |
| Business-Banking | 27 | 5.6 |
| Agriculture | 13 | 3.8 |

| C. Religion | Number | Mean |
|---|---|---|
| Friends | 1 | 10.0 |
| Jewish | 1 | 10.0 |
| Seventh Day Baptist | 1 | 10.0 |
| Protestant | 4 | 8.5 |
| Roman Catholic | 13 | 8.2 |
| Episcopal | 11 | 7.3 |
| Presbyterian | 8 | 7.3 |
| Unitarian | 4 | 6.5 |
| Lutheran | 5 | 6.2 |
| Disciples of Christ | 2 | 6.0 |
| Mormon | 4 | 6.0 |
| Congressional | 8 | 5.6 |
| Methodist | 10 | 3.5 |
| Reformed | 1 | 3.0 |
| Baptist | 8 | 2.3 |

Only data on senators with scale scores of 1 and above have been presented. The data on age, occupation, and religion appeared in the *Congressional Quarterly Almanac*, 86th Cong., 2d Sess., 1960. Age is of
January 1, 1960. Since some senators list more than one occupation, the
number in Part B of the table is greater than 82.

ment has acted positively to secure enforcement of rights for minority groups and
other less privileged citizens.[10]

In terms of occupational background, senators in the professions—law, jour-
nalism, and teaching—show greater support for integration than their colleagues
in business and particularly in agriculture. This finding corresponds with results
obtained from national sample survey data. V. O. Key has reported that professional people, as compared with businessmen, clerks, and farmers, tend to favor
greater federal governmental action to secure school integration.[11]

Among the major Protestant denominations, Episcopalian and Presbyterian
senators vote more frequently for integration than do Methodists and Baptists.
Lutherans and Congregationalists occupy an intermediate position. Roman Catholics senators support civil rights legislation more consistently than any of these

major Protestant groups. Senators from minority denominations, like the Friends, Jews, Seventh Day Baptists, Unitarians, Disciples of Christ, Mormons, and "non-denominational" Protestants, have scores above the mean for the total Senate population. In general, this finding agrees with conclusions reached in studies of the social attitudes of religious groups in the American population. We may consider Congregationalists, Presbyterians, and Episcopalians as conservative on economic issues and relatively liberal on non-economic issues, like civil rights. The opposite trend holds for Baptists and Methodists. However, in contrast to the general population, Catholics in the Senate support integration more consistently than members of major Protestant denominations.[12]

According to a study made by the Survey Research Center of the University of Michigan, viewpoints held by a representative to Congress and constituents in his district most nearly agree on the issue of Negro rights.[13] Using data from the scalogram, we have attempted to discover what relationships exist between senators' scale scores and the type state those senators represent. Parts A-D of Table IV compare four socioeconomic characteristics of states with senators' mean scores. In general, the population per square mile is positively related to senators' votes on civil rights issues. Senators from more densely populated states cast more votes in favor of legislation to enforce integration. However, senators from states averaging 51 to 75 people per square mile (Missouri, New Hampshire, and Wisconsin) have higher means than those representing states with between 76 and 100 population per square mile (California, Hawaii, Kentucky, Tennessee, and West Virginia). There is a similar positive relationship between percentage of state urbanized and mean scores. However, senators from moderately urbanized states (Iowa, Maine, New Hampshire, Tennessee, and Wyoming) have the lowest means.

The percentage of Negroes living in a state is somewhat related to the population per square mile and degree of urbanization. The eleven most urbanized and densely populated states, i.e., California, Connecticut, Illinois, Massachusetts, Maryland, Michigan, New Jersey, New York, Ohio, Pennsylvania, and Rhode Island, all have Negro populations greater than 2 per cent of the total population. In all except the three New England states—Connecticut, Massachusetts, and Rhode Island—Negroes form over 5 per cent of the population. Senators from these eleven states have a mean of 8.4. As the percentage of Negroes in a state increases from 0 to 10, the mean scores of senators representing those states also rise. Constituents from states with over 10 per cent Negroes tend to elect senators much less favorably inclined toward civil rights legislation. These states include Delaware, Illinois, Maryland, Tennessee, and Texas.[14]

Senators from wealthier states give greater support to civil rights bills than senators from poorer states. There is a direct inverse relationship between a state's percentage of incomes under $3,000 and senators' mean scores. The wealthiest states include California, Connecticut, Hawaii, Massachusetts, Nevada, New Jersey, and New York; their senators, evenly distributed between Republicans and Democrats, vote most consistently for protection of Negro rights. Excepting Nevada, these seven states are highly urbanized and densely populated.[15]

The political characteristics of a state, especially the degree of party competition, bear a strong relationship to senatorial voting on civil rights issues. In general, the greater the party competition within a state, the higher the mean score of senators representing that state. This relationship holds true even when the percentage of Negroes remains constant. Senators elected from competitive two-party

TABLE IV. RELATIONSHIP BETWEEN SCALE SCORES AND CHARACTERISTICS OF STATE REPRESENTED BY SENATOR

| A. People/Sq. Mile | Number | Mean |
|---|---|---|
| 1– 25 | 26 | 5.5 |
| 26– 50 | 16 | 5.7 |
| 51– 75 | 6 | 7.0 |
| 76–100 | 10 | 6.4 |
| 101 and above | 24 | 7.5 |

| B. % Urban | Number | Mean |
|---|---|---|
| 31–40 | 10 | 5.6 |
| 41–50 | 6 | 5.8 |
| 51–60 | 12 | 3.4 |
| 61–70 | 22 | 6.5 |
| 71–80 | 20 | 7.3 |
| 81–90 | 12 | 8.3 |

| C. % Negroes | Number | Mean |
|---|---|---|
| 0–1.9 | 32 | 6.1 |
| 2–3.9 | 12 | 6.2 |
| 4–5.9 | 12 | 6.6 |
| 6–7.9 | 6 | 6.7 |
| 8–9.9 | 10 | 9.7 |
| 10 and above | 10 | 3.4 |

| D. % Incomes under $3,000 | Number | Mean |
|---|---|---|
| 10–14 | 14 | 8.4 |
| 15–19 | 32 | 7.1 |
| 20–24 | 16 | 5.4 |
| 25–29 | 10 | 4.6 |
| 30–34 | 6 | 4.3 |
| 35–39 | 4 | 3.8 |

| E. Party Dominance of State Average Party Strength in Percentages | Number | Mean | % NEGROES | | | | |
|---|---|---|---|---|---|---|---|
| | | | 0–1.9 | 2–3.9 | 4–5.9 | 6–7.9 | 8–9.9 |
| | | | Means | | | | |
| 50–53 | 38 | 7.4 | 7.3 | 8.2 | 7.9 | 10.0 | 9.5 |
| 54–57 | 24 | 6.5 | 6.2 | 4.8 | 4.5 | 6.5 | 10.0 |
| 58–61 | 8 | 4.4 | 4.7 | — | — | 3.5 | — |
| 62–65 | 10 | 4.5 | 4.5 | 6.2 | — | — | — |

| F. Senators' Margin of Electoral Victory % of Votes Won | Number | Mean |
|---|---|---|
| 50–54 | 34 | 7.4 |
| 55–59 | 25 | 5.6 |
| 60–64 | 10 | 5.2 |
| 65–69 | 3 | 8.3 |
| 70–74 | 3 | 5.0 |
| 75 and above | 4 | 4.8 |

TABLE IV (continued)

| G. Geographic Region | Number | Mean |
|---|---|---|
| North Atlantic | 6 | 10.0 |
| Pacific | 10 | 9.6 |
| Lake | 8 | 7.9 |
| New England | 12 | 6.4 |
| Border | 12 | 5.3 |
| Rocky Mountains | 16 | 5.2 |
| Great Plains | 14 | 4.8 |
| South | 4 | 2.2 |

In this table senators voting 0 have been omitted from consideration. Data on population/sq. mile, % urban, and % incomes under $3,000 come from U.S. Bureau of the Census, *County and City Data Book, 1962* (Washington, D.C.: U.S. Government Printing Office, 1962), pp. 2—3. Data on % Negroes appear in U.S. Bureau of the Census, *U.S. Census of Population 1960, U.S. Summary: General Population Characteristics* (Washington, D.C.: U.S. Government Printing Office, 1962), pp. I—164. The data on party dominance of state appear in Edward F. Cox, "The Measurement of Party Strength," *Western Political Quarterly*, 13 (December 1960), 1035—42. The term "average party strength" refers to the average percentage of votes won by the dominant party. Cox considered only national contests for President, senator, and representative. Data on margins of electoral victory can be found in the *Congressional Quarterly Almanac*, 86th Cong., 2d Sess., 1960. The classification of states into geographic regions is based upon George L. Grassmuck, *Sectional Biases in Congress on Foreign Policy* (Baltimore: Johns Hopkins Press, 1951), pp. 4—10. Contrary to Grassmuck's classification, Delaware has been included within the Border states.

states, where average party strength is under 55 per cent, give greatest support to integration; they have a mean of 7.2. Senators from generally Democratic states have a mean score (6.7) higher than those from generally Republican states (mean of 5.3). Senators representing safely Republican states (Vermont, North Dakota, Nebraska, and New Hampshire) and safely Democratic states (the eleven southern states) have the lowest means, 3.9 and 0.4, respectively.

To a large extent, a senator's margin of electoral victory reflects the degree of party dominance within a state. As the margin of electoral victory increases, the senators' mean scores decrease. Contrary to this inverse relationship, however, senators who have margins of electoral victory from 65 to 69 per cent show greatest support for enforcement of integration; these three senators are Symington, Aiken, and Jackson.

The geographic regions throughout the United States comprise clusters of states with distinctive political and socioeconomic characteristics. Senators from the North Atlantic and Pacific Coast states most consistently favor integration. New York, New Jersey, and Pennsylvania, the states in the North Atlantic region, are politically competitive, highly urbanized, densely populated, and wealthy; here Negroes constitute around 8 per cent of the total population. Senators from the five Pacific Coast states, Alaska, California, Hawaii, Oregon, and Washington, are, except Kuchel and Fong, Democrats who favor positive state action to improve the conditions of minority groups.[16] The Lake region includes Illinois, Indiana, Michigan, and Ohio; these states are politically competitive, highly urbanized, densely populated, and wealthy; Negroes comprise over 6 per cent of the population. Seventy-five per cent of the senators from these states are Democrats. Outside the South, senators from the Great Plains, Rocky Mountain, and Border states vote least often for civil rights measures. The Great Plains states include Iowa, Kansas, Minnesota, Nebraska, North Dakota, South Dakota, and Wisconsin; these states are mainly represented by conservative Republicans who feel less disposed to use the action of the federal government to enforce rights of minority groups. The Rocky Mountain states—Arizona, Colorado, Idaho, Montana, Nevada, New Mexico, Utah, and Wyoming—have mixed representation: eleven Democrats and five Republicans served in the Senate in 1960. These eight states contain a relatively small percentage of Negroes (average of 1.7). Finally, senators elected from Delaware, Kentucky, Maryland, Missouri, Oklahoma, and West Virginia have voting records on integration which reflect the more southern mores of constituents in these six Border states.

We can confirm the significance of a state's characteristics as an influence on senatorial voting by comparing the scale scores of senators from the same state. In the case of two-thirds of the states, there is no more than one point difference in the two senators' scores. In only eleven states did constituents elect senators who diverge from each other by four points or more.[17] In most cases, the Democrat, the younger senator, and the senator with the lesser seniority vote more consistently to enforce integration. Thus, in seven of these states, the two senators belong to different parties, with the Democrat always having the higher score. In nine of these eleven states, the older senator and the senator with greater seniority obtain the lower score.

As well as isolating regularities in the voting behavior of individual senators, the Guttman scalogram identifies those senators who vote inconsistently; their votes do not fit into a perfectly cumulative scale pattern. The most striking characteristic of the inconsistent voters is that they make the most moderate responses to civil rights issues. Of the thirty-one senators who have a non-cumulative voting pattern, twenty received a scale score of from 8 to 4. The more strongly a senator holds civil rights attitudes, the more consistently he votes. Senators making the highest (9, 10) and lowest (3, 2, 1, 0) scores have the most cumulative voting patterns. We may hypothesize that the moderates (scores of 8, 7, 6, 5, 4) are most disposed toward compromise. Because they want to secure the passage of some legislation, they do not vote consistently pro- or anti-integration. In their view, "extreme" stands may damage the hope of securing any civil rights law. Thus, the desire for compromise may partially account for the lack of wholly consistent voting patterns.

As shown in Table V, members of both political parties voted with equal consistency. Thirty-one per cent of the Republican senators and 31 per cent of the Democratic group have non-cumulative scale patterns. Non-southern senators with both the least and greatest seniority have more non-cumulative voting patterns than senators serving from six to twenty years. Increasing age also brings increasingly inconsistent voting. Older senators over seventy-five cast the most inconsistent votes. Finally, senators from the New England and Rocky Mountain regions vote substantially more inconsistently than their colleagues from the North Atlantic, Pacific, and Great Plains states.

TABLE V. CHARACTERISTICS OF SENATORS MAKING NON-SCALE RESPONSES

| A. *Party Affiliation* | *Total Number* | *Number of Inconsistent Voters* | *Percentage of Inconsistent Voters* |
|---|---|---|---|
| Democratic | 65 | 20 | 31 |
| Republican | 35 | 11 | 31 |

| B. *Number of Years in Senate* | *Total Number* | *Number of Inconsistent Voters* | *Percentage of Inconsistent Voters* |
|---|---|---|---|
| 1– 5 | 31 | 15 | 48 |
| 6–10 | 24 | 9 | 38 |
| 11–15 | 14 | 2 | 14 |
| 16–20 | 7 | 1 | 14 |
| 20 and more | 6 | 4 | 67 |

| C. *Age in Years* | *Total Number* | *Number of Inconsistent Voters* | *Percentage of Inconsistent Voters* |
|---|---|---|---|
| 35–44 | 8 | 2 | 25 |
| 45–54 | 20 | 7 | 35 |
| 55–64 | 34 | 12 | 35 |
| 65–74 | 14 | 6 | 43 |
| 75 and above | 6 | 4 | 67 |

| D. *Geographic Region* | *Total Number* | *Number of Inconsistent Voters* | *Percentage of Inconsistent Voters* |
|---|---|---|---|
| Great Plains | 14 | 2 | 14 |
| North Atlantic | 6 | 1 | 17 |
| Pacific | 10 | 4 | 20 |
| Lake | 8 | 2 | 25 |
| Border | 12 | 4 | 33 |
| Rocky Mountains | 16 | 9 | 56 |
| New England | 12 | 7 | 58 |

Except in Part A of this table, data on senators with scale scores of 0 have been omitted.

## Summary and Conclusion

By using the techniques of Guttman scale analysis, we have demonstrated that in 1960 various civil rights roll calls had a common core of meaning for senators. The scalogram provided order and precision to complex voting behavior; it clearly differentiated the attitudes various groups hold toward the enforcement of integration. Through mean scores, we indicated certain relationships between beliefs about civil rights and other relevant variables.

Table VI summarizes the relationship between scale scores for the one hundred senators and senators' party, state, and personal background. Democrats cluster around more extreme scores (10 to 0), whereas Republicans make more moderate scores (6, 5, 4). Those with moderate scores tend to be somewhat older than those with higher or lower scores. There is a general inverse relationship between number of years in the Senate and scale scores. Senators with greatest seniority come predominantly from one-party states, while senators more in support of civil rights

TABLE VI. SUMMARY OF RELATIONSHIP BETWEEN SCALE SCORES AND SENATOR'S PARTY, STATE, AND PERSONAL BACKGROUND

| | SCALE SCORES | | | | |
|---|---|---|---|---|---|
| | 10 | 9—8—7 | 6—5—4 | 3—2—1 | 0 |
| Party | | | | | |
| % Democrats | 38 | 8 | 11 | 15 | 28 |
| % Republicans | 14 | 14 | 26 | 46 | 0 |
| Age in Years | 54 | 56 | 65 | 59 | 60 |
| Number of Years in Senate | 6 | 4 | 12 | 12 | 15 |
| % Average Party Strength | 53 | 54 | 59 | 57 | 81 |
| % Margin of Electoral Victory | 56 | 57 | 59 | 59 | 90 |
| People/Sq. Mile | 212 | 137 | 79 | 91 | 72 |
| % Urban | 71 | 65 | 56 | 60 | 47 |
| % Negroes | 5 | 4.8 | 2.2 | 5.6 | 28 |
| % Incomes under $3,000 | 17 | 17 | 24 | 23 | 38 |

legislation are mainly elected from competitive, two-party states. Moreover, as senators' margins of electoral victory increase, they become less sympathetic toward protection of Negro rights.

When we compare scale scores with characteristics of a state, we find that those senators scoring 3, 2, and 1 deviate from the predicted relationships. These senators come from slightly more politically competitive, densely populated, highly urbanized, and wealthy states than senators scoring 6, 5, and 4. The scores of Senators Saltonstall of Massachusetts, Dirksen of Illinois, Butler of Maryland, and Frear and Williams of Delaware seem to explain this divergence from the expected relationships. These four states have an average party strength of 50.2 per cent, 344 persons per square mile, 76 per cent urban, and 14 per cent incomes under $3,000. Except Massachusetts, these states have more than 10 per cent Negroes among their total population. Senators from states with the largest concentration of Negroes have the most extreme scores. In states where Negroes constitute the least percentage of the population, senators have the most moderate scores (6, 5, 4). The southern states are the least politically competitive, densely populated, urbanized, and wealthy; their constituents elect senators strongly opposed to integration. In contrast, senators most willing to support civil rights legislation come from the most politically competitive, densely populated, urbanized, and wealthy states.

In order to fully understand legislative voting behavior, we must not assume that certain external factors, like political party, occupation, religion, and political and socioeconomic characteristics of a state's population, influence a senator in a simple, direct fashion. These various group influences are mediated by certain "intervening variables" which create, strengthen, and modify behavior. Intervening factors, such as the senator's appraisal of the issue, his standards of judgment, biases, whims, and emotions, as well as his ideological predispositions, account for how a senator perceives and selects among the multiplicity of influences. As Senator Paul Douglas has commented, the issues before the Senate appear very complex, and the senator's individual conscience finally determines how he will vote on a particular roll call.[18] This reason partially explains the lack of perfect reproducibility in the scalogram and the failure to discover consistent relationships between the group influences and mean scale scores. Despite this qualification, however, the findings uncovered by Guttman scale techniques do provide important insights into the patterns of voting behavior and into some significant variables which influence senatorial votes on civil rights issues.

## NOTES

1. Donald E. Stokes, "Spatial Models of Party Competition," *American Political Science Review,* 57 (June 1963), 373.

2. In the national sample, 35% agreed strongly that the national government should remain aloof from the school segregation problem, whereas 29% felt strongly that the government should not stay out of the question. See V. O. Key, Jr., *Public Opinion and American Democracy* (New York: Knopf, 1961), pp. 211, 228–29.

3. The most comprehensive presentation of Guttman scaling procedures appears in Louis Guttman, "A Basis for Scaling Qualitative Data," *American Sociological Review,* 9 (April 1944), 139–50 and in Louis Guttman, "The Basis for Scalogram Analysis," *Measurement and Prediction,* ed. Samuel A. Stouffer *et al.* (Princeton: Princeton University Press, 1950), pp. 60–90. Scale analyses in the field of political behavior include Duncan MacRae, Jr., *Dimensions of Congressional Voting* (Berkeley and Los Angeles: University of California Press, 1958); George M. Belknap, "Scaling Legislative Behavior," *Legislative Behavior: A Reader in Theory and Research,* ed. John C. Wahlke and Heinz Eulau (Glencoe: Free Press, 1959), pp. 388–99; S. Sidney Ulmer, "Scaling Judicial Cases: A Methodological Note," *The American Behavioral Scientist,* 4 (April 1961), 31–34; Glendon A. Schubert, *Quantitative Analysis of Judicial Behavior* (Glencoe: Free Press, 1960).

4. I proceeded according to the assumption of William H. Riker, who has hypothesized, "The most significant roll call possible is one in which (1) all members vote and (2) the difference between the majority and minority is the minimum possible under the voting rules." See William H. Riker, "A Method for Determining the Significance of Roll Call Votes in Voting Bodies," *Legislative Behavior,* p. 379.

5. See Andrew F. Henry, "A Method of Classifying Non-Scale Response Patterns in a Guttman Scale," *Public Opinion Quarterly,* 16 (Summer 1952), 94. The mean score for those senators voting consistently is 4.7.

6. According to Louis Guttman, "The Basis for Scalogram Analysis," *loc. cit.,* p. 77, the coefficient of reproducibility should be at least .90. Neither respondents with the highest scale scores nor those with the lowest scores should comprise more than 20% of the total population. See Bert F. Green, "Attitude Measurement," *Handbook of Social Psychology,* ed. Gardner Lindzey (Cambridge: Addison-Wesley, 1954), I, 356.

7. These findings correspond to results obtained in a national field study of political beliefs of American leaders and followers. Democratic leaders tended to give significantly greater support to the enforcement of integration than Republican leaders. The difference between Democratic and Republican followers was insignificant at the .01 level. Of 24 issues, both Democratic and Republican followers were least united on the issue of enforcing integration. Democratic leaders were least united on the farm supports issue and next least united on integration. Republican leaders were least united on three issues other than civil rights. See Herbert McClosky, Paul J. Hoffman, and Rosemary O'Hara, "Issue Conflict and Consensus among Party Leaders and Followers," *American Political Science Review,* 54 (June 1960), 422, 425.

8. See Donald R. Matthews and James W. Prothro, "Social and Economic Factors and Negro Voter Registration in the South," *American Political Science Review,* 57 (March 1963), 28–30; Donald R. Matthews and James W. Prothro, "Political Factors and Negro Voter Registration in the South," *American Political Science Review,* 57 (June 1963), 356. According to V. O. Key, the Southern Democratic senators are united aganist Republicans and non-Southern Democrats only on the issue of opposition to federal intervention in race relations. Key has also shown that the race issue has little importance in Texas politics. Moreover, in Tennessee Negroes have had the right to vote in the cities, and political officials provide more public services to Negroes than in other southern states. See V. O. Key, Jr., *Southern Politics* (New York: Vintage Books, 1949), pp. 352, 74–75, 254.

9. Since the Democratic senators from the South vote consistently against civil rights bills, in the remaining sections of the paper we will consider only those 82 non-southern senators with a scale score above 0.

10. Sample surveys conducted by the American Institute of Public Opinion also reveal the greater opposition of older people to integration. In 1958 respondents were asked if they approved or disapproved of a two-and-a-half-year delay in integrating white and Negro students in the Little Rock schools. Replies by age were as follows:

|  | *Approve* | *Disapprove* |
|---|---|---|
| 21–29 years | 45% | 55% |
| 30–39 | 46 | 54 |
| 40–49 | 53 | 47 |
| 50–59 | 54 | 46 |
| 60 and over | 59 | 41 |

Northern Democrats were least likely and Southern Democrats most likely to approve a delay. Republicans took an intermediate position.

|  | *Approve* | *Disapprove* |
|---|---|---|
| Northern Democrats | 40% | 60% |
| Republicans | 50 | 50 |
| Southern Democrats | 82 | 18 |

In 1961 respondents were asked if they would vote their party's nominee for President, if he were a well-qualified Negro. Older persons were more likely to refuse to vote for the Negro candidate.

|  | *Yes* | *No* | *Don't Know* |
|---|---|---|---|
| 21–29 years | 54% | 34% | 12% |
| 30–49 | 58 | 37 | 5 |
| 50 and over | 42 | 48 | 10 |

For these reports, see Hazel Gaudet Erskine, "The Polls: Race Relations," *Public Opinion Quarterly,* 26 (Spring 1962), 142, 148.

11. See Key, *Public Opinion and American Democracy,* p. 136.

12. Wesley and Beverly Allinsmith, "Religious Affiliation and Politico-Economic Attitudes: A Study of Eight Major U.S. Religious Groups," *Public Opinion and Propaganda,* ed. Daniel Katz *et al.* (New York: Dryden, 1954), pp. 151–58. In a sample survey of the Detroit area, Gerhard Lenski found that for those Detroit residents born outside the South, white Catholics were more likely than white Protestants to advocate segregatèd schools. Among both middle- and working-class white Protestants, Methodists and Baptists were less likely to favor integrated

schools than Episcopalians, Presbyterians, and Lutherans. See Gerhard Lenski, *The Religious Factor* (2d ed. rev.; Garden City: Anchor Books, 1963), pp. 164, 397.

13. In the late 1950's, the correlation between a representative's congressional roll-call votes and his constituents' attitudes was nearly 0.6 on the civil rights issue, compared with 0.3 on social and economic welfare questions and −0.09 on the matter of support for American involvement in foreign affairs. See Warren E. Miller and Donald E. Stokes, "Constituency Influence in Congress," *American Political Science Review,* 57 (March 1963), 49. Lewis Froman indicates that Democratic representatives have more liberal voting records than Republican representatives because the former come from more liberal constituencies, as measured by a district's percentage non-white population, average population per square mile, percentage urban, and percentage owner-occupied dwelling units. I have used similar measures to classify state characteristics. See Lewis A. Froman, Jr., "Inter-Party Constituency Differences and Congressional Voting Behavior," *American Political Science Review,* 57 (March 1963), 58–59.

14. Matthews and Prothro, "Social and Economic Factors and Negro Voter Registration in the South," *loc. cit.,* have found that in southern *counties* with more than 30% Negroes, registration rates of Negroes decline sharply. Our data indicate that nationally constituents in *states* having more than 12% Negro tend to elect senators hostile to Negro rights. These states include Maryland and Delaware, as well as the eleven southern states of the old Confederacy.

15. These findings confirm those of national sample surveys which indicate that people in wealthier occupations—professions and business—are more in favor of school integration than skilled and unskilled workers. See Key, *Public Opinion and American Democracy,* pp. 135–36. On the basis of the Detroit area study, Gerhard Lenski also reports that the middle classes prefer integrated housing and schools more than do the lower classes. See Lenski, *op. cit.,* pp. 324, 397.

16. According to Key, *Public Opinion and American Democracy,* p. 108, constituents in the Far West show more acceptance of government intervention in the economy and greater support for civil liberties.

17. The specific figures comparing scores of senators from the same state are as follows:

| Point Difference: | 0 | 1 | 2 | 3 | 4 | 5 | 6 | 7 | 8 |
|---|---|---|---|---|---|---|---|---|---|
| Number of States: | 25 | 8 | 1 | 5 | 2 | 2 | 2 | 3 | 2 |

18. Paul H. Douglas, "A Senator's Vote: A Searching of the Soul," *New York Times Magazine,* April 30, 1950, p. 44.

# 22. Dimensions of Voting Behavior in a One-Party State Legislature[*]

### SAMUEL C. PATTERSON

Two-party competitive politics may be a desirable ideal toward which to strive, but it is clearly not a pervasive phenomenon in the United States. Republican dominance in some states of the upper Northeast and Middle West and Democratic dominance in the states of the South make uni-partisanship characteristic of politics, particularly at the level of state offices, in much of this country. Yet, understandably, much of our explanation of the political behavior of elected representatives is supported by data in political systems or subsystems where party is a relevant variable. Where two parties are highly competitive in the legislature, and on issues where conflicting positions are held by legislators, party has much to do with the conflicts which occur.

State legislatures in which there is no real party competition may be classified as either nonpartisan by design, as in Minnesota [1] and Nebraska, or nonpartisan by virtue of the overwhelming dominance of one party. That is, a legislature in which one party has an overwhelming majority may be viewed as a special case of the nonpartisan legislature. In some, factionalism may partially substitute for partisanship.[2] In others, the voting of legislators may not be manifestly collectively organized and may appear to be highly diffuse.

The following analysis deals with a state legislature of the latter sort—the 1959 session of the Oklahoma House of Representatives. Democratic legislators had a very large majority (110 Democrats, 9 Republicans), the few Republicans did not oppose the Democrats in any important ways as a group,[3] and there were no visible, persistent, and highly organized factional combinations on the Democratic side. Here was a state legislature in which party played virtually no role at all and legislative conflict could not be explained by the existence of intraparty factionalism. The research problem was twofold: what behavioral uniformities could be observed in the voting of members of a one-party legislature, and what correlates best explained those uniformities?

### Scale Analysis of Oklahoma House Roll Calls

The research technique which best captures underlying uniformities or dimensions of legislative voting behavior is scale analysis. This tool of analysis has been delineated adequately elsewhere.[4] Suffice it to say that the objective of scale analysis

[*] From *The Public Opinion Quarterly,* Vol. 26 (1962), pp. 185–200. Reprinted by permission.

is to determine, in connection with a logically related set of roll calls (universe of content), whether the pattern of voting by members of the legislature conforms to the general model illustrated below. If so, the researcher has ordered legislators on a continuum with respect to that universe of content, so that, in terms of the adequacy of the fit of voting behavior to the model (measured by the coefficient of reproducibility), the member's votes can be reproduced from his scale score, and it can be argued that in all probability one dominant factor, or dimension, produced the voting pattern for those issues.

GENERAL MODEL OF CUMULATIVE SCALE TYPES

| Scale Type | Score | Positive Votes | | | | | Negative Votes | | | | |
|---|---|---|---|---|---|---|---|---|---|---|---|
| | | $a$ | $b$ | $c$ | $d$ | $e$ | $a_1$ | $b_1$ | $c_1$ | $d_1$ | $e_1$ |
| A | 5 | X | X | X | X | X | | | | | |
| B | 4 | | X | X | X | X | X | | | | |
| C | 3 | | | X | X | X | X | X | | | |
| D | 2 | | | | X | X | X | X | X | | |
| E | 1 | | | | | X | X | X | X | X | |
| F | 0 | | | | | | X | X | X | X | X |

This general approach was applied to the 1959 Oklahoma House by means of the following specific procedures:

1. All roll call votes for the session were examined. A roll call is required on final passage in the Oklahoma House. The 127 roll calls on which there was some conflict (where at least 10 per cent of the members voted against the remainder) were selected for further analysis.

2. The 127 conflicting roll calls were categorized on the basis of their content. In the absence of other criteria, and in view of the fact that more inclusive categories did not seem justified by preliminary observation and analysis, universes of content were assigned on the basis of traditional breakdowns of areas of concern to state government. At the beginning, thirteen such content areas were identified. At a later stage a universe identified as the "Governor's program" was added. The roll call votes for each of the 119 members of the House were tabulated for the issues in each content area. These universes, and the total number of roll calls for each, are shown in Table 1.

3. Each content area was examined to determine whether or not the roll calls therein fitted the criteria of a cumulative scale. Of the preliminary universes of content identified in Table 1, 7 were found to produce acceptable scales, 3 produced quasi-scales, and 4 were not scalable. Decisions concerning the handling of scale errors and absences followed consistent and fairly well established standards. As it seemed desirable to keep the scales as "pure" as possible and the number of roll calls in any given content area was relatively small, contrived items were not employed. Of course, this made it difficult to reduce the number of nonscale types. Some items did not fit a given scale, and all unused roll calls were evaluated to determine whether they would fit one of the scales. Of those universes of content producing scales, all are characterized by coefficients of reproducibility well above 90 per cent, and the adequacy of these scales does not seem open to serious doubt.

4. Members were assigned scale scores based upon their positive responses for

TABLE 1. UNIVERSES OF CONTENT, NUMBER OF ROLL CALLS IN EACH CATEGORY, AND RESULT OF SCALE ANALYSIS FOR THE 1959 OKLAHOMA HOUSE OF REPRESENTATIVES

| Universe of Content | Number of Roll Calls | Result of Analysis |
|---|---|---|
| Appropriations | 11 | Scale; C.R. = .95 |
| Business regulation | 10 | Quasi-scale |
| Campaigns and elections | 7 | Scale; C.R. = .94 |
| Conservation | 6 | Quasi-scale |
| County affairs | 6 | Not scalable |
| Crimes and punishments | 6 | Quasi-scale |
| Labor and welfare | 10 | Scale; C.R. = .95 |
| Public morals | 9 | Scale; C.R. = .95 |
| Regulation of the professions | 8 | Not scalable |
| Schools | 8 | Scale; C.R. = .93 |
| State officials and employees | 9 | Not scalable |
| Taxation | 10 | Scale; C.R. = .94 |
| Transportation | 17 | Not scalable |
| Governor's program | 7 | Scale; C.R. = .95 |
| Miscellaneous | 3 | Not scalable |
| Total | 127 | |

each of the seven scales. Again, standard procedures were employed in the assignment of scale scores.

The end product of the scale analysis was an ordering of members of the 1959 House on seven different dimensions. The contents of these seven dimensions for the Oklahoma House need to be described briefly.

*Governor's Program Scale.* This scale developed from seven issues from the program announced by the Governor prior to the session under study. A diversity of proposals dealing with state care of orphans, withholding taxes, care of crippled children, reorganization of the highway commission, central state purchasing, apportionment of funds for education, teachers' salaries, and a highway code are associated with this dimension. The dimension involved is support for the Governor.

*Labor and Welfare Scale.* This consisted of issues related to workmen's compensation, unemployment compensation, state public assistance, and protection of health in industrial and railway establishments.

*Schools Scale.* This dealt with issues related to payment and appointment of state aid to public schools, student transfers, duties of county school superintendents, and payment of school claims for materials, supplies, equipment, and services.

*Campaigns and Elections Scale.* This consisted of bills providing a variety of regulations on political campaigns and elections, such as requiring a nomination deposit, identifying printed campaign material, regulating procedures for voting machines, permitting selection of presidential electors at party conventions, prohibiting candidates or their relatives or employees from serving on county or precinct election boards, and proposing that candidates for presidential elector not participate in run-off primary elections.

*Public Morals Scale.* This contained items involving state regulation of public morality and conduct: permitting horse racing and pari-mutuel betting, forbidding the sale of beer after midnight and on Sunday, repealing prohibition of alcoholic beverages, making it a misdemeanor to sell or trade motor vehicles on Sunday, regulating the carrying of firearms, permitting state courts to set aside divorce decrees under certain circumstances, regulating marriages of underage persons, and making it a felony to sell alcoholic beverages containing more than 3.2 per cent alcohol (the "bone dry" proposal).

*Appropriations Scale.* This consisted of bills appropriating state funds for a variety of purposes: the state Highway Department, the control of predatory animals by the Wildlife Conservation Commission, the Planning and Resources Board, the state Bureau of Investigation, and the construction and maintenance of a hospital for mentally retarded children by the state Board of Public Affairs.

*Taxation Scale.* This consisted of proposals increasing the depletion allowable for oil and gas production for income tax purposes, regulating expenditures for advertising by tax assessors, increasing the gasoline tax, permitting cities of a certain size to levy local taxes under certain conditions, permitting the withholding of income taxes from income, and authorizing an additional county ad valorem tax for county health departments.

Among the content areas which did not produce scales, where one dominant dimension did not emerge on the basis of which all members could be ordered, were highways and transportation, county government, and state officials. Here local interests and demands are so heterogeneous that ordering on a single dimension would be unlikely.

### Relationships Among Scales

Conflict in the voting behavior of members of the Oklahoma House was not random and chaotic. On the contrary, on the basis of seven well-defined dimensions, the behavior of House members was so highly patterned that it fitted the relatively rigorous requirements of the cumulative scale. In order to determine whether or not these seven distinct dimensions were related to one another, rank-order correlation coefficients were computed between them. Table 2 shows this array. It is striking to note the extent to which these scales were only slightly related. Only the Governor's program scale was associated with other scales to any extent.

It is difficult to evaluate the meaning of these correlation coefficients beyond the general impression that these scales represented independent and more or less unrelated dimensions of voting behavior in the Oklahoma House. MacRae found higher relationships among scales for the 81st Congress.[5] It may be that cumulative scales for legislative bodies where party is a relevant organizing principle for

TABLE 2. RELATION OF DIMENSIONS OF VOTING BEHAVIOR OF OKLAHOMA HOUSE
MEMBERS, BY RANK-ORDER CORRELATIONS *

| Scale | Governor's Program | Labor and Welfare | Schools | Campaigns and Elections | Public Morals | Appro- priations | Taxation |
|---|---|---|---|---|---|---|---|
| Governor's program | | −.02 | +.01 | +.18 | +.28 | +.21 | +.31 |
| Labor and welfare | −.02 | | −.03 | −.09 | −.12 | −.16 | −.13 |
| Schools | +.01 | −.03 | | +.09 | −.02 | −.07 | −.08 |
| Campaigns and elections | +.18 | −.09 | +.09 | | +.18 | +.00 | |
| Public morals | +.28 | −.12 | −.02 | +.18 | | −.06 | +.01 |
| Appropriations | +.21 | −.16 | −.07 | +.00 | −.06 | | +.05 |
| Taxation | +.31 | −.13 | −.08 | +.01 | +.05 | +.12 | +.12 |

* The statistic employed was Kendall's *tau* corrected for tied ranks.

behavior are more likely to be related (that is, to intersect in some important ways) than in a legislature where party is not an available reference group for members. In the absence of partisan organization, one-party state legislators appear to respond to different sets of issues in essentially unrelated ways.

If the positions of members of the 1959 Oklahoma House on seven separate dimensions were more or less unrelated, if alignments of members in conflict on different sets of issues differed, how can these scales be explained? It seems most likely that the salient referents for members of a one-party, nonfactional legislature in relation to the dimensions of their voting behavior are different from those in a two-party legislature. The hypothetical correlates of voting behavior in the Oklahoma House which were examined from the available data were (1) the characteristics of members' constituencies in terms of political competitiveness, rural-urban differences, and constituents' socio-economic status, and (2) the structure of the House, in terms of leadership and committee groupings. Analysis of the seven scales for the Oklahoma House indicated that different correlates of scale position were relevant for different scales.

### Dimensions Related to the Political Competitiveness
### of Legislative Districts

The Governor's program scale is of special interest, since it ordered members on a continuum from low to high gubernatorial support. Both House leaders and new members tended to have higher Governor's program scale scores than nonleaders and old-timers. That legislative leaders should have higher scores on this scale than nonleaders can be accounted for by the direct role of the Oklahoma Governor, under most circumstances, in organizing the legislature.[6] In the 1959 session the Governor's known supporters were selected to the key positions of legislative leadership. The higher support for the Governor's program among new members is a consequence of the fact that new members tended to be elected from more highly competitive house districts than old-timers. Competitiveness between parties

TABLE 3. RELATION OF POSITION ON THE GOVERNOR'S PROGRAM SCALE AND THE CAMPAIGN AND ELECTION SCALE TO THE POLITICAL COMPETITIVENESS OF HOUSE DISTRICTS (IN PER CENT)

| | Political Competitivenss of Districts | | |
|---|---|---|---|
| Scale Score | Highly Competitive* (23) | Semi-competitive† (66) | Non-competitive‡ (30) |
| Governor's program: | | | |
| 6−7 (pro Governor) | 69.6 | 42.4 | 36.7 |
| 4−5 | 17.4 | 28.8 | 36.7 |
| 0−3 (anti-Governor) | 12.9 | 19.7 | 20.0 |
| Not classified | 0.0 | 9.1 | 6.7 |
| Total | 99.9 | 100.0 | 100.1 |
| Campaigns and elections: | | | |
| 5−6 (support for regulation) | 73.9 | 51.5 | 46.7 |
| 3−4 | 17.4 | 18.2 | 20.0 |
| 0−2 (opposition to regulation) | 4.3 | 16.7 | 26.7 |
| Not classified | 4.3 | 13.6 | 6.7 |
| Total | 99.9 | 100.0 | 100.1 |

*Counties and districts in which both parties won at least one election to the House of Representatives between 1952 and 1958, and counties and districts where each party won at least 40 per cent of the vote in 50 per cent of the elections during that period.

†Counties and districts of one-party dominance, but where the minor party contested at least 25 per cent of the elections to the House between 1952 and 1958.

‡Counties in which there were no general election contests for House seats between 1952 and 1958.

in the member's district tended to bear a relationship to scale position on the Governor's program scale (see Table 3). House members from highly competitive two-party districts tended to have higher scale scores than members from non-competitive, one-party districts. The differences among members representing districts which varied in terms of political competitiveness were most distinctive in the high scale positions. Nearly 70 per cent of the members elected from two-party competitive districts received high (6 to 7) scale scores, while only 42 per cent of those members elected from semi-competitive districts, and 37 per cent of those elected from one-party districts, fell into high scale positions.

A significant relationship between the political competitiveness of legislative districts and scale position also was demonstrated in connection with the campaigns and elections scale. High scores on this scale denoted members who supported restrictions on compaigns and efforts to ensure high standards of campaign conduct, as well as regulation of the honesty and democratic character of elections. One might logically anticipate that these issues would be more salient and have a higher value for members elected from politically competitive districts than for members chosen from politically stagnant districts involving an extremely low level of conflict for public office. As Table 3 shows, members elected from highly competitive districts tended to have higher campaigns and elections scale scores than members from one-party districts. Seventy-four per cent of the members from highly competitive districts supported legislation regulating campaigns and elections more closely, while only 47 per cent of the members from one-party districts supported such legislation.

On the basis of other dimensions, however, the political competitiveness of House districts did not discriminate well among members. And the political competitiveness of legislative districts in Oklahoma was not highly related to the rural-urban division, although it was not entirely independent of it.

### Dimensions Related to Rural-Urban Differences

Legislative behavior is frequently interpreted in terms of the rural-urban ecological differences in legislators' constituencies. In some Northern two-party states, rural-urban differences in legislative districts function to reinforce party differences in the legislature.[7] It might be expected that, in the absence of partisanship in the Oklahoma House, rural-urban differences would become an important source of legislative conflict. On the basis of the seven underlying dimensions of voting behavior identified for Oklahoma House members, generalizations about rural-urban differences must be carefully qualified. Except for the appropriations and taxation scales, discussed below, metropolitan legislators tended to have higher scale positions than members from all other districts.[8] But differences among urban, rural small-town (semi-rural), and rural districts varied from scale to scale. In general, rural districts elected legislators who scored higher on these scales than either urban or rural small-town members. That is, rural members' scale positions resembled those of metropolitan members more than did urban members' scale positions. For the most part, rural-urban explanations were not very satisfactory for these scales beyond indicating the difference between metropolitan members and legislators from urban, small-town, and rural constituencies.[9] One exception to this generalization arose in connection with the public morals scale.

Those legislators with high scale positions on the public morals scale supported legislation designed to enlarge the freedom of public conduct and opposed legislation to restrict it, in connection with proposals to amplify or strengthen Sunday laws, restrict the use of alcoholic beverages, or permit gambling. Position on this scale was not highly related to the proportion of Baptists (the largest and most militantly prohibitionist church in the state) in legislative districts, a relationship which was hypothesized. The rural-urban difference among scale positions was, however, most definitive for the public morals scale (see Table 4). Metropolitan legislators scored high on this scale by a much larger proportion than members from urban, semi-rural, or rural districts. Fifty-two per cent of the metropolitan members occupied high positions on this scale. In the case of the public morals scale, as with others, rural small-town districts tended more than others to elect legislators who scored low on the scale. The higher than expected scale positions for rural members was the result of the existence of two distinguishable kinds of rural ecological area in the state: the poor rural southeast, and the wealthy rural northwest. Members from the relatively wealthier northeastern counties, close to "wet" Kansas counties, were more inclined to receive high scale scores than southeastern, more heavily Baptist, rural counties. The socio-economic status of constitu-

TABLE 4. RELATION OF POSITION ON THE PUBLIC MORALS
SCALE TO THE RURAL-URBAN CHARACTERISTICS OF HOUSE
DISTRICTS (IN PER CENT)

| Public Morals<br>Scale Score | Rural-Urban Characteristics of Districts | | | |
|---|---|---|---|---|
| | Metro*<br>(23) | Urban†<br>(28) | Semi-rural‡<br>(50) | Rural§<br>(18) |
| 4–5 (high) | 52.2 | 28.6 | 22.0 | 16.7 |
| 2–3 | 30.4 | 60.7 | 56.0 | 61.1 |
| 0–1 (low) | 13.0 | 10.7 | 18.0 | 11.1 |
| Not classified | 4.3 | 0.0 | 4.0 | 11.1 |
| Total | 99.9 | 100.0 | 100.0 | 100.0 |

  * All districts in Standard Metropolitan Areas.
  † All districts with urban aggregates of 2,500 or more and
a ratio of urban population of more than 55 per cent.
  ‡ All districts with urban aggregates of 2,500 or more and
a ratio of urban population of less than 55 per cent.
  § All districts without an urban aggregate of 2,500 or more
population.

ents in rural districts largely accounted for the distribution of rural members on
this scale, but in this case the rural-urban comparisons discriminated for all members better than socio-economic status alone.

### The Metropolitan-Rural Coalition on Taxation Legislation

More than was the case with any of the other dimensions of voting behavior in
the House, the taxation scale illustrated a pattern of legislative behavior best
accounted for in terms of a fairly persistent coalition between metropolitan and
rural-farm representatives. Distinctions among members in different scale positions
on the taxation scale did not develop on the basis of the socio-economic make-up
of their constituencies, the political competitiveness of districts, or the committee
structure of the House. Additionally, there was not a direct relationship between
taxation scale position and the rural-urban continuum. As Table 5 shows, a very
high proportion both of metropolitan and rural members occupied high (5–6)
scale positions on this scale. Almost 61 per cent of the metropolitan members and
72 per cent of the rural members scored high, while only 32 per cent of the urban
legislators and 44 per cent of the rural small-town members were in the high scale
categories. A much larger proportion of the urban and small-town members were
in the middle and low scale ranges than were metropolitan and rural representatives.

While both metropolitan and rural members proportionately occupied higher
scale positions on some other scales, notably the schools scale, in every other
case some other variable seemed to have better explanatory power in terms of
hypothetically accounting for the dimension. In the case of the schools scale, an
index of socio-economic status of constituents better discriminated among members in different scale positions.

The taxation scale, on the other hand, seemed to illustrate best a fairly persistent

TABLE 5. RELATION OF POSITION ON THE TAXATION SCALE
TO THE RURAL-URBAN CHARACTERISTICS OF HOUSE DIS-
TRICTS (IN PER CENT)

| Taxation Scale Score | Rural-Urban Characteristics of Districts* | | | |
|---|---|---|---|---|
| | Metro (23) | Urban (28) | Semi-rural (50) | Rural (18) |
| 5–6 (high) | 60.9 | 32.1 | 44.0 | 72.2 |
| 3–4 | 21.7 | 42.9 | 40.0 | 16.7 |
| 0–2 (low) | 0.0 | 17.9 | 6.0 | 5.6 |
| Not classified | 17.4 | 7.1 | 10.0 | 5.6 |
| Total | 100.0 | 100.0 | 100.0 | 100.1 |

*Definitions are in the footnote to Table 4.

and overriding metropolitan-rural combination, a coalition on tax measures which can be reasonably inferred from the issues making up the scale. Metropolitan members were in the minority in the House and disadvantaged by an apportionment rigged in favor of rural, and especially rural small-town, parts of the state. The taxation scale suggested a fairly straightforward coalition in the House based upon the support by metropolitan members of tax legislation designed primarily to benefit rural areas (e.g., distributing gasoline tax increases on the basis of county road mileage, providing an additional gasoline tax increase for improvement of rural roads, and permitting an additional tax levy for the support of cooperative county libraries), in return for rural support of tax legislation favoring metropolitan areas (e.g., permitting a city located in a county having 325,000 inhabitants to levy local taxes for revenue purposes under certain conditions, providing withholding tax legislation amenable to metropolitan interests, and increasing the depletion allowable for oil and gas production for income tax purposes). Since most of the items in the taxation scale would have involved a tax burden, or general tax policy, applicable to all, but would have been of differential benefit to metropolitan and rural areas, it was reasonable that urban and small-town representatives were in lower positions on the scale.

### Socio-Economic Status of Constituents and the Public Education Dimension

In the case of the schools scale, the socio-economic characteristics of members' constituents, measured by the percentage of constituents who earned $5,000 a year or more, best discriminated among occupants of scale positions (see Table 6). A very large proportion (86 per cent) of legislators whose constituents were proportionately high in socio-economic status had high scale scores, and a substantial proportion (45 per cent) of legislators representing constituents characterized by low socio-economic status had low scores on the schools scale. Public education has a high value among Oklahomans, especially in the quantitative sense, and support by legislators for schools appeared to be more highly related to the socio-economic status of constituents than to other variables. Other scales were not consistently related to socio-economic status.

TABLE 6. RELATION OF POSITION ON THE SCHOOLS SCALE TO THE
SOCIO-ECONOMIC STATUS OF MEMBERS' CONSTITUENTS

| Schools Scale Score | Per Cent of Constituents Earning $5,000 or More* | | | |
|---|---|---|---|---|
| | 0—4.9 (20) | 5.0—9.8 (44) | 10.0—19.9 (33) | 20.0 above (22) |
| 0—2 (low) | 45.0 | 11.4 | 3.0 | 4.5 |
| 3—4 | 5.0 | 22.7 | 15.2 | 9.1 |
| 5—6 (high) | 25.0 | 54.5 | 63.6 | 86.4 |
| Not classified | 25.0 | 11.4 | 18.2 | 0.0 |
| Total | 100.0 | 100.0 | 100.0 | 100.0 |

*From County and City Data Book, 1956, U.S. Bureau of the
Census, 1957. Income data are for 1949.

## Dimensions Related to Legislative Committee Membership

A different focus was needed to account for the ordering of Oklahoma House members on the dimension representing support for legislation dealing with labor benefits and welfare legislation. The proportion of manual workers in the Oklahoma labor force is relatively low, and labor unionization is not widely distributed in the population. There is not a wide basis for constituency support for legislation assisting working people in Oklahoma. The labor and welfare scale was not distinctly related to measures of possible constituency support. Perhaps the inclusion of only one welfare issue in the scale accounts in part for the fact that it was not consistently related to the percentage of recipients of public assistance in House districts. When members' scale positions were compared with the percentage employed in manufacturing in House districts, there was some discernible difference between members from districts with the highest proportions employed in manufacturing and all others, but the relationship was not striking.

Observation of legislative politics in Oklahoma with regard to labor issues suggests the crucial importance of lobbying by labor representatives in the absence of grass-roots support on a wide scale for pro-labor legislation.[10] That labor unions have been moderately successful (so-called "right to work" legislation has never been enacted in Oklahoma) is perhaps the result of friendly House committee treatment of labor legislation. In the case of the labor and welfare scale, the legislative committee appeared to constitute the most discriminating basis for scale position. As Table 7 indicates, members of the House Committees on Labor Relations and Social Welfare tended to occupy high scale positions by a much larger proportion than either House leaders or members who did not serve on these two committees. Sixty-five per cent of the members of the two House committees concerned with these issues occupied high scale positions, while only about 41 per cent of nonmembers and House leaders received high scale scores. A higher proportion of nonmembers had medium and low scale scores than did committee members. The tendency for committee members to vote together was clearly illustrated by this scale, and in this case the legislative committee seemed to be the critical reference group for legislators in their voting behavior.

TABLE 7. RELATION OF POSITION ON THE LABOR AND WELFARE SCALE TO MEMBERSHIP ON THE HOUSE LABOR RELATIONS AND SOCIAL WELFARE COMMITTEES (IN PER CENT)

| Labor and Welfare Scale Score | Member of Labor Relations and Social Welfare Committees (20) | House Leader* (46) | Rank-and-file Member (53) |
|---|---|---|---|
| 5–6 (high) | 65.0 | 41.3 | 41.5 |
| 3–4 | 15.0 | 37.0 | 32.1 |
| 0–2 (low) | 5.0 | 13.0 | 17.0 |
| Not classified | 15.0 | 8.7 | 9.4 |
| Total | 100.0 | 100.0 | 100.0 |

*Includes officers of the majority party elected by the Caucus; chairmen of all legislative standin committees except Labor Relations, Social Welfare, Engrossed and Enrolled Bills, and House Administration; and members of the General Conference on Appropriations.

The most crucial areas of legislative policy making frequently are in allocation of public funds and arrangements for gathering revenues. The importance of appropriations and taxation measures to the effective operation of state government makes it likely that gubernatorial pressures are most operative in these areas of legislation. The taxation scale was more highly related to the Governor's program scale than were other scales, and the appropriations scale was relatively highly related to the Governor's program scale (see Table 2). While the correlation coefficient between the appropriations and taxation scales was +.12, and thus a tendency to support appropriations was somewhat related to a tendency to support increased taxation, a comparison of these two scales indicates that a number of members favored increased appropriations but opposed increased taxes, within the terms of the issues included in these scales.

The appropriations scale was not distinctly related to constituency characteristics in terms of socio-economic status, rural-urban differences (unlike the taxation scale), or political competitiveness. This scale, like the labor and welfare scale, appeared to be particularly related to the committee subgroup structure of the legislative body. The compromises and negotiations over the allocation of public funds represented by this scale seem to have been made by the members of the committee ultimately responsible for the formulation of legislative policy on appropriations. As Table 8 indicates, a very substantial proportion of the members of the General Conference Committee on Appropriations (a permanent joint conference committee, House members of which were appointed early in the session) occupied high (4–5) positions on the appropriations scale, and in this respect they are to be distinguished from other House leaders, and from rank-and-file members. Nearly three-quarters of the members of the Conference Committee had high scale scores, and none occupied low scale positions. Only 38 per cent of the other House leaders and 31 per cent of the nonleaders had high scores, while 16 per cent of the other House leaders and 19 per cent of the rank-and-file occupied low scale positions. Position on the appropriations scale thus seems clearly to be related to

TABLE 8. RELATION OF POSITION ON THE APPROPRIATIONS SCALE TO
MEMBERSHIP ON THE GENERAL CONFERENCE COMMITTEE (IN PER
CENT)

| Appropriations Scale Score | Member of General Conference Committee on Appropriations (15) | House Leader* (32) | Rank-and-file Member (72) |
|---|---|---|---|
| 4–5 (high) | 73.3 | 37.5 | 30.6 |
| 2–3 | 26.7 | 40.6 | 37.5 |
| 0–1 (low) | 0.0 | 15.6 | 19.4 |
| Not classified | 0.0 | 6.3 | 12.5 |
| Total | 100.0 | 100.0 | 100.0 |

*Includes officers of the majority party elected by the Caucus,
and chairmen of all legislative standing committees except Engrossed
and Enrolled Bills and House Administration and those who were also
members of the General Conference Committee on Appropriations.

membership on the General Conference Committee, and in all probability this
scale was more nearly associated with the structure of the House than with constituency variables. A similar association did not pertain with respect to the regular
House Standing Committee on Appropriations and Budget, suggesting the crucial
policy-making position regarding appropriations held by the General Conference
Committee. The appropriations dimension was likely to be ordered to a considerable degree in terms of the decisions of that committee.

## Conclusion

This analysis of the dimensions of voting behavior of members of the 1959
session of the Oklahoma House of Representatives has endeavored to demonstrate
some of the consequences of one-party politics in a state legislature. It has been
suggested that, in the absence of party as a reference group for the legislator, the
dimensions of his voting behavior tend to be only slightly related. It has been shown
that within seven dimensions of voting in the Oklahoma House on issues that fitted
the requirements of a cumulative scale, members' behavior was highly consistent,
but that from one of these dimensions to another it was more or less unrelated.

It has been suggested, further, that if members' voting behavior on seven identifiable dimensions was not significantly related, these scales were likely to be
functions of different correlates. It was found that the Governor's program scale
and the campaigns and elections scale were related to the political competitiveness
of House districts. The schools scale was found to be related uniquely to the socio-
economic status of the representative's constituents, while the public morals scale
was found to be best related to the rural-urban characteristics of his district. The
labor and welfare scale and the appropriations scale were found to be related
most discriminatingly to the committee structure of the House, with the relevant
committee members scoring higher than nonmembers. Finally, in the case of the
taxation scale it was found that the correlates relevant for other scales did not
supply sufficient explanation, and that ordering on this scale seemed best explained

in terms of a metropolitan-rural coalition with respect to the specific issues making up the scale.

There are significant differences between partisan and nonpartisan legislative bodies. Where party organization or even stable factional alignments are not available to the legislator to refer to for voting standards, the patterns of voting in the legislature are likely to be compartmentalized. And, in the absence of party as a reference group, the legislator is likely, consciously or unconsciously, to respond to different pressures in different voting areas.

## NOTES

1. The results of nonpartisanship in the Minnesota legislature have been assessed briefly by Charles R. Adrian. See his "Some General Characteristics of Non-partisan Elections," *American Political Science Review,* Vol. 46, 1952, pp. 766–776; and more extensively by G. Theodore Mitau, *Politics in Minnesota,* Minneapolis, University of Minnesota Press, 1960, pp. 57–79.

2. Key analyzes factionalism in Southern politics, but only a minimum of attention is given to its ramifications in Southern legislatures. See V. O. Key, Jr., *Southern Politics in State and Nation,* New York, Knopf, 1950. Some consideration of legislative factionalism in Alabama is to be found in Murray C. Havens, *City Versus Farm?* University, Ala., University of Alabama, Bureau of Public Administration, 1957.

3. Republicans advanced no candidate for Speaker, voted for the Democratic candidate, and generally endeavored to avoid identification as Republicans.

4. Scale analysis as a sociological technique has had wide application, and the bibliography is large and well known. It has been applied recently to legislative roll call votes by Duncan MacRae, George Belknap, Douglas Price, and Charles Farris. See: George M. Belknap, "A Method of Analyzing Legislative Behavior," *Midwest Journal of Political Science,* Vol. 2, 1958, pp. 377–402; Duncan MacRae, Jr., "Roll Call Votes and Leadership," *Public Opinion Quarterly,* Vol. 20, 1956, pp. 543–558, and *Dimensions of Congressional Voting,* Berkeley, Calif., University of California Press, 1958; Hugh Douglas Price, "Are Southern Democrats Different? An Application of Scale Analysis to Senate Voting Patterns," in Nelson W. Polsby, Robert A. Dentler and Paul A. Smith (eds.), *Politics and Social Life,* Boston, Houghton Mifflin, 1963, pp. 740–756; and Charles D. Farris, "A Method of Determining Ideological Groups in Congress," *Journal of Politics,* Vol. 20, 1958, pp. 308–338. MacRae, in his *Dimensions of Congressional Voting,* provides detailed methodological guidance for the researcher, upon which I have relied heavily.

5. MacRae, *Dimensions of Congressional Voting,* p. 250.

6. See MacRae's findings on leadership and "organization loyalty" in the Massachusetts House of Representatives in "Roll Call Votes and Leadership," pp. 550–552.

7. See Malcolm E. Jewell, "Party Voting in American State Legislatures," *American Political Science Review,* Vol. 49, 1955, pp. 773–791; and William J. Keefe, "Comparative Study of the Role of Political Parties in State Legislatures," *Western Political Quarterly,* Vol. 9, 1956, pp. 726–742. Some students seem to be saying these days that rural-urban differences in politics are inconsequential, or becoming so. See, for instance, Robert S. Friedman, "The Urban-Rural Conflict Revisited," *Western Political Quarterly,* Vol. 14, 1961, pp. 481–495. It seems more likely that rural-urban differences are important, but more so on some kinds of issues than others, and more so in some parts of the country than others.

8. See footnote to Table 4 for definitions of metropolitan, urban, semi-rural, and rural districts, from which members were elected.

9. It is interesting to compare David R. Derge, "Metropolitan and Outstate Alignments in Illinois and Missouri Legislative Delegations," *American Political Science Review,* Vol. 52, 1958, pp. 1051–1065.

10. See Samuel C. Patterson, "The Role of the Lobbyist: The Case of Oklahoma," *Journal of Politics,* Vol. 25, 1963, pp. 72–92.

# Part VII

# Research

# Introduction

IF ONE were to line up on his bookshelf all the books, monographs, brief research reports, and articles which he could find having to do with American legislatures, he would have a fairly extensive library. This library would include a considerable collection of material on legislative history, especially narratives describing the enactment of various kinds of legislation. It would include procedural descriptions detailing the written rules and practices of national and state legislatures. It would include biographical and autobiographical accounts of the lives and times of notable legislators. It would include a large prescriptive literature—discussions of legislative ailments and proposals for reform. These contributions to the library would make up its largest part. The bulk of writing about American legislatures has been primarily narrative, descriptive, or hortatory.

Modern legislative research has a different orientation. In the last fifteen years, research on legislative systems has become more scientific, and thus more rigorous and systematic. As much as any other segment of political science, legislative research has been infiltrated by the influences of behavioral models, strategy, and technology. Less effort has been devoted to descriptive narratives, and much more to interpretive and explanatory investigations based upon systematic, and often quantitative, data. The pioneering work of George H. Haynes and A. L. Lowell just after the turn of the century, and of Paul Hasbrouck, Stuart A. Rice, and Herman C. Beyle in the late 1920's and early 1930's has been recognized and emulated in recent research. Legislative research has become much more sophisticated in its theoretical basis and technology, assisted by the applications of systems, role, and functional analysis and the development of models of decision-making behavior with analogues in the analytical techniques of cluster analysis, scaling, and factor analysis.

The attributes of modern legislative research have been set forth quite succinctly by Eulau and Hinckley in the following way:

> First, the newer studies are most distinctive for their reliance on the individual legislator's behavior—broadly interpreted as including not only his acts but also his orientations to actions—as the empirical unit of analysis. Using the individual actor as the micro-unit of inquiry turns research in quite new directions. The legislature is now seen as a macro-unit that divisible by N and analyzable in terms of all possible influences on and relations among $n_1$, $n_2$, $n_3$, . . . N.[1]

Empirical investigations have moved away from focusing entirely upon formal legislative structure and procedure, and now tend to focus on the motivations and behavior of legislators. Structural properties of the legislative system are viewed in terms of their effects upon behavior. Generalizations and comparisons at the macroscopic level can now be built upon analyses of individual legislative behavior. The motivations and orientations of legislators have been fairly widely investigated utilizing the technique of systematic interviewing; this technique is discussed in the contribution by Hunt, Crane, and Wahlke. Decision-making behavior has been analyzed by using the data of roll-call votes, and this is the empirical basis for the paper in this section by MacRae.

> Second, although continuing to accept legislation as a core function, the newer studies, by asking questions about informal behavioral patterns and latent functions as well as about the consequences of these patterns and functions for structural arrangements, orient research toward the discovery of behavioral and institutional phenomena that formal analysis cannot possibly discern.[1]

Some of the earlier selections in this anthology illustrate the increasing concern of research in legislative behavior with informal legislative structures and unwritten rules of the game (norms). In this section, Wahlke deals briefly with the very important theoretical problem of the functional contribution, or capability, of legislative systems *vis-à-vis* the larger political system. He cogently points out the vital nexus of theory and research in creating a more scientifically useful theory of legislative systems. Both Wahlke and Jewell stress, in somewhat different ways, the important role comparative analysis plays in more adequate understanding of the operation of legislative systems.

> Finally, the newer studies attempt to purge legislative research of its earlier overcommitment to evaluative judgment and a premature policy orientation, and to concentrate instead on testing hypotheses about legislative behavior and functions and on building viable empirical theory.[1]

This does not mean that the legislative analyst is never concerned about making evaluations of legislative institutions, or that he eschews any interest in public policy. Empirical political research is a requisite for effective change in legislative institutions, if change is to be seen mainly as planned or manipulated institutional adjustment. Legislative change is itself a significant subject for systematic investigation; we know unfortunately little about environmental adaptations of legislative systems. Legislative policy outputs provide important variables for research, and we need to do much more research on the determinants of policy outputs, and on the political consequences of legislative policy.

### NOTE

1. Heinz Eulau and Katherine Hinckley, "Legislative Institutions and Processes," in James A. Robinson (ed.), *Political Science Annual 1966,* Vol. 1 (Indianapolis, 1966), pp. 86–87. The above quotations all come from these pages.

# 23. Behavioral Analyses of Representative Bodies[*]

JOHN C. WAHLKE

This paper undertakes to consider where behavioral study of representative bodies appears to be going and what problems are involved in getting there. But, "Where to start the chronicle and what to include? Few legislative studies bear a behavioral label and many are significant only as suggestive prototypes." [1] The relevant literature displays the same diversity in topics studied and in techniques of research which characterizes political and social study in general. For here, as in the more inclusive fields, the adjective "behavioral" designates an approach and not a body of theory or knowledge. The field of inquiry can perhaps be delimited with sufficient precision for present purposes, however, if the term "behavioral studies" is taken to refer to analyses whose data directly concern those human beings known as representatives, the persons who constitute the various representative bodies historically known to man.

### Varieties of Behavioral Analysis

The works marked out by such a definition appear to fall into three generally distinct types which differ both in the questions they seek to answer and in the methods of data collection and analysis they use. They are also distinct in that works in one category tend to make references primarily to other works in the same category and to relate less often to works in the others.

*The Character and Recruitment of Representatives.* One variety of study often erroneously thought to be distinctively "behavioral" is that which ascertains certain demographic characteristics of the membership of particular representative bodies. The character of representatives' constituencies, for example, was the object of attention as early as 1895.[2] Since that time descriptions of various representative bodies in terms of representatives' age, sex, tenure, occupation, religion, ethnic origin, social class, and similar characteristics have become so numerous and familiar, especially in America, that some legislatures regularly publish such information about their own membership.[3] A closely related but more ambitious line of effort is that represented by the *History of Parliament* project, which, following the earlier work of Sir Lewis Namier,[4] attempts to "record the names, and . . . the careers of the persons elected to serve in Parliament from the reign

* From *Essays in the Behavioral Study of Politics,* ed. by Austin Ranney (Urbana, 1962), pp. 173–190. Reprinted by permission of the University of Illinois Press.

of Edward I to a date as far into the nineteenth century as circumstances may permit." [5] A more recent subtype of the variety of study in question is that which explores career-configurations or general political-attitude configurations of persons who become or aspire to be representatives.[6] Although such studies often range very widely in their attempts to relate career- or attitude-patterns to various antecedent or causal factors and although they frequently share some of the characteristics of the next variety of study to be considered, they may be said to conclude usually by tabulating various patterns as "characteristics" of the membership of the membership of specific representative bodies.

The chief point to be noted about all the sorts of study here discussed is that they tend to be purely descriptive. The reader of the statistics is ordinarily left to infer for himself what the facts presented have to do with the structure, functioning or performance of the representative body, or the behavior of the members described. The case for amassing quantities of such descriptive information about the careers and the demographic characteristics of representatives is best argued by W. O. Aydelotte, who foresees the possibility of discerning in these numerous data (chiefly by statistical methods) "revealing correlations." [7]

For such data to be most useful, however, more is needed than simple tabulations for particular representative bodies or simple intercorrelations among one or more of the characteristics surveyed. Logically, two sorts of hypotheses are needed: first, hypotheses concerning the circumstances which lead to the presence or absence of representatives with certain characteristics; second, and more important, hypotheses concerning the consequences of variations in these characteristics for the behavior of individual legislators and, thereby, for the working of the representative body.

What appear to be hypotheses of this second sort are often encountered. For example, it has been said that lawyers more than representatives from other occupations act as brokers, or "professional representers," or, alternatively, that they act as "precedent-mongers" and conservers of the legal *status quo*.[8] A more complex example is provided by the assertion that political integration of local government units with central government is better promoted where many representatives in the central government have had prior experience in local government offices.[9] So commonplace that they are hardly recognized as hypotheses of this sort are the beliefs implicit in innumerable studies that representatives from rural areas act as agents of farmers, that representatives from working-class occupations act as agents of the working class, or that representatives from managerial and entrepreneurial occupations act as spokesmen for business interests. In fact, propositions such as these are generally guesses put forward to justify presentation of the descriptive factual information; they rarely function as hypotheses to be tested by the research which is being reported.[10]

*Motivations and Behavior of Individual Representatives.* A second variety of research is less concerned with what representatives are than with what they do and why they do it. Works of this variety seek explanations of the actions of representatives in the form of general propositions about their behavior as individuals. With some exceptions, they do not ordinarily refer to the characteristics discussed in the preceding category in making their explanations.

A few analysts have attempted to examine representatives' actions in the light of theories and principles of general psychology. John B. McConaughy's assessment of representatives' personality characteristics,[11] for example, suggests that one important psychological hypothesis about political behavior (Harold Lasswell's, that a prevailing psychological mechanism in the behavior of politicians is displacement of feelings of personal inadequacy) probably does not hold for representatives generally. But this study has never been replicated for members of other representative bodies nor extended beyond McConaughy's small sample. Similarly, Garland C. Routt's application of hypotheses taken from theories of group dynamics to study of the interactions among representatives on the floor in one legislature[12] has not been followed up by others.

Instead of working within some explicit psychological framework, most analysts in this category attempt, without psychological trappings, to measure the proportionate influence of various political forces or factors suspected to influence representatives' individual decisions. A number of studies, for example, describe the ways representatives receive and react to information from various sources, such as mass media, letters from constituents, or public opinion polls.[13] Others describe the relationships of representatives to their political parties,[14] to their constituencies,[15] to pressure groups,[16] to other actors, and to such abstract influence as their cultural environment.[17] Some analysts concentrate upon a particular problem, such as the dilemmas of the representative who is also a leader of an interest group.[18] A very important group of more recent studies consists of those which examine the group life of the representative body in terms of its members' perceptions of the norms of the group.[19] And closely related to these are studies of the formation of personal friendship and other cliques within the larger body [20] or of informal structures of authority such as develop, for example, around subject-matter experts within the representative body.[21]

The findings of all these and similar studies, viewed individually, are highly informative; collectively they span a wide range of representatives' behavior. But they use such a diversity of terms and concepts and focus on such a variety of questions that it is very difficult to cumulate them into any concise and coherent statement of the present status of knowledge. One major reason for this difficulty is the common failure to be guided by some carefully formulated and clearly recognized model of the representative actor, which failure, in turn, promotes the implicit use of a great variety of models. The most familiar of these are the classical "rational-man" model (the representative individually measuring proposed courses of actions against an objective standard of the public interest), the social-class-interest model (the representative acting according to the dictates of norms and values acquired by virtue of his class status), and the simple pressure-politics model (the representative passively moving according to the mechanical combination of forces which happen to impinge on him). Future research could profit from specification of a psychological theory or model sufficiently general to accommodate the great diversity of research interests displayed in this field and sufficiently reliable to be generally accepted as a framework for future research.

One promising line of development is suggested by the fact that the basic terms and concepts used to date seem to refer not just to gross physical actions of representatives ("behavior" in the technical sense of that word in Watsonian psychological theory) but to their attitudes, judgments, and perceptions concerning the persons and forces in their political world. Several provocative works have pursued inquiry in this direction more directly and more generally than most of those previously discussed.[22] Further pursuing this line of reasoning and investigations, some analysts (the writer included) have reached the conclusion that role-theory, as set forth in social-psychological and sociological literature, promises to be both a means of systematizing the great quantities of information already set forth and a powerful theoretical weapon for future research.[23]

*Decisions by Representative Bodies.* A third (and most numerous) variety of analyses focuses upon the actions with members of a given body engage in simultaneously and collectively. Instead of microcosmic examinations of patterns of behavior of the individual representative, these studies undertake a macrocosmic examination of patterns found in aggregates of actions by component individuals at particular points in time. They rarely seek or specify the individual psychological mechanism bringing about a given pattern of actions for the collectivity of representatives. On the whole, they display more careful formulation of hypotheses and greater methodological sophistication than do most analyses.

In one way or another, almost all these studies involve the attempt to discover and measure the influence of the various factors productive of cleavage in representative bodies, i.e., the determinants of collective decisions. Earliest in time and easily most numerous of all works in this category are those which assess the significance of political parties.[24] More recent studies, of which Julius Turner's [25] is probably the best-known example, attempt not merely to measure the influence of party but to compare it with the influence of other factors. Thus investigation has been pushed beyond the examination of party and constituency pressure to the examination of sectional bases of cleavage, including urban-rural influences,[26] cleavages stemming from the activity of pressure groups,[27] from members' relationships to their party leadership or their state delegations,[28] and from ideological and policy-interest differences among members,[29] to name only a few of the topics covered by the most significant works of recent years.

Increasingly, such studies seek not merely to assess the amount of influence exerted by one or another factor but to investigate the circumstances under which their influence varies. Among the circumstances investigated and found significant are the degree of interparty competition in representatives' districts,[30] the character of the issue facing the representatives,[31] the majority or minority status of the parties,[32] the institutional structure of the legislative party,[33] the socio-economic characteristics of representatives' constituencies,[34] and various combinations of these.

These studies frequently sharpen and amplify the meaning of commonly used concepts. MacRae's analysis of congressional voting, for example, demonstrates the importance of distinguishing between economics and civil-rights liberalism and suggests that congressional liberalism-conservatism is explained better in terms of politics than personality.[35] Both MacRae and Truman [36] push analysis of party-cohesion well beyond simple numerical comparison of the opposing parties' cohesion and explore the nature and stability of intraparty divisions as well as the types and extent of interparty cleavage.

There is an obvious relationship of interest between studies of the influence of such factors as party, constituency, and pressure group on the decisions of representative bodies and studies of individuals' patterns of response to the same entities. Search for the causes of different patterns of group action tends to overlap or link up with the search for the bases of individuals' behavior even more clearly. For example, to understand why constituents' interests and ideology should outweigh party demands for organizational loyalty as a factor influencing the representative body's actions, it is necessary to speculate about the psychological mechanism through which these forces affect the behavior of the individual representative.[37] The same can be said of the desire to learn whether the influence of constituency comes about through "pressure" applied to representatives or through political selection of representatives typical of their districts.[38] Works which approach questions in this way are not easily classifiable exclusively as studies of either individual behavior or group action; they contribute to knowledge on both accounts. They also suggest further why development of psychological models of the individual representative is essential to future research.

Questions concerning the political model of the representative body are more pertinent, however, to the variety of studies being discussed. The most common model is a loose conception of a "decision-making process," wherein decisions at each step along the way are the product of forces or pressures, injected into the system. The findings of many an analysis, therefore, offer little more than a snapshot of the particular constellation of forces or pressures which happen to be exerted at whatever time the analysis is made. But there is a strong tendency toward converting concern with "process" in a loose sense into concern with structure in a more precise sense. More recent studies appear less concerned with comprehending why each particular decision comes out as it does or with predicting successfully the outcome of each future decision than with determining the general framework within which all decisions are made. The finding that southern congressmen's positions on racial issues are arrived at on a state-wide basis instead of on the basis of their individual constituencies' stands,[39] for example, is a bit of structural information in this sense. It does not tell us whether or not Congress will have to decide on some racial issue or what it will decide, but it does tell us something about *how* it will decide *if* it faces such an issue. Likewise, Truman's exploration of the ways in which party leadership groups mediate the various influences affecting the work of Congress [40] tells us about something that is relatively permanent in the system that is Congress.

In short, studies of the decision-making process in representative bodies are usually more than mere inventories of the quanta of force expended in dividing the body for purposes of decision. They are more likely to resemble blueprints, however sketchy, of structures of authority and channels through which power and influence flow. Before pursuing the implications of this proposition, it will be helpful to consider some questions about methodology raised by the foregoing thumbnail sketch of recent research.

### Methodological Problems

Perhaps because the literature is extremely heterogeneous with respect to methods and techniques of research, questions of methodology often receive explicit and exhaustive attention from analysts, both in separate sections on methodology in various research reports and in articles or monographs dealing only with questions of methodology.[41] But for the long run methodological problems are neither the most difficult nor the most critical to be faced.

*Types and Sources of Data.* The requirement (by definition) that the data of behavioral studies consist ultimately of some record of the specific actions or characteristics of specific human beings is neither rigorous nor restrictive. It does not single out any particular class of actions as the only legitimate object of research attention nor does it specify that data about representatives' actions be drawn from any one particular source.

Records of roll-call votes have so far been the most widely used source of data, and roll-call voting has therefore been the class of actions most thoroughly inspected. Analyses of the third type discussed above rely principally upon such data, but analysis of representatives' individual behavior often make inferences from the same. On the other hand, data from official journals and reports concerning related actions, such as speeches and motions in debate, sponsorship of bills, resolutions and amendments, or conduct in committee and in hearings, which constitute one of the most frequently used sources of data for studies of representatives' individual behavior and the most common source for studies of their demographic characteristics, are ordinarily used in analysis of the action of representative bodies only for background information or illustrative purposes. The record of actions provided by newspapers and other secondary sources, however, has been very little used by any analysts, one good and probably sufficient reason being the wholly unsystematic and (for purposes of analysis) inadequate attention paid by these sources to the manifold activities of representatives and representative bodies.

Few would deny that the formal actions of voting and related forms of participation in the representative body's more visible official activities are a critically important class of actions. On the other hand, a major reason for past concentration upon these has no doubt been their easy accessibility to data collectors. Unquestionably research must take into account a greater variety of actions by the representative actors.

Direct and systematic *observation* of activities to this end has been used in at least one case as the chief source of data,[42] and in some cases as one of several major sources,[43] and in others as a source of background information.[44] The limitations of this data source are obvious. The legislature is a finite body of men engaging in a series of actions which, though not infinite, are certainly innumerable. They cannot all be observed simultaneously, let alone recorded for future analysis. And representatives' behavior includes a large class of actions—the often-mentioned "backroom deals," secret interchanges, communications by tone and gesture, etc.—which are forever inaccessible to any observing analyst.

An increasingly important source of data about representatives' behavior is *systematic interviews* with the representatives themselves. From representatives' responses (verbal actions) analysts can make two sorts of inference about other characteristics or behavior: informational (did or did not some particular representatives do such and such?) and attitudinal (do or do not particular representatives think, feel, or perceive a certain way?). Particularly the second usage is becoming more frequent, not only in the study of American representative bodies [45] but in both Western and non-Western bodies elsewhere.[46] One advantage of this data source is that it can yield bases for inferences about many classes of actions for which either no data whatever or only still more indirect data are provided by the other sources described. That interviews provide data from which inferences are made rather than direct data about the behavior to be analyzed is not really a unique feature of this data source. In a strict sense, *all* data provide only bases for inferences. Moreover, the experience of all who have used this method of data collection testifies that many frequent objections—representatives will not talk, sophistication of respondents is unjustifiably presumed, words have no relation to behavior, etc.—while they call attention to pitfalls to which researchers must be alert, are insufficiently grounded to justify refusing to consider the use of interviews at all.

It seems almost platitudinous to say that all the above-mentioned sources of data have their legitimate place in future research, that researchers, whatever source they use, should recognize the limitations of their data as well as their potentialities, or that there is need for the exercise of still greater ingenuity in discovering and utilizing new sources of data. But it is imperative to recognize that any thought of some day finding ways to amass data about every action of every representative is quixotic. It is also unnecessary. Productive analysis does not proceed from collecting "*all* the facts"; it begins when the analyst, guided by some theoretical conception and purpose, knows *what* kinds of facts he needs and then finds appropriate methods for collecting and analyzing the data he has found necessary to his purposes.

*Techniques of Analysis.* Just as the term "behavioral study of representative bodies" is occasionally taken to refer to some particular type or source of data, so also it is sometimes erroneously identified with particular (especially mathematical) techniques of analyzing its data. It is true that such techniques as *scale analysis* and *factor analysis* find increasing use in behavioral studies.[47] It is also true that behavioral analyses tend to rely on increasingly rigorous *statistical techniques,* although the prevailing standards and techniques are not really as new or as sophisticated as is sometimes thought.[48] In most cases, these techniques have made possible findings which probably could not have been reached by less quantitative methods. In most cases, their mathematical character provides us with standards for judging how reliable and conclusive the findings are. But, while adequacy of research techniques to research objects and high standards of evidence and proof are characteristic of many analyses, these characteristics do not, themselves, constitute "behavioral study."

In the same way, the term should not be confused with a particular type of analysis, such as the *case study* or the *comparative study,* the *developmental* or the *cross-sectional study.* Each of these is represented in the arsenal of behavioral studies.[49] In each case, the type of analysis is dictated by considerations of research strategy (questions to be attacked) and not just by research economics (availability of time, personnel, and money). In each case, the limits of generalization from a particular study are set by the type of analysis chosen.

In general, it would appear that comparative analysis is becoming more frequent, though case studies are not becoming less so, but that relatively little attention is yet being given to developmental, as distinguished from cross-sectional, questions. Although the causes for this pattern of emphasis no doubt lie partly in mundane considerations of mechanical feasibility, they probably stem even more from theoretical problems. Once theoretical clarification brings out the questions which research must answer, problems of methodology become essentially technical questions about the adequacy of means to ends. Solving those problems will undoubtedly require the invention of new tools and devices as well as mastery of existing ones. But it also goes without saying that the tools will not operate themselves, nor will they produce if used by mechanics untrained in the objectives to be served by their use.

### Theoretical Problems

In other words, it is the theoretical problems facing behavioral study of representative bodies which are ultimately the most important and most difficult to solve. They all involve making clear the long-run objectives shared by all research in the field. To avoid possible misinterpretations of the discussion which follows, it should be said immediately that "solving" the theoretical problems does not require choosing among mutually exclusive alternatives. It does, however, require clarity about the nature of the alternatives, about their relation to one another, and about the relation of any given piece of research to them.

*Politics and Behavior: Psychology or Political Science?* By studying the behavior of representatives, one can learn something about the political behavior of human beings. Does a desire for power operate differently when men act in this particular institutional context than when they act in others? In what ways? Why do some men satisfy that desire by seeking representative office while others satisfy it in other ways? By the same token, studying the behavior of representatives can contribute to the understanding of human behavior even more generally. What gratifications does the holding of representative office provide men? What ego needs are served by different types of behavior in that office? The answers to such questions take the form of propositions which hold true for all human individuals. The ultimate aim is to learn how and why people act.

Our sketchy review of the literature shows that, contrary to the beliefs of some, few analysts of representative bodies have been concerned to discover universalistic propositions about political behavior. Still fewer have sought general psychological laws. The concern of almost all has been with the consequences of behavior which follows certain laws or principles, not with its causes. How does that behavior affect the distribution of power and authority in society? How does it affect (and how is it affected by) the political institutions which embody power and authority and through whose working other values are distributed?

It would therefore seem that the analyst of representative bodies can work best when he is able to start from a model embodying acceptable and general psychological propositions. He ordinarily will use that model to arrive ultimately at propositions which are of a quite different order. In the imperfect world of research, however, where labor must be divided, "psychological" research aimed at the production of models or the establishment of general propositions about political behavior can be a welcome ally of the analyst of representative bodies. The fundamental requirement is only that each researcher know what he seeks, how it relates to what others seek, and how reliable his findings are.

*Politics, History and Political Theory: Uniqueness and Generality.* David Truman's statement about his congressional case study is applicable to legislative sutdy in general: its objective "is not history, not description of the unique elements in a stream of events, but identification of the features . . . that are basic and permanent." [50] But a critical question not squarely faced by analysis to date is, "basic and permanent features" of what? Of each particular system individually and uniquely? Of groups of similar systems? But what does "similar" mean in this case?

Of all representative bodies in all times. If so, what differentiates "representative" bodies from other bodies of men?

The tradition of political science since Plato and Aristotle has been to aim at the highest level of generalization. It may therefore be suggested that the long-run objective of analysis of representative bodies is understanding of "*the* representative body." In other words, one cardinal standard for evaluating any study is its contribution to the development of a general theory of representative bodies.

Analytical energy and talent have so far been concentrated on comprehensive understanding of single systems as unique entities. Even comparative studies have usually been limited in their aims, seeking out the unique characteristics of the bodies compared more often than analyzing features shared by all of them as representative bodies. Even so, it is possible to detect a trend toward recognizing the more general theoretical objectives of analysis.

The particular direction of the trend has already been obliquely suggested; it is toward increasing concern with institutional aspects of the representative body. This is manifested, for example, by the effort to describe norms and informal structures of the representative group [51] or to discover patterns and channels of influence which are stable over long periods of time.[52] It is manifested by the effort to link "psychological" understanding of representatives' behavior to understanding of the structures of decision-making processes through such theories and concepts as that of role." [53] Terms like "power," "process," and "institution" are beginning to take on more precise meanings; their theoretical relationships to one another are becoming more clear.

Conceptual clarification at this level seems the most pressing need if the requisite theoretical progress is to be made. To make that progress requires also that more and more representative bodies, in all cultures and at all levels of government, be subjected to comparative analysis. This does not mean that intensive analysis of particular individual systems is *passé*. The areas of our ignorance about many representative bodies is vast. Nor does it mean that more ambitious comparative analysis should be postponed until we are provided with some acceptable general theory. Theory and research necessarily progress in lock step, not independently of each other. It does mean that progress will be most rapid where analysis, comparative or individual-system, aims at contributing to the development of general political theory.

*Politics and Sociology: System and Function.* The preceding remarks can be summarized as follows: behavioral analyses have made and promise to make still further substantial contributions to our understanding of the internal workings of representative bodies as a type of political institution. They lead beyond realistic description of the structure and processes of particular institutionalized groups to investigation of the differential consequences to all representative institutions of various forms of power and influence brought to bear on them, of the conditions of stability, and of the causes of changes in institutional structure and to other important questions of a general theoretical nature.

One other point requires conceptual and theoretical clarification which probably cannot be provided by behavioral analysis of representative bodies alone. This concerns the function and purpose of representative bodies in the larger political and social systems of which they are a part. Such concepts as "legislation" and "representation" are of crucial significance here. They must be given precise meaning in terms of a general political or social theory if they are to direct attention to the relevant aspects of representatives' behavior. Indeed, unless they are precisely defined from a theoretical standpoint, it is impossible to know what bodies qualify as objects of analysis by students of "representative" bodies. Only on the basis of clear theory on this point can analysts know what it is about representative bodies they should compare, even if they have no doubts about which bodies are representative ones and which of them they wish to subject to comparative study. Beyond such obvious political concepts and questions lie still more abstract concepts of general sociological theory, such as the origins and the management of conflict and tension in society,[54] to which also analyses of representative bodies must ultimately be relevant.

This kind of theoretical problem, of course, faces all students of government and not just "behavioral" ones. But it is incumbent on behavioral analysts to recognize that they are responsible, like all other students, for utilizing and ultimately helping to develop theory at this level, too.

## Conclusion

The main points we have covered can be summarized very briefly. (1) "Behavioral study of representative bodies" should not be identified with any particular methodology or methodological school. (2) Analyses of this kind have contributed greatly to our knowledge of how particular representative bodies work, but their ultimate objective is knowledge of a more general nature. (3) The knowledge sought is knowledge about government and politics, not general psychology. (4) The problems most immediately facing such analyses involve articulating "psychologist" and decision-process studies into a coherent attack on questions about the institutional character of representative bodies, a contribution to development of a general theory of representative bodies. (5) Progress toward such a theory requires articulation of behavioral analyses with political theory in a still more general sense, particularly with respect to the political functions of representation and legislation. (6) Problems of methodology can be dealt with as individual technical problems in proportion as theoretical problems are solved.

In reality, none of these problems will ever be "solved" in the sense that knowledge about representative bodies will be complete and final. Behavioral research aspires to knowledge which, though it may increase in generality and probable truth, will always be fragmentary and hypothetical. To some, this prospect may appear to condemn researchers to a labor of Sisyphus. If so, there is some comfort in the thought that we do not know certainly that our stone must periodically roll back on us forever. But we must still resign ourselves to knowing that the basic tools of future researchers will remain that of their forebears: minds which are finite and human.

## NOTES

1. N. Meller, "Legislative Behavior Research," *Western Political Quarterly,* Vol. 13 (1960), p. 134. Professor Meller's article provides an excellent review of the most relevant literature. See also J. C. Wahlke and H. Eulau, eds., *Legislative Behavior: A Reader in Theory and Research* (Glencoe, Ill.: The Free Press, 1959).

2. G. H. Haynes, "Representation in New England Legislatures," *Annals of the American Academy of Political and Social Science*, Vol. 6 (1895), pp. 58–71.

3. A convenient listing and discussion of the most important of these studies can be found in Meller, *op. cit.*, pp.141–43. Meller notes that the characteristics studied include, in one case, the cranial capacity of the representatives' heads.

4. L. B. Namier, *The Structure of Politics at the Accession of George III*, 2 vols. (London: Macmillan and Co., 1929).

5. F. M. Stenton, "The History of Parliament," *London Times Literary Supplement*, January 6, 1956. See also G. P. Judd, *Members of Parliament: 1734–1832* (New Haven, Conn.: Yale University Press, 1955).

6. H. Eulau *et al.*, "The Political Socialization of American State Legislators," *Midwest Journal of Political Science*, Vol. 3 (1959), pp. 188–206, and "Career Perspectives of American State Legislators," in D. Marvick, ed., *Political Decision-Makers* (Glencoe, Ill.: The Free Press, 1960).

7. W. O. Aydelotte, "A Statistical Analysis of the Parliament of 1841: Some Problems of Method," *Bulletin of the Institute of Historical Research*, Vol. 27 (1954), p. 141.

8. C. S. Hyneman, "Who Makes Our Laws?" *Political Science Quarterly*, Vol. 55 (1940), pp. 556–81.

9. W. J. M. Mackenzie, "Local Government in Parliament," *Public Administration*, Vol. 32 (1954), pp. 409–23.

10. See, however, D. R. Matthews, *The Social Background of Political Decision-Makers* (Garden City, N.Y.: Doubleday and Co., 1954), chaps. 1, 2, and 5, for an excellent discussion of relevant theories and hypotheses which might be applied. See also his "U.S. Senators and the Class Structure," *Public Opinion Quarterly*, Vol. 18 (1954), pp. 5–22.

11. J. B. McConaughy, "Certain Personality Factors of State Legislators in South Carolina," *American Political Science Review*, Vol. 44 (1950), pp. 897–903.

12. G. C. Routt, "Interpersonal Relationships and the Legislative Process, *Annals of the American Academy of Political and Social Science*, Vol. 195 (1938), pp. 129–36.

13. Meller, *op. cit.*, discusses most of these.

14. D. MacRae, Jr., "Roll-Call Votes and Leadership," *Public Opinion Quarterly*, Vol. 20 (1956), pp. 543–58.

15. L. A. Dexter, "The Representative and His District," *Human Organization*, Vol. 16 (1957), pp. 2–13; H. Eulau *et al.*, "The Role of the Representative: Some Empirical Observations on the Theory of Edmund Burke," *American Political Science Review*, Vol. 53 (1959), pp. 742–56; W. W. Crane, Jr., "Do Representatives Represent?" *Journal of Politics*, Vol. 22 (1960), pp. 295–99.

16. W. W. Crane, Jr., "A Test of the Effectiveness of Interest Group Pressures on Legislators," *Southwestern Social Science Quarterly*, Vol. 41 (1960), pp. 335–40; J. C. Wahlke *et al.*, "American State Legislators' Role Orientations Toward Pressure Group," *Journal of Politics*, Vol. 22 (1960), pp. 203–27.

17. E. A. Shils, "The Legislator and His Environment," *University of Chicago Law Review*, Vol. 18 (1951), pp. 571–84.

18. J. H. Millett, "The Role of an Interest Group Leader in the House of Commons," *Western Political Quarterly*, Vol. 9 (1956), pp. 915–26.

19. R. K. Huitt, "The Morse Committee Assignment Controversy: A Study in Senate Norms," *American Political Science Review*, Vol. 51 (1957), pp. 313–29; D. R. Matthews, *U.S. Senators and Their World* (Chapel Hill: The University of North Carolina Press, 1960), chap. 5.

20. S. C. Patterson, "Patterns of Interpersonal Relations in a Legislative Group," *Public Opinion Quarterly*, Vol. 23 (1959), pp. 101–109.

21. W. Buchanan *et al.*, "The Legislator as Specialist," *Western Political Quarterly*, Vol. 13 (1960), pp. 636–51.

22. R. K. Huitt, "The Congressional Committee: A Case Study," *American Political Science Review*, Vol. 48 (1954), pp. 340–65; O. Garceau and C. Silverman, "A Pressure Group and the Pressured: A Case Report," *American Political Science Review*, Vol. 48 (1954), pp. 672–91; C. Silverman, "The Legislator's View of the Legislative Process," *Public Opinion Quarterly*, Vol. 18 (1954), pp. 180–90.

23. J. C. Wahlke *et al.*, *The Legislative System: Explorations in Legislative Behavior* (New York: John Wiley & Sons, Inc., 1962), chap. 1; Eulau *et al.*, "The Role of the Representative"; Wahlke *et al.*, "American State Legislators' Role Orientations."

24. A. L. Lowell, "The Influence of Party Upon Legislation in England and America," *Annual Report of the American Historical Association* (1901), Vol. 1, pp. 321–43. For a convenient listing of the many works appearing subsequently, see Meller, *op. cit.*, pp. 146–47.

25. J. Turner, *Party and Constituency: Pressures on Congress* (Baltimore: The Johns Hopkins Press, 1951). See also D. MacRae, Jr., "The Relation Between Roll-Call Votes and Constituencies in the Massachusetts House of Representatives," *American Political Science Review*, Vol. 46 (1952), pp. 1046–55, and "The Role of the State Legislator in Massachusetts," *American Sociological Review*, Vol. 19 (1954), pp. 185–94.

26. See the listing in Meller, *op. cit.*, p. 146.

27. *Ibid.*, pp. 147–48.

28. D. B. Truman, *The Congressional Party: A Case Study* (New York: John Wiley & Sons, Inc., 1959).

29. D. MacRae, Jr., *The Dimensions of Congressional Voting* (Berkeley and Los Angeles: University of California Press, 1958).

30. *Ibid.*, pp. 284–89; MacRae, "Roll-Call Votes and Constituencies."

31. W. W. Crane, Jr., *The Legislative Struggle in Wisconsin* (unpublished Ph.D. dissertation, University of Wisconsin, 1959); MacRae, *The Dimensions of Congressional Voting*.

32. Truman, *op. cit.*, especially pp. 285ff.

33. *Ibid.*, pp. 94–144, 193–246.

34. MacRae, "Roll-Call Votes and Constituencies."

35. MacRae, *The Dimensions of Congressional Voting*, p. 231.

36. *Ibid.;* Truman, *op. cit.*

37. MacRae, "Roll-Call Votes and Leadership."

38. MacRae, *The Dimensions of Congressional Voting*, p. 256.

39. *Ibid.*, p. 270.

40. Truman, *op. cit.*, pp. 193–246. See also Wahlke and Eulau, eds., *op. cit.*, pp. 355–413.

41. MacRae, *The Dimensions of Congressional Voting*, pp. 298–382; Truman, *op. cit.*, pp. 10–14, 320–30; D. MacRae, Jr., "Some Underlying Variables in Legislative Roll-Call Votes," *Public Opinion Quarterly*, Vol. 18 (1954), pp. 191–96.

42. Routt, *op. cit.*

43. Crane, *The Legislative Struggle in Wisconsin*.

44. Truman, *op. cit.;* Buchanan *et al.*, *op. cit.;* Eulau *et al.*, *op. cit.;* Wahlke *et al.*, *op. cit.*

45. S. C. Patterson, *Toward a Theory of Legislative Behavior: The Wisconsin State Assemblymen as Actors in a Legislative System* (unpublished Ph.D. dissertation, University of Wisconsin, 1958); Crane, *The Legislative Struggle in Wisconsin;* Buchanan *et al.*, *op. cit.;* Wahlke *et al.*, *op. cit.;* Eulau *et al.*, *op. cit.*

46. Professor Norman Meller has used this method in the Marshall Islands. Mr. William H. Hunt in 1960 completed intensive interviews with selected members of the French National Assembly. Also see Wilder W. Crane, Jr., *The Legislature of Lower Austria* (London, 1961).

47. MacRae's *Dimensions of Congressional Voting,* representing the most extensive use of scale analysis to date, contains a discussion of that method in relation to alternative approaches, pp. 298–312. George M. Belknap, "A Method for Analyzing Legislative Behavior," *Midwest Journal of Political Science,* Vol. 2 (1958), pp. 377–402, explains the use of this method in considerable detail. Factor analyses have been much less frequent. For an example of this technique, see H. B. Carlson and W. Harrell, "Voting Groups Among Leading Congressmen Obtained by Means of the Inverted Factor Technique," *Journal of Social Psychology,* Vol. 16 (1942), pp. 51–61.

48. The concept of a "party vote" devised by Lowell, *op. cit.,* is still used regularly with only minor modifications. Truman's analysis, *op. cit.,* follows a method devised by Stuart Rice and Herman Beyle over thirty years ago: H. C. Beyle, *Identification and Analysis of Attribute Cluster Blocs* (Chicago: University of Chicago Press, 1931). The index of party cohesion was developed by Rice even earlier: S. A. Rice, "The Behavior of Legislative Groups," *Political Science Quarterly,* Vol. 40 (1925), pp. 60–72.

49. The works of Buchanan, Eulau, and Wahlke cited above are all part of a comparative study of legislators in California, New Jersey, Ohio, and Tennessee conducted by them and Professor LeRoy C. Ferguson with the aid of a grant from the Social Science Research Council having as one of its major purposes the promotion of comparative study. Other examples of comparative study are found chiefly but by no means exclusively in analyses of party voting in representative bodies. Examples of developmental study are found mainly among analyses of various characteristics of legislators: Namier, *op. cit.;* A. W. Martin, "The Legislative Assembly of New South Wales, 1856–1900," *Australian Journal of Politics and History,* Vol. 2 (1956), pp. 46–67.

50. Truman, *op. cit.,* p. 15. Note the similarity of MacRae's comment: ". . . even the most transient issues can be used to illuminate more lasting problems, for we may abstract from each issue to consider the procedural, tactical, and strategic features of the political system within which it is posed," *The Dimensions of Congressional Voting,* p. 212.

51. See p. 386.

52. See pp. 388–389.

53. See note 23.

54. Professor Heinz Eulau is presently engaged in research in this area.

# 24. Comparative Research in State Legislative Politics*

MALCOLM E. JEWELL

The field of legislative politics, like other closely related aspects of American state politics, offers one of the richest, most fertile fields for research in comparative government and politics. Do not misunderstand my use of the term "rich." I am not suggesting that the foundations are likely to offer grants for study in Austin or Atlanta comparable to those available for students embarking for Rangoon or Nairobi. I am suggesting that the opportunities for truly comparative studies at the state level are great, that some of the techniques developed by students of foreign comparative government can be utilized in this study, and that the results may have interest beyond the borders of American states. The minimal expense and the relative accessability of research data are obvious reasons for encouraging research at the state level. But there are equally important if less obvious reasons. One of the most frustrating problems confronting the student of comparative politics is the difficulty of measuring a few variables when a large number of others are beyond his control; this problem is minimized in the study of state politics. The political cultures in Louisiana and Mississippi are similar enough to permit meaningful contrasts between bifactional and multifactional political systems. Illinois and Michigan have two-party systems that are similar enough to make possible some judgments about the effects of two different systems of legislative apportionment. Some of the states are undergoing political change rapidly enough to shed light on the causes and consequences of two-party politics and the effect of primaries on political systems.

Despite these logistical and scholarly temptations, until recently there were relatively few safaris into the fields of comparative state politics, and most of these followed well-trodden paths where game was scarce and produced only a few familiar specimens. I think we can find four rather obvious reasons for this small research yield:

(1) Most studies were formal ones, often prepared for the use of legislators, covering primarily legal technicalities—the rules and procedures of legislative bodies, for example.

(2) Students of state government tended to be reformers, who concentrated their attention on those aspects that needed change, in their judgment. We have

* This paper was presented at a Conference on Research in Legislative Politics of the New York Legislative Internship Program in 1964, and appears here in print for the first time.

literally hundreds of studies of malapportionment, but little analysis of the relation of legislators to constituents; we have numerous studies emphasizing that committees are too numerous, but little information on variations in the functions of committees from state to state.

(3) Those students who ventured into the study of politics often found it easier to write about colorful politicians and political skulduggery than to wrestle with the difficult task of comparing political systems and practices among states.

(4) Surprisingly few of the experts on state government and politics were knowledgeable about more than a few states or sought to carry out research that crossed state lines.

We have no difficulty tracing the revival of comparative study in state politics to its source. The date was 1949, the event was the publication of *Southern Politics.* In this work, in his *American State Politics,* and through the works of his students, V. O. Key not only provided much of our knowledge but suggested most of the hypotheses that are still being tested concerning state politics. Directly or indirectly he inspired the comparative studies of New England and the Border States, as well as individual studies of Florida, Louisiana, Texas, Indiana, Pennsylvania, and Wisconsin, to name some of the best.[1] It is true, as Professor H. D. Price has asserted, that those who have followed Key have left some geographic areas virtually unexplored and have often added little to the conceptualizations suggested by Key.[2] But even those studies covering a single state have contributed to comparative analysis because they have often used similar methodological tools and have answered the same questions. The emphasis on parties, elections, and the nature of political competition has often left other aspects of political systems obscure. Nevertheless, most of the studies I have mentioned dealt, at least briefly, with legislative and gubernatorial politics.

The most significant study of comparative legislative politics is *The Legislative System,* in which Professor Wahlke and his associates devote particular attention to the analysis of legislative roles within the contrasting political systems of four states.[3] Studies in depth of legislative politics have appeared in Illinois, Florida, and California.[4] Though diverse in approach, these studies may be suggestive in the planning of research designs for comparative study. Comparative analysis of gubernatorial politics is in its infancy, with Coleman Ransone's volumes providing descriptive analysis that crosses state lines. In very few states—notably Illinois and Massachusetts—do we have research in depth on the governor of a single state.[5]

In addition to studies focused on the political or legislative system of a state or group of states, we have a growing number of studies dealing with narrower aspects of legislative politics.[6] The best known and most numerous are based on roll call analysis, but research is being done on the governor, committees, norms and roles, and legislative elections, to name some examples. Though usually limited to a single state, this research is shedding factual light on some of the most obscure corners in the legislative process. More important, perhaps, some of the research is methodologically imaginative; it is preparing the way for more ambitious and valuable comparative analysis. One practical liability is that some of this research remains obscure, hidden away in graduate theses or university bureau publications that sometimes lack adequate distribution to interested scholars. A more serious liability is that this research work is often undertaken without any visible conceptual framework.

The growing pace of legislative research has made the creation of conceptual frameworks not only possible, but necessary if we are going to move from particular facts to even a modest level of generalization. The purposes of this paper are to review and restate the conceptual framework best suited for legislative research, to suggest some priorities for filling in the vast gaps in our knowledge, and to offer a few comments on methodology.

## Legislative and Political Systems

It is useful to begin by recognizing that in each state there is a distinct political system, consisting of a number of sub-systems: the legislature, the judiciary, the administration (governor and bureaucracy), the electoral system (including parties and other groups functioning like parties), and the system of opinion-leadership and interest-representation. There is extensive overlapping of these sub-systems; legislators are constantly interacting with the actors in other sub-systems. Legislative rolls are determined not only by the norms of the legislature itself but by the expectations of these other actors: governors, lobbyists, constituents, and the rest. At the risk of repeating the obvious, I want to point out that most of the role conflicts and contrasting choices of roles that are probed so thoroughly in *The Legislative System* would be meaningless if the legislature were a castle surrounded by a moat, if the legislators were not constantly looking outward as well as inward for the sources of their roles.

If the legislature cannot be torn loose from the interrelated sub-systems for research purposes, we must recognize the value of studying a legislature within the context of its entire political system. Professor Price has suggested that priority be given, not to the study of separate institutions or their component parts, but to description and analysis of whole state political systems.[7] Although probably no existing study is comprehensive enough to fit his standards, the greatest value of the best single-state political studies (already cited) is that they do comprehend the whole political system, however briefly the legislature—and other sub-systems—may be treated. (Likewise, the greatest fault of most formal studies of legislatures is that they treat the legislature in isolation.) The authors of *The Legislative System* contrast the role structures that they found in the four states being studied. The recent theorists of comparative government talk convincingly in terms of comparing and classifying political systems. Comprehensive studies of the political system in each of several states would add immeasurably to our understanding of the legislative sub-system and its exact place in the larger system.

The argument for focusing attention on the political system does not depend only on the implications that we can draw from role analysis or the popularity of such an approach in foreign comparative studies. Anyone who closely examines the way roles are selected, power is distributed, and decisions are made from one state legislature to another must recognize great differences—differences that appear to be rooted in the political system itself. There are obvious differences among the political systems of New York, Tennessee, Louisiana, and California which have an impact on the legislature itself. The contrasts among legislators are concealed by the similarity of nomenclature—terms such as caucus, speaker, and rules committee. But the caucus in New York bears little resemblance to one in Tennessee; the speakers in Texas, South Carolina, and New Jersey differ in their functions, power, and method of selection; and the Kentucky rules committee is not quite like that in any other state.

Obviously our objective is not to describe fifty different political systems; this is no answer to the student who is frustrated by the difficulties of adequately describing fifty legislative systems. Our objective must be to find the similarities and differences that will enable us to define the major categories of systems. My contention is that the most meaningful differences among legislatures are a consequence of differences among political systems. It is no easy task to define categories of political systems that have analytical utility. Such definition is impossible in a factual vacuum, and it is risky as long as the scarcity of facts remains acute in so many states. This is one reason for emphasizing our need for hard data of every kind about state politics, even data that lacks a conceptual framework or appears ill-suited for comparative analysis.

What characteristics of political systems can we use for definitional purposes? If we look at characteristics associated with the components (or sub-systems) of the political system, we can eliminate the judiciary because of its relative isolation and both the bureaucracy and interest groups because they do not seem to vary much from one political system to another. Some characteristics of the legislative system (size, experience of members, quality of staff services) have little impact on the political system; those characteristics that do (such as party cohesion and legislative leadership) appear for the most part to be dependent variables—dependent on other components of the political system. I would define categories of political systems in terms of their electoral systems (parties or factions) and their chief executives.

### A Three-Dimensional Classification of Political Systems

Efforts to define categories of electoral systems have been focused almost entirely on party competition and have resulted in disagreements over the offices, time periods, and standards to be used in measurement.[8] If we focus our attention on the political system, it becomes clear that we need to measure not only the level of competition but also the strength or cohesion of parties or of factions within a one-party system. I would define competition in terms of the closeness of competition for and alternation in control of the governorship, because it is the most important *state* office and because legislative control is distorted by malapportionment. Any time period that is chosen is arbitrary and imperfect; I would tend to stress the most recent years (because the degree of competition is changing rapidly), and would certainly include no more than the period since World War Two.

I would distinguish between two groups of political systems having a competitive two-party system; the criterion for distinction would be the cohesive strength of the parties. Characteristically in one group we would find legislative parties in which voting cohesion was relatively high, the leadership had political roles, and the party was an important reference group for legislators. The party organization at the state level, and in some urban areas, would be strong and disciplined and would influence if not control the nominating process. Perhaps most important, the parties would be relatively homogeneous in the interests that they represented. In the second group of two-party states we would find the party to be less significant, both in the legislature and in the electoral (and particularly nominating) process; in most of these states the party would also have a lower level of homogeneity. A third group of state political systems are those in transition from a single-party to a two-party system. The emerging party is likely to have a cohesive strength (particularly if it is newly emergent) that may force a measure of discipline on a previously splintered dominant party. The fourth and fifth categories are one-party state systems, the former being ones in which factions have some of the continuity and perform some of the functions of a party either in the legislative or the electoral system. (This is essentially the distinction Key made between bifactional and multifactional systems, with the single faction considered as an imperfect form of bifactionalism.)

An appraisal of the governorship adds another dimension to the classification of political systems. The governor is potentially a key figure in the legislative system, the leader of his party, chief administrator, and the focal point of public attention and group pressures. Moreover, there are important variations in the power available to and the legislative and political roles played by a governor. Constitutional and statutory provisions give some governors much greater control than others over the administration and the budget. Variations in the terms of office affect every aspect of a governor's authority. In some states the governor assumes a strong legislative role in response to the customary expectations of both legislators and the public; in other states, an effort to do so flies in the face of political norms. Where political parties are strong the governor may, or may not, be able to use his party authority to further his objectives.

I suggest a division of governors into two classifications: *strong* and *weak*. These categories may lack sophistication but not simplicity. It is a simplicity born of desperation because any attempt at precision would produce a multitude of classifications defeating our purpose. Some governors clearly fit one of these categories; others occupy an uncertain middle ground and must be arbitrarily classified. Some governors have both outstanding strengths and weaknesses—for example, those in Pennsylvania and Indiana, who have only a single term but have unusually large patronage resources. It is also important to emphasize that, within the limits imposed by law and—more vaguely—by custom, governors have some choice of the role they will play. There are examples of governors who have chosen a much stronger legislative or partisan role than their predecessors and, in so doing, have significantly affected the entire political system. (Governor Brown of California and Governor Collins of Florida are just two examples.)

We now have a two-dimensional system for classifying political systems. Since our primary interest is the legislature, I think it is necessary to add a third dimension, one particularly pertinent to the legislature. For both strong and weak governors, we should distinguish between those who ordinarily can and those who cannot command a legislative majority on issues of greatest concern to them. Obviously this is a fragile distinction, sometimes varying within brief time spans, and in a two-party system often differing for Democratic and Republican governors. Yet, so central is the governor's legislative role in many states that this distinction appears essential. A strong governor, almost by definition, will seek a legislative majority on many issues; but even a weak governor may aspire to legislative leadership—and consequently seek a majority—on some issues.

I have used the single criterion of a governor's legislative majority for the sake of simplicity, but this term has different meanings in two-party and one-party states.

In a state with two strong parties the governor's most dependable source of legislative support is his own party. Most such governors would be classified as strong (although the Massachusetts governor is an exception because of his short term and lack of control over the administration). Where the parties are strong, it makes a great deal of difference whether the governor's party has or has not a majority in both houses. If it does, he usually is in a commanding position; if it does not, he must be constantly prepared to bargain with the opposition leadership and his tactics must be much less partisan. In some states, like New York and Michigan, a Republican governor can always count on a loyal majority and a Democratic governor always faces an opposition majority. In other states, like Rhode Island and Massachusetts governors of both parties have become used to divided government. The primary cause of divided government is malapportionment, but the concentration of voters geographically, the effects of mid-term elections, and the obstacles facing a traditionally weaker party all contribute to the likelihood of divided government. In states with weak parties, it makes some difference—but not so much—whether a governor has a legislative majority. Weak parties are associated, but not perfectly, with weak governors. In a state where a second party is emerging to challenge the dominant one, the fact of this growing competition may provide the governor of the dominant party with a more cohesive legislative majority than has been customary in the past. The governor of the newly emerging party is most unlikely to have a legislative majority.

In a one-party state the governor normally lacks both a dependable, cohesive party majority and a cohesive opposition party. Where strong factions are found within the legislature, as is true in just a few states, the governor is likely to be identified with a majority faction, which may be more or less cohesive. In the absence of parties or factions, a strong governor can often use the resources of his office to mobilize legislative support for his program; in the absence of an opposition group, he often has a high degree of success. A weak governor, unable or unwilling to play a strong legislative role, may find that his policies coincide with those of a legislative majority (as in South Carolina) or he may find that the legislative majority represents interests frequently in conflict with those to which he is responsible (as in Florida).

Table 1 is designed to put this three dimensional classification of political systems into clearer perspective and to illustrate its utility by placing certain states into categories. In given instances the classification of states is certainly open to debate; this ambiguity illustrates both the imperfection of the classifications and the inadequacy of our knowledge (or at least mine) concerning many state systems.

We have produced a classification that formally reduces the categories of political systems from fifty to twenty, but the five categories of electoral systems dominate the classification. Moreover, a closer look at the table shows that most political systems presently existing or likely to exist are clustered into a few categories. Most systems with strong, competitive parties have strong governors; where the two parties are weaker, the governor is likely to be weaker. In a one-party state it is unlikely for a cohesive legislative majority to appear that is in opposition to the governor, particularly if he is a strong governor, in terms of constitutional power and custom. It seems likely that most states will continue to be found in no more than ten of the categories shown in Table 1.

The search for precise explanations of why particular political systems have developed in specific states is an elusive one, but certain general patterns seem

TABLE 1. A CLASSIFICATION OF STATE POLITICAL SYSTEMS

| Competitiveness and Organization of Parties | Governor's Strength and Relationship to Legislature | | | |
|---|---|---|---|---|
| | Strong Governor | | Weak Governor | |
| | Legislative Majority | Legislative Minority | Legislative Majority | Legislative Minority |
| Two strong, competitive parties | N.Y. (R) N.J. (R) Mich. (R) Conn. (R) Pa. (R) Ill. (R) Ohio (R) Ind. (R) R.I. (R) Wis. (R) | N.Y. (D) N.J. (D) Mich. (D) Conn. (D) Pa. (D) Ill. (D) Ohio (D) Ind. (D) R.I. (D) Wis. (D) | | Mass. |
| Two weak but competitive parties | Calif. Oregon | | Iowa (R) Missouri Kansas (R) | Iowa (D) Kansas (D) Nevada |
| One party dominant; second party emerging | Kentucky Tennessee Okla. (D) Md. (D) | Okla. (R) Md. (R) | N.C. Vermont (R) | Arizona Vermont (D) |
| Single party with factions | Louisiana Virginia | | Texas Minn. (R) | Minn. (D) |
| Single party without factions | Alabama Georgia | | S.C. | Florida |

clear, patterns that help to explain the clustering of systems into a few categories. The systems with two strong, competitive parties are found in the industrial states of the Northeast and Midwest, where each party is relatively homogeneous. The Democrats represent metropolitan, lower income, and ethnic interests; the Republicans represent rural and small-town as well as prosperous suburban interests. The New Deal realignment in national politics is reflected in the state political systems. Moreover, the strong governor appears not only as a product of strong political organizations, but also as a response to demands for positive governmental programs to meet the complex needs of highly urban-industrial states. Weaker, but competitive parties are found further West, where the parties lack both homogeneity of interest and traditional voter loyalties. Governors have been slower to adopt a strong legislative role in states where the demands on state government have been fewer. The historical origins of the one-party systems are well known, as are the trends, both North and South, toward the development of two-party systems.

## Research in Political Systems

If this has been not merely an exercise in taxonomy, it should provide guidance for research in the legislative process. If we agree that the legislative system can be best understood within the context of the larger political system, it becomes necessary to accumulate enough knowledge about each state political system to place it accurately within one of the categories we have defined (categories that can be refined as we learn more). Comparative legislative studies should be made within this framework; studies of legislatures in similar political systems should be distinguished from those covering legislatures in different political systems. A study of the majority leader, for example, might be confined to two-party states and might be devoted to showing how his role differs in states with strong and weak governors and in states where the majority party is and is not also the administration party. Another aspect of such a study, presumably, would be to determine whether the leader's role was consistent enough within each category to make contrasts between categories meaningful.

One area of research which contributes to our understanding of legislatures concerns changes in political systems. First we need to know more about what causes these changes. The revival of Democratic parties in northern Republican states is a delayed response to the political revolution that accompanied the New Deal. The emergence of Republican parties in southern and border states is related to growing industrialization, disillusionment with national Democratic party policies, and the appeal of national Republican candidates. Why has the rate of two-party development varied so much from state to state? Why did strong two-party competition come more rapidly in Rhode Island than in Pennsylvania, or in Maryland ahead of Virginia? The states in transition to a two-party system offer great opportunities for research into the requisites for party competition. What circumstances make it possible for a governor to assume a strong legislative or partisan role in a state where precedent is against him? Alternatively, why do some governors abandon the strong roles of their predecessors? The effect of malapportionment on divided government is obvious, but we know little about the other causes, such as the nature of legislative elections in the middle of a governor's term.

Students of the legislative processes are less interested in what causes changes in political systems than in how these changes affect the legislature. When a two-party system emerges in Kentucky and, more slowly, in Florida, when radical changes occur in the apportionment of Oklahoma and Connecticut, when the governor's term is lengthened in Ohio or his powers are increased in Michigan—when these and comparable changes occur in the political system what changes can be observed in the legislative system? More than in any other time period within memory, political systems are in flux, and the opportunities for observing the consequences in the legislatures are correspondingly great. The study of a single legislature in transition can often contribute as much to our knowledge as a comparison between legislatures in different states; it has the advantage of holding constant some of the variables that change when we move from state to state.

William Buchanan's recent volume, *Legislative Partisanship,* is probably the best study of a legislature in transition. By contrasting the California Assembly during its nonpartisan era with the more partisan Assembly of recent years, he is able to evaluate the functions of parties for a legislative system. He concludes: "Without parties the legislature can operate successfully. The public cannot." [9] He also provides insight into the causes of partisan revival; these did not spring from within the legislature but from outside forces, such as Governor Brown and the Democratic clubs. He also noted the effect of growing partisanship on the method of leadership selection, roll call patterns, and a variety of legislative roles.

This kind of analysis can be repeated, and enlarged upon, in other states where a two-party system is emerging, in the plains states and in the border and a few southern states, for example. We have evidence that this trend has sparked stronger and more frequent party alignments on roll calls, but we know little else. Is it true in general, as is suggested by experience in a few states, that party consciousness is likely to become apparent first in the emerging minority party? Is solid party unity in voting on Speaker's contests a prime requisite for strong legislative parties, as Buchanan suggests? How quickly and how inevitably does the Speaker become a party leader and not merely a presiding officer? Does the caucus usually assume greater importance, and is there evidence to support the thesis that the caucus is utilized more by an emerging second party than by parties that have become well established in a two-party system? An emerging second party is likely to develop party consciousness and cohesion if it becomes either the majority party or the administration party; which factor is of greater importance for this purpose?

No aspect of legislative studies stands in greater need of research than the governor's legislative role. During the last decade several states have lengthened the governor's term from two to four years; this must have affected his relations to the legislature, but we do not know exactly how. In the relatively rare cases where his constitutional or budgetary powers are enlarged, we should look for some effect on the legislature. The usual reason for reclassifying a political system in terms of gubernatorial strength is that a new governor brings to the office a different concept of his legislative role or new techniques for fulfilling this role. In seeking to explain why some states have strong governors and others have weak ones, we are often confronted with the answer, "That's just the way it's done in this state." Governors in some states do not have the legacy of a Roosevelt or Dewey, a La-Follette, or a Wilson. How does a governor change custom? How does he try to change the expectations of legislators and public concerning his role? What is the position of a weak governor in a state with a tradition of strong governors? Does this create a power vacuum in the legislature?

In addition to answers for these broader questions, we need specific, comprehensive evidence about the variety of techniques used by governors. Simple factual information is in short supply in nearly every state. How much patronage does a governor have, and how does he use it? How does he determine the number of bills to include in his program? How often does he meet with his legislative leaders, and how often does he bypass them to deal with rank-and-file members? Does he use state or local party officials as allies in seeking to win legislative votes? Does he try to influence the selection of legislative leaders, and if not, why not? To what extent does he use his many opportunities for public speeches to generate support for his legislative program, and if not at all, why not? It would not take much imagination to extend this list of pertinent questions for several pages. In many states the governor's influence on the legislative process is as great as the President's influence, and in some it is greater. Yet the casual reader of headlines is likely to be more aware of this influence than the student who reads the available literature on state government in many states.

Another important change in the political systems of many states is occurring at present, the judicially inspired revision of the apportionment system. In a few states its effects will be minor, but in most the effects will be substantial and in a few they may be drastic. Obviously we are interested in the directly evident effects on partisan majorities and on the bills that are passed. But there are many other changes that we ought to anticipate, at least as possibilities. New York is a good example of a state in which the political system and the legislative sub-system might be substantially changed by the kind of apportionment that some of us expect to be required eventually by the courts. Will a party like the New York Democrats that becomes a majority after reapportionment have as much difficulty shedding its "minority complex" as the Republican congressional party did during the Eisenhower Administration? Will metropolitan delegations vote more often as a bloc when their numerical strength increases? Will reapportionment in some states increase the number of safe districts or the number of marginal districts, and how will this affect legislators' roles and voting records? How will the governor's tactics change in those states where divided government becomes the exception instead of the rule?

### Legislative Elections and Representation

Studies of the electoral process, whether based on statistics, observations of campaigns, or survey research data, have been focused on national and statewide elections to the almost total neglect of legislative elections. First, statistics on legislative elections need to be compiled, and they are sometimes scattered in courthouses across the states or buried in incomplete newspaper files. Scrutiny of such statistics, once they have been excavated from oblivion, can provide more complete answers concerning the extent of competition for legislative offices. Several persons have followed Key's lead in measuring competition and seeking its causes,[10] and I have tried to explain variations in southern legislative primary competition. The elusive question of presidential coattails has commanded attention in the literature but almost no attention has been devoted to gubernatorial coattails in legislative elections. Closely related is the question of straight-party voting for legislators in multi-member districts; examination of a few states suggests that it is usually high enough to elect complete party slates in such districts.

Case studies of congressional and local campaigns are becoming more numerous; we need comparable studies of legislative campaigns. Where does the candidate get his funds? Does he coast along with the party's campaign, or does he spend his evenings hopefully ringing doorbells? Does he ever mention issues, and if so, under what circumstances? We should recognize the enormous variation in the environment of political campaigns. The state senator who represents all of Los Angeles county, the group of legislators who conduct a joint campaign running at large in Denver, and the legislator who represents a Vermont village face vastly different problems in carrying out a campaign. More than a few case studies are needed to portray this variety. More than case studies, however, we need comprehensive studies that cover particular aspects of legislative campaigns. Frank Sorauf, in his study of Pennsylvania titled *Party and Representation*, provides data (using a 50 per cent sample of House districts) on the background, recruitment, and organizational endorsement of legislative candidates in the 1958 election.[11] The study is based largely on several hundred field interviews and illustrates the wealth of information that can be obtained by anyone willing to carry out state political research in depth. Two or three comparable studies in states with similar political systems would make possible a high order of generalization about the election of legislators in two-party states.

We also need survey research data on legislative elections. Our ignorance concerning the perceptions and motivations of those who vote for legislative candidates is almost total. The Survey Research Center's data, shows that in congressional elections voters usually vote according to their party affiliation, sometimes deviating because of a presidential candidate or their greater knowledge of a congressional candidate in the other party. It shows that knowledge of congressional candidates rarely pertains to issues or voting records.[12] I suspect that similar conclusions would be reached from a study of legislative elections, but we have no evidence. Are legislative candidates actually closer to the voters and more likely to be personally known by them; or are they less visible than congressional candidates because of greater turnover or less publicity in the press? If party affiliation is the dominant factor in legislative elections, what determines the vote in primaries? To what extent do party organizations make endorsements in legislative races? In Pennsylvania, Sorauf found that such endorsements occurred in two-thirds of the primaries, and were usually made publicly. Would organizational endorsements be so frequent in New York? A more difficult question to answer is how often the voters know about these endorsements in primaries and how often they are influenced by them.

The study of roles in *The Legislative System* provides the essential starting point for any research into the nature of representation.[13] The distinction between the focus of representation (district or state) and the style of representation (trustees, politicos, and delegates) and the categories within each are useful. It is helpful to know that legislators make these distinctions, and that they are most likely to view themselves as trustees. It seems to me that we must regard these descriptions as stereotypes, useful because they suggest the legislator's state of mind as he weighs the demands made on him by persons and groups that may or may not be conflicting. In a sense, I think, all legislators are politicos. I agree with Frank Sorauf's conclusion in Pennsylvania: "The average legislator appears, then, to make no firm commitment to constituency, party, or self. Their demands on him and their sanctions over him shift from issue to issue. Both the shifting political demands and the finely balanced equities of choice force him to choose only tentatively and cautiously, one issue at a time." [14]

What we need now is much more data on the contacts between legislators and constituent interests. One characteristic of trustees is that they feel ill-informed about constituent views on most issues. It becomes necessary to find out how much mail and how many calls and visits legislators get on various types of bills. On the same or comparable issues, are these contacts greater in certain types of districts (urban or rural) or for certain types of legislators (veteran or freshmen)? If a large proportion of these contacts are inspired by interest groups, it is possible that the legislators hear more from constituents about relatively trivial bills pertaining to narrow interests and less about issues of obviously greater public importance. What is the legislator's attitude toward mail? Is he as perceptive as congressmen in recognizing pressure mail and as quick as congressmen to discount the importance of such mail? Compared to the congressman, the legislator is closer to his constituents, but he is less visible and deals with less well known issues over a briefer period of time. Our stereotypes about legislative-constituent communication are usually based on Congress; any meaningful generalizations at the state legislative level must await the accumulation of factual evidence.

One of the most ambitious and significant studies of the representational process is that undertaken by the Survey Research Center at Michigan in 1958 to measure the relationships among a congressman's voting record, his own attitudes, his perception of constituent attitudes, and actual constituent attitudes.[15] This is a difficult and expensive undertaking but one worthy of duplication, in whole or in part, at the state level. Studies along this line might clarify the confusion evident in roll call studies about the effect that the closeness of an electoral margin has on a legislator's voting behavior. Is the legislator from a close district particularly sensitive to constituent pressures (as some roll calls studies show) or is this more likely to be true (as the Michigan study suggests) for legislators from safe districts, who are more likely to perceive constituent views accurately? The Michigan study also shows that any such investigation must distinguish among various categories of issues. A study of legislative perceptions of and attitude toward constituent views might usefully distinguish among three categories of legislators: those who intend to retire after a term or two, those who are becoming career legislators, and those who plan to use the legislature as a stepping stone to statewide office and consequently have a potential statewide constituency.

### Legislative Leadership Structure

One of the most important and variable legislative norms concerns the choice and tenure of leaders, particularly the Speaker. The Speaker is chosen, de facto, by the governor in Kentucky and Alabama; in Illinois the governor has intervened even in the opposition party's choice of a speaker; but in many states the governor takes no part in the selection. Speakers in South Carolina and Rhode Island serve indefinitely, but in New Jersey the position is rotated annually. In some states the position appears to be an inherited one, and any competition for the stepping-stone positions is obscured from public view. In Texas and California, however, there is prolonged, open competition for the job. We need, first, specific information on customary practices. If possible, it would be useful to know how customs have become established; they do not seem to be rooted in the political systems or in other aspects of the legislative system. More important, how does the method of choice affect the leader's role, his political resources, his influence on other legislators? David Truman has described the peculiar position of congressional leaders in the administration party who must serve two masters: the President and the congressional party.[16] At the state level we have examples of legislative leaders who owe their position entirely to the governor, and others who are entirely independent of him.

A few state legislatures resemble the national House; a few senior members hold the positions of power, including key committee chairmanships. More often seniority seems to be less important or even irrelevant. What qualities, other than seniority, characterize the men who gain the leadership posts? Are previous elective positions, certain occupations (such as lawyer), or security of tenure factors that are taken into account in the choice of leaders? The characteristics of the average legislator are becoming well known, but we know little about leaders. We lack biographical studies and analyses of leadership techniques comparable to those at the national level that won admiration for Lyndon Johnson's skills as majority leader. The contrast between Johnson and Mansfield leads to the suggestion that we need to know how much the functions of state legislative positions vary with changes in personnel.

### Legislative Roll Call Behavior

The value of roll call data in legislative research is, or should be, beyond dispute. As David Truman has said, "Roll call votes . . . have the great advantage of being 'hard' data. Like statistics on elections, they represent acts the facts of whose occurrence is not subject to dispute." [17] Several words of warning should be added at once. Some roll calls at the state level are inaccurate, but they usually do record accurately the size of any dissenting group. Unanimous and nearly unanimous roll calls are so numerous in many states that most students have omitted these from their research in order to make the studies manageable and comparable from state to state. Such discrimination seems essential although it has a distorting effect and eliminates a few important bills. We must recognize that the most significant decisions on bills may not be visible in the roll call stage. A negative decision in committee or caucus may bar a bill from the floor; a compromise at an earlier stage may produce a deceptively high level of voting agreement. This does not invalidate the roll call as a focus for research; it simply emphasizes the need— however difficult—of investigating more thoroughly the committees, caucuses, and other arenas in which legislative decisions are made. It is this kind of evidence that interns and other observer-participants are uniquely qualified to gather.

The classification of political systems, developed earlier, serves as the framework for distinguishing between two categories of legislative voting: in some states (those with two competitive parties that are strong or at least not very weak) party alignments occur more regularly than any other kind of alignment. In other states it is rare to find any kind of alignment (urban-rural, regional, factional) occurring on roll calls with any consistency from issue to issue or session to session. In other words, there is a basic distinction to be made between states in which the party is a significant reference group for legislators and those in which it is not.

During the last decade there has been a rapid increase both in the number of roll call studies and in the sophistication of the statistical tools used for measurement. There remains much work that can be done, and the technique used need not be a complicated one. The choice of technique depends on the precise purpose of the study; if one of the more complex techniques seems advisable, there are available both examples of the technique and computing equipment to make it feasible.

It seems to me that relatively simple techniques are highly useful for comparative purposes. It is simple, if laborious, to calculate the proportion of non-unanimous roll calls on which the two parties took opposite sides, the proportion of roll calls on which there was a party vote (the two parties opposed and each with a high index of cohesion), and the proportion of high cohesion roll calls—or an average index of cohesion—for each party. Once these or similar calculations have been made, it is feasible to make comparisons between parties, from one time period to another in a state, or from state to state. At present such basic data is available for only a few sessions in about half of the two-party states; we have only limited—and conflicting—evidence about the differences in cohesion of majority and minority, or administration and opposition, parties.[18]

In only a few states do the roll calls of most bills follow party lines. In most two-party states the party becomes a reference group on only certain categories of issues. In general, these are likely to include bills involving the governor's prestige and program, bills involving socioeconomic or "liberal-conservative" issues on which the parties are likely to have taken a stand, and bills affecting the narrow interests of the parties. Through the skillful use of questionnaires, observation, and analysis we ought to be able to learn with much greater precision which bills produce party alignments and why. Has the governor taken a stand on the bill, was it in one party's platform, was it discussed in caucus, is a prominent member of one party sponsoring the bill? Wilder Crane's Ph.D. dissertation is the most intensive effort yet made to discover the reasons for legislators' votes on a selected number of roll calls through questionnaires. Crane discovered that many legislators do not perceive as party issues roll calls that result in party alignments. Crane's research suggests the need for caution in explaining voting alignments, but I think that it also neglects the unconscious political factors influencing the vote and places too much weight on legislators' self-analysis. (I suspect that many legislators are reluctant to admit that their vote was motivated by partisan factors.) [19]

On any roll call in a two-party state that provides evidence of some, but less than perfect, party cohesion, we want to know which legislators did not follow party lines. This requires analysis of legislators and their districts. Research in a number of states suggests several variables that must be watched: Legislators from districts most typical of the party (in the sense of leading in those qualities that distinguish Democratic from Republican districts) are likely to be most loyal to the party. There is conflicting evidence concerning the effect of safe or precarious electoral margins on loyalty and very little evidence about differences between veteran members and freshmen. We know little about the voting behavior of legislators playing various roles or having greater or lesser contact with constituents. Too often in the past the research has stressed the effect of only one, or occasionally two, of these factors on voting behavior. The use of techniques of multiple and partial correlation would provide us with a clearer impression of the weight of various factors.[20]

In one-party states and a few with weak two-party systems, party is virtually never a reference group for legislators. The student who is trying to find some pattern in the roll call voting must explore more widely and must usually rely more heavily on evidence other than roll calls to provide clues to voting patterns. Various legislators may follow the governor's lead on bills that he supports and on other bills turn to a variety of sources for voting cues: pressure groups, legislative leadership, committees, or others. The analysis of roll call voting in such states must be undertaken with a minimum of preconceptions and a willingness to explore any reasonable trail. The research techniques used must be compatible with this approach.

No single technique of roll call analysis is an all-purpose tool. I have suggested the advantage of simple techniques for comparative purposes. In order to measure party voting on various groups of issues, it may be sufficient to apply these simple indexes of cohesion and party voting to each of the groups of roll calls. A more precise way of measuring positions on groups of bills is the scaling technique.

Whenever party cohesion is weak or disappears, the scale assumes greater importance as a device for discovering what voting patterns exist. Samuel Patterson used it in Oklahoma, for example, to determine that in that one-party state there were recognizable patterns on at least seven groups of issues but that these scales represented independent and largely unrelated dimensions of voting behavior.[21] Once the scales have been developed, it becomes possible to measure the characteristics of legislators and/or districts at either end of the scales; here again statistical techniques using multiple variables would provide greater accuracy.

David Truman and John Grumm (studying, respectively, Congress and the Kansas legislature) have pioneered in the use of bloc analysis to measure roll call voting. (Grumm has also used the somewhat more esoteric technique of factor analysis.)[22] Truman used this technique to define blocs within the Democratic and Republican parties, and Grumm used it to define blocs in the Kansas legislature and determine how closely they coincided with parties. The method, with some variations, involves measuring—through the use of computers—how frequently each pair of legislators votes together and constructing matrixes or diagrams that show what blocs can be formed by grouping those who vote most consistently together. In a state legislature where simpler methods demonstrate the existence of strong, cohesive parties, these techniques seem to have the least advantage. They do appear useful for identifying and describing blocs or factions that exist within a party. Their greatest utility, it would seem, would be in identifying blocs in a one-party legislature. One advantage of bloc analysis is that it is objective; it does not start from any assumptions about the location or strength of blocs. It is useful, of course, only with regard to roll calls on which there is a substantial level of disagreement in the legislature. If there is reason to believe that voting patterns differ sharply on several groups of issues, bloc analysis might be modified by dividing the roll calls into several groups according to subject matter and constructing a separate matrix for each group. Unless there is some reason to expect that blocs exist, on most bills or on certain categories of bills that are separately investigated, the technique of bloc analysis may prove to be frustrating.

Roll call analysis may have monopolized the attention of legislative students to the neglect of other subjects, but the topic is one that still leaves room for extensive explorations. In these explorations, we need to recognize the importance of party cohesion in some states and the importance of distinguishing between states where party is and is not a major factor through the use of clear, simple measuring sticks. There is no urgent need for more complex statistical devices, but there is a need to use those that we have more widely, more imaginatively, and with greater care and precision. It is worth bearing in mind that, however precise and sophisticated the methodological tools, roll calls will always be a crude kind of data, uneven in importance, sometimes inaccurate, and never a complete record of legislative decision-making. This is an appropriate place to suggest as well that roll call will become more useful when it is tied more closely to other forms of legislative research.

## Notes

1. Duane Lockard, *New England State Politics* (Princeton, N.J., 1959); John Fenton, *Politics in the Border States* (New Orleans, 1957); H. D. Price, *The Negro and Southern Politics* (New York, 1957); Allan P. Sindler, *Huey Long's Louisiana* (Baltimore, 1956); Clifton McCleskey, *The Government and Politics of Texas*

(Boston, 1963); Frank Sorauf, *Party and Representation* (New York, 1963); Leon D. Epstein, *Politics in Wisconsin* (Madison, 1958).

2. H. D. Price, "Comparative Analysis in State and Local Politics: Potential and Problems" (Unpublished paper, 1963 annual meeting, APSA).

3. John C. Wahlke, Heinz Eulau, William Buchanan, LeRoy C. Ferguson, *The Legislative System* (New York, 1962).

4. Gilbert Y. Steiner and Samuel K. Gove, *Legislative Politics in Illinois* (Urbana, 1960); William C. Havard and Loren P. Beth, *The Politics of Mis-Representation* (Baton Rouge, 1962); William Buchanan, *Legislative Partisanship* (Berkeley and Los Angeles, 1963).

5. Coleman Ransone, *The Office of Governor in the United States* (University, Ala., 1958) and *The Office of Governor in the South* (University, Ala., 1951); Institute of Government and Public Affairs, University of Illinois, *The Office of Governor* (Urbana, 1963).

6. See Norman Meller, "Legislative Behavior Research," *Western Political Quarterly*, Vol. 13 (1960), pp. 131–153.

7. Price, "Comparative Analysis in State and Local Politics."

8. See, for example, Duane Lockard, *The Politics of State and Local Government* (New York, 1963), pp. 179–189; Austin Ranney and Willmoore Kendall, "The American Party Systems," *American Political Science Review*, Vol. 48 (1954), p. 477; Joseph A. Schlesinger, "A Two-Dimensional Scheme for Classifying the States According to Degree of Interparty Competition," *American Political Science Review*, Vol. 49 (1955), p. 1120.

9. Buchanan, *op. cit.*, p. 148.

10. See citations in Jewell, *The State Legislature* (New York, 1962), pp. 33–45, 134.

11. Sorauf, *op. cit.*, ch. 5.

12. Donald E. Stokes and Warren E. Miller, "Party Government and the Saliency of Congress," *Public Opinion Quarterly*, Vol. 26 (1962), pp. 531–546.

13. Wahlke *et al.*, *op. cit.*, chs. 12 and 13.

14. Sorauf, *op. cit.*, p. 126.

15. Preliminary reports on this research include Warren E. Miller and Donald E. Stokes, "Constituency Influence in Congress," *American Political Science Review*, Vol. 57 (1963), pp. 45–56, and papers presented at annual APSA meetings in 1961 and 1962.

16. David Truman, *The Congressioanl Party* (New York, 1959), pp. 289–308.

17. *Ibid.*, p. 12.

18. See Jewell, *The State Legislature*, p. 52.

19. Wilder Crane, "The Legislative Struggle in Wisconsin: Decision-Making in the 1957 Wisconsin Assembly" (Ph.D. dissertation, University of Wisconsin, Madison, 1959). A study of party voting in Missouri takes into account the issues that were discussed in caucus; see George D. Young, "The Role of Political Parties in the Missouri House of Representatives" (Ph.D. dissertation, University of Missouri, Columbia, 1958).

20. For an excellent example, see Thomas A. Flinn, "Party Responsibility in the States: Some Causal Factors," *American Political Science Review*, Vol. 58 (1964), pp. 60–71.

21. Samuel C. Patterson, "Dimensions of Voting Behavior in a One-Party State Legislature," *Public Opinion Quarterly*, Vol. 26 (1962), pp. 185–200.

22. Truman, *op. cit.*; John Grumm, "The Systematic Analysis of Blocs in the Study of Legislative Behavior" *Western Political Quarterly*, Vol. 18 (1965), pp. 350–362, and "A Factor Analysis of Legislative Behavior," *Midwest Journal of Political Science*, Vol. 7 (1963), pp. 336–356.

# 25. Interviewing Political Elites in Cross-Cultural Comparative Research*

WILLIAM H. HUNT, WILDER W. CRANE, and JOHN C. WAHLKE

Despite increasing use of public opinion research in many corners of the world,[1] there remains a widespread belief that survey techniques are peculiarly appropriate to the American scene, particularly when the object of study is the public office-holder. Beyond the shores of North America, it is said, local habits and mores either incline people to resist interviewing or structure their thought in such a way as to preclude getting reliable data from them, or both. The utility of survey techniques for comparative research among political elites spanning cultural boundaries would therefore be severely limited. A comparison of the authors' individual experiences in three separate but related research projects leads to some tentative conclusions about this belief.

All three projects applied survey techniques to the study of institutionalized groups rather than to the study of a sample of a general population. The earliest of these, in which Wahlke was a participant, interviewed 474 of the 504 members who in 1957 constituted the legislatures of California, New Jersey, Ohio, and Tennessee.[2] Hunt's study involved interviews in 1960 with a stratified random sample of seventy-six members of the French National Assembly, drawn from three parties (U.N.R., M.R.P., and S.F.I.O.), and seventy-four party federal secretaries corresponding, where possible, to the departments of the deputies selected.[3] Crane sought interviews during the summer of 1960 with all fifty-six members of the unicameral legislature of Lower Austria.[4]

The American State Legislative Research Project investigated the role concepts of legislators. The French study utilized some questions drawn from this project, but used others too, including some from Gross, Mason, and MacEachern's study of the school superintendency role in the United States.[5] Austrian interviews originally followed a direct translation of the American state legislatures schedule; after interviews were begun, several questions were added to elicit further information on legislators' errand-running functions. The three studies provide an admirable basis for comparison, therefore, since they dealt with a common subject matter, interviewed analogous populations, and utilized instruments which were in two cases practically identical and in the third case substantially parallel.

* From *The American Journal of Sociology,* Vol. 70 (1964), pp. 59–68. Reprinted by permission of The University of Chicago Press.

## The Problem of Access

The problem of access is often stressed in non-American contexts and in this country as well. Experience in these three projects suggests that degree of access and difficulties encountered were a function of institutional rather than cultural factors.

The initial step toward gaining access in all three cases was a letter describing the project and soliciting the co-operation of each prospective respondent. In Austria, this step alone was an effective means of access in almost all cases. In France, more than three hundred letters were sent to prospective responden's. Yet it still required the utmost ingenuity and effort to track down a portion of those sought and to pin them down to an interview once they were found. Letters and follow-up visits to the Palais Bourbon, where deputies may be paged, proved to be the most essential access tools. Ultimately, the process of gaining access in a few cases involved the interviewer's loitering in the vicinity of the Palais Bourbon in hopes of buttonholing respondents.

Experience among American legislators more nearly resembled that in France than that in Austria, although there was considerable variation among the four American states. In two states, the researchers were introduced by the speaker of the chamber either by the reading of a letter (Ohio house) or directly in person (Tennessee senate and house). The "web" technique was principally used in California, New Jersey, and in the small Ohio senate, the researchers relying upon informal interpersonal contacts between themselves and prospective respondents and among the respondents interviewed and their friends as means of gaining access. In Ohio and Tennessee, it was common practice for interviewers to "work the floor" in search of respondents, since it was there that they were most available.

The vital importance of familiarity with the institutional context of interviewing is suggested by the difference between the simplicity and ease of access to less important Austrian state legislators and the difficulty and complexity of access to busier French national legislators, as well as by the variety of techniques needed to gain access in the six cases (four American, two European). The differences in experience here clearly reflect institutional more than cultural differences. Much of the French and American difficulty, for example, is traceable to simple lack of office and communication facilities for legislators: most deputies in Paris can be reached only by mail addressed to the Palais Bourbon; of the Americans, only California legislators had genuine offices, with secretaries to help fix appointments for them.

Experience in both America and Europe was consistent with Robinson's conclusion about interviewing American congressmen: there is greater resistance to granting an appointment than to giving a satisfactory interview.[6] In a number of cases where American legislators agreed somewhat reluctantly or impatiently to grant a few minutes of their time, they rapidly became so interested in the process of answering the questions that it was difficult to terminate the interview. Similarly in France, the common warning that a respondent could talk for "just a quarter of an hour" was usually forgotten once the interview was under way.

In Austria there were striking and instructive differences in the *initial* co-operativeness of the respondents. Socialists were, without exception, immediately prepared to co-operate in answering questions. Business and worker representatives of the Peoples party were also generally co-operative from the beginning, but the fifteen farmer representatives of the Peoples party were almost all *initially* suspicious, the two refusals being from this faction. Once the formal part of the interview was finished, however, and the interviewer's pen put aside, most of those in this faction insisted on continuing the discussion for some time. The pattern came to be that those who were initially most reluctant were those whom it was most difficult to leave.

Contrary to the Austrian experience, French Socialists were the least accessible of the three party groups, although Socialists and M.R.P. deputies seemed to be the most co-operative once the interviews were under way. American interviewers reported no systematic differences between parties with respect to ease of access. The tentative conclusion in all three cases is that subcultural differences in basic attitudes and outlook make for greater differences in access within each system than broader cultural differences among the various systems of the Western world. In any case, it is important to emphasize that relative ease or difficulty of access was by no means predictive of a respondent's ultimate co-operation or frankness in the course of the interview.

The problem of access was successfully met in all three instances, as shown by Table 1. Only three legislators in California, three in Ohio, and two in Tennessee

TABLE 1. INTERVIEWS AND FAILURES TO INTERVIEW

| | UNITED STATES (N=504) | | FRANCE (N=76) | | AUSTRIA (N=56) | |
|---|---|---|---|---|---|---|
| | No. | Per Cent | No. | Per Cent | No. | Per Cent |
| Refused outright | 8 | . . . . | 3 | . . . . | 2 | . . . . |
| Evaded, without clear refusal | 14 | . . . . | 7 | . . . . | 0 | . . . . |
| Died or hospitalized | 2 | . . . . | 2 | . . . . | 1 | . . . . |
| Contact failure | 6 | . . . . | 2 | . . . . | 0 | . . . . |
| Total not interviewed | 30 | (6) | 14 | (18) | 3 | (5) |
| Total interviewed | 474 | (94) | 62 | (82) | 53 | (95) |

refused outright to be interviewed; all legislators in New Jersey were interviewed. One each of the California, Ohio, and Tennessee refusers demonstrated hostility to academic research; none of the French or Austrian refusers did. The Austrian speaker explained his refusal to be interviewed as due to his belief that expressing opinions was contrary to his role as an impartial presiding officer. The figure for French non-interviews is based on the *original* sample drawn for French deputies. Substitutes were interviewed in ten of the fourteen cases; subsequent tables in this paper report on seventy-five deputies who were interviewed, including substitutes, and three deputies included in the sample of federal secretaries.[7]

## Conduct of Interviews

*Interview Staff.* The possible distortion of interview results occasioned by particular characteristics of the interview staff is a familiar problem. In America it was thought the problem might arise from differences in status between interviewer and respondent, particularly between student interviewers and legislators. As the professional status of the junior staff was questioned in only a few instances, the American researchers concluded that on the whole both senior and junior interviewers faced the same difficulties, and that the respective advantages of one over the other were offset by corresponding difficulties.

In Europe, the crucial question concerning interview staff was nationality. All French interviewing was done by one American, while in Austria, thirty-five interviews were conducted by an American, fourteen by an American and an Austrian together, and four by an Austrian alone.

American nationality was a definite advantage in gaining access in both European countries. A request from an American aroused curiosity and the feeling that one must be cordial to foreigners, as illustrated by the comment of one French deputy: "If you had not been an American, I would not have received you. We are so busy, but, in my opinion, one should do everything possible to solidify links between Americans and Frenchmen, and particularly I am happy to receive a *young* American." Despite the fact that Crane's Austrian assistant was a junior judge in a Viennese lower court and thus had the advantages of an academic title and judicial non-partisanship, his presence, whether alone or in the company of an American, sometimes created problems by arousing the suspicions of his countrymen.

While American nationality may facilitate interviewers' gaining access in Europe, it is uncertain whether interviewers of different nationalities will obtain similar results. The fact that the interviewer is a foreigner may actuate perceptions that he is an impartial researcher who will protect respondents' anonymity. On the other hand, respondents may slur over esoteric details because they believe the foreigner will not understand them. In both France and Austria some respondents tended to instruct the interviewer about general and obvious aspects of their countries' politics and to waste time by chastising American foreign or racial policies. When Crane's Austrian assistant was present, the time wasted in lectures on elementary Austrian politics was reduced, but respondents' diatribes on American policies, directed at the foreign member of the interviewing team, were not eliminated. With regard to the candor of respondents, it is Hunt's impression that deputies spoke more freely and candidly to him than they would have to a French interviewer. Crane, however, found no clear pattern of differences between interviews that involved an Austrian assistant and those that did not. Some of the most candid interviews were obtained in both circumstances.

Viewed together, experiences in the three projects suggest that more flexibility in choosing interview staffs is possible than is generally believed. Interviewing difficulties vary with the different kinds of status relationships between interviewer and respondent, but the general magnitude of such problems appears to be no greater in Europe than in America. Regardless of locale and of the particular status difference, the proper instruction of interviewers would go far toward eliminating such problems before they arise.

*Location of Interviews.* In all three projects, the place of interview was a function of the institutional structure and practices of the legislature under examination. Table 2 shows the differences among the three countries but does not reveal the

TABLE 2. PLACE OF INTERVIEWS

| | PER CENT | | |
|---|---|---|---|
| | UNITED STATES (*N=474*) | FRANCE (*N=75*) | AUSTRIA (*N=53*) |
| Capitol building | 62 | 76 | 32 |
| Respondent's place of business | 20 | 2.5 | 47 |
| Respondent's home | 7 | 8 | 17 |
| Hotels, restuarants | 9 | 11 | 4 |
| Miscellaneous other places, or combinations of the above | 2 | 2.5 | 0 |
| *Total* | 100 | 100 | 100 |

corresponding variation among the four American states. Thus, in geographically small New Jersey, where the legislature meets only one day a week, it was necessary and possible to conduct most interviews in respondents' homes or offices. Ohio's large legislature and greater traveling distances demanded the completion of most interviews within the legislative session and in the legislative chambers. This was feasible due to Ohio's comparatively long session, but Tennessee's short legislative session (eleven weeks) made it necessary to secure about half the interviews by extensive and sometimes difficult travel. The geography of France would have created similar difficulties, but the practices of the Assembly allowed most interviews to be conducted in Paris. The adjournment of the Lower Austrian Legislature in early summer, however, required that Crane travel to about two-thirds of his respondents' homes or offices.

Privacy and freedom from interruption were available in varying degrees at each interview site. With due allowance for extreme variations in particular cases, the consensus of interviewers in both America and Europe is that interviews conducted in homes and offices were more satisfactory than those conducted on the floor or in the lounges of the capitol. There was, in general, little cultural variation in the problems of interview site.

*Respondents' Co-operativeness.* An initial indication of the generally high level of co-operation in all three projects is the amount of time legislators were willing to devote to the interviews. The average interview required approximately 1½ hours, the shortest lasting ½ hour and the longest about 5 hours. French interviews varied in length between ½ hour and 3¼ hours, with a median of 1⅓ hours, while Austrian interviews ranged from 1 to 3 hours, the average being 1½ hours. With interviews of such length it was sometimes necessary to meet respondents several times in order to obtain complete results. That substantial proportions of French and American legislators were willing to submit to second and even third rounds of intensive interviewing is an additional indication of respondents' co-operation in these two nations.

A more direct measure of respondents' co-operativeness is provided by the interviewers' rating of each respondent, entered on the interview schedule immediately upon completion of the interview. Table 3 shows that remarkably few respondents

TABLE 3. INTERVIEWERS' RATINGS OF RESPONDENTS' CO-OPERATIVENESS

| | PER CENT | | |
|---|---|---|---|
| | UNITED STATES (N=474) | FRANCE (N=75) | AUSTRIA (N=53) |
| Very co-operative | 45 | 64 | 36 |
| Co-operative | 45 | 23 | 49 |
| Not very co-operative | 8 | 9 | 13 |
| Very unco-operative | 1 | 4 | 2 |
| Not recorded | 1 | 0 | 0 |
| Total | 100 | 100 | 100 |

in either Europe or America were judged unco-operative. The measure is, of course, a highly subjective one. The critical distinction is that between "co-operative" and "not very co-operative," since all interviewers used as their standard here the adequacy of responses for the purposes of the project. The three groups are very similar in the proportions which were rated something less than co-operative. The distinction between "co-operative" and "very co-operative" is more difficult to draw. The relatively high proportion of French respondents rated "very co-operative" may reflect the use of thirteen substitutes in the French sample as contrasted with the use in the American and Austrian projects of the total population. However, the researcher in France was generally impressed by the efforts of French legislators to keep appointments despite their busy schedules. Some deputies returned to Paris a day early after the week end, while others did not go home on a week end, in order to co-operate with the interviewer.

Although Robinson has concluded that the interview is likely to be "of little therapeutic value" to an American congressman,[8] many respondents in these three projects, particularly the French legislators, seemed to enjoy immensely the opportunity to vent their personal opinions and values. The authors feel that this may partially explain the high degree of co-operation exhibited in many cases.

*Respondents' Candor.* Interviewers' ratings of respondents' candor constitute perhaps an even more subjective measure than ratings of co-operation, but the results, summarized in Table 4, are interesting. Again one notes the generally similar proportions of respondents adjudged to be something less than frank, and again the French respondents rank somewhat higher than others. It is significant that more French than other respondents called special attention to their desire to speak frankly. One claimed that "if the party were to learn all that I've told you, they'd kick me out the back door." Other respondents thought their own candor was unique: "Now I think that my colleagues probably haven't been completely candid with you. In any case, I'm going to tell you what they wouldn't dare have told you."

The experience in Austria was quite similar, despite the interviewers' expectations

TABLE 4. INTERVIEWERS' RATINGS OF RESPONDENTS'
FRANKNESS

|  | PER CENT | | |
|---|---|---|---|
|  | UNITED STATES (N=474) | FRANCE (N=75) | AUSTRIA (N=53) |
| Very frank | 33 | 59 | 34 |
| Frank | 52 | 25 | 55 |
| Not very frank | 12 | 9 | 11 |
| Very evasive | 2 | 7 | 0 |
| Not recorded | 1 | 0 | 0 |
| Total | 100 | 100 | 100 |

of respondent reticence due to Austria's violent political history. Many Austrian legislators described their official roles in the Dollfuss-Schuschnigg dictatorship, others their Nazi affiliations. Many specifically maintained they had talked frankly and demanded repeated assurances that their replies would be treated confidentially. Like French respondents, a number believed they were unique in speaking candidly.

In all three projects, candor was revealed most clearly in the freedom with which respondents named not only colleagues they liked and respected but those they did not. Observation, as well as internal checks between replies of different respondents, suggests that even though they were sometimes poorly informed about some subjects they discussed, most of them tried to speak frankly and openly.

*European Respondents' Reactions to "Behavioral Research."* Although both the French and Austrian projects were successful in securing most of the interviews sought, European respondents' reactions to certain types of questions do reflect cultural patterns which pose problems for comparative behavioral research. The most obvious instance of this is the general European suspicion of check-list or scale-item questions. For example, a question used in the American study which asked respondents to indicate their relative interest in international, national, state, and local politics had to be omitted in France because respondents refused to make such rankings. Only 60 per cent of all French respondents answered all five yes-no-type questions composing a scale of affect for interest groups. Almost none of the respondents refused to verbalize, usually at some length, on the *subject matter* of such questions, but a relatively high proportion could not be persuaded to answer in the customary and familiar form used in almost all American surveys. The Austrian experience was practically identical.

In both European countries there was some resistance to the very notion of using precoded questions to obtain data. There were complaints that such devices were "too brutal," that they provided no opportunity for considering "nuances," or that respondents had "personal positions" with regard to politics that would not fit into the categories provided. Many respondents insisted on verbalizing their answers in addition to marking the answer sheets and then, in their excitement, forgot to mark the appropriate columns. Securing answers under such circumstances was not easy, but it is Hunt's conclusion, in disagreement with Lerner, that such methods and questions can be used in France if sufficient attention is given to adjusting them to French conditions.[9] By patient listening and constant probing, the interviewer can succeed in obtaining codable data. The resistance described seems to be more to the "American gimmick" than to the actual process of answering the questions.

A comparison of Austrian and Californian experience with check-list questions provides strong evidence of the degree of cultural difference in this respect. When it became clear that asking these questions inordinately prolonged Austrian interviews, it was decided to leave them (with a stamped return envelope) for respondents to complete at their leisure. The mere thirty-three that were returned in no sense constitute a representative sample.[10] When the identical procedure was adopted in California, however, only 3 of 113 respondents failed to return the questionnaire.

Some of the resistance to the mechanics of check-list and scale-item-type questions can perhaps be traced to mere unfamiliarity with them. Europeans are not so accustomed as Americans to frequent public references to Gallup polls and consumer surveys. Neither are they accustomed in their schools to the use of multiple-choice examinations, which probably help condition Americans to these devices.

But most of the resistance probably runs much deeper than this. Among educated Europeans, it reflects a bias in favor of "humanistic" and against "quantitative" or "scientific" modes of thinking about social and human problems which is by no means foreign to American culture. The explanation offered by European respondents in resisting check-list and similar questions sounds much like many American complaints about modern "social science." Consider the following, written by an Austrian legislator:

> I regret that, after consideration of the questionnaire, I am not in a position to transmit it in the form sought by you. I am certainly a person who enjoys making decisions with clear judgments in political questions. However, I cannot with a clear conscience answer with a short "yes" or "no," for every "yes" has its "however," and every "no" its "if." I would therefore have to give to each of your questions a limiting or expanding commentary. I am of the opinion that one could not begin anything at all with such statistics, which lead very often to false evaluations and mistaken conclusions.

Such attitudes complicate the job of the researcher. They make it extremely difficult to use in Europe certain standard instruments and measures which have been proved valid and reliable in American research. But it can hardly be emphasized too strongly that European resistance is more to the *form* of certain questions than to the basic assumptions of behavioral research. While such attitudes may preclude the use of some rigidly precoded questions, they do not prohibit the use of carefully structured questions which yield more than sufficient data to be coded in rigorously defined categories and subjected to quantitative analysis. The Austrian and French demonstration that it is possible to secure frank and full answers to intensive questioning is undoubtedly more significant than their demonstration of the inutility of particular devices which may often legitimately be labeled "gimmicks" by American researchers as well as by European respondents.

## Equivalance and Comparability of Data

One problem on which experience in the three projects can offer only the most impressionistic evidence concerns the possible distortion of concepts and ideas in translation from one language to another or the possible uniqueness of concepts and connotations in a given culture. In some apparently very simple cases where genuinely comparable findings were sought, language differences made it difficult to obtain clear conceptual equivalance. For example, it was not possible to find a French equivalent for "may or may not" as a check-list response.[11] Similarly, even native French persons asked to help in translating interview questions could think of no discreet way to ask respondents their religious views. After twenty-four interviews, however, a formula was found which was used successfully in all subsequent interviews and which elicited mail replies from twenty-one of the twenty-four not originally asked the question.[12] In Austria, the most difficult expression to translate was "rules of the game" (referring to unwritten norms of legislative behavior). After using an elaborate description of the concept in the first few interviews, it was found that the Austrian legislators had an obvious expression for it: *"ungeschriebene Gesetze"* ("unwritten laws"). The same expression was used in France (*"règles non-écrites"*).

There were, of course, more complex problems than those of simple translation. For example, the French conceptions of "interest groups," "pressure groups," and "lobbies" have quite different connotations from the same American terms. Again, a French "political friend" is a very special kind of friend, with the result that a question dealing with legislators' friendship relations in the chamber was perhaps the most difficult and indiscreet of all questions asked in France. The question was omitted in Austria after the first few interviews.

The Austrian study encountered fewer problems of this kind, but it had some conspicuous failures which reflect the necessity for thorough knowledge of institutions as a precondition for effective behavioral research. Some questions (taken by simple translation from the American interview schedule) were totally irrelevant for Austrian legislators. For example, questions on legislative decision-making, such as how legislators make up their minds how to vote, are meaningless to legislators who have no "free votes" and who act almost entirely as decision-legitimizers. The few questions which served in America to construct a scale of legislators' ideology were all questions on which Austrian legislators were unanimous, suggesting that ideological cleavage, if any, is specific to political systems rather than global in character.

On the whole, the problem of translating concepts from one culture to another, whether at the simple level of transliteration or at a more complex conceptual level, was solved in the light of researchers' experience and understanding of the particular system and culture they were studying. This means that "operational equivalence" was perhaps less common than "conceptual equivalence" in those instances where direct comparability was explicitly sought. It is the feeling of the researchers that conceptual equivalence presented a few difficult but not insurmountable problems. One would, of course, anticipate more difficulty on this score where cultural differences are greater than those among the three Western cases involved here.[13]

## Summary and Conclusions

The mere fact that extensive interviews were completed in three diverse settings with comparable instruments and objectives is in itself worth reporting. Even the American researchers were occasionally faced with the reaction commonly encountered by Hunt and Crane and reported earlier by Lerner: "There was universal doubt about the value and the feasibility of the enterprise." [14] But in each case access was gained and intensive interviews were completed. Conducting the interviews presented no really new problems, either with respect to staff, to location, or to maintaining rapport.

More important, the interviews yielded data of more than satisfactory quality as well as sufficient quantity. The reluctance of European respondents to answer the more "gimmicky" type of question did not extend to answering questions in general, even highly structured ones. In France and Austria, as in America, the interviews rather easily provided data on political socialization and career lines. Few respondents were at all hesitant to tell when they first became interested in politics, what positions they had held, how they became legislators, or to describe clearly their family, social, and educational backgrounds. In all three cases, the interviews provided a wealth of data concerning legislators' perceptions, attitudes, and role concepts, although in a form less easy to analyze, perhaps, than the other data.

An often-overlooked advantage of the systematic interview which impressed researchers in all three projects is its capacity for providing direct, observational knowledge of the kinds of institutional factors which were once the sole concern of political scientists. Where many interviews are conducted at the scene of institutional activity, the interviewer becomes also an intimate and constant observer.

But there is a reverse side to this coin. Experience in all three projects strongly recommends some prior understanding of the institutional environment to be studied. Such knowledge, of course, facilitates comprehension of respondents' replies. But more important still, it enables the interviewer to ask intelligent probing questions and to assume the kind of interviewer role that seems most suited to the type of population studied in these three projects. The interview in these cases is most productive when it is a two-way conversation. It is not just that European politicians resist giving simple responses to an inanimate research instrument; American as well as European legislators seem to appreciate an intelligent and informed interviewer whom they can take into their confidence and with whom they can explore questions suggested by, but not included in, the interview schedule.

Nevertheless, those who interviewed in America and Europe are agreed that their most valuable asset was the rigidly structured and uniform interview schedule. Even where a question was inappropriate to a particular state or country, it was found that "no answer" responses were significant from a comparative point of view. Moreover, the structured questionnaire was an important rapport-building device in all three cases. Particularly in Europe it was found that placing personal and biographical questions at the beginning served to relax respondents and involve them in the interview. The fact that possibly indiscreet or inapplicable questions could be read from a standard form was also a valuable asset, since it tended to lead respondents to blame someone other than the interviewer for possible embarrassment and thus to increase their tolerance for the process of being interviewed.

Despite the problems described in this article, therefore, the authors must conclude that systematic, structured interviews are a useful tool for genuinely comparative behavioral research among European as well as American political elites.

## NOTES

1. See, e.g., G. Katona, "Survey Research in Germany," *Public Opinion Quarterly,* XVII (1954), 471–80; W. Phillips Davison (ed.), "Twenty Years of Public Opinion Research," *Public Opinion Quarterly,* Vol. XXI, No. 1 (Spring, 1957), entire issue; and the following articles in *Public Opinion Quarterly,* Vol. XXII (1958): E. C. Wilson, "Problems of Survey Research in Modernizing Areas"; L. and S. H. Rudolph, "Surveys in India: Field Experience in Madras State"; and M. Ralis *et al.,* "Applicability of Survey Techniques in Northern India."

2. John C. Wahlke, Heinz Eulau, William Buchanan, and Leroy C. Ferguson, *The Legislative System: Explorations in Legislative Behavior* (New York: John Wiley & Sons, 1962). The study was supported by individual grants to the four authors from the Social Science Research Council, which also gave some funds to the group collectively for certain common expenses. In addition, Wahlke was aided by the Institute for Research in the Social Sciences of Vanderbilt University.

3. The French study, tentatively entitled "Effects of Legislative Roles upon Party Cohesion," was supported by a Research Training Fellowship from the Social Science Research Council. In addition, financial assistance during the analysis stage was received from Funds for Small Grants To Support Research in Public Affairs provided to Vanderbilt University and Wabash College by the Ford Foundation. The present article deals only with the interviews with legislators and excludes those with federal secretaries.

4. The Austrian study was aided by a grant from Vanderbilt University's Institute for Research in the Social Sciences. Reports on this study are Wilder Crane, *The Legislature of Lower Austria* (London: Hansard, 1961) and "The Errand-running Function of Austrian Legislators," *Parliamentary Affairs,* Vol. 15 (1962), 160–69.

5. Neal Gross, Ward S. Mason, and Alexander W. MacEachern, *Explorations in Role Analysis: Studies of the School Superintendency Role* (New York: John Wiley & Sons, 1958).

6. James A. Robinson, "Survey Interviewing among Members of Congress," *Public Opinion Quarterly,* XXIV (1960), 137. Another recent article on interviewing American congressmen is Charles O. Jones, "Notes on Interviewing Members of the House of Representatives," *Public Opinion Quarterly,* XXIV (1960), 404–6.

7. Hunt is confident that, had two more months been available for interviewing, the number of deputies interviewed from the original sample would have been increased considerably. Pressed for time, he simply used substitutes to provide his stratified sample of the three parties.

8. *Op. cit.,* p. 133.

9. Daniel Lerner, "Interviewing Frenchmen," *American Journal of Sociology,* LXII (1956), 187–94. Lerner describes how he was compelled to move from a "highly structured questionnaire" to a "minimally directive dialogue" with a "highly participant interviewer." Lerner notes that "this transformation of the schedule reduced the utility of precoding and other mechanical devices for assuring uniform reporting" (p. 194).

10. The thirty-three respondents who did fill out the check lists were nineteen Socialists and fourteen members of the Peoples party. A further breakdown by faction of those co-operating by filling out the return parallels very closely the rankings of the various groups in terms of access (discussed earlier): Socialists,

76 per cent; Peoples Party Workers League, 62 per cent; Peoples Party Business League, 50 per cent; Peoples Party Farmers League, 33 per cent.

11. The five categories of response to items dealing with deputy role definitions were (1) "Dois absolument" ("Absolutely must"); (2) "Devrais plutôt" ("Preferably should"); (3) "Pourrais ou pourrais ne pas" ("Might or might not"); (4) "Ne devrais plutôt pas" ("Preferably should not"); and (5) "Ne dois absolument pas" ("Absolutely must not").

12. The question was finally asked as follows: "En ce qui concerne les idées religieuses, est-ce que vous vous considérez catholique, catholique pratiquant, ou autre chose?" ("Regarding religious ideas, do you consider yourself to be a Catholic, a church-going Catholic, or something else?")

13. H. P. Phillips, "Problems of Translation and Meaning in Field Work," *Human Organization,* XVII (1960), 184–92.

14. Lerner, *op. cit.,* p. 187.

# 26. A Method for Identifying Issues and Factions from Legislative Votes *

DUNCAN MACRAE, JR.

Roll-call votes are being used increasingly to throw light on various aspects of the legislative process. As long as these votes are neither simply unanimous nor cast purely on party lines, they contain information that can often be rendered more intelligible by the simplification or condensation of many votes into fewer variables or dimensions. The researcher interested in a particular legislative decision can thus profit by seeing whether it exemplifies a more general and repeated type of occurrence. The techniques of analysis used in studying legislative votes are broadly applicable to collegial bodies of many sorts, including municipal, state, and national legislative bodies; party congresses and conventions; the U.S. Supreme Court; and the United Nations General Assembly.[1]

Two major questions have been asked which lead to the search for different kinds of simplifying variables in this analysis. One concerns the *issues* that divide a given group of legislators at a given time, *i.e.*, what general matters are being argued about? The second concerns the *subgroups* of legislators within the group selected for study: what are the blocs, factions, cliques, and the like, whose more persistent existence is reflected by the division on a given vote?

These two questions are closely related. In factor or cluster analysis, they correspond to the analysis of roll calls and of legislators,[2] respectively, with the aim of finding clusters of related roll calls or of legislators who vote similarly. Alternatively, they correspond to the study of factor loadings of roll calls as opposed to the factor scores of legislators. The Beyle-Rice bloc analysis of legislative votes, more recently used by Truman,[3] is one approach to the second question. In cumulative (Guttman) scaling, the end-product is a simultaneous ordering of roll calls and of legislators; roll calls constitute cutting points between ordered categories, and legislators are distinguished by their placement in these categories.

The purpose of this paper is to present a method of analysis that throws light on both these questions. This method starts from cumulative scaling, but modifies it so as to make its results less dependent on preliminary hypotheses and more comparable with those of factor and cluster analysis. Other modifications of conventional scaling procedures are then introduced to reveal certain types of blocs or factions more clearly. Illustrative data are presented to show the types of inference that can be made.

Let us first reconsider the aims of roll-call analysis. To say that we are looking

* From *The American Political Science Review*, Vol. 59 (1965), pp. 909–926. Reprinted by permission.

for issue dimensions, or for subgroups of legislators, does not specify the task accurately enough. It is crucial, in the first place, that the issue dimensions not be forced to be orthogonal, *i.e.*, independent of one another. A central problem in the delineation of issue dimensions is that of comparing one issue-structure with another. These comparisons rest partly on the discovery of different issues in roll calls that took place at different times; but they also depend in an important degree on our opportunity to observe differences in the degree of association of given issues with one another, in contrast with that between either different subgroups (*e.g.*, parties) or different times. Thus the increasing use of computer programs for principal component analysis and orthogonal rotation of factors, though it has some advantages, has the great disadvantage of obscuring these contrasts.[4] Oblique rotation of factors, when it becomes more generally available to political scientists, will avoid this particular problem; but the method proposed here is a simpler means to the same end.

To say that we are looking for blocs is also an insufficient statement of the problem. Blocs may vote together on particular issues, *e.g.*, the "farm bloc." There are of course general divisions within legislatures, such as inter-party divisions, or within parties, such as the North-South split in the Democratic party; but not all blocs or factions have this character. To avoid prejudging this question, and to reveal issue-oriented blocs more clearly, we propose to identify the sets of roll calls on which similar divisions occur, and only *then* to look for blocs as they may exist on each such set.[5] This procedure also makes the resulting picture less dependent on the number of roll calls that take place on a given issue; for if a given division is repeated many times (*e.g.*, in tactical struggles over civil rights), the apparent bloc structure may give undue weight to this division if all roll calls are counted alike.

### *I. Cumulative Scaling and Coefficients of Association*

We begin with procedures for cumulative scaling, which have been used extensively for the analysis of legislative votes.[6] This method was originally developed by Guttman for the analysis of answers to attitude questions designed by the researcher.[7] Compared with factor analysis, it has the advantage of making fewer assumptions about linearity, cardinality, and (as we shall use it) the homogeneity of attitude continua; its underlying logic can be explained in non-quantitative terms.

The cumulative scaling model we shall use may be described first in the "perfect scale" case. For this initial exposition, we make the following simplifying assumptions and definitions:

1. On every roll call, all legislators of the group being studied cast votes in which they choose between two alternatives.[8] Unanimous votes of the group are omitted from the analysis.
2. On each roll call, votes are classified as "+" or "−" in such a way that "+" on every roll call is positively associated with "+" on every other.
3. The proportion of "+" votes on a given roll call, among all "+" and "−" votes on that roll call, will be called $p_+$.
4. We arrange the roll calls in descending sequence of $p_+$ and assume that there are no ties. Each legislator's "response pattern" is defined as his

sequence of votes, classified as "+" or "−" and ordered in this sequence of roll calls.

5. A perfect scale pattern may then be defined as a response pattern in which no "−" response is ever followed by a "+". A perfect scale is a set of items for which the legislators under study all have perfect scale patterns.

For example, if four roll calls formed a perfect scale, then every response pattern would fall into one of five types: $----$, $+---$, $++--$, $+++-$, or $++++$. These response patterns may be designated by the "scale scores" 0, 1, 2, 3, 4, corresponding to their numbers of "+" votes. If the legislators who vote in these five patterns are placed in five categories in the order shown, the divisions ("cutting points") between the categories are the four roll calls, in descending order of $p_+$. Thus the scale ranks roll calls and legislators together. The value of $p_+$ for each roll call gives the proportion of all legislators who are to the right of that roll call.

So far we have said nothing about absences, "error" votes, or the meaning of the votes and scales in conceptual terms. These questions will be dealt with next.

We first consider certain limited problems of missing data and "errors," to illustrate ways in which cumulative scaling differs from other types of multivariate analysis, particularly factor analysis. When missing data (e.g., absences) occur in what otherwise would be a perfect scale type, and when they do not introduce ambiguity into the decision as to what that scale type would be, they may be replaced by hypothetical votes that "would have been cast"; for example, the response pattern $+-O O O$ (O = non-response) would become $+----$ and $O O O+-$ would become $++++-$. And when a response (+ or −) differing from that in a perfect scale type could be altered in only one way to produce a perfect scale type, this change is conventionally made; if the response pattern was $-+++$, this would become $++++$, and if it was $---+$ this would become $----$.

These observations show that in the treatment of departures from perfect scale types, cumulative scaling does not treat all responses as interchangeable. A "+" vote on a roll call on which the +'s are a small minority (one with low $p_+$) is not treated the same as a "+" vote when they are a large majority. This distinction between items in different places on the scale will be important to us in interpreting scales.[9]

The fact that not all roll calls need to be treated alike is further illustrated by a finding that sometimes occurs in the scale analysis of legislative votes: the issue involved in roll calls at one end of the continuum is sometimes recognizably different from that at the other. For example, a "liberalism-conservatism" scale for the Democrats in the 81st Congress had several roll calls at one end (on which only a small liberal minority dissented), dealing with communism and civil liberties; items of this sort did not appear elsewhere on the scale.[10] This sort of divergence in content between roll calls in different ranges of $p_+$ can reveal the fusion of special issues into more general ones, the legislative tactics and strategy of the period being studied, or the relations among blocs or groups.

This possible heterogeneity of content within a scale points to a modification of conventional scaling procedures that will make them more appropriate to legislative analysis. Guttman scaling was initially devised to weed out badly chosen items in a set of attitude questions designed by an investigator to reflect a single underlying continuum or concept. The set of "all possible questions of the same content" that might exemplify this concept, was designated by Guttman as the "universe of attributes." [11] When cumulative scaling has been applied to legislative votes, the procedure has usually begun with the selection of a set of roll calls judged to deal with a given general issue. Scaling has been viewed as a procedure for selecting within this set. But the investigator is more liable to errors of judgment with roll calls than with questionnaire items; he may fail to group issues as the legislators did, or even ignore certain issues. Moreover, in searching for issues or attitudes he may overlook certain bloc divisions that were not easily identifiable by common issue content, but which could nevertheless be revealed by the same procedures.

The method proposed here—to search for clusters of similar votes regardless of content—is therefore more empirical and less dependent on preliminary hypotheses or conceptual considerations than Guttman's approach. In making this change, we contend that the structure of legislative votes is a datum for the investigator to discover, not to create. Differences in content of scales at different values of $p_+$ are important legislative facts that should not be obscured by method.

Our empiricism cannot be unbounded, however; otherwise it might lead to such absurdities as the selection of an arbitrary group of legislators simply in order to eliminate "error" votes, or the assemblage of a meaningless collection of roll calls for which the legislators in question had scalable votes. The aim of our research is to make general statements about legislative processes. These statements involve concepts and relations between them. Concepts acquire significance by virtue of

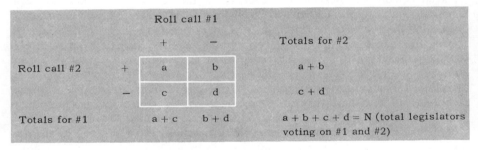

FIGURE 1. Fourfold Table

entering into multiple relations or multiple, empirically concordant, definitions.[12] Thus the reduction of a concept to a single operational definition would negate our central aim.

For this reason one must provide additional definitions of "issue" and "bloc," to test whether an empirical cluster of roll calls, or the divisions of legislators on it, represents either of these concepts. Issues will be recognized here from the content of the roll calls involved; a cluster of roll calls may include more than one issue, and an issue may appear in more than one cluster. Blocs will be recognized from characteristics of the groups of legislators separated by a cluster of roll calls—in this paper, chiefly the state and region of their districts. Either of these definitions could easily be extended, while remaining consistent with the concept in question, if other types of information were included in the study.

If bases of legislative division are to be sought through empirical search of a heterogeneous collection of roll calls, the study of overall response patterns (long sequences of +'s and −'s) is an inefficient way to do this. It is easier to compare each roll call with each other. This procedure was presented (for questionnaire items) by Toby and Toby.[13] Each item is considered as a dichotomy, and each pair of items yields a fourfold table, such as that in Figure 1. When the two roll calls in question have the relationship of two items in a perfect scale, one cell of the fourfold table will be empty. Suppose that, in Figure 1, roll call #1 has the higher value of $p_+$. It will then precede roll call #2 in the sequence of descending $p_+$ described above. But from the definition of a perfect scale pattern, given above, no "−" is ever followed by a "+". Therefore no "−" on roll call #1 will be followed by a "+" on roll call #2, and cell $b$ of the table will be empty. This cell is conventionally known as the "zero box."

We then examine all the fourfold tables generated by comparing each roll call under study with each other. As long as the scale criterion is met perfectly, only the presence of zeros in the appropriate cells need to be noted; but in actuality, some degree of "error" or departure from the scale model is usually considered acceptable. We then use some criterion to assess the adequacy or scalability of each fourfold table, and define a scale cluster as a set of roll calls, all pairs of which meet this criterion. This procedure was followed by Toby and Toby, with the criterion that the proportion of cases (legislators) in the "zero box" not exceed ten per cent of the total number of cases in the table.[14] This criterion was consistent with the original rationale of error assessment in Guttman scaling, according to which each "error," or vote which departed from the scale model, was to be counted equally in assessing the adequacy of the scale. This notion has been embodied in the coefficient of reproducibility and in other proposed indices for measuring the adequacy of scales.[15]

One may argue, however, that "errors" between two items far apart in $p_+$ should be given particular weight; these would correspond to a legislator's voting first with a group at one extreme, and then with one on the opposite extreme. One would then wish to substitute for the equal counting of errors an unequal counting, depending on the distance between the items $(c-b)/N$.[16] The author has previously done this by means of an exponential model based on latent-structure analysis.[17]

This unequal counting, as well as other advantages, can be obtained by the use of Yule's Q-coefficient.[18] For a fourfold table as shown in Figure 1, $Q = (ad-bc)/(ad+bc)$. This coefficient has several desirable properties:

a. For a perfect scale relationship between the two items in question, it attains the value $+1.0$.

b. If the two categories ($+$ and $−$) of one of the items are reversed, Q changes only its sign.

c. As the table departs from a perfect scale relationship, the error is effectively measured by the product $bc$. The use of Q weights the number of errors, $b$, in approximate proportion to the difference in values of $p_+$ between the two items $(c-b)/N$,[19] in relation to the produce $ad$.

d. The use of Q does not presuppose quantitative attitude continua, either manifest or latent, but can be justified in terms of pairwise rankings of legislators and the probability that these rankings will be consistent between two items.[20]

Each fourfold table may then be classified as "scalable" or not "scalable," depending on whether the corresponding value of Q attains a specified minimum value. This classification is analogous to similar procedures based on the proportion of cases in the zero box, or on a constant in the exponential model. A dichotomous set of relations of this kind can then be examined for clusters, such that within each cluster all pairs of items are mutually scalable, and no further items can be added.[21] The task of searching for such clusters is greatly simplified if they are required to be mutually exclusive; this also avoids some artifactual relations between clusters. The particular procedures used will be described in the next section.

The procedure described so far does not depend on the minimum value of Q which is chosen as necessary for scalability. But because we are interested in placing legislators in relation to response patterns that fit the cumulative-scale model, we normally set a relatively high threshold value. If the incidence of error is too high, the assignment of scale scores to response patterns becomes difficult. The simplest way to realize the advantages of the scale model is to consider only data that have relatively little error. This choice concentrates our attention on certain types of roll calls at the expense of others; in factor-analytic terms, we concentrate on those with pure loadings on the oblique rotated axes, and with high communalities.[22] It is of course possible (though not conventional) to set one value of the error threshold in identifying bases of division, and another in choosing subsets of roll calls for placing legislators on scales.

## II. Locating Clusters in the Q-Matrix

The basic tool for this analysis is a matrix of Q-coefficients between pairs of roll calls, produced by a computer program.[23] Because we are concerned only with values of Q that exceed a specified minimum value, we omit from the matrix all lower values, and thus facilitate the visual search for clusters. Table I shows an illustrative Q-matrix for Republicans in the House of Representatives in the 84th Congress (1955–56).

Each row, and the corresponding column, corresponds to a roll call, identified by the year (1955 or 1956) and the sequence number used by the *Congressional Quarterly*.[24] Originally all the 102 roll calls on which the Republicans had at least seven per cent dissidence were analyzed in this fashion; but for reasons of space, only the 31 that fell into scale clusters are shown in Table I.[25] Values of Q in the table are multiplied by 10. The "positive" vote on each roll call was provisionally chosen as that vote associated with the Republican party, as contrasted with the Democrats; the one roll call in the table for which this polarity was reversed is marked with a dagger (†). The threshold value of Q chosen for this study is .8; this value was chosen as high enough to separate distinct issues, but low enough to include a sufficient number of roll calls in the scale clusters to permit inferences about them.

We define a scalable cluster as a set of roll calls, all of whose pairs have associations of at least .8. Such clusters may be found in the matrix by search for symmetrical patterns such as those shown in Table I. When such a cluster exists, the roll calls in it may be indicated by enclosing their diagonal elements in boxes which mark the corresponding rows and columns. Wherever one of these rows

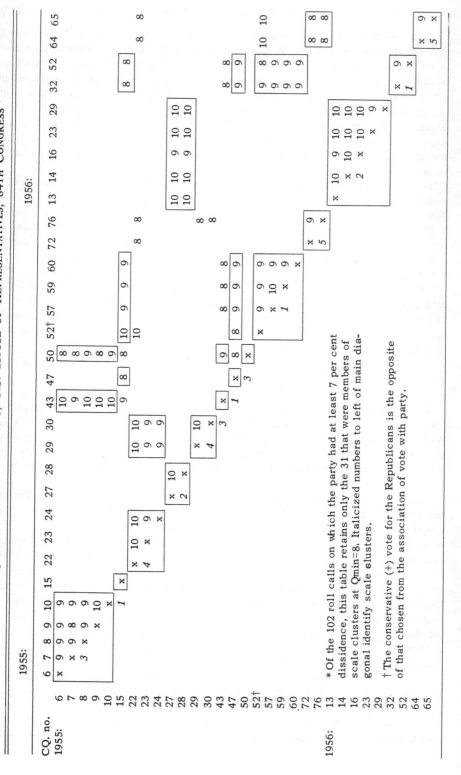

\* Of the 102 roll calls on which the party had at least 7 per cent dissidence, this table retains only the 31 that were members of scale clusters at Qmin=8. Italicized numbers to left of main diagonal identify scale slusters.

† The conservative (+) vote for the Republicans is the opposite of that chosen from the association of vote with party.

intersects another column belonging to the same cluster, the value of Q at the intersection must be at least .8; these intersections are also enclosed in rectangular boxes in Table I. Since the matrix is symmetrical, we need examine only the upper triangular part. The largest cluster in Table I is marked *"1";* of the eight items in the cluster, seven dealt with foreign aid and one with the debt limit. The debate on the last item included reference to foreign aid.

After the identification of the first cluster, two general procedures are available for finding further distinct clusters. One is to proceed as in factor analysis, and to compute residual associations before repeating the procedure; this method has been used in a set of computer programs designed by Tryon.[26] A second procedure involves treating each association in the matrix simply as a dichotomous variable; a special case of this type, which is the procedure used here, involves deleting the roll calls in the first cluster from the matrix, and repeating the procedure on the reduced matrix.[27] This decision assigns each roll call to no more than one cluster. It also insures that the actual votes, rather than some mathematical function of them, will meet the same tests for scalability in all clusters and thus permit comparable placements of legislators.

The two next largest clusters among the remaining roll calls in Table I (including seven each) are labeled *2* and *3*. All the roll calls in cluster 2 dealt with agricultural issues. Cluster 3 dealt with reciprocal trade; one item in the group (5-43) [28] almost entered cluster 1, but 5-52 was preferred to it as completing an eight-item cluster with higher average Q. Cluster 4 (5 items) dealt with the pay of postal employees. Cluster 5 included four items dealing with housing and atomic power. Item 5-22 could have entered cluster 5 as well as 4, but the five-item cluster 4 as shown had higher average Q and was preferred on this basis. We terminate the search for clusters with groups of four roll calls.[29]

Of these clusters, numbers 1–4 dealt with clearly recognizable issues, of greater or lesser generality. Cluster 5 may have dealt with the more general "welfare state" issue. None, according to criteria we shall specify below, corresponded to a major bloc division in the Republican party.

Clusters enable us to identify recurrent bases of division in a legislature, and to list the legislators who occupied particular places in such divisions. In looking for clusters we ask general questions and get general answers. The method of cluster analysis that we have described sometimes leads to close decisions in allocating roll calls to clusters. But the identification of the basis of division, and the placement of legislators, are not usually greatly altered by moving a few roll calls into or out of a major cluster.

If we wish to trace roll calls on particular bills and to find what more general divisions they exemplify, another approach is available. We may build initial scales from roll calls related to the bills in question. These scales, or individual roll calls of interest, may then be examined in relation to the more general scales, or to other roll calls in the Q-matrix. In this way the particular bills may be placed in a wider context.

## III. The Placement of Legislators on Scales

Once a cluster of roll calls is found, the legislators under study may be located according to their relative favorableness or unfavorableness to the positions considered positive on those roll calls. They may be assigned scores in terms of the conformity of their response patterns with perfect scale patterns. These scores give further information about the meanings of the scales, by identifying extreme legislators on a single scale or deviants in the relation between two scales. Distinctions between bases of division may then be studied with the aid of these legislators' views, as expressed in debates, other communications, or (for contemporary studies) interviews. Legislators' positions on scales may also be related to other relevant variables, such as constituency or career characteristics.

We shall sketch the procedure for placement of legislators briefly, since their positions will be used here only to clarify the relations between scales. It is assumed that positive polarities have been chosen consistently for the roll calls in the cluster. The next step in the procedure is to arrange the roll calls in the cluster in descending order of $p_+$, and to group them into sets marking off approximately equal intervals in the range of $p_+$ from 1 to 0. Not every roll call will become a separate cutting point on the scale, since we permit considerable non-scale response between two items with values of $p_+$ close together. Instead, we use "contrived items," each consisting of two or more actual roll calls; the legislator's "vote" on such an item is considered to correspond to the preponderant vote on the component roll calls.[30] An objective procedure is followed for assigning each roll call to a contrived (or ordinary) scale item.[31] Legislators' response patterns on these contrived items are then assigned scale scores in terms of their resemblance to perfect scale patterns.[32]

The associations between legislators' scores on pairs of scales measure the associations between the scales. From the Q-matrix one can estimate these associations by noting whether there are many high Q's between roll calls in one cluster and those in another. But a more precise answer to this question is possible in terms of the associations between legislators' positions on pairs of scales. The index of association we shall use is Goodman and Kruskal's gamma.[33] This index includes Q as a special case, if applied to a fourfold table. Gamma (or Q) measures the probability that a pair of individuals in the table will be ranked consistently on the two variables. In a fourfold table, for example, each dichotomy (horizontal or vertical) may be considered as a ranking of all legislators, though with a great many ties. The only pairs of legislators about whom we can clearly say that the information in the two rankings is consistent or inconsistent, are those who occupy different rows and different columns in the table. If their places in the table are to the upper left and lower right, respectively, these two rankings are consistent; the number of ways in which such a pair might be drawn (in the fourfold table in Figure 1) is $ad$. If their places are on the upper right and lower left relative to one another, their rankings are inconsistent, and the number of possible inconsistent pairs is $bc$. Thus the coefficient $Q = (ad-bc)/(ad+bc)$ measures the number of consistent pairs minus inconsistent pairs divided by the total number of pairs about which a judgment of consistency might be made. The same expression may be obtained by reasoning in probability terms.

The index gamma is obtained by a straightforward extension of this reasoning to any larger table comparing two sets of ranked categories. The terms in gamma corresponding to $ad$ and $bc$ are simply the sums of a number of such products of cell entries.[34]

The associations between scale positions for Republicans in the 84th Congress, corresponding to the scales discussed above, will be shown below in Table III. It will be seen there that foreign and domestic issues arrayed the Republicans quite differently at that time, and that agricultural issues were separate from both.

## IV. The Interpretation of Scale Clusters

The example we have presented involves a set of relatively clear and distinct issues, easily recognizable from inspection of the substance of the legislation involved in the corresponding roll calls. Not all sets of clusters are quite so clear, however, and additional principles of interpretation must be introduced before we can proceed to compare the divisions of the two parties in various Congresses.

Our aim in interpreting clusters, as suggested above, is to center attention on bases of legislative division that can each be recognized by a variety of approaches —whether by various statistical methods, classification of issues or blocs by informed observers, or relations with outside variables. The procedure that we proposed for defining clusters can in fact yield two clusters that deal with much the same issue, or it can combine two apparently different issues in the same cluster. The ways in which this can happen, and procedures for interpretation, may be indicated by reference to a previous analysis of the 81st Congress.[35]

This previous analysis differed from the present one in three principal respects: it started from conceptual definition of issue clusters, rather than purely empirical definition; it used a different model for assessing the scalability of a pair of items from the corresponding four-fold table; and it set a more stringent error threshold for accepting a pair of items as mutually scalable. In spite of these differences, the broad lines of interpretation resulting from that study are sustained by re-analysis following the method proposed here. Table II presents the relations between the scales identified in the former study and those found in the re-analysis.

The main similarity between the results of the two analyses is that certain issues are represented by very similar scales, completely distinct from others, in both studies. Foreign aid is completely distinct from domestic issues for both Republicans and Democrats; no roll call that appeared in a foreign-aid scale in one analysis appeared in a domestic scale in the other. For the Republicans the re-analysis produces two foreign-aid scales (columns 3 and 7) rather than one, apparently involving a distinction between economic and military aid. For the Democrats there is only a single foreign-aid scale. Agricultural issues also form a completely distinct scale for the Republicans in both analyses (though they do not, in the re-analysis, for the Democrats[36]). This distinctness of issues is thus a clear and consistent finding with respect to variations of method, if not (as we shall see) with respect to time.

A second similarity is that for the Republicans, domestic issues other than agriculture tend to be divided into two types, which we shall call urban and non-urban. Urban issues are those with a special appeal, on the liberal side, to representatives with urban constituencies—primarily housing and civil rights. Non-urban issues are ones on which a Republican might experience district pressure to vote on the liberal side without representing an urban district; principal examples are labor relations, social security, taxation, natural resources, and civil servants' pay.[37]

In analyzing this distinction, however, we observe that the scales in question are no longer perfectly separate in the two analyses. Among the roll calls in the "welfare state" scale of the earlier analysis, five fell in new scale 1, none in new 2; and

## TABLE II. COMPARISON OF FORMER SCALES AND NEW SCALES, 81ST CONGRESS

### A. Republicans
Distribution of Roll Calls in Old and New Scales

| | New Scale No. and Subject | | | | | | | | | |
|---|---|---|---|---|---|---|---|---|---|---|
| | 1 Urban | 2 Non-urban | 3 Foreign aid | 4 (Patron-age) | 5 Urban | 6 Agricul-ture | 7 Foreign aid | 8 D.C. revenue | None | Total |
| *Old Scale* | | | | | | | | | | |
| Welfare state | 5 | – | – | 1 | 2 | – | – | – | 6 | 14 |
| Race relations | 9 | 4 | – | – | 2 | – | – | – | 6 | 21 |
| Labor relations | 1 | 7 | – | 1 | – | – | – | – | 2 | 11 |
| Foreign aid | – | – | 8 | – | – | – | 3 | – | 3 | 14 |
| Cotton-peanuts | – | – | – | – | – | 4 | – | – | 1 | 15 |
| Parity-oleo | – | – | – | – | – | – | – | – | 4 | 4 |
| None | 7 | 6 | 1 | 6 | 4 | 3 | 3 | 6 | | |
| *Total†* | 22 | 17 | 9 | 8 | 8 | 7 | 6 | 6 | | |

Associations ($\gamma$) Between Old and New Scales*

| | | | | | | | | |
|---|---|---|---|---|---|---|---|---|
| Welfare state | 77 | 77 | 54 | 46 | *81* | −12 | 47 | 52 |
| Race relations | *80* | *71* | 41 | 40 | *83* | −08 | 35 | 56 |
| Labor relations | 59 | *83* | 10 | 59 | 57 | 18 | 08 | 69 |
| Foreign aid | 61 | 31 | *97* | 10 | 51 | 19 | *82* | 09 |
| Cotton-peanuts | 06 | 11 | 15 | 07 | 09 | *89* | 12 | −16 |
| Parity-oleo | 37 | 09 | 63 | 20 | 38 | 44 | 38 | 02 |

### B. Democrats
Distribution of Roll Calls in Old and New Scales

| | New Scale No. and Subject | | | | | | | |
|---|---|---|---|---|---|---|---|---|
| | 1 Domestic | 2 Foreign aid | 3 (Commu-nism) | 4 (Rural) | 5 Pricing | 6 Housing | None | Total |
| *Old Scale* | | | | | | | | |
| Welfare state | 23 | – | 3 | – | – | 3 | 5 | 34 |
| Race relations | 24 | – | 1 | 1 | – | 1 | 3 | 30 |
| Foreign aid | – | 9 | – | – | – | – | 2 | 11 |
| Agriculture | 2 | – | 1 | 1 | – | – | 3 | 7 |
| Oleo | – | – | – | – | – | – | 3 | 7 |
| None | 23 | 5 | 4 | 6 | 5 | 1 | | |
| *Total†* | 70 | 14 | 9 | 8 | 5 | 5 | | |

Associations ($\gamma$) Between Old and New Scales*

| | | | | | | |
|---|---|---|---|---|---|---|
| Welfare state | *89* | 56 | *84* | 70 | 39 | *80* |
| Race relations | *95* | 57 | *86* | 75 | 32 | *83* |
| Foreign aid | 48 | *96* | 44 | 36 | 24 | 33 |
| Agriculture | 85 | *71* | *83* | 79 | 27 | 70 |
| Oleo | −19 | 19 | 19 | 11 | 41 | 14 |

† Including a few roll calls assigned to more than one scale in the previous study (*op. cit.*, pp. 324–331).

* With polarity of former scales reversed. Decimal point is omitted.

for the earlier "labor relations" scale, almost the converse was true (one and seven respectively). But roll calls from the former "race relations" scale fell more evenly in both. Moreover, roll calls in these three old scales were also found in new scales 4 and 5. We must therefore reconcile disparities between conceptual and empirical definition of clusters.

For the Republicans, Scale 5 ranked the members of the party in a way that was associated highly with that of Scale 1 ($\gamma = +.86$; see Table III). Moreover, seven of its eight roll calls dealt with bills that were also involved (at other legislative stages) in Scale 1.[38] In addition, its associations with other scales of the former analysis (Table II) and of the re-analysis (Table III) were nearly identical with those of Scale 1. We therefore regard Scale 5 as an artifact of the method of clustering used, and not distinct in issue content from Scale 1. We shall refer to such a scale as a "shadow" scale. This is not to deny the possibility of discovering meaningful (though small) differences in legislators' rankings on the two scales, by detailed analysis; but since we have not discovered them, we consider these scales to measure essentially the same thing. A similar problem also arises for the two foreign-aid scales (3 and 7) found for the Republicans in the re-analysis.

The converse problem arises for the Democrats: two conceptually distinct areas of legislation, corresponding to the "welfare state" (Fair Deal) and "race relations" scales, merge in one dominant scale in the re-analysis. This new combined scale ("domestic") is highly associated with both old scales ($\gamma = +.89$ and $+.95$, Table II). The two former scales were highly associated with one another as well ($\gamma = +.84$)[39] and had similar patterns of association with the other new scales. One might ask, then, whether these two areas of legislation should be considered the same or different for the Democrats at that time. This question may be answered in two ways. First, the *issues* are clearly distinct, and it should be regarded as an empirical statement, not a definition of a new "issue," that they elicited similar voting patterns in that Congress. If they did not do so at other times (and this sort of change did occur for foreign aid), then we need not change our definitions of issues from one period to another in order to describe this change. For this purpose, conceptual definition clearly assumes primacy.[40]

On the other hand, it is equally clear that similar groups of Democratic congressmen were opposing one another on the Fair Deal and on civil rights or race relations.[41] Basic to this opposition was the North-South split in the party. For analysis of blocs or factions, then, we must recognize that these two major issues were in a sense "the same." This reasoning will be elaborated below when we discuss the relations between scales and factions.

In spite of the problems that result from the application of rigid statistical rules for cluster identification, these rules have definite advantages. In the first place, an empirical search reveals issues that might not have been hypothesized by the researchers. Not only are unexpected issues seen (*e.g.,* clusters have been found dealing with veterans' affairs, with public power in the West, and with public lands), but different bases of division are found for different parties and periods. Some of these issues could have been found, to be sure, by empirical search within narrower "preliminary universes of content," such as that of domestic nationwide issues. But the conceptual procedure risks a lack of objectivity in relation to various investigators' notions of how issues should be classified. This may bias any conclusions reached about the change of issues over time, if the researcher identifies

# TABLE III. ASSOCIATION BETWEEN SCALES IN FIVE CONGRESSES *

## Republicans

### 80th

| | | 4 | 1 | 6 | 5 | 2 | 7 | 3 |
|---|---|---|---|---|---|---|---|---|
| Foreign aid | 4 | x | 86 | 56 | 60 | 04 | -42 | -49 |
| Foreign aid | 1 | | x | 73 | 67 | 01 | -42 | -45 |
| Draft | 6 | | | x | 56 | -29 | -58 | -52 |
| Housing | 5 | | | | x | -30 | -50 | -55 |
| Public lands | 2 | | | | | x | 61 | 42 |
| Rural | 7 | | | | | | x | 70 |
| Agriculture | 3 | | | | | | | x |

### 81st

| | | 3 | 7 | 1 | 5 | 2 | 8 | 6 | 4 |
|---|---|---|---|---|---|---|---|---|---|
| Foreign aid | 3 | x | 83 | 64 | 52 | 27 | 05 | -16 | -09 |
| Foreign aid | 7 | | x | 58 | 47 | 24 | 11 | -21 | 00 |
| Urban | 1 | | | x | 86 | 72 | 48 | -05 | -41 |
| Urban | 5 | | | | x | 77 | 52 | -14 | -41 |
| Non-urban | 2 | | | | | x | 84 | 18 | -60 |
| DC revenue | 8 | | | | | | x | 17 | -42 |
| Agriculture | 6 | | | | | | | x | 17 |
| (Patronage) | 4 | | | | | | | | x |

### 83rd

| | | 1 | 3 | 2 | 5 | 4 |
|---|---|---|---|---|---|---|
| Foreign aid | 1 | x | 60 | 26 | -34 | -70 |
| Urban | 3 | | x | 82 | 04 | -79 |
| Non-urban | 2 | | | x | 13 | -33 |
| Rural | 5 | | | | x | 24 |
| Immigration ) | 4 | | | | | x |

## Democrats

### 80th

| | | 4 | 6 | 2 | 1 | 5 | 3 |
|---|---|---|---|---|---|---|---|
| (Draft) | 4 | x | 71 | -38 | -65 | -64 | -64 |
| Foreign aid | 6 | | x | 37 | 36 | 38 | 22 |
| Taxes | 2 | | | x | 55 | 56 | 62 |
| Domestic | 1 | | | | x | 79 | 77 |
| Public lands | 5 | | | | | x | 73 |
| Rural & communism | 3 | | | | | | x |

### 81st

| | | 2 | 1 | 3 | 6 | 5 | 4 |
|---|---|---|---|---|---|---|---|
| Foreign aid | 2 | x | 63 | 56 | 42 | 13 | -48 |
| Domestic | 1 | | x | 87 | 88 | 35 | -81 |
| (Communism) | 3 | | | x | 82 | 38 | -77 |
| Housing | 6 | | | | x | 52 | -77 |
| Pricing | 5 | | | | | x | -24 |
| (Rural) | 4 | | | | | | x |

### 83rd

| | | 2 | 1 | 7 | 5 | 3 | 6 | 4 | 8 |
|---|---|---|---|---|---|---|---|---|---|
| Foreign aid | 2 | x | 78 | 62 | 49 | 14 | 14 | -11 | -76 |
| General | 1 | | x | 81 | 68 | 70 | 32 | 05 | -83 |
| (Border probs.) | 7 | | | x | 59 | 57 | 22 | 11 | -70 |
| Domestic | 5 | | | | x | 56 | 32 | 21 | -65 |
| Domestic | 3 | | | | | x | 44 | 01 | -63 |
| Fiscal | 6 | | | | | | x | 12 | -12 |
| Foreign trade | 4 | | | | | | | x | 06 |
| Domestic | 8 | | | | | | | | x |

## Republicans

### 84th

| | 3 | 1 | 5 | 4 | 2 |
|---|---|---|---|---|---|
| Foreign trade 3 | x | 57 | −12 | −18 | −03 |
| Foreign aid 1 | | x | 32 | 06 | −28 |
| (Urban) 5 | | | x | 62 | −01 |
| Postal pay 4 | | | | x | −05 |
| Agriculture 2 | | | | | x |

### 87th

| | 3 | 1 | 6 | 4 | 2 | 5 |
|---|---|---|---|---|---|---|
| General 3 | x | 74 | 63 | 56 | 47 | −02 |
| Foreign aid 1 | | x | 61 | 69 | 55 | 00 |
| (Procedural) 6 | | | x | 53 | 63 | 00 |
| Domestic 4 | | | | x | 83 | 11 |
| Domestic 2 | | | | | x | 06 |
| Agriculture 5 | | | | | | x |

## Democrats

### 84th

| | 1 | 3 | 5 | 6 | 4 | 2 |
|---|---|---|---|---|---|---|
| General 1 | x | 86 | 79 | 73 | 19 | −40 |
| Domestic 3 | | x | 74 | 61 | 22 | −23 |
| Contracts 5 | | | x | 59 | 16 | −17 |
| Regional 6 | | | | x | 00 | −70 |
| Foreign trade 4 | | | | | x | −22 |
| Agriculture 2 | | | | | | x |

### 87th

| | 1 | 3 | 2 | 7 | 4 | 5 | 6 |
|---|---|---|---|---|---|---|---|
| General 1 | x | 86 | 85 | 55 | 41 | 65 | −15 |
| Kennedy projs. 3 | | x | 90 | 59 | 56 | 55 | −10 |
| (Bureaucracy) 2 | | | x | 57 | 70 | 62 | 06 |
| (Patronage) 7 | | | | x | 38 | 54 | 27 |
| Hanford 4 | | | | | x | 30 | −45 |
| Agriculture 5 | | | | | | x | 58 |
| Sugar 6 | | | | | | | x |

* Associations are gammas with decimal point omitted. "General" scales include both foreign and domestic issues; "domestic" include both urban and non-urban. Parentheses enclosing a title indicate that fewer than 80% of the items in the scale in question conform to the title category.

the issues at each period on the basis of a preliminary subjective selection of roll calls.

A second advantage of empirical search is that it is well suited to discovery of bases of legislative division that are *not* centered about issues. One such example is the distinction between divisions, in a parliamentary system, that center about issues and those that center about the fate of the cabinet.[42] Another such example is the use of clusters of roll calls to delineate blocs and factions.

## V. Postwar Issues in the House of Representatives

We may now apply the method to a substantive problem: the tracing of issues in the House of Representatives in the two postwar decades. We choose for analysis five Congresses, involving four combinations of party control of the Presidency and Congress: the 80th (D,R control respectively), the 81st (D,D), the 83d (R,R), the 84th (R,D), and the 87th (D,D). The 87th Congress (D,D) is added to permit examination of temporal trends. Associations between the scales found in these Congresses, for each party separately, are shown in Table III.

Consider first the table of associations for the Republicans in the 84th Congress (next to last table in the left-hand column). The five scales for which associations are shown in Table III are the same ones that were identified in the Q-matrix of Table I. Scale 1, dealing with foreign aid, has relatively low associations with all the other scales except that for foreign trade (Scale 3); this association was foreshadowed by several high values of Q between roll calls in the two scales in Table I. The two other scales that form a separate grouping deal with domestic matters: Scales 4 (postal pay) and 5 (welfare state; here classed as "urban"). Scale 2 (agriculture) is relatively independent of the other four.

The table of associations we have just discussed illustrates several general principles of presentation in Table III. First, groups of scales, all of which have values of gamma of at least .5 with one another, are enclosed in rectangles to indicate their membership in "higher-order clusters." Second, the "positive" votes chosen for each scale are those on which the Republicans proportionally exceeded the Democrats in the majority of the roll calls in the scale in question.[43] Thus the "agriculture" scale for the Republicans in the 84th Congress has small negative associations with all the other scales, because the segment of the party voting with the Democrats (in favor of price supports) tended to be the most conservative (*i.e.,* to oppose the Democrats most) on other issues. Third, the various scales (rows and columns) are arranged in such an order as to bring their highest positive associations near the diagonal, rather than according to size of cluster (which their serial numbers indicate).

These last two principles throw into relief four scales on which inter-party alignments—often relating to the President's position—were reversed in relation to intra-party divisions. In each case the reversal is revealed by a set of high negative associations between the scale in question and others, placing the scale in a higher-order cluster. First is the Democrats' scale on the draft in the 80th Congress (#4), which we shall discuss below. Second was their "rural" scale in the 81st Congress (#4), on which urban liberals joined Republicans to oppose the Southerners' acreage allotments for cotton and peanuts, as well as the Truman Administration's cutback in postal services. This latter economy move by the Administration also led to polarity reversal on the Republicans' scale #4, though with lower negative associations.[44] In the 83d Congress two more reversals occurred, as one such scale appeared for each party (#4 for the Republicans and #8 for the Democrats) when the Eisenhower administration took liberal stands backed by most of the Republicans, drawing liberal support but conservative opposition.

By placing closely associated scales near one another in each table, we arrange issues in a sequence that is broadly similar across parties and Congresses. The issue of foreign aid can usually be placed at one end of such a sequence, and we place it first (top row and left column) where possible. The first scale in nearly every case either deals primarily with foreign aid or combines foreign and domestic issues ("general"). At the other end of the sequence is usually a scale dealing with agriculture or agricultural interests. Between are scales dealing with a variety of domestic issues. When the issue of foreign trade appears, it is sometimes quite independent of the rest, as for Democrats under Eisenhower; sometimes closely related to foreign aid, as for the Republicans in the 84th Congress; and sometimes merged in a general scale, as for the Republicans in the 87th Congress.

In every table for the Republicans, two or more scales involving domestic issues can be found that differ in their degree of association with both foreign aid and agricultural or rural issues; domestic issues more closely associated with foreign aid tend to be less closely associated with aid to agriculture. In most cases, the former scales are recognizably concentrated on urban issues and the latter on non-urban issues (as defined above). Thus the diversity of division we observed for the Republicans in the 81st Congress is a more general characteristic of that Congressional party.

Throughout the Congresses studied, the Democrats in the House tended to be divided in a more unitary way than the Republicans.[45] Agricultural issues never merged with others in the principal higher-order cluster for the Republicans, while they merged for the Democrats in the 80th and 87th Congresses, and were so closely related to other domestic issues in the 81st and 83d Congresses that no separate agriculture scale appeared. Similarly, foreign aid twice failed by wide margins to fit into a domestic higher-order cluster for the Republicans (81st and 84th Congresses), while for the Democrats the two failures (81st and 83d Congresses) were by much narrower margins. Finally, the proportion of roll calls in the Q-matrix which entered the leading scale cluster was always higher for the Democrats than for the Republicans, as will be shown in Table IV below.

Comparing Congresses, we can see evidence of a greater consistency of division within the Democratic party on various issues in the 87th Congress than in the previous ones. Among the Democrats there was a steady trend toward consistency, which can be traced in the relation between foreign and domestic issues. In retrospect, the voting patterns of the 80th Congress appear particularly inconsistent. At that time American foreign policy was taking a new direction, as exemplified by Truman's program of aid to Greece and Turkey, and the continuation of the draft in peace time; the wartime alliance with the Soviet Union was being reversed. Support for Truman's policy was stronger, proportionately, from his own party than from the Republicans; yet, within the Democratic party, factional alignments were reversed. The small group of Democrats who opposed these policies tended to come from the left of the political spectrum, while the Republicans who opposed were from the right. This alignment explains the fact that for the Democrats at that time, all the associations of the "draft" scale (#4; including the vote on passage of Greek-Turkish aid) with domestic issues were negative. This scale did

TABLE IV. INCLUSIVENESS OF LEADING SCALE CLUSTERS

| Congress | REPUBLICANS | | | DEMOCRATS | | |
| --- | --- | --- | --- | --- | --- | --- |
| | Subject of first cluster | Per cent of all roll calls in this cluster (%) | Total roll calls in matrix | Subject of first cluster | Per cent of all roll calls in this cluster (%) | Total roll calls in matrix |
| 79 | Domestic | 10 | 136 | Domestic | 36 | 139 |
| 80 | Foreign aid | 14 | 73 | Domestic | 29 | 103 |
| 81 | Urban | 12 | 181 | Domestic | 38 | 176 |
| 82 | Domestic | 26 | 138 | Domestic | 28 | 139 |
| 83 | Foreign aid | 14 | 77 | General | 19 | 104 |
| 84 | Foreign aid | 8 | 102 | General | 22 | 85 |
| 85 | Non-urban | 11 | 144 | Domestic | 32 | 136 |
| 86 | Domestic | 13 | 130 | Domestic | 37 | 127 |
| 87 | Foreign aid | 12 | 159 | General | 41 | 150 |
| 88 | General | 13 | 150 | General | 51 | 144 |

enter into a higher-order cluster that reflected an underlying constancy of division within the party; but it was not consistent with the other scales in relation to inter-party alignments, or to the President's position. The associations between foreign aid and domestic issues were also low.[46]

This state of affairs did not last long. Foreign aid was still distinct from issues in the 81st Congress, but the left wings of both parties then tended to support it more consistently. And with the succeeding years, the convergence between the alignments on foreign and domestic issues became such that by the 87th Congress the Democrats revealed a "general" scale, combining foreign and domestic issues. The Republicans had such a scale as well, but it was less dominant and the coalescence of issues over time was less pronounced for them.

In this transition, party control of Presidency and Congress does not seem to have played the dominant role. The particular policies that Presidents urged on Congress, from Greek-Turkish aid to trade and agricultural policies, may well account for important changes in the configuration of issues. But the *general* degree of organization of issues seems to have been more a constant difference between the legislative parties in the House, and for the Democrats to have shown a trend over time toward consistency, than to have been altered and reversed by changes in party control. The differences shown in Table III do not easily fit the latter hypothesis.

## VI. The Voting Patterns of Blocs and Parties

In addition to the identification of issues, our procedure can also aid in the identification of certain types of blocs or factions. The Q-matrix provides two sorts of relevant evidence: the allocation of roll calls among clusters and the distribution of $p_+$ in these clusters. While a uniform distribution of $p_+$ was considered best in Guttman's initial procedure, the actual nonuniform distributions observed in legislative analysis provide useful information about the bloc divisions. If a group of legislators is regularly divided into two opposing blocs, this will be revealed by a corresponding scale cluster in which the cutting points ($p_+$) are concentrated in a narrow range. The same phenomenon will result if a minority bloc repeatedly splits off from the remainder of the larger group; in this case the values of $p_+$ will be concentrated nearer the extremes (0 or 1), and we shall be more likely to say that a single "bloc" was involved than that there were two opposing blocs. If two mutually exclusive minority blocs (*e.g.*, small left and right wings) split repeatedly from the main segment of a party, but not at the same time, this fact will be revealed by a single scale cluster with two concentrations of values of $p_+$ near the two extremes.

If concentrations of $p_+$ of this kind are observed in scale clusters that are general in content, we infer that if blocs exist they are effective over a wide range of legislative subject-matter; if they are observed in clusters that are narrowly restricted in subject matter, we infer that the blocs are issue-specific. Clearly this distinction is one that should be allowed to arise out of the data, rather than being imposed by restrictive assumptions or models. Presumably the deepest cleavages within a party, or the divisions between parties that tend to set one whole party against another, will be characterized *both* by very general scale clusters (containing roll calls on a great variety of topics), and by a narrow concentration of cutting points ($p_+$).

In the House of Representatives in recent years, a bloc division of this sort has been more prevalent among the Democrats than among the Republicans. One way to show this is to compute the proportion of all roll calls in a Q-matrix which enter the first or largest cluster; Table IV shows this proportion for each party in ten recent Congresses. In every case the proportion is higher for the Democrats than for the Republicans. The subjects of the leading clusters also help to explain the difference between the parties; in four Congresses the leading cluster for the Republicans concerned foreign aid, while the leading cluster for the Democrats always included domestic issues. This difference in subject-matter is due to the greater diversity of cleavages in the Republican party, not to its being divided on fewer domestic issues. Not only were various domestic issues, including agricultural issues, more distinct for the Republicans in terms of relations among scales; but, as another manifestation of the same variety of division, roll calls were less concentrated in any particular cluster.

Some effects of party control of the presidency and congress can be seen in Table IV, for the Democrats but not for the Republicans. The Democrats' most inclusive leading scale clusters were observed in the 88th, 87th, 81st, 86th, and 79th Congresses, and their least in the 83d, 84th, 82d, 80th, and 85th. Of the first five, four were Congresses in which the Democrats controlled both congress and the presidency; of the last five, the lowest (83d) was the one instance in which the Republicans controlled both, while three others involved "truncated majorities" in which the party controlling congress did not control the presidency. Thus Democratic control of both branches seems to have made the Democrats' divisions more consistent. The two exceptions can also be explained plausibly. The 86th Congress was the third of a series of truncated Democratic majorities, and one preceding a presidential election which the Democrats had hopes of winning; the Democratic leadership in congress was putting forward its own policies and not merely opposing the president. Conversely, in the 82d Congress, in spite of nominal Democratic control, the coalition of Republicans and Southern Democrats had asserted its control from the opening of the first session; [47] of all the Congresses in this series with nominal Democratic control, this was the one with least Democratic strength. Moreover, a presidential election was approaching and Republican prospects seemed favorable. Some Democratic congressmen may have decided to vote in terms of the particular appeals of legislation for their districts, rather than the general appeals of President Truman, who was having difficulty with his programs. In this sense the political configuration of the 82d Congress may have resembled that of the 80th.

The proportion of roll calls in the leading scale for the Republicans shows far less clear association with party control. The unusually high figure for the 82d Congress may be attributed to repeated divisions of the party on a series of roll calls on amendments to the Defense Production Act, which constituted nearly half of the roll calls in their leading scale. Bills on this subject were introduced in 1951 and 1952, each time with an open rule permitting numerous amendments. These amendments were used to embarrass the Truman Administration; and possibly the prospects of electoral victory in 1952 induced most Republicans to join forces in support of the diverse amendments opposing governmental controls.

The dominant scales found for the Democrats are such as might have resulted from division of the party into blocs; and their greater dominance, when the Northern Democrats controlled the legislative program, suggests that the bloc division within the party was heightened at those times. But before reaching such a conclusion, we must ask whether the division was a deep one or merely set off a few dissidents at one extreme. For this reason, as well as others, we must study the distribution of $p_+$ among the roll calls in each leading scale cluster.

The distribution of $p_+$ within a scale is a useful datum concerning the repeated divisions of the set of legislators being studied. The Democrats' leading scales do show the concentration of values of $p_+$ that might have resulted from division of the party into two blocs; the dispersion of $p_+$ in these scales (semi-interquartile range) varied from .07 to .12 in the ten Congresses studied. If cutting points had been uniformly distributed over the permitted range (from .07 to .93), the corresponding dispersion would have been .22, about twice as great.

Not surprisingly, the Democrats' dominant scale invariably arrayed Northern urban congressmen at one end and Southerners at the other. But the median value of $p_+$ did not always divide the party precisely into Northern and Southern wings; for while the proportion of Southerners [48] varied between .36 and .55 over the period studied (86th and 80th Congresses respectively), the median value of $p_+$ varied from .18 to .68. When the South was proportionally strong within the party, it tended to gain the votes of some middle-of-the-road Democrats as well; while in recent Congresses (85th through 88th) the South was not only proportionally weaker but also tended to lose votes from within its own group. Whether this change corresponds to a change in the boundaries of social groupings in the party— i.e., of blocs as revealed by evidence other than similarity of voting—requires further testing. If our identification of blocs is correct, we should expect Border-state Democrats, and some Southerners, to have interacted more in recent years with their Northern party colleagues. It is also possible, however, that the inclusion of foreign aid in the dominant scale in recent years has moved the dividing point farther toward the conservative, or Southern, end.

While the Republicans' leading scales were less dominant than the Democrats', they too showed concentrations of $p_+$. Most often their divisions tended to set off a small liberal faction, as the Democrats' set off a conservative minority. But in the

79th and 81st Congresses the Republicans' leading scale revealed minority factions at both extremes.[49] The properties of the Republicans' leading scales are harder to describe with assurance, however, because for that party one or more scale clusters were often close rivals of the largest; and depending on whether domestic or foreign issues were involved, the distributions of $p_+$ were quite different.

The observed concentrations of $p_+$ might be thought to result from legislative strategists' decisions to bring certain bills to the floor, or the willingness of committees to allow them to come up, or the insistence of interested minorities on the yeas and nays. But these factors still permit minorities at either extreme of a party to vote separately on roll calls; votes on passage and on conference reports characteristically set off small minorities of the opposition, and in the 79th, 80th, and 81st Congresses, minorities on the side controlling the House were also frequently set off on roll calls. Until further analysis yields alternative explanations for the observed concentrations of $p_+$, we shall regard them as reflecting actual social groupings within the parties, i.e., blocs.

The division between the parties themselves also constitutes a useful test of our method of bloc identification. If the same procedure we have described is applied to the entire membership of the House, the proportion of roll calls in the leading cluster is higher than for either party alone in the 83d Congress, but lower in the 87th.[50] Thus in a legislature where the parties have relatively weak internal discipline, as they do in the United States Congress, the divisions within the parties can be considered as apparently comparable with the divisions between them. If we wish to speak of a "multi-party system" in Congress, we should make the necessary quantitative distinctions between the "parties."

It is also possible, conversely, for a deep legislative cleavage to cut across party lines. This possibility is illustrated in the votes of the French Radicals from 1956 to 1958. By late 1956, after the fall of the Mollet cabinet and the investiture of Maurice Bourgès-Maunoury, a deep split had developed in the parliamentary party, centering about support for, and opposition to, Pierre Mendès-France. This division existed in the UDSR as well. When these two parties were scaled together, the main cluster reflected this division.[51] Of 22 roll calls under the Mollet cabinet, only one fell in the main cluster; of those under the subsequent cabinets, 58 per cent did. Within this cluster, the semi-interquartile range of $p_+$ was only .10. Thus this division into two blocs, while it crossed party lines and was not itself reflected in a formal division between parties, was deeper and more consistent than that between the two major parties in the U. S. House of Representatives.

We can now evaluate the propriety of scaling two or more parties together. If the investigator wishes to reveal a major bi-factional cleavage, he should study the votes of both factions together and examine the major scale cluster as an indication of the cleavage. If more than two factions combine in shifting patterns of coalition, like those of the Fourth French Republic, this method will best reveal cleavages if only two major factions or parties are studied at one time. On the other hand, if one wishes to reveal the diversity of issues that divide a legislative body, there may be advantages in studying the individual factions separately and examining their internal divisions. This might entail separate studies of individual parties or of major factions within a party. The method we have presented may make it possible to identify such factions empirically without the need of assumptions such as a geographical or historical definition of the "South." [52]

## VII. Summary

The method proposed here for identifying issues and factions modifies the customary procedures of cumulative (Guttman) scaling in several ways:

(1) It searches for clusters of similar roll calls by empirical examination of pairwise relationships.

(2) Each possible pair of roll calls is evaluated for scalability in relation to a threshold value of Yule's Q-coefficient, and "errors" or departures from the scale model are thus weighted unequally. Because Q is a coefficient of association, the results are more comparable with those of factor and cluster analysis.

(3) It is no longer assumed that each scale need correspond to a single issue-continuum. Instead, the possibility of combination of issues by factional opposition is considered, and variations of issues among different ranges of $p_+$ may be interpreted.

(4) A non-uniform distribution of $p_+$ in a scale cluster is taken as a useful datum revealing factional structure, rather than simply an inconvenience in the selection of scale items.

These modifications, though not altering the scaling procedure fundamentally, serve an important purpose: to adapt it to the particular needs of legislative analysis, as against questionnaire analysis. Modification (2), which relates scale analysis more closely to other methods, may also have value in other applications.

Results from this relatively empirical method agree fairly well with those of a previous study of the 81st Congress based on an initial conceptual grouping of roll calls.

Substantive results for postwar issues in the U. S. House of Representatives, and other selected data, are presented to illustrate the utility of the method. During this period the Democratic party in the House was more consistently divided than the Republican. The degree of organization of the internal cleavages of the Democratic party increased from the 80th to the 87th Congress. Party control of the presidency and congress was related to the degree of dominance of the Democrats' major scale, but not to the Republicans', and not clearly to the general degree of organization of intra-party divisions. Particular legislative programs of individual presidents did, however, find their counterparts in the relations between scales.

In terms of the dominance of a major scale cluster, the degree of bi-factional division of a legislative body, a group of parties, or a single party may be regarded as a continuous variable. Inter-party divisions find their place on this continuum. In the House of Representatives, the inter-party division is not always dominant, as the North-South cleavage among the Democrats approaches it in degree of dominance. The division within the French Radical party and UDSR in 1956–58, however, was more completely dominant in the votes of that period than the division between the parties in the U. S. House of Representatives.

Although this empirical method gives rise to artifactual "shadow" scales duplicating others in content, additional information permits the identification of such scales. In particular, all scales or higher-order clusters found in this study, which have associations ($\gamma$) no greater than .5 with outside scales, have clearly recognizable and distinct issue content.

The Q-matrix can be analyzed without resort to the particular clustering techniques presented here. The data it contains are very close to the fourfold tables themselves. The relation between individual roll calls of interest to the investigator and major issues or bloc divisions can thus be revealed, and those that have little such relation can be studied separately.

This method has the great advantage of simplicity. It requires little more for its understanding than a knowledge of the properties of Q and $\gamma$. No knowledge of matrix algebra or multidimensional geometry is required. The method uses computers, but it is relatively easy for the user to understand completely the operations that the computer performs on the data. Some of the disadvantages of the method could undoubtedly be reduced by greater technical sophistication; however, it is presented as a useful step toward the fuller exploitation of legislative voting records.

## NOTES

1. Representative articles are S. C. Patterson, "Legislative Leadership and Political Ideology," *Public Opinion Quarterly,* Vol. 27 (1963), pp. 399–410; L. N. Rieselbach, "The Demography of the Congressional Vote on Foreign Aid, 1939–1958," *American Political Science Review,* Vol. 58 (1964), pp. 577–588; G. R. Schubert, "The 1960 Term of the Supreme Court—A Psychological Analysis," *ibid.,* Vol. 56 (1962), pp. 90–107; H. R. Alker, Jr., "Dimensions of Conflict in the General Assembly," *ibid.,* Vol. 58 (1964), pp. 642–657; F. Munger and J. Blackhurst, "Factionalism in the National Conventions, 1940–1964; An Analysis of Ideological Consistency in State Delegation Voting," *Journal of Politics,* Vol. 27 (1965), pp. 375–394.

2. The term "roll call" will be used to refer to any division of legislators into two opposing groups on a political issue—including, for example, whip polls and discharge petitions. "Legislators" will refer to members of bodies (or groupings such as state delegations) analyzable in the ways proposed.

3. H. C. Beyle, *Identification and Analysis of Attribute-Cluster Blocs* (Chicago, 1931); S. A. Rice, *Quantitative Methods in Politics* (New York, 1928), ch. 16; D. B. Truman, *The Congressional Party* (New York, 1959).

4. Most analyses of political data published so far, using analytic rotation by computers, to the author's knowledge, have used orthogonal rotation. Schubert's study (*op. cit.,* pp. 96–97) is an important exception; he rotates to oblique axes based on Guttman scales, and avoids orthogonal rotation on grounds similar to those presented here. Another exception is J. G. Grumm, "A Factor Analysis of Legislative Behavior," *Midwest Journal of Political Science,* Vol. 7 (1963), pp. 336–356.

5. In so doing, we no longer assume that such a set of roll calls must be restricted to a single issue. This meets to some extent the criticism of A. Lijphart in "The Analysis of Bloc Voting in the General Assembly: A Critique and a Proposal," *American Political Science Review,* Vol. 57 (1963), pp. 904–905.

6. For a recent example, see Rieselbach, *op. cit.;* for a more detailed exposition of reasoning and procedures, see D. MacRae, Jr., *Dimensions of Congressional Voting,* University of California Publications in Sociology and Social Institutions, Vol. 1 #3 (1958), pp. 203–333.

7. L. Guttman, "The Basis for Scalogram Analysis," ch. 3 in S. A. Stouffer *et al., Measurement and Prediction* (Princeton, 1950).

8. Voting systems with three alternatives (*e.g.*, abstention) may often be analyzed by converting a trichotomy into two dichotomies. Votes for a multiplicity of unordered alternatives (as in a Presidential nominating convention) are less easily treated in this way.

9. In factor analysis it is conventional to form factor scores by adding the weighted contributions of items loaded on a given factor; this procedure treats items as interchangeable, in the sense considered here. Schubert, in assigning scores on cumulative scales, also uses an additive procedure (*op. cit.*); this may be appropriate for matching scales with factors, but it is not the procedure that we propose here.

10. MacRae, *Dimensions* . . . , *op. cit.*, p. 228.

11. Guttman, *op. cit.*, pp. 80ff.

12. For further treatment of the last two points see A. Kaplan, *The Conduct of Inquiry* (San Francisco, 1964), pp. 41, 50.

13. J. Toby and M. L. Toby, "A Method of Selecting Dichotomous Items by Cross-Tabulation," ch. 15 in M. W. Riley, J. W. Riley, Jr., and J. Toby, *Sociological Studies in Scale Analysis* (New Brunswick, 1954).

14. *Op. cit.*, p. 343. It was also required that the numbers of cases in cells *a* and *d* each be at least twice that in the "zero box."

15. See, for example, H. Menzel, "A New Coefficient for Scale Analysis," *Public Opinion Quarterly,* Vol. 17 (1953), pp. 268–280; E. F. Borgatta, "An Error Ratio for Scalogram Analysis," *ibid.*, Vol. 19 (1955), pp. 96–100.

16. It can be seen from Figure 1 that for roll call #1, $p_+ = (a+c)/N$, and for roll call #2, $p_+ = (a+b)/N$. The difference is $(c-b)/N$. If roll call #1 has the higher $p_+$, this difference will be positive.

17. See D. MacRae, Jr., "An Exponential Model for Assessing Fourfold Tables," *Sociometry,* Vol. 19 (1956), pp. 84–94. This method was used in *Dimensions* . . . , *op. cit.*

18. See G. U. Yule, *Introduction to the Theory of Statistics* (London, 1911), p. 38.

19. This approximation is good as long as *c* is much larger than *b*.

20. See L. A. Goodman and W. H. Kruskal, "Measures of Association for Cross Classifications," *Journal of the American Statistical Association,* Vol. 49 (1954), pp. 723–764. An alternative line of reasoning which leads to similar formulations is put forward in M. G. Kendall, *Rank Correlation Methods* (London, 3d ed., 1962), pp. 3–5. In comparing two rankings, Kendall counts the number of pairs of elements that are ranked consistently, and the number ranked inconsistently, out of all possible such pairs. With either of these approaches, it would be possible to assess a fourfold table not only in terms of the proportional consistency of the rankings it provides (as measured by Q), but also in terms of the proportion of rankings about which a judgment of consistency may be made. If this latter proportion is low (*i.e.*, the proportion of ties is high), as in tables with extreme values of $p_+$, the table may be given less emphasis in interpretation.

21. Computer programs for carrying out this operation are discussed in R. E. Bonner, "On Some Clustering Techniques," *IBM Journal of Research and Development,* Vol. 8 (1964), pp. 22–32. A related program was written by F. K. Bamberger for the Univac I, and used in exploratory research by the author. A similar program was written for the IBM 7094 at Chicago by R. Axelrod. These programs were costly in computer time, however; the clusters reported here therefore were obtained from the Q-matrix by paper-and-pencil methods, which are believed reliable up to a matrix size of about 150 items.

22. In the House of Representatives, the votes ignored by this choice tend to include a disproportionate number of questions affecting particular areas of the

country, such as the appointment of judges for a particular district, the movement of an Army installation from one place to another, or the treatment of an industry whose production and markets are highly localized.

23. See D. MacRae, Jr., "IBM 1401 Q-Matrix and Editing Programs for Legislative Votes," *Behavioral Science*, Vol. 10 (1965), p. 324. For each pair of roll calls, only those legislators voting on both are counted in the calculation.

24. These numbers are used to identify the roll calls in the *Congressional Quarterly Almanac*, Vols. 11, 12 (Washington, 1955, 1956).

25. The actual computer printout also indicates the value of $p_+$, and the provisional "positive" vote (yea or nay), on each roll call. This preserves all the information in the individual fourfold tables except for the distribution of nonvoting.

26. See R. C. Tryon and D. E. Bailey, *Cluster and Factor Analysis* (in preparation). Reference is made to this method in D. MacRae, Jr., "Cluster Analysis of Congressional Votes with the BC TRY System," *Western Political Quarterly* (in press). See also Tryon and Bailey, "The BC TRY Computer System of Cluster and Factor Analysis," *Multivariate Behavioral Research*, Vol. 1 (1966), pp. 95–111.

27. More elaborate procedures of the second type are presented in Bonner, *op. cit.* In the procedure used here, ties between clusters of equal size are resolved in favor of the cluster with highest average Q.

28. To designate roll calls by number, we precede the *Congressional Quarterly* number by the last digit of the year (5 or 6).

29. In general, we terminate after the first six scales and ties, if all possible scales containing as few as six roll calls have been found.

30. This procedure was proposed in S. A. Stouffer *et al.*, "A Technique for Improving Cumulative Scales," *Public Opinion Quarterly*, Vol. 16 (1952), pp. 273–291.

31. In the descending sequence of values of $p_+$, any interval of .10 or greater is first marked off as a division point. Then each sequence of values of $p_+$ between these division points, or at the end of the overall sequence, is further divided if it spans a range of $p_+$ greater than .15. This division is made by specifying further division points, equally spaced, with intervals as near to .10 as possible. The roll calls falling between each pair of division points then constitute a contrived (or if only one, an ordinary) item. This procedure, while useful for placing legislators, discards information provided by the distribution of $p_+$.

32. The detailed procedures are essentially the same as those specified in Mac-Rae, *Dimensions* . . . , pp. 321–322.

33. Goodman and Kruskal, *op. cit.*, pp. 749–751.

34. For an elementary discussion of gamma, how to calculate it, and its relation to Q, see M. Zelditch, *A Basic Course in Sociological Statistics* (New York, 1959), pp. 180–186.

35. MacRae, *Dimensions* . . . , *op. cit.*

36. This finding is consistent with the high associations between the former agriculture scale and the former welfare-state and race-relations scales ($\gamma = +.70$, $+.79$ resp.).

37. This distinction was shown to be related to the rural or urban character of constituencies in *Dimensions* . . . , *op. cit.*, pp. 266–268.

38. Further evidence of this overlap arose in the process of cluster identification. A number of roll calls in Scale 1 could equally well have been placed in Cluster 5; they were simply assigned to Cluster 1 by the preference which our rules give to larger clusters. Moreover, a change in the minimum Q also transferred items from one cluster to another.

39. This was also pointed out in *Dimensions* . . . , *op. cit.*, pp. 251–252.

40. This position was taken by Guttman when he introduced the scaling technique. See *Measurement and Prediction, op. cit.*, pp. 72, 84, 85.

41. The two issues were *not* similar in this sense for the two parties combined, however; the Republicans were generally more favorable to civil rights than the Democrats.

42. See D. MacRae, Jr., "Intraparty Divisions and Cabinet Coalitions in the Fourth French Republic," *Comparative Studies in Society and History,* Vol. 5 (1963), pp. 164–211.

43. The principal exception to this rule concerns votes on civil rights, on which the Democrats generally voted more conservatively. The polarities on civil rights roll calls were reversed before application of the rule. Scale #5 for the Republicans in the 80th Congress was assigned a polarity consistent with its higher-order cluster; the two of its four roll calls whose polarities were thus reversed were on Republican bills opposed by Democrats and conservative Republicans.

44. The polarity of Scales #4 for the Republicans and #4 for the Democrats is reversed in Table 3 relative to Table 2. This is because in the previous study, polarities were chosen for intra-party consistency, while they are chosen here to show the relations between internal divisions and interparty differences.

45. For domestic issues, this difference between the parties has also been observed in another study of this period: David R. Mayhew, "Democrats and Republicans in the U. S. House of Representatives: A Study of Intra-Party Coalition Patterns in the Postwar Period," Ph.D. dissertation, Harvard, 1963, esp. ch. 6.

46. This low association is partly due to the inclusion of Marcantonio and Isacson (ALP, NY) together with the Democrats; on Scale 6, they joined a small group of conservatives in opposing foreign aid.

47. See F. M. Riddick, "The Eighty-Second Congress: First Session," *Western Political Quarterly,* Vol. 5 (1952), pp. 106, 108; *Congressional Quarterly Almanac,* Vol. 8 (Washington, 1952), pp. 58–59.

48. Representatives from the eleven former Confederate states.

49. Bloc analysis of the parties in the 81st Congress also showed the Republicans to be divided into more and smaller subgroups than the Democrats. See D. B. Truman, *The Congressional Party, op. cit.*

50. The proportions of roll calls in the leading scale, if the parties are combined and the same procedures followed as for a single party, are .27 for the 83d Congress and .35 for the 87th. The division between the parties at the median $p_+$ appears, however, only when the dominant scale is a domestic one.

51. Details of sampling are reported in MacRae, "Intraparty Divisions . . .," *op. cit.* The results given here differ from those in that reference in that a minimum level of $Q = .8$ was used for comparability with the Congressional data presented here.

52. This is of course an aim of the Beyle-Rice method, as pointed out by D. B. Truman, *op. cit.*

# Bibliographical Note

Two recent general books are available on American legislative behavior: Malcolm E. Jewell and Samuel C. Patterson, *The Legislative Process in the United States* (New York, 1966), and William J. Keefe and Morris S. Ogul, *The American Legislative Process* (Englewood Cliffs, N.J.: 1968). In addition, students will find useful the collections on Congress and the American state legislatures which provided the working papers for the American Assembly sessions in 1964 and 1966. The papers on Congress, edited by David B. Truman, are in *The Congress and America's Future* (Englewood Cliffs, N.J.: 1965). State legislatures are dealt with in the American Assembly collection edited by Alexander Heard, *State Legislatures in American Politics* (Englewood Cliffs, N.J., 1966).

REPRESENTATION: Three excellent studies are available on the general concept of representation. In the first, *Representative and Responsible Government* (London, 1964), A. H. Birch focuses upon the unfolding of representative government in Britain. Hanna F. Pitkin deals very admirably with the development and concept of political representation, analyzing the contributions of theorists like Hobbes, Bentham, and Burke, in *The Concept of Representation* (Berkeley and Los Angeles, 1967). Finally, the papers in Nomes X, the yearbook of the American Society for Political and Legal Philosophy—*Representation* (New York, 1968)— edited by J. Roland Pennock and John W. Chapman, are very useful. The development of political representation in the United States is the subject of Alfred de Grazia's seminal study, *Public and Republic* (New York, 1951). The special problems of congressional districting and state legislative apportionment have evoked a voluminous literature, but the best references are Andrew Hacker, *Congressional Districting: The Issue of Equal Representation* (Washington, D.C., 1964), and Gordon E. Baker, *The Reapportionment Revolution* (New York, 1966).

ACTORS: Donald R. Matthews' *U.S. Senators and Their World* (Chapel Hill, 1960) remains the major analysis of congressional recruitment. In *Party and Representation* (New York, 1963), Frank J. Sorauf has focused on legislative elections in Pennsylvania, and Malcolm E. Jewell has surveyed southern legislative elections in *Legislative Representation in the Contemporary South* (Durham, N.C., 1967). Elections to the U.S. House of Representatives over the last half a century are analyzed by Milton C. Cummings, Jr. in *Congressmen and the Electorate* (New York, 1966), and the political effects of electoral laws on legislative representation are interestingly examined by Douglas Rae in *The Political Consequences of Electoral Laws* (New Haven, 1967). The status of legislative office in the overall recruitment process is explored by Joseph A. Schlesinger in *Ambition and Politics* (Chicago, 1966). Finally, Heinz Eulau and John D. Sprague analyze the careers of lawyer-legislators in *Lawyers in Politics* (Indianapolis, 1964). The everyday life of congressmen is explored by Charles L. Clapp in *The Congressman* (Washington, D.C., 1963), a part of which is included in this anthology, and

449

by Donald G. Tacheron and Morris K. Udall in *The Job of the Congressman* (Indianapolis, 1966).

STRUCTURE: Although it is dated in some respects, the best single book on congressional structure in general is George B. Galloway's *The Legislative Process in Congress* (New York, 1953). A reasonably comparable volume on the structure and procedure of state legislatures is Belle Zeller's *American State Legislatures* (New York, 1954). Among a variety of studies of congressional committees are: David N. Farnsworth, *The Senate Committee on Foreign Relations* (Urbana, 1961); James A. Robinson, *The House Rules Committee* (Indianapolis, 1963); and, on the Joint Committee on Atomic Energy, Harold P. Green and Alan Rosenthal, *Government of the Atom* (New York, 1963). For an experimental analysis of the internal processes of committees, see James D. Barber, *Power in Committees* (Chicago, 1966). Major studies of legislative party structures are: David B. Truman, *The Congressional Party* (New York, 1959); Charles O. Jones, *Party and Policy-Making* (New Brunswick, N.J., 1964); and, in the case of one very unusual and interesting state, William Buchanan, *Legislative Partisanship: The Deviant Case of California* (Berkeley and Los Angeles, 1963). Congressional party leadership is analyzed by Randall B. Ripley in *Party Leaders in the House of Representatives* (Washington, D.C., 1967), and congressional floor procedure by Lewis A. Froman, Jr. in *The Congressional Process* (Boston, 1967).

EXPECTATIONS AND PERCEPTIONS: The major investigation of legislative expectations and perceptions is that by John C. Wahlke, Heinz Eulau, William Buchanan, and LeRoy C. Ferguson, *The Legislative System* (New York, 1962), which is based upon extensive legislative interviews in Ohio, California, New Jersey, and Tennessee. A different, but compatible, analysis of Connecticut freshmen legislators is James D. Barber, *The Lawmakers* (New Haven, 1965). A seminal piece of research on the nature and implications of expectations and perceptions in a committee subsystem, focusing upon the appropriations committees of Congress, is Richard F. Fenno, Jr., *The Power of the Purse* (Boston, 1966). Congressmen's perspectives on legislative reform are subjected to systematic analysis by Roger H. Davidson, David M. Kovenock, and Michael K. O'Leary in *Congress in Crisis* (Belmont, California, 1966).

COMMUNICATION: The major attempts to deal with the legislative system in communications terms are three: Lester W. Milbrath, *The Washington Lobbyist* (Chicago, 1963), based upon interviews with a sample of 100 Washington lobbyists; James A. Robinson, *Congress and Foreign Policy-Making* (Homewood, Illinois, 1967), based upon extensive interviews with members of Congress; and, Raymond A. Bauer, Ithiel de Sola Pool, and Lewis A. Dexter, *American Business and Public Policy* (New York, 1967), a study utilizing public opinion polls and congressional interviews in connection with foreign trade legislation.

ACTION: There are three classic studies of congressional voting behavior. The earliest, Julius Turner, *Party and Constituency* (Baltimore, 1951) used Rice-Beyle indices of cohesion and likeness to analyze the relative effects of party loyalty and constituency pressure on voting. The other two were analyses of the 81st Congress: David B. Truman's *The Congressional Party* (New York, 1959), and Duncan MacRae, Jr.'s *Dimensions of Congressional Voting* (Berkeley and Los Angeles, 1958). Truman analyzed congressional roll-call votes using cluster-bloc analysis, while MacRae's principal method was cumulative scale analysis. Two studies illustrate longitudinal analysis of congressional voting behavior: David

R. Mayhew, *Party Loyalty Among Congressmen* (Cambridge, 1966), and Leroy N. Rieselbach; *The Roots of Isolationism* (Indianapolis, 1966). The classic case study of the enactment of a particular bill is Stephen K. Bailey, *Congress Makes a Law* (New York, 1950), which traces the steps in the passage of the Employment Act of 1946. The passage of the labor union reform act in 1959 is dealt with by Samuel C. Patterson in *Labor Lobbying and Labor Reform* (Indianapolis, 1966). On the state legislative side, Wayne L. Francis has investigated legislative decision-making in the fifty states based on data from mailed questionnaires returned from legislators in his *Legislative Issues in the Fifty States* (Chicago, 1967).

RESEARCH: Specific sections on research problems and developments are included in a number of the volumes already cited, especially the books by Jewell and Patterson and by Wahlke, Eulau, Buchanan, and Ferguson. A helpful research guide is included in Roland Young's *The American Congress* (New York, 1958). Charles O. Jones and Randall B. Ripley have assembled a useful guide to research on congressional parties—*The Role of Political Parties in Congress* (Tucson, 1966). The manual on *Legislative Roll-Call Analysis* (Evanston, Illinois, 1966) by Lee F. Anderson, Meredith W. Watts, Jr., and Allen R. Wilcox is very valuable. As legislative research becomes more comparative in its focus, researchers will find the major new comparative investigations helpful, including Gerhard Lowenberg, *Parliament in the German Political System* (Ithaca, N.Y., 1967); Allan Kornberg, *Canadian Legislative Behavior* (New York, 1967); and Frederic Debuyst, *La Fonction Parlementaire en Belgique* (Brussels, 1966). Legislative behavior in Italy is the subject of research by Gordon J. DiRenzo, *Personality, Power and Politics* (Notre Dame, Indiana, 1967), and Giovanni Sartori, *Il Parlamento Italiano* (Naples, 1963). Austin Ranney's *Pathways to Parliament* (London, 1965) is a very good analysis of recruitment of parliamentary candidates in Britain. The parliament of the French Fourth Republic has been studied by Duncan MacRae, Jr. in *Parliament, Parties, and Society in France* (New York, 1967), and of the Fifth Republic by Philip M. Williams in *The French Parliament* (London, 1968). In addition, there are some interesting materials in Éliane Guichard-Ayoub, Charles Roig, and Jean Grangé, *Études sur le Parlement de la Ve République* (Paris, 1965). Research on Asian, African, or Latin American representative bodies is rare, but see Dario Canton, *El Parlamento Argentino en Épocas de Cambio* (Buenos Aires, 1966).